Guide to Security Considerations and Practices for Rare Book, Manuscript, and Special Collection Libraries

Compiled & Edited by
Everett C. Wilkie, Jr.

Chicago | Association of College & Research Libraries |

The paper used in this publication meets the minimum requirements of American National Standard for Information Sciences–Permanence of Paper for Printed Library Materials, ANSI Z39.48-1992. ∞

Library of Congress Cataloging-in-Publication Data

Guide to security considerations and practices for rare book, manuscript, and special collection libraries / compiled & edited by Everett C. Wilkie, Jr.
    p. cm.
  Includes index.
  ISBN 978-0-8389-8592-2 (pbk. : alk. paper) -- ISBN 978-0-8389-9336-1 (epdf) -- ISBN 978-0-8389-9337-8 (ebook) -- ISBN 978-0-8389-9338-5 (kindle) 1. Rare book libraries--Security measures--United States. 2. Libraries--Security measures--United States. 3. Archives--Security measures--United States. 4. Libraries--Special collections. 5. Book thefts--Prevention. I. Wilkie, Everett C.
  Z679.6.G85 2011
  025.8'2--dc23
                      2011025370

Cover Illustrations:
Map image: Courtesy Dorothy Sloan—Rare Books, Austin, TX
Other images: Courtesy Courtenay Place, Wellington, ca 1939, photographed by Sydney Charles Smith. S C Smith Collection, Reference No: 1/2-048351-G Alexander Turnbull Library, Wellington, New Zealand.

Printed in the United States of America.

15 14 13 12 11 5 4 3 2 1

In Memory of
William A. Moffett
(1933-1995)

TABLE OF CONTENTS

Preface

Everett C. Wilkie, Jr.

This book is in some respects the result of certain dissatisfactions. The Security Committee of Rare Books and Manuscripts Section (RBMS) of the Association of College & Research Libraries (ACRL) for several decades now has revised and kept in print both its *Guidelines for the Security of Rare Books, Manuscripts, and Other Special Collections* and *Guidelines Regarding Thefts in Libraries*, both of which are now superseded by its *2009 Guidelines Regarding Security and Theft in Special Collections*. Those documents are supplemented by the Section's *Guidelines on the Selection of General Collection Materials for Transfer to Special Collections*, which, although a security document, is not promulgated by the Security Committee itself but rather by task forces. Those documents have been kept current as circumstances have changed and different considerations have come to the fore.

Because they are guidelines, however, they sometimes lack a level of specificity needed to implement their recommendations properly. ACRL guidelines are purposely general in keeping with the Association's philosophy and mission. Thus, one cannot necessarily expect to find in a security guideline any detailed discussion of, say, a CCTV system, although it may be a recommended feature of a library security program. Because numerous people over the years approached others and me with questions about implementing some of the general recommendations in the guidelines and actually expressing regret that the guidelines were not more specific and detailed, I approached the RBMS Security Committee, of which I was chair

at the time, with a suggestion that we write a more detailed security manual. The suggestion was enthusiastically endorsed by the committee, and we began researching, gathering material, and writing the chapters. This work is the result of those efforts, although it should not be considered an official publication of the RBMS. The section's guidelines gave the impetus for it, but the section was not officially involved in writing or vetting the text.

Despite our ambitions, this work is not a complete guide to security in special collections settings. We have concentrated almost entirely on the prevention and resolution of thefts to the exclusion of more general security considerations, such as fire safety. Most special collections librarians agree that a total security program encompasses numerous aspects, including disaster planning and conservation concerns, and various writers on the subject of security have argued persuasively that many of these elements must be included in a total security program. Trinkhaus-Randall, painting with a broad brush, remarks on the need to "consider the whole picture which includes the theft and mutilation of materials; environmental conditions; disaster preparedness and recovery; care and handling; storage; education and training; conservation; preservation photocopying, microfilming and scanning; proper day-to-day photocopying; and preservation surveys" (O'Neill, p. 92). One can hardly argue against the idea that a manuscript lost to fire, flood, or total physical deterioration is as gone and useless as one permanently lost to theft. We have hereinafter, however, concentrated on the problem of thefts to the exclusion of others, although we do not doubt the importance of the considerations we have chosen not to address.

Most writers on special collections security also agree that security recommendations do not resemble Spandex©. In other words, there is no such thing as one size fits all. Because of various factors at different institutions, what may be appropriate and practical for one place is not in another. The inherent tension between security and other needs is described by Foley, who favors factoring security situations heavily into an institution's calculations: "Not only do many of the items in special collection repositories have high monetary value, they carry great historical value as well. The public's ability to access these historic documents cannot really be measured monetarily. If cost-benefit analyses are done in purely financial terms, it is not just the repositories that will lose. All of us will lose. Bland and other criminals have taught valuable lessons about the importance of securing the historical record, but those lessons are for naught if we continue to ignore them" (Foley p. 28). Although we have gone full throttle and usually tried to portray ideal security situations, obviously no library would be able to implement everything described or suggested hereinafter. No library, despite all efforts, has ever created or will ever enjoy a 100% airtight security system. Some of the passages in this work may appear dictatorial, prescriptive, or even as pronouncements of the "Library Security Nanny". We recognize that but feel we must nevertheless recommend what we consider to be best practices.

This manual is also out of date in some respects. Despite our efforts to describe current practices and capabilities, some aspects of library security develop so quickly that a printed manual is something of a plodding document that cannot ever be completely current. Changes, especially in security systems such as access control, occur almost on a yearly basis. Advances in other areas, such as profiling and cataloguing systems, also change the security landscape in dramatic ways. Despite the potential anachronisms, we hope this is a text that will serve as a guide to security considerations that any rare book, manuscript, or special collections library might entertain. A good deal of useful security information is also available on the Internet, although regrettably some of it is transient. Some sites that we identified early on in our research have already disappeared. We have, nevertheless, frequently cited URLs as sources of information but have preferred to find print sources for that information when possible. Some information is available only on the Internet, however, and over time probably all of our URL citations may become useless. If you are reading this text twenty years after it was first published, you are probably looking at a very different electronic world than the one in 2011, and much of the information available to us may have vanished or been moved.

Although some overlap and redundancy inevitably exists among chapters, we intend each chapter to be a self-contained discussion. In other words, although one will find some mention of cataloguing systems spread elsewhere, the main discussion of that topic will be in the chapter devoted to it. Unlike a narrative, this is not a text meant to be read from beginning to end. Because security considerations have numerous permutations, however, themes will run through various chapters.

One limitation here is that although the problem of library thefts is pandemic and international, we have in most respects confined ourselves to security discussions relevant to the United States only. Many of our recommendations could be used in practically any setting; others, however, are probably useful only in this country. Any serious attempt to have broadened this manual to include practically every possibility in any country would have made the task impossible. A second limitation is that this text is not intended primarily to serve the needs of archivists, a profession that already has several security publications. A good deal of what is said hereinafter could, of course, be applied to archives, and their experiences with security have informed our discussions. Their special circumstances, which are sometimes different from special collections libraries, have not, however, been systematically addressed.

Acknowledgements

This text is the work of many hands—those who have come before us and whose works are cited throughout; those whose names are printed herein as the authors; and others who gave assistance, advice, and criticism as the text was being developed. We would like especially to thank Elizabeth Johnson (Indiana University), Saundra Taylor (formerly of Indiana University), Travis McDade (University of Illinois), Margaret VanDoren (formerly DEA), Arnette Payne (Creigthon University), Denny Bumb (OCLC), Mary Elizabeth Wilkie (University of North Carolina), trooper Gary Rozzell (Texas Department of Public Safety), and Barbara Holcomb (Simsbury Bank). Todd Fell (Yale University), a former RBMS Security Committee member, saved the writers considerable aggravation and time by locating and providing copies of needed articles, some of them quite obscure. Fell, Alvan Bregman, and the late Heather Lloyd nurtured the RBMS "Incidents of Theft List," conceived by Susan M. Allen, by compiling contributions to it, all for several years each, which has served as a rich resource. Leslie Overstreet (Smithsonian Institution), one of the stalwarts behind the success of "Reading Room Security and Beyond," a workshop at 39th RBMS Preconference in Washington, DC, 22 June 1998, also provided valuable assistance. Special thanks must also be extended to Pat Taylor, librarian of the Lakeshore Branch of the Llano County Public Library (TX), and her predecessor, Mary A. Warren. They and their colleagues unfailingly provided copies of needed books through interlibrary loan and delivered them to rural Texas.

Dozens of others too numerous to name have also added to this manual by doing such things as answering surveys and questions posed to them personally. Although not named specifically, they have all contributed to this text and merit our gratitude.

~May 2011

Introduction

Anne Marie Lane

Any library...any time...anybody

After the 1999 publication of Bruce A. Shuman's *Library Security and Safety Handbook: Prevention, Policies, and Procedures*, it would have been ideal if thefts dwindled because of new precautions and heightened awareness. Sadly, that has not happen, so this book is another attempt to persuade library staff and administrators, particularly those in special collections, to confront that threat. Of course, the security of libraries and their holdings is not a new concern; it has always been a problem. Some have always wanted to have "pieces of the past," for which many are willing to pay high prices and take great risks. One difference now, however, is that online auction sites allow thieves to sell the objects quickly, which contributes to escalating worldwide theft of library, archival, and museum objects.

The simple fact–for all types of libraries–is that if books, manuscripts, maps, and other materials are stolen, they are no longer available for patron research or enjoyment. Those are losses of cultural heritage. Also, the institutions incur financial losses, not just the value of the missing items, but the replacement costs—if replacements can even be found. Certainly, one cannot replace unique manuscripts. An additional complication in detection is that thieves may not take whole books, but slice out valuable old maps and illustrations. Since the books appear to still be present in the libraries, it is not until they are examined later that the damage is discovered.

A likely scenario in college or school libraries is that of students going through vandalism or shoplifting phases. In institutions where big-ticket items are housed, thefts occasionally have taken place as night break-ins or as armed robberies. In those instances, the institutions were probably surveyed before hand, with attention given to aspects like the presence or absence of security cameras, guards, locked or unlocked areas, understaffing, and lax or strict rules. Occasionally, in situations of betrayed trust, the thefts can actually be "in-house." For whatever reasons, some student assistants, volunteers, staff, curators, archivists, librarians, and administrators find themselves tempted to steal. Those are the cases that are the most disheartening.

In special collections libraries, the usual scenario is that of amateur or professional rare book and manuscript thieves who know exactly what items they want, and who have searched catalogues to know which institutions have them. These people sometimes gain the confidence of library staff by conducting themselves as personable booklovers or knowledgeable researchers. Then, after looking at the materials, they hide the desired objects on their person and boldly walk out the door. It appears that sometimes such thieves are actually working for others who desire specific items. Other times they sell the items themselves on the antiquarian market for profit. In some cases, the stolen objects are found in their homes because they simply want to possess them.

Some thieves are not caught, and the material is never recovered. Other thieves are apprehended–especially if the library staff is quick to report the losses to the police, to other libraries, to local antiquarian booksellers, and others. Despite potential institutional embarrassment, that is a critical step. It is important because thefts can be solved if someone recognizes a stolen object being offered for sale by someone on the Internet, to an auction house, or to a bookseller. Booksellers are often very helpful allies in these situations. Punishment does vary by state. To see what individual state laws say about library theft–if they specify at all–see the RBMS Security Committee's online listing at www.rbms.info/committees/security/state_laws.

To find out more about individual cases, the RBMS Security Committee's online summary of international library theft reports, from 1987 to the present, is at www.rbms.info/committees/security/theft_reports/. The site can be searched by year or by keyword. The last feature is useful when one is trying to track the names of specific thieves or institutions, especially if the incident occurred in one year, but the person did not stand trial until years later.

The RBMS Security Committee's theft reports are disturbing evidence of the pressing need for library staff to enforce effective security measures, especially in protecting special collections of great historical and financial value. Those theft reports demonstrate how *any library* can find itself vulnerable at *any time* from practically *anybody*.

Why Security?

Everett C. Wilkie, Jr.

> Every great book has been stolen at least once. That's how we know it's a great book.
> ~*Attributed to A.S.W. Rosenbach*

Unlike most people and the weather, rare book and manuscript librarians not only talk about security, but they also actually try to do something about it. Security issues emerged late in the last century and early in this one as one of the more pressing problems facing institutions holding rare and unique materials as wave after wave of thefts, some of them spectacular generating spectacular wide media attention, washed over them. No longer content to hush up the losses in hopes that word of them did not spread, several institutions responded in a vocal, aggressive way to the thieves, some of whom were actually sent to prison because of the thefts. The legacy of the late William Moffett, who was practically the first modern librarian to try to run a rare book thief to earth, grew stronger as more of his colleagues decided it better to follow his example to attempt to make the public aware of such thefts and of their costs in cultural and economic losses. As a result, not only were law enforcement officers, prosecutors, and judges convinced that the thieves were a real threat to society, many in the media and the wider public became sympathetic, as the popularity of such publications as W. Thomas Taylor's *Texfake* (1991), Nicholas Basbanes' *A Gentle Madness* (1995), Miles Harvey's *Island of Lost Maps* (2001), and Kim Martineau's articles on E. Forbes Smiley in the Hartford Courant (2007) demonstrate. No longer is a book or manuscript stolen from a special collections library just a special type of "overdue book."

Such a climate made special collections library security programs more of a priority than they had ever been. Many institutions examined their security programs and initiated changes. Such decisions, however, are complicated. The decision to implement a serious security program in a special collections library involves complex determinations concerning pecuniary, property, privacy, and people considerations. Those considerations apply to everything from new patron registration forms to an access control system to a marking program. Successfully addressing each of these will determine in large measure if a security program accomplishes its goal of preserving materials from theft or damage and of recovering them if they are alienated somehow.

Probably the greatest deterrent to a successful security program is the pecuniary consideration. Although all the money in the world will not ensure the success of a security program, the lack of enough of it probably will. Even the most basic services, such as a burglar alarm system, require an initial and ongoing outlay of funds. More complex systems, such as detailed special collections cataloguing, access control, and CCTV, can cost thousands of dollars in start-up and ongoing costs. Systems integrating several security functions can cost even more. Persuading an institution's administration that such outlays are necessary, especially if no serious incident has ever happened at it, can be difficult. While it is probably true that most institutions have a basic physical security system, such as a burglar alarm, few are able to muster or to commit the resources necessary to protect against the wide array of threats that can be posed by thieves. When one factors in other expenditures such as personnel time, overhead, and indirect costs, even implementing a computerized patron registration system or a shelf reading program can be expensive. Less expensive improvements, such as creating new and better patron registration materials or new charge slips, can involve expenses beyond the budgets of some institutions. Even a security program that depends on nothing but the eyes and ears of library personnel must somehow come up with the funds to pay those people.

Property is a complex issue in a security scenario. Reduced to its basic level, property in this context usually means the institution's books, manuscripts, archives, maps, artifacts, and other such materials. Most repositories, however, have more property at stake than is readily apparent. One often overlooked area involves data, especially that in on-line catalogues, and access to it. Another is financial materials or other administrative records, such as patron registration, financial archives, and accession records. Computers are often another type of vulnerable property. Numerous institutions in their considerations of securing their property fail to consider all the types of special collections property they could potentially lose, including those embodied solely in electronic form. As any law enforcement officer can attest, almost anything can be stolen, and usually someone is out there with a creative way and the will to do just that.

A security program will always entail a loss of somebody's privacy. In many ways, privacy issues can be controversial ones in implementing any security system, especially those involving access control and CCTV. On any level, though, almost any security system is going to make some record of what somebody is doing, even if it is something so basic as recording that John cut off the alarm system at 8:05 a.m. instead of 8:00 a.m. More aggressive systems can record practically everything a person does on the premises during the day. Usually it is the level of privacy that becomes an issue, or rather the level of loss of privacy. Even very basic security procedures such as registering patrons require them to surrender personal information about themselves. Whereas almost any person may walk into a public library, consult materials, photocopy them, and leave in perfect anonymity, such a case is rarely true in a special collections setting. Background checks may require employees to surrender a good deal of personal information, for example. Privacy issues will need to be weighed heavily in any security consideration and can sometimes prove controversial.

People are really the only element that matter in a security system. Individuals make the choices that lead to thefts, and other individuals make the choices that stop them. If the former group were not a problem, the latter group could sleep well at night. The sum of individual attitudes often comprises an institution's security outlook; in other cases, it is the force of a dominant personality or a strong leader that does so. In reality, all security decisions are psychological, much like one's choice of a spouse–often illogical and filled with component parts of intellectual appreciation, despair, joy, and gut reactions. A security systems salesperson once called on a convenience store run by a middle-aged Korean couple. The husband was not interested in a security system, stating that he was an ex-colonel in the Republic of Korea Army and had no fear of "punks." When asked if he was present at all times and if his diminutive wife shared his prowess, his eyes clouded for a moment with doubt, and he purchased a system with a panic button for her. That incident is a typical microcosm of the types of thinking and reactions that will enter into any consideration of a security system, whether for a convenience store or a special collections repository.

Security is fundamentally an attitude. No librarian involved in security wants to embody Togo's famous maxim: "We have met the enemy and he is us." An institution through its personnel, equipment, and procedures either does or does not embody security to some degree. All the good intentions and equipment in the world will make little security difference if the will to act, for example, is lacking. Thus, each employee in an institution from library pages to board members must ask themselves personally, "Why security?" That same question must also be asked by users themselves, who often bear the brunt of security measures. It is not so much the posing of the question that raises the problems; it is the answers to it.

We hope in this volume not only to raise some questions but also to provide some potential answers. In the end, however, any influence our efforts have on security will rest with individuals working at hundreds of libraries across the nation entrusted with safeguarding our mutual cultural heritage and who hold security in their hands.

General Considerations

Everett C. Wilkie, Jr.

And while the sun and moon endure
Luck's a chance, but trouble's sure,
I'd face it as a wise man would,
And train for ill and not for good.
~*A. E. Housman*

Institutional preparations before a theft are the most important measures to prevent thefts and to facilitate recovering stolen materials. The basic problem is that the special collections library, whether a stand-alone entity or part of a larger institution, must have coordinated policies agreed upon by the entire organization, including any governing board. Confusing, contradictory attitudes and actions not only facilitate thieves but also make recovery efforts more difficult if not downright embarrassing publicly.[1] For any effective security program to be workable, the engagement and cooperation of the uppermost levels of administration are necessary.

The most basic decision—and one that is ironically sometimes the most difficult to achieve—is that the institution must take security considerations seriously in the first place. In a climate where scarce resources are often thought to be better allocated towards cataloguing, exhibitions, or acquisitions, security is sometimes given short shrift on the theory and hope that nothing untoward will ever happen. Although nearly every library will have a disaster plan for prevention and recovery from events such as water pipes bursting, many institutions are ill-prepared for thefts, either to prevent them or to follow up if one happens. As Susan M. Allen correctly remarks:

> For a number of years I have argued that the theft or mutilation of books, archival materials, and/or manuscripts from a library or archive is a disaster much like an earthquake or a fire. It is likely to sneak upon you quietly and without notice. The resulting disaster from theft or mutilation may be as devastating as any natural disaster for an institution's collections and staff morale. Just as water-soaked materials caused by a hurricane or flood are certain to be lost forever if timely action is not taken to treat them, so stolen materials will be lost forever if timely action is not taken to attempt to recover them and to stop the thief from any future activity. It would be well to ask questions about theft and incorporate theft into a disaster plan as an unfortunate circumstance to rank with those of a more natural origin.[2]

In more general terms, Trinkhaus-Randall describes the permeation of staff life that security should assume, an attitude that should originate in the upper levels of administration:

> Since security should be a component of every staff person's position description and should be addressed in all interviews of potential staff persons, it should be at least partially ingrained in each person's modus operandi. Security is not just fancy locks,

motion detectors, fire alarms, sprinklers and other fire suppression devices; it is a state of mind that should permeate a repository's operations. All the fancy devices in the world will serve little if the policies, procedures, and activities of the repository are lax and present a "devil-may-care" attitude to researchers.[3]

Although such things as floods cannot necessarily be prevented, many thefts can be stopped, and the library needs to do all it can to prevent them. That attitude needs to be preceded, however, by the realization that *any* special collections library has items someone is going to want to steal and that sooner or later someone will probably show up to do just that.

The most basic administrative step in special collections security is that every institution must have one person in charge of overall security. This person is normally referred to as the Library Security Officer (LSO), and administration should be urged to appoint one and to set up a program of library security. The LSO may be drawn from any department of the library. As logical as it may seem, for example, that a curator would fulfill this function, other personnel from such places as acquisitions, cataloguing, and conservation also fulfill the role in some instances. The chief professional attributes of an LSO are that s/he must be aware of current security practices and be creative about implementing them in the institution, knowing there will be constraints on what can be done. No matter what this person's position in the organization, s/he must be in a position to manage changes, make decisions that will be enforced, and have access to fiscal resources to implement security decisions. It does little good to have an LSO whose only authority is that of persuasion and who does not command the confidence and cooperation of

those higher up in the administration. An LSO who is window dressing is about as effective as a dummy camera or a toothless guard dog. Any LSO needs, nevertheless, to take this statement as both a mantra and a guide: "Preventing theft in libraries is a difficult and complicated problem."[4]

The LSO would ideally chair a security group for the institution, whose members would need to be drawn from various departments and activities, such as acquisitions, public relations, cataloguing, or maintenance. Every aspect of a rare book and manuscript library has some potential security problem, and the committee needs to be as representative as possible of the institution itself so that potential vulnerabilities are not overlooked. The chief administrative officer of the institution also needs to be a member and to attend the meetings. This committee would be the one in charge of making security decisions, recommending changes, and planning for reactions to theft. Ideally, it would document all security concerns and decisions, and provide a written security guide for the library.[5] Failure to formulate a written security policy is a basic security lapse.

Several constituencies will concern the LSO. First, the LSO and the committee need to be proactive in making contact with the people who will investigate thefts. The time to become acquainted with the proper law enforcement agencies is before a theft occurs, not after. Depending on the library's situation, that agency may be the campus security service, the town's police force, the sheriff's department, or another specialized police organization. Those agencies are usually quite willing to visit the library to share mutual concerns and to make security recommendations. Every library should be on speaking terms with the people who will be called upon to help in case of theft and should make every effort to educate them about the seriousness of such incidents.[6] If at all possible, the LSO should make the acquaintance of someone at command level in the responding department.

A second group with whom the library needs to make regular contact is any physical security consultants the library uses. Normally, this would be the company that provides the institution's physical security barriers, such as burglar alarms or access control systems. Such people are often quite well versed in the latest security products and can recommend changes and upgrades as appropriate. They can also do limited security surveys to determine gaps in coverage, usually at no charge. Recommendations from these consultants should be taken seriously. Unfortunately, one of the stumbling blocks often encountered here is the need to spend money to provide physical security. Lack of will to spend money in this area often forces the library to limp along on outmoded, insufficient equipment, or no equipment at all. Despite society's often ingrained suspicion of salespeople, no reputable security company will make unreasonable or unnecessary recommendations for expenditures merely to line its own pockets. One must bear in mind, however, that good security apparatus is neither free nor necessarily cheap.

A third group the library needs to contact is an outside security consultant. A general security survey should be undertaken and repeated at various intervals, say, after a major renovation or after a decade has lapsed. Such a survey will probably take several days but should result in a written document that will inform the library's security decisions. Because such people have usually seen numerous library operations, they are often in a position to bring viewpoints and judgments not obvious to library staff. Their qualifications and references should, however, be carefully checked before they are allowed to do any work.[7]

A fourth group the library needs to contact is the antiquarian book trade. If there is a theft, the library's materials may quickly end up in the hands of booksellers; thus, at a minimum the library needs a personal acquaintance with those in its immediate area insofar as possible and with those farther afield who deal in materials such as the library owns. The library may also need to employ these people periodically to make appraisals of its materials. Such appraisals are useful since they highlight materials that may need special attention because of their commercial value and so that if they are stolen an accurate idea of their value can be readily communicated to law enforcement. That value often has a bearing on the type of investigation launched or whether an arrest is affected on the spot.[8]

A subgroup of the antiquarian book trade that also needs to concern the library are auction houses. Establishing relationships with the major houses is usually difficult since they are often involved only in selling materials. Distressingly, several of them have been involved in selling materials of dubious origins. On-line auction venues are even more problematic since there is no real oversight of consignments. Some institutions have established programs whereby monitors watch certain auctions for troublesome materials. At the very least, if the library has suffered a theft, auction venues should be carefully watched, a job made somewhat easier by the fact that most catalogues are now available free electronically.

A fifth group, often overlooked in larger institutions, are the general library staff and any other staff, such as maintenance people or contractors, who work in the library. The LSO and the committee need to communicate routinely with those important constituencies to impress upon them the importance of good security and to inform them of security measures being implemented and the reasons for them. Brief presentations at general staff meetings, for example, are one way to inform and encourage cooperation and interest. All staff are the first line of security for any institution and should never be overlooked. If renovation work is planned, the library's security policies must be rethought somewhat and explained clearly to architects, contractors, and others. Finally, the library will need to consider restraints and problems that may be presented by union contracts and other such labor negotiating instruments. Searching bags and belongings when employees exit a building, for example, can be controversial.

Aside from being on good terms with various important constituencies, the LSO and the security committee also have the tasks of ranking actions necessary for security and advocating personnel and funding to accomplish them. Those actions will vary by institution. For example, if the library has no special collections cataloguing backlog, the priority might be establishing a systematic shelf-reading program. If the institution has never applied ownership marks to its materials, doing so might become a priority. Such decisions can often involve difficult compromises. Some argue, for example, when the discussion involves cataloguing, "Less is more."[9] That point of view states that it is more important to have a cataloguing record, no matter how brief, than to delay cataloguing materials because standards are so high that work cannot be accomplished rapidly, leaving materials sitting in a backlog untouched, unknown, unused, and at risk of being stolen. Because large backlogs are a security hazard, the LSO might find herself or himself up against the cataloguing department in trying to balance the need for speed as opposed to thoroughness. A proposal to search the general stacks for special materials that should be transferred might also involve considerable time and expense.[10] Many library activities have security implications not always obvious to others, and the LSO should be regularly consulted on proposed projects and activities.[11]

A vigorous LSO and a strong security committee can work in many positive ways to raise awareness of security issues to the library administration. Thefts often have repercussions beyond mere loss of materials. Any administrator, if nothing else, wants to avoid the public embarrassment and staff demoralization a theft would cause. In some cases, library thefts have caused staff members to be demoted, reassigned, or fired. Administrators need to be convinced that it is far simpler, cheaper, and easier to invest in adequate security measures and to ensure that those measures are funded sufficiently to make them effective, while recognizing, nonetheless, that no security system is foolproof.[12]

If all preparations have been made before a security breach, the same must be made in the eventualities that a theft is discovered either in progress or after the fact. The former situation is no doubt the more challenging because the threat is real and present. If the LSO and security committee have done their work properly, there will be arrangements in place to deal with a theft in progress. The most basic decision involved in this instance is whether to call law enforcement to the scene. That decision, above all others, requires some type of administrative approval before it becomes necessary, and should be discussed thoroughly with management and a plan of action agreed upon. A library needs to also be familiar with its own state laws concerning thefts, which often govern what actions a library may take if it suspects a theft is occurring. Deciding what to do is one of the important decisions that must be made if a theft is in progress. It is far too late to worry about the situation if a patron is walking out the door with a manuscript but one has no idea if one can legally detain the person.

As a corollary, deciding what to do if the theft proves to be genuine is also a serious administrative consideration. After the Johns Hopkins Library apprehended Gilbert Bland, he was released immediately upon payment of damages for a sum that was decided on and paid on the spot. That proved to be a mistake. At the very least, if a thief is reasonably believed to have stolen library materials, s/he should be detained and his/her identity confirmed. That aspect of thefts is one of the reasons law enforcement should be familiar with the library and its holdings and that appraisals of materials should be in hand. Such a procedure, however, requires the cooperation and understanding of both the library administration and other entities, such as counsel, to implement. A discussion of what to do when confronted by an active thief is one that the library needs to have made well before a decision has to be made on the spot.[13] To their credit, for example, Yale police arrested Smiley when library staff said the institution would press charges.[14] The library does need to bear in mind, however, that any decision to arrest a suspect lies with the police officer.

What to do after a theft is another aspect of security that needs to be considered well beforehand. In the past, many libraries concealed thefts, but such a procedure is no longer conscionable. Professional guidelines recommend that thefts be given publicity, not only to stop further depredations but also to educate the public about the problem. For example, despite the fact that Johns Hopkins released Bland, their subsequent publicity about his activities brought an abrupt end to his career and alerted other libraries to his activities.[15] In any case, however, the library needs administrative support for whatever course of action it chooses to pursue, whether it is to conceal the incident or to publicize it.[16] If the institution has a public relations department, that entity will also need to part of the planning well before the fact.

Administrators also need the will to act upon internal security breaches. Staff or volunteers who ignore or short-circuit security measures need to be dealt with firmly, and upper level administra-

tors need to understand that any such disciplinary actions are not based on whim or caprice. In the case of convicted book thief Mimi Meyer at the University of Texas–Austin, she was dismissed after it was discovered she had a book in her office that she had taken from the stacks without proper documentation.[17] That action probably saved the library further losses, as it turned out later.

Building administrative support for adequate special collection security measures can, regrettably, be a hard sell. Faced with the need to upgrade the on-line catalogue or fund an adequate shelf-reading scheme for special collections, few administrators are going to choose the latter. In some cases, the LSO may be cut off from governing bodies, such as a board of trustees or the provost, and have no opportunity to present security concerns directly to them. In many ways, the attitude is systemic and inherited. Almost no library school or any other post-graduate institute teaches students systematically about security and its importance, preferring instead to educate them about such topics as "Internet Issues and Future Initiatives" or "Managing Serials in an Electronic Age." Rarely a word in any of it is to be found about how to hold on to what you have and the importance of doing so. Indeed, most library school students graduate without ever having had a single whiff of security subjects or how to value books, although they should be required. As Thompson, discussing thefts from public library shelves of valuable books, wryly remarks, "Many choice items might be enjoying a better fate today if our library schools had given a bit more instruction in this type of diagnostics."[18] In an ironic twist to the situation, one of the reasons such courses are not taught is precisely because they have not been emphasized for so long that there are few people left qualified to teach them, even if there were demand for them.[19] An analysis of rare book and special collections job ads that appeared on Exlibris over the past several years has not re-vealed a single one, for example, that required any substantial knowledge of security, most preferring such things as "knowledge of OCLC and Voyager" and "excellent communication skills." It is little wonder that we are now faced with a generation of administrators who believe adequate security is an unnecessary expense or a bother, to be ignored in favor of more glamorous programs such as electronic serials, until their hands get slammed in the door by a theft from their library. While not discounting the many things necessary to the modern library, the most important role that an LSO and a security committee can assume is to educate administrators and others about the vital role of security in the proper functioning of the library system and the institution. As Gill remarks, any successful security program is going to depend on "the senior management team showing strong support for the security operation."[20]

Although perhaps somewhat arcane, special-ized topics, everybody who works in special collec-tions, from the administration on down, needs to be generally familiar with "Concept of Risk" and "Risk Management." The latter is defined as "the systematic process of managing an organization's risk exposures to achieve its objectives in a man-ner consistent with public interest, human safety, environmental factors, and the law. It consists of the planning, organizing, leading, coordinating, and controlling activities undertaken with the intent of providing an efficient *pre-loss plan* that minimizes the adverse impact of risk on the organization's resources, earnings, and cash flows" (emphasis added).[21] The concept of risk management is a well-studied topic in the business and insurance worlds and of great concern to governing bodies in those environments. Although not very much applied in library settings, the concepts inherent in it would probably prevent many security problems from

arising in the first place if administrators applied them to special collections. Among problems po-tentially avoided by a competent risk management plan are "Excessive time spent by managers and boards in dealing with unanticipated losses, thus detracting from other important concerns," and "Deterioration of public image and loss of custom-ers because of actions offending societal norms."[22] Those problems certainly occur after every major library theft, as the machinations and problems fol-lowing the Spiegelman and Smiley fallouts clearly demonstrate. As the American Risk and Insurance Association concludes, "Simply buying insurance has not solved risk management problems for de-cades."[23] Courses in risk management are usually readily available at any major university, and if nothing else, an institution's insurance company may be happy to instruct staff and administration on the concept and to undertake surveys that ana-lyze an institution's security risks.[24]

The "Concept of Risk" is a widely discussed idea positing in one instance that people do not evaluate risk in rational, statistical terms, a fallacy that gener-ally does not intrude on the thinking of institutions such as insurance companies. A person will often perceive risk in emotional terms rather than ratio-nal ones, for instance. A common example of such thinking is the person afraid to fly who would rather drive to a destination, although the former mode of transportation is by far safer and more reliable, and carries much less statistical risk. As quizzical as it may seem, for example, "as the number of li-brarians increases, the magnitude of the crime and disruption also tends to increase," a proposition that seems almost counterintuitive but which serves as a classic example of proper risk analysis.[25] In special collections libraries, faulty lines of thinking often get translated into such statements as, "We've never had any problems here before," "We've always done it this way," or "Nobody would steal from us."

Such thinking is complacent and dangerous, and the LSO should seek to educate administrators that any library, including this one, is at risk for theft. Seeking to raise the administration's awareness of this issue can be a complicated process, but basically the strategy should be to demonstrate that thefts happen and that they can happen in this library, too, unless measures are taken to forestall the event. As Keller remarks,

> Work with your local police and fire officials, your security consultant or even some of your security contractors and vendors, to compile statistics that may support your case that risk is real. Think of creative ways…which re-state risk in a manner your boss can understand. Most important, make your boss aware that risk CAN be managed. Too many people tend to ignore–or hide from–risks that they feel they can't control. They feel that if they ignore a risk, it will go away. They are aware that a problem exists and that there will be consequences if the disaster occurs. But they kid themselves about the likelihood of the problem occurring. By identifying the risk and assessing the criticality of the risk occurring, you can target risks objectively. Which risk is more likely to occur? Which has the greatest impact if it does occur? This process helps you decide where to devote limited resources and offers your boss a real solution to the problem of managing risks.[26]

The Library Administration and Management Association places the evaluation of risk squarely in the hands of the library's administration, stating that "Library Directors" should be responsible for "anticipating, and taking measures to prevent predictable losses such as minor vandalism, injuries, theft of library materials or library user property, utility interruptions, and the non-return of items borrowed from the collection" and should seek external consultation to identify "any high threat sites within the library and any collections, furnishings, or equipment with unusually high value in order to anticipate and prevent security program inadequacies."[27] Raising the administrator's awareness of such responsibilities is something that the LSO should undertake.[28]

Numerous institutions have purchased insurance to cover collections losses from all sources, including thefts. As hinted at above, however, the mere fact that one has purchased insurance should not make one all the more complacent in regards to collections security and risk management. In fact, if insurance is in place, the institution should be all the more vigilant to prevent any losses. In some cases, the total monetary value of special collections seems to exceed already the total value of all the library's general collections.[29] A properly planned security program that correctly contemplates risk management will provide for periodic updates of the monetary value of special collections and provide adequate insurance for them before the need arises.[30] Although one often hears the arguments that special collections are "priceless," "cannot be replaced," and "cannot be valued," such arguments are specious. Monetary values can, in fact, be placed on any special collection item by a competent appraiser, despite whatever priceless intellectual value the item may have and despite the fact that there can never be duplicate of it.[31] If some huge disaster or theft befalls the library, the institution is going to be far better off if it can, for example, receive a settlement of $1,000,000, even if it cannot replace some of the unique materials lost. Such an amount of money would at least enable the library to relaunch an acquisition program immediately rather than merely staring down a black hole with no funds to make up the loss.[32]

Conclusion

E. Forbes Smiley plundered nearly $3,000,000 worth of materials, and even that was a mere pittance of the total value of materials at the institutions from which he stole. He was preceded by James Shinn, Stephen C. Blumberg, Daniel Spiegelman, and a host of others. Allen reported in 1997 that of all thefts reported between 1987–1994 that 12% were from public libraries; 21% from research libraries, state historical societies, archives, and museums; 46% from academic libraries; and 21% from book-sellers and private collectors. She also reported a sharp spike in thefts between 1991–1994. Although conceding that better reporting may be responsible for the statistical rise, Allen concludes, "this trend is still not one that anyone would wish to see."[33] Even investments in security of only a small fraction of the amount Smiley and the others stole would go a long way towards preserving our common heritage. Building institutional administrative support for adequate security measures is one of the more daunting tasks facing those in the rare book and manuscript profession and, regrettably, one of the more difficult. In too many instances, thieves do more than LSO's can to justify security's ways to man.[34]

NOTES

1. See, for example, Bill Panagopulos, "More re Jefferson Davis-Transylvania U. Theft" (Exlibris, 23 May 2008).

2. Susan M. Allen, "Preventing Theft in Academic Libraries and Special Collections," *Library & Archival Security*, v. 14, #1 (1997): 29–30. See also Allen's article, "Theft in Libraries or Archives," *C&RL News* 51 (1990): 939–43

3. Gregor Thrinkhaus-Randall, "Library and Archival Security: Policies and Procedures to Protect Holdings from Theft and Damage," in Robert K. O'Neill, ed., *Management of Library and Archival Security: From the Outside Looking In* (New York & London: Haworth, 1998), 111.

4. Allen, "Preventing," 42. Robert B. Burke and Sam Adeloye, *A Manual of Basic Museum Security* (Leicester: International Council of Museums, 1986), briefly discuss the functions and responsibilities of a chief security officer: "Every museum should have a staff member appointed as its chief security officer–even if this employee must be designated to act as chief security officer in addition to other duties. The chief security officer would be charged with planning, organizing, coordinating, and controlling all permanent and incidental security measures and would be consulted on all matters having any influence on security, such as special exhibitions, renovations, and the appointment of new staff and would advise the museum director in all matters of security. To ease decision making and to keep responsibilities clear, there should be a direct line of authority from the museum director to the chief security officer. The security chief should maintain constant communications not only with the museum director, but also with other key museum staff members" (7). On the other hand, Pamela Cravey, *Protecting Library Staff, Users, Collections, and Facilities: A How-To-Do-It Manual* (New York & London: Neal-Schuman, 2001), suggests that there be two LSO's in libraries with a separate special collections department (110–111).

5. Vincent A. Totka, Jr., "Preventing Patron Theft in the Archives: Legal Perspectives and Problems," *American Archivist* 56 (Fall 1993), discovered that of the institutions he surveyed, *"none"* of the repositories had a written security policy" (original emphasis; 666).

6. This point is forcefully made by Bryan Hanley, "Crime Prevention," Australian Institute of Criminology. Art Crime, Protecting Art, Protecting Artists, and Protecting Consumers Conference (2–3 December 1999): 6. : http://www.aic.gov.au/conferences/artcrime/hanleycp.pdf.

7. See Steven R. Keller, "Hiring a Consultant: Clearing up Cloudy Skies" (1998): http://www.museum-security.org/consult.html and John J. Fay, ed., *Encyclopedia of Security Management*, 2nd ed. (Burlington: Butterworth-Heinemann, 2007), 467–73.

8. Hanley urges that institutions "Regularly assess and update the value of property. Current values of property if stolen or damaged are very important in criminal prosecution…" (5).

9. For a recent statement of this argument, see Mark A. Greene and Dennis Meissner. "More Product, Less Process: Revamping Traditional Archival Processing," *American Archivist* 68 (2005): 208–63.

10. See ACRL *Guidelines on the Selection of General Collection Materials for Transfer to Special Collections* (Chicago: ACRL, 2008). http://www.ala.org/ala/acrl/acrlstandards/selectransfer.cfm.

11. A list of potential security-related concerns is suggested in RBMS/ACRL *Guidelines Regarding Thefts in Libraries* (Chicago: ACRL, 2003), section G.

12. Even if all materials are eventually recovered, every successful theft proves to be highly embarrassing, if nothing else. See, for example, the reported reactions of the staff in Poland's Jagiellonian Library as reported in: Monica Scislowska, "Rare Books Stolen from University in Poland: Missing Manuscripts Humiliate Famous School," seattlepi.com (13 November 1999) http://seattlepi.nwsource.com/national/pole13.shtml.

13. See the 8 December 1995 message from Cynthia H. Requardt of Johns Hopkins University in which the school's reasoning for releasing Gilbert Bland was explained (http://palimpsest.stanford.edu/byform/mailing-lists/exlibris/1995/12/msg00054.html). At the subsequent RBMS 1998 "Reading Room Security and Beyond" security conference in Washington, DC, a member of Johns Hopkins University counsel gave more detailed reasons for the decision to release Bland in exchange for immediate restitution. One of those reasons was that the Baltimore police could hardly have been persuaded to arrest him, given the number of other, more serious crimes with which they had to deal.

14. Email to author, 20 July 2007.

15. See the 7 December 1995 Exlibris message from Cynthia H. Requardt of Johns Hopkins University in which Bland's identity was announced and warning given about his activities (http://palimpsest.stanford.edu/byform/mailing-lists/exlibris/1995/12/msg00046.html). This was the message that alerted the library community to this thief and led to his arrest.

16. The library world was shocked to discover that British book thief Farhad Hakimzadeh, convicted of stealing from the British Library, had already been caught stealing materials at the Royal Asiatic Society twelve years before, a theft that had been kept quiet by mutual agreement between him and the library. See Sandra Laville, "Book World's Silence Helps Tome Raiders," *The Guardian* (2 February 2009).: http://www.guardian.co.uk/uk/2009/feb/02/antiquarian-book-theft-library-crime.

17. Based on personal conversations with HRHRC staff, 2006.

18. Lawrence S. Thompson, *Bibliokleptomania* (Berkeley: Peacock, 1968), 33.

19. ACRL *Competencies for Special Collections Professionals* (Chicago: ACRL, 2008) does state in section II, "Fundamental Competencies," that all special collections librarians should have an "Understanding of security and preservation needs of original objects, both in storage and during use." Ironically, however, later in the document under section III, "Specialized competencies," only those in public service are required to have any knowledge of security. Those in the areas of "Management, Supervision, and Administration" are required to have "Knowledge of physical environments and facilities optimal for long-term preservation, security, and use of special collections materials." Otherwise the word "security" does not appear in the document, and despite wide agreement that security is an aspect of practically everyone's work in special collections, those working, for example, in "Promotion and Outreach," "Technology," and "Processing and Cataloguing" do not seem to require any such specialized knowledge as it affects their activities. One exception to the lack of security training is Travis McDade's course, "Rare Books, Crime, and Punishment," offered through the Midwest Book and Manuscript Studies program. In 1992, an SAA preconference workshop entitled "Security in Archives and Manuscripts Respositories" was met with such enthusiasm that it was cancelled for lack of interest. On the other hand, a 1998 RBMS Preconference seminar on thefts held in the wake of the Bland thefts was over-subscribed. Such contradictory outcomes seem to be a reflection of the unfortunate ebb and flo of responses to security risks, which seem to run in cycles rather than being a consistent concern.

20. Martin Gill, "Security in Libraries: Matching Responses to Risks," *Liber Quarterly* 18 (September 2008): 102.

21. American Risk and Insurance Association, "Risk Management." http://www.museum-security.org/riskmanagement-insurance.html. That phrasing is just one of many. For other definitions, see Mary Breighner, William Payton, and Jeanne M. Drewes, *Risk and Insurance Management Manual for Libraries* (Chicago: American Library Association, 2005), 2.

22. Gill 102

23. Ibid

24. Some such courses are even available on-line. In May, 2008, for example, Solinet offered such a course entitled "Risk Management: Knowing Your Responsibility."

25. Alan Jay Lincoln, *Crime in the Library" A Study of Patterns, Impact, and Security* (New York & London: Bowker, 1984), 117. It is also true that larger libraries have more materials to steal. Another unwelcome risk of increased library electronic security was the rise of materials mutilations as thieves sought to defeat such measures. See S. B. Watstein, "Book Multilation: An

Unwelcome Byproduct of Electronic Security Systems," *Library & Archival Security* 5 (1983): 11–33.

26. Seth R. Keller, "Understanding Risks." http://www.museum-security.org/keller/la.html.

27. *Library Security Guidelines Document*, June 7, 2001," (Chicago: American Library Association, 2007). http://www.ala.org/ala/lama/lamapublications/librarysecurity.htm#loss.

28. At the very least, all library administrators should be familiar with Mary Breighner, William Payton, and Jeanne M. Drewes, *Risk and Insurance Management Manual for Libraries* (Chicago: American Library Association, 2005). See also Bruce A. Shuman, *Library Security and Safety Handbook: Prevention, Policies, and Procedures* (Chicago: American Library Association, 1999), 109–48. For a recent overview and analysis of faulty thinking patterns, see Dan Ariely, *Predictably Irrational: The Hidden Forces that Shape our Decisions* (New York: Harper, 2008), passim.

29. An informal survey done in December, 2007, asked librarians whose special collections were part of a larger institution's holdings (e.g., college and university libraries) if that situation could be true at their libraries. Several were quite positive that the monetary value of special collections already outweighed that of the general collections. Others noted that since special collections continued to collect real materials eventually the monetary value of those collections would also overhaul the equivalent value of the general library collections, especially since more and more of the latter were being built on electronic resources that the library does not actually own but to which it only purchases access. Writing against a background of an institution where acquisition funds are apparently not hedged in by endowment and donor restrictions, William H. Wisner, *Wither the Postmodern Library? Libraries, Technology, and Education in the Information Age* (Jefferson & London: McFarland, 2000), laments: "And of course there is now little extra money remaining to buy books, in the social sciences or any other discipline. After spending so much on technology, you'd have to have the oratorical powers of Cicero to squeeze another dime out of the powers that be" (15). In a development that may spread, David Abel, "Welcome to the Library: Say Good-bye to Books," Boston.com (2 September 2009), reports that Cushing Academy, a prep school, has decided to do away with almost all of its books to concentrate on electronic resources of various kinds. The only physical books the library will retain are some children's books and some rare books. Part of the rationale for that action was that the school's studies indicated almost no students were using the 20,000 books. http://www.boston.com/news/local/massachusetts/articles/2009/09/04/a_library_without_the_books/.

30. Breighner, Payton & Drewes recommend that special collections materials be appraised separately because, "By their nature, these items present unique problems when trying to establish values" (27–28). Because of some of the problems inherent in dealing with loss of unique or very valuable materials, they also recommend, "It is critical to focus on protection rather than insurance for these library assets" (71).

31. Breighner, Payton, & Drewes observe in relation to such materials, "When an item is irreplacable and there is no ready market for similar items, the value may be purely arbitrary and may depend on whether the proposed value is reasonable and how much premium the library is willing to pay for insurance" (71).

32. William H. Walters, "Journal Prices, Book Acquisitions, and Sustainable College Library Collections," *College & Research Libraries* 69(November 2008), convincingly argues that one strategy to help "undergraduate colleges build and maintain sustainable library collections" is to "emphasize books rather than journals" (580). Breighner, Payton & Drewes argue that it is important to determine appraised, base-line values *before* a loss occurs (89).

33. Allen, "Preventing," 31–32.

34. In many cases, the aftermath of a major theft sets off a round of probably long-deferred security upgrades that, had they been in place earlier, might have prevented the theft in the first place. Bland confessed to the University of Delaware police, for example, that he did not steal from places with CCTV systems. After Smiley's thefts were discovered, the Boston Public Library spent about $200,000 on security enhancements. See Jenna Russell, "Stolen Maps Find their Way back to Library's Collection," *Boston Globe*, 2 January 2008. http://www.boston.com/news/local/articles/2008/01/02/stolen_rare_maps_find_their_way_back_to_librarys_collection/.

Background Checks

Everett C. Wilkie, Jr. (with contributions from Margaret Tufts Tenney)

Better background checks would help a good deal.
~*Shuman*

While not obviously directly related to the daily operation of rare book or manuscript libraries, the issue of background checks is one pertinent to their security. Almost anybody associated with or with access to materials can steal or mutilate them. Experiences at major American and European institutions unfortunately prove that volunteers and staff members of any rank may be security risks.[1] While it is important to develop an environment of trust between administration and staff employees of special collections libraries, it is vital to realize that this atmosphere may not be a deterrent to significant incidents of theft or vandalism.[2] Since one's judgment of other people may be mistaken, it is wise to develop and enforce written, objective policies and procedures that maximize the safety of rare and special materials and to employ them during the hiring process and periodically over an employee's tenure.[3] As Lincoln properly observes, such checks are "low cost security options."[4] Despite their popularity, however, such checks should be used with caution. A botched one can have serious consequences for the both the institution and the individual.[5]

Every employee of any institution will be subject to some type of background check, even if it so minimal as a personal interview for ten minutes. In a special collections setting, where perhaps extremely valuable materials are at risk, there might be more thorough checks instituted, especially for professional and para-professional staff with ready access to materials. Regrettably, such checks will probably not be done for people such as volunteers, interns, or student workers, although they should be, since experience proves such people also steal materials.[6] Other significant figures associated with the library, such as board members, should also be subjected to such checks but rarely are.

Background checks at their simplest level seek to document a person's trustworthiness for the position about to be assumed. Any number of checks might be performed, some of them controversial and invasive. Many aspects of such checks are controlled or limited by state and federal laws or institutional policy. What an institution chooses to do, therefore, will be a matter of local choice almost exclusively. It may even choose not to perform some checks that it would otherwise be allowed to do if it so elected. In most cases, an applicant's informed consent must be obtained.[7] In almost no case, however, should people be hired merely on the basis of the employer's instincts or feelings about the candidate.[8]

The gamut of such investigations includes the following, among others:

1. Personal statements by applicant
2. Fingerprinting

3. Criminal background check
4. Credit check
5. Investigative consumer report
6. Drug test
7. Polygraph
8. Bonding
9. Psychological Assessment

1. Personal Statements by Applicant

These statements are those included in the cover letter and in the application and its attachments, such as a resume or transcripts. Those documents contain statements about what applicants are saying about themselves and should all be carefully verified since a dishonest or misleading statement at this level is perhaps a direct falsehood. Especially sensitive are the matters of education, employment, and references. Education for all hires should be confirmed by requiring official copies of all transcripts to be sent to the employer at the employer's expense. All employment listed on the application should be verified. Finally, references should be contacted and their evaluations sought. Any discrepancies should be resolved, especially since they may be perfectly innocent on the applicant's part. In many special collections venues, this basic process is about as far as it goes in background checks and is generally applied only to salaried employees.

The nosiness of applications varies wildly. Some ask few pertinent security questions; others ask many. Of special concern to any special collections is going to be whether the applicant has ever been convicted of a crime beyond such matters as parking tickets or minor traffic violations. There should also be a question asking if the applicant has ever been convicted of a crime of "moral turpitude," which does include drunk driving, among darker crimes. A positive answer to any of those questions should not necessarily preclude a candidate from consideration, however. A person convicted

of minor marijuana possession back in 1972 is not necessarily disqualified from a position of trust. A person convicted of embezzlement five years ago may present quite a different problem. As important as it is to inquire about a crime that resulted in conviction, one should be certain to ask if the person is on parole or currently under indictment for anything, although not yet tried or convicted. (See Appendix IV.) Another important question concerns military service; if an applicant has ever been in the military, a copy of the discharge certificate should be required to make sure the discharge was honorable, especially if the institution gives veteran points in the hiring process.

When interviewing prospective employees it is imperative to determine how invested the applicant is or may become in local and professional communities. Student workers, for example, should be asked questions about their studies and school-related activities, about their career plans, and memberships in student associations. The interview should be structured to gain information about the person's background, future plans, and attitudes toward the library's collections. All applicants can be asked about their reasons for wanting to work at the institution. Ethical conflicts—for example, if the applicant is a book or manuscripts collector or dealer—should be considered.

2. Fingerprinting

Fingerprints are a basic way law enforcement tracks people since each person has a unique set of them. Obtaining fingerprints for every person who works in special collections, even volunteers and students, is a wise practice. It is a widely held misconception that obtaining fingerprints results in a record that is held by law enforcement agencies. Such is not the case. Many police departments, for example, hold sessions so that parents can have children fingerprinted, but the prints are returned to the parents and never become useful to law enforcement unless occasion arises for their use, whereupon the parents then supply them. Every hospital takes prints of newborns, none of which are ever turned over to law enforcement agencies unless a need arises. In the case of special collections, having those prints available can be useful in a wide range of applications, from theft investigations to internal security procedures, such as access control systems. If a library intends to conduct criminal background checks on applicants, obtaining them might be necessary. If fingerprints are taken, they must be made by someone qualified to do so.[9]

3. Criminal Background Checks

Criminal background checks are usually conducted by a law enforcement agency or a private firm for the institution. Such checks review criminal convictions on file at various jurisdictions to see if a person has ever been convicted of a crime. More and more, it is being recommended that even such persons as volunteers be subjected to the process, a concern that has arisen in part from problems in the child care industry. Such checks, depending on their thoroughness, will sometimes require fingerprints for checking by the police and will include a name check. Usually as part of this process a so-called Department of Motor Vehicles check is run against the applicant's driver's license. Other parts of such a check might include investigation to determine if an applicant is on a sex offenders registry. These checks are among the more common ones performed in special collections as part of the hiring process.[10]

An adjunct investigation to a criminal background check is a county civil court records check, which may reveal controversial items not of a criminal nature. It should reveal such things as lawsuits filed against or by the applicant and tax liens that have been filed against the applicant. This type of check is almost never used in a special collections

environment, and some of the information will be revealed in a typical credit check, anyway.

4. Credit Checks

Of all the types of background checks, credit checks are among the more common and controversial. One school holds that a person with sound credit is per force more dependable; another holds that such situations as financial disarray have little to do with such matters since the situation could have arisen from any number of factors, such as a serious illness or divorce, none of which are specifically reflected on the report itself.[11] A credit check is probably one of the more invasive checks possible, since it will reveal perhaps deeply personal matters to the institution. Arguably, however, it is plausible that a person with financial problems is more likely to steal to help alleviate such difficulties, although that viewpoint ignores the obvious argument that thieves may have good credit scores because they steal to pay their bills on time. In lieu of an entire credit check, an institution may obtain just an applicant's FICO© score, which is a rough indicator of credit worthiness but does not reveal any financial specifics.[12] One aspect of a credit check is that it is sometimes useful for confirming an applicant's address history. If credit reports are obtained on potential employees, it is vital that they be reviewed by financial experts who can correctly interpret them. In some cases, however, credit checks are useless. Because adverse reports, even bankruptcies, are removed after several years have passed, the credit check is of limited utility and may not reveal the behaviors of a person who may have, for example, defaulted several times.[13] Credit reports received by employers are modified to remove birthdates, spouse's name, and actual account numbers.

In general, for special collections security purposes, credit checks are probably dubious instruments with little predictive value, although they are commonly employed in this venue. Unlike insurance companies and banks, libraries have never developed models that predict a person's behavior in a library situation based on a credit report. Insurance companies are confident, for example, that their special statistical models can predict a person's potential for losses. Banks are equally confident that a credit report and score will accurately predict a person's behavior if a loan is granted. Libraries have no such model, so one must wonder what predictive value a credit report could have. Without knowing for certain, one may conjecture that Clive Driver probably had a good credit rating and that Benjamin Johnson probably had a mediocre one, given his age. Both stole from their libraries, however.

Close adjuncts to a classic credit report are the Consumer Report and the Employment Credit Report, both performed to reveal financial information of a type not shown by a credit check. In these types of investigation, one contacts a clearinghouse company that keeps track of bad checks, bank overdraws, liens, aliases, and other such problems with individual accounts. A pattern of financial difficulties of this nature may indicate yet other sources of concern for the library in the hiring process. Depending on which type of report is ordered, the report will also reveal other things such as irregularities with driver's license or social security numbers. Services that provide these types of checks are, for example, ChexSystems, DPPS, and the three major credit reporting bureaus.

5. Investigative Consumer Report

As defined by the Fair Credit Reporting Act, Section 603, "The term 'investigative consumer report' means a consumer report or portion thereof in which information on a consumer's character, general reputation, personal characteristics, or mode of living is obtained through personal interviews with neighbors, friends, or associates of the consumer reported on or with others with whom he is acquainted or who may have knowledge concerning any such items of information. However, such information shall not include specific factual information on a consumer's credit record obtained directly from a creditor of the consumer or from a consumer reporting agency when such information was obtained directly from a creditor of the consumer or from the consumer." Personal investigations of applicants involve hiring an outside agency to check on a person in a fairly public way. The desired result is a report that reveals personal aspects of an applicant not likely to be revealed by any other method. Such an investigation usually involves people who literally do such things as go talk to an applicant's friends and former neighbors, for example, to ask them questions about the applicant's demeanor, lifestyle, and other such matters. Typically they may also be combined with other investigations, such as criminal background or DMV checks. Numerous agencies are willing to perform these tasks, although the reports are hedged with special rules regarding their use.[14]

6. Drug Tests

Although widely used in some business situations, drug tests seem to be rare in the special collections environment. Because drug use can cloud judgment and lead to financial pressures to support drug habits, employers would seem to be correct in wanting to know this information about their employees on an on-going, continuing basis. On the other hand, many adequately-paid recreational drug users are not likely to be breaking into houses or stealing books to support their habits. If drug tests are given, they are always given by surprise. What an institution might do with such information, especially if a test is positive, is a matter of choice. In some venues, any positive test is cause for dismissal; in others, it is only a matter of caution.[15]

7. Polygraphs

A polygraph, or so-called lie detector test, is a controversial test usually hedged about with legal concerns. If one is given at hiring, the only point of it would be to determine an applicant's truthfulness by having him or her respond to general questions, the answers to which are already supposedly known and often provided on the application. The test, however, can be loaded to determine different parameters. A common question, for example, is "Have you ever stolen from your employer?" That is a question to which almost everyone would have to answer "Yes" since an act so small as even taking home a legal pad would technically constitute theft. After a theft, however, having consent to such a test might be useful in solving the crime. Despite whatever virtues it may have, a polygraph will probably remain a very rare tool in special collections. The results of such tests are generally not admissible as evidence in a court, and private entities are in most cases barred from requiring them.[16] If an institution wishes to give such a test, there are paper-and-pen versions available that test many of the same parameters.

8. Bonding

The process of bonding an employee is that of buying a specialized insurance policy, usually called a fidelity bond, to pay any damage or loss caused by that employee's dishonesty. In other words, if a bonded employee steals a $50,000 manuscript, the bonding agency will reimburse the institution for that loss. Obtaining such coverage on employees will usually require background checks of the employee involved and may entail a review of the institution's security practices. Coverage is normally available for anyone working in the library, even volunteers. People with the following problems are usually not bondable, however: an ex-offender with a record of arrest, conviction or imprisonment; anyone who has ever been on parole or probation; anyone who has any police record; an ex-addict who has been rehabilitated through treatment for alcohol or drug abuse; people with poor credit records or who have declared bankruptcy; a person dishonorably discharged from the military; and persons lacking a work history. Bonding seems to be rare in special collections settings, although sometimes terms of grants require bonding of staff as a condition of acceptance and in some cases certain trustees must be bonded.[17]

9. Psychological Assessment

Psychological assessment is a tool often used in other venues but almost never in a special collections environment, although it might be employed to advantage to predict behaviors in certain situations. Many such tests exist but the most common ones are those that seek to predict behavior and to uncover covert attitudes and feelings. Some occupations, such as law enforcement officers, 911 dispatchers, seminary students, and airline pilots, are often subjected to such tests.[18] They are very rarely used in special collections, however. As with most such tests, the person's informed consent is required.

General Considerations

If special collections is part of a larger institution such as a college or university, the supervisor must be certain that institutional human resources offices are aware of and come to share their special security concerns. The library security officer or library administration should be called on to support security clearance requests for all individuals hired to work in special collections or who will come in contact with collection materials during the course of their workday, including interns, students, and volunteers, who often have access to sensitive items such as keycards and computer passwords.[19]

Ideally all security clearances should be completed before a new employee begins working. While background checks can be expensive, administrative support should be sought to work their cost into each fiscal year budget as a staffing expense. Legal rulings regarding background searches will vary by state or even by institution and need to be addressed in concert with the institution's human resources or legal departments.

If the cost of pursuing background checks on prospective employees is prohibitive, employees and volunteers must be supervised especially closely. Volunteers working in or around collection materials should have well-defined tasks, be monitored by a staff member at all times, and be strictly limited to the number of areas to which they may have access. Supervisors must be active in communicating with their staff, offering and soliciting advice on issues and concerns. Supervisors should also be aware of the temper of each staff member to be able to spot a disgruntled employee. (See Appendix I for a model statement.)

A gaping hole in special collections security is the presence of people in the library who do not actually work for the library and over whom the library has only marginal control and authority. The most common examples of such persons are maintenance staff, security guards, workers, and outside contractors, all of whom probably work for an entity other than the library itself, especially if the library is a stand-alone institution with no affiliation with a larger unit, such as a university. If at all possible, the library should insist that all such persons, before they are allowed to perform work in the library, have some type of background checks to ensure their reliability and honesty. Although the library might not necessarily be privy to the results of such checks, the assurance that they have been performed should be sought. (See Appendix II below.)[20]

Another special problem faced by special collections occurs in larger institutions wherein the rare book library and its collection share cataloguing tasks and systems with other units. In some cases, people outside special collections can access any cataloguing record of any other unit. In other words, it is possible for a student cataloguer in the main library to access and alter rare book and manuscript cataloguing records. For that reason, it is important that special collections attempt to exert influence on the security procedures employed before such people are hired by any library unit if they will have such access or if they will access rare materials outside the confines of the special collections unit itself. A parallel problem is also presented by acquisitions units who handle special collections materials. (See Chapter 8)

Finally, the library is faced with Juvenal's conundrum: "Sed quis custodiet ipsos custodes?" In other words, the library must be certain that the people performing its background checks are themselves above reproach and have been subjected to the most rigorous checks possible. As LAMA recommends: "The library director should require that all persons managing background checks and investigations undergo advance background checks known as a 'full field' investigation, to be conducted and analyzed by a professional consultant or local police officials, not by staff from an umbrella organization who may have concerns or controls that may affect the data or the outcome. The person or persons conducting these investigations need simply to report the result of the investigation against the advanced level acceptance standards above, keeping the information permanently on file. No one involved in the background check process at the library is exempt from it."[21]

Unfortunately, the great security unknowns in today's special collections setting are the patron's themselves, who are usually allowed access to materials after providing minimal information about themselves, which may not even include a social security number or verification of their identity other than the ID card they present. Although no library seems to perform them on patrons, it is perfectly possible to secure a criminal background check, among other checks, on any patron almost instantly. Numerous firms offer that service, which is completed entirely on-line and requires just a few minutes from start to finish. Costs vary, however, depending on the scope of the search.

Once an institution has set down this road, it should continue. Little permanent good is achieved by obtaining such things as credit reports and drug tests at hiring but then not obtaining them at regular intervals to be sure problems have not arisen in the meantime. Theoretically, if an event such as a bad debt would disqualify a person at hiring, it would also be a disqualifying event for continued employment. If one institutes a program of background checks, it is important that they be performed not just for new hires but for everyone who works in the library, even employees of long standing. Some employers perform fresh checks every time an employee is considered for promotion, which should be a minimum threshold. Oth-

ers perform them on a regular basis, say, every five years, on all personnel.[22]

Any potential problems revealed by background checks should be brought to the person's attention and the person given an opportunity to explain any concerns. Sometimes problems arise in a person's past or personal life for any number of perfectly innocent reasons, such as serious illness, divorce, or identity theft. The institution should be careful not to reject arbitrarily an employee who may be otherwise well suited to perform the duties required. As one commentator noted, "The presence of one or even multiple risk factors does not necessarily lead to dishonest behavior."[23] It goes without saying that the results of any such inquiries and the employee's responses to them must be kept utterly confidential and available only to administrators who have a genuine need to know them. Under no circumstances should they be kept on a computer, especially one hooked to the Internet.[24] Any computer files should be printed out, deleted from the computer, and the print-outs kept in a secure location. Records obtained for people who are not employed should probably be destroyed, although legal counsel's advice should be sought on that matter for any pertinent statutory considerations.

Appendix I: CSO Undercover
Hard Questions About Background Checks

> I thought we had a good relationship with human resources—
> until the time came to implement a background check program.
>
> ~Anonymous

Every CSO has experienced that rare security project that takes life quickly and moves with a force of its own. The project seems to leave port without you. You wake up at night thinking through what might have been missed, trying to take solace in the rapid progress.

That, at least, is preferable to the project that just can't get under way—like my efforts to develop a background check program. Doing this can be a real challenge at a company that has operated for decades without anything more than a rudimentary screening to verify the accuracy of an applicant's education and work history. For those who must wrestle with this type of challenge, there is dangerous shoal water all around you.

It started when, as an outgrowth of our nation's new understanding of risk after 9/11, my industry self-administered a set of standards regarding background checks. The inherent problem with a collective industry wide approach, though, is that it typically results in watered-down standards language with little direction. The room for company interpretation undermines the objective of demonstrating to Congress that the private sector can police itself, and it leaves CSOs in a precarious position, with few tools to help us overcome institutional obstacles.

I am the optimist, though, and my team and I rushed to work with key stakeholders, including human resources, legal and corporate compliance. I remember feeling good about how the project was being formulated. We had worked effectively enough with human resources on projects in the past, and it seemed like we were all speaking the same language.

The feeling would soon change. The artifacts of each organization's beliefs began to manifest themselves in missed milestones, unclear language and documents that could never shake their "draft" marking. The project started to feel like the little ship that couldn't. Every time we set sail, the S.S. Human Resources tugboat took us back to port.

Meanwhile, the security group had been given the required leeway to institute contractual requirements to manage risk with our partners and suppliers. It got so bad that the window washers contracted to clean our corporate headquarters had more stringent background checks and requirements than our own employees, who were operating processes that make up a portion of the nation's critical infrastructure.

Compromise is a necessary tactic. The hard part is drawing lines that preserve the intent of a given program. Let's take a look at why drawing those lines was harder than I expected and, in the end, impossible.

Hard question #1: Do the circumstances of a crime matter?

The trouble started when the human resources department's selected project manager was the company's diversity manager. I respect individuals and their diverse backgrounds, but I didn't anticipate, for instance, a discussion that certain felonies might sometimes be acceptable.

Acceptable? For security professionals, it can be hard to see the patterns exhibited by felons and not link them to missing qualities like integrity. We see those who are found guilty of serious crimes as missing the necessary qualities to support trust. I had the idea that any felony might disqualify employment.

Others who are less exposed to rap sheets, however, seemed to view the crimes as possibly resulting from particular circumstances and, therefore, less likely to be repeated. Human resources wanted to pick small windows for applicable criminal findings, with the basic belief that people can change and should get another chance. I was made to feel like an insensitive and nonhuman security thug.

My group and I had some theories about why this was happening—the most likely one being that others in the group either identified with individuals who had records or felt guilty about having themselves committed a crime of some sort. I wasn't trying to judge anyone, but I did want to assist the company in deciding whether or not to extend a privilege (employment) to someone. I would offer examples that would get everyone to say, "Yes, that makes sense." But within minutes, the HR reps' common beliefs would reassert, and they would argue that a single bad decision (for example, felonious assault) doesn't always mean an engineer can't be a good engineer.

Hard question #2: How do you conduct a background investigation?

There are several methods for obtaining background information. They include:

- typical employee screening and application verification process
- county records check, based on a legal name or identifier, for criminal offenses
- state criminal records check based on an identifier

- state fingerprint check
- multistate fingerprint check
- national, FBI-conducted background check (where possible)

The beginning of the list is filled with flawed processes that provide only a limited amount of information. If you were found guilty of a felony, for example, what are the chances you would still live in or seek employment in the same county? Unfortunately, the methods at the beginning of the list are also the easier ones to execute.

I, like most security professionals, prefer the slightly more costly but more comprehensive state-based fingerprint check, in states where it is available. (The most comprehensive method—a national, FBI-conducted background check—is available only for specific jobs in regulated industries.) But human resources basically thought that any check would be good enough for the voluntary standards.

Hard question #3: What are disqualifying offenses?

Most states have specific requirements detailing what felonies can result in a negative adjudication based on jobs or roles. For instance, a school-bus driver must not have been found guilty of any violent crimes or crimes that involved children. Our team, however, couldn't even agree on how much time had to pass before a felony would not disqualify a job candidate, so developing a list of disqualifying offenses was going to be really tough. To make matters worse, job descriptions had not been defined well enough to help identify disqualifying factors by role.

Hard question #4: How do you implement the program?

After we made some headway in defining potential disqualifying offenses (marked "draft," of course), reconciling the cost of the services and arguing enough to know where everyone stood on the time limit for past crimes, the big, ugly issue came up. I remember the meeting to this day.

The human resources project team wanted to cut the estimated cost of implementing the program. The dollar amount equaled the cost of background checks for the number of employees currently on staff who had access to critical assets. The manager sat back and said, "Well, of course, you don't propose running a check on our current employees, do you? We might have to move a large number of people out of their current roles."

Time to dig the holes and insert our heads into the ground.

The way I saw it, you had to check your existing staff, or the program had no value. The standards were meant for a cadre of people who had the means to be very disruptive and damaging—those people who were in the jobs already, as well as those who might be hired in the future. The risk was now, not over the next 20 years.

Time for More Research

By this point, I could see that the project was taking on water and appeared to be sinking. This time I proposed we go back to the table and draft more

stringent disqualifying offenses. I argued that a simpler system would be easier to manage and execute against.

I looked around and found the response I anticipated: We need to benchmark the industry. The security team already had done that, but this time the benchmarking would be done by each executive involved.

Slowly but surely we all came back to the table with variable results relying on small sample sets. The industry had a wide field—from companies that maintained three full-time employees to conduct background investigations and manage a strict adjudication process, to companies that conduct checks with no disqualifying guidelines, to companies that did absolutely nothing.

We were back where we started. Well, one thing was different. I had a different view of the private sector's ability to police itself. I know you should be careful what you wish for. But with a stricter standard, there would have been less room for interpretation—and CSOs like me wouldn't have to struggle between what is more effective or in the spirit of the standards, versus what is simply easier for the corporation or more culturally and politically acceptable.

Appendix II: Know Your Employee

By Bob King, Senior Extension Educator

**Cornell University
Cooperative Extension
Monroe County**

Cornell Cooperative Extension
Monroe County

Gaining as much knowledge as possible about an employee is important for morale, profit, and security considerations. Paying attention to employee financial, emotional, or personal motivations—and sharing feedback with employees—can dramatically improve morale, communication, and profitability.

An employee's perception of whether you have a genuine interest about their job performance and welfare can have a much larger impact on morale and productivity than factors such as training and technology. Even more so, we are now entering into an era of liability and security concerns that requires many of us to gain additional and more in-depth information about employees before, during, and after they have been hired.

Before hiring a potential employee, ask about education, work history, and personal interests. Conduct a background check. That's more than checking their references; it's also seeking out whether they have a criminal history, traffic violations, or something else that may prove to be a red flag. If you are concerned about an individual's criminal history because of the requirements of the job, local law enforcement authorities may be able to help with this task.

Criminal background checks can be done by a local law enforcement agency but only for arrests made by that agency within their jurisdiction and by their own personnel. Consequently, other law enforcement agencies may need to be contacted in order to account for other geographical areas and/or jurisdictions where the potential employee may have lived or worked.

Background checks require complete information. This includes full name, social security number, date of birth, and any known aliases. Generally, local law enforcement agencies also require a signed waiver by the potential employee in order to allow the requested information to be released to a potential employer. The processing fee is nominal and can be as low as $5. Remember if you have a bad feeling about someone, move on to the next candidate.

Once employed, get to know your employee; ask relevant but nonintrusive questions on a somewhat regular basis. Encourage dialogue in order to determine a person's behavior. Behavioral changes may be an indicator of drug use, personal problems, psychological issues, etc. Also keep track of an individual's progress on confidential matters, loss prevention concerns, and traffic violations. Confidential agreements are becoming commonplace and may be used to ensure confidential information remains undisclosed. Periodic checks on drivers' license records are also becoming more commonplace and may prevent you from having an employee driving your vehicles with a suspended drivers' license. Many automobile insurers provide this service upon request.

When an employee leaves, make sure to find out why and where they are going. Keep the lines of communication open. Do this as part of an exit interview so you can find out how to contact past employees about financial matters, such as W2s, and on other issues such as criminal mischief and inventory shrinkage that may impact your business after they have left.

Source: Offices of the Sheriff–Monroe, Livingston and Wyoming Counties; New York State Police—Troop E. http://counties.cce.cornell.edu/Monroe/ag/2002%20Know%20Your%20Employee.htm. Reprinted by permission.

Appendix III: No Background Checks Slated Despite Arrests

By Brook Corwin, Staff Writer, August 30, 2001

In the wake of the arrests of two Carolina Dining Services employees, officials say there are no plans to institute background checks on CDS employees.

University police arrested two CDS employees on felony charges in the past two weeks.

Aramark Corp., a service management company and the food service provider for UNC-Chapel Hill, hires all CDS employees without running background checks, said UNC and Aramark officials.

But several other schools with Aramark contracts, including East Carolina University and Duke University, have required the company by contract to run background checks on all employees it hires to work at the university.

Ira Simon, CDS administrator, said UNC-CH has never requested that Aramark do background checks because of its confidence in Aramark's standard hiring procedure.

"Aramark is a very reputable company," he said. "Part of the reason we selected them was that they had success at their other universities."

Simon said that because UNC-CH did not specifically ask Aramark to conduct background checks when the 10-year contract was signed in May, the corporation is under no obligation to do so.

And Simon said he still trusts the quality of Aramark's human resource department despite the arrests. "I thought they handled it as efficiently and effectively as they could have," he said. "I honestly think Aramark is very conscientious about their hiring practices."

But officials at other schools with Aramark contracts are more adamant about the necessity of background checks.

"All applicants have to survive a background check in order to work in any department on our campus," said Jim Wulforst, the director of dining services at Duke. "You have to protect the living environment of the faculty and students. It's always been a regular practice and something we're very picky about."

Jim Mullen, director of employment services at ECU, said his school instituted a policy last December that also requires background checks for all ECU employees, including dining service employees hired by Aramark.

Mullen said ECU used to run background checks only for certain "sensitive" positions that had direct contact with students, a hiring policy similar to the one UNC-CH currently uses. "We didn't want to single out any group, so we expanded the checks to everyone, and it has worked out well," Mullen said.

All UNC-CH Aramark officials declined to comment on the matter.

But Aramark officials at UNC-Greensboro and UNC-Wilmington both said, like UNC-CH, their schools do not require them to run background checks.

"We work with universities very closely, and they did not stipulate a need for background checks," said J.P. Fesperman, who serves as the assistant food director at UNC-W.

Sam Zamrick, Food Services director for UNC-G, said background checks are not needed at UNC-G because Aramark has been the food service provider at the school for 38 years and mostly has long-term employees.

But he added that for a school such as UNC-CH, which hired Aramark last spring, it might be important to do background checks until the company is established. "Depending on your situation and location, criminal checks could be appropriate for a school," Zamrick said. "You're going to have a lot of staff turnover in the beginning."

Appendix IV: Consent to Criminal Background Check

STAFFORD MUNICIPAL SCHOOL DISTRICT
CONSENT TO PERFORM CRIMINAL HISTORY BACKGROUND CHECK IN COMPLIANCE WITH THE
FCRA (FAIR CREDIT REPORTING ACT)

Date: _____

_____

Last Name   First Name   Middle Initial

_____

Maiden and / or Other Last Names Used

_____

City   County   State

_____

Date of Birth**   Social Security Number**

_____

Sex**   Race**

I, _____, am an applicant for employment with Stafford Municipal School District and have been advised that as a part of the application process, the employer conducts a criminal history background check. I do hereby consent to the employer use of any information provided during the application process in performing the criminal history check. The employer has informed me that I have the right to review and challenge any negative information that would adversely impact a decision to offer employment. In addition, I have been informed that I will have a reasonable opportunity to clear up any mistaken information reported within a reasonable time frame established within the sole discretion of the employer. Under the fair Credit Reporting Act, I have been advised that upon request I will be provided the name, address, and telephone number of the reporting agency as well as the nature, substance and source of all information.

*AS SHOWN ON THE ORIGINAL APPLICATION
**TO BE USED ONLY FOR CRIMINAL HISTORY SEARCHES, AND NOT A PART OF THE PERSONNEL FILE.
The following are my responses to questions about my criminal record history (if any) with descriptions to any question with a YES answer:

1. Have you ever been convicted or plead guilty before a court of any federal, state, or municipal criminal offense? (Excluding minor traffic violations)
❏ Yes ❏ No
If YES, please provide an explanation below:

_____

_____

_____

2. Have you ever-received deferred adjudication or similar disposition for any federal, state or municipal criminal offense? ❑ Yes ❑ No
If YES, please provide an explanation below:

_____

_____

3. Have you ever-received probation or community supervision for any federal, state, or municipal criminal offense? ❑ Yes ❑ No
If YES, please provide an explanation below:

_____

_____

4. Have you ever been convicted of any criminal offense in a country outside the jurisdiction of the United States? ❑ Yes ❑ No
If YES, please provide an explanation below:

_____

_____

5. As of the date of this authorization, do you have any pending criminal charges against you? ❑ Yes ❑ No
If YES, please provide an explanation below:

_____

_____

THIS SECTION IS TO BE USED TO LIST ALL COUNTIES AND STATES OF RESIDENCE SINCE AGE 18 OR HIGH SCHOOL GRADUATION. YOU MUST BE SPECIFIC ABOUT DATES OF RESIDENCE. I HEREBY CERTIFY THAT ALL INFORMATION PROVIDED IN THIS AUTHORIZATION IS TRUE, CORRECT AND COMPLETE. I UNDERSTAND THAT IF ANY INFORMATION PROVES TO BE INCORRECT OR INCOMPLETE THAT GROUNDS FOR THE CANCELING OF ANY AND ALL OFFERS OF EMPLOYMENT WILL EXIST AND MAY BE USED AT THE DISCRETION OF THE EMPLOYER.

CITY/TOWN	COUNTY	STATE	DATES FROM	TO

Applicant (Print Name) _____

Applicant Signature _____Date _____

Appendix VI: Is Harvard Checking Employees' Records?

Marios V. Broustas

The arrest of a former University library worker as the infamous Widener slasher has focused attention on Harvard's decision not to require background checks for many of its lower level employees.

Stephen L. Womack was arrested and arraigned this week on charges that he allegedly destroyed millions of dollars worth of books. He is sitting in a Cambridge jail cell today even as police continue their investigation into the 42-year-old Arlington resident's background and his possible motive for the crime.

In the past four years, Womack, a part-time library employee from 1990 to 1992, has stolen books from Northeastern University, tried to extort money from that university and threatened to blow up a bank if ransom money was not left for him at Widener, according to police. He also sent letters saying he would blow up libraries at Northeastern and at Harvard if they did not fire all their Jewish employees.

In announcing Womack's arrest this week, University officials described the suspect as a lone must of sorts. They said there was no reason for Harvard to overreact and impose new checks on its employees.

"We're very glad this disturbed individual has been caught," said Joe Wrinn, acting director of the Harvard News Office. "We're glad it's over."

Harvard College Librarian Richard De Gennaro, in fact, explicitly said that the University should not require background checks for library employees.

"This person obviously has mental problems, and you don't make policy based on that," he said Thursday. "This is just one person who happened to be a very bad apple."

But if Harvard had looked into Womack's past, they might have discovered that he had a decade-long history of mutilating books, according to officials at the Lexington Public Library. Wikje Feteris,

a librarian there, said this week that Womack had taken out hundreds of books there, and returned only the covers.

Harvard Police Chief Paul E. Johnson said yesterday that employee background checks should be instituted in many parts of the University.

"Anybody who works for Harvard should be scrutinized carefully," Johnson said. "It would make my job easier because the possibility of these things happening would be reduced to some extent."

In addition, Johnson said that by developing extensive information on employees, Harvard could make it easier to solve complicated cases of employee theft.

In the Womack case, for instance, University officers had little background information available on the former library employee because Harvard had never bothered to ask for it.

Even though police had suspected an inside job from the time books were first found slashed in 1990, it took nearly four years, hours of Federal Bureau of Investigation assistance and a tip from Northeastern to crack the case.

"When you get into these investigations," Johnson said, "it is considerably more substantial [to have background information]."

Other Cases

Harvard officials attempted to emphasize the uniqueness of the Womack case. But police are currently investigating at least one other slashing case in which a University affiliate may be a suspect.

In fact, some of the biggest recent robberies on campus have been inside jobs, not break-ins. And Harvard continues to put employees without background checks in contact with some of its most valuable holdings.

Including the Womack case, a substantial amount of Harvard property has been stolen or damaged by three different University workers since May 1993.

James A. Hogue, a Harvard Extension School student and casual employee of the Mineralogical Museum, was arrested on May 10, 1993, for stealing nearly $100,000 in precious gems, minerals and other property from that museum.

"This is one of the largest, if not the largest recovery dollar-wise in the history of the department." Harvard Police Lt. John F. Rooney told The Crimson at the time.

That summer, Harvard police broke another case of employee theft. A volunteer at the Museum of Comparative Zoology was discovered to have stolen rare objects, including fossilized insects, from a collection there.

Johnson has cautioned that other universities have also been unable to do sufficient background checks. Before coming to the Extension School, Hogue, now 34, managed to enroll at Princeton University in 1988 under the alias "Alexi Indris-Santana," according to the Associated Press.

Applying under the cover story that he was a self-educated farm hand, "Santana" earned a $20,000 scholarship from the school.

Hogue had previously been enrolled, under his real name, in the University of Wyoming. After two years there, he transferred to Austin (Tex.) Community College.

In 1987, Hogue stole thousands of dollars worth of bicycle parts in California. He was arrested a year later in Utah, where he served six months in a state prison and a second six months in a halfway house before he broke parole and left the state, according to a May 1993 story in the Harvard *Gazette*.

In the summer of 1992, while Hogue worked at the New Jersey electronics firm Roscom, he stole at least $600 in electronics equipment.

Despite his past, Hogue was able to enroll in the Extension School under his real name. In turn, his status as a student helped him get a job with the Mineralogical museum.

He gained access to the stolen property through his work as a "casual employee" of the museum, according to Carl A. Francis, associate curator of the Mineralogical Museum.

With that access, he stockpiled gold, silver, rubies, opals and more than 100 other precious and non-precious gems and minerals during a period of nine months. He also picked up a microscope valued at $10,000.

Harvard police, including Sgt. Kathleen Stanford and Det. Richard Mederos, both of whom investigated the Womack case, finally cornered Hogue in his home in May 1993. There they found the jewels, the microscope and the equipment he stole from the New Jersey electronics firm.

Hogue pled guilty that December to one count of larceny over $250. Middlesex County Superior Court Judge Robert Barron sentenced him to one year in prison, with an additional three-year suspended sentence tacked on.

Hogue was sent to Cedar Junction prison in Walpole, Mass. Officials at the facility said yesterday that he is no longer being held there.

Hogue is now believed to be serving a five-year sentence in New Jersey on a warrant for leaving Utah under a false alias, according to reports in *The Daily Princetonian* and *The Peninsula Times-Tribune* last year.

Upgrading Security

Harvard museum officials now claim that a case similar to the Hogue heist could not happen again.

Frances A. Beane, deputy director for finance and administration in the University art museums, said yesterday that Hogue's thefts barely outpaced improvements to Harvard's security in the museums.

"When [the Hogue thefts] happened, we were in the process of upgrading the entire security system," Beane said.

In recent months, the University has used a grant from the National Endowment for the Arts to improve security. A crime similar to Hogue's now cannot occur, Beane said.

While some employees know how the museums' security systems work, workers are not allowed to go into a room or gallery without a fellow employee in tow, Beane said.

"It would be impossible for a security person to take something out of the gallery," Beane said.

Still, the art museums continue to hire employees without doing background checks. "We do not have a process for doing security checks for all our staffs," Beane said.

James Cuno, the Cabot director of the University art museums, said the extent of the background checks on employees depends on the responsibilities given to each individual.

"It differs according to the position the person has, how close to sensitive materials they are," he said. "Secondly, if they are security staff there is a different kind of background check than if they are curatorial staff."

An Inside Job

Still, a smart employee with knowledge of an internal security system can foil even the most sophisticated surveillance, police said.

That, at least, is what happened in the Womack case, according to police.

Womack, who worked as a library assistant, evaded not only numerous surveillance cameras but also officers who took turns doing stakeouts in the stacks. Routine door checkers also did not appear to present a problem for the suspect.

Targeting books on religious subjects, Womack used a knife and his hands to rip out pages. Instead of sneaking the book or torn pages out of the library, he copied the books onto microfilm.

When he was caught, Womack allegedly had 300 rolls of microfilm. Each roll had approximately 15 different texts.

Johnson said the Widener slasher had been on the department's "short list" of the 20 most wanted suspects as early as 1991. Harvard police spent more than $50,000 on expensive closed-circuit TVs and video recording equipment. Some cameras were even set up to look like books.

The slasher, however, was able to elude police monitoring devices and was never seen exiting the library with stolen items.

Ultimately, Harvard's investigation took four years and cost hundreds of thousands of dollars. But it was information developed by the Northeastern University police which broke the case.

During a monthly meeting of officials from local university police departments. Northeastern officers mentioned that they had experienced a series of book thefts and mutilations at their libraries. The perpetrator often left threatening notes.

Harvard police investigators at the meeting immediately suspected a connection to the slasher, who had left several notes at the University. One note said he would continue cutting out the insides of books "until the voices tell me to stop."

After an intense few weeks of investigating the case 12 hours per day, police identified Womack as a suspect.

At his home in Arlington Wednesday, authorities said they found a cache of stolen books, manuscripts, typewriters, photography equipment, cutting implements and other objects allegedly stolen from the University.

All had been taken while Womack was being paid to do Harvard's work.

"Anyone who works for Harvard should be scrutinized carefully," Harvard Police Chief Paul E. Johnson said.

http://www.thecrimson.com/article.aspx?ref=228062. 12/17/1994, Reprinted by permission

NOTES

1. For published reports see the RBMS "Incidents of Theft" list under the Security Committee at: http://www.rbms.info.

2. The Historical Society of Pennsylvania in a ten-year period from about 1987–1997 suffered the loss of millions of dollars worth of its museum collections because of thefts by long-time janitor Earnest Medford, who in turn sold them to George Csizmazia, an electrical contractor who had done work at the Society. In 1996 security guard Joseph Anastasio at the University of Bridgeport Library pled guilty to stealing manuscripts from the library's collections and selling them to collectors.

3. One supervisor at a state institution remarked: "We have had folks that were guilty of theft, embezzling, etc. It is good to know and we obviously don't hire those folks" (email to author, 13 July 2007).

4. Alan Jay Lincoln, "Low Cost Security Options: Background Checks," *Library & Archival Security*, vol. 9, nos 3–4 (1989): 107. In the U.S. background checks are governed by several federal laws: Civil Rights Act of 1964 (Title VII), Employee Polygraph Protection Act, Fair Credit Reporting Act, Equal Employment Opportunity Act, Americans with Disabilities Act, and Equal Employment Opportunity Act. Various state laws and local regulations may also come into play.

5. See Sarah D. Scalet, "Good (and Bad) Background Checks," Csooline.com (1 August 2004). http://www.csoonline.com/article/219483/Good_and_Bad_Background_Checks?page=1.

6. Institutions almost never conduct criminal background checks on students admitted. Other checks, such as confirming education, are invariably performed, however. Thus, a library can in general not depend on the fact that a student has been vetted by the institution before being admitted.

7. An important exception to this rule occurs if the employer itself conducts the background checks. In that case, the employer is exempt from the notice and consent provisions of federal law and the potential employee does not have to be provided with any information concerning the hiring decision. Basically the same rules apply if an employer conducts a so-called "employee misconduct investigation." For various potential levels of background checks depending on an employee's responsibilities, see Library Administration and Management Association, *Library Security Guidelines Document, June 7, 2001,* (Chicago: American Library Association, 2007), "Appendix B: Staff Pre-employment Screening Guidelines." http://www.ala.org/ala/lama/lamapublications/librarysecurity.htm.

8. Bruce A, Shuman, *Library Security and Safety Handbook: Prevention, Policies, and Procedures* (Chicago: American Library Association, 1999), 193–94 correctly warns against this practice.

9. Although fingerprints can be taken by those with little or no experience in doing so using so-called inkless systems, in this case it is imperative that they be taken by someone qualified to take them using black ink.

10. For a clear example of the consequences of failing to do criminal background checks, see Brooke Olson, "Material Stolen from Archives," http://www.museum-security.org/bermeo.html, wherein is recounted the story of thief Robert Bermeo, who, although once convicted of theft from a store, was hired by an institution from whom he also stole over $1 million worth of materials. The institution failed to do a background check.

11. For a typical review of this controversy, see Mary Challender, "Does Bad Credit Signal a Bad Employee?" *Des Moines Register* (13 June 2004). http://desmoinesregister.com/apps/pbcs.dll/article?AID=/20040613/OPINION01/406130307/1036

12. FICO (anagram for Fair Isaac CO) is just one type of such a score, although a widely used one. The exact mechanism for determining the score is a secret; one is, thus, subjecting the applicant to the judgment of others rather than the judgment of the institution itself.

13. If a position pays $75,000 or more, credit checks can go back indefinitely.

14. One disclosure form states that the scope of such an investigation may include: "In the event an investigative consumer report is conducted, I understand such information may be obtained by personal interviews with my acquaintances or associates or with others whom I am acquainted or who may have knowledge concerning my character, general reputation, personal characteristics or standard of living. I understand such information may also be obtained through direct or indirect contact with former employers, schools, financial institutions, landlords and public agencies or other persons who may have such knowledge."

15. A wide variety of drug tests are available, depending on what the institution wishes to learn about applicants and employees. For example, a typical NIDA-5 test for such substances as cannabinoids can be supplemented by tests for oxycodon, a widely abused drug. Testing of head hair is the most informative method since it will reveal drug use for up to the past ninety days. On the spot tests include urine and saliva. Of course, there are companies that offer solutions to allow candidates to beat those tests.

16. For a review of issues with polygraph tests, see *The Polygraph and Lie Detection* (Washington: National Academies Press, 2003). The 1988 Employee Polygraph Protection Act severely limited the ability of private employers to use such tests. For the future of such tests, see Polly Shulman, "Liar Liar Pants on Fire," Popsci.com [e. g. *Popular Science Magazine*] (July 2002), at: http://www.popsci.com/popsci/medicine/1080c4522fa84010vgnvcm1000004eecbccdrcrd.html.

17. For a brief discussion of bonds, see Mary Breighner, William Payton, and Jeanne M. Drewes, *Risk and Insurance Management Manual for Libraries* (Chicago: ALA, 2005), 73–74.

18. Such testing for law enforcement personnel is fairly well developed and widely required. See, for example, Cary D. Rostow and Robert D. Davis, *A Handbook for Psychological Fitness-for-Duty Evaluations in Law Enforcement* (New York: Haworth, 2004).

19. In some larger institutions, volunteers, for example, are often vetted through an independent office that screens all volunteers, no matter where they work on campus. In that case, the library must make sure that office is aware of its security requirements for such workers.

20. For guidelines concerning control of outsides contractors working in a museum or special collections area, see Patrick Boylan, "Security Guidelines when Using Outside Contractors," Museums and Heritage Organisation Policy Statements Series. http://www.museum-security.org/articles.html#contractors. Miriam B. Kahn, *The Library Security and Safety Guide to Prevention, Planning, and Response* (Chicago: ALA, 2008), advises in the case of outside workers: "Talk to the security department to learn if there are background checks the institution runs before hiring contractors" (76).

21. LAMA, Appendix B.

22. Librarians working at extremely secure facilities such as military bases can often be subjected to routine, ongoing checks involving such procedures as random drug tests and having their cars checked by police dogs.

23. Goshen College, Campus Crime Prevention Programs, *Library Safety & Security: A Comprehensive Manual for Library Administrators and Police and Security Officers* (Goshen: Campus Crime Prevention Programs, 1992), 79.

24. Instances of personal data being illegally retrieved from computers are almost too widespread to require comment. In one instance, the Bancroft Library's patron registration records may have been compromised; in April, 2006, the University of Texas McCombs School of Business had nearly 200,000 personal records compromised, including social security numbers.

General Building Considerations

Everett C. Wilkie, Jr.

> Once a building has been constructed, the damage has been done.
> —*Fischer & Green*

Security considerations need to be incorporated into all phases of building management and design, whether one is examining an existing structure, planning a new one, or remodelling one. Although every type of building, from a stand-alone nineteenth-century house to a modern special collections facility inside a university library will have various considerations, certain security principles will apply to each type of building and program.

Conflicting considerations often come into play, however. As Atlas remarks, the modern architectural dictum that form follow function is often reversed, with emphasis being placed on form to the detriment of function, which can compromise security.[1] Libraries seem peculiarly subject to such thinking because of the desire to make them appear open and inviting. In the case of special collections, that thinking can be problematic, especially when renovations are planned. Atlas concludes, "Making a building secure when it was not originally designed to be secure is an expensive proposition."[2] Agreeing with Atlas about excessive retrofitting expenses, Fischer and Green succinctly conclude, "Once a building has been constructed, the damage has been done."[3]

This chapter includes some general considerations along with some specific recommendations for various specialized situations with the assumption that the institution is being burglarized after

hours.[4] Specific security systems and problems particular to reading rooms are discussed in other chapters.[5]

Security is usually considered in either zones or concentric circles (See figs 3.1 and 3.2). In other words, security starts from the outside and works its way in until it reaches the most critical areas of the library in need of most protection. Theoretically, by the time a person has penetrated the most critical area s/he will have supposedly passed through so many alarms that the attempt will have been detected and frustrated.[6]

Detective Sergeant Bryan Hanley of the Queensland, Australia, Police Service, offers these four succinct observations on general building security:

1) **Natural Surveillance** which is effected by design that aims to increase the ability to observe potential offenders. It is characterised by features that maximise visibility of people at all times. It includes the ability to see into and be seen from parking areas, building entrances, verandas, doors, windows as well as pedestrian friendly footpaths and streets.

2) **Territorial Reinforcement** is effected by physical design that creates or extends an area of influence and control. Where employed it results in an increased sense of territorial control which deters potential offenders. It is characterised by

Figure 3.1

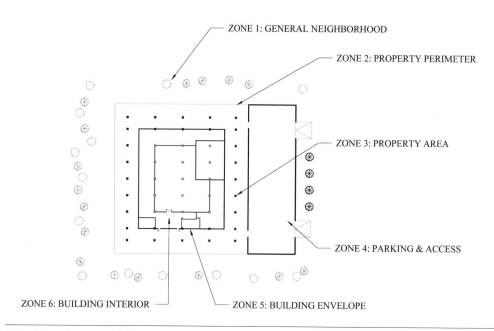

ZONE 1: GENERAL NEIGHBORHOOD

ZONE 2: PROPERTY PERIMETER

ZONE 3: PROPERTY AREA

ZONE 4: PARKING & ACCESS

ZONE 6: BUILDING INTERIOR

ZONE 5: BUILDING ENVELOPE

Critical Premises Security Points (Courtesy Sara Alicia Costa, Ocurrente Design)

Figure 3.2

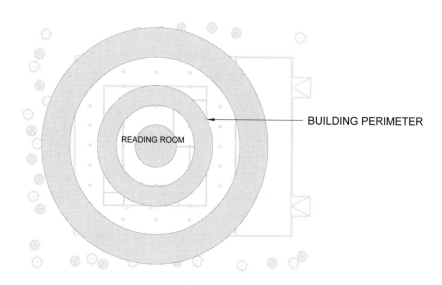

BUILDING PERIMETER

READING ROOM

Security Zone Concentric Circles
Security Is Increased as Target Is Approached (Courtesy Sara Alicia Costa, Ocurrente Design)

features that define property lines. It establishes and delineates boundaries distinguishing between private and public space using landscaping techniques including planting, pavement design, gates and appropriate fencing.

3) **Natural Access Control** is effected by design that aims to decrease the opportunity to commit crime by denying access to crime targets and creating in offenders a heightened sense of risk. It is created by designing streets, footpaths, building entrances and gateways to clearly indicate public routes and discourage access to private areas with structural elements.

4) **Target Hardening** is effected by design features that prohibit entry or access such as window locks and dead bolts for doors.[7]

Although the discussion that follows below is somewhat more discursive than the brief points given above, Hadley's points are valid, especially for outside appearances. The same ideas may also be applied inside a building. For instance, it is a good security measure if a person has clearly indicated to him or her, by either signage, design, or access, that when entering special collections he or she is entering a special area unlike the rest of the library or other the campus buildings.

The first areas that need to be examined are the grounds on which the institution sits. Preferably, at least some of the outer areas will be quite visible from nearby streets, an important consideration in the casual detection of illegal activity by the police and public. As lovely as shrubbery and other plantings can be, they should not be so heavy that they obscure views of windows and doors. At night, the grounds should never be in the dark but brightly lit, a classic, first line of defense against thieves, who generally prefer darkness. Lighting should make all doors and windows visible. If deemed appropriate, a barrier can be erected around the structure, although it should be of a type that can be seen through, such as a

fence. Solid walls are rarely a good security choice since they usually do not stop thieves and can even help hide their activities. In some situations, it may be wise to have the grounds and exterior covered by CCTV monitored off-site after hours.

Once one reaches the building itself, the first items one should consider are openings–including all openings, not just the obvious windows and doors. HVAC connections, for example, are classic openings sometimes exploited, as are such structures as skylights and roof access hatches. Anything that can be removed or opened to provide an entryway needs to be looked at carefully. Even nearby manhole covers, if not secured, can offer a way inside the building.

One normally considers doors the first line of defense, although they are not necessarily what a thief will try to breach. In any case, doors will ideally be made of metal, be hung in metal frames, and of maximum duty rating. Hinges should face inside the building. In some cases, doors must open out rather than in, as required by most fire codes for exterior doors.[8] If that is the case, hinges should be altered so they cannot be removed or damaged or designed so the door cannot be shifted off of them. Glass doors should be fitted with shatter-resistant plate glass. Older wooden doors, which must often be retained for historical or aesthetic reasons, present a particular weakness since almost all of them are fairly readily defeated. Average garage doors are also easily defeated since they can readily be sawn through and should be replaced with metal roll-up doors. At the very least, all exterior doors should trip at least two alarms if they are disturbed.

Apart from the door structure itself, the locking system employed on it will be the next weakness.[9] Exterior doors equipped with dead bolt locks should have long bolts that are structured to prevent sawing.[10] Such locks would preferably be of the high-security type with special keys that cannot be duplicated by a locksmith and cannot be picked. If possible, both sides of the lock should have keyways, although life safety considerations may prevent that alternative. Such locks should have special strike plates secured to the building frame itself by long screws. Some consideration should also be given to the position of the lock in the door. Placing locks higher or lower than usual frustrates those who attempt to kick a door in. Some doors are locked to the floor, which is a fairly secure system that offers some advantages over securing the lock into the door frame. The bolt itself should be covered by a protective metal plate (an astragal) to prevent easy access to it from the outside (see figs 3.3 & 3.4). (Preferably, the institution will fit out its doors with an access control system having electric strikes, which are extremely strong and can help secure even wooden doors.) In the rare cases

where one has sliding patio doors, they should be secured in such a way to prevent their being opened or lifted from their tracks. Metal framed plate glass doors equipped with magnetic locks will fail under assault well before the lock itself. Finally, if a door has large exterior handles, such as those sometimes seen on glass entry doors, they should be designed to fail before the door frame or the lock.[11]

Other openings are probably considered sealed, although they may be successfully breached. One common weakness is a roof hatch that allows access from the inside to the outside. Because it is usually out of sight, it can be a favorite target since thieves can linger over the opening with reduced chances of detection. The same consideration applies to skylights and other decorative roof openings, which are often in areas not readily observable from the outside. Occasionally, thieves will remove such

Figure 3.3

Full-length Astragal (Used by permission)

Figure 3.4

Astragal Guarding a Lock (Used by permission)

things as rooftop HVAC equipment or exhaust fans to obtain access. Another potential opening is an air conditioning unit installed in a window or through a wall. The units are easily pushed inside and ideally would be protected by a metal cage. The best protection against such breaches is the institution's alarm system.

Windows are probably the next likely point of access if a thief decides to forego entry through a door or other opening. A standard recommendation for securing them is to use shatterproof glass. If one decides to adopt that course, s/he must be sure that the window frame and mullions will survive assault. All the shatterproof glass in the world will make little difference in a flimsy, nineteenth-century, double hung window that can be readily removed by a few well-place pulls with a crowbar. Windows must also have secure locking systems.

Many modern windows are built into the walls and will not open at all (see fig. 3.5). Older wooden windows should be pinned from the inside, at the very least. Unfortunately, there is no real way to stop someone from defeating a double-hung window; one can only make the task as difficult as possible. Again, adequate alarm systems are one's best protection against window breaches, and all windows should be protected by at least two devices, such as a motion detector and glass break detector or shock detector and motion detector. One must be careful in considering window security, however, to ensure that occupants can escape through them if need be. For that reason, bars are controversial. Not only do they delay police and firefighters, they can trap people inside. Finally, second-story or higher windows are also vulnerable. They should all be secured as if they were on the first floor.[12]

Figure 3.5

Highly Secure Special Collections Windows (Courtesy the Lilly Library)

An often overlooked problem is presented by walls and roof structures. These are sometimes breached to avoid visible doors and windows as entry points. In other words, the thieves merely punch a hole through the building's outer shell. Although this is a situation that can be detected while in progress by a proper security system, such an arrangement is normally so expensive that most institutions cannot afford it. A less expensive arrangement is adequate volumetric protection of all spaces.[13]

Exterior service panels are also items that need attention; although they perhaps cannot be used for entry, they can be tampered with. Outside circuit breaker boxes, for example, should be locked and if possible alarmed so that notification is sent if they are opened. Of more concern, however, is the service entrance for the telephone system. The box containing those wires is normally quite flimsy and easily opened with simple tools. If the institution cannot bury both its phone and electrical wires and bring its service entrances inside the walls, the alarm system should definitely be equipped with a radio or cellular backup notification system, a feature that should be standard in every alarm system but often is not.[14]

Once one has moved inside the structure, some of the same problems await. Even windows or glass can again become security issues. The most frequently encountered interior barrier, however, are doors, most of which are less robust than the building's exterior doors. In evaluating doors, it is helpful to consider what it is intended to protect. A door to a secretary's office may not necessarily need to be as stout as a door leading to a special collections area or the stacks. For critical interior doors, however, many of the same considerations apply as would be considered for an outside door, and they probably should be of the same type and quality with the same locks. When the library is closed for the day, every door that can be locked should be locked, even if it leads to a non-critical area. The purpose of such a policy is to throw as many barriers as possible in a thief's way. Again, those doors should be protected by a dual layer of alarms. In an ideal situation, all doors into any stack area would be alarmed at all times, even when the building is open, and entered through an access control system that shunts the alarm when a door is properly opened.

Although glass is used inside structures, rarely is it in the form of windows. More than likely, the glass will be in the form of walls or partitions. Those structures again require the same types of treatment as outside glass, including being very robust to resist shattering. In the cases of interior glass partitions, life safety issues rarely intrude since they are not normally considered a potential escape route.

The institution's interior walls present even more security considerations than its exterior ones. Generally, interior partitions are relatively flimsy and easily breached by battering. Plaster, sheetrock, and simple concrete block walls can all be defeated in mere minutes.[15] Any special collections area located inside a larger structure needs to pay careful attention to its own interior walls to ensure that if someone attempts to breach them an alarm will sound. Again, multiple alarm devices inside a special area are essential.

The institution's ceilings also present weaknesses, especially if they are modern drop ceilings, or plaster and sheetrock, which can be defeated readily.[16] In such cases, a thief could enter an adjoining, perhaps unalarmed space, punch through the ceiling on that side, go through or over the partition wall, and break through the ceiling in the special

collections area. This type of intrusion is especially troublesome since the thief, once in the ceiling, may have access to the area's alarm wiring, as well. At a minimum all exterior spaces, such as halls, adjacent to special collections walls should be covered by alarm devices to prevent someone from approaching them undetected. In very secure installations, the area between the deck and the drop ceiling is protected by motion detectors.

Threats are also presented by various other openings into the special collections area. Those will usually consist of HVAC ducts and other utility chases and entrances. Because some of these ducts are relatively large, it is possible for a person to enter the special collections area through them. Air returns tend to be more than adequate for a person to come through them.[17] All such openings should be physically barred by grills or some other barrier.[18]

Elevators, including dumb waiters, present special considerations. If the building is equipped with one, its shaft is a potential entry point or hiding place for a thief who intends to steal materials after hours. In no case should an elevator be left in operating condition once a building closes, but rather should be taken to a designated floor and locked to prevent operation. The doors should be alarmed in case they are closed or opened. Any elevator that serves the stacks or other sensitive areas, such as a conservation lab, should be operable by keys or access cards only for those floors. Similar considerations apply to dumb waiters.[19]

Without question, the strongest part of any special collection's area will be its vault, and if a person has managed to reach this part of the library, s/he should be faced with a substantial obstacle that will require a lot of time to defeat. As with any vault, however, if a thief has enough time, s/he will be able to enter it eventually. One tactic employed by some institutions is to shield the main vault door with an ante-room, which is itself extremely difficult to penetrate.[20] In general, vault walls should be so difficult to penetrate that any thief will attempt first to defeat the door. Any other opening into the vault, such as HVAC flues, should be physically blocked.

An ancillary consideration to surveying the building is to obtain a complete set of scale drawings for the structure showing all walls, HVAC systems, electrical systems, alarm systems, etc. In many ways, such plans are more revealing of security problems that a physical examination of the premises would be. As part of any security survey, those plans should be consulted. As with any confidential information about the library, the plans should be closely guarded and not made available publicly. Any publicly available floor plan of the library, such as one on the library's web site, should be altered so that the precise location of special collections stack areas is not shown. Care should also be taken not to share physical information by other inadvertent means, such as shelf marks or elevator and door signage. A shelf mark that has a location such as "Sixth Floor, Room 203" gives a potential thief information that should not be available. Staff should not discuss details of the building layout with the public. Libraries should communicate to entities, such as the physical plant department or the institution's architects, that premise plans should not be shared casually with just anyone who has no real need to consult them. Superseded plans that will not be securely archived should be destroyed. Adjunct materials, such as alarm system manuals or operating procedures, should be likewise secured.[21]

Every library should be periodically surveyed by security professionals, architects, law enforcement, and insurance specialists to identify potential weaknesses and strengths. As conscientious as most librarians may be, they are not necessarily specialists in architecture and security. The field of physical security systems changes rapidly from year to year, and numerous new products are always being added to the market, some of which may be appropriate for an institution to consider. If the institution, however, never invites specialists to inspect its property, none of these newer systems or techniques will ever come to its attention. Thieves are always inventing ingenious new ways to accomplish their deeds, and the security industry seeks to foil them by countermeasures. At the very least, the library should not hesitate to take advantage of some of the security measures that may in fact prevent thieves before they ever start and may defeat them if they do.

In some ways, book and manuscript thieves are less than creative. By repeated attacks on obvious targets such as large research libraries, they provoke ever heightening security measures in such institutions, making them increasingly difficult objects. In their lack of imagination and understanding, they often fail to investigate or comprehend the relative riches that lie in surrounding, smaller entities that present far softer targets, protected sometimes by simple burglar alarm systems intended merely for home use that offer minimal protection. Blumberg, for example, could have taken everything he stole at the Connecticut State Library from other libraries within fifty miles of that institution. At one of them, he could have found most of the 271 books he stole on the other side of a hidden, exterior brick wall in an otherwise unalarmed space. As more and more protection is afforded larger institutions, thieves will seek easier targets, as they always do. The rise of Internet resources has also made more obvious where likely targets are. Even the smallest institutions often have their holdings publicly available on-line, and booksellers list their wares on various Internet services. Thus, smaller institutions and other potential victims, such as booksellers, who often have woefully under-protected premises, need to take steps to examine their places of operation to ensure that thieves do not find them easy prey as they expand their searches for materials to steal.

NOTES

1. Randall I. Atlas, "Architectural Security: Integrating Security with Design," in John J. Fay, ed., *Encyclopedia of Security Management*, 2nd ed. (Burlington: Butterworth-Heinemann, 2007), 445.

2. P. 445.

3. Robert J. Fischer and Gion Green, *Introduction to Security*, 7th ed. (Boston: Butterworth-Heinemann, 2007), 189.

4. Burglary is not so remote a possibility as it may seem. Stephen C. Blumberg, for example, was a skilled intruder whose methods are still not completely understood.

5. Several authors discuss general security considerations. See, for example, Alan Jay Lincoln, *Crime in the Library: A Study of Patterns, Impact, and Security* (New York & London: Bowker, 1984), 136–161 and J. Stephen Huntsberry, "Viva Blumberg: Lessons Learned," *Proceedings of the National on Cultural Property Protection and International Conference on Museum Security: "Cultural Property Protection from the Ground Up"* http://www.museum-security.org/blumberg-huntsberry.htm.

6. See, for example, "The Security Bullseye" illustration in Robert B. Burke and Sam Adeloye, *A Manual of Basic Museum Security* (Leicester: International Council of Museums, 1986), 22, and "The Four Lines of Protection" in Don T. Cherry, *Total Facility Control* (Boston: Butterworth-Heinemann, 1986), 100.

7. "Crime Prevention," Australian Institute of Criminology, Art Crime: Protecting Art, Protecting Artists, and Protecting Consumers Conference (2-3 December 1999:3–4. http://www.aic.gov.au/conferences/artcrime/hanleycp.pdf.

8. Kicking in a door is relatively simple. Defeating a door that opens outward, however, is a more complicated and difficult process.

9. For an overview of lock standards in this situation, see American National Standards Institute & Builders Hardware Manufacturers Association, *A.156.5-2001, Auxiliary Locks and Associated Products.*

10. Such locks have a free-floating, hardened steel cylinder inside the deadbolt itself. The cylinder rotates beneath the saw stroke, thereby preventing the bolt from being sawn in half.

11. In some cases, thieves have defeated outward opening doors by attaching chains or cables to the handles and pulling the doors out of their frames by means of a power winch or driving off in a vehicle. All doors at grade level should be protected by bollards to prevent someone from driving a vehicle into them.

12. See Bond, W. H., "The Gutenberg Caper," *Harvard Magazine* (March/April 1986): 42-8 for an instance in which an upper story window was used in an attempted burglary in 1969. At a major Southern university several decades ago, it was discovered that persons unknown were throwing books from a window in the rare books reading room on an upper story and then retrieving them from the bushes later.

13. To detect attacks on the perimeter while they are in progress, an institution would have to have an extensive system of shock detectors, which probably represents a prohibitive expense. A more economical solution is a system of motion detectors that protects all interior spaces. Although such a system will not detect an attack in progress, it should detect an intruder once s/he enters the space.

14. It bears repeating here that if phone lines are cut, the event is not treated as a burglar alarm but rather as a loss of signal. The security company will not call the police in such a case but will attempt to reach a staff member instead.

15. All concrete block walls enclosing special collections areas should have vertical rebar supports in them and be filled with an appropriate material, such as pea gravel. Ideally, partition walls between special collections and other areas should be made of at least concrete block or brick rather than mere sheetrock.

16. A story recently appeared about a burglar who hid in drop ceilings only to emerge after hours to steal drugs from in-store pharmacies. See Betsy Lehndorff, "Denver Pharmacy Burglar Strikes from Above," *Rocky Mountain News* (7 September 2007). http://www.rockymountainnews.com/drmn/local/article/0,1299,DRMN_15_5692592,00.html. The author knows personally of several other instances in which burglars have come through roofs at various times and by various means.

17. A total of 96 square inches is considered adequate for a person to pass through. See U.S. Army, Information Security Program, *AR 380-5*, Appendix H, "Classified Document and Materiel Storage Standards and Information" (Washington, 1988). http://www.marcorsyscom.usmc.mil/sites/ia/References/training/IASO%20Training/Army/AR%20380-5/preface.htm.

18. Blumberg used such weaknesses much to his advantage. See Nicholas A. Basbanes, *A Gentle Madness: Bibliophiles, Bibliomanes, and the Eternal Passion for Books* (New York: Henry Holt, 1995), 471–72, 480.

19. Blumberg exploited the opportunities offered by elevator shafts in at least one unnamed California library (Basbanes, p. 480).

Spiegelman gained access to Columbia's special collections area by means of a dumb waiter shaft. See Travis McDade, *The Book Thief: the True Crimes of Daniel Spiegelman* (Westport: Praeger, 2006), 14–18.

20.   Ante-rooms are also good ideas for sparing wear and tear on the door and locking mechanism. Usually with an ante-room, the vault door would be opened at the beginning of the day and left in that position, but with the vault entrance blocked by an access door (U. S. Army).

21.   Such a blunder happened when Blumberg was casing Henry H. Clifford's home and discovered a copy of the house's alarm manual in the crawl space (Basbanes, 494).

Reading Room Design for Security

Jeffrey D. Marshall

In a well-conducted man-of-war every thing is in its place, and there is a place for every thing.

~ *Frederick Marryat*

Librarians and archivists who have the opportunity to participate in the planning of a new or remodeled reading room may face many conflicting needs and expectations. Administrators and the public may view the reading room as the showcase of the library, distinguished more for its appearance than its functionality. Ease of access, not security, may be the architect's preconception of functionality. Reading rooms may have to serve as exhibit or reception rooms as well. The design of the reading room must take these needs and expectations into account, and when conflicting uses cannot be eliminated they must be mitigated by design and by appropriate policies and procedures (see figs 4.1–4.4.)

Quite often the architect will be reporting to a senior administrator, someone whose responsibilities may include multiple buildings. The administrator may have little understanding of Special Collections/Archives security needs and how those might conflict with programmatic priorities. The library building committee or representative might have little or no opportunity to educate senior administrators. Therefore, developing rapport and beginning an ongoing conversation with the architect are vital first steps in ensuring that security will be a paramount consideration. If certain features of a proposed design come into question,

it is the architect who will have to answer, and he or she should be ready and willing to do so.[1]

The Security Zone

Collection storage areas typically receive the greatest attention when it comes to security, but are usually the easiest to protect. Stack areas are

Figure 4.1

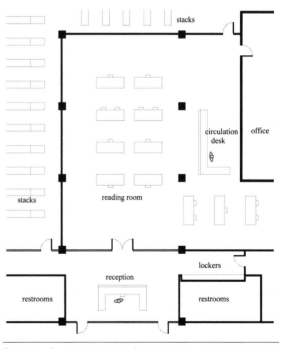

Scenario 1 (Courtesy Sara Alicia Costa, Ocurrente Design)

Figure 4.2

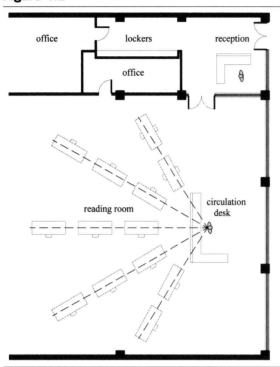

Scenario 2: Highly Secure Reading Room
(Courtesy Sara Alicia Costa, Ocurrente Design)

Figure 4.3

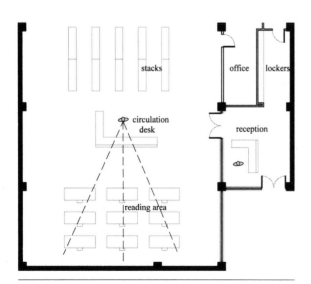

Scenario 3 (Courtesy Sara Alicia Costa, Ocurrente Design)

almost always securely locked, accessible only to staff, and have limited access points. The reading room presents greater security challenges. It will be accessible to users during certain hours and may be accessible to departmental staff, outside staff, and custodians at any time. To minimize the opportunities for theft, designers should carefully consider what activities are appropriate within the reading room security zone, and what activities should be confined to areas outside of the zone. However those activities are delineated, the transition from one zone to another needs to be defined by a wall or checkpoint.[2]

Before the point of entry to the reading room, users should have access to an area large enough to hold coats, umbrellas, brief cases, bags, backpacks, and laptop cases. Restrooms and public elevators must also be located outside the security zone. Designers need to be aware that those with mobility challenges will also require access to lockers and restrooms outside the security zone. User services must, of course, go hand-in-hand with effective procedures. For example, if the storage of briefcases in lockers outside the reading room is merely available but not mandatory, the presence of lockers has no positive impact on security.

Controlled Access to the Reading Room

If possible, researchers and staff should have only one point of entry to the library. (Emergency exits must not open from outside.) The entryway, ideally, is an area separate from the reading room, through which all must pass. The reading room may have a second locked door controlled by staff members both from the registration desk in the vestibule and from the reading room. Some libraries may consider this second door unnecessary, and may even combine the registration function with reference. Either way, the registration desk serves as the

Figure 4.4

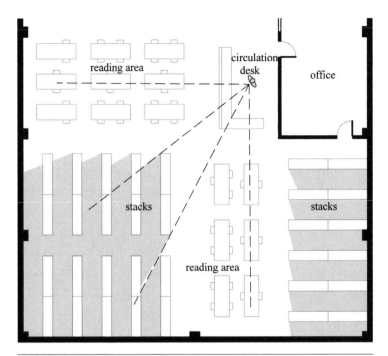

reading area

circulation desk

office

stacks

stacks

reading area

Scenario 4: Note that Monitoring Activity in Stacks Is Blocked
(Courtesy Sara Alicia Costa, Ocurrente Design)

the reading room security zone. In this case, separate security measures and procedures must include the protection of security information (alarm codes and details of security infrastructure), keys, and collection materials that may be temporarily located outside the security zone. Rare materials should not be removed for examination or processing and left in an area less secure than the reading room or storage area.

Detection portals will need to be positioned at an exit if any materials are security-stripped. While magnetic and other detection devices are not currently in wide use for most Special Collections materials, new technologies may make tagging of these materials more practical, thus requiring a monitoring station at the exit.

point of control, where trained staff determine that persons entering or exiting are not carrying inappropriate materials. The layout of this area of first and last contact should ensure that staff confront (cordially, of course) every user at entry and exit.

An uncomfortably high proportion of thefts in special collections departments, archives, and museums are committed by staff. Although eliminating the risk of an inside job is impossible, requiring staff to use the same entrance to the building is a minimal prevention step. If a separate staff door is available for reading room entrance and exit, it should be visible from the desk.

If staff offices are accessible directly from the reading room, the entryway to the reading room might be the only point of access to the offices, although this arrangement can quickly become tedious if large numbers of staff are involved. It may not always be possible to locate offices within

Design of User Space

When entering the reading room, the user should encounter the reading room supervisor before having an opportunity to take a seat. The placement of the supervisor's desk should therefore be near the door, but more importantly, it should be positioned to give a clear view of all reader desks. Some recommend that the supervisor's desk be elevated to improve sight lines, but perhaps more important is a design that maximizes the supervisor's mobility and ability to communicate with users. A rectangular or square room without ells is the easiest to configure for observation.[3] To maintain lines of sight, the reading room should have no pillars to interrupt sight lines or spaces that are hidden from direct observation. If pillars are present, user desks should not be placed behind them or other visual obstructions, and "dead spaces" should be made inaccessible. Ceiling or wall-mounted mirrors and

CCTV systems may permit observation of areas that are otherwise difficult to see.[4]

Determining the right size for the reading room can be difficult, especially if the room is to be made available for non-research uses. The larger the room, the more difficult it will be to supervise all users. Designers may want to consider moveable partitions as long as they do not obstruct surveillance or create hidden spaces. Ideally, a second staff member should be available to supervise the room from a different angle if more than a handful of researchers are present.

Desks should be arranged so that the supervisor faces every user or can see down the entire length of the tables (and can do so without leaving his or her station); in no case should a researcher be able to work with his back to the supervisor or in such a way that boxes, laptops, or other objects obscure the supervisor's view of the materials in use. It is best to have one researcher per table; some tables may need to be large enough to accommodate large-format materials. Researcher tables should not have drawers. If task lighting is provided, the units should be of a size and design that will not obscure the supervisor's view.[5]

The presence of low-security, open stack collections within the reading room presents a special difficulty. Reference collections and other secondary sources are valuable aids to research. When present in the reading room, those materials should be arranged so as to leave no unobservable areas; e.g. bookcases should be arranged against walls, not in parallel stacks. The supervisor may be tempted to treat users working with open stack materials with a lesser degree of caution, although such an attitude should be discouraged since many reference books are now rarer and more expensive than the materials they document. Despite the temptation to provide separate areas for the examination of reference materials, this is not wise. Researchers, such as those collating an eighteenth-century book or comparing an original manuscript with a printed transcription of it, will invariably want both the reference book and the rare material at the same time. A better strategy is to ensure that the reading room is designed so that all materials are given equitable surveillance and care.

Some special collections libraries, particularly those serving undergraduate students, need to accommodate groups working on research projects or whole classes who have come for presentations. These activities are best conducted outside of the reading room but under direct supervision of the librarian (and faculty member or teaching assistant). Besides creating a distraction to other researchers, groups present many challenges to direct observation. Designers may want to include a classroom or group study area adjacent to and accessible only from the reading room. If so, the same security considerations must be applied. If valuable materials can be used in the study room (which should be locked when not in use), a supervisor and surveillance cameras should be present. Glass walls may permit observation from the reading room, but that should not be considered sufficient. Any barrier between the supervisor and the patron creates a delay in the supervisor's reaction to inappropriate activities.

Proximity to Collections and Finding Aids

The point of retrieval of materials is another area of concern. Ideally, collection storage areas should be adjacent to and accessible only through the reading room and, if necessary, a secure loading dock area. An entrance to the stacks from a point other than the reading room could also serve as an unintended exit for persons unauthorized to use it. Very often, a large proportion of collections must be stored off-site, and procedures will have to be developed to provide security during transportation. To ensure that patrons do not have access to collection storage areas, it is advisable to have a keyed door between the reading room and the stacks. In some libraries, materials are handed through a window directly to reading room staff so that there is little or no foot traffic between stacks and reading room. This arrangement may limit other design considerations, however, and a locking door to the stacks should be equally effective. The reading room staff should have locking cabinets near the supervisor's desk to store any materials that cannot be returned immediately to the stacks. These may also be useful for storing items to be reproduced.

As mentioned above, reference and secondary source materials may be present in the reading room and should be shelved so that they are easily observable. Any paper finding aids, card catalogs, or computer terminals should also be arranged in such a way as to permit easy observation.

Surveillance

The types of CCTV equipment and their placement can be contentious issues when designing a library. Sometimes the number of cameras required to cover a space entirely can be daunting, and the sheer mass of them is sometimes considered unattractive. In renovated historical structures, aesthetic considerations often come into play. Placement of monitors needs to be decided on early in the process. Wherever they are placed, design considerations to accommodate them will have to be taken into account. In some cases there may be direct conflict between CCTV security needs and the desire for a space that is not littered with cameras and other paraphernalia.

No security step is more effective in preventing or recovering from a theft as direct observation of the patron, but CCTV systems have become common adjuncts to human eyes. Ideally, the design of the reading room should allow 400% observation; i.e. observation of patrons at all times by two staff members and by CCTV cameras from two different angles. To cover all areas of the reading room, this may mean mounting numerous cameras at different locations. The design of the reading room must take into consideration the limits of human observation and surveillance cameras.

Surveillance cameras serve three distinct purposes: deterrence, real-time observation, and recording of evidence.[6] Deterrence can be achieved even with non-functioning cameras, but expert thieves can spot dummies and such cameras may create legal liabilities. In addition, the fact that cameras are not operational may become known to patrons and may produce an unhealthy attitude toward security among staff. Real-time observation by CCTV is highly recommended, but should not be considered "a substitute for direct staff observation."[7]

Few libraries can afford trained personnel to watch video monitors. While CCTV provides additional points of observation, the quality of the images will never be as good as human observation. If the video monitor cannot be watched at all times, it is even more important to have a system that records the images. Besides providing a back-up when suspicious activities are discovered after the fact, recorded evidence of a theft is often crucial to prosecution and recovery.

The quality of cameras and the images they record vary greatly. The crucial evidence recorded by the camera may be the proof of the presence of an individual rather than the act of theft itself, and this may be achieved with less than top-shelf equipment. Because the detection of theft often occurs long after the event, images ought to be stored for several decades if not permanently. Digital recordings do not require as much space to store as video recordings, but both media present preservation challenges that must be factored into the choice of technology.

In addition to monitoring readers' tables, cameras should be placed at all exits, including emergency exits. Cameras can be installed so that they activate only when the exit is used, or they may be activated by motion detectors. In all cases, recording equipment needs to capture the date and time continuously while in operation. (See Chapter 7 .)

Doors, Windows, and Alarm Systems

Building codes, fire codes, and the Americans with Disabilities Act dictate the placement of doors in public facilities and limit the kinds of locking devices that can be used. Deadbolt locks provide the best security and can be paired with interior crash bars or similar devices to allow rapid evacuation in an emergency. Electronic locking systems that require the entry of a code, card swipe, or biometric information can be very effective, permitting heavily-bolted doors to be easily opened by authorized personnel. Any doors that patrons are permitted to open may need to have automated opening devices for the disabled.

Windows can present climate control challenges as well as security risks. If the reading room is to have windows they should be sealed and either shielded or made of shatter-proof material. They can also be equipped with sensors to alert police in case of breakage. Doors should be equipped with alarms that staff can arm when the reading room is closed or that can be activated by a timer. A wide variety of motion detection systems is available for interior detection, and these systems, when reliably linked directly to a police station or reputable security company, are very effective. All alarm systems should be tested periodically, and it is important to ensure that a backup power supply is immediately available in case the power goes out. Alarm systems can be retrofitted to any space, but understanding the limitations of both the space and the system to be implemented is an essential part of planning.[8] (See Chapter 6.)

Conclusion

Whether designing a new reading room, renovating an existing space, or simply retrofitting an active room for improved security, librarians and archivists must consider the floor plan and the configuration of architectural features as the first building block of security. Where architectural obstacles to security cannot be avoided, technology should be designed to mitigate security threats. In all cases, reading room design is just the beginning of security, which can only be made effective through careful policies and procedures.

NOTES

1. For a good summary of the issues involved in working with architects and contractors, see Thomas P. Wilsted, *Planning New and Remodeled Archival Facilities* (Chicago: Society of American Archivists, 2007), 53–68.
2. The concept of functionally-defined security zones is mentioned by Wolf Buchmann in "Preservation: Buildings and Equipment," *Journal of the Society of Archivists* 20 (April 1999): 5–23.
3. Richard Strassberg, "The Final Barrier: Security Consideration in Restricted Access Reading Rooms," in Laura B. Cohen, ed., *Reference Services for Archives and Manuscripts* (New York: Haworth Press, 1997), 52.
4. Mary Boone Bowling and Richard Strassberg, "Security in the Reading Room: A Society of American Archivists Web Seminar" (Chicago: Society of American Archivists, 2005), 3. This and subsequent page numbers refer to the printed PowerPoint© excerpt, but the compact disk should be consulted for the full discussion.
5. Ibid., 5. One potential deterrent to thieves is glass-top reading tables. Such tables are probably effective, however, only with CCTV cameras that look directly down on the researcher.
6. Gregor Trinkaus-Randall, *Protecting Your Collections: A Manual of Archival Security* (Chicago: Society of American Archivists, 1995), 43.
7. Bowling and Strassberg, 5. The ensuing points largely follow Bowling's and Strassberg's web seminar discussion.
8. Trinkaus-Randall provides a detailed, though now somewhat dated overview of locks, alarms, and surveillance equipment (43–59).

Access Control Systems

Everett C. Wilkie, Jr.

> Nothing is more important in reducing risks of theft, injury, and mitigation of liability than controlling ingress and egress at your facilities.
> ~*A Plus Identification & Security*

Access control systems range all the way from the extremely simple to the very complex. Such systems are very old. A drawbridge is an example of such a system. So, too, is a simple latchstring that could be pulled inside a cabin door at night. So is any type of lock. The advent of electronics has vastly changed the access control landscape. Today, almost everyone has seen a modern access control system based on an electric strike, some type of reader, and some type of key, such as a card. Despite the great level of security such systems afford, libraries have been slow to adopt them. It is regrettable that almost any hotel has better access control than most rare book and manuscript libraries.[1]

What It Does

Access control systems govern *who* can pass into a space, into *which* space one may pass, and *when* one may do so. They typically control a pedestrian door, although they can be configured to control just about anything that can be opened or closed, or turned off and on. Some systems are very small, controlling only a few doors and a few people. Others are sizable, controlling dozens of doors and thousands of people. Their complexity ranges from systems controlled by central computers to those that control a single stand-alone lock opened by a keypad. This chapter does not address every pos-sible type of access control system. Precisely what type of system a library installs will be a matter of negotiation with a security company, of budget constraints, of purpose of the system, and of comfort level. The purpose of this chapter is to review only some types of systems and to offer suggestions concerning their implementation.

Although specific discussions of such matters are beyond the scope of this guide, the library should bear in mind that some access control systems have powerful capabilities for interaction with the institution's CCTV, resource management, and burglar alarm systems. They also have considerable interest for building and personnel managers in matters concerning energy use and tracking staff attendance and movement. Your security company should be able to explain these capabilities to you in some detail.

An Important Caveat

A library should never install any sort of access control system without the consent of the authority having jurisdiction (AHJ), which is usually the local fire marshal. Access control systems often have serious implications for life safety, and although such life safety issues are generally beyond the scope of this guide, in this instance they cannot be avoided. Do not even put so much as a combination lockset on a supply closet without the AHJ's approval.

Failure to obtain this approval could expose the library to severe financial and criminal penalties. If someone is injured or killed in a fire because of an unapproved access control device, the institution is going to be caught between a rock and a hard place.[2]

System Components

All access control systems, from the simplest to the most complex, grant access based on knowledge, possession, or physical trait, and more complex systems use a combination of these. In a system based on knowledge, the user must know something, usually a combination, before the lock will open. In a system based on possession, the user must have something, perhaps a card of some type, before the system will operate. In a system using a physical trait, the user must have a personal characteristic, such as a certain finger print, to operate the system. Commonly, the first two types are referred to as "dumb," since they will operate for anyone with the required knowledge or item, whether the person is supposed to possess it or not. The last system is referred to as "smart," since it will operate only for the proper person.

Every access control system consists of four elements: 1) a lock; 2) a key; 3) a reader; and 4) a controller. The first element is the device, including the door strike, that secures the door to the frame and prevents it from being opened freely. The second element is the device presented to the lock in an attempt to operate it. The third element is the device that receives information from the key and determines if it fits the lock. The fourth element is the device that decides if the lock should be released. Even something as simple as a front door lock on an apartment contains all four elements.

Locks and Controllers

Most libraries are protected by standard mechanical locks, the simplest level of access control and the most universal protection system in use. These devices consist of a lock in the door that is secured to the strike in the doorframe by a piece of protruding metal. The device is operated by inserting the proper key, which allows the pins to fall, which in turn allows the plug to rotate, thus withdrawing the piece of metal from the strike. Such protection is fairly inadequate and can be easily defeated. Many such locks can be easily picked. Because they are small, keys are easily stolen and most are also easily duplicated. Even those stamped "Do Not Duplicate" are protected only by the warning on them and the integrity of the locksmith to whom they are presented for duplication. Often, one key opens every lock in the building or special collections area. The locks are also subject to being opened readily by bump keys, which can be made to open dozens of locks with a single device.[3]

If a library is unwilling to install a modern access control system, it should then consider switching at least some locks to proprietary keyways or so-called Extra Security locks. In such locks, the keys themselves usually cannot be duplicated by anyone without assistance from the manufacturer. The keys are extremely complicated, often with double faces, and cannot be copied by the average locksmith, who will have neither the proper blanks nor the proper cutting machinery. The manufacturer will limit from whom it will accept an order for new keys. Such locks are also extremely difficult if not impossible to pick. Finally, such locks often have other added security features, such as resistance to being drilled. Because they still rely on keys, however, they are subject to compromise if a key is stolen.[4]

Libraries might also consider reinforcing doors and their frames. There are several relatively inexpensive hardware applications that will strengthen doors and locks against physical attack. There are even nearly indestructible locking hinges available.

Almost any locksmith can install such devices. Such measures are particularly appropriate if the library has wooden doors and frames. As Dixon remarks, "Locks, however, are only as secure as the quality of the materials and the building techniques used to construct the door, cabinet, or window to which they are attached."[5]

If a library depends on mechanical locks for protection, it should have some procedures and safeguards in place. At the very least, all keys should be accounted for in writing. Every staff member who has a key should be required to sign for it when it is issued, and its return should also be recorded. In this instance, it is important to account for all keys. Does the campus security force have keys? Are there keys stored in the Knox box on the outside of the building? Do any trustees have keys? Are keys issued to maintenance and service personnel? Are there keys just lying around in desk drawers? Extra keys should be secured in a proper key safe.

Consideration should also be given to establishing different levels of access by altering the keyways on certain locks and restricting to whom keys for those locks are issued. Even in very small institutions, it is rarely a good idea to have all locks with identical keyways that can all be opened by one key. Does everybody really need to be able to get into the Curator's office at all hours? Does the volunteer who comes in on Saturdays to process manuscript collections need to get into the book stacks? Some people will undoubtedly need a master key that will open practically all the locks in the library. Such master keys, however, should be issued only to a very few senior staff members.[6]

Staff possession of keys should also be subject to certain considerations. In some institutions, many staff members pick up their keys at the beginning of the day and are required to turn them back in when they leave at the end of work every day. Staff should be warned against ever giving the institu-tion's keys to anyone else, even their spouses. If the library's keys are on the same key ring as the house and car keys, they should be on a separate ring that can be removed before the other keys on the ring are lent to another. Staff should also be required to keep their keys in their personal possession at all times when the institution is open. Keys should never be left lying on desk tops, in desk drawers, or in purses. Finally, for the staff member's own personal protection and the institution's security, there should be no identifying information on any key or attached to the key ring itself.

The loss of a key is a serious matter that usually requires action on the library's part. Even so much as its overnight disappearance should be cause for concern.[7] Correcting the situation caused by a lost or misplaced key will require promptly rekeying some or all of the library's locks to render the problematic key unusable. Rekeying can be expensive, but security should not be compromised by ignoring the lost key and hoping for the best. The necessity for rekeying is one of the powerful arguments for a modern access control system, wherein such a loss can be immediately dealt with little additional expense.

Another drawback of conventional locks is that they leave no record of who operated them. Although modern access control systems are not perfect in that regard, it is impossible to operate many of them anonymously. Unless the library is filming every door with a CCTV system, one will never probably never know exactly who opened a given mechanical door lock and compromised security.

Finally, it would seem to be painfully obvious, but it needs to be pointed out that mechanical locks do no good if they are not locked. Some institutions do not lock all doors equipped with locks when they close for the day. One of the chief values of a lock is that is slows a thief or vandal because s/he must take time to somehow defeat it, even if the attempt eventually succeeds. Slowing the actions of a thief is an important security consideration. There is little reason to ease the person's task by leaving locks unlocked. Libraries will lock the stacks but leave the computer room open. Thieves come in all stripes; not all steal books or manuscripts. Any library needs to take full advantage of the locks it does have. A parallel consideration, if a library uses spring locks, is the decision to alter some devices so that they can never be left unlocked. In other words, the proper key will open the lock but it cannot be left in an unlocked state once the door is closed. Many libraries have this feature on locks controlling access to the stacks, although these types of locks in general are relatively insecure.[8]

The next level of access control is represented by surface mounted, stand-alone locks that are operated by some type of card or keypad. Such devices work like a traditional mechanical lock so far as their locking mechanisms are concerned. It is the method of opening them that is different. The key is sometimes a plastic card with a magnetic strip on it. The strip holds information that the lock reads. If the card is authorized for that lock, the bolt may be withdrawn. Almost everyone has encountered such a device in a hotel or motel. Some such locks use a keypad into which a series of numbers must be entered in the proper sequence before the lock will open.[9]

Such locks offer several advantages over traditional mechanical locks. They are virtually impossible to pick. Lost cards are usually easily removed from operation, and acceptable combinations can readily be changed. Finally, if the door is closed, there is no option to leave it unlocked. Despite those advantages, there are some drawbacks, especially to those operated by a keypad. Persistent thieves given enough time can often ascertain the correct combination for such a lock. Keypads are also sub-

ject to being observed, and thieves can sometimes obtain a combination merely by watching someone enter his or her code.[10] Some simple devices will allow only one operational sequence (e. g., a card or a combination but not both). With those locks operated by cards, as in traditional locking systems, a valid card will release the lock for anyone who has it. Finally, cards can also be lost, although making lost cards inoperative is usually a relatively simple procedure.

If a library is considering such locks, it needs to inquire carefully about several features of such a system. The first area of concern should be how many users each lock can accommodate as some can hold only a few codes. Many users with the same code present a security problem. Second, some such locks can hold event logs. The library should inquire if this feature is available, and, if so, how many events the log can hold and how the log is printed out. If this feature is available, the log should periodically be printed and kept permanently. Third, the library must be very cautious to inquire into the procedure for the removing unauthorized users. Some systems use proximity readers that respond to small, encoded tags the user holds up to the lock. In some of them, a tag cannot be removed from the system unless it is present for presentation to the reader. In other words, if a staff member leaves abruptly taking the tag, the library will have no way of disabling that particular tag. Finally, some such locks have a keyway that can be used to override the lock, which again raises the problems associated with traditional mechanical locks.

A more sophisticated type of access control system is one that uses a reader (or keypad) to operate an electric strike, electromagnetic lock (called a mag lock, for short), or a solenoid bolt. In this case, the reader is mounted near the door rather than on it and does not contain the locking mechanism itself. In the case of an electric strike, the door frame contains a specialized, powered strike that holds a gate that is normally closed. When the reader recognizes a proper card, power to the gate is temporarily dropped and the door can be opened. It is possible to use the library's existing locks with such a system since only the strike is replaced. In the case of a mag lock, the door is held shut by a powerful electromagnet to which power is interrupted when an authorized code is detected by the reader. Such locks are common on plate glass doors into which conventional electronic strikes cannot be installed.[11] A solenoid bolt features a mechanism that withdraws a bolt when an authorized code is presented to the reader. Many of these systems are computer driven and can handle hundreds of users, even for just a single door. Although the installation of such a system might seem like overkill, one should be seriously considered by any library contemplating adding or upgrading access control.

Using a keypad to address the lock has the same drawbacks here as it does with using them in a stand-alone system. One of these difficulties, having a third party steal an access code by observing a user, can be obviated by some modern digital keypads. With such keypads, the order of the numbers on the pad is scrambled every time the device is used. Thus, if Mary's number was 1234, when she entered the combination on the pad, it would appear to an observer that the number was really 9652 because the numbers 1234 would appear for the nonce in those positions. The next time she operated the keypad, the numbers would be in yet different positions.

Some such systems use readers that are addressed by cards. Many combinations of types of cards and readers exist, but some combinations have significant drawbacks. The most vulnerable type is the system that depends on bar codes. The chief drawback to such systems is that the reader is easily fooled by a forgery. Some readers will open the lock when they are presented with a photocopy of the bar code. If known, usable bar codes can also be duplicated on computer printers. For those reasons, bar code systems should be avoided and have lost popularity in recent years, despite the development of bi-directional encoding.

A step up from bar code systems are those that use magnetic cards. In such a system, the card has a magnetic strip encoded with information necessary to operate the lock, much like a typical credit card. Although a technology superior to bar codes, such cards are subject to failure because the information encoded in the magnetic strip may be corrupted by physical wear or exposure to a magnetic field. Another significant drawback is the magnetic strip itself. Because the strip has physical limitations on how much information it can hold, it is possible that several cards exist that will open the same door. In other words, in issuing millions of cards, manufacturers are forced to reuse codes, thereby resulting in some cards that are identical. The possibility is remote that a duplicate card would ever be presented to your reader, but the issue is of some concern to the security industry and clients should be advised of the problem. Finally, the information on the card can be captured by third parties and replicated on another card that will function exactly as the original.

A fairly secure and trouble free card and reader system is one employing Wiegand technology where encoding is placed in wires embedded in the card. The information on the wires is almost impossible to duplicate, and new cards are available only from the manufacturer. The cards never wear out and are relatively immune to damage. They are, for example, immune to magnetic fields. Most Wiegand cards are proximity cards, which means they merely need to be held within a few inches of the reader to operate it.[12] This feature can be a convenience if one's hands are full. This system is an excellent technology for card reader systems. Nevertheless, it has become so popular that duplicate cards are possible. Some resellers offer proprietary cards to ensure each one is unique, although they probably should be avoided.[13]

"Smart cards" are a technology that has become popular in recent years and the use of which will probably spread to numerous venues, even the local Laundromat. Unlike other cards, these cards contain a computer chip that is read by the reader and that can contain various information about the user. They are becoming increasingly common on college and university campuses, especially for student use, because of the wide variety of information they can hold. For a library's purposes, they do offer significant advantages over more traditional technology for access control. One important feature smart cards have, for example, is the ability to hold biometric information. Thus, even if Mary's card fell into the wrong hands, unlike other cards it would not work because the image of Mary's iris stored on the card would not match the iris of the person trying to use the card. Finally, the "card" need not be a card at all; the chip can be installed in various devices, such as a key ring. In a more far-flung application, the small devices can even be implanted under a user's skin. The cards can be coupled with RFID systems to provide contactless access.

The most secure system is one that uses biometric readers. These readers compare a body part to stored information. If the two items match, the lock is released. Body parts most commonly used are finger-print, palm print, the face, or retina. Whichever one is chosen is scanned into a storage device, where it is kept for comparison when a user attempts to pass through a protected door. Such technology is highly reliable and provides a great level of security. There certainly is little concern here about losing an access control device or having it duplicated. It can be defeated, however. A staff member could be forced under duress, for example, to place his or her hand onto the reader. Some institutions use biometrics in combination with other access control methods, such as also requiring a pin, achieving a level of redundancy that might be considered necessary for areas such as vaults. Their chief advantage is that they positively identify who is being let into an area, a level of certainty that cannot be achieved with other systems unless the door is being watched somehow. Although prices for such systems have declined in recent years, they are still relatively expensive.[14]

An important, but sometimes overlooked aspect of card systems is that the locks also can usually be opened with a key. In many cases, far too many staff members are given keys in addition to their cards. In such a situation, the recording features of an access control system become useless, since the use of keys cannot be captured by the system. If an institution uses a card control system, it should strictly control who has keys and keep that number of people to a bare minimum. Even those who have keys should be disallowed from operating the lock with them except in cases of genuine necessity.[15]

Finally, if the library is considering installing a new or replacing an old system, it should strongly consider proximity cards, which have the most reliable record and the fewest problems. Proximity systems are not as subject to either failure or compromise as others that depend on different technologies. Some predict that proximity systems will eventually be the only card access systems available.

Stand-Alone vs. Computerized Systems

Stand-alone access control systems have limitations not encountered in more muscular, computerized systems. To take full advantage of an access control system, the library should have a system that controls who can open a door, when they can open the door, and which door they can open. It should also provide a record of all transactions at every reader. The simpler surface mounted access control locks are sometimes incapable of controlling all functions or of providing adequate transaction records. For example, they sometimes cannot control when a door may be opened. In such an instance, one can issue Mary a combination that opens the front door and the stacks door, but one cannot tell the system that Mary can't open those doors on July 4th or after 5:00 p.m. Many do not have a memory chip to store transactions. Those that do often have limits on the amount of information stored and cumbersome processes for viewing the information or for printing it out.

Computerized systems obviate such difficulties by providing means to control every aspect of access. Using a standard PC, such systems can configure cards and their readers so that Mary, for example, can open only the front door, the stacks door, and the break room door between the hours of 9:00 a.m–5:00 p.m. on days when the library is regularly open. It will record every instance when Mary opened those doors and will also record her attempts to enter other controlled areas, like the conservation lab or vault, for which she has not been granted access. Another important feature of such access control systems is that they can control access on both sides of a door, an arrangement that can be quite clumsy with a lesser system. Finally, such systems can easily sound an alarm of some sort if a protected door is deliberately or accidentally left ajar.[16] If at all possible, this is the type of system a library should install.

Two types of systems are run by computers. In both types, all authorized users, authorization levels, and cards are entered into the main computer. In one type, all decisions concerning the system's operation are made by the main computer. In the other, processing is distributed and all decisions are made by individual units controlling just a few

doors. When either system is operating normally, there is little difference in their capabilities. If, however, in the first type of system the main computer crashes or is turned off, the system runs in what is called "degraded mode." In that mode, the system will honor any system card presented to a reader no matter what its authorizations. In the second type of system, however, even if the main computer crashes or is turned off, the readers will honor only proper cards, because all decisions are made by the individual control units. Usually, however, if the individual control unit fails, these systems also operate in the degraded mode.

One problem that will have to be addressed in computer-driven systems is the possibility of power failure. If a failure is so prolonged that all power to the doors is lost, the system will operate in one of two modes. The first is called "fail safe."; in that scenario, all the doors will be open. The second is called "fail secure"; in that one, all the doors will be locked. In reality, the library may have no choice in the matter, since many AHJs require that the fail safe mode be employed. Note that this choice normally has no bearing on a person's ability to exit a space.

System Configurations

Cables and their installation in an electronic access control system will depend on many factors, and the library should not concern itself with those matters, as they should be handled exclusively by the security company designing and installing the system. The overall configuration of the system, however, might be of some concern to the library. Four possible configurations exist, as outlined below. Each has its advantages and its problems.

Star or Home-run

In this system, every controller is connected directly to the main control unit. This type of system may be relatively expensive if the main control unit cannot be centrally located. It is, however, extremely reliable and robust. Obviously, if one of the controllers or its wiring has problems, that situation will not affect the operation of any of the others.

Daisy Chain

In this configuration, the main control unit communicates with all the controllers by a single circuit. The advantage of this cabling method is that it can be used over long distances since each controller usually has a signal booster incorporated. Its chief disadvantage is that trouble on one controller may affect all the others between it and the control unit.

Trunk

In this configuration, all controllers are hooked to a pair of wires. In many respects this is the easiest system to install and modify, since controllers can be added or subtracted easily. It is also highly reliable because problems with one controller will not affect other controllers on the system. If, however, a trunk wire is damaged, all controllers beyond the damaged point will not function properly. As with the ring system, this configuration has powerful communications capabilities. Because of the primary importance of the trunk wire, the library might consider putting it in conduit.

Ring

This is a combination of the star and trunk configurations. In this case, each controller is wired to a loop that goes from the main control unit, past each controller connected to the loop, and back to the central control unit. As with the star configuration, problems with one controller do not affect any of the others. Obviously, however, a problem with the main circuit might degrade the performance of the entire system. This configuration does, on the other hand, allow a system take advantage of

communications bandwidth in a way that neither the star nor daisy chain configuration does.

Shunts

An important feature of a computerized access control system is that it can be tied into the intrusion detection system. With such an access control system, doors can always be left armed. For example, the stacks door can always be left armed to guard against unauthorized entry or exit even when the library is open. This capability is achieved by means of device called a shunt. If a controlled door is left armed at all times, the presentation to the reader of an authorized card, for example, will cause the shunt to bypass the alarm, allowing the door to be opened without sending the security system into alarm. If the door is otherwise opened, an alarm will sound. Doors may be protected on both sides if desired. In other words, a person cannot pass a door in either direction without presenting a valid code that unlocks the door.[17]

Elevators

Any elevator in the special collections area should have an access control system to prevent its unauthorized operation. In many instances this control is provided by some sort of keying system. Such systems suffer from the same drawbacks as any access control system that depends on traditional locks. Elevators are easily controlled by access control systems using technologies more sophisticated than actual keys.

Testing

No matter what type of access control system the library chooses, it should routinely be challenged. For example, as part of security system checks, controllers should be presented with bogus cards, bogus codes, or bogus handprints. Such testing ensures that the system is operating properly. If the system uses a computer, it, too, should be challenged; bogus passwords, for example, should be presented to it to ensure that it will not operate under such conditions. Finally, all doors with access control should be periodically tested by pulling on them, as that is the only way to know if the door is actually locked. In this instance, it pays to use one's imagination to try to figure out ways to defeat the system. Only in that way can potential security problems be revealed. Such testing should be done quarterly by library staff apart from any periodic testing and maintenance done by the security company.

The Negatives

A good access control system is an important security feature. Although there are compelling reasons for installing a highly sophisticated system, there may in fact be factors that militate against it. An ornate library in a historic house, for example, may not be willing to disfigure its interior with card readers or electric strikes, which are rarely graceful architectural elements in such a setting. In that situation, proprietary keyways may be the only realistic option. Budget considerations may also be a factor. Although prices continue to drop, an adequate access control system is not exactly cheap, even though it is probably cheaper than the replacement of a Vesalius or a First Folio and the embarrassment of explaining why they are missing. Some institutions may also feel that an access control system implies spying on staff. After all, the systems can do precisely that—record a person's comings and goings. The installation of such systems can also involve bruised feelings and resentment. In issuing access levels, administrators are forced to make judgments concerning a person's movements, which decisions can be interpreted by staff as distrust or denigration. It may not make Mary happy that she can no longer just wander into the conservation lab. Finally, the

installation of such a system will put an added burden on staff. The access control system is an important component of library security, and staff can compromise it by carelessness or by failure to follow procedures. Compromising security by lending an access card to an unauthorized staff member should have serious consequences. Those are repercussions for which the library administration should be prepared.

As with patron registration and circulation records, events captured by the access control system need to be kept for a very long time, decades if not permanently. In cases of insider theft, such records may prove invaluable in solving the crime. Storing the data, however, requires the commitment of computer resources. If a library installs an access control system, it should insist that the system be able to capture and hold all data without loss and be prepared to preserve that data for decades. No computer controlling an access control system should ever be connected to the Internet.

Contracts

Many of the observations about contracts made in the chapter "Burglar Alarm Systems" will also apply to a contract for an access control system. Only considerations special to access control systems will be covered here.

As with burglar alarms, if there is a service contract on the system, the security company should be responsible for every aspect of the system, including all wiring. Of particular concern with an access control system are the electric strikes. In many instances, the security firm will subcontract their supply and installation. Despite that arrangement, the library should ensure that the security company itself is responsible for them if they should fail. Do not accept a situation where those devices are warranted by a third-party company or have maintenance restrictions placed on them.

The library should also inquire about procedures for ordering new cards. Usually the security company orders the cards from the manufacturer and supplies them to the library. Although it usually will not be specified in the contract, the library needs to know how much lead time is required to secure new cards as it may be as much as several weeks. The library should also obtain from the security company information on precisely what type of card its system uses, including the manufacturer and the card's technical specifications. Technology changes rapidly, and it is nearly impossible to ascertain the technical parameters of a card just by looking at it. An electronic access control system will last for years, but as it ages, cards for it may, like parts for a '37 Buick, become harder to find. Because of that situation, the library needs to have very precise information about the type of card its system uses.

In access control systems that necessitate a computer, the library may be facing a serious decision. In all cases the security company will provide the software necessary to operate the system and the proper training for library personnel to use it. Problems arise when the software is installed on a library-owned computer. Although security companies will supply the necessary specifications for the computer needed to operate the system (e.g., disk space needed, memory, etc.), they will sometimes not guarantee that the system will work properly unless it is installed as the only system on a computer supplied by the security company itself. The company's reluctance to otherwise warrant the system's operation is understandable. Over time, a library may make modifications to its own computer, such as adding programs. Such modifications may interfere with the operation of the access control system. If the library installs the system on a computer supplied by the security company, the company is completely on the hook if it fails to operate the system properly. The drawback to such an arrangement is that the security company is rarely able to provide the computer at a price comparable to that for which it could be purchased on the open market. On the positive side, such an arrangement isolates the access control system from other library computers and reduces the possibility that the system can be hacked. It bears repeating that in no instance should operating software for the access control system be mounted on a computer with Internet access.

Several components of electronic access control systems are sensitive to various kinds of interference from their surroundings. If the interference is severe enough, parts of the access control system may fail. Although the library may reasonably expect that a newly installed access control system will work as intended, the library must not expect the security company to correct gratis problems introduced by new construction or remodeling. It is always a wise idea to have the security company review any construction plans, especially wiring diagrams, to ensure that the access control equipment will not be interfered with. Running a 220v electrical line down the same tray holding access control cables is a type of situation that should be avoided.

Finally, the contract should include a provision for checking and cleaning the system annually. Access control systems will probably show normal wear and tear over the years and should be routinely monitored to make sure all their components are still functioning properly.

Conclusion

Controlling access to library space is an important consideration of which any library is aware, even if it employs only garden-variety locks. At the very least, any library will secure its main entrance doors when it closes for the day, the simplest form of access control. Given the alarming losses to library collections both from inside and outside theft, it would seem prudent for libraries to consider upgrading the methods whereby they allow access to their facilities and collections. As prices for these systems fall while their capabilities rise, libraries need to consider adding them as part of their overall security program.

NOTES

1. This area of technology is changing rapidly, so much so that some of the information presented here may be out of date by the time it is published. For a brief overview of the history of electronic locks, see John J. Fay, ed., *Encyclopedia of Security Management*, 2nd ed (Burlington: Butterworth-Heinemann, 2007), 312–13.

2. This caveat does not apply to the installation of ordinary door locks that lock a door only from the outside. Installation of double deadbolts, however, may need to be approved by the AHJ.

3. Blumberg is believed to have used copies of stolen keys or the keys themselves to have entered at least nine libraries between 1986–88. See Nicholas Basbanes, *A Gentle Madness: Bibliophiles, Bibliomanes, and the Eternal Passion for Books* (New York: Holt, 1995), 513.

4. See "Proprietary Keyways," *Focus on Security*. For a basic overview of locks, see Leon Dixon, "Keys & Locks: Technical Aspects of Locking Devices," *1999 National Conference on Cultural Property Protection Proceedings: Cultural Property Protection from the Ground Up* [Washington: Smithsonian Institution, 1999], 130–133. http://www.museum-security.org/locks-and-keys.htm.

5. Dixon, 130.

6. For a review of issues and procedures involved in planning a keying system, see Shankle & Shankle, *Comprehensive Manual of Locksmithing*, 307–345.

7. The notorious book thief Stephen Blumberg in one instance stole a ring of keys while the library was open, had them duplicated overnight, and then sneaked them back in after the library opened the next day. He then used the duplicate keys to break in.

8. Dixon notes, "Unfortunately, it is easy to open a spring bolt from the outside with the use of a celluloid or thin metal strip…. Even a young person can master this trick and for this reason the lock is considered a low security device offering little real protection" (132). For a brief overview of various locking mechanisms, see Gregor Trinkhaus-Randall, *Protecting Your Collections: A Manual of Archival Security* (Chicago: Society of American Archivists, 1995), 43–47.

9. Such surface mounted locks may present some ADA compliance issues because of the configuration of their handles.

10. In a system with only one or very few codes, care must be taken to routinely clean the keypad or buttons. Over time, dirt and oil from fingers build up on them, thereby considerably enhancing a person's ability to decipher the code by leaving a physical indication of which numbers are being used.

11. In addition to the invariable life safety considerations such locks present, they have the disadvantage that if an intruder can somehow interrupt the power supply, they no longer hold.

12. Proximity cards owe their origin to radio frequency identification (RFID) originally developed for use in pet collars. In this application, the RFID-equipped collar would allow a pet door to open for the animal wearing the collar but keep it closed against other animals, such as raccoons, not wearing the device.

13. Most libraries are not large enough that the issue of "bits" will not be of concern. The more bits a card can handle, the more unique cards can be issued. Initially, cards were 26-bit, but that number has risen to 37-bit, which will allow for millions of unique cards. The possibility that someone outside the library will have a duplicate card that will operate the library's system is remote. A parallel problem that no amount of bits will solve is issuing cards to outsiders, such as vendors or contractors, without assigning the card to a specific person. Doing so compromises security badly. See Morawski, 65–66.

14. Biometric readers are subject to sometimes unique considerations. For example, if the library has a staff member so heavily afflicted with arthritis that the person cannot readily extend the fingers, it probably is unwise to select a palm print reader. Most other biometric readers have similar considerations.

15. Ton Kremers, "…and the Curator Did It," *Rogues Gallery: An Investigation into Art Theft*, AXA Art Conference, November 1, 2005, 9, reports that in the case of the Dutch Army Museum, "There was an electronic access control system but at the same time staff were also in possession of keys. At random they used their keys or their electronic cards to enter the depositories.

So, the electronic history of access was useless. Besides, this history was erased weekly from the digital files." Ed Morawski, *How to Defeat Burglar Alarms—Not!: Dispelling Hollywood Myths* (N. p., 2007), remarks: "It is highly recommended that whatever type of locks you install, do *not* distribute any hard keys" (60).

16. Doors with access control systems on them are almost always also supplied with door closers to ensure that they are not left open.

17. Leaving a controlled space usually involves a "request to exit" function. In some case, this may be nothing more than pushing on a paddle that operates the lock from the inside. In other cases, it may require pressing a button. In the most sophisticated systems, a person is required to operate a reader because both sides of the door are protected.

CH6

Burglar Alarm Systems

Everett C. Wilkie, Jr.

> "A modern alarm system is extremely hard to defeat"
> ~ *Mowarski*

A wide range of burglar alarms systems is available. Such systems are more accurately called intrusion detection systems because their real function is to detect unauthorized entry into a protected space, whether the person is a burglar or not. The intruder may, for example, be a staff member who has innocently entered an area off limits to him or her. The intrusion detection system exists to detect the event and warn the proper personnel of such unauthorized entries.

In general, a burglar alarm system is the most common anti-theft device found in special collections libraries except for the librarians themselves. Even if a library lacks more sophisticated systems, they will have one, even if it is elementary. Given the fact that both Blumberg and Spielgelman were prolific burglars who between them stole from many libraries, an investment in an adequate burglar alarm system would seem a relatively cheap prevention. Unfortunately, the alarms in the institutions they pillaged were not sophisticated enough to detect their activities. Finally, one cannot prove a negative, so it is impossible to say how many burglaries intrusion alarms have prevented.[1]

In selecting an intrusion detection system, the library must consider many factors. In the discussion that follows, emphasis is placed on the capabilities and defects of certain equipment commonly used in such applications. The actual design and operation of a system will depend almost entirely on local requirements and needs. The discussion is hardly exhaustive and does not attempt to cover every consideration that must be borne in mind in this connection or every available device. It does, however, attempt to address many of the problems and considerations common to the installation and use of any intrusion detection system.[2]

Monitoring

Numerous scenarios exist to monitor a system, from a central station to a small audible alarm that rings only on the premises and does not notify anybody in particular that an intrusion has occurred. The choice of what type of monitoring is provided, however, is one of the critical choices that an institution faces. For a security system to stand any real chance of alerting authorities to an intrusion, it needs to be monitored by a central station. Installing a system that sounds only a local alarm or uses a telephone to call the curator at home can be a grave miscalculation and should be undertaken only under the most unusual circumstances. Increasingly, systems that directly call the local police from the premises are becoming illegal.

Central station monitoring systems are equipped to receive an intrusion alert at any time the system is armed and to alert authorities to the intrusion. If one chooses a central station system, it is important that the station be UL certified and a member of the Central Station Alarm Association. The UL certification and membership in the Association indicate that the central station meets rigorous standards for its profession.[3]

If one decides to install a system monitored by a central station, one should ask the company how many central station monitoring facilities it has. Most will have only one station to receive and process signals, and that single station may be a very long way from the premises. Obviously, if something happens to that single station, an alarm is not going to be processed in a timely fashion. UL certification will ensure that the station has the necessary systems (e.g., battery backups, generators, trained personnel, etc.) but will not ensure that the station may not for some reason be able to receive your alarm; thus, redundancy is important. The more central stations a security company has, the better the level of the protection will be. (In some applications, systems are actually monitored by two separate companies.) One can imagine the problem posed, for example, by a security company with only a single monitoring station that was flooded in New Orleans after Katrina.

The institution should also inquire whether the security company owns its own monitoring facility or if the monitoring contract will be passed off to a third party. If a third party is to monitor the system, the institution should be cautious. In case of problems, the security firm may have little leverage with the third party's central station. The institution could also find itself in the midst of a scenario in which the monitoring company blames the institution or the security company; the security company blames the institution and the monitoring company; and the institution does not know whom to blame. Such scenarios are avoided if the security company owns the monitoring facility.

Another crucial consideration is how your alarm system will communicate with the central station. Numerous ways to communicate are recognized as standard, almost all of which employ phone lines. It is probably best, however, to avoid the so-called direct wire system and adopt one of the other communication standards. Line supervision should also be incorporated. A line supervision system is capable of detecting tampering with the phone circuits and is an important adjunct to the communication system itself. Both multiplex and derived local channel systems inherently provide line security because of their design and operating features.

No matter how sophisticated the communication system, its Achilles' Heel is the phone line. If something happens to break the line of communication between the library and the central station, the latter will not receive any signals. It is a common misconception that the failure of the phone line triggers an alarm at the central station. More likely, it will trigger what is called a supervisory or communications failure signal. Central station personnel have no way of knowing, of course, what caused the communication loss. It could be a backhoe operator who dug up a phone line, an automobile accident that took out a phone pole, or trouble with the phone company's computers. Because of that uncertainty, they do not summon law enforcement; instead they attempt to call someone on the institution's call list to report the problem. Finally, such signals are given low priority. They are dealt with only after all signals of higher priority, such as fire, burglar, or panic, have been processed.

Because practically all thieves know that an alarm system communicates over the phone lines, it is becoming increasingly common for them to sever the phone lines before they break in. Even if the library's phone lines are underground, there is likely an above-ground service entrance on the outside that can be attacked. Because of those weaknesses, strong consideration should be given to either a radio or cellular backup system. Such systems are almost impossible for an intruder to defeat, and ensure that an alarm signal is transmitted even if the library's phone lines are compromised for any reason, such as an ice storm. Such a service is not available in all areas of the country, but if it is, strong consideration should be given to installing it. If the security company with which you are negotiating does not offer the service, it may be time to keep looking, bearing in mind that the service may not be available in your area at all.[4]

In some instances, central station monitoring per se may not be allowed, such as with large institutions having their own police or security forces that operate their own monitoring centers. Such centers are called Proprietary and often offer excellent levels of protection. One of their chief advantages is that the monitoring personnel can directly dispatch security officers to the scene. A second advantage is that the communication path between the library and the monitoring center is likely very short and highly reliable. Finally, monitoring center personnel may be intimately familiar with the area in a way that those in a remote center could never be,. That knowledge allows the response to be better fitted to the particular situation. Only under unusual circumstances, however, should an institution engage in an arrangement with a third-party security company in which the first response to an alarm is the dispatch of a so-called runner employed by or under contract to the security company.[5]

Some modern systems allow the intrusion system to be monitored or altered over the Internet by the owner. Such systems should probably be used cautiously since they are subject to potential hacking and other compromises, such as stolen passwords.

Wiring Systems

It would seem arcane that any librarian would actually have to worry about the type of wiring used in an intrusion detection system. Although the actual wire used should be of no concern, how a system will be wired should be an object of curiosity. (See "System Configurations" in the Access Control Systems chapter.)

Two basic wiring systems are typical: home run and trunk. In the former, each device is wired separately to the control panel on its own circuit. In other words, if there are four door contacts on the system, each one is wired separately. In the latter, one trunk line is run and each of the four door contacts is wired into the central trunk line. Either wiring pattern is highly reliable and offers excellent protection. In either scenario, if the first door contact somehow fails, the others are not compromised.

In an effort to cut the price of their systems, some companies configure circuits in what is called a daisy chain configuration. In such a configuration involving four door contacts, the first contact will be wired to the control panel, the second one wired to the first, and so on until all four contacts are connected by one common circuit. Unlike the other two circuits, however, this type of configuration is fraught with problems. If for some reason the first door contact fails, its failure compromises all the other door contacts and leaves the premises with no protection anywhere on that circuit. Surprisingly, this type of wiring configuration is neither illegal nor substandard—it is to be avoided, however. In an institution's negotiations with a security company for installation of a system, that type of wiring should be specifically banned by the institution.

Several features increase line security. Almost all security systems are surface wired, which is standard practice. For a greater degree of security or where more protection for the wire itself is desired, the wiring may be put into conduit. Better line security can also be achieved by installing line monitoring devices that are extremely difficult to defeat, such as diodes that allow current to flow in only one direction. At the very least, the institution should insist that end of line resistors be installed so the circuits can be constantly monitored by the control panel.

Although hard-wired devices are preferable, a wide variety of wireless devices are available. These communicate with the control set by radio waves and function exactly as their hard-wired equivalents. In some instances, it is either impractical or aesthetically unappealing to run visible wire. In such cases, consideration may be given to wireless devices, bearing in mind, however, that their communication path with the control set is more easily compromised than with devices that transmit signals over hard-wired circuits. Unlike hard-wired devices, which draw their power from the circuit, wireless devices are powered by batteries that need to be changed periodically. If wireless devices are used, the control panel should routinely interrogate them to be sure they are functioning and that their batteries are charged. UL standards require that the devices be checked at least once a hour.

Alarm Initiating Devices

An alarm initiating device is an instrument that detects an intrusion and sends a signal to the control unit, which then activates local alarm signals such as a horn or lights and transmits a signal to the central station, if one is monitoring the system. Numerous devices exist for a wide variety of applications, some of them quite esoteric and rarely encountered in most rare book and manuscript libraries.

An important concept concerning alarm initiating devices is that of "normally open/normally closed." That phrase refers to the system's electrical configuration. Almost all fire detection equipment,

such as a smoke detector, is on normally open circuits. In other words, when the device is not in alarm, the control panel sends electrical current out to the device and monitors the return voltage. Because the electrical circuit in the device is normally open, the panel does not expect to detect any return voltage. If the device goes into alarm, however, the circuit closes, the control panel detects the fact that current is being returned, and the alarm is sounded.

Almost all intrusion detection devices are normally closed. The control panel sends a current out to the device and expects in a normal condition to receive back a known amount of current. Thus, when intrusion detection devices are not in alarm, a current flows through a normally closed circuit. If, however, the device goes into alarm, the circuit is broken, the current being received by the panel drops, and the alarm is sounded. This concept explains why an intrusion detection system cannot be set until all protected doors, for example, are closed. If any device is open, the control panel will detect the lack of current on the circuit and signal the problem.

Perimeter Protection

Perimeter detection devices are alarm initiating devices intended to sound an alarm when the perimeter of a structure is breached. The most commonly protected entrances are windows and doors, although protection can also be provided for things such as walls, ceilings, or fences. Some such sensors are referred to as line detection devices.

Door Contacts

The door contact is probably the best known perimeter protection device. Most contacts consist of a magnet attached to or inserted in the protected door and a switch that is attached to or inserted into the door-frame. The switch is wired to the alarm control unit. The switch contains two very small, overlapping slivers of flexible metal called reeds. When the door is closed, the reeds are held together by the magnet and the circuit is closed. If the door is opened, the magnet is removed and the reeds separate, opening the circuit. Although door contacts can be ordered in various degrees of sensitivity, a typical gap of 3 inches is tolerated before the reeds are released. That gap is necessary to accommodate ill-fitting doors, for example, and to allow for other factors, such as wind pushing on a door. Door contacts are *always* installed on the protected side of the door.

The two most common types of reed door contacts are surface and recessed. Each works identically. Some institutions, for aesthetic reasons prefer recessed contacts, which are hidden in the frame and door. Surface contacts, despite their lack of aesthetics, are more easily installed and serviced and less likely to come loose since they are screwed to the mounting surfaces instead of being merely inserted. In some situations in which wire cannot be run inside the walls to the door frame, surface contacts may be the only choice. Surface contacts, however, are more easily damaged by accident since they are not protected by the door and frame. Door contacts are available in either wired or wireless configurations.

A more secure type of contact is called a "balanced" contact. Theoretically, it is possible to defeat door contacts by introducing magnets that hold the reeds closed even though the door is wide open. Balanced contacts are tuned to a specific magnetic force; thus, if a foreign magnet is introduced, they go into alarm. Such contacts are, however, considerably more expensive than the usual everyday door contacts found in most installations. They do offer superior protection.

Other types of door contacts exist for various other applications. Two such typical contacts are roller ball and plunger, used to protect pedestrian doors. Those are usually mounted on the hinge side of the door and are practically invisible unless the door is thrown wide open. They can be easily defeated, however.[6] One application, often overlooked, is the provision of a plunger for the door on the cabinet holding the control set, which should be alarmed to prevent unauthorized access to the circuits. For large overhead doors in such areas as receiving and shipping, specialized contacts exist to protect such openings.

Glass Break Detectors

A cheap glass break detector is probably more trouble than it can ever be worth. Although the concept of protecting against intrusion by warning of a breaking window is laudable, perhaps no perimeter protection device has ever produced so many false alarms. In some institutions they have caused so many false alarms that they have been disconnected. Advances in the technology employed in the devices, however, have improved them markedly in the past several years. Because they are practically the only perimeter protection device that transmits an alarm signal while an intruder is still outside, they add valuable time to personnel response.[7]

All such devices detect the vibration and/or frequency caused by breaking glass.[8] Regrettably, older devices, which were usually only acoustic, were subject to problems. Chief among those problems was that loud noises would cause them to go into alarm. Passing trucks, thunderclaps, and low-flying planes are just some examples of the types of noise sources that would trigger older units. Another problem was that their sensitivity was unreliable. Because there are many types of glazing material, from heavy plate glass to fragile eighteenth-century panes, the one-size-fits-all approach of earlier detectors caused them to malfunction. They simply would fail to go into alarm because they did not correctly interpret the frequency of the glass when it was shattered. Thus, in selecting glass break detectors, it is important to install a type tuned properly to the characteristics of the glass it is protecting. Obviously, if a library has several different types of glass that need protection, some care must be given to this problem.[9]

Good modern glass break detectors are two-stage devices (acoustic and seismic or piezoelectric) that sense the two separate events involved in glass breakage. If, for example, an intruder threw a brick against a plate glass window, two events would happen almost simultaneously: first, the brick's striking the window would produce a pressure wave as the glass bowed slightly inward beneath the blow, producing an alarm on the seismic side; and second, if the brick were thrown hard enough, the glass would shatter, with a signature sound peculiar to the type of plate glass, producing an alarm on the acoustic side. Modern glass break detectors avoid false alarms by measuring both events. One circuit (seismic) in the detector senses the pressure wave while another (acoustic) detects the signature of shattering glass. The detector must perceive both events in order of occurrence before it will go into alarm. Thus, if the thief fails to throw the brick hard enough to shatter the glass, the detector does not go into alarm.

Once glass break detectors are installed, care must be taken not to compromise them as any alteration of the protected glass can cause the detector to fail. If the glazing is replaced, for example, the characteristics of the new glass may not be the ones to which the detector is tuned. Another common problem is redecoration; so if items such as drapes, curtains, or blinds are installed on protected windows, the glass break detector may not signal an event because of the obstruction they cause. Finally, even installing or moving exhibition cases, especially if they are moved near protected windows,

may compromise protection. If any modifications are made to the space where glass break detection is installed, it is prudent to consult with your security company both before and after such activities.

One particular caution needs to be considered with modern glass break detectors: they look outward, not inward. They are not designed to detect glass breakage inside a space. In other words, just dropping and shattering a drinking glass or coffee mug inside a protected room will not set them off, but unfortunately, neither will someone pounding on an exhibition case with a hammer.

Finally, all such glass break detectors will reliably cover only a certain amount of space. First, they work only within a certain range (measured in feet) of the glass to be protected. If glass to be protected is on the outer perimeter of a device's range, it is probably better to install a second one than to hope that just the one will do the job. Glass break detectors are also directional. In other words, like motion detectors, they have a certain arc (measured in degrees) in which they operate. This arc can vary from a few degrees to 360. Designing a system that adequately protects all the glass around a space needs to take into consideration both the range and arc of various devices. If either variable is miscalculated, protection will be compromised.

Shock Detectors

Shock detectors, also called vibration detectors, are activated by abnormal vibration. Depending on the type of detector, they can be used to protect any surface subject to being battered, including walls and other structural elements. They can be used, for example, instead of glass break detectors to protect windows and will go into alarm when a window is merely struck but not broken. The most common use of such devices in a rare books and manuscripts environment will probably be to protect exhibition cases. Discrete but effective, shock detectors offer excellent protection against someone's trying to break into a case. If such devices are used in exhibition cases, however, they should never be disarmed. When the intrusion detection system is inactivated at the beginning of the day, the circuits on which these devices reside should remain armed. These devices can also be used to protect walls from penetration. Finally, in addition to the plunger mentioned above in connection with the cabinet containing the control set, the cabinet should also be equipped with a shock detector.[10]

Volumetric Protection

Called volumetric, area, or space protection devices, such equipment is intended to monitor a fairly large, open area as opposed to an opening, such as a door or window. Although they can be used to monitor openings, they are normally considered supplemental devices used as "traps" to back up perimeter devices. Because they can be defeated in certain circumstances, it is probably not wise to use them as the sole protection for openings. Some of these devices should be highly visible; others should be quite difficult to detect[11]

The most common types of volumetric protection devices are microwave, photoelectric, ultrasonic, passive infrared, radar ranging, and audio. Microwave units are rarely used in rare books and special collections application because their beams pass through both glass and gypsum walls, thereby creating the possibility of false alarms occasioned by movement outside the protected space and each such device has its own advantages and disadvantages. As an aside, if the device resembles what most people envision when they hear the term "motion detector" (i.e., it has a lens), be sure to inquire if it is tightly sealed. Flies, roaches, spiders, and other small critters can cause false alarms if they get inside the device.

The photoelectric device (called an "active" device) is the stuff of movie legend. When the jewel thief approaches the case in which the prize resides, he usually blows smoke that reveals the paths of the beams. (This technique does not work in real life because the beams are usually infrared, invisible to the human eye.) In this application, a light source is aimed at a receiver or a reflector. If the transmission of the beam is interrupted, the device goes into alarm. Applications suitable for these devices are fairly unusual in rare book and manuscript libraries. Because they project a great distance, they are useful as supplemental protection along walls and banks of doors. They are line-of-sight devices, however, and the beam cannot be blocked by anything. If they are mounted on brackets, they can also become misaligned if anything bumps their components. If their presence is known, they are easy to defeat by merely crawling under or stepping over them. In some applications attempts are made to mitigate that problem by installing several beams at various heights.

"Passive" infrared devices (PIRs) use light differential to detect intrusions. Because all objects emit infrared energy, the PIRs can create a reference level for a space. If someone enters a protected space, his or her body causes the background infrared energy level to change, which is detected by the device and an alarm initiated. Such devices are not subject to as many false alarms as ultrasonic devices but do have their problems. They can be affected, for example, by sources that produce cold or heat. Thus, if they are protecting an area that contains a refrigerator, just the heat of running the compressor and motor can cause the detector to go into alarm. The two most common sources of false alarms, however, are sunlight and car headlights. Passive PIRs should be positioned so that they are affected by neither, which usually means they should not look out windows.

Ultrasonic devices use the Doppler shift to provide protection. A transmitter in the device floods the area to be protected with inaudible sound waves and a receiver in the unit samples the reflected waves. If they are the same frequency as those that leave the transmitter, no alarm is sounded. Any movement inside the protected area causes the return frequency to change, and this change will cause the device to initiate an alarm. As foolproof as this system may seem, it is susceptible to false alarms and failures. Such events as air movement caused by an HVAC system, moving fan blades, or hanging objects that move will all cause the device to go into alarm. The space that such devices protect should, therefore, not be subject to alterations or extreme air currents. They are not suitable for such areas as a public foyer in which banners and balloons might be hung. In other, more stable areas, such as offices or stack areas, they provide good protection. Finally, if a library has a rodent problem, ultrasonic devices are probably not a good choice since the animals' movements may cause these devices to go into alarm.[12] Generally, these devices are no longer in use, although they are sometimes still found in older installations.

Some modern detectors are so-called combination or dual units that combine PIR and microwave in a single device. Before the device will initiate an alarm, both sides of the detector must be tripped within a certain time limit. Thus, if the HVAC system comes on and starts moving a banner around, the infrared side will probably not be affected. Alternatively, if the refrigerator begins to run, the microwave side will be unaffected. In either case, no alarm will sound. These devices provide a high level of protection with a lower incidence of false alarms and should probably, all factors being equal, be the ones installed. Most such devices will also ignore any body weighing less than 60 pounds, thereby avoiding false alarms triggered by rodents or other small animals. Care must be taken to carefully adjust the microwave

side, however, since those rays pass through objects into adjoining spaces.

Audio devices listen for sound. They are usually configured to a preset level, and if the ambient noise level exceeds the threshold, an alarm is initiated. Some systems are supplemented with microphones that allow a central-station operator to listen in, as well. Although such a system would seem to have advantages, it is rarely as reliable as others. It is subject to being tripped by loud noises from any source and may not detect intruders who are very quiet. As desirable as having an operator listen in may seem, that possibility is also fraught with problems because a human must interpret what is being heard and that interpretation may be erroneous. In one instance, an operator listened in to a premise that had an alarm condition but was unable to correctly interpret what was being heard and delayed calling the police. What the operator heard was a fire in progress, and when he eventually became concerned enough to call the police, the officer finally sent to the scene found the place engulfed in flames. Removing the human element from alarm interpretation is probably a sounder procedure.

A specialized type of volumetric detector is the range-controlled radar (RCR) device, which combines a radar beam and another form of protection (usually PIR) in one device. The chief advantage of an RCR device is that its range can be deliberately limited, the only volumetric device with this capability. If one had a window, for example, in an exterior passageway, such a device would be a useful adjunct to a glass break detector. It could be pointed directly at the window but its range could be limited to, say, 6 feet, and any movement beyond 6 feet would not be detected. Such detectors are also basically immune to the movement of small animals, such as dogs and rats, so long as they do not come within 6 feet of the device. One can see examples of this type of device every day in establishments that have automatic door openers.

Another specialized type of volumetric device is a long-range PIR detector. Unlike other volumetric devices, which usually spread their coverage over 45 degrees, a long range device concentrates its beam but can project it up to 200 feet, far beyond the effective range of other PIR devices. Such a device is useful in protecting long spaces. For example, if one had a row of offices off a common hallway but did not wish to protect each office, a long range PIR could be configured to look down the hallway. In that case, if an intruder exited an office into the hallway, an alarm would be initiated. Such devices could also be used to look down row after row of stacks, thereby making it impossible for someone to hide in the stacks after closing. Unlike a photoelectric device, long-range PIRs have a narrow beam that floods a space from floor to ceiling. Such devices cannot be defeated by stepping over them, for example.

A third type of specialized volumetric detector is a 360-degree device. Such devices are usually combination units mounted in the center of the ceiling rather than in a corner, although they may be mounted there as well. The chief advantage of such a device is that it can protect a fairly voluminous area all by itself. These detectors are commonly used to protect large spaces such as reading rooms, exhibition galleries, or open areas with cubicles in them. Their major limitation is that they can be mounted only so high off the floor, so they are of limited use in spaces with high ceilings.

Personal Protection

Any device carried by a person or activated at will is an independent device, sometimes referred to as a "panic" or "hold-up" alarm. Some of these devices are meant to be carried by an individual and are usually some sort of pendant with a button; in all cases they depend on wireless communication with the control set. Other types can be hard-wired to a desk, the floor, or some other fixture. In the case of special collections libraries, it is probably a good idea to have the reference desk in the reading room equipped with such an alarm in case the attendant needs to summon help in an emergency. If there is another desk covering the main entrance, an alarm should be placed there, as well. Normally, all such signals are immediately processed by the alarm system and go directly to the top of the call screen in the central monitoring system. Although incidents of actual assault and violence are rare in special collections settings, other incidents, such as a theft in progress, may make the need to promptly summon help essential.

If such devices are employed, the library should insist that any alarm sent *not* be verified before it is acted upon. In some cases, especially those involving medical home alerts, the monitoring station will attempt to verify that the signal is a genuine emergency rather than an inadvertent alarm. Such procedures usually involve trying to make contact with the user before assistance is dispatched, and only if contact fails will aid be sent. In the case of special collections libraries, the response to such an alarm should be immediate without verification, although the library should make it a policy that these alarms will not be used for medical emergencies. As with all components of the alarm system, the devices should be routinely tested.[13]

Annunciation Devices

Annunciation devices are instruments that give either audible and/or visible notification on the premises that the intrusion detection system is in alarm and are the first indicators to openly signal the alarm condition. Generally, such devices consist of various types of sounders and lights. Although a security system can be configured so that it does not have any annunciation devices or so that the devices do not sound or illuminate, it is a standard security recommendation that the annunciation devices always sound or illuminate on the premises. This alerts any intruder that his or her presence has been detected, and the loud noise can cause panic, confusion, and haste, all of which might work to shorten the intrusion. Sounders are also set at a pitch that is intended to be irritating to the ears without causing any real damage. Despite the idea that a silent alarm system does not alert a thief and therefore the police may catch him or her unawares, most thieves seem to assume that the alarm system has been tripped, even if there are no outward indicators that such is the case.[14]

There should be a sufficient number of annunciation devices installed to cover the entire premises, as they cannot do their job properly if they are too few. For example, if someone breaks into the stacks and the nearest annunciation device is two floors above in the reading room, one of the chief purposes for having such devices is compromised. The devices should at a minimum be able to flood the entirety of the protected premises with sound, as does a fire alarm system.

Whether annunciation devices should also be mounted outside is a question that has no certain answer. Some security authorities believe that sounders and flashing lights on the exterior increase the chance that a passing police officer will notice the alarm condition and stop to investigate, but most of the evidence for such possibilities seems to be anecdotal. If such devices are mounted on the exterior, they should be either inaccessible or armored, preferably both, and each container holding a device should also be equipped with a shock and tamper detector. It is common for thieves to try to destroy exterior annunciation devices before they attempt to break in. If the system sounds only locally it is vital that the exterior annunciation devices be heavily protected.

Batteries

After the phone line, batteries are the weakest component of a security system. All intrusion detection systems are required to have batteries that will power the system for a certain time in case of power failure. The minimum battery life required is 4 hours. Consideration should be given to upgrading the batteries to those with a longer capacity. If the institution suffers an extended power failure, the security system will go dead after the batteries completely discharge, leaving no protection. If an institution has a reserve source of power, such as a generator, the security system circuit should be wired into it so the system will stay armed in case of an extended power failure.[15]

Power Supplies

Most alarm systems use DC power they draw through a converter from the library's electrical system.[16] Every system contains a power supply that it uses to power all devices on the system. Although your security company will calculate the power needed by your system, mistakes are occasionally made and too small a supply may be installed. The strength of the supply is especially crucial in the area of powering annunciation devices, which consume a relatively large amount of current in alarm. Before the system is accepted as installed, it should be put into alarm to ensure that all sounders are operating at full strength, that all lights are flashing at the proper brightness, that all keypads are functional, and that all detection devices on the system are working.

Control Sets

The control set is the brains of an intrusion detection system. All detection devices are wired into it, it contains the device that sends the alarm signal to the monitoring facility and it initiates warning devices, such as sirens, horns, and lights in an alarm condition.

Control sets offering different levels of sophistication are available. In general, a library should install the most sophisticated control set it can afford that meets its needs. Special attention must be paid to the expansion capacities of the set. If one installs a set that barely meets one's needs, any future expansion of the system may compromise security by overloading the control set, and the library may even be forced to purchase a new one. At the very minimum, the control set should have the capacity for 16 hard-wired devices and the capability to add 8 wireless ones, even if one does not use all that capability at first.

Any control set used by an institution, even if it is an historic house, should be UL listed for commercial use. Control sets meant for residential use, although also certified by UL, are unsatisfactory for use by an institution and should be avoided. In negotiations with any security company, the institution should make it plain that it will not accept a control set intended primarily for residential use.

The choice of phone line configuration is also of some concern. The control set should have the capability of operating two phone dialers instead of just one, especially if it is using a Digital Alarm Communicator System. If possible, the control set should have its own dedicated line separate from the institution's phone system, which insulates the system from problems that occur with the institution's phone system. If the control set does use the institution's phone system, it is vital to ensure that the control set's dialer is first in line and can seize a phone line immediately, even if all are in use. In no case should the alarm's dialer be connected to a phone system that will not dial in case of a power failure. The integrity of the connection should be tested after *any* work is done on the institution's phones.

The control set should also have the capability of performing certain administrative functions.

One such function is the ability to provide opening/closing reports, which provide a record of who turned the system off or on and when the action was taken. They may be provided on a scheduled basis by the central station or printed off immediately or on demand at the premises. The control set should also be capable of storing and dumping an event log. An event log is particularly important in case of a break-in because it records exactly when the intrusion occurred and which devices were activated. The number of events that a control set can store varies. Some can hold hundreds; others just a few.

Some consideration needs to be given to the number of users who can address and manipulate the control set. Some control sets can accommodate hundreds of user codes; others only a few. Great care must be taken to install a control set that can accommodate everyone who will be able to use the system now and those who might be added to staff in the future. Few situations lead to security confusion faster than two staff members who have to share the same code because the control set is too small to hold any more user codes. Thought must be given to identifying *everybody* who will need to use the system; do not forget custodial or maintenance workers who may need access to the premises when the institution is closed and the security system is set. Although it is possible in some instances to upgrade various features of a control set, it is usually impossible to increase the number of user codes.

The control set should be able to accommodate different levels of authority over its functions. For example, only certain people using their code should be able to add or subtract users in the system, change the prearranged opening and closing times, or bypass devices. There may be areas, such as vaults or exhibition cases, that only certain people should be able to disarm. The control set should be sophisticated enough to accommodate those various security levels.

Finally, some thought needs to be given to the physical security of the control set. The actual control set circuits are enclosed in a metal cabinet, and this cabinet should have a lock, a shock sensor, a water sensor, and a door contact to detect any attack made on it. It is preferable that it be installed in a secure, locked room that has its own security protection, including a water sensor on the floor, and, if possible, it should be protected from electrical vagaries, including lightning and nearby machinery, which can damage or interfere with its components. It should not be installed in a basement, especially if the area is prone to flooding and should not be installed below or near any fresh water or waste water pipes.

Zones

The term "zone" has two meanings in relation to an intrusion detection system. Its first meaning refers to the layout of the premises themselves. The various areas being protected are often referred to as "zones." Its second meaning applies to the control set. Some control sets have "zones," which are the physical connections of security devices it can accommodate. In discussions with security companies, it is important that the two meanings of "zone" be used accurately to avoid misunderstandings. When a security salesperson states, "We'll put that area on its own zone," s/he may not mean what one thinks is meant.

Premise Zones

It is useful to think of an institution in physical zones when planning for a security system. Doing so removes the temptation to concentrate overly on individual doors and windows, for example, and forces one to consider the institution's layout and its required security in larger terms. Such thinking also tends to reinforce the habit of reviewing zones in terms of their functions, which will to some extent influence security measures.

In reviewing and analyzing an institution's zones, some thought must be given at first to identifying areas that need great levels of security. In a large institution not every area will need the same level of protection. For example, although the main entrance and back door need to be alarmed, they probably would not require the same level of protection as the stacks or a vault. An administrator's office may need some protection (or none), but it may not require the same level of protection as a curator's, conservator's or cataloguer's office, where rare materials are likely to be left out overnight or over the weekend. In a small library, it may be desirable to afford all areas the same level of protection.

Second, careful consideration should be given to the physical layout of the building and routes by which an area might be broken into. In this instance, one must think unconventionally. An average person trying to break into a room would probably consider first how to defeat the door. A thief, on the other hand, may not take such an approach, as s/he is more likely to remove a sidelight, come over the wall from an adjoining space, or simply punch through a sheetrock wall. Such considerations will influence security levels and prompt questions such as: Is it enough to protect an area with just a door contact or should the contact be supplemented with a volumetric detector that can trap an intruder who bypasses the door? Should the path to the area be alarmed so that detection is achieved before an intruder can reach the space? Is it really possible that a person could enter through an air duct? In considering such scenarios, it is useful to enlist the cooperation of local law enforcement agencies, who, if they have not have seen it all, have probably seen more such activity than the average librarian.[17]

Third, the uses of and activities in a space will influence security decisions. Far too many institutions have systems that are either completely on or completely off. For example, if an evening reception is taking place in the reading room, the entire institution is without alarm protection because the system is configured so that the entire system is either on or off. In effect, the institution as a whole is just one premise zone. Areas such as offices, the stacks, and the vault, where nobody has any business being at the time, are left without protection for as long as the reception lasts. If possible, consideration should be given to having a security system that is capable of being disarmed in sections so that after-hours activities, for example, do not compromise the security of the entire building.

Fourth, some zones may not necessarily be spaces at all but may rather be objects, such as exhibit cases or paintings, and such specialized concerns should be addressed in designing a security system. It may be desirable, for example, that the protection for them not be dropped when the institution opens for the day, but can be dropped only by a special code that controls only the control set zones into which the devices protecting them are wired. Other specialized areas that need similar consideration are roof hatches, sky lights, the control set housing, and elevators.

Control Set Zones

The number of zones that exist in a control set has a direct bearing on the level of protection that can be achieved and on the police response to any alarm. Translating the zones identified as part of the premises into the zones available on the control set should be approached cautiously to ensure that the desired protection is in fact realized. Control sets utilizing zones are those wired in the "home run" configuration.

A control set with eight zones can accommodate at least eight devices being wired into it with a separate circuit for each device. A set with 100 zones can accommodate at least 100 such devices.

Most modern control sets have expansion capabilities, allowing for the addition of more zones if the need arises. All sets, however, have an upper limit to the number of zones they can accommodate. No control set is infinitely expandable.

In an ideal configuration, each protection device would be on its own zone, and this configuration should be the institution's goal. Such an arrangement provides several advantages. First, it makes identifying problems and servicing the system much easier. If, for example, three devices are wired into the same zone, it is more difficult to determine which device is causing problems. If only a door contact is wired into zone 2, the problem circuit and device are immediately isolated. Second, this configuration can have important ramifications for the level of protection provided. For instance, if a zone is causing difficulties and must be bypassed before the alarm can be set, it is far preferable that there be only one device on that zone. If all the door contacts and the one volumetric device protecting the reading room are all on one zone and that zone has to be bypassed, the reading room is left with no protection until the problem is repaired.

The most important advantage of having each device wired to its own zone, however, is the effect that the arrangement has on the police response to an alarm. When an alarm is received at a central station, the operator knows exactly which zone has gone into alarm because this is communicated by the control set when the alarm is sent. All the zones have a written description that also shows on the operator's computer screen. If, as in the previous example, all the reading room protection devices are wired into one zone, all the zone information the operator will probably see is "Reading Room," which is all the information that can be relayed to the police. Such information is better than nothing but it really does not tell the responding officer where to go or what part of the building has been breached.

If, on the other hand, each device is wired into its own zone, the information relayed to the central station operator is far more useful. It probably reads something like "North Door Contact" or "Glass Break South Side." Such precise descriptions allow the operator to communicate exactly to the police where the intrusion has occurred. Not only does such precise information enable the police officer to respond immediately to the part of the building where the intrusion has taken place, but it also protects the officer by relaying to him or her precisely where a threat is likely to be encountered once the premises are reached.[18]

Individually wiring each device into its own zone can also be of material importance in trying to figure out the events of a theft. When an intruder sets off a security device, that information is relayed by the control set to the central station; the dialer then hangs up. If, however, yet another device is tripped, the control set again calls the central station and will call repeatedly so long as devices are being tripped. Such a sequence of events is obviously of great interest to the police responding to the alarm. On the other hand, it is also of great interest to the librarian. There will be a significant security difference between a sequence that reads "Reading Room Motion" and then "North Door Contact" and one that reads "North Door Contact" and then "Reading Room Motion." In the latter instance, someone has broken in. In the former instance the implication is strong that someone was hiding on the premises when the library closed for the day. Such information is impossible to ascertain when the only report received by the central station says merely, "Reading Room."

Finally, in deciding how many zones may be needed on the control set, it is important to bear in mind that modern control sets can accommodate a large variety of devices, including water sensors, high/low temperature sensors, and carbon mon-

oxide detectors. Although these devices do not cause an intrusion alarm if they are tripped, they do require zones inside the control set. If they are to be added to the control set, enough zones must be provided for them, as well.

The concept of zones has no validity in control sets that use trunk wires. The limiting factors with such control sets are how many trunk wires the set can accommodate and how many devices can be linked to each trunk. Such control sets are often used in large systems that may require hundreds of detection devices. Such sets are just as capable of pinpointing alarm points as a set using individual zones. In such sets, each detection device has its own unique identifier that the control set recognizes. Thus, even if a dozen devices are attached to one trunk, the control set will know that the door contact on the north door is the device that has gone into alarm. It can also discriminate among wireless devices.

A final consideration that is related to the concept of zones is control set partitions. Most control sets have at least two partitions. It is this capability that allows, for example, all the perimeter detection devices to remain armed while the inside devices are ignored. That is the situation when someone presses the "Stay" button to work late. If the library deems it desirable to leave certain areas of the library alarmed while others are cut off, it needs to ensure that the control set will have enough partitions to accommodate various scenarios.

Staff and the Security System

No intrusion detection system is capable of running itself entirely. It requires that from time to time library staff tell it what to do. Such commands might consist of telling the system to arm or disarm itself, to bypass a troubled circuit, or to cease sounding an alarm. Some staff members will have access to the system by necessity; others will need access only as a convenience. Who has access to the system and what any individual can instruct a system to do should be given careful thought. Implementing solutions to these concerns will involve the security company, who will have to program the system to your specifications.

Depending on the sophistication of the system, several actions are possible, all of which concern establishing a person's clearance level: 1) arming and disarming the system; 2) silencing alarms; 3) entering and deleting authorized users; 4) changing closing and opening times; and 5) bypassing alarm circuits. Each action is fraught with its own security considerations.

Codes have special considerations. All operations on the system should require an individual code to be entered. All systems perforce require a code to be entered to disarm them. Not all require such a code to arm them, however. Under no circumstances should a person just be able to push an "Away" or "Stay" button to arm the system. All codes should also be unique to an individual; no two individuals should ever have the same code. All codes should be random. Avoid assigning codes in sequence such as 1234, 1235, 1236, 1237, etc. Finally, staff members who have codes assigned should be instructed never to reveal them to anyone else. That policy is for the protection of not only the library but also of the individual staff member.

A person's level of clearance refers to the actions that he or she may require the system to take. Establishing a person's clearance level is a function that should be restricted to only a few senior staff members. On a practical level, consideration needs to be given to the access that should be allowed to any given individual. Should a reference librarian, for example, be allowed to disarm the vault? Should the secretary be allowed to disarm the stack areas? Should a volunteer be allowed to enter the conservation lab? Should X, Y, or Z be allowed on the premises when they are normally closed? Some compromise between absolute security and practical considerations is probably in order in determining a person's clearance level, but the actual decision involving a staff member's clearance level should be in the hands of very few people.

Arming and disarming the system is the most basic function that staff will perform and is probably the one for which most staff will be authorized. As a practical matter, anyone who potentially will have to open or close the library will need this level of access. Some thought needs to be given to this potential pool of people. For example, will custodial staff need to enter the library at odd hours? What about maintenance workers responding to an emergency? What about the intern who needs to work on the manuscript processing project on Saturday mornings? There is nothing inherently wrong with giving any person permission to arm and disarm the system, so long as the process is carefully controlled and monitored. As an aside, it should be noted that there is never any reason to give a police officer such a code and that alarm repair personnel have their own codes and do not need to know any individual's code to perform their work.

The responsibility of silencing alarms should be as restricted as possible. As a practical consideration, however, anyone who has authority to arm or disarm the system probably needs the authority to silence an alarm by resetting the system. People are sometimes careless and set off the alarm system unintentionally. For example, they can't remember their code and spend time fumbling through their belongings trying to find it. While they're looking, the pre-set delay elapses and the system goes into alarm. In such a situation it seems far-fetched to summon someone in authority to report to the scene. What level of authorization this situation will require is a matter of institutional judgment.

Entering and deleting authorized users should be severely restricted to only a few people. There should be only a single code for this purpose and ideally only a few people should possess it. It should be borne in mind that the code that allows entering and deleting authorized users is probably the same as the master code for the system, which allows its holder to do almost anything. As a practical matter, however, the code will probably have to be known to a few senior staff members. If, for example, the only holder of the code is on vacation and a person needs to be deleted from the system, a security problem is created because of the inability to immediately delete the departed staff member's code. Some compromise between absolute security and practical considerations is probably in order in this situation.

Changing opening and closing times is a serious issue. Establishing these times with the central station is a procedure that needs to be worked out. Without a schedule, the central station staff cannot determine if the premises are properly secured when they are supposed to be. On the other hand, events such as evening or weekend programs may require that the normal closing time be altered. Also, there are probably some staff members who will need to have access to the premises at any time. All such events are violations of the institution's established schedule and will trigger concern at the central station if not properly accounted for. Usually, a staff member's ability to alter or violate the established schedule is a matter of clearance level. Only those staff members with a genuine need to alter the schedule's parameters should have codes that allow them to do so. A potential thief, for example, would be in a position to do great damage if he or she could somehow set back the closing time to midnight, thus allowing several undetected hours to rummage the collections.

Bypassing alarm circuits is a regrettable action that must sometimes be taken. This situation almost invariably occurs when a staff member at the end of the day tries to arm the system, only to be told that zone 2, for example, will not arm. Only the most senior staff members should be able to bypass a non-functioning zone, although that consideration is tempered by the number of people who have authority to arm the system. In the end, the institution will have to make judgments about an individual user's discretion before allowing him or her to bypass a defective zone. Any individual who is able to bypass a non-functioning zone should be trusted to make wise decisions about the security compromise involved in the action. Some institutions do not allow such discretion and require staff members to remain on the premises until a repair person comes to correct the problem, even if it means spending the night.[19]

All staff involved with the operation of the intrusion detection system need to be instructed in its use and its capabilities. Such instruction, however, should be conducted on a need-to-know basis. Advanced instruction in the system's operation should be conducted by your security company and should be available to all senior staff members who will have overall responsibility for the system's operation. The security company's lessons should cover all user aspects of the system. A user manual should also be provided for reference, although this manual is a high-security item and access to it should be restricted. Senior staff, in turn, should instruct other staff in the system's operation, including hands-on demonstrations about how the system operates. Information that staff members do not need to know about the system, depending on their authorization level, should be withheld from them. Any subsequent modifications or alterations to the system should also be reviewed by the security company with senior staff and then with others as appropriate.

One access code that nobody on the library staff will ever know is the "installer's code." This is a code used by security company installers and repair personnel to manipulate the system as is necessary for them to perform their jobs. Its identity is known only to the security company and need not concern library staff. The only practical consequence of its existence is that it does occupy one code slot in the control set. Thus, if your control set will accommodate eight codes, it will in fact accommodate only seven user codes because one slot is taken up by the installer's code.

Finally, some systems can be armed and disarmed with a remote control. Although such an arrangement is often used with home security systems, it should not be employed in a library. Anyone in possession of the remote can successfully disarm the system without a code; the remote is the equivalent of a master key. If a situation arises in which such a device seems desirable, such as an employee confined to a wheelchair who cannot reach the keypad, consideration should be given to alternate measures, such as lowering the keypad itself.

Relations with the Central Station

Your security company's central station, if you have chosen that option for monitoring, is the one entity with which your institution will have daily contact, even if it is only electronic. The services that a central station can provide vary, and library staff will have to make some decisions concerning those.

Initially, the library will have to provide the central station with a call list. The call list should include, in order, the persons to be notified in case of an incident at the library. All available phone numbers, including pagers and cell phones, should be provided as part of the information on the list. This list should be kept accurate, which is the library's responsibility. If staff members leave or are added or if phone numbers change, those circumstances need to reflected in the call list. The library should also periodically request from the central station a

copy of its call list to ensure that the information in it is timely and accurate. The list should be reviewed every time there is a change to it. In case of an incident, central station personnel will start at the top of the list and attempt to call people until someone answers. Obviously, the longer the list, the greater the chance of success for making timely contact. Staff members on the call list should be warned that they cannot have their home phone system set to block calls from the alarm company.

The order of persons on the call list needs some careful consideration by library staff. The persons high on the list should probably be the ones with the highest level of authority to take action in an emergency and who have the proper clearance level to deal with the system. The order of the list does not necessarily have to reflect the library's chain of command, however. The first person can be the Head of Maintenance. It could also be the most appropriate senior staff member who lives closest to the premises. Whoever this person is, s/he must have authority to spend money on the spot, an authority that the first few people on the call list should also have. In an emergency, the person might need to call locksmiths, carpenters, glaziers, or alarm company personnel to the premises to repair damage that would prevent the building from being secured or further damaged.[20]

The most fundamental function of the central station is to monitor the system in various ways. The crucial function is to receive alarms and take the action that you specify in response to them. After a central station receives an alarm, its personnel usually have two options, one of which you will specify: 1) call the police and then call designated staff people; or 2) just call designated staff people. Neither of these options should be rejected out of hand, depending on the institution's situation.

By far the safer option is to have the central station call the police when an alarm is received.

Not only does this procedure ensure a timely police response, but it also allows the central station to communicate directly to the police the information they have in hand about the emergency (e.g., which security point has been breached). Valuable time can be wasted if the central station has to take time going down a call list trying to reach a staff member, who for various reasons (e.g., on vacation, away at a conference, on the phone, in the shower) may not be available to take the call. It is not unheard of for central station personnel to go through an entire call list and not get an answer from any of the people on it. If a security company has a policy that it always tries to reach the subscriber first, that company should not be employed. Calling the police first must always be an option.

For various reasons, some institutions prefer that central station personnel first try to contact people on the call list. A library with a long history of false alarms, for example, may prefer this option on the theory that the alarm is probably not genuine. Others feel that the time lost in first contacting a library personnel member, especially if the call list is short, may not necessarily jeopardize the institution and that it is more important that a staff member be contacted first so s/he can promptly report to the scene.[21] If this option is chosen, it is vital that the central station call the police after one unsuccessful pass through the call list. One problem with dispatching only staff members in response to an alarm is that they may come into contact with dangerous people once they reach the scene.

One important detail sometimes overlooked is the correct phone number for the alarm company to call for law enforcement response. Remember that the central station cannot call 911; it must have a number that can be reached from its location. The institution should check with its local law enforcement agency to ensure that it knows the correct police agency to summon and that the proper number (or numbers) are provided to the monitoring station. In small towns, unincorporated areas, or large institutions, identifying the proper responding agency can be problematic.

The central station can also provide the library with a wide variety of reports on system activity, although most of those reports have to be specified as an option; they do not come standard. The most basic such report is an opening/closing report. The central station keeps a computer record of every time the system is armed and disarmed and who performed the action. Periodically, usually once every two weeks, the report is printed and sent to the institution. In some configurations, the institution can print its own reports, either in batch mode or in real time. These reports can be quite significant, especially in cases of insider thefts. They should be provided for and kept indefinitely. Contrary to popular belief, the central station cannot tell you who closed the library June 3 two years ago. One needs one's own report for that information.

One aspect that the central station can also monitor is "no close/no open/irregular open-close" activity. To use this service, the library must provide the central station with a schedule of its regular opening and closing times and all exceptions, such as weekends and holidays. The schedule is entered into the central station's computer. If any deviation from it is noted, the central station attempts to contact someone on the call list, usually after first attempting to call the premises. Some important wrinkles in this service are possible, however. First, if the library is supposed to close at 6:00 p.m. or open at 8:30 a.m., some time, often an hour, is going to elapse before the central station begins to call. That precaution is to allow for sometimes normal delays. Second, these signals are relatively low priority. They will be dealt with by the central station as time allows only after all more pressing signals, such as fire, burglary, or panic, have been handled. Third, a staff member with the proper security clearance can alter the times from the premises themselves without resulting in any action being taken by the central station. Finally, a staff member with the proper security clearance can also open and close the premises at will, again without resulting in any action being taken by the central station. As with opening and closing reports, all this activity should be logged and kept as a permanent report.

The central station can also monitor so-called supervisory alarms, which are not considered emergencies and are all reported to people on the call list. Some of these conditions will be monitored automatically as part of basic services. For example, the central station will know if communication has been lost with the control panel and will attempt to report the condition. If any specialized devices, such as water detectors, are incorporated into the system, the central station can monitor them, too. As with other non-emergency signals, these types of alarms are dealt with only after all more pressing alarms have been taken care of.

The central station can also provide the library with an event log of all activity on the system. Unlike opening and closing reports, these logs contain records of everything, including specifics of system response when it goes into alarm and any supervisory alerts. If possible, these logs should be acquired in printed form and kept permanently. In some cases, the institution can print its own. Of course, if the institution is receiving an event log, it will not need some other reports, such as opening/closing, because these will be subsumed in the event log.

Depending on the type of transmission system used, the central station will also supervise the integrity of the communication lines on a fairly constant basis. As a minimum, UL requirements are that the central station communicate with the control set at least daily if communications use a Digital Alarm Communicator System. This is usually satisfied by the receipt of opening and closing signals. Many communication systems automatically provide line supervision. It is a good idea to receive an explanation from your security company of what type of line supervision will be employed with your system.

In an effort to reduce false alarms, which cost society millions of dollars a year, the central station may also provide alarm verification before calling authorities to the scene.[22] Although there are various ways of determining if an alarm is genuine, one common way is to wait until two devices have been tripped. The design of a system will guide the library's decision about whether it wants alarms verified first. For example, if the library is equipped with only door contacts on the outside doors and no internal traps, verification is probably not a wise option. A burglar forcing the back door will probably not open another door contact. This service and the central station's policy should be discussed with the security company.

Finally, the central station is probably the first place you will call in case of trouble with your system. If you are having difficulty getting the alarm to set, for example, and have tried everything you know to do to remedy the problem, you will probably call the central station for assistance. You will also call them if you wish to test your system so that they will know to ignore any alarms until they are told otherwise. The central station's phone number should be in the possession of everyone who can use the security system. It should not, however, be posted publicly. As careful as central station personnel are, they can sometimes be gulled. There is no need to give an intruder an edge by having the central station's number posted on the control set.

Contracts

The contract you sign with the security company will have many provisions. You should review the installation contract carefully to be sure that you understand all its terms and that it provides for the services you want. In general, it is unwise to forego a subsequent maintenance and service contract, even if you purchase the system outright. If you have your system certified as a UL system, you will have to have such a contract to obtain and keep that certification. Remember that the signed contract is the only document that matters; no matter what a salesperson may say, it is the language of the contract that is binding.

The central decision about the contract will be whether to purchase the system outright or allow it to remain the property of the security company. In general, it is a poor idea to purchase any security equipment outright. Many security companies rapidly lose interest in the customer and the system if they no longer have a financial stake in the equipment. If the security company says that purchase is the only option, that should raise a red flag. If the security company owns the equipment, it is often easier to get upgrades and other work done at no added expense.

The second decision about the contract will be whether it includes service and maintenance. Although an institution is usually under no obligation to accept such a contract, even if the system remains the property of the security company, declining one is probably a poor idea. Service contracts, especially if the system remains the security company's property, will likely ensure prompt attention to problems. It will also ensure that if equipment fails through no fault of the institution that it will be replaced at no additional expense. Institutions that have no service contracts are exposed to a situation where repairs are made on a time and materials basis when the warranty expires, usually after 90 days. Replacing components under those circumstances can be hideously expensive and a genuine shock to the budget.

Maintenance and service contracts have several provisions that often lead to misunderstandings. Some of the more common sources of confusion are addressed below.

The contract will undoubtedly include language to the effect that the security company will "endeavor" or "attempt" to summon authorities in case an alarm is received by the central station. No security company will guarantee that they can reach authorities, and the contract will specifically shield them from any action on your part in case they do not. Just as you may make a telephone call and for some reason not get connected, the central station is subject to the same vagaries. For that reason, among others, the security company cannot guarantee it will contact authorities.

Hours of repair services are also subject to negotiation. Most service contracts allow for service calls at no additional expense during regular business hours. If your system needs service outside those hours, there is usually an extra charge for that service. In some cases, you may as part of your contract specify that you want 24-hour service. There is usually an extra charge added to your payment for that provision. Whether to elect such expanded service will be a matter of institutional preference. No matter what the library's decision concerning this provision may be, the library should ensure that the security company can in fact provide 24-hour service.

Accidents, vandalism, and acts of God also lead to confusion. The contract will contain language stating that the security company is not liable for damage to the equipment from those sources. As part of the service contract, almost all companies will replace at no extra charge a device that simply quits working for no apparent reason. However, if staff is putting in an exhibition and someone accidentally rams the end of a 2x4 into a keypad, the security company is not liable for that damage and will charge for a replacement. Also, burglars will often damage equipment in an effort to defeat the alarm system. It is not unusual for them to smash keypads, sounders, and motion detectors. In those situations, the library would be expected to recover its costs from its insurance company or the person who caused the damage.

Special note needs to be taken of lighting and power surges. You should discuss with your security company measures you can take to insulate the control set from them.[23] It is not unheard of for an entire system to be destroyed by lightning. Because the control set is the only device on the system connected directly to the building's electrical supply, it is especially vulnerable to power fluctuations. The control set is also by far the most expensive piece of equipment in the entire system. If it is ruined by lightning, the institution will have to pay for a new one. (Because of advances in self-diagnostics of control sets, there is rarely any doubt if electrical fluctuations have done the damage, even if none is visible.) It is also important not to overlook phone and data lines, which should also have surge protection.[24]

Consideration must also be given to precisely which components of a system are covered by the service contract. Normally, there is at least a 90-day materials and labor warranty on a system. After that period, the covered items are governed by the contract. It is important to ensure that the service contract covers *every* component of the system, including the wiring, and not just some of them. The most common exemption in service contracts is the batteries. Such an exemption should be unacceptable to the institution. The batteries in both the control set and any wireless devices are going to fail sooner or later. The responsibility for replacing them should be shouldered by the security company as part of the service contract.

Most contracts also include language that states the installed security devices are not warranted as being fit for any particular purpose. That language does not mean that a motion detector will not function as a motion detector. It merely means that is all it will do. One common misconception, for example, is that motion detectors will detect fire. That expectation is precisely the type of application excluded by language concerning fitness for any particular purpose. There have been instances where a fire did in fact set off a motion detector resulting in the police's being dispatched to the scene expecting a burglary but only to discover a fire instead. The only reason the motion detector went off in the first place, however, was that it was melted by heat and its circuit opened as a result.

It is an important concept to bear in mind that a security system is not a replacement for insurance and is not intended to function as insurance. Security systems are sold on the basis of the equipment installed and the services desired by the institution. Identical systems will cost the same in a high-crime, combat zone as they do in a low-crime, high-brow neighborhood. Security companies do not rate risks. Because of that, almost all contracts contain an exclusion that severely limits the security company's financial liability, even if they are at fault for a loss.

If a maintenance contract is purchased, it should include an annual cleaning, inspection, and testing of the entire system. Especially important in this regard is cleaning the volumetric devices. Their performance degrades if the curtains and lenses in them become dusty or are compromised by other factors, such as spider webs in them. The library staff also has some responsibility in regards to maintenance. Once a month, at least, the staff should test the entire system and all its components. Such a procedure normally involves taking the system off line, setting it, and then testing each component as necessary to be sure it is working properly. There simply is no way, for example, to test if a motion detector is working except by testing it in this way.

Finally, the security company should provide the library with a set of as-built drawings once the system is completed. These drawings should be based on accurate, complete floors plans provided by the library. The drawings should show the placement of all system components and locations of wiring runs. Such drawings are invaluable when maintenance questions arise, especially if the problem involves wiring. They are also important for analyzing further security needs. The drawings are themselves high security items, should be kept in a secure location, and made available only to those with a need to know their contents.

Conclusion

There is no such thing as a one-size-fits-all burglar alarm system and no such thing as a system that cannot be defeated. What equipment and services one needs will be determined by the physical aspects of the library, the required comfort level, and the various activities that have to be accounted for. In this chapter, we have tried to address some of the most common concerns and to suggest other, perhaps obscure, considerations that can have influence on a library's security considerations. Although there is no substitute for a staff dedicated to security, staff input should be guided by consultations with a reliable security company that will be able to transform needs into technical reality and genuine protection.

NOTES

1. In the case of Blumberg's planned burglary of Henry Clifford's home, the burglar alarm system certainly frustrated the plot. Even though Blumberg actually found the plans to the system, he was unable to defeat it and abandoned the entrerprise. See *Nicholas Basbanes, A Gentle Madness: Bibliophiles, Bibliomanes, and the Eternal Passion for Books* (New York: Holt, 1995), 494.

2. This area of technology is changing rapidly, so much so that some of the information presented here may be out of date by the time it is published.

3. Central stations that monitor fire systems are perforce UL certified. If your company does not monitor fire signals, further questioning is in order about their UL certification.

4. In early 2008, some analog cellular backups ceased working when the federal government shut down the bandwidth on which they worked. Such users would need to upgrade to digital cellular service.

5. More jurisdictions have adopted so-called verified response to alarms before a police officer will respond. In such a scheme, the alarm must be verified by a third party, such as a neighbor reporting the alarm, the owner, or the alarm company by some secondary means, such as a CCTV system. In many cases, the typical arrangement is indeed a security company runner, so the situation may be unavoidable. Ed Morawski, *How to Defeat Burglar Alarms—Not!: Dispelling Hollywood Myths* (N. p., 2007), explains that sometimes employing runners is not necessarily a bad idea (81).

6. Morawski remarks of such contacts, " If you value your security—don't ever allow contacts like this to be installed" (24).

7. Other devices that can go into alarm when an intruder is still outside include pressure mats and alarmed screens. Note that glass break detectors protect only glass. Other protections have to be used for Plexiglas©, plastic, and other non-glass glazings.

8. Foil strips are generally no longer used.

9. Devices exist to test that glass break detectors are properly tuned and in working order. The old trick of clapping one's hands loudly to see if the detector responds is never an adequate test.

10. Neither glass break nor shock detectors are likely to detect such things as bullets and BBs fired through windows.

11. Daniel Spiegelman was apparently able to wander at leisure through the Columbia University rare book stacks and vaults because the area was protected only by perimeter alarms and had no traps. See Travis McDade, *The Book Thief: The True Crimes of Daniel Spiegelman* (Westport: Praeger, 2006), 1–21.

12. Morawski does not recommend use of these devices (38–39).

13. Testing is particularly crucial in the case of these devices because any alarm they activate will usually be silent. The person will have to trust that they have worked.

14. Holdup or panic alarms are almost always silent. The silence is based on the premise that if such an alarm is necessary, the person initiating it is in some physical danger and that noise might agitate the assailant.

15. Any maintenance contract for a security system should include replacing the batteries as part of the basic monthly charge. Beware of maintenance contracts that do not cover all batteries in a system.

16. If at all possible, the control set should draw its power from a dedicated circuit with nothing else on it. The circuit should be protected, if possible, by GFI and surge protection.

17. In New Zealand at the Auckland University Library thieves stole materials by gaining entrance through an unprotected window. See *New Zealand Herald*, January 6, 2007. McDade narrates how Spiegelman took advantage of an unalarmed, unused dumb waiter to gain access at Columbia, an entry point that seems to have escaped the notice of everyone, including the police (14–16).

18. In deciding how to label zones, it is important that the labels make sense to someone, like a police officer, who has absolutely no knowledge of the premises. This is especially true of describing perimeter devices. Avoid generic labels like "Glass Break" and "Reading Room" if at all possible. Labels should read more like "North Door" or "Glass East Side." Even when labeling interior spaces, it is best to avoid designations such as "Room 211", which mean nothing to anyone but staff; try to locate the space with something more descriptive of where it actually is, such as "Northeast Corner Office."

19. If the institution has such a policy, it is only humane that they also have a 24-hour emergency service agreement with the security company.

20. Although outside the scope of this guide, a proper emergency procedures plan will have already addressed some of these problems before the need arises. For example, arrangements should have long been made with people such as locksmiths and carpenters for emergency repair services. It is also a good idea to check one's hazard insurance policy. Many insurance companies will pay reasonable expenses to make emergency repairs or to secure property against further damage.

21. Some caution is necessary here. It is possible that the alerted staff member may arrive at the premises before the police. If that situation occurs, under no circumstances should the staff member enter the premises until the police arrive. An utterly hilarious incident involving such a situation is related by A. C. Greene involving Marshall Terry. When called by the security company to report an incident at a house he was babysitting, Terry arrived to be met by a police officer. After introducing himself as Marshall Terry, he was told by the police officer, "Pleased to meet you, marshal; you take the front and I'll take the back."

22. For a discussion of this problem, see Rana Sampson, *False Burglar Alarms*, 2d ed. (Washington: U. S. Department of Justice, Center for Problem-Oriented Policing, 2007). http://www.popcenter.org/problems/false_alarms/1. Sampson estimates that in 2002 alone U. S. police forces responded to 36,000,000 burglar alarms at a cost of $1.8 billion.

23. At the very least, consideration should be given to installing lightning rods on the structure just as a general safety measure.

24. See Del Williams, "Suppressing a Surging Issue: A Simple Solution for a Complex Problem," *Security Products* (July 2002): 24–25.

Closed Circuit Television Systems

Everett C. Wilkie, Jr.

> Used in conjunction with other methods and strategies, CCTV can be very effective;
> but beware, as a stand-alone crime prevention tool, it is a non-starter.
>
> ~ *CD Associates*

Closed circuit television systems (CCTV) are common today. They may be found in office buildings, in convenience stores, and on city streets. The only component of the system normally visible to the casual observer is the camera. The entire system, however, is often a complex connection of cameras, lens, wires, monitors, and recording devices. The systems, if designed properly, can offer an excellent method of observing activity and recording events, especially those that go unnoted by human observers at the time they happen.

Despite the great security advantages CCTV systems seem to offer, their use in rare book and manuscript libraries is fairly limited.[1] One question that needs to be frankly addressed concerns the efficacy of CCTV systems in a special collections setting. Hardly any question exists in the minds of those in the business and law enforcement worlds that CCTV systems are effective in both preventing and solving crimes, as their extensive employment in those venues would indicate; but how efficient are CCTV systems in a special collections setting? Although CCTV systems are widely recommended in library and archival literature, no real studies have been done in special collections environments, so anecdotal evidence will have to suffice. Eight instances in the past decade are instructive:

1. In the case of Gilbert Bland, in his confession to the University of Delaware police he stated that he avoided libraries with CCTV systems installed.

2. In the case of E. Forbes Smiley at Yale University, the fact that he was cutting maps from books was confirmed by CCTV surveillance, although its presence did not seem to deter him.

3. In the case of Daniel Lorello at the New York State Archives, he stated that in late 2007 he accelerated his thefts because he heard that a CCTV system would be installed in his library.

4. In the case of Stephen L. Womack at Harvard University, who mutilated numerous volumes in the Widener Library, CCTV systems installed for the express purpose of catching him were successfully evaded by the suspect.

5. In the case of an auction house, it was discovered that someone had stolen a map from the storage area while the auction was in progress, but the incident was captured on CCTV. After an auction-room announcement to that effect, the map was surreptitiously returned by the thief, which was also caught on tape.

6. In the case of Melvyn Perry, who stole from

the British Library, a CCTV system was installed after his thefts became known. The system was instrumental in subsequently convicting J. P. Bellwood of thefts from the library.[2]

7. In the case of Farhad Hakimzadeh, who stole from the British Library and other institutions, it is believed he deliberately positioned himself in the reading room to avoid the CCTV camera views.[3]

8. In the case of the strong-armed robbery at Translyvania University in 2004, the defendants checked first to be sure there were no cameras in the library.[4]

Although anecdotal, those instances offer evidence that some thieves fear CCTV systems, that they are capable of preventing thefts (however imperfectly), and that they can provide evidence used to apprehend and convict thieves. Special collections libraries should, therefore, consider installing them to secure their collections as part of an overall security program. In few cases, however, will CCTV systems make a real security difference unless they are properly designed, installed, maintained, and monitored.[5]

CCTV systems are complicated systems, and entire books have been written on their components, their installations, and their advantages. Some systems can control scores of cameras, although such a large application is not likely in a special collections setting. The discussion below is not intended to be a comprehensive, technical discussion of all the various aspects of even a simple CCTV system, but rather to address large issues that may be of interest to a librarian contemplating or using such a system. As one commenter remarked, "While the technical workings of cameras, lenses, and cabling are very important to someone in the installation and service industry, the average security manager could not care less whether a

1/2-inch or a 1/3-inch format camera is used. What is important to the security manager is adequate coverage and good picture quality."[6] That approach is somewhat similar to the one here.

System Components

All CCTV systems consist of at least a camera body, a lens, a camera mount, a transmission device, a monitor, and in most systems a recording device. Those with more than one camera usually include a device to switch between the cameras and to send video to the recording device. All of those components are available in various levels of complexity and capabilities, and the decisions that are made concerning them will determine how well the system functions for the purposes desired. The following discussion is intended to review various aspects of those components.

Camera Bodies and Lens

The camera body is the part that contains the imager and has attached to it the lens, the mounts, and wires for transmission of images and receipt of power to operate it. The most basic decision concerning the camera is whether it should be color or black and white. Color cameras used to be the more expensive option, and although that situation is still somewhat true, color cameras have dropped dramatically in price. Color cameras record many details and some evidence that simply cannot be captured by black and white units. The superiority of color is illustrated by the fact that all drivers' licenses and other such ID cards have color pictures of the bearer. The color camera's chief disadvantage is that it does not capture images so well in low light as a black and white camera, although this difference has narrowed markedly in recent years. If low light is a concern, there are cameras that record in both color and black and white depending on the light level.

All analog CCTV cameras output 30 frames a second. On the other hand, cameras put out various numbers of horizontal TV lines (TVL), and the institution should inquire about the camera's TVL capabilities. 300 TVL will give a somewhat poor view of the scene, while 500 TVL will render an excellent view. The library should buy as high a resolution as possible, and one should bear in mind that the monitor should be compatible with the cameras. It does little good to buy a monitor that will display only 300 TVL if the cameras are sending 500 TVL.

Cameras come in sizes referred to as 1/6″, 1/4″, 1/3″, 1/2″, 2/3″, and 1″, although sizes over 1/3″ are becoming less common as the capabilities of the smaller sizes are improved. (Those measurements refer to the size of the imager and not to the size of the camera body itself.[7]) Most interior applications do not require cameras larger than 1/2″; greater sizes are usually reserved for surveilling large outdoor areas such a parking lots. In general, staff need not concern themselves with the size of the imager, so long as it can be combined with a lens that produces the desired view. One thing that should concern staff, however, is pixel density. The only real concern here is how many pixels come out the end of the system rather than how many the camera is sending, the two not necessarily being equivalent. Another thing that should be addressed is to ensure that the lens fitted to the camera body is one intended for use with the imager. If the lens and imager are mismatched, the view will not be correct, A circular image on the monitor is an indication of a mismatch; it means the lens is too small.

Lenses are available in a wide variety of sizes and focal lengths, which can be either fixed or variable. If a reading room is rearranged or remodeled, the view previously provided by a particular camera may no longer be sufficient, so it is probably best to avoid cameras that do not allow for changing the lens. Experience with a system will also sometimes reveal the desirability of altering a view, and often the easiest way to correct those situations is to change the lens. Some newer lenses are varifocal allowing the installer to adjust the focal length to between, say, 3-8 millimeters. Such a lens might obviate the need for buying another lens later, if the institution chooses to pay the extra initial expense for it.

A fixed lens will provide only one view. The focal length of the lens, its distance from the point being observed, and the imager size combine to determine the field of view and an alteration in any one of those three elements will change the field of view. The focal length usually ranges from 1 to 400 millimeters. Determining the field of view of each camera should concern the librarian, and care should be taken to ensure that the field of view is the one desired. If one desires just a general view of the reading room, that will require one combination. If, on the other hand, one desires a tight view of the manuscript reading table or the vault door, that will require another combination. Your security firm representative should be able to supply you with an inexpensive device that will allow you to make such calculations on your own; calculators are also available on the Internet (see fig 7.1). A more sophisticated device for determining views is an optical viewfinder. One literally looks through this device, adjusts it so that the desired view is seen, and then reads the proper settings from its reference rings. It is also possible to experiment by having your security firm bring out several cameras and lenses so that you can determine how various combinations work. Finally, a specialized type of camera usually with a fixed lens is a pin-hole camera, normally reserved for undercover work or in situations where secrecy in observation is required.

If the view needs to be changed in real time, you will need a zoom lens, but the equipment required

Figure 7.1

Inexpensive Camera View Determiner (Used by permission)

to operate such a lens is more complicated than that required for a fixed lens. The zoom feature does allow the operator to focus on suspicious activity and allows the camera to provide several views, from the general to the specific. In other words, it is possible with one such lens to monitor the entire reading room and then change the view to closely monitor just one table. An intermediate option is a fixed lens that can be adjusted from, say 3–8 MM. Although such a lens cannot be operated remotely, it does offer the advantage of providing a wider or tighter view by employing a mere adjustment instead of a new lens. To change the view, however, somebody is probably going to have to climb a ladder.

Depending on the type of camera, the zoom function can be digital or optical and both provide good service, although there are important differences in the type of images they provide. An optical camera works like any conventional magnifying device such as a telescope or microscope in that it actually magnifies what it is looking at. In other words, until the resolution range of the lens is reached, the image is an actual magnified piece of the object being observed and, therefore, it is truthful and captures details accurately. On the other hand, a digital zoom is not really a magnified image

at all. A digitally zoomed image is merely one that has been electronically enlarged to provide a bigger image. No more detail than is in the original image is provided; a part of the image is just made larger. The effect is the same as looking at a photograph through a loupe; there is no better resolution than the underlying photograph provides. Although it is a remote possibility, with a digital zoom a library might not capture critical details with sufficient clarity.

Two optional features allow cameras to adjust to varying light conditions. An auto iris is a device that allows the camera to adjust to varying light levels by automatically adjusting the F-stop. If the light level in a space falls, for example, the auto iris will lower the F-stop to allow more light into the imager. A useful adjunct to an auto iris is a back light correction (BLC) circuit, which automatically adjusts the view if the light behind the subject is so bright that the subject itself is dark. Although the library may anticipate that light levels will remain constant, it should obtain cameras with those features. Doing so will ensure that the cameras will function over a wide range of lighting conditions. Any camera pointed at a door or window should have BLC.

It cannot be overly emphasized, however, that no camera/lens combination exists that can cover every possible lighting/viewing situation so some compromise may be necessary.

Mounts

Camera mounts, including enclosures attached to them, range all the way from simple brackets to those designed to resist being shot with heavy caliber handguns. Cameras can also be concealed in a variety of enclosures, such as pictures, clocks, smoke detectors, sprinkler heads, clock radios, exit signs, and motion detectors. (Pinhole cameras have no mounts; they are inserted directly through a wall or ceiling.) In most applications, cameras are visible, and a sizable segment of the security industry believes that having cameras highly visible is a deterrent, as is obvious in every bank. The major drawback of having cameras too visible is that the situation allows a thief to make some rough calculation of their field of view. To make it plain that an institution has a CCTV system but yet defeat a thief's attempts to calculate the system's capabilities, many institutions now mount their cameras in domes or housings. Not only does practically everybody know what is in the domes, but the domes also render the camera invisible. Domes are also more aesthetically pleasing than having cameras dangling everywhere.

A term that one sometimes hears in relation to CCTV systems is "PTZ," an acronym for "Pan, Tilt, Zoom." The last of those terms properly refers to the capabilities of a camera lens; the first two refer to the capabilities of the mount. The reason that they are all lumped together is that the three capabilities are often found together, although that situation need not necessarily be the case. In a mount that will pan and tilt, motors move the camera, even one with a fixed lens, from side to side (pan) and up and down (tilt). This capability allows the operator to adjust the view as necessary. In other words, if the operator sees something suspicious in the lower left hand portion of the monitor screen, he or she can move the camera to the left and down to get a better view. To take full advantage of that capability, the movable mount is often coupled with a zoom lens on the camera. Finally, a pan and tilt mount can usually be programmed to move automatically; the operator can immediately interrupt the programmed movement, however, should the need arise.

Dome Cameras

So-called dome cameras combine in one unit a specialized camera and a specialized mounting system. They are almost ubiquitous (see fig 7.2). These cameras accurately reflect the PTZ acronym because almost all of them incorporate those features in one unit and, unlike other cameras have the ability to be pointed almost anywhere at will. The camera itself will pan horizontally through 360 degrees of arc and tilt vertically through nearly 180 degrees of arc. Normally mounted under a dome on a ceiling, one unit can sometimes adequately cover an entire space and can be programmed to observe various parameters. One popular feature is the "guard tour", where the camera periodically moves itself to cover the entire room; it can also be programmed to follow movement. Finally, they can be tied into the library's intrusion detection system. If they sense movement when the alarm is set, they not only can trip the alarm system but they also can begin following the movement they detect. Most

Figure 7.2

Transmission Tower in the Middle of Nowhere. Note Dome Camera on Mast (Used by permission)

dome cameras are available with either varifocal optical lens or digital zoom.

The biggest drawback to dome cameras is that because the unit generally contains only one camera it can point in only one direction at one time. Thus, the camera may be pointed away from an event when it occurs. In this sense, a system of fixed cameras that covers an entire area among them is a superior solution for ensuring that nothing important is missed. To address this shortcoming, dome units are available with four cameras, each covering roughly 90 degrees of arc. Such units, however, lack the PTZ features as the cameras are normally fixed.

Transmission Systems

The two methods of transmitting the image to the monitor are referred to as either guided or unguided systems. In the former, some type of cable or wire is used; in the latter, the signals are transmitted through the air.

A popular choice for transmission method is coaxial cable, but as reliable as coaxial cable is, it does have some drawbacks. It is relatively inflexible and cannot be bent neatly around corners; its transmission properties can be interfered with by nearby electrical fields; and because the entire length of the cable must be properly shielded, any defect in the shield caused either by poor manufacturing or an installation accident will degrade its transmission quality. Finally, the length that a cable can be reliably run is limited because the signal will degrade if it has to travel too far between the camera and receiving equipment.

An alternative to coaxial cable is fiber optic cable, although it is a more expensive option. Despite its greater expense, it is far lighter, more easily manipulated, and is immune to electrical interference, including lightning strikes, because the signal is composed of light. It does not need to be shielded, and fiber optic cable was once called "by far the most effective method of sending CCTV signals over any distance."[8] Its chief disadvantage is that it takes considerable care and skill to correctly connect it.

A third transmission choice is twisted pair lines. The main advantage of this system is that the power to operate the cameras and the signal transmission are contained in a single wire run, thereby reducing expense. Cable runs can also be longer than coaxial cable with no loss in picture quality.[9]

A final method for sending signals is a wireless transmitter of some type. Once rare, this method is becoming more common. It finds one application in covert cameras, such as those hidden in a clock radio, that transmit by ultra-high frequency (UHF) radio transmission. The range of these transmitters has improved markedly in the past several years, and it is not unusual to find those that can transmit signals several miles. Other types of wireless transmission include infrared and microwaves, although these applications will likely be fairly rare in rare book and manuscript libraries. The chief security problem with UHF is that anyone can intercept the signals.

Whatever type of transmission system is chosen, one needs to keep in mind Harwood's observations on their pertinent considerations: "For guided transmission, which uses wires or cables, the medium is more important. For unguided or wireless transmission, the signal is more important."[10]

Monitors

Monitors, which display the view transmitted by the camera, come in various sizes. Although all monitors perform basically the same function, the choice of this one piece of equipment will to a great degree determine how well the library likes its CCTV system and the effectiveness of it. Depending on the cameras chosen, the monitor will be either color or black and white. (A color monitor will work with a black and white system; a black and white monitor will not work with a color system). The chief mistake institutions make in the selection of a monitor is to buy one that is too small. For instance, a typical 9" monitor, though inexpensive, is simply too small to allow the operator to view what is happening with any real certainty. When a monitor is divided into several screens, its size becomes even more critical. Often the images in each screen are all too small to allow the operator to discriminate between innocent and nefarious activity. If a library discovers that its monitor is too small, it should not hesitate to install a larger one. Color monitors are superior because they are more interesting to watch and do not bore the operator as so readily as a black and white screen. One should bear in mind that almost everyone has become accustomed to color TV and will likely find watching a black and white monitor excruciating. If space is a problem, flat screen monitors are available; they have a smaller footprint than a conventional monitor incorporating a cathode ray tube (CRT) and will probably replace CRTs entirely.

Monitors incorporating a CRT have two features that need to concern the library: screen size and resolution. Screen size refers to the viewing area measured diagonally; resolution refers to the number of horizontal TV (HTV) lines the screen will display. In general, these two measurements are in rough proportion to each other. In other words, the larger the diagonal measurement, the more horizontal lines the monitor will need to display for an adequate picture. Because of the complexity of processing color signals, black and white monitors will usually offer more horizontal lines. The largest black and white monitors can have as many as 1000 horizontal lines. Color monitors, on the other hand, rarely rise to that level. The more horizontal TV lines of resolution, the clearer the picture. One should be careful to ensure that the monitor chosen will display the camera output as it is hardly wise to buy a monitor that will display

only 300 HTV lines when the cameras are sending 500 HTV lines.

Flat screen monitors, all of which are color, are also referred to by screen size and resolution. Screen size is measured the same as a conventional monitor. Resolution, however, is referred to by both the horizontal and vertical number of TV lines the monitor will display, which is the usual way to refer to CRTs on computer systems. In general, the higher the numbers the better the picture. Unlike CRTs, which display their best picture at the center of the screen with some loss towards the edges, flat screen monitors display the same quality picture over the entire screen. Flat screen monitors for CCTV systems are usually powered by direct current rather than the alternating current required for a CRT. Because they lack a CRT, flat screen monitors can also be easier to watch, especially under fluorescent lights, which can exaggerate the flicker of the CRT. Finally, some models are wireless, allowing for great flexibility in monitor placement.

The placement of monitors in relation to those being surveilled is of some concern. Although one sees places of business where a monitor is in plain view, in a library this is rarely a wise placement. Being able to observe the monitor gives a potential thief an excellent idea of what the cameras are watching and allows him or her to see when the monitors are not being watched. Monitors should not be placed where they can be observed by the persons being watched, an arrangement that can nearly always be implemented. If, for example, it is desirable to have a monitor at the reference desk, it should be mounted beneath the desk and viewed through a glass surface rather than being set on top of the desk.

Recording Devices

Although it is possible to have a CCTV system that does not include a recording device, omitting such a component is a poor security decision. If a situation is not observed when it happens, no record will be left of it if there is no device to record the images being sent from the cameras. One once-common recording device is a video cassette recorder (VCR), but this piece of equipment is plagued with problems. The tapes they use are subject to many of the same problems that bedevil any VCR, principally breaking or wearing out. Finally, all tapes reach their end, making the management of the tapes of some concern since a new tape needs to be inserted every day and the previous day's tape stored. Archived tapes should be kept under lock and key. It is a matter of continual debate how long these tapes need to be kept but similarly to all security related library records, they probably should be maintained indefinitely. Despite the fact that thefts may not emerge until years later, as a practical matter few libraries are in a position to keep more than a few weeks' worth.[11] Given advances in CCTV technology, the VCR is rapidly going the way of the dinosaur and probably will not even be an option in the future. So despite their long history, such devices cannot be recommended for a new installation.[12]

An alternate choice is a digital recorder, which uses a hard disk to record images. Such recorders have been gaining popularity in recent years, and it is a common prediction in the security industry that VCRs will at some point no longer be available for commercial CCTV systems. Because there is theoretically almost no upper limit on how much information the disk can hold, it does not have the same limitations as a VCR tape. For example, a digital recorder with an 80GB drive will hold 7.5 pictures per second for about 170 hours; a VCR in 168 hour mode will hold only one picture every .7 seconds. Put another way, a digital recording device with an 80GB drive in 160 hour mode recording one picture per second in standard resolution will go for over 90 days before it fills up; a VCR set to the same specifications would fill up after 160 hours. The devices are mechanically simpler than a VCR and not as subject to breakdown or malfunction. The information on them can be manipulated just as that found in any electronic file; it can be burned into a CD, transferred to a ZIP drive, stored on another computer, or printed out.[13] Those possibilities alleviate the storage problems encountered with VCR tapes, and because the images are digital, they do not degrade over time or when copied. The information on the disk is also available randomly.[14] Some digital systems allow remote viewing, and if one can establish an Internet connection, the images can be viewed either in real time or in an historical mode from, say, home or a motel room. On the negative side, as with any computer drive, they are subject to malfunctions such as hacking or crashes.[15] The latest wrinkle in remote viewing involves cameras with their own IP addresses that may be addressed remotely in real time. Again, however, such cameras can also be compromised by hackers.[16]

Whatever type of storage device is selected, it should be secured from damage or theft by putting the device in a locked box, which should be bolted down. This box, if possible, should be in an alarmed area, and the box itself should be alarmed. If a locked box is not possible, at the very least, nobody should be able to approach the recording device without being filmed by the CCTV system. Thieves are quite aware of a CCTV system's capabilities and will often try to steal the VCR tape or other media to cover their tracks.

Switching and Multiplexing Devices

No matter how large the system, it is theoretically possible to attach each camera to its own monitor. If a system has more than one camera, a device is usually installed to allow the changing of views on the monitor and to tell the recording device what to store. This device is actually the brains of the system, and selection of this device is a crucial decision that will determine to a large extent what the operator sees and what images are captured by the storage device. All the leads from the cameras are wired into this device, which is then in turn wired to the monitor(s) and recording device(s). No matter which device one chooses, it is important that it have the capability, at least, to insert a time and date stamp on all images. Preferably, it should also have a text inserter that allows for camera identification (e.g., "Back Door," "Reading Room South.")

A sequential switcher is the simplest and is encountered usually in systems that contain four or fewer cameras. This type of switcher rotates among the cameras at a fixed interval, giving a full-screen display of each camera image. The obvious drawback to this arrangement is that if something is happening on Camera 4, it may be a little while before that camera's image appears on the monitor. In other words, if the dwell time is set to 10 seconds per camera, it will be 30 seconds before camera 4 is seen again once the image from camera 1 starts to display. If one does install a system with a sequential switcher, it is vital that the switcher not be the type that records only the image on the monitor screen. If, for example, the operator, noting something suspicious, selects one camera out of four to stay on the screen, in some systems the other three cameras are not being recorded. Installing a switcher with such a serious limitation has security implications that should be carefully weighed. If the switcher does not have that limitation, there is no reason that a small CCTV system cannot be successfully operated with one.

The next step up is a matrix switcher. Its chief disadvantage is that it, too, can display only one camera at a time. The chief advantage of a matrix switcher is that it can combine inputs with various outputs, such as a monitor. If, for example, the operator wishes to view camera 2 only, by pressing the proper button the images from that camera could be sent to either of two monitors while the other monitor could continue to display the other cameras as before. Systems using matrix switchers can be easily expanded if they are modular. In reality, however, there is an upper practical limit to how many cameras a single operator can realistically handle. Any system over 16 cameras using a matrix switcher is probably stretching the physical limits of a single operator. If the library installs a matrix switcher and needs the capability to control cameras remotely, be sure that such a capability is possible with the switcher selected as simpler units may not have it.

The next type of device is a quad splitter. As the name implies, this device can divide the screen into four sections, each of which displays one camera view. Some newer units use the same technology to divide the screen into multiple sections or to rotate the first four cameras onto the screen, and then the next four, then back to the first four, etc. The chief disadvantage of a quad splitter is that the images on the screen can be hard to see adequately, with a resultant loss in security surveillance. Most units, however, will allow the operator to send a particular camera to full screen if necessary. Needless to say, too small a monitor servicing a quad splitter is a disaster. Some quad splitters are sold as part of the cabinet that holds the monitor but this arrangement, while reducing costs, has some implications. First, if the library decides it needs a larger monitor, it will have to replace the entire unit, including the quad splitter. Second, if any part of the unit needs repair, the entire device may have to be removed from the premises. Be sure, if this type of unit is selected, to inquire carefully about replacement policies while the unit is out for repairs.

If a switcher is a corporate jet, a multiplexer is an F-16 Eagle. The advantages of a multiplexer (called a MUX) are numerous. The one that attracts most favorable comment is its ability to offer a wide variety of screen displays on the monitor, even picture-in-picture. MUXs are available in a wide variety of abilities, and these should be inquired into carefully. One capability that the library should consider is the MUX's ability to play back images from a recording device while still displaying live images on the monitor and recording them on a second storage device, an important feature. If an operator sees something suspicious, it is a significant advantage to be able to review the suspicious activity while continuing to observe the activity live. Almost all MUXs allow for remote manipulation of cameras. Finally, some MUXs can automatically detect the VCR's recording speed and adjust their output accordingly. This capability prevents the MUX from overwhelming the tape because an operator forgot to reset the system before leaving for the weekend. When coupled with a digital storage device, a MUX offers excellent security. Even the simplest multiplexer has tremendous advantages over even a sophisticated switcher. If at all possible, it should be the choice in a conventional CCTV system.

Internet Protocol Systems

Because of advances in computer technology, it is now possible to bypass conventional configurations that use separate monitors, recording devices, and switchers/multiplexers with digital cameras that run over Internet Protocol systems (IP systems). One type of system is mounted entirely on PCs, with the camera leads all running directly to boards in the computer or transmitted wirelessly through the Internet. The PC acts as the monitor, recording device, and switcher/multiplexer. Although once in relative infancy, this type of system will probably become standard. The library should seriously consider such an arrangement, but if the library

does select such a system, the computer on which it is mounted should probably not be used for any other purpose, and some thought should be given before connecting to the Internet.

IP systems offer some advantages over traditional analog technology. First, images from the camera can be viewed from any place with an Internet connection. In other words, one could be in Istanbul and view activities in real time at a library in Kansas. Historical video would also be available. Second, IP camera resolution is often close to that provided by analog cameras. Third, IP cameras can be trained. If, for example, a camera is focused on an expensive manuscript in an exhibition case, it can recognize if the object is no longer in its view and alert security personnel. (Apparently no experiments have been done, however, to see if a camera can detect a substitution.) The cameras can also detect motion and function as part of an intrusion system.[17]

What You See Is What You Get

A CCTV system cannot capture what it cannot see or record. Determining precisely the type of information the library wants captured is an important decision and influences almost every aspect of the system the library will select. As Morawski remarks, "You can't get information out of nothing."[18] Thinking about desired results is an important exercise. Matchett observes, "When designing a camera system, the most important part of the procedure takes place well before any system component is selected."[19]

A basic consideration is whether to select a digital or analog system. The former is the type usually being flogged by the security industry as the wave of the future and as a methodology superior to analog. The library should be cautious, however, because this choice can involve some critical decisions, the consequences of which may not become evident until the images are needed as evidence. Because a digital signal is so dense with information, systems must anticipate the next image or in turn strip part of the image away before it is sent to the storage device. If digital systems were unable to perform such functions, their output would overwhelm practically any storage system. The problem with a digital system is that by altering the image in any way, it makes it theoretically possible for a defense attorney to argue that the image being displayed is not the actual image at all. For some frames, that argument would be correct. No such problems arise, however, with analog systems. Any image sent by an analog system to a storage device is an actual image that has not been subjected to any electronic altering or correcting. It is also important to bear in mind that usually during a demonstration of a system, what one usually sees is the direct output of the camera to the monitor, not the image that would be displayed if the system were hooked to a recording/playback device.

Six Mistakes

Libraries often make six critical mistakes in choosing and operating their systems. The first mistake is not to record all the time. In some institutions, at the end of the day the recording device is shut down, thereby leaving the library with no record, no matter how dim, of what happens overnight. In a variation of that scenario, the recording device is too small to store several days worth of images. Thus, even if the recording device is left operating Friday evening, it runs out of capacity or begins to overwrite on Saturday morning and thus does not capture all activity over the rest of the weekend. It is vital that the library record all information from all cameras all the time, especially during periods when the library is closed. One would believe it obvious that the system should at least be recording whenever the library is open, but such is not always

the case. When E. Forbes Smiley, for example, was first suspected at Yale, the CCTV system was not operating and had to be turned on. The system was not operating because apparently some patrons objected to it because of privacy concerns. No library should ever cave in to such considerations.

A second mistake is to make no provision for any recording capacity in darkness. Special collections librarians' aversion to light almost compels them to plunge the library at the end of the day into as near to total darkness as can be achieved. If the library has a CCTV system however, doing so can be a crucial error. Extremely low light compromises some cameras' ability to capture images clearly. If possible, compromise between the desire for turning off lights and the necessity of providing light for the cameras should be considered. Modern cameras can capture images successfully at fairly low light levels, often as low as 0.0003 lux for some of the newer black and white units. Some experimentation with the cameras and the lights may reveal a compromise that will allow the library to get serviceable images in such situations.[20]

One solution to providing serviceable images when the library is closed and in darkness is to use built-in infrared illumination as a light source (see fig 7.3). Cameras that function with infrared light have come down in price drastically in the last few years. They require no special arrangements and can be installed on any system right along with conventional cameras. During normal lighting conditions, they function as any other camera. In darkness, however, the infrared lights illuminate automatically and the camera begins to record in black and white mode. Infrared cameras are rated at 0.0 lux. The chief drawback to such units is that, unless the infrared illuminator is a flood, the range is usually not beyond 50 feet.[21] The presence of even one such unit can significantly enhance a CCTV system, however.

Figure 7.3

Color Camera with Infrared Lights (Used by permission)

The third critical mistake made by libraries with their CCTV systems is failing to provide for thorough coverage. Almost every library will agree on the necessity of watching patron reading room activity and provide for that to some degree. Many, however, stop there. People passing in and out of stack doors, in and out of vaults, in and of elevators, or in and out of delivery doors are never recorded, despite the fact that these areas are critical to a library's security, particularly in the case of insider theft or a break-in after hours. The activities of desk attendants are also rarely monitored, although those persons are crucial elements in security. In deciding on coverage, a library needs to consider carefully the possibilities for security breaches and insofar as possible monitor the activities and places where such breaches are likely or possible.

A fourth mistake is to install a system inadequate to the task. Any number of reasons may cause such a situation to arise. A common one is money. The library should realize, however, given the flexibility of modern CCTV systems, that there

is rarely any reason to have to install a full-blown system all at once. If a library needs eight cameras, for example, so long as the basic equipment will eventually operate eight cameras, there is no need to install all eight at once. The process can be spread out over several years and budget cycles. Simply throwing up a cheesy, four-camera system with a tiny black and white monitor and calling it a day because that is all that can be afforded at the moment is a failure of security planning and budgeting.

A fifth mistake is not to have cameras that record fast enough to capture "slight of hand" incidents, which are common in such venues as gambling casinos but obviously also found in rare book libraries. The Yale video of E. Forbes Smiley cutting maps from books, for example, was so slow that it basically did not detect his activities. To record reading room activities, libraries should consider systems with recording rates on demand of between 120 and 480 frames per second. It should be noted though, that such recording rates rapidly consume available recording space.

A sixth mistake is to provide for no redundancy in the system or its servicing. Redundancy is a complicated matter that can be taken to extremes, as it necessarily is on the Space Shuttle or a commercial airliner. In the library's case, however, some consideration needs to be given to contingencies and how redundancy might help prevent security lapses. For example, it might be a wise idea to purchase at least one extra camera body that could be installed quickly if a camera breaks down, and the security company cannot provide a replacement off the shelf. Other redundancies might be contemplated for such equipment as a multiplexer. Although the one you installed might hold x cameras, if Social Science does vacate that adjoining space and you get it, you might now need y cameras. The multiplexer you chose should be able to be adequately expanded or bussed to a new one to accommodate the new cameras you will be installing. Finally, a library might want to consider duplicate cable runs to some critical cameras. If the cable path for the camera watching the vault is damaged, it is a far simpler and faster matter to hook up an existing second cable than to install another run.[22]

Regrettably, another reason for an inadequate CCTV system may lie in the library's relationship to a parent institution, such as a government entity or a university. In such cases, the library may have little choice except to take what it is given, no matter how adequate or inadequate the system might be. The library will not be in the position of going itself into the marketplace to seek a system that will answer its security concerns. It may be at the mercy of whatever recommendation is made by the campus security force, for example. Alternately, the parent institution may have an exclusive contract with a security company to provide CCTV equipment for the entire institution, thereby leaving the library with no choice of vendors, even if the company's equipment is not what the library needs. The library may also find itself subject to the aesthetic sense of the institution's architect, without whose approval nothing can be done. In such situations, the library has little choice but to negotiate as best it can for what it needs. If the system proposed is clearly going to be inadequate, the library might consider declining it. Once it is installed, that is probably going to be it for many years.[23] As Fay points out in his discussion of applying technology to security situations, "Very important also is to get the solution right the first time because retrofitting can be costly."[24]

The Purposes of Surveillance

The four purposes of CCTV surveillance are monitoring, detection, recognition, and identification. Depending on the purposes to which information captured from the CCTV system will be put, each of those purposes will to a great degree determine what views the library chooses for its system. Each of those purposes is reflected in what one sees on the monitor screen and what is recorded, and were developed to apply to general surveillance situations, such as parking lots.

For monitoring purposes a person should not occupy less than 10% of the monitor screen height. This is actually a fairly tiny image that will allow the operator to do little more that verify a person's presence in an area.

For detection purposes a person should not occupy less than 30% of the monitor screen height. Again, this image is fairly small but should be large enough to allow the operator to identify some characteristics of a person.

For recognition purposes a person should not occupy less that 50% of the monitor screen height. At that resolution, an operator should be able to identify a person with reasonable certainty. The view should be able to discriminate clearly such things as dress, accoutrement, hair style, etc.

For identification purposes a person should not occupy less than 120% of the monitor screen height. This amount of resolution can generally be achieved only with a zoom lens. At this level of resolution, there should be no doubt about a person's identity, dress, or activity.

Translating these surveillance levels into practical library uses is an issue with which every library will have to grapple. Different views may be required for different security levels. A fairly common mistake that libraries make, however, is to provide for a view that really does not satisfy security requirements. This mistake is usually incorporated physically by too few cameras recording views that lack critical details. In libraries, because distances between the cameras and the scene being recorded are usually so short, recognition will probably be achieved. What will not be achieved, however, is the capture of detrimental activities, such as razoring plates from books. It is to that area that libraries need to give consideration in implementing a CCTV system. Capturing such activity probably requires that the system be able to operate as needed in the identification mode, which usually will require a zoom lens. Other areas of security may reflect different realities. It is, for example, desirable to capture for recognition purposes all persons entering and leaving a vault. It is not desirable, however, that the picture be so good that the operator or anyone else reviewing the video be able to discern the vault combination. At the very least, the library should avoid reading room views where the surveillance level rises only to the detection level. Such views are rarely useful either for detection or later prosecution.

A CCTV system also offers the opportunity to provide sound recording of events, and your security firm may ask if the library wishes to install sound recording capability, a common feature, especially in business applications. Some cameras come equipped with built-in microphones. Stand-alone systems are commonly referred to as Laurae (pronounced lah rew') systems, after the company that popularized them. The chief advantage of the latter system is that microphones can be placed anywhere. In either case, the sound is recorded on the storage device along with its corresponding video. One advantage of a sound system is that it would capture a thief's lies concerning his or her purpose for using the library. The map thief Gilbert Bland, for example, lied repeatedly about his research purposes to gain access to materials. A sound recording system would have captured his deceits in a way a CCTV system alone could not.

If a library is considering installing a sound recording system, however, it needs to ensure that the system is legal. Such systems are firmly hedged about with restrictions and in many instances may be patently illegal invasions of privacy. Before a library installs such a system it should check with legal counsel and with local law enforcement agencies. Installing an illegal sound recording system can have significant legal consequences for a library and its personnel.[25]

The Operator

Throughout this chapter "the operator" has been referred to. For a CCTV system to be truly effective an operator must be employed. An operator's job is to monitor the system, note suspicious activity, watch that activity, be sure it is properly recorded, and notify the proper staff that the activity is taking place. Without such a person, the CCTV system is not performing at full capacity. The sad fact is that most libraries don't employ one. Typical library practice is to scatter monitors in various places hoping that someone, who is usually busy doing some other task, might notice something amiss. It is everybody's but nobody's job to surveille the premises via the CCTV system. Such an arrangement usually compromises security.

Even if the library cannot employ an operator, it can sometimes make arrangements that approach the ideal. For example, if the reading room attendant cannot really see the reading room adequately, other persons could be assigned in rotation to watch the reading room via the CCTV system when a reader is present. Such an arrangement not only improves security by having someone actually watch the scene, but it also gives several staff members experience with system operations and capabilities. Watching readers via the CCTV system also has important conservation implications, because the operator can also watch for activities such as using pens and using materials as writing surfaces.

The Downside

As important as CCTV systems can be for library security, they are not without their problems. A significant issue for most libraries is going to be the expense of installing and maintaining the system. Although CCTV system prices have dropped as their capabilities have risen, an adequate system is still probably going to represent a significant sum of money. Even if only part of a system is installed with the idea that it will be expanded in future years, the price of installing all the equipment necessary in that scenario might make the library hesitate. Second, there may be staff resistance to the idea of a CCTV system. Staff rarely objects when the only ones being surveilled are readers; however, if, the system is also intended to monitor staff activities, some questions may arise. No matter how noble a purpose is ascribed to the CCTV system, some people are probably going to conclude that its main purpose is to spy on them. To some people, a CCTV system is the ultimate tool of Big Brother.[26] Third, once installed the system is going to require staff time to maintain and operate. Someone has to be in charge of the system, watch it for maintenance problems, see that those problems are addressed, and do other activities, such as changing and storing VCR tapes. All that has to be done in addition to actually watching the monitor. In a library with a small staff, such a reallocation of resources may be something of a strain. That problem is somewhat offset, however, by the fact that the CCTV system in effect adds several sets of eyes to watch for security concerns. If an untoward event occurs, it is always possible that the CCTV system caught what everybody else missed at the time.

Operational and privacy issues need to be addressed. Without wishing to recommend that even more documentation be generated by a library, it is probably best that policies and procedures for the CCTV system be written. Topics that might be addressed include the system's purpose, who will be responsible for it, its security functions, and whatever privacy issues need to be resolved. Although many libraries and government agencies lack such policies in the U.S., some idea of what one might contain may be gleaned from those in force in New South Wales.[27] In some situations, there may also be legal issues involved with a CCTV system, and those should be checked with counsel.

Although any library would probably believe that its CCTV system is intended primarily to watch for damage to or theft of library materials, the installation of such a system also has other security considerations. There is a developing body of case law that holds that the owner/operator of a CCTV system may be liable for violations of personal security. In other words, if Mary is assaulted at the back door being surveilled by a CCTV system, Mary may have some action against the library because nobody noticed the activity and called the police or came to her aid. Such liability increases exponentially if Mary lies outside unnoticed for 20 minutes bleeding from a knife wound, especially if the entire incident proves to be captured on the recording device. A library needs to consider such possibilities carefully when it decides to install a CCTV system.[28]

Contracts

Many of the observations about contracts made in the chapter "Burglar Alarm Systems" (q. v.) will also apply to a contract for a CCTV system. Only considerations special to CCTV systems will be covered here.

As with burglar alarms, if there is a service contract on the system, the security company should be responsible for every aspect of the system, including all wiring. If the library uses a VCR as a recording device, the institution should inquire closely about repair/replacement policies as the machine will eventually fail. When it does, the library wants to ensure that the security company will promptly provide a replacement while the original unit is out for repairs. Some provisions for its routine maintenance should also be agreed upon. In no case should a VCR running 24 hours a day go beyond a year without a thorough maintenance routine, including replacing worn parts, being performed. The cost of this maintenance can be built into the maintenance contract or assumed by the library on an annual basis. VCRs can fail suddenly—and usually at precisely the wrong time and in precisely the wrong way. A well-maintained unit is going to be more reliable than one that has not seen maintenance in three years. Even though it may be a little more expensive to do so, the library should probably purchase all VCR tapes through the security company. In that way, if a tape damages the machine, the security company cannot blame the problem on the library. Monitors also fail and repair/replacement policies for those devices should also be inquired into.

One aspect of the system for which the security company is not really responsible–nor should it be–is the camera views. This aspect of the system should have been thoroughly reviewed and tested prior to installation of the system. If the library later decides it does not like the view it is receiving from a particular camera, it is not the security company's responsibility to reposition the camera or to provide such things as new camera bodies and lens to correct it for free, assuming that the company properly installed what was requested in the first place. Of course, if the view is somehow technically incorrect (e.g., static, smeared), that is the security company's responsibility.

Without question, problems with camera views constitute fertile fields from which spring many arguments between customers and security companies, and the library needs to be as careful as

possible in such matters. In some cases, however, it may be nearly impossible to test a view. If eight cameras are to be installed at various points in a 20' ceiling, getting views before actual installation is going to be a somewhat cumbersome if not courageous act. If the security firm uses an optical viewfinder to allow the library to select its views, someone from the library is probably going to have to sign off on the list of views selected prior to installation. If that procedure is used and the views are not satisfactory, the library probably does not have a leg to stand on if the views are insufficient and need to be changed.

All components of a CCTV system also fall under the exclusion of fitness for a particular purposes. That exclusion does not mean, for example, that a camera will not function as a camera. It means merely that a camera will do only that and that nothing more should be expected of it. Some people believe that cameras will detect fire, especially those units that are programmed to follow movement and trigger the burglar alarm if any is detected. They reason that the smoke and flames move; thus, the camera should have sounded the alarm. Although one might reasonably expect a camera to capture images of the fire in progress, the camera is not warranted to be fit for the purpose of detecting a fire and sounding an alarm.

The Future: A Caveat

Some of the difficulty writing about and describing current CCTV systems is that some of the information is obsolete soon after it appears in print. As Sentry Security Systems correctly observes: "The days of expensive time lapse VCR's, multiplexers, splitters and monitors are numbered. Today, this expensive and performance-limited equipment is replaced by computer technology resulting in better recording quality, control and functionality as well as remote viewing. All these enhanced features are often available for a lower price and lower total cost of ownership."[29] Thus, a library interested in installing a CCTV system needs to inquire carefully into current possibilities and emerging technologies. Although current technologies are still adequate, valid, and proven, emerging ones may be a better choice.

NOTES

1. This area of technology is changing rapidly, so much so that some of the information here may be out of date by the time it is published.

2. See Chris Fleet, "Report of the 'Responding to Theft Seminar' Held at the National Library of Wales on 25 April 2002." http://www.maphistory.info/aberseminar.html.

3. See "Jail for Stealing Pages from Rare Books." http://uk.news.yahoo.com/4/20090116/tuk-jail-for-stealing-pages-from-rare-bo-dba1618.html.

4. United States Court of Appeals. Sixth Circuit. "United States of America, Plaintiff-Appellee/Cross Applicant v. Charles Thomas Allen, II, et al., Defendants-Appellants/Cross-Appellees," 3.

5. The use of CCTV systems is a relatively recent development. Alice Harrison Bahr, *Book Theft and Library Security Systems, 1979–79* (White Plains: Knowledge Industry Publication, 1979) reported that CCTV systems were a "less obvious" remedy for reducing thefts, and that one such system in a public library designed to prevent pilferage was considered controversial. She concluded, "Video monitors are still used by libraries, but for security problems other than those connected with collection loss" (97–98). Just a few years prior, Burns Security Institute, *National Survey on Library Security* (Briarcliff Manor: Burns Security Institute, [1973]), did not even ask the libraries it surveyed about CCTV systems.

6. Alan R. Matchett, *CCTV for Security Professionals* (Boston: Butterworth-Heinemann, 2003), xi.

7. The imager is sometimes referred to as a CCD, an acronym for "charged couple device," one of several types of solid state imagers. The imager sizes (1/4", 1/2", etc.) do not refer to the actual size of the imager itself.

8. Cieszynski, Joe, *Closed Circuit Television* (Oxford: Newnes, 2001), 22.

9. Signals can also be transmitted over phone lines. Unless the system is running over an ISDN line, however, the picture quality will probably not be satisfactory.

10. Emily Harwood, *Digital CCTV: A Security Professional's Guide* (Boston: Butterworth-Heinemann, 2008), 111. She discusses both systems in detail (111–146).

11. The National Archives retention schedules suggest destroying "routine" surveillance tapes after six months, for example. See *General Records Schedule 21 Audiovisual Records,* Transmittal 8 (December 1998). http://www.archives.gov/records-mgmt/ardor/grs21.html.

12. Harwood presciently entitles her chapter on recording devices, "From VTRs to VCRs, DVRs, and NVRs" (197–204).

13 Obtaining a print from a VCR tape requires a specialized and expensive printer.

14. Harwood by her title alone clearly indicates the way the CCTV industry is moving. In support of her preference for digital systems, she remarks: " There are many reasons to switch to digital for security surveillance and recording applications. Probably the strongest reason is that digital information can be stored and retrieved with virtually no degradation, meaning that with digital images, copies are as good as originals. When a digital recording is copied, it is a clone, not a replica" (x).

15. A somewhat hybrid recording device is one that uses either digital tape or a disk drive and tape. Such devices often hold 30–40MB of information and far outstrip the capacities of a conventional VCR.

16. Hardwood touches on problems with digital signals, which, like any other digital image, are subject to manipulation and alteration in ways that are difficult to accomplish with analog formats. She discusses various methods to validate and secure digital images (224–224).

17. For a brief overview of such possibilities, see Ed Morawski, *How to Defeat Burglar Alarms—Not!: Dispelling Hollywood Myths* (N. p., 2007), 51–56.

18. P. 57.

19. P. 25. Although speaking of outside CCTV systems, he further observes, "If the wrong type of camera is selected or the wrong location is selected, the view from the camera can easily be less than desirable" (207).

20. Bright sunlight is about 10,000 lux; a full moon produces about 0.1 lux. As technology improves, conventional cameras can produce serviceable images with less light. The newest cameras can function in 0.0003 lux, which is about the amount of light on a clear, starlit night.

21. Sometimes circumstances make it impossible to use cameras with built-in infrared illuminators. For example, cameras may be mounted on a ceiling that is 30 feet high or may watch an area over 50 feet wide. In such cases other options, such as infrared flood lights, are available.

22. See Matchett, 31–34.

23. Although this same situation might well arise in relation to both burglar alarm and access control systems, it is a particularly troubling scenario in relation to CCTV systems, which generally have far more options and possibilities than either burglar alarm or access control systems.

24. John J. Fay, ed., *Encyclopedia of Security Management*, 2nd ed. (Burlington: Butterworth-Heninemann, 2007), 59.

25. See, for example, Cara Anna, "Company admits it sold illegal audio bugs," *Austin American-Statesman*, (28 November 2002), D: 1.

26. For a brief description of the problems involved in getting approvals to install a CCTV system in the Royal Library of Sweden, see Tomas Lidman, "Crime and Crime Prevention Measures in the Royal Library, Stockholm, 2002–2002," *Liber Quarterly* 12 (2002): 314.

27. Privacy Committee of New South Wales, *Invisible Eyes: Report on Video Surveillance in the Workplace* 67 (September, 1995). http://www.austlii.edu.au/au/other/privacy/video.

28. Such considerations argue against ever installing dummy cameras, which create the same expectation of security but actually do absolutely nothing.

29. Sentry Security Systems Inc. Web site at: http://www.cctvsentry.com/. (The quoted statement is no longer available on the web site.)

Special Circumstances

Everett C. Wilkie, Jr.

> Ice is forming on the tips of my wings,
> Unheeded warnings, I thought I thought of everything.
> ~ *Pink Floyd*

Despite the quotidian circumstances that generally face rare books and special collections libraries, special circumstances do arise that require some alteration of security procedures either to waive or tighten them. In some cases, the library is literally not in total control of its materials or of those who have access to them. As nervous as such circumstances may make the custodian, sometimes they cannot be helped and must be accommodated. Some of the more common situations and their security implications are discussed below.

Materials Lent for Exhibition

Great amounts of materials–rare, common, expensive, or cheap–are exchanged between institutions for exhibition purposes. The entire world of exhibitions would probably grind to a halt or be considerably impoverished if peers did not cooperate with one another's exhibition plans. When a library surrenders an object for exhibition at another venue, however, it is taking a leap of faith that the borrowing institution will care for the item and return it in the same condition in which it was lent, taking reasonable precautions to ensure that it is not stolen or damaged. The lending institution need not necessarily go entirely on faith, however, and a few propositions for the borrower are not out of the question.

ACRL has published guidelines for borrowing and lending materials.[1] From a security aspect, only some of their provisions are pertinent. In general, the two situations that present major security problems are transport and the exhibition itself.

Transportation of an item to and from the exhibition venue offers opportunities for items to go astray or be stolen. Despite the fact that the lending institution does not wish to lose any materials, some reasonableness is required. If the institution is lending their third copy of a piece of nineteenth-century sheet music, common carriers such as FedEx or the postal service might be adequate. If the item is a rare thirteenth-century illuminated French missal on vellum, more stringent transportation requirements might come into play. The four most common transportation scenarios are the following:

1) United States Postal Service. This method of transportation seems to be generally unfavored in museum and library circles and is rarely used. If it is, the only acceptable method is registered mail. Unfortunately, because of the audit procedures, this method is slow, even if relatively secure, and it cannot be tracked on the fly. If the item does vanish, the USPS can generally determine the last person who handled it, however. Another USPS option is Express Mail, which can generally deliver overnight to most major locations in the U.S. Although not signed for, each piece of Express Mail is scanned at

every delivery point and can be tracked in general. Generous, real insurance is also available for items sent by the USPS.[2]

2) Commercial carriers, such as FedEx, UPS, and DHL seem to be considered safer and more reliable than the USPS, although they have no equivalent to registered mail. Once a parcel goes into the system, it is scanned at every point but no personal record of who actually handled the item is maintained, much like Express mail. Insurance considerations with commercial carriers are also hedged with numerous conditions, and sometimes valuable items are excluded from full coverage. Regrettably, disappearances from commercial carrier systems are sometimes reported.[3] Such disappearances are investigated by the shipper's investigators, regular law enforcement, or perhaps the FBI rather than by U.S. Postal Inspectors. Care must be taken when numerous packages are delivered at one drop by commercial carriers, in which case a single signature by someone in the shipping department may authorize the bulk receipt of a large number of items. Since the carrier is absolved of responsibility with the signature, and the individual items may not have been checked (or even counted), there will be no way of accounting for a package that may be listed on the waybill but not found subsequently.[4]

The use of the USPS or commercial carriers should be considered only for items of fairly minimal value. If an irreplaceable or extremely valuable item is to be shipped, the methods below should probably be used.

3) Fine arts carrier. Several such carriers exist and offer a range of services, from mere pick-up and delivery to packing and crating. Their advantage is that they operate a dedicated transportation system with bonded drivers and crews who do nothing but move fine arts materials in their own equipment. Usually once an item is loaded onto a truck, it does not come off or change hands until it reaches its destination, a distinction that does not apply to any other commercial transportation option. In general, this method is true point-to-point transportation with no intervening hand-offs and is quite secure. However, it is quite a bit more expensive than options 1 or 2 above.

4) Courier. A courier is an individual who picks up an item at point A and physically delivers it to point B without ever letting it out of his or her possession. Such a method is appropriate if the item being lent is relatively valuable and easily transportable. It probably will not be appropriate for a two-volume Gutenberg Bible on vellum, for example. In most cases, if this option is chosen, a library staff member will be the courier rather than a third party. In some cases, the lending institution may insist that the courier not finally relinquish the item until he or she can witness it installed and secured in the exhibition case; the courier may also need to be present when the item on loan is removed from the installation and repacked. Despite the apparent lavishness of this method, it can actually be quite a bit cheaper than option 3.[5]

Both the lending and borrowing institution need to bear in mind that all transportation and insurance costs are to be borne by the borrowing library or museum. Although it does not pay to be unreasonable by insisting, for example, that a $15 piece of sheet music be transported by courier, it is reasonable to insist that more valuable materials be treated accordingly.

Before an item is delivered to the venue, the lending institution will naturally be concerned about security at the borrowing library, since it will have little control over that aspect of the exhibition. At the very least, the borrowing library should be willing to provide the lender a detailed explanation of its security arrangements while the object will be in its possession.[6] If the lending library's object is extremely valuable, it is not unreasonable that the library insist on a site visit to inspect the venue to resolve lingering security doubts. Again, this trip is something the borrowing institution should pay for but upon which the lender should insist only under special circumstances.

The ACRL *Guidelines* suggest that the following security matters be ascertained before materials are sent for loan:

> Describe how items on exhibition will be properly safeguarded against theft or damage. Describe the exhibition cases and locks and the method by which framed items are mounted on the wall. Describe the intrusion alarm system in the exhibition area. If security staff are employed, give the number of security staff employed and the number on duty at any time. Indicate the days and hours that the exhibition will be regularly open. Indicate whether food and drink are ever allowed in the exhibition area, whether the space is rented to outside organizations, and if any other use is made of the space other than for exhibition viewing.[7]

In some cases, such situations are ironic. As one curator remarked after looking over her own security checklist she was preparing to send to a borrowing institution, "According to this, we couldn't even borrow our own materials."[8] In any case, the lending institution should satisfy itself that the materials will be at least as secure while on loan as they would be in their home collection.

Materials on Interlibrary Loan

In response to perceived building pressure to create a document governing potential interlibrary loan of rare materials, RBMS and ACRL created a guideline for lending materials on ILL.[9] Most of the security considerations that apply to lending materials for exhibition apply to lending them for use in another library's reading room by a patron, although the big difference is that someone will actually be using the material rather than viewing it in an exhibition case. Despite the ambitious program and ideas laid out in the document, apparently few institutions are willing to lend materials to another institution for this purpose.

If a library is willing to lend materials, certain caveats might be in order. First, it is probably a poor idea to lend unique or otherwise irreplaceable items or collections. Especially in the case of manuscripts, microfilms, copies, or scans should probably be provided instead. Second, if at all possible and despite the suggestion in the *Guidelines* that materials be sent through normal inter-library loan channels, the lending library should probably insist that the borrowing library's special collections take direct possession of the items from a commercial shipping firm, such as FedEx, and that the materials be returned the same way.[10] Especially in the case of large institutions, items sent through the mail will probably be processed through a general mail sorting facility, whereupon track of them will be lost.[11] Third, it is undeniable that the lending library loses control of its materials and is taking a leap of faith that the borrowers will secure and treat its materials properly, a faith that can regrettably be misplaced. A few lending institutions have reported that they believe their books to have been photocopied, for example, even though they were not supposed to be, with resultant wear and tear.[12] Fourth, it is also probably a bad practice to lend original materials for which surrogates are readily available.

Renovations and Moves

If a library is being renovated or moved and the activity involves the special collections area, an entirely new set of risks not normally associated with everyday operations come into play. The library must be highly alert to potential problems posed by the presence of people over whom the library has little control and who are often at liberty to come and go as their jobs require. Renovation and moving projects come in so many varieties, from small to extensive, that nothing more than general caveats can be given about them. Each individual library will need to undertake careful planning depending on the extent and nature of the project.[13]

In the best of all possible renovation worlds, the library would simply move its collections to storage or another venue until construction is completed, even if it means loss of access to certain parts of the collections. That is the strategy that the Bancroft Library chose when its main building was retrofitted for earthquake protection and otherwise renovated.[14] Some collections were still available but many of them were in inaccessible storage. On the other hand, the John Carter Brown Library remained open during its renovation; it could store its materials in existing stacks while construction of a new wing was under way.[15] The Hargrett Library at the University of Georgia adopted a hybrid scheme, closing for several weeks in 1999 to move collections to another area in the library and then reopening in the temporary space while its permanent space was undergoing work.[16] In another scenario, The Connecticut Historical Society moved its manuscript collection to another part of the building while its stacks were being renovated, although the collection was not available during that time.[17] The William Andrews Clark Library, however, closed down its stacks from 2005–2008, and material was unavailable to researchers during its mold remediation project.[18] The idea of closing the library for any length of time during a major renovation can strike administrators with horror, and great efforts are made to keep some of the collections accessible. Considerations such as having to suspend fellowship programs or otherwise inconvenience a library's researchers often weigh heavily. How to keep displaced employees employed, especially if they are under union contracts, can also be a problem. Whether such efforts are wise from a security standpoint is a judgment call.[19]

Although the library will have little control over people performing renovation work, it should if at all possible seek assurances that all workers have undergone criminal background checks. Such a check should be the minimum threshold for any worker on the premises. Second, the library should also seek assurances that workers will never be on the premises when they are closed, which might involve some rearranging of staff schedules. Construction work normally begins at 7:00 a.m., usually well before most libraries open for the day. If at all possible, at least one library staff member should be present at the beginning and end of the work day. Third, the library should ensure that work does not interfere with the operations of its alarm systems and that they can be set at the end of every day. Construction details, therefore, need to be coordinated with the library's security company to be sure protection is not compromised. Fourth, the library should insist that no construction workers be allowed to have keys, access cards, or alarm codes. Library staff alone should have those privileges. Fifth, the library should, consistent with worker safety, also insist that all workers display visible ID cards issued for the project. In some instances, it is too easy for an outsider to wander in wearing a hard hat and begin looking around.[20] Any worker without a proper ID card should be cause for suspicion. Arrangements should be made in advance so that workers know they must show the contents of all pockets and tool cases whenever exiting the library, and visual inspections should be routinely performed at check-points.

When collections are moved temporarily to off-site storage or to a new facility, certain security considerations will come into play. If collections are moved to another building on campus, the library will perhaps be able to exercise more control over who has access and under what circumstances. It is possible, for example, to arrange for a situation in which only special collections staff and a few others, such as emergency personnel, have access. Such an arrangement would be ideal. On the other hand, collections may be packed and moved by a commercial firm, in which case the library will have less control over access. In such a scenario, the library should examine any proposed storage space, make inquiries about security systems, and ascertain which members of the storage firm will have access to the storage area and under what circumstances. The library should insist that as few people as possible be allowed into the storage area. Ideally, the library's collection would be in a separate part of the facility rather than mixed in with other collections.[21]

One special collections library that moved its materials to commercial off-site storage during renovations described the arrangements in this way, which seems very close to ideal, in response to a series of questions posed to the librarian.

How much do you know about the security of your collections while they are in storage?
Security was a concern, so we grilled the companies that bid on the job about it. Not just in the storage end, but also the packing/moving end. I'm pretty satisfied. The one we went with moved the **** collection from **** to the **** without problems, so I'm not too worried. Plus, we are heavily insured.

Have you seen the space?
Yes. It is nice enough. A former factory/warehouse; it is clean and has good climate control (definitely better than ours).

Is the space alarmed?
Yes. Burglar, fire, water, temp/RH. It is also about a block from both the police and fire departments. And they have a pretty good disaster plan (better than ours, I would say). I am also going to hide some temp/RH data loggers in the space to independently check that.

How many people would have access to your materials?
About a half dozen including myself and other library staff. There is an on-site librarian, her assistant, the head of ****; it has keycard access and they are the only ones who will have cards. We will be informed if repairmen or others need access. And the movers when the books are being unloaded. Once the books are in there, though, it will be very limited access.

Will they be segregated from the other materials in storage or mixed in?
Segregated. Most of our books will be on a different floor than those of other libraries stored at the same facility. The special collections will be in a separate locked room (with its own climate control) on the main floor adjacent to the on-site librarian's office.

Are they sealed in cartons or containers of some sort or just arranged on open shelves?
Boxed, palletized, and wrapped. Special collections items are in acid free boxes inside plastic containers with a security seal in a separate locked room.[22]

Any collection move or on-site renovation is going to present a variety of security concerns based on individual library circumstances, collections, budgets, and staff. In all cases, however, a prime directive should be that the library not lose anything to theft during the transition.

Permanent Off-Site Storage

As collections have grown far beyond the ability of libraries to contain them all properly, numerous institutions have turned to building off-site storage facilities, an arrangement that presents its own set of security problems for the rare books library. If at all possible, rare books and special collections libraries should seek to be exempted from having to move their own materials into such a facility, but often the situation is unavoidable. If a library simply must store part of its collections off site, certain decision-making principles would apply.

First, insofar as possible only materials of low financial value should be moved off-site. The selection process should be precise, avoiding moving entire sections of call numbers, for example, unless the classification contains mostly low-value books, like modern novels. Second, materials that are easily vandalized without leaving any obvious external evidence of the process should also be retained. Such a consideration would imply, for example, that color plate books or collections of separate illuminated manuscript leaves are poor candidates for transfer. If manuscript collections are to be included in the transfer, they should not be ones that have any highly valuable materials in them and, if at all possible, the cartons should be banded or otherwise sealed up to prevent tampering. Likewise, collections of easily removed and concealed ephemera, such as postcards or trade cards, should probably not be transferred. Third, one should avoid the temptation to think "large." Although it is simpler by far to clear six feet of shelf space by moving one large set rather than clearing another six feet by removing numerous individual items, careful consideration should be given to whether expediency is the better choice.[23] Some large sets contain valuable materials, such as plates or other illustrations. Fourth, in few cases should cataloguing backlogs or otherwise unprocessed materials be moved to regular storage. If such collections are put into storage, they should be sequestered so that only special collections staff has access to them.

The library should be most concerned, however, with the security arrangements in place at the storage facility and while its materials are being transported. Of course, the facility should have burglar alarms at a very minimum. Of greater concern will be who has access to the library's materials and how the materials are stored in the building. First, anyone working in the storage facility or with access to it, such as maintenance workers, should all pass appropriate background checks. Second, the facility should not be available for access to any workers except during regular hours. If the facility closes at 5 p.m. on Friday and does not reopen until 7 a.m. on Monday, nobody should be in it during those intervening weekend hours except during emergencies.

Transportation to and from the facility will also be an issue. Materials should be transported only by designated people who should not stop at any intermediate point between the special collections library and the storage facility. In other words, delivery routes should be arranged so that special collections is the first delivery point and the last pick-up point on any run. No particular attention should be drawn to rare materials in transit. We know of one case in which the remote storage facility boldly indicated that the contents of the transport box were "Highly Valuable," thus calling special attention to itself. Since material in remote storage should not be of the first importance or value, a sensible but not obsessive rigor should be accorded to them. All material requested from remote storage should be reassessed for value and artifactual significance before being sent back.[24]

The audit trail for special collections materials should also be clear and unambiguous. It is important that retrieval, acceptance, discharge, and reshelving records include the identity of the person responsible at every stage of the process. Such records should be kept in duplicate at the storage facility and at the library itself. (In the best of all possible worlds, only special collections staff would retrieve and reshelve materials in storage, but that procedure is usually impracticable.)

Books in the General Stacks

A common situation in any large, older library is that books of great value may be housed in the general stacks and available for circulation or otherwise useable without supervision of any sort. In some cases, high-value materials have been identified by the library staff and sequestered within the stacks themselves, usually in areas cordoned off by wire cages, special rooms, or some other such barrier that prevents free access.[25] Nevertheless, such materials are often available for unfettered circulation if a special request for them is made. Merely restricting free access to them does not necessarily mean that they receive any further special treatment in the greater scheme of things. A sad fact is that at almost any major university with a large research library the only investment an enterprising, ambitious student need make in an education fund is the price of a pack of single-edge razor blades.

Such considerations have prompted numerous libraries to undertake stack surveys to identify materials that either should be moved to special collections or housed in more secure locations in the general stacks, as outlined in the ACRL/RBMS *Guidelines on the Selection of General Collection Materials for Transfer to Special Collections*.[26] Unfortunately, two painful realities are that many books identified in such surveys are in condition too poor for inclusion in special collections (but hardly too poor for surreptitious on-line sale) or that the special collections area is too small to hold all the candidates. The latter situation, especially, leaves special collections

facing the problem of books it *should* have but cannot accommodate. In effect, the special collections unit cannot exercise proper vigilance over such materials, although it should.

Despite whatever space constraints a special collections library may face, it should nevertheless seek to have an appropriate survey of the general stacks undertaken. If nothing else, only after such a survey can the level and extent of the potential risks be identified and quantified. If they are extensive, certain security measures can be taken. The first of those is to restrict circulation. A library could establish a general policy, for example, that no item printed before 1850 can leave the building and may be consulted only on-site.[27] At the very least, if possible, any valuable or vulnerable material should be sequestered in the stacks and unavailable for general, unfettered access. An extension of such policies might indicate that the requested item would be retrieved from the stacks and consulted only in the special collections reading room, although it technically would be part of the general collection. An alternative is to move higher-value items to remote storage, if available, and have them delivered to special collections when needed.[28] In any case, libraries need to identify and protect such valuable or rare materials from loss or vandalism.

In considering projects to read general collections stacks for rare materials, something of a long view is required, and the appraisal process should be repeated periodically, perhaps every decade. A project last done in 1985, for example, is badly out of date. Materials that previously had low interest or little commercial value can rise in both areas significantly over time and therefore become attractive targets for thieves. Thus, as with shelf reading projects, a commitment to constantly review general library holdings is required to avoid having valuable materials slip through the cracks. One might also consider that perhaps someday the special collections area may be enlarged to the extent that it can accommodate all the rare materials previously identified in the open stacks; an accurate listing of such materials, therefore, would be useful in such an instance. Despite whatever long visions one may have, however, short-term considerations may abort any project. Examining shelves and collections for valuable items is a detailed process that will involve a lot of staff time. Also, any movement of materials will also likely involve cataloguing resources to reclassify materials. Making materials secure may also involve capital costs for construction or renovation. Despite those costs, periodic surveys of the general stacks collections, especially in large university libraries, are reasonable precautions to identify and prevent losses of valuable materials.[29]

Off-Site Projects

Sometimes special collections materials must leave the premises for scanning, microfilming, or conservation. Larger institutions often are often able to accomplish such procedures in-house, meaning that the materials may not need to go very far and may not even leave the library. Rarely will they need to leave the campus. Although any of those scenarios raises conservation concerns, the special collections unit will want to have in place an audit system that accounts for the whereabouts of all items at all times. Even if the processing is done in the library or somewhere else on campus, special collections will also be concerned about security at whatever venue the work is being performed. For example, all such places should have adequate locks or access control systems and burglar alarms. If possible, there should be a secure place such as a special cabinet where materials can be locked up when not in use. In no case should special collections materials ever be left unattended or unsecured. Explaining such requirements to other personnel doing, for

example, scanning work is an important component of such projects, and enlisting their understanding and cooperation is vital. As with the special collections area itself, it is important for library personnel to know who has access to such spaces and when. Once again, serious consideration needs to be given to the transport of rare book materials to and from the project sites.

Numerous projects will require, however, that materials leave the special collections library entirely and be sent off-site to a commercial processor. That situation is especially true with microfilming, which is becoming a scarce service on university and college campuses. Unless the project is quite large, companies are usually not willing to set up their equipment and operators on-site. In such a case, it is helpful to think about the company and its activities in much the same way one would consider a decision to lend materials for exhibition. Many of the same concerns would apply, especially those concerning access and security arrangements. Some firms are quite used to handling rare materials and have made adequate provisions for security. On the other hand, others are primarily commercial and may not be able to satisfy real security requirements. Into whose hands special collections materials are going when they leave the premises is a genuine concern, and the library should carefully investigate security arrangements at the commercial vendor's premises.[30]

Sending materials out for conservation treatment is usually less of a security concern than other types of off-site activities, since most conservators and conservation labs are well aware of security requirements and have them in place. Of course, any in-house library facility should also be in a similar position. If a library is contemplating using a new off-site conservator, inquiries will need to be made about security arrangements, especially burglar alarms and access to the materials. Because of the nature of some conservation work, it is impracti-cable to lock up materials in cabinets, etc., overnight or when nobody is around. Thus, total premises security will be of special concern to the library. If possible, at some point a library staff member should visit the conservator's premises to confirm security arrangements in person and discuss secu-rity preferences. In no case should materials be sent to a conservator in whose security arrangements the library has little faith.

Off-Site Acquisitions and Cataloguing

As departments have become centralized, some special collections libraries no longer have their acquisition and cataloguing done within their unit but rather have them done at another department in the library or in another library building alto-gether. In other words, although special collections may order a book, it is delivered first to a central acquisition facility and then perhaps to a separate cataloguing department rather than directly to special collections itself. Such arrangements create numerous security concerns.

If an item goes to cataloguing in a separate department, it is running a gamut of security con-cerns. Sometimes the personnel who catalogue special collections materials in such scenarios have no special arrangements for enhanced security of the items they are processing. Their desks are sometimes in open spaces or cubicles with no spe-cial protection afforded them. Materials, therefore, often lie uncontrolled in plain sight, even when the cataloguer is not present. Sometimes there are no arrangements for securing materials at night or during breaks, again leaving materials vulnerable. At the very least, the special collections library should strive to ensure that its materials are never out of the direct control of the cataloguer working on them and that they are secured from unauthor-ized access at all times.[31] Audit trails should also be established between special collections and cataloguing to ensure that materials are always accounted for when they are sent to be catalogued and when they are finally returned to be shelved.[32] It is in the cataloguing department's self interest to ensure that all special collections books are always accounted for until they are sent to be shelved since suspicion will immediately fall on them if an item goes missing while in their custody.

One odd aberration to off-site cataloguing oc-curs with individual manuscripts, manuscript col-lections, and archives. It seems in some instances that such materials almost never are sent to off-site processing but are sorted and described by the special collections department itself. Centralized cataloguing units seem to lack the training or in-terest to process such collections and normally end up with just a finding aid or other description from which they then create an on-line record without ever actually handling the materials, much the same as the Library of Congress creates NUCMC records for various institutions. Thus, it would seem that such collections are not necessarily exposed to many of the security problems presented by their printed counterparts.

Many of the same considerations would apply to a central acquisition department that processes receipts and payments. Chief among the acquisitions problems is that someone else in the library may ac-tually handle the material before special collections staff has a chance to do so. Such scenarios create opportunities for materials to disappear or be com-promised, especially if all tracking data are lost once a package enters the institution's delivery system. If possible, the special collections unit should make arrangements so that all materials ordered by it are shipped directly to it and not opened by anyone else first. That way curators can assure that the items are as described and complete. Only then should it be released for acquisition processing or cataloguing.[33]

Especially in the case of acquisitions, no bill should ever be paid until, at a minimum, the special collections department has examined the item and approved the invoice. A proper accounting procedure should be established and strictly followed, including a selected audit of special collections expenditures on a yearly basis.[34]

We Will Not Be Keeping It

One specialized type of acquisition often overlooked and historically abused is gifts.[35] In this situation, no money changes hands, so only a modest audit trail exists, usually consisting of just a written receipt. Such transactions usually fall outside the scope of a regular financial audit, as well. In a sound system, all gifts would be received directly by the special collections unit, which would inventory the materials, and would be signed for by two people rather than just one before being sent for any further processing. Preferably, only those items to be added permanently to the collections should be accepted, thereby reducing the amount of extraneous but potentially desirable material that passes through the system. If the materials are subsequently sent through the acquisitions system, a paper trail of the donation will have been created and should follow the items until they are returned for shelving.

An atypical kind of gift is the one given to the library for its benefit with no intention that it will ever be added to the collections. In other words, donors will sometimes give a library materials with the full understanding that they will be swapped to booksellers for credit or sold and the proceeds used for such things as conservation or acquisition funds. In the case of such materials, they will never be sent to an acquisitions or cataloguing unit and must, therefore, be strictly segregated from all other library materials until they are all disposed of. A detailed inventory of the material should be prepared so that the library will always know what it was given and be able to identify any losses in the meantime.

A corollary type of material often in limbo is that scheduled for deaccession at some point. Such material may languish on the shelves uninventoried for years before it is sold. Such troves of undescribed materials provide opportunity for potential thefts. In some cases, the material to be deaccessioned has never been accounted for it the first place, much less catalogued. Although such materials often constitute the dredges of the collection, in other cases much rich material is present.[36] At the very least, since a complete inventory of such materials may be lacking or impossible to create, access to potential deaccessions should be strictly limited. Far better, of course, is an actual written inventory, although in some cases that is plausibly impossible.

Missing Items

Missing items fall into two categories: 1) those known to be stolen, and 2) those that cannot be found. In the former case any type of searching for the items will go on outside the institution, probably by monitoring the market to see if they show up for sale anywhere. What concerns us here is the second category.

As Norman Maclean points out, "There is no better way in this world to lose something forever than to misfile it in a big library."[37] If an item cannot be found, the typical librarian's instinct, in absence of any other evidence, is to conclude that it has been misshelved or misfiled somehow and that it probably has not been stolen, a conclusion that is probably true in the majority of circumstances. Unfortunately, no real guidelines exist to guide decisions about the point at which a librarian should become suspicious of theft, and most such decisions are perforce based on many factors, such as the librarian's level of suspicion, the specific circumstances surrounding the disappearance, the library's overall level of security, and any evidence that might lead to suspicions. Given the wide range of circumstances that could appertain to missing materials, no recommendations applicable in all instances can be made. At some point, however, the librarian will have to decide whether to chalk the disappearance up to unknown factors or to report it as either stolen or at least missing under mysterious circumstances.[38]

One mistake that librarians make in relation to missing materials is to fail to really search, as, say, the police would if they showed up at the library with a search warrant looking for the missing book. Many librarians adopt a thought process that posits something like, "Where might this book have been misshelved?" and then begin a process of elimination by looking for mistakes that might have been caused by shelving the item in the correct call number order but in the wrong size, mixing up some aspect of the call number, or mistakenly shelving the item in the right area but just on the wrong shelf. Such mental acrobatics may not lead to the discovery of the missing item, which might require a more extensive search. In a genuine search, the entire library would be examined, including going down all shelves, through offices, file cabinets, and other storage areas such as closets, just as the police would do if they were searching for a marijuana stash. Only after the premises have been thoroughly searched in a systematic way may one be relatively sure the item is really gone. The following story of a "missing" manuscript illustrates the value of a real search:

> A year or two ago, we were "missing" a small, bound, boxed, medieval manuscript, handsome, early and doubtless valuable. We knew it had been used several times in the few months leading up to its "disappearance"

because it has been the subject of an assignment by one of our medievalists. We looked, and looked. It *should* have been located on the highest, extra-wide, shelf of a section in our vault, but there were ample reasons to believe it might have been mis-shelved in a number of creative ways. Finally, one day, one of our tallest student assistants, shelved another manuscript on the top shelf and discovered the "missing" item pushed to the rear of the shelf and mostly resting in the space between it and a "backing" shelf (on the other side of the section of shelving). Given the size of the item and the configuration of the shelving, only someone tall enough to essentially "see" the actual contents of the top shelf (nearly seven feet from the floor) would have spotted the thing. Those of us who are more "height-challenged" would never likely have ever seen it unless we had some reason to crawl up on a ladder to inspect (or dust) that top shelf.[39]

Few librarians have the luxury of genuine searches, however, and in many libraries such searches would require months and months and would probably be justified only in cases of items of great value. Even if done thoroughly, such searches may fail. (See Appendix I below.)

In August, 2008, a brief survey was conducted asking libraries about their policies concerning missing items. The survey questions and the compiled/edited responses from the thirteen responding libraries follow (some responses add up to more than thirteen because of multiple possibilities; some add up to fewer because of no response):

1) Do you have missing items, either books or manuscripts?

Most respondents had both categories of items missing, although two had only missing books.

2) How did you discover they were missing (use all that apply)?
    a. Called to reading room but could not be located (10)
    b. Needed for some other purpose (e.g., exhibition, class use) but could not be located (8)
    c. Discovered missing during shelf reading (7)
    d. Contacted by third party (e.g., bookseller, law enforcement) (4)
    e. Other (6)

3) Who conducts searches for missing materials?
In almost all cases, this responsibility escalates from junior to more senior staff. Often pages or other para-professional staff do initial searches, with other, more senior members becoming involved if they are unsuccessful. At four institutions, however, curators do all the searching.

4) How many times and how often do you search before you give up?
Four institutions answered "Depends" based on various criteria, such as rarity or importance. Three institutions search 2–3 times, and one 5–6. Three institutions responded that they never stop searching. The institutions that cease active searches seem resigned to the idea that the item is probably permanently missing if their searches are fruitless.

5) Does your search procedure involve going back through circulation records to determine the last time the item was used?
Nine libraries look at these records; three do not; and one does depending on the circumstances.

6) Do you have any formal procedures for conducting searches?
Six libraries have procedures of some sort; seven do not.

7) If so, are they written down?
The same six libraries in #6 with formal procedures have written them down; the other seven have not.

8) What percentage of missing items do you eventually locate by searching or shelf reading?
Five libraries do not have statistics to document their recovery rate. The other libraries report success rates between 20% and 95%, with the majority reporting success rates of between 70%–90%.

9) What percentage of missing items do you locate by serendipity?
The same five libraries lacking statistics in #8 have no statistics on this. The other libraries report varying degrees of luck, from finding 1% of missing items to about 15%. One library, which obviously has a staff member who rummages a lot, reported finding about 75% of its missing items by luck while in the process of other activities.

10) Do you have any criteria to determine when you conclude a missing item is most likely stolen?
Only one library had such criteria, and that was based on staff opinions only.

11) Have you ever had a theft from your collections?
Two libraries reported no known thefts; the other eleven reported known thefts at various times, some decades old.

12) If so, it was done by:
    a. Burglar (3)
    b. Researcher (5)
    c. Insider (8)
    d. Don't know (3)

13) Do you suspect any items you cannot find are because of an unsolved theft?

Four libraries answered Yes; five libraries answered No; and four were not sure.

14) How large is your special collections library or the specific unit for which you are reporting (estimates are OK)?
   a. Printed Materials (e.g., books, maps, broadsides, etc.)
   b. Manuscripts (number, linear feet—any measurement is fine)

Without giving specifics, institutions reporting ranged from quite large with over 250,000 books and large manuscript collections to smaller entities with only about 25,000 books and 1,000 manuscripts.

15) Are you a stand-alone library or part of a larger entity?
Four of the libraries are stand-alone institutions.

Discussion

Aside from the conclusion that most libraries probably have materials they cannot readily locate, the advantages of actually doing repeated searches for materials seem obvious. Although some things are found by serendipity, searches produce better results, even if they are not always successful, no matter what the size of the library. Library size seems to make no difference in search failure or success. Presumably, the situation evens itself out. In other words, a large library with 250,000 books may have more places where an item could be mislaid, but probably has more people available for searching, so it is at no disadvantage compared to a smaller library with fewer places to search but having fewer people to do so. It also seems clear that the responding librarians, in light of any other evidence to the contrary, are hesitant to conclude that an item has been stolen, an attitude that may make insider theft more difficult to consider or detect. Finally, there does not seem to be any difference in success rate among libraries that have written search policies, although one librarian did remark that some of the "legacy" instructions were useful for newer people who were less familiar with the many ways an item could go missing. Written guidance would seem important, however, to ensure that each search is done methodically.

Conclusion

Many of the procedures suggested above are designed to reduce instances of insider thefts, which are always made easier if material is unaccounted for at any point or is within the exclusive control of just one person. Unfortunately, all the situations discussed above are ripe for materials to disappear at any unguarded moment through insider thefts, by outsiders who see an opportunity to steal an item, or inadvertent loss. Despite the added burdens of paperwork and other audit procedures, an institution on the whole is wise to employ as many security procedures as possible within its workflow. Unfortunately, such suggestions do not always meet with either cooperation or approval. For example, one curator, whose materials are catalogued in a centralized library unit, noted that security suggestions have been met with "bruised egos, opposition, and non-support from our Director."[40] Such situations are unfortunate and expose special collections materials to loss or damage and the institution to potential public embarrassment. Insofar as possible, the entire institution should cooperate with the security measures necessary to ensure the protection of its special collections materials at all times.

Appendix I: A Failed Search

While employed by a prominent historical society as its head librarian, it was brought to my attention in 1994 that our copy of an extremely rare and valuable pamphlet was missing and had not been seen since it was in an exhibition a couple of years previously. Since it was a slim volume, easily mis-shelved, nothing nefarious was believed to have happened. Later, however, the head cataloguer brought to my attention another rare, early work that he had discovered by chance shelved among the regular book collection rather than with the imprints, where it should have been. At that point suspicions soared, and a quick examination of the early imprints collection, with the use of the shelf list, revealed that seven early works, worth over $100,000 at the time, were missing. Oddly, however, none of them had been called to the reading room in recent years, so that type of theft did not seem a real possibility. The books were reported stolen to both the ABAA and to Exlibris.

At that point, it was decided that a two-prong approach would be used to locate the missing items since we seemed to be dealing possibly with a case of sabotage rather than an actual theft. In the first instance, all library staff were delegated for one day a week to read the rare book shelves against the shelf list. The shelving for regular books was inspected item by item instead of against the shelf list. Those procedures revealed some misshelved books, some of which had been missing for years. More alarmingly, one of the missing items was discovered shelved with items slated for deaccessioning.

As a corollary to the stack search, a thorough search of the 65,000 square foot building was instituted. In the process every area was gone through, including all staff offices, all desks, all file cabinets, and all storage areas. Even furniture on exhibition had drawers opened. Those searches were done totally surreptitiously with no notice to staff.

A frustrating lacuna in the search was the two floors of manuscript stacks. These consisted of hundreds of linear feet of mostly Hollinger boxes and cases. If a person were intent on hiding materials, that would be the place to do it. Of course, it was utterly impossible that every box could be opened and examined, so this area was really not searched thoroughly.

The police were also called in, and suspicions initially fell upon a former intern who had shown a special interest in early Americana of the type that was missing. After questioning this person for two hours, however, the detective reported that he did not believe the person to be a viable suspect. Having no more to go on, the police investigation ended.

In the meantime, the current director had resigned. In the inter-regnum, the rarest of the missing pamphlets surfaced under mysterious circumstances, having been found lying in plain sight on a shelf in the book stacks.

The new director hired a private detective to continue the investigation. Despite interviewing all library staff, this man produced no useful results. His suggestion to monitor the stacks with hidden cameras was not acted upon, to our dismay as it turned out. One day the stack supervisor came to me and told me she had something she wanted me to see. Down in the second book stacks level sat the rest of the missing books on a reshelving station with an unrelated note on them in an unknown hand, again all in plain sight. A check of the alarm system records did not reveal any unusual closings or openings. At that point, we regretted the decision not to use the hidden cameras.

With that, the case was resolved, although we never figured out who deliberately disturbed the books. We were all merely thankful that they had not been stolen and that we had them back again. For all we knew, of course, the last batch of missing books had actually been removed from the premises and then returned. The process, however, is a case study in the potential failures and successes of an actual systematic library search for missing items.

Used by permission

NOTES

1. See American Library Association. Association of College & Research Libraries. *Guidelines for Borrowing and Lending Special Collections Materials for Exhibition.* Chicago: ACRL, 2008. http://www.ala.org/ala/acrl/acrlstandards/borrowguide.cfm.

2. Northeast Document Conservation Center, *Packing and Shipping*, Preservation Leaflet 4.12 (Andover: NEDCC), recommends registered mail as the preferred way to ship "art and artifacts of moderate size and value."

3. Ton Cremers, "…and the Curator Did It," *Rogues Gallery: An Investigation into Art Theft*, AXA Conference, November 1, 2005, reports two recent incidents in which employees of shipping or warehousing companies stole goods consigned to their employers, including one person who stole over 130 items from commercial storage (7–8).

4. In one case, a valuable book being delivered among other packages to a library in fact was signed for but not specifically accounted for by the university mail room and subsequently was found to have vanished. Email to author, December, 2007.

5. This method is not foolproof, however. One library lost materials in transit when the courier was robbed of the shipment. See Exlibris, 22 March 2008. NEDCC recommends, "The best way to transport an irreplaceable document, book, or work of art on paper is to pack it securely and deliver it yourself."

6. The American Association of Museums has created a model facilities report. It may be found at http://www.aam-us.org.

7. *Guidelines for Borrowing*, section C.4.

8 Overheard by the author.

9. See American Library Association. Association of College & Research Libraries. *Guidelines for the Interlibrary Loan of Rare and Unique Materials* (Chicago: ACRL, 2008). http://www.ala.org/ala/acrl/acrlstandards/rareguidelines.cfm.

10. *Guidelines for the Interlibrary Loan*, section B.1.

11. Note that even in the case of registered mail, accountability stops as soon as the USPS delivers the item to the institution. Tracking will probably not be done inside the institution's own delivery system.

12. Emails to author, November, 2007. It would seem to go without saying that the borrowing library should strictly honor any conditions on the loan imposed by the lender.

13. For case studies that demonstrate the vagaries of moving collections, see *Moving Archives: The Experiences of Eleven Archivists*, ed. John Newman and Walter Jones (Lanham & Oxford: Scarecrow, 2002).

14. See Kathleen Maclay, "Bancroft Library Reduces Hours in Preparation for Move, Retrofit" (18 March 2005). http://www.berkeley.edu/news/media/releases/2005/03/18_librarymove.shtml.

15. Based on personal knowledge and interviews with staff.

16. See Sheila McAlister, "Hargrett Library to Close for Renovations," Exlibris, 10 February 1999.

17. Email to author, July, 2007.

18. See UCLA, College of Letters and Science, "An Academic Gem Returns" (4 January 2008). http://www.college.ucla.edu/news/08/clark-library.html.

19. Walter Jones, "University of Utah," in *Moving Archives*, remarks that providing reference service during that institution's move proved so problematic that it was abandoned (20–21).

20. This type of activity is an old security salesperson trick but can be used by anybody to gain access to a site. The preferred garb is professional dress, a clipboard, and a white hard hat, since that is the color typically worn by engineers. Almost nobody on a construction site will challenge such a person. Todd Welch, "Oregon Historical Society," in *Moving Archives*, reports one method for readily identifying library staff members: "The library move team was given special blue T-shirts and hot-pink name badges for identification and security purposes…" (111).

21. A similar situation appertains when collections are moved permanently from one facility to another with no intermediate storage. Lisa Backman, "The Cable Center," in *Moving Archives*, notes, "There must be someone with the movers at all times.... Most importantly, it is a matter of security having a staff member with the movers at all times. No one likes to admit that items can go missing, but items can and do go missing" (5–6). For an example of a move within a facility from one area to another, see Jones in *Moving Archives*, 17–26.

22. Email to author, December, 2007. Used by permission. Note that packing materials in wrapped pallets allows for ready detection of any intrusions. The pallets should all be accounted for at delivery to the warehouse and when they are returned to special collections. If at all possible, a specific list of the contents of each pallet should also be created.

23. Large sets in storage create multiple headaches, especially if they are called out of storage for use. If a patron, for example, cannot ascertain which volume the desired information is in, the entire set will probably have to be called, a procedure that would be far simpler if the set were retained in special collections. One can imagine the logistical problems with a patron looking for topics in Diderot's *Encyclopédie*, for example, if the set is in storage. The wear and tear on large sets when they are moved can also be considerable.

24. For an overview of considerations pertinent to sending special collections materials to storage, see Mary C. LaFogg and Christine Weideman, "Special Collections," in Danuta A. Nitecki and Curtis L. Kendrick, eds, *Library Off-Site Shelving: Guide for High-Density Facilities* (Englewood: Libraries Unlimited, 2001), 205–218.

25. In many older libraries in both Europe and the U.S. the general stacks will be full of older, valuable books that have been sitting there since the day they were acquired from their original publishers, often centuries ago.

26. Chicago: ACRL, 2008.

27. Such materials would obviously also be unavailable for ILL.

28. So many possible permutations of such situations exist that it is impossible to sort all of them out. If the special collections library, for example, is contained in the main library building, having special materials delivered there for use is an option. If it is a separate facility, however, such a procedure becomes problematic.

29. After Gilbert Bland's thefts in the early 1990's were revealed, several institutions moved their older U. S. government serial sets to sequestered locations. The sets contain fairly valuable maps, which Bland targeted. Most of the sets resided in open stacks prior to his thefts. Despite that, in February, 2005, Western Washington University reported yet another significant theft from its serial set, involving the loss of nearly 650 pages of materials, almost all of it maps. See Robert Lopresti, "Map Theft News," Exlibris electronic discussion list, 11 January 2008, and his "Map Theft News 2," Exlibris, 14 January, 2008.

30. In one horror story back in the 1980s, a historical society sent a volume of bound newspapers to be microfilmed to a vendor recommended by a sister society, who was ordering the films and for whom the vendor was doing the work gratis. When the newspapers came back, they had been razored out of the binding and two issues were missing.

31. Such arrangements are also for cataloguers' protection and protect them against suspicion should an incident of theft or vandalism arise.

32. In some hybrid arrangements, cataloguers work on the materials in special collections but the items never leave the department. Although this procedure was feasible when cataloguers were using printed work sheets, the advent of direct inputting of records has caused this system to fade. Although on-line systems allow for tracking the whereabouts of items, a printed record is preferable since on-line systems can often be accessed and altered by many people.

33. Odd situations can arise if special collections materials are sent first to an acquisitions unit. In the case of one university that processed some acquisitions through a central department, their books would sometimes be stamped with university ownership marks by mistake, thereby basically defacing them.

34. In such cases, it is vital that the auditor not only sample the payment system, h/she should also ask to see representative items associated with invoices. Although the payment procedures may look entirely regular, it is still possible that the item was skimmed off and never made into the collections.

35. Cremers.

36. See for example, Swann Galleries, *Medicine—Including Books from the Library of Doctor Henry Dolger and a Selection of Instruments, Natural History, Featuring Ornithological Books from the Watkinson Library, Trinity College, Hartford, Connecticut* (New York: Swann Galleries, 1989), for an example of a library deaccession with rich holdings.

37. *Young Men & Fire* (Chicago & London: University of Chicago Press, 1992), 147.

38. Exactly where to report missing items is a long-standing problem, and there is still no central place to make such reports since the demise of BAMBAM. RBMS maintains a section on its web site for such reports and both ABAA and ILAB will accept them, although in the latter's case the reports are not publicly available. In all those instances, the reports are intended to be for stolen items and not necessarily those that merely cannot be found. See the RBMS web site for a list of places to report thefts. A more recent development is the creation of Missingmaterials.org, where anyone can create records for both stolen and missing materials.

39. Email to author, 29 August 2008. The incident is illustrative, however, of how an actual search of the suspect shelf might have solved the problem promptly as opposed to concentrating on the "number of creative ways" the item could have been mis-shelved.

40. Email to author, December, 2007. The writer did note, however, that in the case of an extremely valuable item, he would insist that cataloguers do their work in special collections itself and would not let the item leave his custody to be catalogued.

Security Guards

Everett C. Wilkie, Jr.

Private security plays the majority role in America in the protection of property, people and assets.

~*Ricci*

One protection measure sometimes employed by libraries is the use of security guards. Employing a security force presents its own range of issues, opportunities, and potential problems. In many cases, the library may have no choice in the matter and must depend on whatever is provided by the parent institution or local government. In most cases, special collections libraries avoid many of the problems that plague more public institutions, such as rowdy patrons or other disruptive persons.[1] On the other hand, the materials they house are often expensive or rare and may be deemed worthy of special protective measures. In general, the use of security guards in the U.S., except for airport screeners, has ironically decreased since the September 11 terrorist attacks in the U.S., although they have been routine fixtures in museums for decades and far outnumber regular police officers.[2]

Because every library is unique and operates under different parameters, sweeping, universally applicable recommendations about security guards are nearly impossible. One may easily recommend, for example, that all patrons present photo identification at registration; to recommend that every reading room have a security guard present is not necessarily a sound or practicable idea, however. The range of problems and potential security services available is wide and has been discussed by various authors.[3] Therefore, in the discussion below, few actual recommendations will be made. Rather, the discussion is confined to central questions that any special collections library might ask concerning a security guard program and some possible answers to them.

A general caveat that would seem to go without saying is that any institution that hires security guards of any stripe must be sure that each one of them has passed a rigorous series of background checks. Unfortunately, especially with guards hired from a contract service, personnel may not be completely vetted, and much may depend on state regulations. In any case, the library should insist that no guard be allowed on its property until satisfactory background checks have been done.[4]

Among the considerations that will come into play are the following.

1) Do we need security guards in the first place?

2) Is the force employed directly by the institution or is it hired from an outside contractor?

3) What powers does the security force have to enforce laws and make arrests?

4) What types of protection will the security force offer?

The answers to each of those questions will depend on the level of security the institution wishes to enjoy and, in some instances, on laws and other policies over which the library may have little, if any, control.

Do we need security guards in the first place?
The answer to this question, of course, drives the answers to the remaining ones. Security guards have become such regular sights in so many locations that there is rarely any controversy associated with their use, especially if they are successful in helping the library fulfill its mission.[5] If, for example, a library is part of a university or college campus, security guards may already be available with no other consideration necessary on the library's part. In that case, the library needs to educate the security force about its particular needs so that they are met.

If the library is an independent, free-standing institution, however, it may wish to consider having its own dedicated security force, although that option is generally feasible only with larger institutions with more elaborate budgets than those of the typical local historical society or smaller research institution. Most in the latter category will probably rely exclusively on local law enforcement or staff for security needs, although again, in such cases, the responding agencies need to be informed about the library and its particular problems.

Another option is to contract for security services on an ad-hoc basis. Many institutions use this option for special events such as meetings, exhibition openings, or other such events when the premises will be subject to greater threats because of the presence of unusually large numbers of people. This option allows the institutions to provide enhanced security only at those times when such is considered desirable. One attractive feature of this type of scenario is that the institution can usually employ off-duty regular police officers for the event if they so choose, thereby providing an enhanced level of protection.

Those institutions that decide to rely on local law enforcement need perforce to pay special attention to their alarm systems. In general, the problem with this scenario is that some alarm systems are not robust and modern enough to thoroughly cover the premises. The expense of installing and maintaining systems that will thoroughly saturate the premises and reduce the probability of an undetected intrusion to almost zero are normally so great that few smaller institutions will undergo the cost. Another consideration is that no matter how excellent alarm systems may be, there will always be gaps in them that can be exploited, both when the institution is open and closed. A third consideration is that sometimes the premises are so convoluted and complex that completely covering the structure would be very difficult. In such a scenario, the institution must weigh the advantages of an upgraded alarm system against those presented by a security force.[6]

The decision to employ a security firm can be guided in many ways by an institutional assessment performed by the library's risk managers from an insurance company or by an outside agency contracted to do an evaluation. Such surveys consider many factors, such as the library's physical vulnerability, the neighborhood in which it is located, and the library's security history. A library in a high-crime area might have different vulnerabilities from those of a library in a remote rural location with almost no crime. Before going much farther down the security road, a library with no security force and an elementary alarm system might wish to pursue the survey option first to determine its security parameters and potential solutions.

At bottom, like other security measures such as burglar alarms, many of the benefits of security guards are intangible because it is almost impossible to prove a negative. As Fay points out, "No one knows for certain the amount of loss that was avoided because a security officer was present as a psychological deterrent or because the officer acted in a particular way to discourage or prevent a criminal act."[7] Despite that issue, it seems unarguable that the presence of security guards can at least hasten the resolution of an incident or prevent a suspect from readily escaping because the guards are already on the scene. One might also argue that security guards might chill the criminal intents of some persons, just as the average person loses the desire to speed when there is a police car in the rear view mirror.

Is the force employed directly by the institution or is it hired from an outside contractor?

Almost all libraries that are part of a larger entity may have this decision made for them, especially if they are affiliated with an institution of higher education. Even in such cases, however, some room for negotiation may exist. If a library falls under the jurisdiction of a campus police force, for example, such a situation does not necessarily preclude the library from contracting with an outside security company to provide protection to the library while it is open to the public or from trying to negotiate a detail devoted exclusively to it. Numerous public libraries employ special guards, even though they technically fall under the aegis of the local police department for basic protection. In other instances, it is possible to persuade the main security agency to dedicate personnel to guard the library, especially if the library's budget can offset the associated expense.

Some debate surrounds the question of whether guards should work directly for the library (i.e., proprietary) or be employed by a contract guard service (CGS). One school holds that guards employed directly by the institution are more loyal and attentive to its needs than those employed from a third party with no vested interest in the library. Such an attitude, of course, discounts the hundreds of guards who will seek to do the best job possible, no matter if they are employed by a CGS, and those companies that seek to provide thoroughly professional services to all their clients. It also discounts the complacency that can set in with an institutional

security force faced with daily, rarely varying routine. Dodson points out that sometimes a CGS arrangement is far better for the institution in terms of costs, performance, and overhead.[8]

An intermediate course adopted by some institutions to supplement regular security forces is the use of trained volunteers, although such people are never intended to go into "any situation where a 'foreseeable chain of events…would result in injury or loss of life.'"[9] Volunteers basically serve as extra eyes and ears for the institution and receive special training in procedures, security systems, building systems, and emergency protocols. They might also receive other specialized training, such as learning CPR. In all cases, however, the role of a volunteer security force "is not to directly enforce Security Department procedures or policies but to provide information to Security personnel that they may follow-up and correct whatever problems have been reported."[10] In all cases, any security volunteer must have a criminal background check.

One middle path rarely taken is to train the library's own staff in the role of security guards. Such training can be quite useful in educating staff about potential problems and their solutions and equips staff in institutions with no guards to be their own eyes, ears, and hands. Because staff have basically the same rights and privileges as the average security guard, training them in the same methods would seem to have merit, even if they are instructed never to act by confronting a thief. Some institutions have a hybrid system in which the security director or a few others have enhanced training and powers but the remainder of the security force has less.[11]

What powers does the security force have to enforce laws and make arrests?

The answer to this question will have deep implications for the library's security program. Security officers are available in three basic forms. The most common is a person, perhaps in uniform, who has no weapons and no arrest powers beyond those of the ordinary citizen. A more uncommon type is a guard, who may be armed and who has certain powers, which may include arrest under certain circumstances. The third type, more uncommon yet, is a guard who is a sworn police officer. The great advantage of the latter two types is that they have probably had more extensive training than the former type and can offer a greater degree of protection in some instances, especially if the use of force comes into play. They can also arrest suspects on the spot, thereby truncating any incident and bringing it to swift conclusion if need be. On the other hand, such guards tend to be far more expensive to employ, both in terms of training and salary. Those considerations will apply whether the guards work directly for the institution or are supplied by an outside service.[12]

One important difference between sworn police officers and security guards is that the former operate under important legal restrictions. Although they have in some respects greater powers than security guards, those powers have limitations. One of the crucial limitations is that questioning by a police officer can be stopped by invoking Miranda rights. On the other hand, security guards operate under no such restrictions and can question suspects freely for any reason, as may any average citizen. Any confession to a security guard is probably valid so long as it was freely made and is also probably above successful legal challenge.[13]

What types of protection will the security force offer?

The security force, no matter what its composition or powers, can be employed in various ways. In the least intrusive system, the force would patrol the premises occasionally during the day and at night. In a more intrusive system, it would visit the reading room and special collections a couple of times a day. In a yet more intrusive system, the force would be apparent all the hours the library and reading room were open, being present at the front desk, in the reading room itself at all times, or performing such duties as checking readers' possessions when they departed the premises. When a building is open, the visible presence of a security guard often seems a good idea.[14] Although one would hope that such a presence would deter thieves, such is not always the case. Charles Merrill Mount stole materials from the Library of Congress and the National Archives, even though both are guarded when open by special police forces. It can also be difficult, it seems, to engage a guard's interest in his or her work. Hezlinga reported that when her library set up a program of having guards in the reading room, resistance was met from the guards themselves: "We put a uniformed security officer in the reading room itself for the rest of the year. This was not a very popular job. Most officers hated it, sitting still for hours, and complaints kept coming in from our security firm."[15] In a system that saturates the premises, guards are present 24 hours a day, seven days a week, even when the library is closed.[16]

The level of protection can vary in any scenario. Almost no problems seem to exist with security guards who are on the premises when the library is open, and numerous institutions successfully employ guards in that fashion. It is when the library is closed that guards seem to be a more appealing idea, especially as a foil to burglars and as a second set of eyes to watch for such emergencies as fires and burst water pipes.[17] Most special collections security guard problems arise when they patrol the premises after all staff have left and the library is closed. Some thefts from institutions have occurred involving security guards after hours. At

Connecticut's Magnus Wahlstrom Library, a guard stole materials while the library was closed.[18] At Boston's Isabella Stewart Gardner Museum, guards were gulled by police impersonators into letting them enter, whereupon the place was robbed.[19] Neither incident could have happened as it did had the guards not been present.

A rather complicated but related service question is whether guards will be armed and with what. Such decisions may affect the resolution of incidents they are called upon to resolve. Fortunately violence in U. S. special collections libraries is extremely rare, so it would seem odd that guards have firearms. On the other hand, a library may also need to consider the neighborhood in which it is located and the instances of crime in the surrounding area. Such considerations might influence thinking. If guards are to be armed, numerous levels of such equipment exist, ranging from batons, to spray, to actual firearms, and to numerous combinations of them. Unless a guard is an actual peace officer, rarely will he or she be similarly equipped with a full panoply of weapons, such as tasers. If guards are to be equipped with firearms, they should undergo stringent training before being given a weapon and being allowed to serve the institution. Unlike the situation with guards and Miranda rights, the situation with firearms is reversed. Regular police have far more latitude in using a firearm than do private individuals.[20]

A Survey

In 2007, an informal survey was conducted of several libraries known to have security guard protection 24 hours a day. Below are the questions posed and the answers to them. The results of this brief survey might serve as a general guide to the experiences and practices of several institutions and enlighten other libraries considering security guard programs.

Security Guard Survey

1) Do your guards have access to the special collections stack areas after hours or just to general areas, such as the reading room or reception areas?

- Library A: The night supervisor has a master key and could go into the library if needed.
- Library B: No.
- Library C: Yes, there is access to the stack area but not the vault.
- Library D: Guards have total access at all times.
- Library E: Do not have access to Rare Books and other special collections areas.
- Library F: Not normally; in emergency can use access cards available when necessary; access cards are locked up.

2) Have you ever suffered any losses that could be attributable to a security guard?

- Library A: Don't know.
- Library B: None that we know of.
- Library C: Not to my knowledge.
- Library D: No.
- Library E: We never have had any losses attributed to them. In fact, I do not think any of them have ever actually been in our closed stacks areas–which are on the Public Safety master key system, but which have an additional combination lock security known only to a limited number of people.
- Library F: None.

3) Do the guards work for your institution directly or are they employed by an outside security firm?

- Library A: Work for the institution.
- Library B: Work directly for the library–prior to 1980 it was a private security firm.
- Library C: Outside security firm.
- Library D: Our guards are part of the University Police Department.

- Library E: Institution.
- Library F: Hybrid. Proprietary people have more substantial duties; contract does general work like patrol galleries.

4) Are your guards sworn police officers, regardless of who employs them?
- Library A: No.
- Library B: No.
- Library C: Guards are trained security officers.
- Library D: No. Our guards act as the eyes and ears of the police officers. They are not to intervene but to call for help.
- Library E: Security officers are sworn officers, but with special powers limited to campus. Campus police officers, on the other hand, have full police powers identical to the city/county police force.
- Library F: No

5) What arrest powers do your guards have?
- Citizen's arrest? (Authority granted by most states that allow any citizen to detain a suspected criminal until the police arrive.)
- Full police powers? (Given to sworn law enforcement officers who can detain and arrest anybody in their jurisdiction.)
- Special police powers? (Similar to full police powers but often restricted to a single locale, such as a library and its adjacent streets or an apartment complex.)
- Library A: Citizen's arrest.
- Library B: None–two supervisors (former police officers) do.
- Library C: Citizen's capability only.
- Library D: None besides those of an ordinary citizen.
- Library E: Security officers are sworn officers, but with special powers limited to campus. Campus police officers, on the other hand, have

full police powers identical to the city/county police force.
- Library F: Citizen's only.

6) Are your guards armed and if so with what? Nightsticks? Handcuffs? Spray? Firearms?
- Library A: No.
- Library B: No.
- Library C: No firearms.
- Library D: Our guards are not armed.
- Library E: Security officers are armed with nightsticks, cuffs and spray. Police officers carry the same arms and firearms as city police.
- Library F: None; only supervisor can be armed.
-

7) Do your guards actually patrol the premises when the library is closed or do they confine themselves to a guard station?
- Library A: They patrol the grounds, but not inside the library.
- Library B: Yes, they patrol.
- Library C: Security rounds are provided on each shift.
- Library D: Yes, our guards have a scheduled patrol.
- Library E: Security officers do patrol some, but have a station in the 24-hour study area and stay close to that post unless more than one officer is on duty.
- Library F: Yes, patrol premises. Outside also.

8) Does the special collections area have its own alarm system that is set when the library is closed? If so, do the guards know how to arm and disarm it?
- Library A: It's all one alarm system, which in the morning is turned off for lower-security areas, but left on in the stacks.
- Library B: No–but it does have locked gates that only security supervisors have keys to.
- Library C: No separate alarm system.

- Library D: Our entire building is alarmed 24/7.
- Library E: The security alarms are armed and monitored remotely at DPS, not within the library.
- Library F: Vaults alarmed 24/7; guards cannot disarm system but can enter in emergency.

9) If guards have after-hours access to stack areas, does your institution have an access control system for those entrances?
- Library A: Yes, they have to swipe their key card.
- Library B: No.
- Library C: Yes.
- Library D: Yes, we have a card access system.
- Library E: No answer.
- Library F: Yes.

10) Have your security guards ever actively helped staff stop a special-collections theft?
- Library A: The bag check guys have caught people going out with reference books. I'm not aware of anything else.
- Library B: No.
- Library C: No.
- Library D: Yes, a staff member suspected a patron of taking a small book out in their pocket. The staff member alerted the guard who stopped the would be thief.
- Library E: No answer.
- Library F: No; never had one.

11) Have your security guards ever, during after-hours, detected or mitigated an emergency, such as a fire or a burst pipe?
- Library A: They have found at least one fire in the art gallery–no fires in the library. We did have one flood in the library a couple of years ago but the guards did not catch it. It wasn't detected until library staff reported to work in the morning.
- Library B: No event has occurred.

- Library C: Yes.
- Library D: Yes, our guards have detected flooding in our basement.
- Library E: Four times within the last five years, security officers have found and reported water leaks. They have called DPS, and DPS in turn has called Physical Plant and appropriate library personnel.
- Library F: Yes–leaks, burst pipes.

12) How long have you had security guards? Can you explain the original rationale for employing them?
- Library A: At least since the 1930's–people have seen pictures.
- Library B: No one readily had this information–as mentioned above, guards have been on staff since 1980; we could not find information regarding when an outside security firm was first hired prior to that date.
- Library C: Approximately 10–12 years. Contracted security staff can provide a better trained security staff, knowledgeable in current best practices.
- Library D: We have had guards from the beginning date our building opened due to the value and rarity of our collection.
- Library E: The concept of security officers is rather new on our campus. Before security officers we had specially trained undergraduate students who patrolled the library and the campus areas during the day and evenings. The opening of our 24-hour study area coincided with the hiring of security officers, but I do not know that the two events were directly connected.
- Library F: Seventy-five years.

Conclusion

The level of security guard protection, who provides it, what is to be provided, and when it is to be provided are complicated issues. Any scenario will involve a set of compromises, and no situation seems to be ideal. Given the various levels of security guard protection available and the scenarios by which it might be provided, each library will have to make its decision based on resources and the possibilities available to it. For example, as desirable as 24-hour security may seem, the parent institution may not be willing to provide it for numerous reasons. On the other hand, an enhanced security presence at such functions as exhibition openings or for two months when an expensive exhibit from another institution is on loan might be possibilities, even if 24-hour security 365 days a year is not feasible. Any situation presents both possibilities and difficulties.

NOTES

1. Violent incidents in public institutions are not far to seek. A single day's reports in March, 2008, brought incidents in which a library director was assaulted and injured and another library besieged by hooligans. On the former, see Chris Foreman, "Greensburg Library Scuffle Injures Director; Police Seek Couple," *Pittsburg Tribune-Review* (14 March 2008). http://www.pittsburghlive.com/x/pittsburghtrib/search/s_557237.html; and for the latter, Adam Morris, Adam. "Gangs Put Library under Siege." *Edinburgh* (Scotland) *Evening News* (17 March 2008). http://news.scotsman.com/latestnews/Gangs-put-library-under-siege.3884348.jp.

2. Paul W. Parfomak, *Guarding America: Security Guards and U.S. Critical Infrastructure Protection* (Washington: Congressional Research Service, 2004), 8, figure 1. http://www.italy.usembassy.gov/pdf/other/RL32670.pdf. Joseph Ricci, *Testimony of Joseph Ricci, CAE Executive Director, National Association of Security Companies (NASCO), Before the House Homeland Security Committee Hearing on "The Direction and Viability of the Federal Protective Service."* [Washington, 2007], points out that there are about 2 million private security guards in all fields but only about 700,000 law enforcement personnel (2). http://homeland.house.gov/Site Documents/2007050111514-01127.pdf.

3. A great deal of detailed information on the actual organization and operation of a security guard program in various venues is presented in Lawrence J. Fennelly, *Museum, Archive, and Library Security*, 3rd ed. (Boston: Butterworth-Heinemann, 1996), 296–312 and Ed Morawski, *How to Defeat Burglar Alarms—Not!: Dispelling Hollywood Myths* (N. p., 2007), 72–75.

4. See "Homeland Security: Guards, Earning Little." CBS News (29 May 2007). http://www.cbsnews.com/stories/2007/05/29/terror/main2860972.shtml. The article notes that Alabama, Colorado, Kansas, Mississippi, Missouri, Nebraska, South Dakota, Kentucky, Wyoming, and Idaho do not regulate the security guard industry, although some locales, such as Boise, do. If states do not regulate security guards, employers are barred from the FBI fingerprint check system. Morawski recommends that institutions be given access to security guard personnel files (75).

5. See Ross Guthrie, "Customer Service? Balancing Security and Customer Service," *Cultural Property Protection from the Ground Up: Proceedings of the National Conference on Cultural Property Protection and International Conference on Museum Security, March 7–11, 1999.* [Washington: Smithsonian Institution, 1999], 71–72. Guthrie correctly touches upon the question of when "customer service" might compromise security (72).

6. In general, engaging the services of a "runner" from a private security company is a bad idea. Not only can it be expensive, it can also be futile. One is better advised to depend on regular law enforcement; in only a few cases should runners be used. One such instance might be if the institution is located in a remote area with thin law enforcement coverage. Even in that case, one must consider whether the runner is likely to arrive before the police. To the contrary, Ed Morawski, *How to Defeat Burglar Alarms—Not!: Dispelling Hollywood Myths* (N. p., 2007), explains that sometimes employing runners is not necessarily a bad idea (81).

7. John J. Fay, ed., *Encyclopedia of Security Management*, 2nd ed. (Burlington: Butterworth-Heinemann, 2007), 53.

8. Minot Dodson, "Why Choose a Contract Guard Service?" *Cultural Property Protection from the Ground Up: Proceedings of the National Conference on Cultural Property Protection and International Conference on Museum Security, March 7–11, 1999.* [Washington: Smithsonian Institution, 1999], 27–28. See Boylan, Patrick, "Security Guidelines when Using Outside Contractors," Museums and Heritage Organization Policy Statements Series. http://www.museum-security.org/articles.html#contractors. See also Robert J. Fischer and Gion Green, *Introduction to Security*, 7th ed (Boston: Butterworth-Heinemann, 2007), 40–43, and Robert

James Fischer and Richard Janoski, *Loss Prevention and Security Procedures: Practical Applications for Contemporary Problems* (Boston: Butterworth-Heinemann, 2000), 135–58 & 177–97 for other discussions of this issue.

9. Matt Gargan, "Options for Staffing a Security Force," *Cultural Property Protection from the Ground Up: Proceedings of the National Conference on Cultural Property Protection and International Conference on Museum Security, March 7–11, 1999.* [Washington: Smithsonian Institution, 1999], 33. Many institutions, such as colleges, also use student security volunteers for various tasks, such as escorting people from the library to their cars after dark. Morawski firmly rejects this idea: "Don't make the mistake of assigning security duties to regular employees either. This is a recipe for disaster" (74).

10. Gargan, 35.

11. See also L. W. Sheridan, "People in Libraries as Security Agents," *Library & Archival Security* 3 (1980): 57–61.

12. See, for example, Norman M. Spain and Gary Lee Elkin, "Private Security Versus Law Enforcement: There Is a Difference," *Security World* 16 (August, 1979): 32, 38, 40.

13. Fennelly, pp. 299–300. For a real world result of such a situation, see Tim McGlone, "Mariners' Museum Archivist Pleads Guilty to Charges Related to Artifacts Theft," Pilotonline.com: http://hamptonroads.com/2008/06/museum-archivist-pleads-guilty-artifacts-theft, wherein a judge ruled that the suspect's confession to museum officials could be allowed because the officials were under no obligation to inform the suspect of his Miranda rights. Nevertheless, real tensions exist between public police and private security guards, as discussed by Fischer and Green (48–51).

14. If a library hires private security guards, care should be taken to determine precisely what types of powers the guards have. In some jurisdictions, they will be limited to making a citizen's arrest. In others, however, guards can be nearly identical to police, including being armed and having arrest powers. The use of such guards can be quite controversial.

15. Els Van Eijck Van Heslinga, "Catch as Catch Can," *Liber Quarterly* 12 (2002): 319.

16. Although without peer in certain situations, police dogs have found little place in library security, even for after-hours patrols.

17. Nicholas A. Basbanes, *A Gentle Madness: Bibliophiles, Bibliomanes, and the Eternal Passion for Books* (New York: Holt, 1995), reports that Blumberg would sometimes time his thefts so that he was removing materials when guards were changing shifts (470).

18. See The *Hartford Courant* (27 November 1996).

19. The crime has never been solved. See Federal Bureau of Investigation, "Theft Notices & Recoveries: Isabella Stewart Gardner Museum." http://www.fbi.gov/hq/cid/arttheft/northamerica/us/isabella/isabella.htm.

20. See Fennelly, 301–302.

Special Collections Reading Rooms

Alvan Bregman and Margaret Tufts Tenney

> The most threatening security element remained the librarians, who issued a box full of correspondence and then checked its contents after it had been used.
>
> *~Lee Israel*

A Special Collections Reading Room (hereinafter "Reading Room") is a space in which rare books, manuscripts and other materials that are scarce, valuable, delicate or particularly subject to theft may be consulted and enjoyed by patrons under secure and controlled conditions. Once a Reading Room has been designated within a library, certain conditions should apply. The most important of these have been outlined in the 2009 ACRL/RBMS *Guidelines Regarding Security and Theft in Special Collections*. It is the purpose of this chapter to elucidate and expand upon the advice concerning Reading Rooms, given in the *Guidelines* so that those setting up a new Reading Room, or running an existing Reading Room, can more readily implement best security practices.

The material kept on open stacks in every library is always subject to theft, and circulating material is subject to accidental loss. In public libraries and other collections where patrons have direct access to library materials, those risks are a part of doing business, and most such libraries expect to replace lost or stolen material on a more-or-less regular basis. But unique or particularly valuable material cannot be readily replaced, and so needs to be protected. In these cases, libraries do best to sequester the material and make it available under special conditions. Expensive reference books, for example, generally do not circulate in public libraries and local history records may also be designated for in-library use only. In addition, libraries of all kinds will find upon examination that they have acquired materials that turn out to be special or even unique. Additionally, there are volumes or items that seemed ordinary when they were acquired but which over time have developed a high market value. For example, a fiction collection may include the first book by a novelist who subsequently wins a major literary prize. The more rare and special material a library has, the more it will need a separate, secure place where patrons can consult this material. In larger libraries, a great mass of rare and valuable material may enter the collection and separate administrative sections are established to manage this material. In all such cases, a Reading Room is requisite (see figs 10.1–10.3.)

Basics

Careful thought should be given to the location of the Reading Room within the library building or special collections department. Ideally, the Reading Room should be a completely self-contained area. If it cannot be walled-in, its boundaries should be designed so that materials in use in the Reading Room cannot be reached by or passed to individuals outside its boundaries. A Reading Room should

Figure 10.1

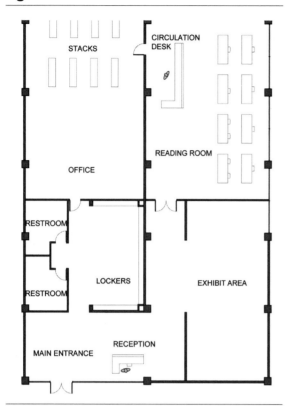

Scenario 1 (Courtesy Sara Alicia Costa, Ocurrente Design)

Figure 10.2

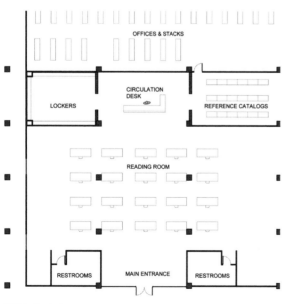

Scenario 2 (Courtesy Sara Alicia Costa, Ocurrente Design)

have a single point of entrance and exit to be used by patrons. Fire codes may require that there be emergency exits within the Reading Room area; if so, these must be alarmed and used only during real emergencies. Where there is access from the Reading Room directly to library stacks, the door should be locked.

There should be a cloakroom or other area outside the Reading Room where patrons and staff can safely deposit personal belongings not needed for research or work. Signs should alert patrons entering the Reading Room that this is an area where special regulations are enforced and where surveillance takes place. For conservation reasons, no food or drink should be allowed in the Reading Room or related work areas.

The Reading Room should be furnished in such a way that sight lines are not impeded. For that reason, extraneous objects should not be placed on tables. A simple set up is preferred, with a monitor's desk and appropriately lit tables where patrons may consult the material they have requested. Shelving units holding reference books should be located along the walls, and should not protrude into the reading area. There should not be alcoves of any kind within the Reading Room, and if there are, they should be off limits to patrons. Seating should be so arranged that bodies or objects do not obstruct surveillance. Patrons should not be so close together that they have access to each other's material, and depending on sight lines and camera placement, should sit facing the same direction. In some facilities surveillance is made more complicated if readers are scattered around the room. (In smaller facilities that will not be a problem.) Under no circumstances should readers themselves determine where they sit; seating should be assigned by the library. Readers who visit for consecutive days should have their seating assignments changed daily.

Figure 10.3

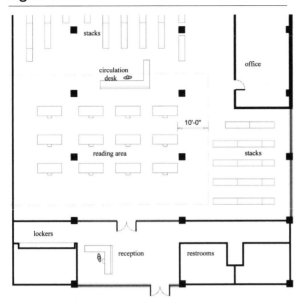

Scenario 3: This Layout Is Fairly Insecure
(Courtesy Sara Alicia Costa, Ocurrente Design)

The Reading Room needs to have a place where supplies can be kept to ensure the safe handling of various kinds of materials. For example, a sufficient variety of book pillows, foam supports, or other kinds of book rests should be on hand. Other supplies may include pencils, colored paper, string and corner weights, magnifying glasses, cold-light sheets or wands, cloth tape measures, calipers, and whatever else might be needed for bibliographical research. There may also be cabinets in which material is kept on hold for patrons. In all cases, those cabinets, if in a public area, need to have locks and be kept secured when not in use.

Reception / Registration of Patrons

A Special Collections Reading Room should ideally have an adjacent or separate room that can be used for Reception. When this is not possible it remains important to maintain the separation of the Reception area and the Reading Room from the general library area in another manner, for example, by using moveable barriers. The Reception area should be visible from the main Reading Room (and vice versa), and both areas should be staffed and/or monitored at all times, allowing the staff in either area to back each other up.

In cases where the reception area is in a separate part of the building not visible from the Reading Room, provision needs to be made for personnel at both posts to communicate with each other concerning patron status and other matters. Reception area personnel need to be able to communicate to Reading Room personnel, for example, what materials a patron has been allowed to bring into the Reading Room (e. g., personal computer, a personal copy of a book to be used for comparison). Alternatively, Reading Room personnel need to be able to communicate to those in the reception area that a patron has turned in all library materials and is at liberty to depart. Ideally, those communications are done in an electronic tracking system, with written check-off lists, pass cards, or some other device that allows disparate areas to check one another.

The Reception area is the place where patrons intending to use the Reading Room can register; where they can be informed of library policies; receive directional assistance; and can securely and conveniently deposit personal belongings, most of which should not be allowed into the Reading Room itself. The library should provide access to and require the use of lockers and a coat closet. Patrons should not be able to reach the lockers from the Reading Room (or vice versa) without passing by the Receptionist, who should be monitoring the area. It is advisable that the lockers be keyed and for day use only. Locker keys should not leave the Library. It should be explained to patrons that their use of lockers enhances their privacy as well as the library's security, as Reading Room or other monitors need not usually examine items in lockers.

Policies and procedures should be in place to address the use of cell phones and digital cameras in the Reading Room. Most institutions will request that they be left in a locker though, increasingly, digital cameras are allowed in the Reading Room with special provisions. Special collections administrators should be aware of the capabilities of new and emerging technology and its consequences regarding Reading Room security and functions.

The staff member(s) scheduled at the Reception desk should have access to a computer, telephone, and preferably other means of contacting security personnel, both within and outside the library. Staff should be trained to recognize when a threat of any kind exists. These may originate from many sources: a patron, another staff member, or the environment. It is also imperative that staff be willing and able to follow an established procedure should a risky security situation occur. Although the detection of a security risk will be a matter of observation, experience and judgment, useful training can often be supplied within an institution either by the Human Resources Department or by the police or security office.

Specific guidelines and procedures regarding security and registration should be established by the institution and should be made available for patrons, either posted in the Reception area, on a website, or available as handouts. It is helpful to provide a separate sheet that patrons can take with them that outlines Reading Room regulations and materials use policy. This will give patrons something to which they can refer if uncertain of procedures. Some institutions also use video orientations.

The initial check-in of patrons should be done before the patron retrieves any materials. Each new patron should register and show photo identification before entering the Reading Room. Some institutions perform that function at the Reception desk or online. There should be enough space at the Reception desk to allow patrons to fill out forms while staff continues to attend to other patrons' comings and goings.[1] Alternately a designated area where registration documentation is filled out could be made available.

The registration document should be kept simple, but should at least contain the questions necessary to establish the patron's full name, current address, permanent address, phone numbers, email address, identification number, and form of photo ID. Photo identification should be current and have the person's name, address and a unique identifying number.[2] A government-issued ID such as a driver's license or passport is preferable, although foreign nationals visitors should always present the latter. Institutions should be extremely cautious about accepting ID issued by any non-governmental entity; that precaution applies especially to college and university ID cards, even those issued by one's own institution.[3] Ideally, the identification card should be copied, preferably in

Figure 10.4

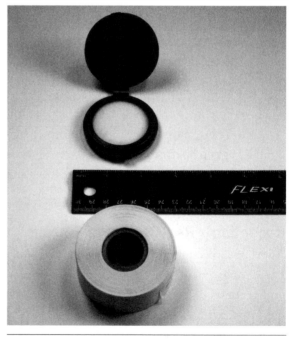

A simple fingerprinting kit. (Used by permission.)

color. In more secure registration procedures, patrons are required to leave a thumbprint on their registration cards and/or to have their pictures taken.[4] In fact, the combination of a picture and a thumbprint is by far the most secure method for positively identifying patrons, and the information could prove vital in cases of theft, especially by a thief who uses a false ID.[5] Special Collections administrators should check with legal counsel about the limits and requirements respecting privacy that may be in place by law or by institutional policy (see fig 10.4).

Registration forms may request or require other information from patrons, such as their institutional affiliation and status (e.g., faculty, student, staff) (see fig 10.5). It is also important to have patrons include the subject, scope, and purpose as well as the expected outcome (project, book, article, film etc.) of their research. If known in advance, patrons should be required to list what collections they will be examining, even though that information will be captured eventually on material requests. If unusual or out-of-scope requests are made during the course of a patron's research, this should warrant the polite attention of staff.

Whether done manually or electronically, there should be a brief agreement statement, to be signed by the patron indicating that he or she understands the policies and regulations of the Reading Room and agrees to abide by them. The registration document should also contain any required statutory notice concerning the state's theft laws; failure to include such a statement and to get the patron's acknowledgement could result in later difficulties. The statement should also contain a clause in which the patron agrees that library staff may search his/her belongings. The patron should sign and date the application and the staff member taking the application should countersign it. Patron information should be updated at regular intervals, e.g., annually, and, if possible, should contain the date

of each visit the patron makes to the collection, what project was worked on, and what material was used. A separate daily log should also be kept either electronically or manually.

This registration information should be retained indefinitely. A patron database or automated special collections management system should be used to allow staff to check and update a patron's record. Each time patrons come into the Reading Room they should sign a log or be checked into a patron registration system where the materials they will be using can be updated. Because of security and privacy issues an institution may decide that personal identification numbers and any payment information should not be retained in an electronic format. It is still possible to keep a written record in paper files at the institution. All registration and circulation records should be securely maintained in a stand-alone database with no Internet access or in paper form in a secure area.[6] Electronic records should be backed up frequently.[7]

On their first visit, patrons should receive a brief orientation to acquaint them with Reading Room procedures, expected patron conduct, and library services that they may request. This not only serves to put the first-time patron at ease about procedures but also reinforces the fact that a special collections Reading Room operates differently from a regular library and that they should expect to be in closer contact with staff. Orientation should include such topics as the location and use of finding aids, catalogs, and reference sources, the handling and care of materials, and duplication policies. A reference interview with a librarian should ensure that a patron sees the right material, saving the patron time and also helping to limit random searches through holdings. The interview helps staff anticipate problems that might otherwise arise only after material is delivered to the patron. For example, it may be possible to provide surrogates of delicate originals or

Figure 10.5

THE WATKINSON LIBRARY/THE TRINITY COLLEGE ARCHIVES
Trinity College
Hartford, Connecticut

Application For User's Card

Name (please print)_____

Local address_____

_____ Tel. no._____

Permanent address_____

_____ Tel. no._____

Student status/job or position title_____

If a candidate for a degree, give name of institution and degree sought_____

_____

Identification (Driver's license, student or faculty I.D., etc.)_____

_____

Research collection of primary use (please check one)   Watkinson Library_____

Trinity College Archives_____

Subject and purpose of research_____

_____

_____

_____

Data from this form will be used to compile statistical and research topic summaries. We
attempt to inform researchers of others with similar research interests.
Do you object to having your name and information about your research
topic made available to others working in the same area?

Yes _____   No _____

I have read, I understand, and I agree to abide by the rules governing the use of the
Watkinson Library/Trinity College Archives as listed on the back of this
form.

Signature_____

Date_____

Approved by_____

Sample Patron Registration Form (Front)
(Courtesy Watkinson Library, Trinity College, Hartford, CT)

of materials checked out for exhibits. In the interests both of security and conservation, patrons should be offered or directed to surrogates (facsimiles, microfilms, online resources, etc.), when these exist, unless there is some specific reason to consult the original.

Once the receptionist has cleared the patron to enter the Reading Room, he or she should be given a clearance slip or other identifying card to present to the Reading Room circulation attendant. This provides a means for the circulation staff to know who is in the Reading Room. When ready to leave, patrons should check out with the circulation desk, be prepared to show what they are taking out, retrieve the clearance slip, and turn it back in to the receptionist.

An institution must decide what will be acceptable for patrons to bring into the Reading Room, and all staff working the Reception area must be aware of and willing to enforce consistently what can and cannot be taken in. Restricted items to be checked include outerwear, hats, bags, and other non-research related belongings. Books, papers and equipment that the patron can show are needed for research should be marked by Reception staff with an identifying stamp or clearance slip so that the materials will be easily identifiable as belonging to the patron. Patrons who wish to take in their computers should leave cases and bags with their other belongings in the Reception area or in a secure area of the Reading Room itself.

Patron dress is also a concern. Shoplifters, for example, often have specially made "booster" clothing to assist them in concealing stolen items. Many institutions ban any items of clothing that could facilitate concealment of items. Especially problematic is any form of outerwear, such as a sweater or jacket, or cargo pants with their numerous pockets. Suit or sport coats are problems because their construction offers numerous places to conceal materials easily. One of the maps that Forbes Smiley stole at Yale, for example, was recovered from the inner pocket of his sport coat. In an ideal situation, patrons would not wear coats or multi-pocket clothing of any type in the Reading Room, but except for outerwear this is almost impossible to enforce.

Laptop computers also present their own set of hazards, in general because of their various drives. If a patron wishes to use a laptop, staff should verify that all the bays, slots and drives on the machine are actual functioning parts and not dummy hiding places. Even real drives can be used to conceal materials: a small daguerreotype, for example, will easily fit in a personal computer memory card slot, and folded manuscripts can readily be shoved into a CD drive slot. At the very least, however, staff should ensure that a patron's laptop has not been deliberately altered. All items should be inspected on the way out. All laptop computers, for example, should be opened to be sure nothing has been concealed between the screen and keyboard.

Patrons and non-staff visitors should be readily distinguishable from staff on sight. The most common way to accomplish this goal is to issue badges to staff and require them to wear them whenever they are on the premises, although they should never be taken out of the building. A second layer of such protection can be accomplished by issuing different badges to patrons and others. In 1979 Bahr reported that having staff wear badges "aroused controversy" in one library and concluded, "Being tagged, watched and searched, after all, is not pleasant. But it serves a purpose...."[8] Since then, however, most of such controversy seems to have faded and security consciousness has been raised: identifying badges at least for staff and outside workers have become routine.

Circulation / Reading Room Regulations

Once patrons have been checked in at Reception and have deposited their belongings in a locker, they can enter the Reading Room. Only staff and registered patrons consulting requested special collection material should be allowed in the Reading Room. Each patron should check in at the circulation/reference desk upon entering and check out upon leaving, so that staff can keep track of who is present and using material. In some cases, the library retains the patron's actual ID card at the desk until s/he has turned in all materials and is ready to leave. In the case of a patron who flees with material, having that card can be critical.

Supervisors should not assign work to Reading Room staff that will draw their attention unduly away from what is going on in the Reading Room. The appearance of vigilance and care makes a large impact on users of the Reading Room. If staff members are not watching or are distracted, those circumstances will provide opportunity for rules to be broken. Moreover, close interaction between staff and patrons helps reinforce in the patron the idea of being in a special collections library and encourages vigilance on the part of staff while deterring would-be thieves. Reading room staff should also be given adequate breaks. Concentrating on surveilling the reading room and patrons for more than two straight hours can lead to mental lapses and potential security problems.

Limitations should be placed on the number of items that may be circulated to a patron at any one time and on any given day. In order to allow circulation staff to monitor material properly, it is especially important to limit the number of loose manuscript materials patrons can have at their desk at any one time. The optimum number will vary, but should be defined by policy (e.g., ten sheets, one folder). For those reasons, among others, material should be organized in small units, e.g., 10 items to a folder, and the number of items ascertained before and after use. Especially important items should have individual folders or containers. Senior

staff should be consulted before any exceptions are granted. Unprocessed collections should not be circulated to patrons without appropriate controls. Those might include allowing the patron access to only a few pages at a time or to being assisted by a curator or archivist. Patrons consulting manuscript material should take notes on colored paper, which the library should provide. Using colored paper makes it easier to spot collection materials mixed in among patron's notes. Colored paper may have a pre-punched hole in it; upon exit, staff can place a pencil through holes and shake the leaves to detect hidden papers.

Staff should be trained in the proper way to handle rare and fragile materials. In turn, trained staff should assess the condition of circulating material to show patrons the proper way to handle them. Staff should be able to answer questions and explain why special handling is important. Material should be removed from enclosures before being given to patrons. If enclosures, such as a Hollinger© box, are to remain with the item, patrons should be given any necessary special instructions regarding handling, contents and order. If possible, circulation staff should also check inside all enclosures when materials are returned to be certain of contents and order.

Visibility and vigilance are very important in maintaining security in the Reading Room. Circulating material must always be visible to the staff. Patrons should be asked to keep all manuscript material flat on top of the table and books should be placed in cradles or on the table top, never in the patron's lap or overhanging the table. String weights should be used to keep books open. Book cradles, archival boxes or stacks of books should not block staff sight lines. Staff should periodically walk around the research area and observe patrons at their tables to check for handling and security issues.

If security cameras are used, they should be placed and angled to maximum effect. Cameras should be at several different locations throughout the room to ensure different angles of observation. Ideally, the camera images should be adjustable so that, when viewed, patrons as well as the materials they have checked out are clearly visible. The ability to zoom in could also be important.

Only staff should move materials into and out of the Reading Room. Patrons should not remove materials from the reading room for any reason. Arrangements for materials to be placed in classrooms within the library or in other parts of the building should be made with the librarian or circulation staff ahead of time, and staff should be responsible for moving collection materials into and out of those areas. An inventory should be made of all material going into and coming out of a library classroom.

Library material should not be left unattended when a patron leaves the Reading Room for a lengthy time (e.g., lunch). There must be controls in place to ensure that patrons do not have access to any material checked out to other patrons. Any material a patron wants to use again should be returned to the circulation desk to be kept on hold under the patron's name and released upon the patron's return. There should be a limit to the number of items that can be kept on hold, and a limit to the length of time that that these items are kept in the Reading Room if not used. Typically, items not expected to be used within one week should be returned to the stacks to be paged again when next needed.

If staff suspects a security problem, they should inform the librarian in charge immediately and building security should be notified. All supervisory staff should have a plan in place for how to approach a suspected security problem and should go over the procedure with on-site security staff. This is very important, especially where campus or institutional police are involved, as there may be limitations on what is and is not permitted when confronting a suspect.

Staffing the Reading Room

Although not every theft from a special collections library is committed by a staff member or volunteer, many are. Hiring for a special collections library reading room should involve security and background checks by the institutional Human Resources department, if there is one, or by library administration (see Chapter 2).

Written policies and procedures for maintaining security in the Reading Room should be in place. All staff should be aware of these policies and procedures, and accountable for maintaining them. Supervisors should make sure that each employee understands the relationship between the handling and care of collection materials and the procedures involved in making materials available to patrons and maintaining security. Staff should be prepared to follow policies and procedures to accomplish a common goal. They should also be able to effectively explain procedures to patrons using the Reading Room.

There are many different reasons an employee might steal. Most cases of theft occur because there is opportunity. It is imperative that staff as well as patrons not be allowed to take purses, briefcases, backpacks, or bulky coats into an area where collection materials are located. The library should provide a secure place for staff members to leave their belongings during the day. This area should be outside the Reading Room and work areas, and can be the same area as for patrons. All staff should be aware that any bags taken into offices or collection areas are subject to search by facility guards or security staff upon request. Some institutions may prefer to have staff open all bags for inspection upon departing the building.

A clear understanding should exist between the Library Security Officer (LSO) and the municipal and/ or institutional police force that serves the institution, as to what can and cannot be expected from the Reading Room guard, if there is one, and police forces. The LSO should act as a liaison with security guards and police to ensure an understanding of the value of the library collections before an incident occurs. Security personnel must also have a clear understanding of what to look for when searching staff bags, as it is often difficult for someone not familiar with the materials housed in a rare books and manuscripts collection to know what to look for and how to recognize materials, particularly if they are unmarked.

Disgruntled employees are often more likely to resort to theft either as a way of acting out or as revenge for imagined or real wrongs on the part of the institution. Staff must be accountable and tasks made as quantifiable as possible. A supervisor should keep good records on staff activities, absences, and assigned task completion both successful and unsuccessful. In most institutions documentation is imperative when considering dismissal of an employee. With proper documentation it may be possible to dismiss a questionable employee before an incident of theft or vandalism occurs.

It is important to realize that all states have different laws covering thefts from libraries. The RBMS Security Committee has published online (http://www.rbms.nd.edu/committees/security/state_laws) a compilation of state laws pertaining to library theft. Because the harmonization and enforcement of such laws is deemed desirable, the ACRL *Guidelines Regarding Thefts in Libraries* includes a "Draft of Model Legislation: Theft and Mutilation of Library Materials."

Classes, Exhibits and Receptions

When Special collections materials are taken from the stacks for exhibits, classes and other events there is a greater chance they can disappear. The more hands materials pass through the greater the chance that somewhere along the way there will be a loss of accountability for the materials. This is particularly true for exhibits, where the person who originally checks out an item may be only the first of many people to handle it before it is checked back in. In those instances it is important to have policies and procedures that can be followed consistently and in which all staff are invested.

Materials checked out for exhibits should be tracked as if they were being circulated in the Reading Room. Policies and procedures should allow for materials to be checked out, prepared for exhibit, exhibited, and returned to the stacks and still be located anywhere in that process. The circulation desk should be able to know what is checked out for exhibit and when to expect these items back. Out slips, call-number flags, manuscript folders and boxes, and special housings should be kept together so they can be readily reunited with their proper material at the close of the exhibit.

Classes, receptions, and meetings where materials are to be displayed require similar procedural care. Ideally the Special Collections library should have a keyed meeting room or classroom where faculty wishing to acquaint their classes with rare materials can meet. Having these separate areas prevents disruption to the patrons in the Reading Room but presents new security challenges. Regardless of what kind of space is used for classes, that space should be considered an extension of the Reading Room as long as materials from the collection are in use.

Site-specific provisions will need to be written to provide for the use and configuration of these spaces. These should include directions and timelines for reserving a room and for requesting the material to be used, and notification of when a curator or other staff member must be present. The regulations should also include information that instructors should pass along to their students to prepare them for using special collections; among those, for example, are procedures for registering and checking personal belongings, and restrictions on what may be taken into the classroom. Relevant forms, handouts and notices should be posted on a website and/or attached.

Those using special collections materials for class or other exhibit purposes should submit a request for materials well ahead of the scheduled event. This is a good opportunity to familiarize the faculty member with the library's relevant policies, procedures and handling guidelines. For classes scheduled to meet regularly during the semester, a staff member should give an introduction on using the facility during the first meeting, offer assistance, and set out ground rules. Ideally, both the professor and all the students in the class should be registered patrons. Ironically, classes are often the one time when library staff does not know the identities of people using materials.

Faculty members should be told that since they are requesting the material, they will be held responsible for its safe return. There should be a limit to the number of items that can be used in a classroom or be put out on display at any one time. The number of items may vary depending on the availability of display space and on the nature and value of the material being used. Library staff should have timely access to the material at the end of each class or event so that all items can be checked in.

The faculty member conducting the class should receive orientation on the proper display, handling and security of materials, even if a curator or other staff member will be present during the class. (It can be awkward for library staff to correct an instructor in front of the class.) In most cases, only a curator, other library staff member or the instructor should handle rare or fragile materials in a classroom setting, although some page-turning by students may be allowed.

Some points that could be included in policies and procedures for using library materials in meet-ing rooms or classrooms associated with the library for classes, receptions or exhibits follow:

1) A special collections staff member or curator must be present if the presenter is not a faculty member (or at all times).

2) A room reservation form should be filled out and signed by the instructor or organizer stating the dates and purpose for using the room, the number of attendees, and whether there is a perceived need for special staff assistance.

3) It is important to have a time line for requesting materials in advance for a class or event. This should be sufficient to allow library staff time to pull the material, consult curators if necessary, and to arrange the material for display, using appropriate supports. This also avoids last minute requests that could create confusion and lead to misplaced items.

4) In a situation where materials are used in a classroom, the instructor will be responsible for the security and proper handling of all materials, unless a staff member is present. Library materials on display for events or in classes should never be handed around for inspection. They must remain on the supports provided. Instead, students or guests may be invited to circulate around the room to get a closer look at particular materials on display.

5) Students or others should be restricted as to what they can bring in to the classroom. If there are books, handouts or paper for notes they should be approved ahead of time. Alternately the institution might provide special paper inside the classroom for instances when notes might be taken.

6) A procedure should be established whereby all students assemble in a lobby or reception area to be led into the classroom together by the professor. That would also apply to the end of class when students should all leave together. This prevents wandering in and out and milling around when materials are out in the rooms. Students should never be left alone in a room with materials.

Conclusion

Because the Reading Room and its extensions are the interfaces between patrons and a library's materials, special attention needs to be given to them. Even the best run and seemingly most secure Reading Rooms and institutions have been subjected to thefts and vandalism of their materials. Regrettably, all the security in the world is not going to stop all the thieves all the time. Reading Room regulations and vigilance will probably do little to stop insider theft. On the other hand, a properly laid-out Reading Room with vigilant staff and a planned environment will be more secure than one poorly designed, chaotic, and disorganized. Security provisions in the Reading Room should make a potential thief believe that trying to steal from your library is not worth the risk. Rigorous keeping of records is important if a library is to recover its materials after a theft.

Reading Room security is not designed to make patrons feel uncomfortable, or invade their sense of privacy, but to ensure the safety of the collections patrons come to use. Although much of the advice provided above is restrictive in nature, we want to emphasize that the ideal Reading Room should be a pleasant, busy and productive place where scholars and interested members of the public can conduct research or find pleasure in examining and reading scarce and special material.

NOTES

1. Pamela Cravey, *Protecting Library Staff, Users, Collections, and Facilities: A How-To-Do-It Manual* (New York & London: Neal Schuman, 2001), suggests that special collections "work primarily from appointments" (p. 111), a procedure that in many instances is simply impractical. No evidence exists that appointments reduce thefts.

2. See Bonnie Hardwick, *The Function and Force of Reader Registration Procedures* (Denver: Society of Colorado Archivists, 1992).

3. Blumberg successfully presented a picture ID that really belonged to Matt McCue, a psychology professor at the University of Minnesota. Unbeknownst to gulled library personnel, the ID was patently fake because it had Blumberg's picture on it. At the time, University of Minnesota faculty ID cards had no pictures on them. See Goshen College, Campus Crime Prevention Programs, *Library Safety & Security: A Comprehensive Manual for Library Administrators and Police and Security Officers* (Goshen: Campus Crime Prevention Programs, 1992), 122.

4. A rarely used but effective method for identifying those who present false identification is to ask to see a credit card or bank ATM card also in the person's name. Although it is a relatively simple matter to create a false identification card, it is quite another matter to create a false credit card, especially in the same name as the ID. The library, of course, would not record any information from the card but merely examine it for comparison sake.

5. Physical fingerprints should be of such quality that they last seventy-five years. One can also take digital fingerprints, although doing so is more expensive and will involve data migration issues.

6. The importance of keeping this computer off the Internet cannot be overemphasized. Exposing such sensitive, critical data to loss, corruption, or hacking is a poor security choice. In 2003, it is believed that the Bancroft Library's patron database may have been compromised. See David Lazarus, "Online Breach at Bancroft," *San Francisco Chronicle* (23 November 2003). Because of such concerns, various computer systems, such as those used to control water treatment plants and nuclear power facilities, are never connected to the Internet, either. Care should be taken that any router to which the machine is connected is not also somehow serving a machine with Internet access.

7. Before discarding paper records in favor of maintaining only electronic ones, the institution should consider the novel ways in which computerized records may be questioned or attacked in ways that do not apply to paper-based records. A dishonest insider thief, for example, could alter automated circulation files to attach a record for a stolen book to an otherwise innocent researcher, a task that would be nearly impossible with paper-based records. Frequent backups minimize the possibility of successful tampering with electronic records.

8. Alice Harrison Bahr, *Book Theft and Library Security Systems, 1978–79* (White Plains: Knowledge Industry Publications, 1979), 88.

Audit Trails

Everett C. Wilkie, Jr.

We used to be assured that books we couldn't find on the shelves were in the pipeline somewhere, being processed. It was only last year that we found out this is not the case. The books are not misshelved, stacked up waiting for cataloging, down at the bindery, sitting in carrels…. The damn stuff's gone.

~Laurence Stone

Materials brought into a rare books or special collections library must be accounted for at all times, from the moment they are ordered to the moment they are deaccessioned and beyond. No matter how one accomplishes this task, the library should be able at any moment to know the precise location and status of any item in its collection. As Kahn remarks, "No matter what routine is for delivery and accession of materials into your collection, you need to create a procedure that tracks the items from the time they enter the building until they are processed for shelving and retrieval by staff members and the public."[1]

Acquisition

When an item is ordered from an antiquarian bookseller, bought in a bookstore, purchased at auction, or donated, a record of the transaction should be immediately created. That record may consist of an invoice or another document, such as a Deed of Gift. With it should be recorded who is involved in the transaction and a description of the material acquired. Any other ancillary documents, such as absentee bidder sheets or bookseller descriptions, should also be preserved. Even if the originals must be surrendered to another office, such as the Bursar, the library should retain copies for its own files. An accession record should also be created soon after the item is received by the library.[2] Those documents are the library's basic proof that it owns an item and should never be discarded.

Cataloguing

One of the Achilles heels of processing incoming materials is that track of them is sometimes lost between acquisition and the time they are made ready for use. In general, materials suffer one of two fates after they enter the library: 1) they are put in a backlog collection; or 2) they are sent to be catalogued. If the former occurs, some record should be made of that fact, a record that should be updated if they are ever fortunate enough to go to stage 2. If materials are sent to be catalogued, a list should be kept and updated as items are processed and put on the shelves ready for use. In too many instances, materials are sent to one place or the other without records being made, thereby creating a rich pool teeming with materials to be surreptitiously fished by unscrupulous insiders. A third but more remote possibility is that materials are sent to conservation before cataloguing. Again, records should be kept of all those items and their progress through the system updated. In all cases, backlogged materials should be segregated and access to them strictly controlled.

Ready for Use

Once materials are catalogued, they presumably

have been entered into the card or online catalogue and are ready for patron use, exhibition, lending, and other purposes. At this stage, a paper or electronic trail of all activity is necessary. Every time an item is removed from the shelf for any reason, a trail of its movements should be created and maintained until it is returned to its proper place, a fact that should also be documented. In the case of reading room use by a researcher, the record should include all the following items (see figs 11.1 & 11.2):

1. The researcher's printed name
2. The researcher's signature
3. The date of the transaction
4. The author of the item (if known)
5. The title of the item or collection
6. The shelf mark
7. The initials of the person paging the material
8. The initials of the person reshelving the material
9. The initials of the person checking the reshelving
10. The unique number of the call slip or transaction record

Figure 11.1

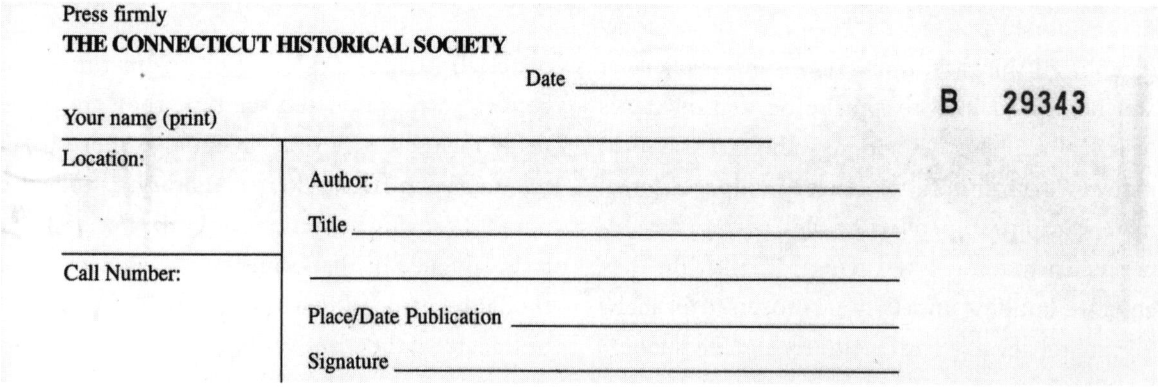

Press firmly
THE CONNECTICUT HISTORICAL SOCIETY
Date ______
B 29343
Your name (print) ______
Location:
Author: ______
Title ______
Call Number:
Place/Date Publication ______
Signature ______

Sample Book Call Slip (Courtesy The Connecticut Historical Society)

Figure 11.2

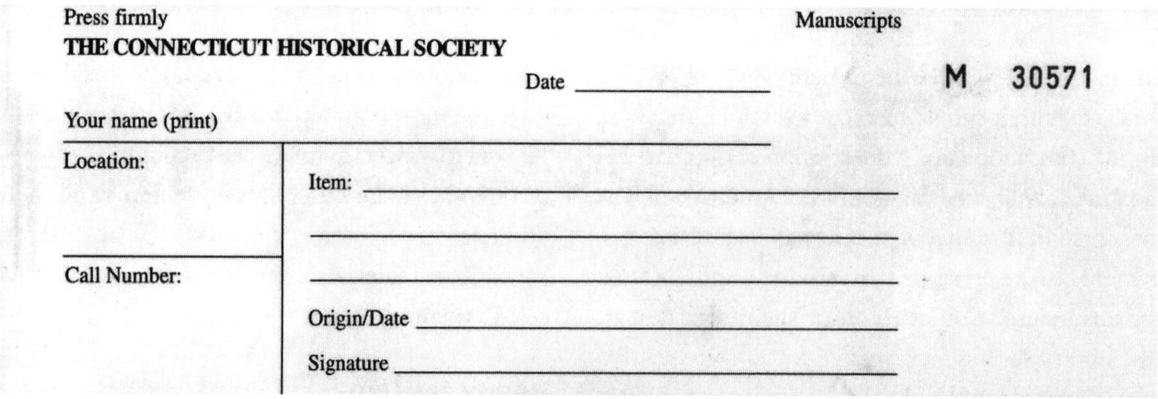

Press firmly
THE CONNECTICUT HISTORICAL SOCIETY
Manuscripts
Date ______
M 30571
Your name (print) ______
Location:
Item: ______
Call Number:
Origin/Date ______
Signature ______

Sample Manuscript Call Slip (Courtesy The Connecticut Historical Society)

The same information may be collected for other uses, such as exhibition or conservation. If the system is paper based, the information should be collected in triplicate for filing by items 1, 3, and 6; in an electronic system supposedly the information can be arranged by any of the elements as needed. The information should be retained permanently; if retained electronically, it should be on a computer not connected to the Internet and the records periodically backed up. In a paper-based system, possibly slightly different forms might be used for either printed or manuscript materials.

All the information listed above can be vital if the library suffers a theft. Numbers 1–3 establish that a particular person was in the library on a given day. Items 4–6 establish that he or she actually used a particular book or manuscript collection. Items 7–8 establish that the item was delivered to the reading room and returned. In addition to the call slip, patrons should also be required to sign a daily log of researchers to confirm items 1 and 3. Needless to say, any item unaccounted for at the end of the day is cause for alarm. A filing system that saves only a patron's name is a gamble because of the possibility of false ID cards and because theft may be discovered by other means. If, for example, a thief has used an alias, but the library cannot determine what name was used, it can probably never find the proper charge slips. On the other hand, if a book is found to be missing a map, one of the only ways a library can determine who used the volume is to be able to search records by shelf mark; recalling who used a certain book perhaps years after a theft is probably fruitless.[3]

Any time an item moves internally, it should also be tracked using the above system. Items sent to conservation, borrowed internally or externally for exhibition, or shelved in an office should all be properly accounted for. Allowing items to be casually moved about is unwise. For example, at the Harry Ransom Humanities Research Center, University of Texas—Austin, volunteer Mimi Meyer was dismissed for having an improperly documented item in her office. As was proven later, she had been stealing from the institution. The library should insist, therefore, that any item moved from its proper place on the shelf be traced and failure to do so treated as a serious matter. In practical terms, such documentation also assists patrons who call for materials that may be in use elsewhere. Obviously, any item sent to off-site storage, to another institution for exhibition, or to a conservator should also be tracked either by checking it out or updating its catalogue record to indicate its present location, as appropriate.

Ideally, when an item is paged for whatever purpose, a marker is left on the shelf in place of the item itself. In the best of all possible worlds, the marker will be a copy of the call slip itself. After the item is reshelved, in a thorough system, another person would go along behind the process with the call slips and verify that the item is really back where it belongs. Only then would the entire marker be removed from the shelf. If at all possible, the people retrieving the materials, reshelving the materials, and checking to be sure the materials are properly reshelved should not be the same person. Stacks should be routinely patrolled for charge slips that seem to be orphans. An item charged out two weeks previously to the reading room but not yet back on the shelf should be cause for concern.

Shelf Reading

One of the more important on-going activities that a rare book and manuscript library can do to ensure collection integrity is to conduct regular shelf reading projects in all collections. Such projects are especially critical to detecting misshelved items, thefts, and substitutions. Unfortunately, shelf reading has long been an unglamorous activity readily neglected.[4] Shuman correctly observes of this vital activity: "Library staff members universally cringe at the very thought of the tiresome chore of inventory shelf reading. Anyone who has performed this odious task knows just how time consuming and boring it is."[5] Those same people, however, expect the janitorial staff to cheerfully mop floors and clean toilets. "Tiresome chore" and "odious task" are relative terms, and no librarian should shirk from this important responsibility. The mere suggestion that librarians would have to be dragged kicking and screaming to this important duty is itself a sad commentary on prevailing security attitudes.

Once an institution has a secure, accurate shelf list, shelf readings should be conducted routinely. Normally, these will involve two people—one to manage the list itself, and another to physically inspect the items on the shelf. Any discrepancy should be noted, reported, and promptly investigated. Any cataloguing problems that come to light (e. g., wrong shelfmark, etc.) should be promptly corrected. It is recommended that shelf readings not follow a predictable pattern but rather that they visit portions of the collection arbitrarily, assuring, however, that the entire collection is at least sampled periodically, assuming it cannot be read in a single cycle. The order of these readings will need to be decided by senior staff but not shared publicly or with others not directly involved in the actual reading process. In all cases, each item should be removed from the shelves and inspected to ensure that it is the actual item listed in the cataloguing record; all items in enclosures should be removed from them for inspection, as well. In the end, the entire collection should eventually be read on an orderly basis, even if that process takes several years.[6]

Although the reading of book collections is a fairly straightforward process, it has its difficulties. In almost no case will a shelf reading project discover if a book has actually been tampered with; it will determine only that the item is physically there and is as basically described. Such features as binding, provenance, bookplates, and other physical features should be inspected. Almost never, however, will the items actually be collated to insure they still are consistent with the cataloguing record. Doing so would so bog down such a project that little would ever be accomplished. On the other hand, shelf readings do, in fact, sometimes uncover depredations. An atlas missing half its maps or a book with its text block removed will be fairly obvious even on casual inspection. In the best scenario, a shelf reading project is a blunt instrument to ensure the collection's basic integrity.

Reading manuscript collections is another matter entirely and fraught with far more difficulties. As a practical matter, about all one can do is ensure that volumes and boxes are on the shelves in the order called for. If a collection description, for example, calls for 25 boxes, one can count to ensure that the requisite number of boxes are present. A more thorough job would entail at least opening the boxes to ensure that the contents appear to be intact. Discovering if specific items are missing from folders and boxes is nearly an impossible task that would require an inordinate amount of time. In many cases, cataloguing records, finding aids, and other lists are inadequate to such a task, anyway, assuming one had the will and leisure to undertake it. One can, however, check to ensure that high-value items are still present, assuming they are noted on the shelf list. If a collection contained, for example, a George Washington letter in box 5, folder 3, the appropriate box and folder could be examined specifically to see if the letter is still present. Other arbitrary samplings of known items can also be taken.

Two important caveats with both book and manuscript collections concern inventory techniques. First, under absolutely no circumstances should an electronic reader be pointed at a bar code and its reading taken for granted. In all instances the physical item should be removed from the shelf and examined to ensure that it is the proper item. Nothing could be simpler for a thief than to steal the proper volume and then replace it with an ersatz one containing a copy of the original bar code.[7] Second, shelf reading personnel in special collections projects do need some specialized instruction in their task. If an item is described in the shelf list as being bound in extra gilt morocco but the item on the shelf is bound in plain calf or cloth, an adequately trained shelf reader should immediately recognize the discrepancy. It would also be helpful if personnel could recognize that the genuine Abraham Lincoln letter has now somehow miraculously turned into a photocopy on old paper. In most cases, it does not pay in such projects to employ the lowest common denominator, such as ill-equipped but sincere freshmen, although they are by far the cheapest labor source. Adequate shelf reading does demand some training and expertise.

Shelf reading is in some ways an instructional and useful activity for various library staff, and each segment of the institution engaged in it will bring its own specialized viewpoints and depart from the process with greater appreciation for the library. If the process is conducted by public services staff, for example, they often come away with highly specialized knowledge of parts of the collection that can be achieved only by examining items individually. Conservation staff frequently can spot many problems that need to be corrected and can arrive at a general idea of the physical status of certain parts of the collection. Cataloguing staff often spot many technical errors that need correction. Manuscript staff usually acquire quite detailed knowledge of an institution's holdings by engaging in shelf reading. Such considerations might lead an institution to suggest that almost every full-time staff member spend at least some time during the year in shelf reading. At one institution, as an added security measure, shelf reading is deliberately assigned to people from outside the unit.[8]

A problematic area for shelf reading programs is a cataloguing backlog. Because materials in such an area are theoretically prone to disappearing without a trace, efforts should be made to insure their presence on the shelves. If done properly, the procedures for adding materials to a backlog should result in at least a brief list of items and their order. If no such list exists, it should be created for future use. If possible, manuscript boxes added to a backlog should be sealed so they cannot be casually opened. Access to such collections should be strictly limited to just a few people.[9] Under proper security conditions, items from backlogs can probably be delivered to researchers in the reading room safely.[10]

Other areas sometimes overlooked in shelf reading programs are staff offices, which should be routinely inventoried to ensure that all the books or other materials in them have either been properly checked out or that their shelving location is the office itself. Materials discovered in an office that have not been properly accounted for should be causes for concern.

Finally, any materials in an off-site storage facility should also be routinely inventoried. Supposedly the library will have an item by item count of all materials so transferred and can use it to conduct the shelf reading. In some cases, however, the only alterations made in cataloguing records might have been to indicate the new location, which presents a complication with a paper-based shelf list. In this instance, an electronic shelf list may prove quite useful if it can be sorted by location. By that method, a specialized list showing only the materials in storage could be generated. The design of some such facilities presents a set of physical challenges not usually encountered in regular stack areas, however.

Despite the fact that no shelf reading program is perfect or will discover all security problems, such a task is a vital part of a security program. In some cases, it can lay to rest concerns regarding theft by discovering misshelved items thought to be missing; it can also raise concerns when items that should be on the shelves are discovered to be absent. (It can also pleasantly reveal items the library did not even know it owned!) The process also has significant implications for public service activities. If nothing else, shelf reading is quite likely to discover misshelved items and restore them to their proper places, thereby improving retrieval rates for the reading room and increasing patron satisfaction. Numerous libraries fund continuous shelf reading projects for the general collections, and special collections should insist that its own collections be included in such processes.

Deaccessioning

The last audit trail a collection item will undergo is deaccessioning, although in many cases this is the most problematic journey an item will face and one that may leave questions perhaps for years. When special collections deaccessions an item, it relinquishes control over it and sends it into the market place in all likelihood. Material is rarely just discarded. In so doing, the library transfers any security or theft problems to those who eventually acquire the article. It is necessary, therefore, that the library keep accurate records of what it has deaccessioned since questions can arise decades later about an item's provenance, especially if the item has library markings remaining on it. At the very least, even in the absence of records, the library should, if possible, indelibly stamp the item as "Sold" or with some other wording that indicates it has been released. If the library cannot bring itself to do so,

as may be the case with a valuable manuscript, the item should be accompanied by written documentation concerning its deaccessioning. Because there is no known method to cancel marks in such a way that a thief could not also duplicate, the library has little choice but to accept its responsibility for record keeping so that it can answer questions if they arise later, which they well may. In no case should a library seek to efface or remove its marks because doing so would probably just raise the suspicion level about the item's origins. Permanently retained deaccession records are the best defense against problems that arise later for both the library and the purchaser. Those records coupled with accurate accession records are also a library's best avenue of authoritative information in case one of its items shows up for sale but has never been deaccessioned, but rather stolen. Access to those records, however, should be strictly controlled so that nobody can create false deaccessions, as has occasionally been done.[11] It goes without saying that dumping a large amount of undocumented material on the market, as has also sometimes been done, is a poor idea.

Stack Access

Stack access is the great undocumented, unaudited road to thefts and is a difficult problem. Although access has probably been restricted since, Burns Security Institute noted in its 1973 survey of public libraries, that of the 240 reporting libraries, 172 had special closed stacks for more valuable materials. Of those 172, all gave access to librarians; 78, to researchers; 51, to writers; 38, to curators; and 38, to others. Some gave access to patrons only under supervision, but others allowed entry to "any responsible library user" or anyone who could "prove a need."[12] In most cases, one can assume that patrons are not given stack access, although this is not always the norm and should not necessarily be the case. Willman Spawn, the great expert on early

American book bindings, was often been given access to special collection stacks because only he knew what was significant. Absolutely no catalogue records existed to identify materials of interest to his research, and only he had the expertise to identify what was significant to it. In his case there was little choice. Others have presented similar dilemmas.

In general, however, only certain staff have stack access. The problem with documenting that access is widespread. In most cases, once a staff member has received authorization to enter the stacks, that access is unfettered and limitless. If one is honest and forthright, one properly checks out materials, leaving the proper call slips in place. If one is not, one simply removes the materials without a trace, a process that is generally not a great challenge and can go undetected for years, even decades.[13] Preventing the problem of unauthorized removal of materials leaves the library with only a few choices; since the normal physical check-out system will be frustrated, other options need to be pursued. Most of those involve some type of physical security feature, such as guards, access control systems or CCTV, all of which can document and monitor activities in the stacks. RFID systems might also play a part in such monitoring, since they can track both the item and the person if both are tagged. In other words, if both the book itself and the staff member's ID card have RFID tags, the system will record that Jane removed from the stacks *Everything You Wanted to Know about Theft*. If she walks out the front door with it, the system may also capture that, but not necessarily, because she may have removed or shielded the RFID tag beforehand. Unfortunately, RFID systems have not proven useful except in the case of general collections books.

Apart from the actual physical monitoring of everybody who enters and leaves the stacks, which is done at few institutions, the library is left with the option of trust, which can be a poor choice, or other monitoring methods. CCTV, access control, and RFID tags all offer some measure of protection in this regard, although all are costly. Stack access remains the great, unaudited unknown in most institutions but is not a problem easily solved. When one considers the large number of people who actually have access to the stacks at all hours—people from staff members to workmen to maintenance staff to security guards—one can appreciate how porous the stacks may actually be.

Conclusion

Although no system will ever perfectly track every item in a rare book and manuscript library, numerous methods, as described above, can be employed to control collections and to help guard against thefts. Many thefts occur in reading rooms, but a distressing number also occur behind the scenes, so any audit system must account for both eventualities. The library needs to document as thoroughly as possible all movements of its materials and of the people who handle them. Any staff member discovered violating the library's auditing rules should at least be counseled on their importance, and repeated violations might call for more serious administrative actions. As with most security practices, audit procedures require the cooperation and understanding of all staff members to be effective and to work as intended.

NOTES

1. Miriam B. Kahn, *The Library Security and Safety Guide to Prevention, Planning, and Response* (Chicago: ALA, 2008), 33.

2. Records of gifts should be audited by a third party and should never be the responsibility of a single individual. At least two people should sign off on gift receipts to prevent insider thefts. Ton Cremers reports that Alexander Polman apparently received

gifts for his institution which he converted for his own use rather than adding them to the collections. "…and the Curator Did It," *Rogues Gallery: An Investigation into Art Theft*, AXA Art Conference, 1 November 2005, 3.

3.   Such records proved vital in the British Library's investigation of Farhad Hakimzadeh, who between 1998–2005 stole considerable material by razoring it out of books. Library staff had to examine over 800 books that had circulated to him. By the time the investigation began, some of the circulation records were a decade old.

4.   For a quick overview of the history of shelf reading projects—or rather the lack of them—see Alan Jay Lincoln, *Crime in the Library: A Study of Patterns, Impact, and Security* (New York & London: Bowker, 1984), 33–35. See also Ralph Munn, "The Problems of Theft and Mutilation," *Library Journal* 60 (1935): 589–592. The Blumberg Survey revealed that this unglamorous activity had an equally checkered history. See Appendix I, questions 6 & 7. Long gaps between shelf-reading projects only help insider thieves accomplish their goals and frustrate recovery efforts.

5.   Bruce A. Shuman, *Library Security and Safety Handbook: Prevention, Policies, and Procedures* (Chicago: American Library Association, 1999), 61.

6.   Some libraries engage in reading the most valuable parts of their collections on a regular basis to make sure they are inventoried at least annually. Others perform mini-surveys on a daily basis of certain selected titles. None of those procedures, however, are adequate substitutes for programs that read the entire collection on a regular basis.

7.   Photocopies of bar codes can read exactly like originals.

8.   Email to author, 16 January 2009.

9.   In some cases, sealing up cartons and boxes is difficult. Some large manuscript collections, particularly those of an archival nature, sometimes arrive at the repository in a confused state in all varieties of containers, from banana boxes to shoe boxes to entire file cabinets. They can be so large that processing them into some kind of order can take years. In such cases, at least access to the materials should be severely restricted.

10.   Delivering unprocessed materials to researchers is a contentious issue. If one does, special safeguards, such as increased surveillance, will be necessary to ensure the collection's integrity. It hardly seems right, however, for a library to take in a collection and then deny it to researchers for years merely because the institution has had no time or personnel to process it.

11.   Clive Driver, for example, created false deaccessioning records at the Rosenbach Library. See Douglas C. McGill, "Museum Says Ex-Chief Sold Off 30 Rare Letters," *New York Times* (22 April 1987). http://query.nytimes.com/gst/fullpage.html?res=9B0DE6DB1F3CF931A15757C0A961948260.

12.   *National Survey on Library Security* (Briarcliff Manor: Burns Security Institute, [1973]), 8.

13.   For numerous examples of such situations, see Cremers, *passim*.

Security and Technical Processing

Elaine Shiner

On two occasions I have been asked,—"Pray, Mr. Babbage, if you put into the machine wrong figures, will the right answers come out?" I am not able rightly to comprehend the kind of confusion of ideas that could provoke such a question.

~*Charles Babbage*

In his 1995 manual of archival security, Trinkaus-Randall described the holistic yet integral nature of archival security: "Security must be considered a basic archival function. At the very least, archivists should be able to envision a security aspect in all the basic tasks that they perform."[1] This point is equally apt for rare book and manuscript libraries. Although security may sometimes seem an overwhelming problem, good security can be achieved incrementally, by considering it as an aspect of every area of library management, from building design and maintenance, to reading room policies, to hiring procedures, to disaster preparedness. With each library function that contains built-in security provisions, the library as a whole becomes more secure. With this principle in mind, let us consider how the technical processing of rare materials can contribute to good library security.

The relationship of good record-keeping policies and habits to library security is so basic that it almost needs no explanation. To protect its collection, a library must know what it owns and must organize that material so that individual items in the collection can be quickly and reliably retrieved or otherwise accounted for. Accurate and secure records deter theft first of all by establishing the existence of library holdings; if a thief is able to destroy all records documenting a stolen book or manuscript, he or she stands a good chance of com-mitting the perfect crime.[2] Records also deter theft by recording each item's location, which prevents library materials from becoming lost. A library in which items from the collection are often misplaced is not a secure library. Good records are also important after a theft has occurred. They can help in estimating the value of a stolen item and may be the only means of establishing ownership of a recovered book or manuscript.

Accession Records

Accession records are brief records of ownership created upon acquisition of an item. They should contain at least an accession number, the author and/or title of the new accession, its date of publication, the initials of the accessioning staff member, and the date. The chief function of an accession record is to document the library's ownership of a particular piece as soon as it enters the library. If the new accession is to be added to a cataloguing backlog, then the accession record may contain additional information, especially any copy-specific information that could aid in uniquely identifying the piece or add to its value. Another important function of accession records is to provide each physical piece in the library's collection with it own unique control number. For example, every volume of a multi-volume work should have its own accession number and every copy of the same edition/issue of a work should have its own accession number. The number should immediately be recorded indelibly on the item. When individual accession numbers are not used, confusion can arise all too easily over how many copies an item a library actually owns, whether the library really owns all the volumes of a set, whether one copy of a work has been de-accessioned, which copy of a work has been de-accessioned, etc. Whenever a rare book and manuscript library cannot be sure of what it owns, a serious security problem exists. (See Fig. 12.1.)

Because accession records are often ephemeral in nature and contain only skeletal information, they should be arranged and recorded so that no one person can ever have access to every instance of the record. Duplicate, updated copies should be kept in various locations to which only a few people have access at any one time. For example, keeping the only copy of accession records on a PC is a dangerous practice. It would be a simple matter for someone to go into record #477665, for example, and exchange the library's copy of Dickens's *Dombey and Son* for a copy of *Martha Stuart at Home* by doing nothing more than changing the record's bibliographical information and then shelving the substitute with the same accession number

after removing the Dickens novel. To thwart such scenarios, duplicate copies of the records should be kept in multiple secure locations. To this day, no more secure accession record has ever been created than that maintained in a clumsy, hand-written or typed accession book, which is extremely hard to alter without leaving any evidence and is easily duplicated.

Temporary Cataloguing

Temporary cataloguing has been used by rare book and manuscript libraries to process books going into a cataloguing backlog. Temporary cataloguing records contain more information than accession records (for instance, authoritative author, title, place, publisher, and date), but much less than full cataloguing records. Temporary cataloguing can be used as an opportunity to collate a new book, documenting its completeness. If a book is discovered to be imperfect, it can be easily returned at the time of sale, but it can be returned only with difficulty, if at all, three or four years later. Temporary cataloguing can be a controversial function. Who is responsible for ensuring that a new accession is "collated and perfect"—the librarian who bought the book or a "temporary cataloguer" in the catalogue department? Unfortunately, this is becoming a moot question. Collection development or acquisitions librarians often have so many new books arriving that collating them is out of the question. Increasingly in rare book catalogue departments even "full-level" cataloguers do not provide signature statements, and may not even provide detailed recordings of foliation/pagination and illustrative matter. In these libraries, librarians never know when they have bought an imperfect copy. The practice of temporary cataloguing may be forsaken in favor of minimal-level or "core" cataloguing, which are considered final steps in processing and may be accomplished much more quickly than full-level

Figure 12.1

> **Johnson, Tom**
> My Life on the Run. NY: Presspress, 1916
> 325 pp., frontis
> Orig green cloth, headcap snagged
> Author's copy with his signature & ink doodle on front pastedown
> Adams, Guns 1418
> Anyman's Bookstore, 2/11/2010 $69.00
> Date created: 6/12/2010
>
> **0211868**

Sample Accession Record

cataloguing. Those two options will be discussed more fully under "Elimination of Backlogs."

Cataloguing

Cataloguers of rare books and manuscripts should strive to record as detailed a description as possible for each item in their collections. Detailed cataloguing records deter theft by documenting the existence in a collection of a unique holding and by recording information that attests to the value of that holding.[3] Knowledge about the value of an item is extremely important as a deterrent to theft, since items known to be extremely valuable can be more securely stored and protected. When a rare books and manuscripts library is ignorant of the value of particular items in its collection, then those items are at risk. Book and manuscript thieves are often extremely clever and well-educated, and, if they are stealing for profit, they are probably well aware of what makes a book or manuscript valuable. In addition to deterring theft, detailed cataloguing records aid in the recovery of stolen materials which have not been marked for ownership by their institutions or whose ownership marks are invisible, inconspicuous, or, even worse, removed.[4]

Nevertheless, cataloguers of all stripes are under pressure to provide "more product, less process."[5] A Library of Congress working group in its discussion on treating rare materials, while not completely retreating from full cataloguing, recommends considering "options for streamlined cataloging" of them.[6] The security danger, of course, is that "streamlined" cataloguing will not be an option but will instead become the standard. The Association of Research Libraries is even more blunt in its statement that full cataloguing needs to be reined in because of access concerns. Although throwing a bone to full cataloguing, the report recommends: "As the managers of special collections repositories address the difficult task of setting priorities, they

need to bear in mind the maxim that some access is better than none and the lack of any online description virtually amounts to no access. They should save perfection in descriptive practices for the most significant material or for that which cannot be described usefully at all without explicit detail. There is no excuse for books not to be described online. Inexpensive processes relying on vendors for sketchy or imperfect metadata is [sic] preferable to the alternative of not exposing the collection to use at all. Imperfect guides should be converted to digital with the least revision possible, focusing on data structure rather than upgrading the descriptive content as a first priority."[7] From a security point of view, "sketchy or imperfect metadata" is the kiss of death, as has been repeatedly demonstrated.

Rare book and manuscript collections should, whenever possible, be catalogued with reference to commonly accepted practices of description for early books and manuscripts. There are of course many good reasons to take the trouble to distinguish between editions, issues, and states of a work, to record signature statements and canceled leaves, to note the presence or absence of errata, booksellers' advertisements, etc., but for security purposes, such information serves to define a unique holding and document its value. For instance, the first issue of a work may be relatively common, while the third may be very rare, and therefore much more valuable. Some issues of a work may be considered incomplete without the bookseller's advertisements. In almost all cases, a perfect copy is more valuable than an incomplete or damaged copy.

For books, it is particularly important to record the number of plates and maps and to describe important illustrative matter. Thieves are particularly interested in plates and maps, which can be surreptitiously removed from books and sold separately. Ideally, plates should be inspected by library staff before and after each use of a book.

However, this is all but impossible in practice, since some books have tens or hundreds of plates. However, if a library discovers that a known thief has used its collection, then the items the thief looked at can be checked against the cataloguing record. If the number of plates has been recorded, it will be easy to discover if any are missing, although, discouragingly, the library might not be able to determine exactly which ones. Too often the situation is similar to the one reported by the Royal Library at the Hague after the discovery of a theft there: "One of the problems in checking all the atlases and books for missing maps was the fact that most of these items have composite descriptions, so it was impossible to decide whether a given map had been missing all along (for instance, had been stolen in the past) or not."[8]

Cataloguing records of rare books and manuscripts should also include any copy-specific information that could uniquely identify an item or affect its value. Such information may include imperfections, binding information, bookplates, former owners' signatures and annotations, presentation inscriptions, and descriptions of papers or objects inserted in or otherwise associated with an item. A precise level of detail is desirable for many reasons, not the least of which is that the library cannot determine properly if an item has been damaged without such information. If, for example, it is noticed upon a book's return that a signature seems to have been cut from the title page, it is vital for the library to know that the signature was there. Failure to record precisely what is in an item can lead to unfortunate situations, such as accusing a perfectly innocent patron of theft when the item suspected to be missing was already absent when the book or manuscript folder was given to the patron in the first place.

Manuscripts present their own set of problems often not inherent in book cataloguing. Single items might well be catalogued at the piece level, as might documents of high value or research interest. The usual fate of most manuscripts, however, is to be processed as a collection with varying degrees of documentation about what the collection actually contains. Smaller collections might be fortunate enough to have a description of every item in it contained in a finding list or inventory. Even the thoroughness of such lists will vary widely, however, depending on the resources a library has at its disposal. Some lists might say, for example, that a folder contains twenty items of correspondence from Joe Schmoe dated between 23 June 1810 and 14 November 1816. A more detailed list might give the correspondents' names and a brief note about contents. An even more detailed list might for each item give the number of pages or leaves, physical characteristics (e.g., torn with loss, stained, etc.), and size, such as might be found in a detailed cataloguing record for a single piece. Rarely, however, will descriptions of large collections rise to the last standard. Although such paucity of description presents an enormous problem in the case of theft, the situation is probably not going to change because of economic factors. Few institutions can actually afford to describe adequately at the piece level the 100,000-item collection of Congressperson Longterm, although it may contain many commercially valuable items, such as signatures from prominent individuals.[9] As a consequence and in recognition of such dangers, most institutions rely on extra vigilance when such collections are used rather than on increased cataloguing detail, the former being the more affordable alternative.

Collections containing separate items such as plates, maps, ephemera, or individual medieval manuscript leaves also present their own set of concerns, apart from those that are found as parts of printed books or codexes, practically none of which are catalogued at the piece level.[10] In the case of separates, however, the library has little choice but to catalogue the individual item or to lump them into a collection and create a collection-level record similar to that created for a manuscript collection. Again, in institutions with large collections of such items, decisions must often be made about how detailed the records will be. Highly valuable items will possibly receive individual treatment at some level. In some fortunate cases, all items are described at that level, but that situation usually appertains in libraries that have a limited collecting scope that concentrates on, for example, one geographical area or one particular cartographer or print maker. Libraries that cast wider nets have bigger problems and greater cataloguing challenges. Ideally, each individual piece would be adequately catalogued so that it could later be identified if it were stolen. Such is rarely the case, however. Many descriptions are old and minimal, so that a library can indeed assert that its copy is missing but cannot prove with certainty that a recovered copy is its own. In the absence of modern, full-level cataloguing records for such items, libraries might wish to consider a visible and secret marking program, so that even if a cataloguing record will not establish provenance, perhaps the marks will. This is also a situation where digitization might be useful as a recovery tool.

Elimination of Backlogs

It is an unfortunate fact that many rare book and manuscript collections have for decades had more money available for acquiring materials than for processing them. As one special collections administrator observed about her university, "Though we have long been known for our collection-building prowess, we have not, over the years, expended equal effort on cataloguing and processing. As a consequence, we have, like many other research institutions, a large hidden collections problem."[11] In addition, many institutions have been the recipients of large donations of still unprocessed collections. While some institutions are now making processing money a condition for accepting donations, it is a relatively recent development and not always a successful ploy.[12] In some institutions, the size of unprocessed collections has reached crisis proportions. The elimination of cataloguing backlogs is an essential step in insuring adequate security for rare book and manuscript collections. Even if a library cannot eliminate its backlog entirely, it should reduce it as much as possible, make its continuing reduction a priority, and try to ensure that it does not grow any larger.[13] At the least, it should make efforts to document it.

One obvious strategy for eliminating cataloguing backlogs in rare book and manuscript collections is to hire and train more rare books and manuscripts cataloguers. Although the difficulties inherent in this approach are well known, cataloguers and heads of technical services in rare book and manuscript collections must attempt to convince their supervisors and higher-level administrators of the critical need for more cataloguers and of the critical connection between cataloguing and collection security (not to mention access), a position that should also be adopted by the Library Security Officer. Even if more rare books and manuscripts cataloguers are hired and trained in the coming decades, however, cataloguers are sure to be under pressure to provide abbreviated cataloguing records quickly and in large numbers. There is an inherent tension in that situation. Abbreviated cataloguing records are much less satisfactory for security purposes and for all the other purposes they serve than are full, detailed records. It is also undeniable, however, that the worst situation is to have no cataloguing at all.[14]

Some rare books and manuscripts libraries are turning to minimal-level or core-level cataloguing to eliminate their backlogs. The Bibliographic Standards Committee of the Rare Books and Manuscripts Section of ACRL has defined a Core Record Standard for Rare Books, which is compatible with DCRB rules.[15] Some rare book collections have made DCRB Core the default standard for all their rare book cataloguing. Although this standard is only minimally acceptable, from a security point of view, it is much better than nothing.

Shelf Lists: Electronic versus Paper Records

A shelf list is a list of a library's holdings in call number or shelfmark order. The shelf list has traditionally been maintained as a card file, often located in the cataloguing department and sometimes copiously annotated by cataloguers and curators. Rare books and manuscripts libraries have traditionally taken care to keep their shelf list catalogues in a secure location to minimize the possibility of tampering and/or the destruction of records. The current recommendation is the following:

> Maintain a shelf list, preferably in paper form for special collections, in a secure area of the library. If the shelf list is electronic, it should be secure from tampering and a backup should be stored off-site. Since the shelf list indicates precisely where each item should be located, and because it contains copy-specific information about special collections materials, its maintenance and security are vital for detecting and recovering thefts.[16]

During the past few decades, as many rare books and manuscripts libraries' holdings have been converted to electronic form and made accessible via OPACs, and more recently, as integrated library system (ILS) vendors have perfected their filing software to allow acceptable shelf listing, many

rare books and manuscripts librarians have come under increasing pressure to close, and in some cases to discard, their paper shelf lists. Shuman, however, points out the critical role of a shelflist in a good security program: "Hand in hand with surveillance goes the shelflist catalog, which many libraries either poorly maintain or have completely abandoned."[17]

In ideal situations, in which electronic records are deemed "secure from tampering" and "duplicated in a backup tape stored off-site," rare book librarians might discard their paper shelf lists with a minimum of anxiety. However, it is doubtful that such an ideal situation exists today for many rare book/manuscript collections.[18]

In the first place, many retrospective conversion projects involving rare books or manuscripts have yielded less than satisfactory results. Collections have often not been fully converted, and the re-con records that do exist may not faithfully represent the data in the card files. In some cases, rare book cataloguing that meticulously recorded pagination and specified edition, issue, or state, has simply been lost through electronic conversion. At the same time, local information from other libraries was often erroneously introduced into many records. Wing or STC numbers, for example, in converted records are sometimes not reliable.[19] In any situation in which converted records fail to faithfully represent the original cataloguing or contain large amounts of false information introduced during conversion, discarding the original cataloguing is simple folly. In such cases, there is little hope that the electronic records will ever be corrected, and there will be no accurate records to check them against if the originals are discarded. The recent merger of OCLC and RLIN has also introduced further issues of quality control.

A second area of concern is the security of electronic records. Although most integrated library systems now have security provisions, it is hard to know whether these measures are adequate for rare book and manuscript collections. Although systems have varying levels of "permissions" to protect catalogue records from deletion by lower-level staff members, it is harder to protect records from tampering. It may be relatively easy, for instance, for someone to purge all information about a second copy. Undoubtedly backups are made of the database, and deletions, and possibly also other changes to records, are tracked through account numbers. But it is often difficult for special collections cataloguing staff to discover pertinent information, such as how long the back-ups are kept and whether the back-ups are searchable in a way that is relevant to their security needs. It can be hard to get LIS staff to talk about system back-ups and security measures. Rare book librarians and LIS staff often simply do not speak the same language, and LIS staff may be wary of talking about security issues to people outside their department. One is thus often faced with a Catch-22, in which security information cannot be divulged because to do so would compromise security.[20]

In their 1995 article[21] Henry Raine and Laura Stalker described a situation in which rare book cataloguers felt increasingly deprived of control over the data they created and isolated from the administrators and computer systems staff who administered and maintained the OPAC. Although there has been some improvement in the display and indexing of rare books and special collections cataloguing records, the gulf in communication probably remains. This gulf may be minimal or non-existent in small, independent rare books and manuscripts libraries that completely control their own on-line systems, but it can be a significant issue for any rare book or manuscript collection that is a department or branch library in a larger entity. The forces driving the evolution of large library cata-

logues may be creating an increasingly unfriendly environment for the standards and values of rare book and manuscript cataloguing. Technical services administrators are under great (and increasing) pressure to control an exploding universe of digital products, with static or decreasing budgets. Cataloguing staff are spread thin, and, of necessity, cataloguing is becoming more machine-driven. On-line catalogues may become bigger in the future, for example, if all state university branch library catalogues merge into a single entity. Merging library catalogues implies merging records and the possibility of loss of information, as has happened with some retrospective conversions. Thus, even rare book cataloguing records created on-line, post-conversion, by a rare book department or branch library could be obliterated through a catalogue merger. In such mega-catalogues, the number of people having the power to alter and delete cataloguing records would be large, and an even larger number of people might gain illicit access to the machines of these empowered staff members.

Finally, hacking is also a possibility. All on-line library systems, especially if Internet-based, are vulnerable to hacking. Again, rare book librarians are usually not in a position to evaluate the seriousness of this threat or to take any role in protecting the on-line system against it. At the very least, any electronic shelf list should be stored on a computer with no Internet connection.

It is clear that although library administrators and LIS departments are aware of data security issues relating to electronic records and are working on them, problems remain. At the same time, on-line library catalogues continue to evolve rapidly in response not only to technological change but also to economic pressures and society's expectation of increasing access. In a technical environment of so much change and uncertainty, it makes sense for rare books and manuscripts librarians to fight to retain control of their cataloguing data through the simple act of ordering shelf list cards as a base line defense against theft or vandalism. Rare books and manuscripts libraries do not contain only "information"; their holdings are also museum objects, some of which have been preserved already for centuries, and are sometimes of immense value. In spite of the promise of increased access to rare collections through digital facsimiles, the objects themselves are likely to become more valuable in the future, not less. The records documenting these objects, our cultural inheritance, also deserve special protection. Administrators of independent rare books and manuscripts libraries with on-line catalogues of high accuracy and completeness, who completely control their own databases, have highly knowledgeable technical services and computer staff, and have high confidence in the ability of their libraries to maintain and protect their electronic records in the future, might consider tossing out their paper shelf lists. But such libraries, if they ex-

ist (and there might be a few), would probably be the last to do so.[22]

Conclusion

Despite the tangled issues presented by cataloguing and bibliographical control, they are not insoluble and not necessarily incompatible with good security practices that can protect a library from theft and assist in recovery if a theft takes place. As alluring as volume and expediency may be, they should be carefully weighed against the institution's need to adequately document its materials and their precise nature. Failure to do so merely opens the library to severe recovery problems if a theft does occur and actually makes thefts easier, especially those of an insider nature. The failure may even allow thefts to go totally undetected or, if suspected, unprovable. Cataloguing documentation is a baseline measure of a library's wealth and health. As such, it should be as accurate and complete as possible.

NOTES

1. Gregor Trinkaus-Randall, *Protecting your Collections: A Manual of Archival Security* (Chicago: Society of American Archivists, 1995).

2. Such a procedure is a favored method in some quarters. As reported by Nicholas Basbanes, *A Gentle Madness: Bibliophiles, Bibliomanes, and the Eternal Passion for Books* (New York: Holt, 1995), curator Robert M. Willingham "not only took valuable items from the rare-book room he supervised but removed, and apparently destroyed, university records that documented their accession" (488).

3. Mary Breighner, William Payton, and Jeanne M. Drewes, *Risk and Insurance Management Manual for Libraries* (Chicago: American Library Association, 2005) argue, "The business of the library is making information available and the key to the business is the online catalog" (40). They further argue that the catalog plays numerous important roles in the library and conclude, "For these reasons, preventing loss of the online catalog is essential" and recommend frequent off-site backups (p. 40).

4. Smiley's prosecutor, Chris Schmeisser, expressed the government's fear that the poor state of library map cataloguing could be used in Smiley's defense. In April Carlucci, "Library Security for Maps: Report on the Program Sponsored by the Map and Geography Round Table of the American Library Association, Held in Washington DC on Sunday, 24 June 2007," *Cartographiti: The Newsletter of the Map Curators' Group of the British Cartographic Society* 79 (Summer 2007): 11–16

5. Mark A. Greene and Dennis Meissner, "More Product, Less Process: Revamping Traditional Archival Processing," *American Archivist* 68 (2005): 208–63.

6. Library of Congress Working Group on the Future of Bibliographic Control, *On the Record* (Washington: Library of Congress, 2008), p. 23. http://www.loc.gov/bibliographic-future/news/lcwg-ontherecord-jan08-final.pdf. The Library of Congress recommendations clearly rested largely on Barbara M. Jones, comp., "Hidden Collections, Scholarly Barriers: Creating Access to Unprocessed Special Collections Materials in North America's Research Libraries," (Association of Research Libraries,

2003). http://www.arl.org/bm~doc/hiddencollswhitepaperjun6.pdf. Jones clearly recognized the tension between access and security (8–9).

7. Association of Research Libraries, *Special Collections in ARL Libraries: A Discussion Report from the ARL Working Group on Special Collections* (Washington: ARL, 2009) 18. http://www.arl.org/bm~doc/scwg-report.pdf.

8. Els Van Eijck Van Heslinga, "Catch as Catch Can," *Liber Quarterly*, 12 (2002): 316. Travis McDade, *The Book Thief: The True Crimes of Daniel Spiegelman* (Westport: Prager, 2006), reports that Columbia, because it failed to completely catalogue an extra-illustrated volume, would never recognize what had been razored from it: "'This is France,' Ashton said, 'The title page was left in here and more maps are here, but I wanted to bring it to illustrate a particular point. These are extra-illustrated volumes. Whether it was Dr. Anderson or someone else, in the 18th century they inserted their own maps in here. These maps do not appear on any index. We can never know exactly what maps were in there. There would have been no reason for us to list them, catalog these separately because they were part of the volume, but we have places where there are stubs, and we know that we have lost not only the maps themselves, but the history of whoever put together this composite atlas, what they put them in, when they put them in'" (p. 145). The same problems bedeviled victim libraries trying to deal with Smiley's thefts, some of which have responded with new programs to more fully describe maps in their books. The 2002 Wales seminar, "Responding to Theft," also noted the importance of accurate cataloguing records in this regard. See Chris Fleet, "Report of the 'Responding to Theft' Seminar, Held at the National Library of Wales on 25 April 2002" http://www.maphistory.info/aberseminar.html.

9. One institution, for example, received a former senator's papers that finally resolved themselves after several years of processing from 1200 received boxes into about 800 cartons containing an estimated 1.25 million items. Processing such a collection at the piece level is obviously impossible for most institutions.

10. For problems and issues that might arise, for example, when fully cataloguing medieval manuscripts, see "Marc Cataloguing for Medieval Manuscripts," *RBML* special issue, ed. Hope Mayo, 6 (1991), and Hope Mayo, "Standards for Description, Indexing and Retrieval in Computerized Catalogs of Medieval Manuscripts," in *The Use of Computers in Cataloging Medieval and Renaissance Manuscripts*, ed. Menso Folkerts and Andreas Kuhne, Algorismus, 4 (Munich, 1990), 19–56. Ephemera present their own set of problems, as discussed in *Descriptive Cataloging of 19th-Century Imprints for Special Collections*, RBML special issue, ed. Stephen J. Zeitz, 7 (1992).

11. Victoria Steele, "Exposing Hidden Collections: The UCLA Experience," *College & Research Libraries News*, 69 (June 2008): 316–317, 331. She goes on to described UCLA's efforts to reduce their backlogs.

12. One library director, when told by the University Librarian to ensure that a gift came with money to process the collection, was overheard to reply, "Oh, sure!" Some donors seem cold to that line of reasoning, apparently thinking that if they have gone to trouble to donate the collection, the institution should be able to catalogue it without further support. Others seem sympathetic and try to help. An informal survey taken in August, 2007, among Exlibris and the Archives list membership, revealed that the respondents had had at best only mixed success in persuading donors to financially support processing. One institution reported that it no longer accepted gifts unless processing money was included. In some cases, donors make matters worse by offering acquisition funds instead of processing monies, thereby practically ensuring that the backlog will continue to grow. (Some public responses to the survey are found in the lists' archives for 30 July–3 August, 2007.) Jones addresses the thorny problem of backlogs, noting that nobody even knows how extensive the problem really is, and proposes strategies for dealing with them (10–12). As she points out, "an unprocessed or under processed collection poses a greater security risk…" (11).

13. In April, 1991, Amherst, MA, police interviewed a college employee who had apparently taken materials from Amherst College's Frost Library's uncatalogued backlog (*Daily Hampshire Gazette*, 25 April 1991). He had an accomplice, Laurence Feldman, at another library who helped sell the materials (*Library Journal*, 15 May 1992). Lawrence S. Thompson, *Bibliokleptomania* (Berkeley: Peacock, 1968), 19–20, recounts the story of Joseph Urdich, who stole materials from a University of Graz backlog, going so far to cover his tracks by "falsifying accession records, substituting uncatalogued books for catalogued ones and giving them shelf marks of older ones…" (19). The only reason he was caught was that his bank became suspicious of his large deposits.

14. Yale's Beinecke Library, for example, recently opened a new manuscript processing facility to reduce its backlog. The facility includes specially designed, flexible space for processing large collections. Additional staff were hired to accelerate cataloguing. See Ellen Doon, "Beinecke Library's New Processing Facility," *Manuscript Repositories Newsletter* (Summer 2007) http://www.archivists.org/saagroups/mss/summer2007.asp

15. The core record for rare books is available on-line at: http://www.loc.gov/catdir/pcc/bibco/coredcrb.html. Other core records descriptors exist for cartographic materials, music, sound recordings, and electronic records.

16. Association of College & Research Libraries, *Guidelines concerning Thefts in Libraries* (Chicago: ACRL, 2009),.

17. Bruce A. Shuman, *Library Security and Safety Handbook: Prevention, Policies, and Procedures* (Chicago: American Library Association, 1999), 61.

18. JSTOR provides a model of a heavily redundant back-up system: "JSTOR also takes very seriously its commitment to preserving the digital copies of the journal content in the archive. To provide protection against loss, we have established redundant data centers, two in the U.S. and one in the U.K. Each one has at least one complete and fully functional copy of the entire archive. The image files are backed up on CD-ROM and on tape. Rotating copies of these tapes are kept at various locations, including an off-site storage facility at OCLC." http://www.jstor.org/about/archive.html

19. In an ironic twist, it is possible that a library may have been able to preserve at least its ownership claim to an item by participation in the ESTC, which records each copy for which it received a report. Although ESTC records are useless for determining the condition or completeness of a particular library's copy, the database does provide fairly concrete evidence of ownership. One library that participated in the project reported an alarming number of missing items, which led it to take further steps to document its collection.

20. Joan Mann, "IT Education's Failure to Deliver Successful Information Systems: Now Is the Time to Address the IT-User Gap," *Journal of Information Technology Education*, 1: 4 (2002): 253–267, extensively analyzes the growing gap between end IT users and those who are specifically educated in the technology. She remarks that the situation "has become such a problem that many organizations are taking matters into their own hands by creating new hybrid positions to bridge the gap" (253). http://jite.org/documents/Vol1/v1n4p253-267.pdf

21. Laura Stalker & Henry Raine, "Rare Book Records in Online Systems," *Rare Books and Manuscripts Librarianship* 11 (1996): 116.

22. William H. Wisner, *Whither the Postmodern Library? Libraries, Technology, and Education in the Information Age* (Jefferson & London: McFarland, 2000), seriously questions the rush into the electronic age: "That momentous technological change will be allowed by world events to continue uninterrupted is an expectation now so rooted in the mind of the common man—not to mention librarians themselves—that these expectations have by degrees been strangely reinscribed as actual duties to fulfill. It is this unexamined and anti-historical conviction which has recently led librarianship down the primrose path of folly: the card catalog, to take but the most stellar example, was discarded by librarians overnight without a shred of discernable regret, remorse, seemliness or—most striking of all—consciousness of what such a sudden loss might mean either to the deep structures of the profession, their historical value, or the impact of such a change on our users…" (12–13). Andrea V. Grimes, "Card Catalogs: Adaptive Reuse Suggestions," Exlibris-L electronic discussion list, 12 August 2009, notes that the San Francisco Public Library kept both its public catalogue and its shelf list.

Marking Rare Book And Manuscript Materials

Everett C. Wilkie, Jr.

> The rarer they are, the less likely they are to mark them.
> ~*William A. Moffett*

Similar to surgery, marking rare book and manuscript materials is planned mutilation for a good cause. The benefits of legibly and clearly marking materials with ownership stamps in rare book and manuscript libraries are well known and appreciated, and need no extended discussion here.[1] Not only can they deter theft, but they can also be instrumental in recovering stolen materials. For those reasons, libraries and individuals have used them for centuries to protect their property. Recent developments in technology and other fields, however, have given libraries numerous marking options beyond what they traditionally had. Recent large-scale thefts, especially of maps, have caused libraries to again examine what they mark and how they mark. In any case, marks will be one of the first lines of recourse if a library has to recover stolen materials. As Bahr remarked in 1979, "Libraries failing to mark valuable materials have paid heavily for this omission."[2] Sadly, Strassberg has been proven wrong in his assertion that "unique treasures are seldom likely to be the game of the professional thief unless the end is 'kidnapping' for ransom" and should not therefore be "sullied" by marks.[3] Experience has proven all too readily that prized treasures are indeed stolen and that unique treasures unsullied by property stamps are instead sullied by razor blades.[4]

Highly Visible Marks

Numerous types of such marks have been applied historically. The most common is the ink stamp. Other types include embossed or perforated stamps, now rarely used. Among historic examples of marks that are no longer used are the marca de fuego and other types of brands, often found on materials of Central and South American derivation.[5] Another type of institutional mark historically encountered but now rarely used is a simple ink manuscript statement of ownership.[6] To increase the effectiveness of such marks, sometimes they are applied multiple times at various places in books, although it is rare to see multiple visible stamps on such items as individual manuscripts, plates, or maps (see fig 13.1). Some libraries put their logos on their bindings. Although doing so would reduce the chances that the entire book would be stolen, it would do little to reduce instances of razoring out plates and maps. As the twentieth century opened, it appears that most libraries decided that a single mark was sufficient, no matter what type was used.[7]

Because they are so highly visible and meant to be deterrents, all such marks are easily discovered by a thief and can be removed with various degrees of success. Embossed marks, for example, can be relaxed and rolled flat.[8] Ink marks can be abraded to the point of illegibility or cut out; some can be dissolved to the point that they are meaningless. Even

Figure 13.1

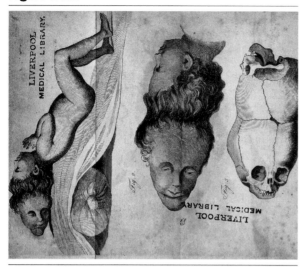

Aggressively stamped plate (Courtesy Bloomsbury Auctions)

marks can be successfully removed with little or no damage. Practically everyone is familiar with the title page that has the upper right corner excised, presumably to remove a previous owner's name.[9] Although the Library of Congress has developed a very secure ink supposedly impervious to being dissolved, any mark applied with it can still be either abraded or excised; the ink, as with ink in general, is not especially suitable for marking some materials, such as those printed on clay-loaded papers or materials not made of paper.[10]

Two commonly encountered problems with ink stamps and embossed stamps are that too few of them are applied and that they are too small. Many libraries, apparently squeamish at the thought of visibly marking materials in the first place, apply only one mark and that mark tends to be fairly small. To present a potential thief with serious problems in removing marks, libraries should mark such things as plates and maps more than once and should use relatively large marks. Certainly no circular mark applied to the verso of a plate or map should be smaller than a U.S. half dollar. Some more aggressive institutions actually put embossed marks in the image or text areas of items, rendering them almost impossible to remove

perforation stamps can be excised. Removing such marks, however, almost always leaves fairly visible evidence that they were there, even if they are no longer legible or present (see figs 13.2, 13.3 and 13.4). Although evidence of removal of such stamps and marks would seem to be cause for suspicion, such is not always the case. Successive owners often have good reasons, not necessarily nefarious, for removing marks. Numerous booksellers over the years, for example, have believed that material, unless the provenance is distinguished, is worth more if the

Figure 13.2

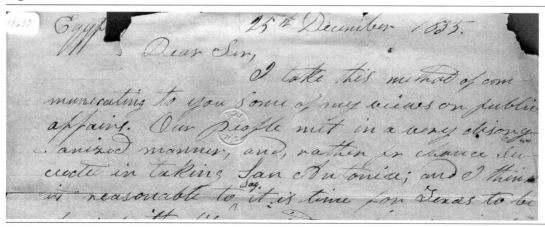

Manuscript with Embossed Stamp Intact (Courtesy Texas State Library and Archives Commission)

Figure 13.3

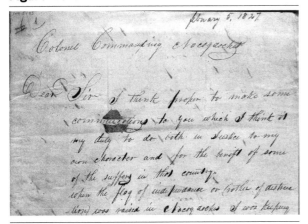

Recovered Manuscript with Embossed Stamp Mutilated
(Courtesy Texas State Library and Archives Commission)

without significantly damaging the piece, thereby reducing its commercial value or raising suspicions about its origin.

A third problem with visible marks is that they are often placed where they can be removed in such a way that little or no evidence is left. Such is the case with marks that are applied in the blank margins of maps or the flyleaves of books, which are relatively simple to remove by trimming without

leaving any obvious evidence. When visible marks are applied, they should be placed so that they cannot be so easily removed.

Despite whatever problems visible marks may present, they should be used as the first line of defense and recovery.[11]

Nearly Invisible Marks

Supplementing visible marks with secret marks is a valid way to protect materials and to increase one's chances of recovering them if they are stolen. Numerous institutions are loath to visibly mark materials because of conservation and aesthetic concerns, reasoning, apparently, that it is preferable to have an unmarked map stolen than it is to have a marked map still in situ protected by a highly visible stamp. The chief problem with secret marks is that they cannot be readily detected by the thief, a bookseller, law enforcement, or another buyer of the material. Thus, they are useful only if the material can be gotten in hand later and examined by the original owner; they have little deterrent value. For that reason, it is recommended that secret

Figure 13.4

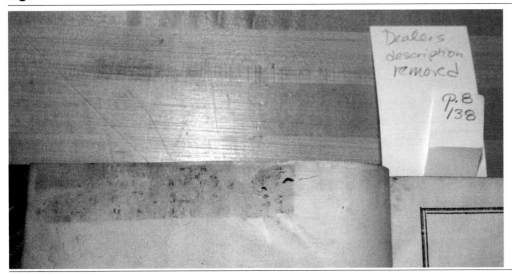

Harry Ransom Humanities Research Center Material with Identifying Evidence Removed.
(Courtesy Pete Smith, Harry Ransom Center)

marks never be used as the only marking method.[12] Yet, all institutions, whether they employ a visible marking program or not, should use some type of secret marking. Just one such mark is strong proof that an item is in fact the institution's property, and modern technology ensures that whatever mark is applied is unique to the institution. Because many of these systems are relatively inexpensive and simple to use, an institution can use more than one on an item to increase chances of recovery.

A general caveat: Nearly invisible marks are so small that the library needs to keep close track of precisely where they are placed on items. Although sometimes not truly invisible, the marks are arcane enough that they are quite difficult to discover if the library does not have accurate records of where they were applied.

Physical Marking Systems

Several methods are currently available for secretly marking materials with unique physical marks.

Meaningless Marks

One type of secret mark is to place a pencil underlining on, say, page 20 of every book, or to place a pin prick on page 3. An alert thief can spot such mark-

Figure 13.5

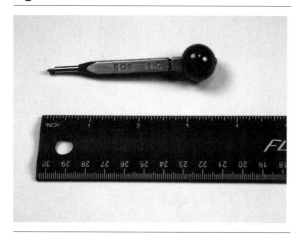

Microtrace Embosser (Used by permission)

ing patterns, and for the most part they are easily defeated once detected. Also, because they are so generic they are rarely of any real use in establishing ownership. A thief could argue, for example, that s/he applied that mark and could even duplicate it in materials stolen from other libraries, thereby undermining its integrity.

Microembosser

A microembosser, sold as Trace Mark©, is a small, hand-held instrument that applies a virtually invisible blind-embossed ownership mark to materials. The lettering comes in four sizes—.010"/.25mm; .012"/.30mm; .016"/.40mm; .018"/.45mm—and the instrument has a capacity of eighteen characters, including spaces (see fig 13.5) . Any of the sizes are appropriate for use on all library materials, although the smallest size possible should be employed. Among a micro-embosser's advantages are that it requires little special training to use, will never wear out, is completely affordable, can be used on even the smallest materials (e. g., miniature books and postage stamps), causes no real damage to materials, can mark practically anything (including metal or wood), and is virtually undetectable with the naked eye. Under magnification, the lettering is easily read, however, but the application should be checked to be sure it is legible. The company registers a library's mark and never issues the same combination of letters to anybody else, so the mark is demonstrably unique, an important issue in recovering stolen materials.

Its chief disadvantage is that if it is discovered it can be partially relaxed by water and a roller on paper-based materials.[13] This technology is in use in various rare book libraries in the United States, and none report any problems with it.

For more description of this technique, see: http://www.microstampusa.com/

Figure 13.6

Individual Microtaggants (Courtesy Microtrace, LLC) Microtaggant® is a Trademark of Microtrace, LLC

Microtaggants

Microtaggants© are inert, plastic club sandwiches that use a scheme of alternating colored layers to provide unique particles for every customer. They are available in sizes as small as 20 microns (i.e., 20 millionths of a meter), a size totally invisible to the naked eye, and millions of combinations are possible (see fig 13.6). When a library orders them, the pattern it receives is unique, registered in the company's database, and is never issued to anyone else. Once applied to materials, the result looks like perhaps a tiny smudge if they are applied in great quantity, but if applied in proper quantity are invisible. Among the advantages of this technology are that it requires no special training to implement, is relatively cheap, can be applied to almost all materials, and is extremely difficult to detect. A small bottle supplied by the manufacturer that applies microtaggants with a brush will make about 5,000 marks 1/8-inch long with approximately 30–40 microtaggants applied in every mark (see fig 13.7).

One disadvantage with microtaggants is that if they are discovered, they can be abraded. The second disadvantage with microtaggants is the commercially supplied carrier. To properly protect materials, microtaggants must be applied in a liquid that dries clear, holding the particles in place. They cannot be sprinkled around dry like salt and pepper. The company cannot vouch that its usual carrier will meet conservation concerns, and tests on the carrier performed by Columbia University seem to indicate that it does alter paper.[14]

Figure 13.7

Microgtaggant Applicator & Bag of Microtaggants. The Bag Holds about 2,000,000 Microtaggants. (Used by permission)

Other potential, more conservation-friendly, carriers might be used, however. The chief features of any carrier are that it must adhere to the material and must dry clear to allow the microtaggants to be viewed if need be. In spring, 2005, the Northeast Document Conservation Center did experiments applying microtaggants of 150–75 microns and 75–44 microns either mixed in various media or applied first loose to the paper and then affixed by applying the media. The four media tested were Liquitex, methyl cellulose, polyvinyl acetate, and Klucel-G. In one case, the microtaggants were applied in enough quantity to make the application visible and then aggressively scraped off using a fingernail, on the assumption that that instrument would probably be available to a thief in a reading room. In the second case, they were applied conservatively and not subsequently disturbed. In the first case, enough microtaggants remained to ensure positive identification of the particles, even after the attempts to abrade them. In the second case, the application was completely invisible to the naked eye, although the microtaggants were apparent under magnification. It would thus appear that they could be successfully applied using media that present few conservation concerns.[15]

Once the microtaggants are applied, it must be verified that they are actually on the material. That process is generally done either by visually inspecting the mark under magnification or by ordering particles that fluoresce under infrared light, which is used to check for their presence. The latter method presents its own set of concerns, however, since a thief could also discover the particles by the same method. On the other hand, the particles may be ordered in what is called infrared to infrared mode, in which they emit no visible light but instead produce noise when interrogated by a special infrared reader that no thief is likely to own. They are then subjected to physical inspection.

For more description of this technique, see: http://www.microtracesolutions.com/

Datadots

Datadots© (or "microdots") are small, inert disks on which is etched a unique code, such as an alphanumeric sequence or a library's name (see fig 13.8). The particles are about the size of a grain of sand. They can also be applied in small amounts to library materials, much as microtaggants are used.[16] Because they are barely visible, they can be selectively applied, placing only one datadot if desired. Once a library orders datadots, the company registers the code and never issues it to anybody else. They are easy to use, require no special training, are relatively cheap, and difficult to detect. Only one need be in place to ensure positive identification. They are, however, larger than microtaggants and potentially more visible to the unaided human eye; the code, however, must be viewed under some magnification to be legible.

As with microtaggants, the problem is that the datadots must be applied in a carrier that dries and

Figure 13.8

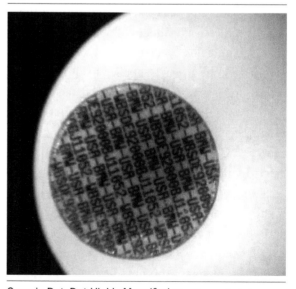

Generic DataDot Highly Magnified (Used by permission)

holds the datadot in place. Again, the conservation concerns with this carrier are unknown, and experiments performed by Columbia University indicate that there are conservation concerns with the commercial carrier. Although no further experiments were done with this material, there is no reason to believe that it could not be applied using the same media identified as appropriate with microtaggants. The company will supply them dry as loose particles. As with microtaggants, they can be abraded if discovered.

For more description of this technique, see: http://www.datadotdna.com/

Invisible Ink

Technically known as steganography, the process of marking materials with invisible ink has a fairly long history in library security and is a method still in use at some institutions, although it is controversial.[17] The ink can be applied by various methods such as a stamp or special pen, and the technology is relatively cheap to acquire and requires no special training to use effectively (see fig 13.9). Modern inks are not soluble in water and resist fading. (Many will fade if exposed directly to the sun for a week or so.) Because the ink is invisible, it can be applied anywhere, including directly on a page of type or an image. Since they are invisible, the markings can also be relatively large. Even if discovered, the inks are difficult to obliterate, and some are virtually impossible to remove without excising them.

The chief problem of such a program is that there must be some method to make the ink visible; a black light, for example, is one method that will make some inks fluoresce. The obvious drawback, therefore, is that a thief can also discover such marks by the same method.[18] Many potential inking schemes are available, however, such as inks that are revealed only when rubbed with a special pen or those that become visible only when rubbed with a coin.[19] Another concern is that the inks are sometimes alcohol based, so some caution must be exercised so that they are not applied inappropriately to materials that might be damaged. They are sometimes not suitable for application to impervious materials such as plastic. The conservation concerns with such inks are unexplored, although one institution that has used invisible ink for decades reports no conservation problems with its formulation, which is proprietary. Finally, it is believed by the Library of Congress that they fade over time, although apparently no extensive tests seem to have been done on the various ink combinations to determine if that is true in all cases. Experiments done by Columbia University indicate that such fading may not be the case.[20] If one uses a marking pen or stamp to apply such ink, one should be careful not to press so hard that a discoverable impression is left in the paper; a light touch is better.

For more description of this technique, see:
http://www.maxmax.com/aSpecialtyInks.htm
http://www.riskreactor.com/Security_Inks/Security_Inks_Main.htm

Figure 13.9

Invisible Ink Pen and Portable Black Light (Used by permission)

Synthetic DNA strands

Synthetic DNA strands are microscopic molecular structures applied to materials and then read by various means, often a laser light at a certain frequency that makes them glow for identification. The identified particles can then be recovered for analysis and comparison to the original DNA supplied to the customer, each of which is a unique combination. This method is a nearly foolproof identification method since the chances of replicating the supplied DNA are about 1 in 33 trillion. Usually the DNA is applied in a carrier in very small amounts, perhaps no bigger than a pin head. Without a laser tuned to the correct frequency, it would be impossible for a thief to detect their presence.

The entire process works something like this:

1. The library orders synthetic DNA strands from a supplier.
2. The supplier manufactures the synthetic DNA, registers it in a database, and supplies the DNA to the library.
3. The library applies the DNA to its materials and records its location.
4. In case of a theft, the suspect material is queried with a laser, which, if it detects the DNA, will make it fluoresce.
5. A sample of the DNA is recovered from the material and analyzed.
6. Depending on the analysis, the DNA is either a correct match or not.

Again, the conservation concerns with the commercially supplied carrier are unknown.

Smart Water Tracer

Smart Water Tracer contains small, microscopic particles with a unique identifying code that is registered in the company's database. Once dry, it is virtually undetectable, although it can be raised by ultraviolet light. The code is, however, able to be read with a microscope on a recovered book, map, or manuscript. Applying the material is simple, in that it consists of merely brushing an object lightly with a small brush, thus depositing hundreds of encoded particles that are extremely difficult to remove entirely.

There are few drawbacks to this technology. It is straightforward, water based, and easy to apply.

For more description of this technique, see: http://www.smartwater.com

Needle Marks

Needle marks are a special kind of perforation stamp but considerably less disfiguring than a normal stamp because the holes are relatively small. They can in fact be made so small as to be nearly invisible. Such marks are somewhat tedious to apply, however, because numerous perforations can be required to achieve the desired level of identification. Historically, needle marks have been applied as the generic marks described above. If a thief detects them, they are easily duplicated in ways to blunt their evidential value. A better system for such marks is that used by the Universal Torah Registry, which supplies a template containing a unique, registered number and a superfine needle with which to perforate the material with the number. Such marks are nearly invisible, can be applied in numerous places, cannot be easily removed, and offer convincing evidence in the case of a theft. Because of the labor involved, however, such a system is probably not practical for large applications, such as marking thousands of books or manuscripts, despite its relative effectiveness.[21]

Misleading Book Plates and Labels

The theory behind this technology is that a thief will almost certainly remove any identifying book plate or other label, such as a call number sticker, but may not be overly concerned about any adhesive residue left behind. The trick here is that the identifying markers are in the adhesive rather than in the label itself. In other words, if so much as a trace of the adhesive remains, it will contain a unique institutional identifier assigned by the manufacturer and registered in a database. Generally, the adhesives cannot easily be dissolved or removed, nor can the labels be easily taken off since they are tamper resistant.

This technology offers several attractive features for security. For example, all bookplates applied to books and all call number stickers could have encoded adhesive. Flat objects such as maps or broadsides could have small stickers affixed to them by the encoded adhesive. If a thief removed them, not only would obvious damage result, any remaining adhesive reside would contain identification of the library of origin. The residue will fluoresce under ultraviolet light.

The main problem with this technology is that the adhesive has not been proven to be sound from a conservation perspective. Otherwise, it is relatively simple and inexpensive to employ and uses the same technology as Smartwater, described above.

For more description of this technique, see: http://www.smartwater.com

Radio Frequency Identification Systems

Radio Frequency Identification (RFID) tags may have some limited use in marking books and other materials as an aid to both preventing theft and identifying stolen materials.[22] RFID tags, also called transponders, can be encoded with data, such as a cataloguing record or an ID code, which can then be read by a remote device (see fig 13.10). RFID tags are available in what are termed "active" and "passive" types, although only the latter is useful for library security. Passive tags do not require an internal energy source, drawing their power from the antenna itself, which excites the tag upon interrogation and causes it to transmit data. Passive tags

are permanently encoded, never wear out, and have no batteries that eventually fail. They are also relatively small, most being about the size of a postage stamp or a quarter coin, and less than the thickness of a sheet of paper. Ranges at which they can be read vary from a few inches up to several yards.

Unlike Achilles, however, conventional RFID tags have more than one weak heel. Despite the small size of the device itself, to work it must have an antenna attached to it. Doing so increases the size of the device. Thus, in actual use, the device cannot readily be concealed in materials, and the only practical way to attach a hidden RFID tag in special collections is either to incorporate it into a bookplate or to affix a bookplate over the top of it. If a thief removes the bookplate, which is highly likely, the tag will be removed as well. Second, an RFID tag can be put to sleep by devices that are small enough to smuggle into a library in a coat pocket; other small devices can also be used to detect their presence. Third, the device can be removed or physically damaged to the point that

Figure 13.10

Types of RFID Tags (Used by permission)

it ceases to function. It is not necessary, however, to destroy the actual device; it can be rendered useless if the antenna is cut.[23] The RFID tags are also subject to being destroyed by static or electromagnetic forces, although they are immune to simple magnets. Because technology is changing so rapidly, future compatibility issues are also a problem. Finally, RFID systems are not cheap. In general, they probably should not be relied on as a front-line secret marking method, although if the RFID tag survives after a theft and can be successfully interrogated, it will provide powerful proof of ownership.

Theoretically, it is possible that currently available RFID tags could be hidden in plain site by attaching them to materials. Thus, they could be adhered to the verso of a map sheet, for example, much as a visible stamp is used. Because the RFID tag would be so plainly visible, however, it would be a simple matter to cut the antenna and/or damage the device itself, thereby rendering it useless. Unfortunately, RFID tags are physically delicate. Also, the conservation problems with the manufacturer-supplied adhesive used to attach them are unknown.

Recent developments in RFID technology, however, offer far more stealth and virtual invisibility. So called powder chips (0.05 x 0.05 millimeters) have been successfully built and are narrower than a human hair. They supposedly have enough storage capacity to hold a 38-digit number; how much more information they can eventually be made to store is unknown. Also, it is uncertain how such small tags could be permanently attached to materials, although some carrier might be used successfully. Despite their small size, these tags are still subject to same forces that could render them inoperable as are their larger counterparts.

For more description of RFID in general, see: http://itp.nyu.edu/everybit/blog/media/rfid-zapper.pdf

Magnetic Strips

These strips, widely used for protecting general collections materials, work by disrupting a magnetic field between two detectors if they have not been demagnetized first and thus sound an audible alarm. In some cases, the strips cannot be demagnetized, and all materials are checked by an attendant before the patron may leave with them.

Despite their popularity elsewhere, magnetic strips have never found wide acceptance in special collections. The adhesive used to attach them present conservation concerns that have never been adequately addressed. The only books for which they are suitable are modern case-bound books, in which the strip can be inserted in the spine. They are unsuitable for use in older bindings or in paperbacks since they must be inserted between leaves of the volume, thereby bringing the adhesive into direct contact with the text leaves. Their presence is readily discovered, either by merely observing the presence of the detectors or by using a device that detects the magnetic field. They are also easily removed, especially when they are inserted between pages.

Magnetic strips probably have no role in special collections marking schemes.

Photographic Systems

Some systems for secret marks do not actually involve any marks at all but rather depend on photographic methods for identifying materials. Such methods are completely uninvasive and do not alter the object in any way, although they can provide some proof that an object belongs to a certain person or institution.

Intrinsic Signature Identification System (ISIS)©

This now-unavailable method from Verification Technologies depends upon the fact that no two objects are utterly the same and that those differences become apparent under sufficient magnification. Because it was a technique with serious security applications, it deserves to be memorialized. Thus, two apparently identical copies of a map, for instance, will appear quite different if the same area on both is compared under high magnification. In this method, increasingly detailed images are captured of a single area of an object. The images are then stored on a computer where they may be accessed via the Internet if need be. If a map, for example, is stolen and a copy recovered that might belong to the original owner, the recovered map can be compared to the file data to see if they are identical. This method is nearly foolproof and almost impossible to defeat since a thief cannot tell by looking at an object if it has been documented by this method. Unlike the other marking technologies discussed above that can be discovered and then altered, this technology is not subject to such vagaries. Conversely, it can also definitely prove that a recovered object does *not* belong to a certain institution.

As sophisticated as this technology was for identifying and recovering material, it was somewhat complicated and relatively expensive to use. All work was done by the company, who stored the images for the customer. Its best application was probably for a few highly valuable items that a library owned that it was completely loathe to alter in any way by stamping or otherwise marking them. Also, because the resulting records were stored on a computer, the data were possibly subject to loss if anything amiss happened to the disk on which they were stored or if the computer was hacked. Finally, it was remotely possible that a thief could alter the very area that was documented, thereby confusing the identification process. To forestall that remote possibility, views were sometimes taken from various places on the object.

Possibly in the future this technology can be revived, especially if the price can be brought down.

PaperPrint©

This system depends on photographing the unique properties of leaves of hand-made paper. Two images are taken, one that shows the surface of the paper and another that shows its interior structure, much as one might see if a piece of paper were put on a light table. The two images are then combined into one (see fig 13.11). The success of this process depends on the fact that no two pieces of hand-made paper and the printing on them can be absolutely identical. The system also records the placement of type or engraving lines on the leaf, thereby providing another unique element for each book. Thus, a print of an area from Copy A will be demonstrably different from the same area of Copy B. The images are stored in a computer database.

The inventor, Ian Christie-Miller, estimates that with his system a trained operator can capture

Figure 13.11

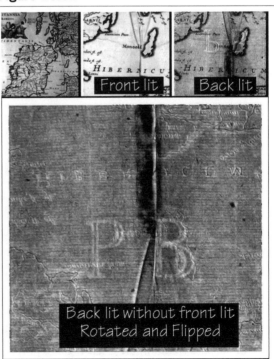

Britannia Romana - Copper Engraving - 1695

Paperprint Image (Courtesy Ian Christie-Miller)

one image approximately every thirty seconds under steps 1–7 as follows:

1. Place light sheet under the item.
2. Take the front-lit image.
3. Turn the light sheet on.
4. Take the back-lit image.
5. Turn the light sheet off.
6. Remove the light sheet.
7. Remove the item.
8. Operator enters data into software.

Step 8 can be variable, depending on the amount of data to be captured.

This technology enjoys many of the same benefits as the ISIS system. No potential thief can ascertain if the book has been documented in this way. Unlike the ISIS system, however, this system is purchased outright by the institution and used on site, making it relatively inexpensive. It also presents the same problems as any database stored on a computer. Its reliability with machine-made, wood pulp paper has not been established, so it does have limited uses. Also, it cannot be used to take images of very large objects in one sitting; such objects must be taken in sections, although theoretically only one section would be required for identification.[24]

For more description of this technique, see: http://www.earlypaper.com/

Other Photographic Systems

Numerous other photographic technologies have been available for years and are routinely used in libraries both as preservation media and security methods. Among them are microfilm, microfiche, photocopies, digital imagery (either by scanning or photography), and conventional photographs. In light of the thefts that have occurred in the past several decades, more interest has been expressed in not only forcing researchers to use surrogates but also on having them in hand to identify stolen materials. As foolproof as a high-quality surrogate might appear for identifying a stolen original, the method is fraught with difficulties and does not always carry the day. A major problem is that the surrogate will invariably not be exactly like the original, even if the latter has been unaltered by the thief. The image, for example, will rarely be the correct size. Also, any alterations in contrast, strength of color, or other factors will make the surrogate appear to be of another copy rather than of the copy the library is investigating. Other physical evidence, such as foxing or tide lines, is easily removed by washing. Finally, in the case of books, crucial evidence is often not recorded. Microfilms, for example, rarely include images of bindings, endpapers, or blank leaves, all of which are necessary to establish the context of the text block. In many cases, the versos of manuscripts or other materials are not recorded.[25]

The case of the Texas State Library and Archives Commission (TSLAC) in relation to several lots sold at Sotheby's 2005 Texana sale (#7994) is an instructive one. For many years, the TSLAC has been aware that hundreds of documents, both manuscript and printed, are missing from the institution, and the belief is that they were probably stolen. After TSLAC staff identified three printed items (lots 23A, 23B, and 27A) in the Sotheby's sale and asked that they be withdrawn, negotiations started with the consignors over returning the items. Despite having fairly good quality copies of two of the items that were made when the items were supposedly in the State's possession, the State was forced to concede that perhaps the items being offered were not the ones depicted in the images. The items had been extensively altered and mutilated, thereby rendering the original images of somewhat dubious evidentiary value.

The existence of surrogates will not necessarily prevent thefts, either. In an ironic twist to their use, it is entirely possible that the very people who should be forced to use them will instead be given access to the originals. Gilbert Bland and E. Forbes Smiley, both now convicted map thieves, were allowed to use originals and undoubtedly could have argued persuasively why they should have been allowed to do so. Any competent thief probably can recite proper reasons for obtaining access to originals. In Bland's case, he stated at one institution that he would be a visiting professor at a local college and wanted to preview the library's materials for class assignments. In Smiley's case, in one library he stated that he wanted to compare the library's originals to his own copies.[26] In both cases, some of the materials they stole were available in facsimiles. Thus, it would appear that one argument against surrogates is that they are often forced on people who would never dream of stealing the originals, but that the originals are instead given to those who have that very intention.[27]

On the other hand, such techniques as microfilming and digital reproduction do offer at least an arguing point for the library and have some advantages. The techniques are relatively harmless to the materials, and the technology to produce them is also well understood and widely available. A potential thief may also be entirely unaware that the images exist and cannot tell from examining an item if it has been documented in this fashion. On the negative side, producing the images can result in considerable expense and time for the institution, both for acquiring and for storing them. They also may fail to persuade others that they offer proof of ownership and may even result in the library's being hoist on its own petard. Finally, such images have no deterrent value, unless the thief is aware they exist. Such techniques are probably better employed as conservation measures to prevent wear and tear on originals rather than as front-line security methods.

New methods are constantly being developed, and the librarian should be alert to developments. For example, Clarkson, et al, announced recently a technique for identifying individual sheets of modern paper using a generic scanner and specialized software.[28] Although the process relies on paper properties long known to rare book librarians, the technique is another example of how to interpret something old in the service of something new. Some such techniques may have library security applications, as does this one.

When to Mark

For any type of security marking system to be effective, it must be applied to materials. All the microembossers in the world do no good if they lie unused in a desk drawer. The problem of exactly when to apply marks is a complicated one, however. Ideally, at least visible stamps would be applied to everything soon after it enters the collections. Because of legal matters, for example, the Library of Congress has for decades promptly stamped all copyright deposit copies it receives. Invisible marks are a slightly different matter, however, since close track must be kept of their whereabouts. In electronic cataloguing systems, perhaps one place to record their location is in a non-public field, although various later migrations to newer systems may render the selected field unusable or worse, visible to the public.[29] That method, however, requires that a cataloguing record be created in the first place, not something necessarily possible if material is added to a backlog. An unmarked item added to a backlog, however, is vulnerable to being stolen without a trace. Libraries may, therefore, wish to develop at least a generic marking system wherein all material that enters the collection is marked in exactly the same place, say, dead center of the verso of the title page or dead center of the verso of a manuscript leaf. When the item is eventually catalogued, that location and/or others can be verified and recorded. In any event, items do need to be marked soon after they are acquired, especially if they are going into a backlog.

Wording of the Mark

Any library considering using one of the secret marking systems that results in a mark consisting of letters (e.g., microembosser, invisible ink) needs to give careful consideration to the actual wording of the mark. In some cases, it is possible to employ a mark that actually results in confusion rather than clarity, thereby complicating efforts to locate the proper library, which may not even be aware material is missing. In the case of Stephen Blumberg, the FBI had some difficulties identifying libraries based on such markings as bookplates or visible stamps because they were ambiguous. In one instance, for example, several books were marked "Cherokee County," which seems clear enough until one realizes that there are numerous counties with the same name in various states. In other cases, such names as Carnegie, Lilly, and Mudd are also shared by numerous libraries. Thus, a library that may have a name used by others needs to do some research into other libraries and arrive at wording that uniquely identifies it as opposed to others with similar names.

Libraries need to also be cautious about being too arcane. A word or group of letters that makes sense to the library may not make sense in another context. Thus, it is recommended that OCLC symbols be avoided. In most cases, it is not obvious what they mean, and it is difficult to relate them to a specific library. For example, the OCLC symbol for the Harriet Beecher Stowe Library in Hartford, CT, is GUX. If someone were to stumble on that mark in a stolen book, only an extraordinary leap of imagination would lead the person to the correct library. If a library intends to use abbreviations to mark its materials, it is probably better off using the symbol assigned to it by the Library of Congress, whose assignments are usually familiar, can be easily referenced, are available on-line, and can often be intuitively deconstructed.[30]

A library needs to also bear in mind that whatever mark it uses may not be needed for 100 years. Thus, in considering what mark to use, library staff should consider that it may need to be interpreted by somebody who has little knowledge of OCLC or Library of Congress symbols, all of which may be long gone and unfamiliar by the time they are needed. If the mark is clearly and simply conceived, it can even be used to trace the present whereabouts of a library, even if it has gone out of existence, as was the case in many library recombinations and absorptions in Kansas that were successfully traced from the Blumberg stash by unequivocal bookplates. Some library symbols have reached the status of being basically timeless and will probably always be recognized (e.g., DLC, AAS, JCB, UCLA), but such is probably not the case with most institutions. (In the case of some Microdots and all Microtaggants, those marks will always be unique though not readily interpretable. It is only important that the library keep accurate records of its marks, even if the company that issued them has been out of business for decades.) In any event, a library needs to give considerable thought to the potential longevity of any mark it chooses and ensure that later generations can decipher it. Finally, as obvious as it may seem, any visible mark needs to be legible; many are not.

Conclusion

Lacking any clear ownership markings, law enforcement agencies proceed on whatever forensic evidence they have available to them to determine ownership. In Smiley's case, wormholes that matched on both the stolen map and the remaining text block were crucial to proving the provenance of one Yale map. In Bland's case, the FBI's forensic examiner was forced to try to match up cut and tear lines on the stubs of both the map and the book from which it was supposedly removed. Even at that, the FBI gave dozens of unattributable maps to the Library of Congress in the end. In Smiley's case, two other complications arose. First, multiple libraries had the same map stolen from them, but the FBI recovered only one copy. None of the libraries could positively identify that copy as theirs. Second, private owners of maps believed to have been stolen resisted returning them unless a library could prove that it was stolen from it. Again, that proved an impossible evidentiary burden for the libraries involved.[31]

As has been demonstrated repeatedly in the last decade or so, recovering stolen materials is complicated by absence of sufficient identification. Lacking clear evidence and proof that a stolen book, plate, manuscript, or map belongs to a certain library, both libraries and law enforcement agencies are frustrated in their efforts to repatriate stolen materials. Libraries need to understand clearly that if they have a Vesalius map stolen and one is recovered by law enforcement, the library is not going to get it back just because it "believes" it to be its copy. Positive forensic proof is required. Such murky situations would be much clearer if materials had unique marks that proved provenance. If a library is so squeamish that it cannot bring itself to mark materials with visible stamps, it should at least consider one of the secret marking systems available to protect its property and assist in its identification and recovery, although such marks have little deterrent value. To amplify one's chances of recovery, perhaps a combination of such secret marks should be applied to ensure the survival of at least one of them. All libraries, no matter what their feelings about visible marks, should use secret ones. Failure to do so only makes thefts easier for those who perpetrate them and recovery more difficult if not impossible for their victims.[32]

NOTES

1. For suggestions on visibly marking materials, see "Appendix 1: Guidelines for Marking Books, Manuscripts, and Other Special Collections Materials," in Association of College & Research Libraries, *Guidelines Regarding Security and Theft in Special Collections* (Chicago: ACRL, 2009).

2. Alice Harrison Bahr, *Book Theft and Library Security Systems, 1978–79* (White Plains: Knowledge Industry Publications, 1979), 107. In replevin actions, one basic legal principle is that the property being claimed must have indicia or ear-marks that clearly distinguish it from all others that may be similar. In 2007–2008, the British Library embarked on an ambitious project to describe in detail and mark over 3,000 of its valuable maps, on which see Kimberly C. Kowal and John Rhatigan, "The British Library's Vulnerable Collection Items Project," *Liber Quarterly* 18 (September 2008): 76–79. http://liber.library.uu.nl/publish/issues/2008-2/index.html?000247.

3. Richard Strassberg, "Library and Archives Security," in Paul N. Banks & Roberta Pilette, *Preservation: Issues and Planning* (Chicago: ALA, 2000), 177.

4. Lack of time and personnel are often given as reasons that special collection materials cannot be marked. Ironically, of course, library administrations have for decades found the wherewithal in money, personnel, and equipment to industriously electronically tag every book that enters the general collections.

5. Although generally considered "quaint" and occasionally noted as present on a cataloguing record, a marca de fuego or other brand is a genuinely good identification stamp that should be recorded by photography. Removed only with great effort, such marks are among the most persistent and stubborn of ownership stamps.

6. The earliest known suggestion for such a system in what became the United States is contained in Thomas Bray's *Proposals For the Encouragement and Promoting of Religion and Learning in the Foreign Plantations*, [London, 1696], Article 5 of which states

that books will be marked with specific ownership indications.

7. Mary Breighner, William Payton, and Jeanne M. Drewes, *Risk and Insurance Management Manual for Libraries* (Chicago: American Library Association, 2005), urge, "Marking materials with a property stamp even on rare and special collections materials is necessary to assure identification of stolen materials" (42). One must contemplate the possibility that in light of recent thefts the institution's risk managers and insurance company may require special collections to visibly mark materials.

8. Embossed marks are actually more difficult to render totally illegible than it would appear. In recent years, the Texas State Library and Archives Commission has recovered numerous documents from which its blind embossed stamp had been removed. In some cases, however, the removal was imperfectly done, and part of the text was still legible. (See their web site at: http://www.tsl.state.tx.us/arc/missingintro.html.) In the case of Harvard University, it recovered embossed materials stolen by José Torres-Carbonnel after an alert bookseller managed to make out the word "Harvard" on a mark that had been only partially flattened, on which see Christopher Reed, "Biblioklepts," *Harvard Magazine* (March–April 1997). One is rather stunned at how cavalier some sellers and buyers seem to be about materials that have evidence of removed markings based on materials one sees offered in the marketplace.

9. The most egregious example of a determined removal of visible stamps that the author has encountered was in a four-volume set of the first edition of Robert Fitzroy, Philip Parker King, and Charles Darwin, *A Narrative of the Surveying Voyages of His Majesty's Ships Adventure and Beagle* (London, 1839). Spread among the four volumes were no less than fifty-three oval ink stamps and several other marks, all of which had been abraded. None of them were legible any longer, but evidence of their removal was quite apparent, especially when the sheets were held up to the light. Map thief E. Forbes Smiley also admitted to removing library marks. Stephen Blumberg removed hundreds of bookplates and other library marks. The remainder of his books seized by the FBI ended up on the auction block, where the condition notes reveal a distressing number of items described as "Removed bookplate and excised lib stamp," etc. See E. Wesley Cowan, *Historic Americana Auction: Remnants of a Gentle Madness, The Stephen C. Blumberg Library of Americana* (Cincinnati: Cowan, 1999), *et passim*. The Cowan sale was unfortunately salted "with a small handful of additional titles from various consignors" (3), the presence of which was not otherwise indicated.

10. Despite problems with older inks, including the fact that they tend to bleed excessively into paper, they have proven resilient and extremely difficult to remove entirely. As Alice C. Hudson, Head of the map division at the New York Public Library, remarked of that library's stamps in the wake of Smiley's thefts: "For years at NYPL we have groaned about our notorious royal blue ownership stamps used since 1911, if not earlier. They bleed through the maps, they bleed when washed or conserved. You know what? Now I loooooove those trashy stamps" (post to Maphist forum, 6 October 2006). The same unstable ink properties also tripped up Robert Willingham. Georgia state crime lab technician James Kelly "identified a blurred oval ink stain on the back of an oversized map taken from Willingham's home as a university library stamp. A portion of the map's cloth backing had been cut away, but enough of the ink had bled through to allow identification." See Nicholas Basbanes, *A Gentle Madness: Bibliophiles, Bibliomanes, and the Eternal Passion for Books* (New York: Holt, 1995), 490. The very faults of such inks are in some ways their virtues.

11. For a brief discussion of problems and advantages of some types of marking schemes, see the Library of Congress, "Ownership Marking of Paper-Based Materials." http://www.loc.gov/preserv/marking.html; "Marking of Materials," *Library & Archival Security* 4 (1982): 47–53; and Ron Lieberman, "Are Rubber Stamps Better than Chains? Security Concerns and the Marking of Books," *College & Undergraduate Libraries* 6 (1999): 77–80.

12. See *Guidelines*, Appendix I.

13. In December, 2007, Green Dragon Bindery did experiments on two pieces of paper, one of which was eighteenth-century hand-made rag paper and the other of which was nineteenth-century machine-made wood pulp paper, both kindly given to me by Bill Reese. Each sheet had two separate Microstamp marks applied to it. Both pieces of paper were washed and bleached. Despite being told where the marks were placed and instructed to attempt to obliterate one of them on each sheet, the bindery still could not totally remove the target marks, which remained partially legible under magnification. The second marks were totally unaltered by being washed and remained completely legible. Thus, it would appear that even if a thief washed a marked sheet, the mark would remain and that mere washing is not sufficient to erase it.

14. The carrier does contain small amounts of xylene, acetone, and ethylbenzene, all of which are required to be listed by the Superfund Amendments and Reauthorization Act, Title III, Section 313 (so-called SARA 313), and are on both the federal Hazardous Air Pollutants (HAP) and the Volatile Hazardous Air Pollutants (VHAP) lists. The carrier contains no known carcinogens, however, and the three substances listed above are common in everyday life, occurring in such things as "Sharpie"

pens, fingernail polish remover, and some household cleaners–all in minute amounts, as is the case here.

15. Microtaggants are also suitable for mixing with printing inks, which implies that one could readily tell a genuine modern first edition from a reprint, forgery, or piracy since only the original publisher would have access to the proper microtaggants.

16. In the future, probably either microtaggants or microdots will be sprayed in quantity by manufacturers on large, valuable items such as cars, boats, trucks, and trailers to assist in identification and theft recovery.

17. Commercial formulae for invisible inks are generally trade secrets, so it is difficult to analyze their chemical composition to determine conservation concerns. In fact, the U.S. government still classifies as secret some invisible ink formulae dating back to WW I. See Katherine Pfleger, "The Formula for Invisible Ink Will Remain Classified as Part of the CIA's Effort to Protect National Security. Really," *St. Petersburg Times* (23 June 1999). http://www.fas.org/sgp/news/1996/06/spt062399.html.

18. Discovering invisible ink marks is not necessarily so simple as it sounds, and one would be hard-pressed to know for an absolute fact that an item is not so marked. Some inks fluoresce under black light; others, under shortwave UV; others, under long-range UV; others require heat. Some inks are undetectable by conventional means and require specialized equipment to reveal them. Thus, even if a thief examined every square inch of a map or book under black light and found no marks, s/he could still not be certain the item was not marked because the ink might not be visible at that wave length.

19. If a library is contemplating using invisible ink, some thought should be given to the technology needed to raise the mark. If one chooses an ink that must be rubbed with a special pen or viewed under a special light, one should consider that a replacement pen, for example, may not be available if the company goes out of business, thereby rendering the mark useless. Such technologies as UV and black light will probably be available for many more decades, if not basically forever.

20. An institution considering invisible ink would probably be well advised to have samples of it tested for fading, paper damage, etc., before adopting it for marking use.

21. See Jewish Community Relations Council of New York, "Universal Torah Registry." http://www.jcrcny.org/html/torah1.html. For a discussion of the problem of stolen Torahs, see Kate Cerve, "Stolen Torahs Stun Congregations, Including One Near St. Louis," *Kansas City Star* (11 July 2008). http://www.kansascity.com/105/story/701961.html.

22. Systems that depend on magnetic detection, such as TattleTape©, have never been deemed suitable for use on special collections materials.

23. If a library places RFID tags under a bookplate, it should embed them in a unpredictable place. Putting them always dead center, for example, is a poor security choice. The devices can be rendered useless by objects so innocuous as a straight pin or a straightened paper clip, which can be used to gouge them out. Placing the devices at unconventional locations, such as the right corner of the bookplate, is a better method. That consideration implies that it is better to place the RFID separately and then position the bookplate over it rather than to order bookplates with the device already built in. Obviously, the smaller the RFID, the better chance it has of escaping destruction.

24. A similar method was used by the British Library to document their maps. See Kowal and Rhatigan, 76–79.

25. For the potential importance of such evidence, see Lee Ann Potter, "On the Other Side: Hidden Treasures Abound on the Backsides of Historic Documents," *Social Education* 68 (October 2004): 376–380; and her "The Flip Side of History," *The Quarterly Journal of the National Archives and Record Administration* 36, (Winter 2004): 6–10.

26. In all bluntness, underlying security gaffes were involved at both institutions. In the first instance, Bland's story was not verified, although it could easily have been. In the second, Smiley was apparently not required to produce his supposed copies of the maps that he wished to compare. In both instances, staff took the thief's story hook, line, and sinker.

27. Given the string of thefts by knowledgeable people such as Shinn, Ploughman, Blumberg (admittedly autodidactic), Bellwood, Bland, and Smiley, one might perhaps be more suspicious of "qualified" people, although there is debate on both sides of the question. Ben Primer remarked, "You have to assume in this business that anyone could be a criminal. The more credentials they have, the more knowledge they have, so they know what is valuable. A researcher with more credentials is almost more dangerous." On the other hand, Paul Needham contends, "In a way, I think people's credentials are irrelevant. Some people are dishonest and most people are not. I am not convinced that this correlates in any way whatsoever with education or knowledge of commercial values." (Both quoted in Ross Liemer, "Yale Map Heist Stirs University Concern," *The Daily Princetonian* 12 October, 2006). Thieves such as Anthony Melnikas, Daniel Cevallos-Tovar, Clive Driver, and Michel Garel seem to have been very knowledgeable and therefore very dangerous. The cases of three anonymous Harvard thieves, all of whom seem to have had specialized knowledge, are discussed in Christopher Reed, "Student, Teacher, Scholar," *Harvard Magazine* (March-April, 1997). Given that the most knowledgeable thieves have apparently caused the most damage, Primer would appear to be cor-

rect. In any case, the combination of specialized knowledge and larcenous intent is not to be underestimated. On the other hand, those with mere revenge in their hearts can also do damage, on which see Christopher Reed, "The Slasher," *Harvard Magazine* (March–April, 1997). Smiley also admitted that part of his motivation was resentment against libraries and librarians by whom he felt slighted.

28. William Clarkson, et al, "Fingerprinting Blank Paper Using Commodity Scanners," Proceedings IEEE Symposium on Security and Privacy (May, 2009). http://citp.princeton.edu/paper/.

29. The safest method for recording locations remains, for better or worse, paper based records not subject to electronic obsolescence. Bearing in mind that one may not need to examine the mark for decades after it has been applied, thought should be given to the best method of rendering its location findable years later.

30. The list is now known as "MARC Code List for Organizations," and the history of various library encoding schemes may be found at http://www.loc.gov/marc/organizations/. This scheme accounts for older, now disused symbols.

31. For a description of the FBI's difficulties in the Bland case and their procedures for identifying maps, see Miles Harvey, "Mr. Bland's Evil Plot to Control the World," *Outside Magazine* (June, 1997). http://www.outside.away.com/magazine/0697/9706bland.html. The observations are also based on conversations between the author and FBI Special Agent Gray, who was in charge of the Bland investigation. A similar procedure was used in convicting Robert M. Willingham by "matching tear patterns and stains" on the books from which he removed prints. See Basbanes, 490.

32. For a somewhat tongue-in-cheek review of security practices in both libraries and the British antiquarian trade and their efforts to recover stolen property, see R. M. Healey, "The Borrowers: High Profile Thefts from Libraries and Dealers Appear to Be on the Increase," *Rare Book Review* (November 2006): 28–32.

Weighing Materials in Rare Book and Manuscript Libraries to Prevent Theft*

Everett C. Wilkie, Jr.

Rare book and manuscript materials have long been and continue to be obvious targets for thieves. No system for completely deterring or detecting such people has ever been devised, despite numerous security improvements over the years and heightened awareness of the problem among custodians of such materials. Many highly effective measures to prevent theft seem obvious and well known. One could, for example, completely collate every book before it was issued to a reader and then re-collate it when it was turned back in. Or, one could completely inventory the contents of a manuscript folder when it was issued and then review the contents leaf by leaf when the folder was returned. Other means of detection and deterrence use CCTV cameras to monitor reading room activities. As effective as such methods might be, they are often not practical, little used, or not employed properly. They are expensive, time consuming, and require more staff than most rare book and manuscript repositories could ever hope to muster. Most reading room security, therefore, continues to depend on staff vigilance as the primary method of deterrence and detection.[1]

A method of detection that is effective, accurate, and relatively inexpensive is offered by weighing materials when they are issued to a reader and then re-weighing them when they are returned. The primary expense in setting up such a system is acquiring the proper scale (or "balance", as the device is technically called) and maintaining it. Appropriate scales are easy to use, give clear indications if something has been removed from or added to a volume or folder, are extremely sensitive, and present few practical problems. The purpose of this chapter is to explore issues and methods surrounding the use of such a system as a deterrent and detection method against theft and vandalism. In part, some of what is proposed here is theoretical. Appropriate scales are sensitive enough to be of real use in detecting theft and vandalism; their use, however, is hardly widespread. The author has knowledge of two major libraries that use this method for detecting such problems, although neither will allow itself to be identified publicly for security reasons. It is hoped that the considerations presented here will induce other libraries to attempt this method so that perhaps better knowledge may be gained about its efficacy.[2]

The Scale

Often used in scientific and industrial settings, where they are referred to as balances, scales are

---

* This chapter first appeared as "Weighing Materials in Rare Book and Manuscript Libraries as a Security Measure against Theft and Vandalism," *RBM: A Journal of Rare Books, Manuscripts, and Cultural Heritage* 7 (Fall 2006): 146–164. It is reprinted here with minor modifications by permission of ACRL.

available with a wide range of features and at various prices. In selecting a scale, the chief consideration for a library is to choose one that will accurately weigh within desired tolerances the majority of materials issued to readers. Although scales are available that will weigh the heaviest items, such as an entire book truck of manuscripts, the primary issue facing libraries in the selection of such a scale is its sensitivity range. Two types of scales are generally available that might be appropriate to rare book and manuscript considerations.

The first type of scale is metric and weighs in grams (hereinafter usually abbreviated gm), a standard scientific measurement equal to one thousandth of a kilogram, itself equal to 2.2046 pounds avoirdupois. (One ounce avoirdupois contains 28 gm.) Even the simplest ones will weigh grams at the hundredths level (i. e., 0.00); many will weigh in milligrams (i. e., 0.000). The second type of scale is avoirdupois and weighs in pounds and ounces. In the United States, practically the only country in the world with a genuine need for such scales, they are used widely for weighing postage or calculating shipping charges. In general, postal scales will weigh to 0.00 ounce, the only practical standard they need to meet in everyday use. On the other hand, they will readily weigh fairly heavy items. Even the simplest postal scale will weigh items up to ten pounds. More sophisticated avoirdupois scales, meant for scientific or industrial use, can weigh down to 0.005 pound (2.27 gm) or even to .001 pound (0.45 gm). (See fig.14.1.)

The chief drawback of an avoirdupois postal scale is that its default setting is so high it fails to weigh at a precise enough interval as compared to a metric scale. Because it needs to weigh only in whole ounces to be useful, it will actually detect small weights, such as a Kleenex® sheet, but will not reflect the actual weight to a precise degree. Such simple scales should probably be avoided despite their attractive price. Because a metric scale weighing in grams will reflect discrepancies with a larger number than an avoirdupois scale, the former is recommended. A gram is a far smaller unit of measure than a pound or even an ounce, and scales measuring that type of weight will perforce reflect larger readings than those weighing avoirdupois, thereby increasing the likelihood of detection. In selecting a scale, one should be careful to choose one that is capable of detecting the desired weights but yet not overly sensitive. A scale that will weigh 1200 gm (about 2 lb 10 oz) at 0.000 is about at the upper level of sensitivity for the weight such a scale will hold. A less sensitive scale that will weigh 8200 (about 18 lb 1 oz) grams will weigh only to a sensitivity of 0.0 gram or one whole gram generally. (See figs 14.2 and 14.3.)

In weighing manuscript folders and most books, a scale that weighs in the hun-

Figure 14.1

A typical avoirdupois postal/shipping scale that will weigh up to 100 lb. Note that the increments are too coarse, however, to be of significant security use. (Courtesy the Lilly Library, Indiana University, Bloomington, IN.)

Figure 14.2						
	#1	#2	#3	#4	#5	#6
Maximum capacity	150 g	300 g	600 g	600 g	1500 g	3000 g
Minimum capacity	—	—	—	—	—	—
Readability	0.005 g	0.01 g	0.02 g	0.01 g	0.05 g	0.1 g
Tare range	Full	Full	Full	Full	Full	Full
Repeatability	0.005 g	0.01 g	0.02 g	0.01 g	0.05 g	0.1 g
Linearity	0.01 g	0.02 g	0.04 g	0.02 g	0.1 g	0.2 g
Stabilization time	3 secs	3 secs	3 secs	3 secs	3 secs	3 secs
Units of measure	gram, hundredweight, pound, ounce, dram, pennyweight, carat, grain					
Interface	RS-232 (1200–9600 baud rate)					
Operating temperature	0°C–40°C					
Power supply	AC power 120VAC or 230VAC, 9V adapter, or 4 dry cell C batteries					
Calibration	Automatic external calibration from keypad					
Display	Backlit LCD 95mm x 25mm					
Draft shield	Yes	Yes	Yes	Yes	Yes	Yes
- Details	Plastic windshield standard					
- Dimensions	155 x 137 x 80 mm					
Pan size	116 mm Ø / 4.6" Ø				144×124 mm / 5.7×4.9"	
Overall dimensions	175×226×63 mm / 6.9×8.9×2.5"					
Gross weight	2 kg / 4.4 lb					
Functions	Weighing, Parts Counting, % Weighing					
Other features	Auto power off. All functions can be enabled/disabled and initial functions can be set.					

Generic example of full specification sheet for metric scales. Note that in the first three lines that as the accommodated weight rises, the sensitivity falls. Also note the various units of measure available on the line entitled "Units of Measure."

dredths of a gram (0.00) up to 4500 gm (about 10 lb) should be adequate; one less sensitive may prove inadequate because it will not be able to detect the removal of small pieces of material, such as a signature from a letter or a bookplate. For larger bound volumes, the situation is somewhat equivalent. If a book weighs 8000 gm (about 17 lb), the most sensitive metric scale available will probably weigh at the 0.0 gm level. That level of sensitivity, however, would probably be sufficient to detect removal of any individual leaves, bearing in mind that such items as atlases have relatively heavy leaves. If one acquires a very robust metric scale that will weigh objects up to 10,000 gm (about 22 lb), the sensitivity

will generally again fall to 1 gm. It may be desirable to acquire two scales of different capacities, one for small items and another for large items.[3]

Some scales are equipped with weighing options that the operator may choose. A scale may be made to weigh in ounces, grams, grains, carats, or any other of a number of weighing schemes if it is ordered with the proper programming. In considering which features to purchase, the institution may find various weighing capacities of interest. If, for example, one has historic gunpowder samples, a scale that can weigh in grains, the standard for such a material, may be desirable. If a collection contains many very small, light-weight items, a

Figure 14.3

Maximum capacity (grams/pounds)	Sensitivity
150 g (.330 lb)	0.001 g
150 g (.330 lb)	0.005 g
210 g (.462 lb)	0.01 g
300 g (.660 lb)	0.01 g
310 g (.683 lb)	0.001 g
410 g (.903 lb)	0.01 g
410 g (.903 lb)	0.001 g
600 g (1.32 lb)	0.02 g
600 g (1.32 lb)	0.01 g
610 g (1.34 lb)	0.01 g
610 g (1.34 lb)	0.1 g
1500 g (3.30 lb)	0.01 g
1500 g (3.30 lb)	0.05 g
2100 g (4.62 lb)	0.1 g
3000 g (6.61 lb)	0.1 g
3100 g (6.83 lb)	0.01 g
4100 g (9.03 lb)	0.1 g
6100 g (13.44 lb)	0.1 g
4100 g (9.03 lb)	1 g
4100 g (9.03 lb)	0.01 g
6100 g (13.44 lb)	1 g
12,000 g (26.45 lb)	1 g

Examples of capacities for metric scales showing accommodated maximum weights and relative sensitivities. Note that scales can vary in sensitivity even when maximum weights are close or identical. (Extracted and condensed from several different specification sheets).

finer tolerance than a gram might also be desirable in such a situation. Before selecting a scale, the institution needs to give some thought to the variety of material it owns and that might be called to the reading room.

Several other considerations also influence one's choice of a scale. Any scale appropriate for weighing books and manuscripts must have an unobstructed flat weighing surface (sometimes called a "pan" or "platform") of adequate size to hold most materials. To produce an accurate weight, it is not necessary that the object being weighed fit entirely on the pan, only that it rest solidly upon it; overhang is acceptable (see below). The pan should be square rather than round. Also, the scale must have some easy way to be calibrated either manually or electronically. To work accurately, the scale needs to be level on a sturdy, flat surface, and special tables are available for that purpose. For ease of levelling, some scales are equipped with a floating ball and adjustable legs. The readout screen will undoubtedly be digital. Another feature common in modern scales is an RSC 232 interface for exporting data to a computer or other device; software is available to automate the export function (see fig. 14 4). In most instances, this interface should be chosen as an option even if there are no immediate plans for its use because it can be used to send weighing data to a computer. Most scales can use a 120V or 230V power supply, preferably conditioned, and most are also equipped with batteries. Because features of scales often cannot be easily altered or upgraded after manufacture, it is important carefully to consider which features the library will need before buying the device.

Security Applications

In practice, the intention is that all materials will be weighed before they are issued to a reader and then re-weighed when returned (see figs 14.5–14.8). Any meaningful discrepancy in the two weights should be cause for concern. As can be seen from Appendix I, any discrepancy shown by a gram scale will probably be large enough to detect, even if only a single leaf has been removed. The larger the proportion of materials removed, the greater the discrepancy will be. This is an important consideration for materials such as large atlases or volumes containing plates, which are often the targets of vandalism. The leaves comprising such volumes are relatively heavy; in fact, to a metric scale weighing at even

Figure 14.4

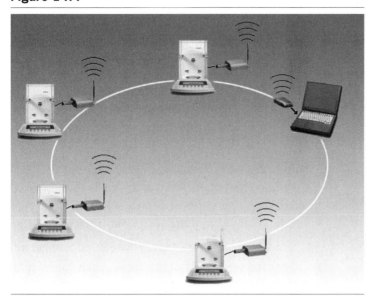

Schematic of a network of scales using Blue Tooth© to communicate weights to a remote computer/device. (Photo Courtesy of Sartorius Corporation.)

one gram, they are huge. The removal of even one of them will result in a large weight discrepancy. (See Appendix II.)[4]

The chief theoretical problem with this system is that a thief will substitute something for what has been removed.[5] Because of repeated experiments the author did using various types of materials, it seems highly unlikely that a thief could accomplish this feat. Especially with older books, the weighing system will probably always defeat the practice of substituting one entire volume for another because it is nearly impossible to match the weight of the substituted volume accurately with the weight of the stolen one. Even such features as book plates and missing pieces of leather on the binding will produce significant weight variances. Attempting to substitute leaves of equivalent weight to the ones removed is also exceedingly difficult to accomplish. For such a procedure to work successfully, the thief would need to know accurately what the removed leaf would weigh so that a proper substitute could be at hand, a number virtually impossible to divine

in advance. The most vulnerable collections to such swapping procedures seem to be modern manuscripts. If they are recent enough, it is possible to obtain paper that is nearly identical to what is to be stolen, substitute it, and not alter the weight of a folder significantly. Even that possibility, however, has proven remote in experiments.[6] Weighing materials also has potentially significant applications in internal security. One could weigh books as they are accessioned if they are to be added to a backlog, thereby establishing a baseline measurement that would be valid until the item is actually catalogued. Any later discrepancy in the weight, especially if an item had not circulated, should give rise to suspicions of insider theft.[7] The procedure also has applications when collections are moved. Items could be weighed before they were moved and then re-weighed when they were reshelved in their new location. Again, any mean-

Figure 14.5

A letter-size folder of modern typescripts. (Courtesy the Lilly Library, Indiana University, Bloomington, IN.)

Figure 14.6

The same letter-size folder of modern typescripts with one removed. Note the reduced weight. (Courtesy the Lilly Library, Indiana University, Bloomington, IN.)

ingful discrepancy would be cause for concern.[8] In situations where large amounts of unprocessed manuscripts are accessioned, an institution would clearly need to wait until a final arrangement had been accomplished before weighing the individual cartons or boxes for this purpose. Even if, however, a researcher were given access to unprocessed ma-

Figure 14.7

A legal-size folder of seventeenth-century manuscripts. (Courtesy the Lilly Library, Indiana University, Bloomington, IN.)

terials, the weighing system would still be effective if unprocessed items were weighed at the time of issue. Weights would, of course, need to be kept current on some items. If an item is sent for conservation, for example, any such procedures are probably going to alter its weight in a meaningful way.

If weighing procedures are instituted, a major consideration is going to be whether patrons know the process is being applied to materials they are using. One school of thought holds that security measures should be obvious and blatant, as is clear in any bank with cameras dangling from every wall. Under such a philosophy, it would seem apparent that the method would be to weigh the item right in front of the user and make no bones about why it is being done. Such a procedure would seem to be the one with the greater deterrent value.[9] Another school holds that security measures should generally be covert and opaque. In that case, the items would probably be weighed outside the view of the user, who would be none the wiser. That procedure would seem to hold more promise for catching an actual thief, although the damage may have already been done. In either case, the patron should never be told the weight. Because of the possibility of false identification, whichever method is chosen, a suspected thief should never be allowed to leave the premises until a meaningful discrepancy is resolved. It is possible a patron is not who s/he appears to be. Another consideration, especially in the US, is that there should be nobody with intervening custody of materials between the patron and the person who does the actual weighing. That consideration also mitigates against weighing items later after a patron has already left.[10]

Practical Considerations

Implementation of a security weighing system involves a learning curve for those involved with its use. As with any security application, not ev-

Figure 14.8

The same legal-size folder of seventeenth-century manuscripts with one removed. Note the reduced weight.
(Courtesy the Lilly Library, Indiana University, Bloomington, IN.)

erything is going to be perfect or problem-free. Just as with considerations for something such as a CCTV surveillance system, the institution will have to balance alternatives to decide if a weighing program is appropriate. Common concerns likely to arise are these:

1) Humidity. Because almost all rare book and manuscript libraries have climate control in both their stacks and reading rooms, weight variations introduced by relative humidity are generally unimportant. Even for those without such controls, it is rarely an issue. Items are weighed at the moment they are issued, and the environment is unlikely to affect them in any meaningful way while they are being used. Even a volume brought from a dry environment into a humidified, climate controlled environment will not quickly absorb a meaningful amount of water from the atmosphere. In fact, it requires days or even weeks for a volume to absorb or lose all the humidity it can hold. In general, concerns about weight changes caused by water loss or absorption are of little concern in this context.[11]

2) Weight discrepancies. Because scales are sensitive, it is possible that there will be weight discrepancies that are not meaningful. In general, a small weight discrepancy to the right of the decimal point will prove to be meaningless in the average book or manuscript folder. Only those to the left of it will matter. Thus, if an item weighs 225.20 gm when issued and upon return weighs 225.10 gm, the difference is probably negligible. If upon return it weighed 220.00 gm, however, that would be cause for concern. It should be noted that any significant increase in weight is also cause for concern because it may indicate something has been substituted for something removed or even that something has been added.[12]

Care should also be taken to ensure that the object when weighed is exactly in the form issued to the patron. If such items as duplicate copies of call slips or call flags are issued with the item, they should probably be removed before the item is weighed so that the weight shown is the item only. In other cases, extraneous materials are sometimes deliberately introduced into collections. A common example of that practice is the use of some type of flag or marker to indicate in manuscript boxes which items are to be photocopied. It would be preferable if photocopy requests could be made without inserting anything extra into a container, but if that is not possible, then all the flags need to be utterly identical so that their extra weight can be accurately accounted for when the box is returned. Introducing such extraneous materials into weighed materials, however, unnecessarily muddies the waters and should be avoided.

3) Pan size. Most scales have a pan large enough to accommodate most books and manuscript folders. For an accurate weight, it is required only that they rest squarely on the pan; orientation on the pan is not a factor. Occasionally, it is possible to encounter a situation in which the item to be weighed is of large size or of such a format that it does not fit on the pan properly. A folio volume of prints still in its original paper wrappers is an example of

such a problem; it may be so limp that it will not properly rest on the pan. In such cases, one may use a piece of stiff material, such as binding board, to support the object. One would first weigh the board separately and record its weight, referred to as the tare. Then one would place the object on the board, which would support it, and calculate the object's weight by subtracting the tare weight. Most scales automate this function and automatically subtract the tare from the weight once the tare is entered. Because some large objects can obscure the readout on small scales, it might be desirable to obtain one with the readout mounted on an arm or one with a remote readout. (see figs 14.9 and 14.10).

4) Installation. All scales are subject to various forces that alter the apparent weight of objects. Some of those are entirely undetectable to human senses but will be detected by the scale. Two forces especially will act negatively on a scale's accuracy. The first is vibration. The unit should, therefore, be located where it is not subject to interference from such things as machinery or passing subway cars. If needed, special tables, which are large, heavy objects (ca 350 lb) usually made of epoxy resin, are available. For more severe cases, vibration damping mounts can be acquired. The second force is the movement of air on the pan. The scale should be located where it is not subject to air rushing from HVAC vents or fans onto the pan, as such a situation will cause the readout to fluctuate and compromise weighing accuracy. One may easily arrive at an appreciation of this problem merely by blowing on the pan and witnessing the effect of air turbulence on the readout. If necessary, the entire unit can be enclosed in a Plexiglas© hood to insulate it from such effects.[13] In any case, the scale must be installed so that the readout is stable and reads 0 when the pan is empty. (See figs 14.11 and 14.12.)

5) What to weigh? Probably not everything needs to be weighed before it is issued. Low value items such as modern reference books might be exempt from the procedure in most institutions. Single sheet items, such as broadsides or separate maps, might also be exempt since any damage to them would be obvious. Any time, however, that a photocopy request is denied, the item, no matter how valuable it is, should be weighed before being returned to the patron, who may decide to remove

Figure 14.9

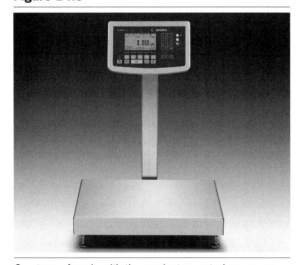

One type of scale with the readout mounted on an arm.
(Photo Courtesy of Sartorius Corporation.)

Figure 14.10

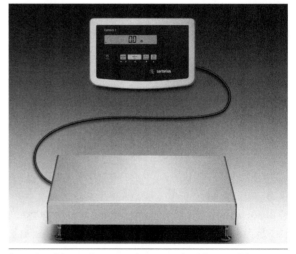

A scale with a remote readout attached by a cable.
(Photo Courtesy of Sartorius Corporation.)

Figure 14.11

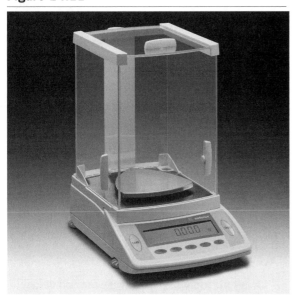

Example of a scale with a hood or draft shield. This particular configuration is an example only; the type of hood is inappropriate for most security applications in a reading room unless one is weighing small, delicate objects. (Photo Courtesy of Sartorius Corporation.)

Figure 14.12

A portable scale with built-in readout. Note the reading, which is caused by air movement on the otherwise empty pan. (Courtesy the Lilly Library, Indiana University, Bloomington, IN.)

the needed leaves rather than undergo the onus of transcribing the information.[14]

A rare but real problem is the substitution of extremely expert facsimiles for original materials, a situation that would most probably occur with broadsides, maps, or other single sheet materials. Such considerations may induce a library to weigh such items; it is difficult, however, to duplicate accurately an original's weight with a facsimile, no matter how excellent the reproduction. (See footnote 2.)[15]

6) Maintenance. Modern scales are robust, designed for extended use, and require little maintenance. The one routine maintenance procedure they will require, however, is calibration to ensure that they remain accurate. Normally calibration is a simple procedure requiring no special training or equipment and done in accordance with the manufacturer's recommendation. Proper instrument maintenance and calibration do, however, have some legal implications, and attention to them is necessary. Maintenance contracts for the devices should probably also be procured.

7) Procedural considerations. Using a scale to weigh materials may involve some procedural changes, especially in regard to manuscript collections. The practice of allowing researchers to have entire book trucks of manuscripts in the reading room would easily defeat the purpose of weighing materials. A scale large enough to weigh such a mass would be so insensitive that it would not detect the removal of single items. If researchers were issued only boxes or folders, however, that were weighed when issued, the scale could probably detect the removal of even something so small as a Post-It© note or signature if the scale weighed at 0.00 gm.

8) The Problem of "when?" A vexing problem involving theft of leaves from books, such as individual maps or plates, is determining when the removal actually happened. If, for example, an atlas is discovered to be missing a map after being used by

Mr. X, suspicion naturally falls on him immediately. The alternate possibility, however, is that the map was already gone when the volume was issued to Mr. X. Because almost no library collates material every time it is used, staff often cannot absolutely be certain that the map was there when Mr. X called it to the reading room and used it. If the item were weighed before being issued, however, the matter would be clearer. If the map were already missing, that lack would be reflected in the initial weight. Weighing materials has implications, therefore, in protecting innocent researchers who just happen to be in the wrong place at the wrong time.

9) What if? Implementing a weighing program is something like buying a firearm for personal protection. One must be willing to use it. Not only must the library regularly weigh all appropriate items issued to readers, but it must also have the will to act upon the results. If a library is not willing to confront a reader who seems to have damaged or stolen library materials, a weighing program will do little good in the end. Some soul searching and the implementation of appropriate procedures should be accomplished before the first item is ever weighed.

Conclusion

Although the idea of weighing objects to determine damage or loss is a relatively new concept in the field of rare books, manuscripts, and special collections, it has been used with success in other venues. It was common practice, for example, that banks would weigh rolls of coins to ensure that a roll did not contain items such as slugs or washers instead of actual coins, and variations of money weighing procedures are still in use today at some banks, security companies, and retail operations.[16] Manufacturers routinely weigh products to ensure quality control. Weighing rare books and manuscripts seems to offer another viable method for preventing thefts and mutilation, although it is admittedly not perfect and must be considered as only one piece of an overall security program.

Every person with custody of rare and valuable materials wishes for a Holy Grail or Magic Bullet of security that will detect every instance of theft and vandalism. No such system has ever been invented, however, so adequate security depends on many methods, each of which is designed to detect only certain acts. As one correspondent, who must remain anonymous, told me: "I retain a healthy respect for the determined, capable, professional thief or fraudster, who I believe could probably circumnavigate our systems, but we have a duty to make life as difficult as possible for them, and to deter the opportunist as well." Weighing materials may find a useful place in our arsenal.

Appendix I. Representative Weights

This appendix is intended to give users some idea of how much objects actually weigh to guide them in deciding what type of scale might be employed in a given library given the nature of the collections. All avoirdupois weights are approximations arrived at mathematically because no proper avoirdupois scale was available for use.

Weights to .00 gram and pounds/ounces of some everyday materials

Material	Pounds	Grams
Photocopy paper (8-1/2" x 11")	0.19 oz	5.43 gm.
100% cotton bond (8-1/2" x 11")	0.16 oz	4.58 gm.
Large Kleenex® sheet	0.04 oz	1.37 gm.
Credit card	0.16 oz	4.60 gm.
Post-It® note (3" x 3")	0.01 oz	0.43 gm.
Business card	0.03 oz	0.99 gm.

Weights to .00 gram and pounds/ounces of some library materials

Tom Clancy. *The Teeth of the Tiger.* NY: Putnam, 2003. 8vo.

741.85 gm (with dust jacket and bookplate) (=1 lb 10 oz)

740.82 gm (with dust jacket but without bookplate) (=1 lb 10 oz)

718.77 gm (without dust jacket or bookplate) (=1 lb 9 oz)

Catalogue of the Everett D. Graff Collection. Chicago: Newberry, 1968. 4to.

1868.19 gm (with dust jacket in Brodart® protector) (=4 lb 1 oz)

1849.00 gm (with dust jacket but without Brodart® protector) (=4 lb 1 oz)

1820.13 gm (without dust jacket or Brodart® protector) (=4 lb)

The Bible School Hymnal. NY & Chicago: Fullar-Meredith, 1907. 8vo.

457.30 gm (all leaves present) (=1.00 lb)

454.14 gm (one leaf removed) (=1.00 lb)

Close-Up USA. Washington: National Geographic Society, 1978. Plastic case containing book, 1 large folded map, 15 smaller folded maps, and scale printed on small Mylar sheet.

1915.03 gm (complete) (=4 lb 4 oz)

1905.93 gm (with only scale removed) (=4 lb 3 oz)

1854.20 gm (1 smaller folded map removed) (=4 lb)

1791.91 gm (2 smaller folded maps removed) (=3 lb 15 oz)

1775.79 gm (large folded map removed) (=3 lb 14 oz)

Bound early nineteenth-century manuscript music book (oblong)

384.97 gm (complete) (=13.57 oz)

382.03 gm (one leaf removed) (=13.47 oz)
379.15 gm (two leaves removed) (=13.37 oz)

Collection of pieces of eighteenth-century Tapa cloth consisting of: one 5.5 x 5-3/4 in piece of dyed, patterned cloth; one 6 x 6-1/4 in piece of dyed, patterned cloth; one 14-1/2 x 14-3/4 in piece of undyed, plain cloth; one 14-1/4 x 14-1/4 in piece of undyed, plain cloth; one 13 x 15 in piece of undyed, plain cloth; one 13 x 37-1/2 in piece of undyed, plain cloth; one 21-1/2 x 37 in piece of undyed, plain cloth. In cloth clamshell case with ms letter.

1817.18 gm.   (Weight of entire collection) (=4 lb)
1811.47 gm.   (Weight with smallest piece removed) (4 lb)
1812.60 gm.   (Weight with ms letter removed) (4 lb)

Weights to .00 gram and pounds/ounces of some heavy library materials
Webster's New Twentieth-Century Dictionary. New York: Publisher's Guild, 1942. 4989.51 gm (11.00 lb)

Harry T. Peters. *Currier & Ives: Printmakers to the American People.* Vol. 1. Garden City: Doubleday, Duran, 1929. Buckram binding. 2676.19 gm (5 lb 14 oz)

Harry T. Peters. *Currier & Ives: Printmakers to the American People.* Vol. 2. Garden City: Doubleday, Duran, 1931. In dust jacket with Mylar protector and original publisher's box. 3628.73 gm (8.00 lb)

Atlas (folio) of James Cook & James King. *A Voyage to the Pacific Ocean.* London: Strahan, etc., 1785. 4535.92 gm (10.00 lb)
Gutenberg Bibles (B42)

Pierpont Morgan Library copies
(Reported in Christopher DeHamel, *The Book: A History of the Bible* [New York: Phaidon, 2001], p. 207n.)
On paper in nineteenth-century binding ca. 30 lb; 13607.77 gm.
On vellum in heavy nineteenth-century binding ca. 50 lb; 22679.62 gm.

University of Texas copy
(Reported on Exlibris, 2 February 2006)
2 vols on paper
Vol I: ca. 14 lb; 6350 gm.
Vol. II: ca. 13 lb 14 oz; 6294 gm.

Legal-size Hollinger Box containing 20th-century typescripts, many on onion-skin paper, in legal-size folders
4309.12 gm (9 lb 8 oz)

Letter-size Hollinger Box containing 20th-century typescripts, memos, etc., in letter-size folders
4535.92 gm (10 lb)

Letter-size Hollinger Box containing 8x10 b&w glossy photographers in folders
6350.29 gm (14 lb)

Envelope of 76 early 19th-century Mexican broadsides (all approximately 32 x 22 cm.)
320.29 gm (11 oz)
316.60 gm (with one removed) (11 oz)

Storage Carton containing Bolivian mss, 1606–1927, but predominantly pre-1826, in legal-size folders
10092.43 gm (22 lb 4 oz)

Appendix II. Materials Vandalized by Gilbert Bland

University of Delaware
John Oldmixon. *Das Britische Reich in America….* Lemgo: Meyer, 1744.
Bland excised Herman Moll, "Eine Neue Charte von America" 21.3 x 48.7 cm
With map 1113.02 gm (2 lb 8 oz)
Without Moll map 1103.96 gm (2 lb 7 oz)

Thomas Jeffreys. *Natural and Civil History of the French Dominions in North & South America….* London: Jeffreys, 1760.
Bland excised "North America from the French of Mr. D'Anville" (47.5 x 57 cm) 22.15 gm (.64 oz)
(Entire volume was too heavy for the small scale being used.)

University of North Carolina at Chapel Hill
Mark Catesby. *The Natural History of Carolina, Florida, and the Bahama Islands….* London: White, 1771. 2 vols.
Bland removed from Vol. 1: "Map of Carolina, Florida, and the Bahama Islands" (52 x 68.5 cm) 47.20 gm (1.6 oz)
(Entire volume was too heavy for the small scale being used.)

NOTES

1. Most of the information in this paragraph is anecdotal. Very little actual research has been done into effective reading room security methods beyond the stage of general recommendations that can be implemented in various ways depending on an institution's circumstances. Even CCTV systems, generally believed to help with deterrence and detection, have had a mixed acceptance. For example, they did not deter map thief E. Forbes Smiley, who stole from reading rooms equipped with them. When suspicions originally fell on smiley in Yale's Beinecke library, the CCTV system was turned off, although Smiley would have had no way of knowing that. For the most current general security guidelines, see ACRL/RBMS *Guidelines Regarding Security and Theft in Special Collections* (Chicago: ACRL, 2009). For a listing of reported library thefts going back to the mid 1980s, see "Incidents of Theft" under the Security Committee at the RBMS home page: www.rbms.info.

2. In preparing this chapter, I was aware of several real-world opportunities to test this system against books that had actually been vandalized. A few libraries, however, flatly refused to allow my experiments or even discuss the matter with me. I was, however, fortunate to discover cooperative libraries that had not reattached maps removed by Gilbert Bland. (See Appendix II for weights of materials vandalized by him.)

3. If the capacity of a scale is exceeded, it will display an error code. It is important to know at which point this code will be displayed. On some scales, it is at about 102% of capacity; on others, it can be as much as 150% of capacity.

4. Dennis East and William G. Myers, "Get the Thief 'Out of the Business': Diary of a Theft," *RBMS* 13 (Fall 1998) describe elaborate measures one thief took to cover the fact he had removed philatelic materials from a manuscript collection (32–33). Weighing the materials before and after use would have instantly detected the removals.

5. This type of behavior was engaged in by a still unidentified thief at the Library Company of Philadelphia in the 1970s. The library's book was eventually recovered from a bookseller. (Based on interviews with Library Company of Philadelphia staff.) Modern books present more problems because they are basically identical. If one had a small pamphlet of poetry printed in 1996 and signed by the author, if a thief substituted an otherwise identical but unsigned copy, the scale probably would not detect it. E. Forbes Smiley was discovered to be in possession of expert facsimile maps, leading to conjectures that he had perhaps substituted facsimiles for the real ones he stole. See William Finnegan, "A Theft in the Library: The Case of the Missing Maps," *The New Yorker* (17 October 2005): 70.

6. Lee Israel, *Can You Ever Forgive Me? Memoirs of a Literary Forger* (New York: Simon & Schuster, 2008), remarks that she substituted her forgeries for genuine articles (97–8). In that case, weighing the folders she used would probably have made no difference. She was nearly defeated, however, by the attendant's vigilance and probably escaped detection only by a stratagem.

7. For a discussion of insider theft and its consequences, see Daniel Traister, "Seduction and Betrayal: An Insider's View of Internal Theft," *Wilson Library Bulletin* 69 (September 1994): 30–33 and Ton Cremers, "Rogues Gallery: An Investigation into Art Theft … and the Curator Did It" (http://www.museum-security.org/insider-theft.pdf). Insider theft is all too common, the most recent incident uncovered being that of volunteer Mimi Meyer at the Harry Ransom Humanities Research Center at the University of Texas, Austin, whose case is summarized by Mark Lisheron, "Book Bandit Rocked Ransom," *Austin American-Statesman*, 1 February 2004. For press releases on other solved insider thefts, see http://palimpsest.stanford.edu/byform/mailing-lists/exlibris/1995/12/msg00101.html; and http://palimpsest.stanford.edu/byform/mailing-lists/exlibris/1998/07/msg00115.html. Obviously, no weighing program will be effective against a staff member who surreptitiously removes entire volumes, as Meyer did.

8. This situation arose recently at Yale University when a student worker hired to help with a move stole some items from the collections while they were in transit. See William Kaempffer and Natatie Missakian, "$2 Million Heist: Hamden Man Suspected in Yale theft," *New Haven Register*, 30 November 2001.

9. In the one library that reports it weighs items in plain sight of patrons, the curator states that many patrons seem oblivious to the procedure and do not seem to realize what is happening.

10. "Chain of custody" is a significant legal concept in this instance. If, for example, Patron X turns a book into Librarian A, who then passes it on to Librarian B, who then passes it on to Librarian C, who actually weighs the book, it could be argued that any missing material might have been removed by Librarians B or C. It is important, therefore, that Librarian A, who takes immediate possession of the book from the patron, do the actual weighing on the spot. In the case of John Hajicek, arrested for supposedly stealing books from a library, he was completely exonerated when he demonstrated that some of the evidence against him could not possibly have been seized at the time of his arrest, a classic case of breaking the chain of custody. See *Columbia* (MO) *Daily Tribune*, 22 April 1995 (http://archive.columbiatribune.com/1995/apr/19950422news13.htm) and 24

April 1995 (http://archive.columbiatribune.com/1995/apr/19950425news16.htm).

11. Conclusion based upon phone conversations with staff of the Image Permanence Institute in 2004. Such considerations will be of concern, however, if items are weighed when accessioned. Because they might well either lose or absorb moisture in the first few weeks after they are brought into the library, an accurate weight might have to wait for several weeks to allow for this process.

12. The notorious John Cockett (aka John Drewe) planted documents in library archival collections, thereby creating false provenance, to make it appear that objects he was selling were genuine. See Jennifer Booth, "Dr. Drewe—A Cautionary Tale," *Art Libraries Journal* 28 (2003): 14–17; and Beth Houghton, "Art Libraries as a Source of False Provenance," World Library and Information Congress: 69th IFLA General Conference and Council, 1–9 August, 2003, Berlin (http://www.ifla.org/IV/ifla69/papers/047e-Houghton.pdf). It was conjectured in some quarters that Samuel Berger, who admitted removing documents from the National Archives, may have also substituted forgeries favorable to President Clinton. See, for example, http://www.captainsquartersblog.com/mt/archives/cat_trousergate.php. For a summary of the Berger controversy, see John F. Harris and Susan Schmidt, "Archives Staff Was Suspicious of Berger; Why Documents Were Missing Is Disputed," *Washington Post* (22 July 2004). In some quarters, the competence of the archivists was questioned, on which see, for example, Fred Kaplan, "Berger with a Side of Secret Documents: Is He a Criminal or a Klutz?" 21 July 2004, on-line at http://slate.msn.com/id/2104138. Henry Putney Beers, *Spanish & Mexican Records of the American Southwest: A Bibliographical Guide to Archive and Manuscript Collections* (Tucson: University of Arizona & Tucson Corral of the Westerners, 1979), discusses an instance from the late nineteenth century in Arizona where land claimant James Addison Peralta-Reavis was proven in court to have introduced forged documents into archival collections to support his fraudulent claim (336). More recently in 2008, the United Kingdom National Archives seem to have been compromised by the introduction of forged documents. See David Leppard, "Forgeries Revealed in the National Archives," Times OnLine (4 May 2008). http://www.timesonline.co.uk/tol/news/uk/article3867853.ece. In this case, the letterheads, supposedly dating from around WW II, were discovered to have been printed on a laser printer, a patent impossibility, among other problems with the documents.

   Special leaves are sometimes removed from otherwise ordinary books. At Yale University in 2005 a thief removed from a book a leaf inscribed and dated by Arthur Conan Doyle (see http://palimpsest.stanford.edu/byform/mailing-lists/exlibris/2005/03/msg00190.html).

13. If one selects a scale to weigh very fine increments, such as grains, it will be vital to provide a hood to insulate the pan from air movements. Appropriate hoods can be fabricated by many firms, including museum exhibition companies.

14. The author has personal knowledge of several such incidents.

15. This is a situation that could be avoided almost entirely by an adequate marking program. (For current marking guidelines, see ACRL/RBMS, *Guidelines*, Appendix I). A plague of expertly (and not-so-expertly) forged documents was unleashed on the Texana market several years ago. For a discussion of the history of those documents, see W. Thomas Taylor, *Texfake: An Account of the Theft and Forgery of Early Texas Printed Documents* (Austin: W. Thomas Taylor, 1991). The general problems of forgeries and both library and booksellers' reactions to the problems they cause are discussed in Pat Bozeman, ed., *Forged Documents: Proceedings of the 1989 Houston Conference* (New Castle: Oak Knoll, 1990), wherein Jennifer Larson, "Obligations of the Dealer: The U. S. Perspective," reports that notorious forger Mark Hoffman in one case substituted a forgery and stole the genuine item at an unnamed library (137). The Folger Shakespeare Library holds several copies of genuine early broadsides and another copy thought to be an expert facsimile of one of them; it, however, refused to allow me to weigh them.

16. That procedure is practicable because in the U. S., coin weights are generally controlled down to the .00 gm level. See U. S. Code, Title 31, Subtitle IV, Chapter 51, Subchapter 2, 5112. Scales specifically designed and programmed to weigh money are still available.

Thieves: Who and Why?

Everett C. Wilkie, Jr.

The only program librarians unanimously find unworkable is the honor system.

~Bahr

Nobody has ever created a usable and recognizable profile of a book or manuscript thief that a librarian could use to positively identify a suspicious person. Thieves have been seen in all varieties, including distinguished professors, long-time trusted library employees, members of the general public, custodial workers, mothers, fathers, the rich, and the poor. Their motives have never been adequately explained or explored, although insight is sometimes shared if the person is arrested and attempts to explain motivations. The reasons for theft are often as myriad as the thieves themselves. Because some of them are never caught, their identities and their motivations cannot be known. The factors that do seem to be constants in all thefts, however, are those known as The Theft Triangle: motive, means, and opportunity.[1] (See fig. 15.1) Any library security program must perforce concentrate on reducing the final element since it has little control over the first two.[2]

John H. Jenkins enumerated five types of thieves and their motivations. His list included: "(1) the kleptomaniac, who cannot keep himself from stealing; (2) the thief who steals for his own personal use; (3) the thief who steals in anger; (4) the casual thief; and (5) the thief who steals for profit."[3] To those, Schröeder adds (1) those who steal to make a political statement; (2) those trying to make a point, such as pointing out defects in an institution's security systems; and (3) those unintentional thieves who get away with materials because of institutional laxity.[4] To those lists, one may also add the extremely rare example of the copycat thief.[5] No doubt other motivations could be added, such as resentment against the library or mental instability, the defense lawyer's darling. Some cases, however, defy explanation. Shenon, discussing the case of Sandy Berger's thefts at NARA, observed that some people who knew Berger "to this day remained perplexed by his crimes."[6]

Precisely who is a threat has also been the subject of conjecture. The types listed above do not, for example, identify which sector of the population is more likely to turn to theft. A kleptoma-

Figure 15.1

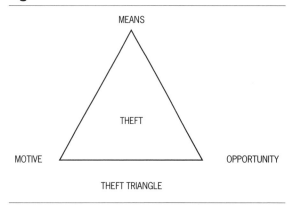

THEFT TRIANGLE

Theft Triangle (Courtesy Sara Alicia Costa, Ocurrente Design)

193

niac or an angry thief could be anybody. In 1968, Thompson confidently stated, "Book thieves may now be classified accurately by profession. Heading the list of professions which have produced notable book thieves is that of the librarian. Close on the heels of the librarian come the clergyman and the scholar. As a big operator, the professional thief ranks considerably behind the librarian and the clergyman."[7] Recent experiences have partly borne him out.[8]

To try to identify thieves by type rather than by motive, an analysis was made of all the appropriate reports in the RBMS Security Committee's Incidents of Theft List, which dates back to 1985.[9] The following table is based on that analysis:

White male	90
White female	10
Insider thefts	33
Outsider thefts	67
White male outsider	64
White male insider	26
White female outsider	4
White female insider	6
Total analyzed thefts	= 100

The following observations emerge from the above statistics:

1) The vast majority of rare book and manuscript thieves are white males, outnumbering female thieves by nearly ten to one. In other words, nearly 100% of thieves are white males.[10]

2) The majority of thefts are done by outsiders (i. e., people with no formal connection to the institution from which they steal).[11]

3) Insider theft is, nevertheless, a significant problem, accounting for nearly 33% of reported thefts. Contrary to sometimes repeated conventional wisdom, however, insider thefts are not more common than those committed by outsiders.[12]

4) White males are more likely to commit thefts in reading rooms; as a percentage of their population, insider thefts by white males constitute only about 33% of all thefts.

5) As a population, females seem more inclined to commit insider thefts, such incidents constituting about 60% of their known activities. They are not so likely to commit outsider thefts.[13]

6) Minority populations present a neglible threat for theft under any circumstances.

Based on other information in the reports, the following conclusions may also be drawn:

7) Almost all thieves act alone. Although there are a few reported instances of collaboration, they are infrequent.

8) Outsider thieves rarely use aliases or false identification, although there are a few instances of that practice. Insider thieves, of course, cannot falsify their identities.

9) Minors seem to present almost no threat. Although the ages of most thieves are unknown and a few are known to be college-age students, those under the age of eighteen are not known to have committed any special collections thefts.

10) Almost all outsider thefts are accomplished in reading rooms. Other types of such thefts, like burglary or smash-and-grab, are extremely rare, which is not to discount their importance. Blumberg and Spiegelman did enormous damage during their careers as burglars, for example.

An adequate security program will, therefore, concentrate its efforts on surveilling white males both in reading rooms and among staff members since they are the ones who seem most likely to commit thefts. On the other hand, female staff members seem to be the ones who should be more carefully supervised inside the library setting itself, since they do not seem to have the same propensity as males for cutting maps out of atlases right in the reading room but prefer to remove materials by other methods, such as smuggling them out the staff door.

Instead of concentrating solely on motivations and types, a library might do well training its staff to identify potential thieves by specific behavior modeling, a technique used widely by police officers and security staff, who are often trained in its practice. The Transportation Safety Administration, for example, employs hundreds of specially trained personnel as part of its "Screening Passengers by Observation Techniques" (SPOT) program at dozens of U.S. airports.[14]

The activity most commonly analyzed is variously called "body language" "paralanguage," or "kinesics." Such techniques seem to have far greater predictive powers than the theoretical analysis of possible motivations or types. Apparently, most potential thieves will give themselves away to a person who knows what to watch for since they have come to the library for the express purpose of stealing materials and are perforce lying. Numerous companies provide training in analyzing body language, and since no liar's pants are likely to spontaneously combust, some training in detecting potential untruths might be a useful preventative.[15]

Several characteristics may mark liars. Identifying those traits might be useful upon both the initial reference interview and upon having to confront someone suspected of theft. Among signs that staff might be trained to observe are:

1) Inappropriate eye contact. Supposedly, liars will tend either to avoid eye contact or maintain eye contact for too long. Darting eyes are cause for suspicion. A corollary of this behavior is someone who looks down when attempting an explanation. People telling the truth will usually look up, even if they do not look you in the eye.

2) Inappropriate touching. Some posit that liars tend to indulge in such activities as covering their mouths, pulling on their ears, or rubbing their noses. Those may all be reactions to stress. The last behavior is the so-called Pinocchio Syndrome.

Supposedly, when people are lying, blood rushes to the nose, causing it to itch. If your patron scratches or touches his or her nose, note that fact. That may be the response to blood rushing to the nose.

3) Inappropriate fidgeting. Liars sometimes fidget, and may tend to shift from one foot to the other. A corollary of this behavior is unsteady hands that shake, although that can also be caused by certain physical conditions or general nervousness.

4) Defensive behavior. A real problem that all liars face is trying to keep their stories straight, particularly the details, especially if they need to repeat them. One might, for example, ask a patron to explain again why s/he needs to use your materials. Someone with nothing to hide will readily repeat the explanation. Someone less than honest may get defensive about having to repeat the story or may mix up details.

5) Defensive body posture. Unless a patron is chilled, s/he will rarely need to cross his or her arms. If, during a reference interview, a patron crosses his or her arms, that should be noted. Note that crossing the legs while sitting probably does not mean anything.

6) Disconnect between a statement and appropriate facial expressions. A liar will often make a positive, cheery statement but then follow it with the expected smile after the statement is completed. An honest person will normally smile, for example, while the statement is being delivered, not after.

None of the behaviors listed above–and they are not nearly the whole catalogue of interesting behaviors–necessarily means a person is up to no good. Perfectly honest people can have some of the same reactions in the right circumstances. A combination of several such behaviors, however, might be cause for suspicion. The opportunity to observe a patron's behavior is a good reason for a reference interview, where reactions might give away a person's real motivations for visiting the library.

A practiced liar and thief, however, will perhaps be well aware of these visual clues and steeled against them. On the other hand, more subtle, involuntary clues cannot usually be hidden by even the most accomplished liars, and staff can be trained in their detection, as well.[16]

Apparently the most powerful deterrent to thieves is the fear that their lies will be found out, so-called detection apprehension. As Ekman points out: "Many factors influence how much detection apprehension will be felt. The first determinant to consider is the liar's belief about his target's skills as a lie catcher. If the target is known to be a pushover, a pussy-cat, there usually won't be much detection apprehension. On the other hand, someone known to be tough to fool, who has a reputation as an expert lie catcher, will instill detection apprehension."[17] Raising the thief's fear of detection apprehension results in contradictions and other signs that the person is not telling the truth.

The demonstration of that concept at work was well displayed in the Smiley case. Smiley easily made his way past the Beinecke's staff and was given books from which he stole maps. Once confronted by the police, however, he collapsed, apparently because he feared quite rightly that he was going to have a harder time lying to them. The crucial incident was when Detective Buonfiglio showed Smiley the E-Xacto© blade that had been recovered from the Beinecke reading room floor by Naomi Saito and wrapped in a tissue by Ellen Cordes, who gave it to the police. Confronted with the evidence, Smiley immediately said the tissue was his and that he had a cold, not knowing that the detective was not the least concerned about the tissue but rather about what it held and knowing also that the tissue never belonged to Smiley in the first place. Smiley apparently became so unnerved that he admitted to knowledge of something that even he knew could not be associated with him in any way and

told an incriminating lie when one was not in the least necessary. He could have with 100% veracity denied any knowledge of the proffered tissue and probably of its contents. As the arresting officer noted, however, when confronted Smiley became "very nervous."[18]

General behavior modelling, as opposed to the specific, seems to hold little promise in detecting a thief beforehand, although librarians must be careful not being gulled by various behaviors or types. Both Blumberg and Bland were widely described as mild-mannered almost to the point of being invisible and attracting no notice. Blumberg even washed, dressed up in better clothes, and carried a briefcase for his "research visits."[19] One thief inspired confidence in reading room staff by pretending to turn in money he had supposedly found, thereby, apparently, succeeding in reducing their suspicions and surveillance efforts. Others, such as Smiley, extruded confidence, grace, and poise. Although one might believe that a potential thief would not wish to draw attention to himself, such is not always the case. Robert Bradford Murphy (aka George Matz and other identities) stole prolifically from the U.S. National Archives by behaving in so rude and eccentric a manner that staff avoided him insofar as possible, thereby facilitating his thefts. As Leab remarks, "His disagreeably aggressive behavior meant that his wishes were met with at each turn. For a period of two or three weeks, Murphy thoroughly, easily and successfully stole at will from this treasure trove."[20] Because all those persons were basically liars, no matter how they behaved in general, other indications might have given them away had staff be alert to them.

Such scenarios strongly suggest that libraries should perhaps train reading room staff in the fundamentals of lie detection. Although reference staff need not be overtly hostile or questioning to a patron, an air of friendly, no-nonsense inquiries about certain aspects of a person's visit and the materials needed for research might do much to deter those who are visiting for less than honorable purposes and make them decide to keep moving.

The damages and repercussions of outsider theft fall on both staff and readers alike, with the greatest brunt probably being borne by the latter, who as a group, innocent and guilty alike, are subjected to ever increasing security measures that restrict access and may cause other inconveniences. The former group is usually subjected to a jarring wake-up call, and consequences can range from discipline to demotion to outright dismissal in addition to added security duties for all staff. As Christine Karatnytsky reports years later after Lee Israel's thefts from the New York Public Library: "This experience, which occurred near the start of my NYPL career, was a painful, shocking lesson, not only for the front-line staff like myself who were duped by this woman and her ilk, but also for the curators. It was they, beginning with George Freedley and continuing with the very dear Paul Myers and Dorothy Swerdlove, who created an institutional culture of personal trust and great good will towards our researchers, especially those, like Israel, who were 'in the business.' (She was very well connected to writers and journalists covering the theatrical beat.) The violation of this spirit of collegiality was difficult to bear, personally and administratively. We all felt betrayed, and the experience has shaped our special collections security policy to this day–sometimes to the dismay of our researchers, not to mention new staff..... It is sad and a little humiliating to revisit this...."[21]

Insider thieves present a more complicated problem since they are usually far more difficult to detect and may carry on their activities in solitude, although that is not necessarily the case. Mimi Meyer and Kathy Wilkerson, for example, had to conduct their thefts while the library was open

because they had no after-hours access. In most cases, such people are above suspicion in the eyes of the world, thereby allowing them to continue their thefts, often for many years. As one person remarked after being told by an FBI agent that his trusted employee was an insider thief, "If he'd told me it was *me* I could not have been more surprised" (original emphasis).[22]

Ton Cremers outlines the characteristics he believes such thieves embody:

1) Most of the time internal thieves have a long working relationship with the institution, varying from some 10 to over 30 years.

2) They are very well trusted and in independent positions–this is true of curators and librarians. Very often they are responsible for the acquisition of new items for the collections, they are recipients of donations, they are responsible for registration, and they have unlimited access to repositories.

3) Often the thieves are valued experts in their profession and therefore beyond any suspicion. The librarian of the French National Library, arrested last year [i. e., 2004], was an international renowned expert of Hebrew manuscripts, and his wife–also arrested–was an expert in Coptic texts and manuscripts. The Danish librarian who was unmasked posthumously last year, was a long-term employee beyond any suspicion.

4) Internal thieves play an important social role. They participate in trade union negotiations, and perform an important role in the professional or private community. The curator of the Army Museum in Delft was very active in trade unions, and was already considering a change in career to become a social worker. The French librarian was a well-known benefactor of an international children's charity.

5) They are the least expected people to be thieves of the collection for which they work.

6) They even participate very actively in solving

the thefts; both in Delft and Paris, the thieves very actively participated in solving the crimes. In Delft this participation was so transparent that it finally led to the arrest of the curator.

7) Insider theft is also a case of swindling. The thieves are never the introvert, remote colleagues with very little contact with co-workers. Contrary, they are more likely the ones communicating with everyone in a seemingly open way. Co-workers are misled as a daily routine. In the Army Museum the director was convinced that his stealing curator was the jewel in the crown of his organisation. He had big plans with this talented man. However, during the investigation this man appeared to be a born liar, and always out to create trust where trust should not be given…. A substantial part of his criminal earnings was invested in several hair implant treatments. His behaviour during the interview I had with him was almost charming. He tried to gain confidence, and every time he was caught lying he was most willing to admit and right away started to build new mystifications.[23]

Such characteristics would seem to apply generally to curators and other senior staff, although the characteristics are hardly foolproof.[24] One convicted curator was described by a colleague as shy and reserved, even "secretive," a profile that hardly fits with Cremers' observations.[25] The profiles of those insiders lower down the ladder are even less clearly delineated. In several cases, former colleagues described them as outgoing and friendly, apparently not the types of personalities that might arouse suspicions.[26] Some others who abused their positions, such as custodians and security guards, are generally nondescript, no evaluation of them being available. Whatever the case, insider thieves are capable of doing great damage, no matter what their stripe.

Insider staff thefts have two special characteristics usually not shared by outsider thefts. First,

although insider thieves are in a minority, they cause often catastrophic losses that dwarf those committed by outsiders. Alexander Polman, who stole from the Dutch Army museum, is estimated to have stolen "over two thousand prints, hundreds of books, and most likely some 20 paintings."[27] Polman almost completely destroyed one rare plate volume, removing forty seven of its sixty seven folio prints, an extent of damage to one volume that probably could not be accomplished in a reading room by a single individual.[28] Frede Møller-Kristensen, the deceased curator of the Danish Royal Library, is known to have taken at least eighty manuscripts and about 600 books, because those had already been sold by his widow and son before police recovered another seventy-five boxes of materials (about 1,500 volumes) from his home.[29] Willingham's depredations, although extensive, could never be determined since he removed many records from the library, including that for the library's eight-volume copy of Pierre-Joseph Redoubté's *Les Liliacées*, of which only two damaged volumes were ever recovered.[30] In another instance at the Texas State Supreme Court, a night janitor stole nineteenth-century case files in the 1970s. The exact number is not known, but is believed to be over a thousand. The files are still showing up in the marketplace decades later.[31] Finally, Yale student worker Benjamin Johnson removed about $2,000,000 worth of materials, some of which he subsequently damaged by cutting out the signatures and selling them separately.[32] Few outsider thieves have ever been known to accomplish such feats at a single institution.

Second, insider thefts or even suspicions thereof sometimes drag the institution into a tangle of incriminations, accusations, and mistrust in a way that no outsider theft can. Their damage often goes well beyond any monetary or collection losses. In the case of the large thefts of manuscript materials by Blumberg at the University of Oregon, the theft was so extensive that it seemed inconceivable that anyone but an insider could have done it. As reported by Nicolas Basbanes, the situation after the theft discovery led to the following events: "In Oregon, meanwhile, sadness turned to outrage, and outrage led to suspicion. 'There was this sense of powerlessness,' [Shannon] Applegate recalled. 'But I was also furious with the university. I felt there had been an incredible betrayal. Scholars aren't even allowed inside those special collections stacks. It seemed it had to be an inside job. We all agreed that was the only way it could have happened. How was it possible to remove what they said was a truckload of documents?' Several university employees were questioned, even a member of the Applegate family was suspected."[33] Cremers reports that after the conviction of Alexander Polman for insider thefts, "we have been able to observe not only the destruction of a fascinating and very rare collection, but also the destruction of working relationships. Now, almost three years after these thefts were discovered there still are a lot of negative emotions and there still is distrust. People blame one another for not noticing the thefts. Some still support the imprisoned curator and regard him as the victim of an imperfect organisation. Others feel a lot of aggression against him."[34] Similar confused and conflicting emotions are also reported by Dan Traister following the insider thefts at the University of Pennsylvania by Kathy Wilkerson.[35]

Monitoring staff and other potential insiders, however, is a difficult proposition, and no known measures will entirely prevent insider theft. Even in highly secure reading rooms, thefts occur; insider thefts are made all the easier by unsupervised access. As tempting as they might seem, Draconian measures are usually impracticable. A library could, for example, state that no staff are allowed on the premises except when the institution is open for regular hours. In reality, such a solution will probably prove unworkable, and in some cases people such as maintenance staff will need to be present either before or after regular hours. A requirement that no staff member ever be in the building alone will also probably prove to be unworkable. In other cases, compromises between security and necessity are possible. Some libraries, for example, allow workers into some areas after hours but do not permit access to sensitive areas such as stacks unless the library is open. Such practices do reduce the opportunities for people to be alone with collections.[36]

Once an institution has gotten past the concept that it need not completely trust anybody, no matter how senior, technology probably provides one solution to the problem of insider thefts. The two main systems that can be used are access control and CCTV. When both those solutions are employed, no staff member is ever really alone and unsupervised. The access control system will record all comings and goings through locked doors into restricted and unrestricted areas, and the CCTV system will record the person's activities, as Daniel Lorello feared. (See his confession below.) Naturally, the saturation level of those systems would need to be quite thorough. Polman put prints into the trunk of his car unobserved before hours, a situation that would have been nearly impossible if the area had been under CCTV surveillance or his access restricted.[37] Needless to say, video evidence might also quickly prove a burglary rather than an insider theft, thereby saving the library needless aggravation and delay. Although covered more extensively in Chapter 12, it is worth mentioning in this context that consistent shelf reading programs and inventories also frustrate insider thefts. Decades between such activities only facilitate those losses. Such arrangements do not necessarily mean that an institution mistrusts any of its staff; they merely indicate that systems are in place to discourage thefts from any quarter.

Regrettably, the bottom line for libraries is that *anybody* can be a thief. As Cremers' analysis would sadly indicate, the more senior a staff member is, the more likely the person will steal, although that theory hardly covers the entire spectrum of insider thieves. Apart from the observation that thieves of any type are more likely to be white males, little guidance can be gleaned about specific populations against which the library should be cautioned. Historically, it would appear that minority populations constitute almost no threat to special collections materials. Other vital statistics about thieves are obscure, however. For example, their ages are rarely known, so one has no idea if a 30-year-old is a bigger threat than a 55-year-old. Until better information can perhaps be developed, a library is well advised to keep a careful watch on anybody who comes into contact with its materials, no matter what his or her role may be.

Appendix I. Daniel Lorello's Confession

LORELLO WAS ARRESTED in 2007 for stealing material from the New York State Library, by which he was employed at the time. Passages in **bold** are printed on the form; everything else is in Lorello's hand. Slightly edited.

Voluntary Statement

State of New York
County of Rensselaer
Date 1-24-08   **Time** 4:45 PM.
Place 53 Van Leuven Dr., South, Rensselaer, N. Y.

I, Daniel Dennis Lorello **address** 53 Van Leuven Dr. South Renssalaer, N. Y. **age** 54 **D. O. B**. — **make the following statement of my own free will.**

I am employed by the New York State Archives in Albany, New York and have been since 1979. I do not recall the first item I took but I think it was in 2002 approximately. I took things on an as needed basis to pay family bills, such as house renovations, car bills, tuition, and my daughter's credit card problem. During the early stages of taking things no one at work ever suspected anything or challenged me at any time. The reason I increased my rate of stealing things was because I learned that surveillance cameras were going to be installed in 2007 and in place by the end of 2007. But the cameras were not installed.

I estimate that I have taken more than 300 or 400 items in 2007 alone. That is when I took most of them. When I sold items I would send them via FedEx, USPS, UPS depending on the buyer's preference. I took money orders, bank checks as payment.

These artifacts were known amongst dealers as shit. I particularly liked items associated with the Revolutionary War, Civil War, Mexican War, Black Americana, WWI, anything related to the Roosevelts, & Jewish items. I took items belonging to all of these wars and ethnic group and sold them on eBay or traded for items which I sold.

I took many items in 2007 because my daughter, ——, unexpectedly ran up a $10,000 credit card bill.

I worked 6:30 A to 2:30 PM in 2007. I estimate that I stole the items 65% of the time between the hours of 6:30 AM to 7:00 AM. I chose that time of day because there was nobody around. 25% of the time I took things during the working day; 10% on weekends and state holidays.

I took the Calhoun letter sometime in 2007. I scanned [it] in 2007 because I thought I was going to sell but changed my mind.

I used the on-line catalogue to pick items/collections. I'd then pick out the items I wanted, placed it in a folder and walked. I was never questioned or challenged.

I estimate that the Attorney General's office recovered approximately 90% of everything I've ever taken.

On 1-23-08 I had the 4 page John C. Calhoun letter at my house at 53 Van Leuven Dr., South, Rennsalaer, N. Y. I first became nervous after a conversation w/ Kathleen Rowe, my boss's boss. She asked me if I knew who "LLD" on eBay was. I knew that it was me. Kathleen Rowe did not know it was me. I worked a full shift that day, leaving work at 2:30 PM, approximately.

On 1-23-08 I went to work at 6:30 AM; stayed until approximately 11:00 AM when I left and drove home. I wrote the letter of apology and returned the Calhoun letter. I did this by driving to Pittsfield, MA, Post Office and paid $14.00 by Express mail. I asked that all be forgiven. The value of the Calhoun letter is really only $600.00. When I saw the eBay bid of $1800.00 I realized it was way too high and I was suspicious of such a high price.

I returned the Currier & Ives Nest Point colored lithograph and the N. Currier colored lithograph of Niagara Falls this morning at 6:50 AM. I placed one in the proper box and one in the next box because Fred Bassett had removed it.

I still have the Belle Boyd appearance broadside. I still have the 1865 Lincoln funeral train time table; E. Anthony Trent affair CDV; unusual Declaration of Independence; super 1865 H. Pope's & Co Sing-Sing prison stereo view.

I am solely responsible for the theft of all these historical documents.

In December 2007 I sold a Davy Crockett almanac 1835 to a man in Colorado for approximately $3200.00. I do my banking at Key Bank on the Concourse and the E. Greenbush Plaza. I divided the money into groups for different projects like home insurance, Christmas, field hockey. I had the Davy Crockett almanac here at my residence at 53 Van Leuven Dr. South, Rennselaer. After I received the check I Priority mailed it to him. The guy liked Davy Crockett almanacs and asked if I had more. I did. I had an 1837 which I sold for $2000.00. So the total received from this man was $5200.

I sold a Poor Richard's almanac in late November or December 2007 for $1001. The buyer was from Connecticut or New Jersey.

The vast majority of my sales were for less than $1000.00

I had an inscribed CDV of Winfield Scott Hancock and sold that for either $2200 or $2400 to ——. This belonged to State Library. —— is an attorney in Schoharie. I sold this item in the summer of 2007. The transaction took place in the bus lot next to the Museum. He gave me cash.

NOTES

1. Robert James Fischer and Richard Janoski, *Loss Prevention and Security Procedures: Practical Applications for Contemporary Problems* (Boston: Butterworth-Heinemann, 2000), list the three elements as motive, desire, and opportunity (63). Martin Gill, "Security in Libraries: Matching Responses to Risks," *Liber Quarterly* 18 September 2008), provides a discussion of what he terms the "seven resources" all thieves must possess to commit a crime (104–105).

2. A library can also reduce motivation by an adequate security program. Both Bland and Lorello admitted, for example, that they feared CCTV systems. On the other hand, Smiley seemed immune to them.

3. John H. Jenkins, *Rare Books and Manuscript Thefts: A Security System for Librarians, Booksellers, and Collectors* (New York: Antiquarian Booksellers Association of America, 1982), [11]. That listing is repeated nearly verbatim without credit by Goshen College, Campus Crime Prevention Programs, *Library Safety & Security: A Comprehensive Manual for Library Administrators and Police and Security Officers* (Goshen: Campus Crime Prevention Programs, 1992), 7. Travis McDade, *The Book Thief: The True Crimes of Daniel Spiegelman* (Westport: Praeger, 2006), notes that Mimi Meyer "stole books to get back at the University of Texas for firing her friend" (23).

4. Schröeder, Margaret, "Special Protection for Special Collections," *Security Management Online*, at: http://www.securitymanagement.com/library/001632.html.

5. "Multiple Map Thief Behind Bars," Thinkspain (12 August 2009), where it is noted that an arrested thief, identified only as Z.V., committed his crimes for the following reason: "The man was prompted to steal historic documents after learning that

ten Ptolemaic maps had been stolen from the National Library in Spain in August 2007, believing that if someone else had done it, he could too." http://www.thinkspain.com/news-spain/16929/multiple-map-thief-behind-bars.

6. Philip Shenon, *The Commission: The Uncensored History of the 9/11 Investigation* (New York: Twelve, 2008), 425.

7. Lawrence C. Thompson, *Bibliokleptomania* (Berkeley: Peacock, 1968), 14–15.

8. See also, Richard Strassberg, "Library and Archives Security," in Paul N. Banks & Roberta Pilette, eds., *Preservation: Issues and Planning* (Chicago: ALA, 2000), 172–175.

9. The list is available at: http://www.rbms.info/committees/security/theft_reports/index.shtml.

10. Unfortunately, no general statistics exist to show what percentage white males constitute of people using special collections or archives. Institutions simply do not seem to collect that type of gender information on registration materials, especially in the current era of political correctness wherein such statistical efforts might be misinterpreted. One institution reported, after doing an ad-hoc, one-month survey for April, 2009, that of the total number of users, 95 were males and 171 were females.

11. Pace the late William Moffet, who opined to Nicholas Basbanes, "Our most serious threat is from 'insider theft.'" Nicholas Basbanes. *A Gentle Madness: Bibliophiles, Bibliomanes, and the Eternal Passion for Books* (New York: Holt, 1995), 488.

12. This statistic is roughly in keeping with Alice Harrison Bahr, "The Thief in our Midst," *Library & Archival Security* 9 (1989): 77–81, who concludes that roughly 25% of library thefts are by staff.

13. As a total of the library population, women far outnumber men, thus statistically raising their insider opportunity. According to United States Department of Labor, "Occupations Ranked by Employment Percentage of Woman and Men," *Occupational Outlook Handbook* (2004), women constituted about 83% of those employed by libraries in the U.S., both in professional and support capacities. http://www.ocouha.com/cur/ooh130501.htm. According to the same source, in the most recent year available (2008–09), that percentage fell to about 81.5%. http://www.bls.gov/cps/cpsaat18.pdf. Brad Oftelie, comp., "Results of the 1997 Survey of the Rare Books and Manuscripts Section (RBMS)" [Chicago: ACRL, 1997] reported that section consists of 64% females ([1]). Available on-line at: http://www.rbms.info/committees/membership_and_professional/rbms-survey97.pdf.

14. See Transportation Safety Administration, "Screening Passengers by Observation Techniques (SPOT)." http://www.tsa.gov/what_we_do/layers/spot/index.shtm; and its "Train Police Officers to Spot Terrorist Related Activity: TSA Designs and Tests Curriculum to Train Police Officers to Spot Terrorist-Related Activity" (6 April 2006). http://www.tsa.gov/press/releases/2006/press_release_0655.shtm. Such concepts are controversial, however. See Carrie Lock, "Deception Detection: Psychologists Try to Learn How to Spot a Liar," *Science News* 166 (31 July 2004): 72. http://www.sciencenews.org/articles/20040731/bob8.asp. Although the era of training CCTV cameras to spot suspicious behaviors is only beginning, it is possible that in the future they could serve to alert staff to problem patrons by modelling their actions.

15. Strassberg discusses some behavioral anomoloies that might also be useful in raising staff suspicions (178).

16. See John J. Fay, ed., *Encyclopedia of Security Management* (Burlington: Butterworth-Heinemann 2007), 161–63 for a useful discussion of the perils and promises of kinesics.

17. Paul Ekman, *Telling Lies: Clues to Deceit in the Marketplace, Politics, and Marriage* (New York & London: Norton, 1985), 49–50. Gill further remarks, "Staff who are alert and give the appearance they will spot something, and guards who appear engaged are a major problem to a thief and these are too often not given the prominence they merit in organisational strategies" (103).

18. See Smiley arrest warrant, Chapter 17, Incident 6. For another instance of police lie detection, see Incident 1 in the same chapter.

19. Basbanes, 482. Blumberg otherwise rarely bathed or changed his clothes (Basbanes, 484).

20. Abigail Leab, "The Saying and the Doing: A Survey of Security and Theft Prevention Measures in U.S. Archives" (Master's thesis, 1998), 10. Also see Donald W. Jackanicz, "Theft at the National Archives: The Murphy Case, 1962–1975," *Library & Archival Security* 10(1990): 23–46, and Philip P. Mason, "Archival Security: New Solutions to an Old Problem," *The American Archivist* 38 (October 1975): 477–92

21. Exlibris discussion list (25 July 2008). The shock that Karantnytsky felt represents a true shift from the culture she describes and which is extensively evoked by Margaret Bingham Stillwell, *Librarians Are Human: Memories In and Out of the Rare-Book World, 1907–1970* (Boston: Colonial Society of Massachusetts, 1973). But even Stilwell had her moments: "Meanwhile the days at the [Annmary Brown] Memorial passed pleasantly, and with a strange mixture of guests. Houdini came in one afternoon, drawn through his interest in astrology to an interest in early printed books treating of that subject. I watched him like a hawk. But happily, he was not a 'collector'" (277).

22. Email to author, 19 November 2007.

23. "...and the Curator Did It," *Rogues Gallery: An Investigation into Art Theft* (AXA Art Conference, 1 November 2005), 3–4. http://www.museum-security.org/insider-theft.pdf.

24. They would certainly seem to apply to Robert Willingham, who was described by several character witnesses as a pillar of his community. See Nicholas Basbanes, *A Gentle Madness: Bibliophiles, Bibliomanes, and the Eternal Passion for Books* (New York: Holt, 1995), 488–89.

25. Email to author, 2007.

26. Emails to author, November, 2007.

27. Cremers, 3.

28. Cremers, 1.

29. Cremers, 6.

30. Basbanes, 489–90.

31. Based on interview with Chris LaPlante, Texas State Archivist, November, 2007. Because the case files are distinctive, the state library has had some success in spotting them in the marketplace and reclaiming them. Those efforts, however have had an unfortunate effect. Now that some dealers are aware of the state's claims, they remove the distinctive filing jackets and sell the manuscripts in small sections rather than all at once. See "Evidence of Ownership Markings," *Missing List: Materials Missing from the Texas State Archives.* http://www.tsl.state.tx.us/arc/markings.html.

32. See Phuoc La, "String of Library Thefts Dates back to '70s," *Yale Herald On-line* (7 December 2001): http://www.yaleherald.com/archive/xxxii/12.07.01/news/p4a.html

33. Basbanes, 478. McDade completes the picture with this horrific conclusion: "The library staff was placed under such heavy suspicion that within a couple of years the four staffers of the collection had left their positions; [Hilary] Cummings left the profession entirely" (25–26).

34. Cremers, 11.

35. "Seduction and Betrayal: An Insider's View of Internal Theft," *Wilson Library Bulletin*, 69 (September 1994): 30–33. McDade also narrates the general erosion of trust in the time immediately following the discoveries of thefts at several institutions (25–27). See also, Edward J. Sozanski, "Theft of Confidence," *Philadelphia Inquirer Magazine* (25 May 1999).

36. Several years ago in response to materials that seemed to be missing, the Library of Congress closed its general stack areas to all but a few people who needed access as part of their duties. Even at that, a recent investigation revealed that as many as 17% of requested materials could not be located, although library officials asserted that the actual percentage of missing materials was closer to 10%. See "Library of Congress Materials 'Unaccounted For,'" *Archival Outlook* (November/December 2007): 13.

37. Cremers, 9. Daniel Lorello stated that he increased the pace of this thefts from the New York state archives when he believed a CCTV system was about to be installed. He also confessed that he came in early and after hours to commit thefts (see above). See Robert Gavin, "Update: State Worker Accused of Stealing Historic Documents." *Times Union* (28 January 2008). http://timesunion.com/AspStories/story.asp?storyID=658903&category=&BCCode=HOME&newsdate=1/28/2008. We nevertheless somewhat agree with Travis McDade, *The Book Thief: The True Crimes of Daniel Spiegelman* (Westport: Praeger, 2006), who concluded: "Even the most sound security and surveillance systems can't prevent thefts by a person with a key to the place and after-hours access" (24).

CH16

Legerdemain
How Did They Do That?

Everett C. Wilkie, Jr.

> We, of course, realize that people will go on trying to steal our property.
> *~Heslinga*

A basic, enduring mystery of most rare books and manuscript thefts is precisely how they were accomplished. The two basic kinds of thefts are outsider thefts, which are accomplished by people who either burglarize the premises or steal from reading rooms; and insider thefts, which involve people with some association with the institution.

Insider thefts, burglaries, and thefts by people such as security guards would seem fairly obvious, although they sometimes seem to happen in plain daylight. In some cases, the thieves simply stole the materials while nobody else was present, as was the case with Blumberg and Spiegelman, who were burglars. In other instances, however, the circumstances of the thefts are more obscure and seem to have happened right in front of potential witnesses. Mimi Meyer, for example, apparently repeatedly walked out of the Harry Ransom Humanities Research Center concealing materials either on her person or in her effects. She had no after-hours access, so all her thefts were accomplished in the presence of others. In the case of Kathy Wilkerson at the University of Pennsylvania, she, too, seems to have walked out of the premises at the end of the day with materials concealed on her person. Denning McTague, an intern at NARA, concealed manuscripts in a legal pad, whereas Benjamin Johnson, a student worker at Yale, seems to have also hid-

den materials on his person. In all those instances, the thefts seem to have occurred in the presence of many potential witnesses. In other cases, the thefts were apparently accomplished when nobody else was around, as was the case at the University of Bridgeport and the Texas State Archives, where personnel stole materials from the libraries during their regular late-night shifts.

Such incidents, however, do not account for the majority of thefts, which occur in reading rooms right under the noses of attendants and other library personnel who are supposedly vigilant.

The techniques of removing materials from reading rooms are limited only by the thief's imagination. Some of them are well known and understood; others are mysteries. They can be used as needed, on individual items and leaves, such as maps, plates, on manuscripts, or on entire volumes. Thieves' dexterity seems amazing. Esko Häkli reports, for example, that Melvin Nelson Perry, about whom library staff was already suspicious, was subjected to the following special arrangements: "The reader was issued with only one volume at a time, and additional staff were placed in the Special Reading Room to keep a close eye on his activities, one of them, in fact, sitting behind him. He also had to show his passport, a requirement which hitherto had not been customary in the library."[1] Even at that, Perry managed to steal six maps.

One security weakness that makes things easier for a thief is unattached materials. One item that Bland stole, for example, was laid into a volume. He didn't even have to bother to cut it out because it was already loose, as was the case with one map Smiley stole.[2] The implication is that libraries need to survey their materials to reattach any loose items that bibliographically should be attached and remove to separate storage items that do not belong in a book. By the same token, one of the reasons manuscript leaves can be readily stolen is that they are often already loose, single sheets of paper.[3]

When faced with an attached single item, the thief has little choice but to remove it. That process is generally accomplished in three ways.

1) Tearing

One way to remove materials from a bound volume is simply to rip them out. That is a hazardous process, however, because the thief risks damaging the materials and the act is anything but subtle. Ripping leaves from a book can also generate noticeable noise. One can assure a clean tear by placing a guide, such as a ruler, vertically along the margin, but that process is so clumsy and obvious that it is apparently not used in reading rooms. Smiley's lawyer stated that his client did indeed remove some maps by tearing them out but also contended that the materials thus removed were so loosely attached that the process was easy.[4] That contention will strike the typical curator as disingenuous since items such as maps and plates are usually quite firmly attached. One does occasionally see maps, for example, on the market that show signs of being ripped out of bound volumes, but one suspects that most items removed in that way are trimmed up to hide the fact.[5] Thief Oliver Fallon apparently did rip leaves from manuscript volumes rather than cut them out.[6]

2) Cutting

Slicing material from a bound volume is a time honored way to steal and apparently the technique preferred by Smiley, who was caught in the act of doing so with an X-acto© blade. Despite the fact that it seems such an act would be obvious, it is apparently very difficult to detect since the movement required to accomplish the removal is fairly small, as is the instrument itself. The most hazardous part of the process is probably the act of concealing the removed leaf rather than the act of removal. Cutting a map or leaf from a book does not require a large blade, for example. Any small, sharp object will normally suffice to cut paper.[7] In the case of books examined after Bland's thefts, it was observed that he apparently was careful to make his first incision strong enough so that he did not have to repeat it. In other words, he used so much pressure that he also sliced into the underlying leaves. Detection of this method is made more difficult if the reader is sitting sideways to the attendant since the book block can be used to partially conceal the movement of cutting the map. Detection would be easier if the researcher were facing the attendant, who then could see straight down the book gutter margin. The blades involved in this technique are so small that they are easily smuggled into a reading room. In grosser cases of this technique, entire text blocks have been sliced from their bindings, although such cases seem usually to happen when the thief has greater leisure, such as in the stacks.[8]

3) Wet String

Another item used for theft and also easily smuggled into a reading room is a piece of cotton string. This technique involves wetting the string by placing it in the mouth for a while, laying the wet string along the gutter margin of the book, closing the book on the wet string, and waiting a few minutes. The saliva in the string migrates to the paper, thereby weakening the fibers and making the leaf easy to extract by pulling on it. Thus, this is actually nothing more than another method of tearing a leaf out, but made easier by weakening the paper first. If done correctly, this method makes no noticeable noise but is more hazardous than cutting since it involves several distinct acts. The string must first be put in the mouth, retrieved, laid in the book, and retrieved again. All those motions provide opportunities for detection. It also takes longer but has the advantage that several strings can be employed at once on different leaves, even in the same volume. A final disadvantage to this method is that it leaves behind copious amounts of DNA that can possibly be recovered and compared to a suspect's DNA. Again, this method is more easily detected if the reader is facing the attendant.

Many other techniques are available to accomplish a theft. Among them are:

Smash and Grab

Although more common in museum settings, this often crude technique involves somehow getting possession of the desired item and then making a run for it while the institution is open for business as opposed to committing after-hours burglary. In December, 1998, thieves forced open a case at England's Durham University Library and made off with numerous valuable items, including a Shakespeare first folio.[9] In another instance, a cased daguerreotype was displayed behind grill work, but an alert thief apparently noticed that if s/he folded the case, the piece would slide through the grill, and thus made away with it. Patrick Bucklew reported that, taking advantage of an unguarded moment, he removed an eight-foot Plexiglas mount from a wall and secreted a displayed scroll in his jacket sleeve.[10] Convicted book thief Rebecca Streeter-Chen removed an atlas from a storage room even though she was accompanied by her two children

at the time. In Salt Lake City, the LDS University Institute of Religion had an entire safe stolen in which were stored two rare Mormon books.[11] Some of those incidents seem to arise generally from opportunity rather than deliberate, planned theft, but all emphasize the importance of having as few unguarded moments as possible in a library.

Substitution

Substitution is a known but somewhat rare occurrence wherein a thief substitutes another volume for the one he wishes to steal. Another such case apparently occurred at the Library Company of Philadelphia, but the details are somewhat vague, and the book was eventually recovered from a bookseller.[12] Somewhat clearer is the case of Donald Lynch, who by substitution stole Chapin Library's copy of a Shakespeare first folio.[13] (See fig 16.1) Smiley was found to be in possession of expertly made facsimile maps, and some have conjectured that he intended to substitute the fakes for the real ones he stole.[14] Facsimile maps were also found in place of genuine maps he had removed. The best documented case of substitution is from the National Maritime Museum in Amsterdam. In that instance, after being alerted by colleagues, library staff discovered the following: "Looking at each piece, only an expert could see how the thefts had been carried out. Our thief had made exact replicas of the maps he wanted to steal, and he had put these replicas back into the atlases in place of the originals. He had also fabricated whole book-bindings and substituted those for the real copies. It turned out that we had several of these 'dummies' in our bookcases!"[15] Lee Israel stole original letters to sell after substituting her own forgeries for them.[16]

Miscellaneous Tricks

The catalogue of the ways in which materials can be removed from libraries is limited only by the

Figure 16.1

Shakespeare Folio Stolen from Chapin College Library
(Used by permission)

thief's ingenuity and imagination. In one case, a woman was stealing books from Brigham Young University by claiming that her metal leg braces were setting off the exit alarms, when in fact it was the security strips in the books doing their job. In another instance, a church was gulled by a so-called parishioner from another church to lend a Bible for an exhibition. The whole story was fabricated, and the Bible disappeared.[17] Some thefts are so mysterious that they boggle the mind and have defied any explanation. The Connecticut State Library, for example, has never solved the mystery of how Blumberg stole nearly 300 books from that institution, although Blumberg is known to have committed burglaries.[18] In another instance, two voluminous reference works with security strips were stolen from the public Reading Room of UCLA's Biomedical Library's History & Special Collections Division: the *Oxford English Dictionary* (1989, 20 vols) and *Paulys Realencyclopaedie der classischen Altertumswissenschaft* (1893–1989, 68 vols), a disappearance that has never been explained or solved.[19] In 2000, a large amount of Oriental material mysteriously

disappeared from a safe at Harvard-Yenching Library, another case that has never been solved.[20] Although this list could be amply enlarged, these instances should be enough to alert the librarian that vigilance is always a necessity and that the materials the library owns are under constant, novel threats, the precise nature of which may be unknown and unanticipated.

The ability to deaccession items is also a potential security hazard. Controls over deaccessioning vary widely, from policies that provide that nothing can be removed without the Board's permission to those that give curators a certain amount of financial leeway so that minor materials may be disposed of without undue administrative burdens. The ways in which materials may be stolen through deaccessioning are myriad. In New Zealand, librarian Karen Dale Churton used her position to steal books and then delete the cataloguing records from the on-line system.[21] Clive Driver of the Rosenbach Library forged documents that made it appear that the material he was selling had been approved for deaccessioning by the library's board. Despite the best of intentions and controls, however, valuable items can still escape by legitimate means. In one case, the first edition of William Brockton Brown's first novel was sold at a library book sale for pennies on the dollar. In another case, a first separate state printing of the U.S. Constitution was disposed of, again for an absurdly low price. Although bad bargains cannot be entirely avoided, the library should seek to ensure that deaccessioning activities are controlled to the extent that nothing valuable can be disposed of under false pretenses. At the very least, such policies should be reduced to writing and any activities audited.

Out the Door

Once the thief has removed the item, s/he must then somehow remove it from the library. If the item is stolen in the reading room, it usually must somehow be secreted or hidden. That may be accomplished in various ways.

The case of Gilbert Bland is somewhat instructive in the mysteries of thieves. Bland stuffed stolen maps into his clothing while sitting in various reading rooms. Some of the materials were, for example, put in his pants. Perhaps that would not be a remarkable situation except for size of some of the maps he stole. One map stolen was a large folded folio on thick paper. When it was recovered, it showed no signs of being folded beyond the original folding; in fact, none of the Bland maps examined show any signs of being folded again, which suggests Bland stole them without folding them into a smaller size for easier concealment. In those particular cases, we are obviously discussing surveillance lapses by library staff. That Bland could have stolen such large maps by putting them in his clothing without some obvious effort on his part to conceal them there is almost inconceivable. If one wishes to get some idea of the logistical problem involved, take a sheet of the local newspaper, fold it in fourths, and then try to hide it in your clothes. That's the equivalent of what Bland managed to do, sometimes sitting in plain sight.[22]

In other cases, materials were also concealed in clothing. In Smiley's case, Yale police recovered one map from the inside pocket of his sport coat. (Other materials were found in his brief case, although he did not have access to that while in the Yale reading room.) Sandy Berger also hid materials in his clothing, as did Dwain Edgar Manske, who stuffed materials in his "pockets, pants, and socks."[23] Bloomberg is reported to have had special clothing with extra pockets in which to conceal materials.[24] Confessed thief and forger Lee Israel admitted to secreting letters in her shoes.[25]

One obvious conclusion from the cases of Bland, Manske, and Smiley is that clothing is rou-tinely used to secret stolen materials. At the very least, no researcher should be allowed in a reading room wearing a coat or cardigan sweater of any sort. Indeed, minimally dressed researchers should be the library's goal.[26] Since the days are long gone when patrons may bring into reading rooms brief cases, purses, or bags, it would seem in most cases that thieves have little choice but to resort to their clothing for concealing materials.

Finally, users taking notes manually should be provided paper for that purpose rather than being allowed to use their own. Workers such as interns and student workers should not be allowed to bring anything into the collections areas and should depart empty-handed at the end of the day, although that will certainly not stop a determined thief who conceals materials otherwise. In the case of Denning McTague, an intern at the National Archives and Record Administration, materials were concealed inside a legal pad and removed when he walked out the door with the pad. He apparently did that repeatedly.[27] Thief Oliver Fallon also hid materials inside a notebook he was allowed to bring into the reading room.[28] Despite the apparent ease, however, of prohibiting researchers from bringing extraneous materials such as notebooks into a reading room, the case is not always so simple as it appears. Researchers will sometimes have valid needs for their own materials. A researcher might want to compare his or her personal copy of a book to the library's copy, for example, or need to compare the published version of a manuscript to the library's original. As easy as flat prohibitions might seem, they are sometimes detrimental to research, and each library will have to make its own decisions in each instance, keeping in mind the security implications of such allowances.[29]

Conclusion

Nothing will ever substitute for vigilance and careful surveillance of users and staff as the primary methods to prevent theft. Although other supplementary measures such as weighing materials and CCTV systems are excellent adjuncts, they depend on humans to operate them properly and to interpret correctly the evidence they capture. Humans are the ones who steal materials, and only other humans will stop them, assuming that they are alerted to the situation by their own observations. In many ways, custodians of materials must learn to think like thieves and be suspicious of the opportunities presented by something so common as a cardigan sweater, a pair of pants, or a legal pad. As security measures continue to increase, thieves' efforts to evade them will likewise become ever more ingenious.

NOTES

1. "Paradise Lost: A Theft from Helsinki University Library." *Liber Quarterly* 2 (2002): 321.

2. Smiley also had no problem removing the map from a copy of John Smith's *Advertisements for the Unexperienced Planters of New England* because, again, the map was merely laid in.

3. The problem of unattached materials is in many cases an instance of where conservation needs intersect security considerations. In the case of the loose map Bland lifted, his problem was made all the easier because the text block had separated from the binding and the first several signatures of the book, including the map, were already loose. His theft would have been made somewhat more difficult had there been money to restore the volume to integrity.

4. That assertion will strike the average curator as somewhat disingenuous since most maps and plates are firmly attached. In one case, one map at Yale was so resistant to being torn out that it was damaged. See William Finnegan, "A Theft in the Library: The Case of the Missing Maps," *The New Yorker* (17 October 2005): 70.

5. The author knows of one instance wherein a patron, frustrated by denial of his photocopy request, simply tore the needed leaves from a modern poetry book right in the reading room. The need to be able to hear a leaf being torn from a volume argues for relatively quiet reading rooms.

6. Paul Thornton, "Academic 'Falls from Grace' by Stealing Church Records," *Edinburgh Evening News* (13 May 2008). http://edinburghnews.scotsman.com/edinburgh/Academic—39falls-from-grace39.4077609.jp.

7. César Ovidio Gómez Rivero, who cut numerous maps from a Ptolemy volume at the National Library in Madrid, used a Stanley knife, which seems an incredibly clumsy, obvious tool for such activity.

8. See, for example, the report of an unknown person who slashed the text blocks from about 150 books in California libraries. See Exlibris, 28 March 1995, via *Chicago Tribune*, and March 26, 1995, via *San Francisco Chronicle*.

9. This case appears to have been partially solved in 2008 with the recovery of the missing Shakespeare. See David Brown, "William Shakespeare Folio Worth £15m Recovered 10 Years After Being Stolen," *The Times* (12 July 2008): http://www.timesonline.co.uk/tol/news/uk/article4316464.ece.

10. "How I Stole a Ming Scroll," *Time* (6 September 2004).

11. Justin Hill. "Books of Mormon May Resurface if Thief Was after Cash. " *Salt Lake City Tribune* (12 April 2006). http://msn-list.te.verweg.com/2006-April/004974.html.

12. Based on interviews with LCP staff, 2006.

13. Lawrence S. Thompson, *Bibliokleptomania* (Berkeley: Peacock, 1968), 34–36. For a fuller accounts, see Robert M. Hitchcock, "Case of a Missing Shakespeare," *Esquire* 16 (December, 1941), and Mark E. Rondeau, "The Bard's Wild Ride: The Almost Forgotten Theft of a Shakespeare First Folio from Williams College." http://www.markrondeau.com/folio.html. This theft is yet another example of the enduring debt that libraries owe the FBI for their assistance in various cases.

14. See Finnegan, who observes: "Under the circumstances, it was disturbing that Smiley was carrying around an unusually good facsimile of an exceptionally valuable map [i.e., Robert Thorne's 1582 *Septentrio Orbis Universalis Descriptio*]. How many curators might be saying that items were accounted for when those items had been replaced by very clever reproductions?" (70).

15. Els Van Eijck Van Heslinga, "Catch as Catch Can," *Liber Quarterly* 12 (2002): 317–318.

16. Lee Israel, *Can You Ever Forgive Me? Memoirs of a Literary Forger* (New York: Simon & Schuster, 2008), 95–104.

17. Exlibris, 3 October 1995.

18. Nicholas Basbanes, *A Gentle Madness: Bibliophiles, Bibliomanes, and the Eternal Passion for Books* (New York: Holt, 1995), 471–73, 475–78, 480.

19. Email to author, 2007.

20. "Yenching Plundered," *Harvard Magazine* (January-February 2001).

21. RBMS Home Page, "Incidents of Theft," April, 2007. http://www.rbms.info/committees/security/theft_reports/index.shtml

22. In one library with physical surveillance problems, Bland apparently deliberately sat where he could not be directly observed.

23. Travis McDade, *The Book Thief: The True Crimes of Daniel Spiegelman* (Westport: Prager, 2006), 33. Philip Shenon, *The Commission: The Uncensored History of the 9/11 Investigation* (New York: Twelve, 2008), reports that one NARA archivist saw Berger in a hallway with documents obviously protruding from his socks and pants (7).

24. Basbanes, 470.

25. Israel, 36 and 97. She did so, however, only *after* removing the material from the reading room.

26. For a somewhat semi-serious discussion of the implications of allowing readers into the reading room dressed in their own clothes, see Honan, William H. "Ideas and Trends: Strip Search before Scholarship." *New York Times* (28 May 1995). : http://query.nytimes.com/gst/fullpage.html?res=990CE0DF103EF93BA15756C0A963958260.

27. RBMS Home Page, "Incidents of Theft," March, 2007.

28. Thornton.

29. If a patron states that s/he wishes to compare the library's copy of an item to one personally owned, the patron should not be allowed to proceed until the personally owned item is presented. Smiley used such a ploy but was never asked to produce his originals. In Berger's case it was, ironically, his own notes on his own legal pad that he needed to steal. Because they concerned classified documents, he could not remove even his own notes from NARA, so he resorted to stealing: "He moved quickly. He ripped off the top fifteen pages of his hand-written notes from the pad, folded them into thirds, and placed them in the inner pockets of his jacket. He left two other pages behind in hopes that would throw the archivist off the trail" (Shenon, 7).

Dealing with a Theft: Before and During

Everett C. Wilkie, Jr.

> Meanwhile, however, librarians should again be aware that Mr. Witherell has demonstrated a long fascination with books–your books–and likes to visit them in libraries–your libraries as well as ours.
>
> *~Dan Traister*

Despite all precautions a library may take, thefts happen. Ranging from major to minor, all thefts and mutilations of materials are serious matters. Although the obvious high-value targets often come to mind, staff needs to bear in mind that there is probably a thief for everything, no matter how inconsequential an item might seem. In one case back in the 1980s, staff at several libraries discovered that the same leaf had been removed from all their copies of a genealogy. That curious discovery was made when one library attempted to get a photocopy replacement leaf for its damaged copy but found that every nearby library it contacted had the same problem. When an intact copy of the book was finally discovered, it turned out that one of the passages in the text cast aspersions on a certain person. It was theorized that an aggrieved descendent was removing as many of the pages as could be located.[1] Although the missing material was not a Ptolemy map, the technique was the same. In light of peccadilloes, both great and small, library staff should never assume that anything is safe.

Before a Theft

Whatever the case, the time to be prepared for a theft is before it happens. Nothing so frustrates any chance of prevention or recovery than a library response that is disorganized, inept, confused, and contradictory.[2] Such a situation might be avoided if the library were better prepared to respond properly to a theft. Among essential steps that every library should take are the following.[3]

1) Appoint a Library Security Officer (LSO). This person is in charge of overall security in the library and in special collections in particular. In a case of theft, the LSO should be the one directing the library's responses, including such tasks as arranging for news conferences, dealing with the media, and communicating with the institution's insurers. S/he should have broad responsibilities for implementing security measures and should also have an authorized deputy in case of absence during an incident.

2) Educate staff in the state's laws concerning library theft. Such state laws vary widely, from practically non-existent to fairly elaborate ones that grant librarians such powers as the ability to physically detain a suspect. In the absence of any specific laws addressing library thefts, the staff needs to know which state laws apply to their situation and what actions they may take under them. That education should be done in part with the cooperation of counsel and local law enforcement, who can better explain various scenarios and potential responses. Improper responses can entail significant legal liabilities.[4]

One scenario that should be clearly reviewed

with staff is the concept of a citizen's arrest since that may well be the underlying principle if library staff restrain a suspected thief in absence of specific legal authority to do so. All states but North Carolina allow such an arrest, although even that state allows an average citizen to detain another under certain circumstances. State laws vary widely on the circumstances pertaining to this situation, so little general advice is available. Again, local counsel and law enforcement should help train staff in the possibilities.[5]

Another legal scenario that may come into play is "shopkeeper's privilege," which also allows certain people to detain suspected thieves under certain circumstances. In some instances, such privileges have been codified under shoplifting laws, which may or may not apply to a library. Once again, the advice of counsel and law enforcement is vital to a proper understanding of the librarian's actions in such a scenario.

3) Decide what type of response will be made if a theft is discovered in progress. Those procedures should be established at the highest institutional level possible to avoid misunderstandings by staff and to properly protect them in case they need to act on a theft. As obvious as it may seem that a librarian would confront a thief, such is not necessarily the case. Some institutions would not allow that course for various reasons, including negative publicity, personal safety, and the possibility of a false accusation.[6] Other institutions might, depending on the circumstances. As inconceivable as it may seem, a library's policy might be to allow a thief to escape uncontested with the institution's Gutenberg Bible. In any case, the actions to be taken in cases of theft should be worked out and made clear well before they are needed.[7]

4) Know whom to call in case of a theft and exactly how to contact them. Depending on the institution's circumstances, the responding agency may be the school's security force, the local police department, the sheriff's office, or the state police, among others. Library staff need to know precisely which agency will respond and approximately how long it will take someone to arrive. It is helpful to have local authorities visit the institution in order to be familiar with it long before any need for their presence arises. As J. Stephen Huntsberry, himself a police officer involved in the Blumberg investigation, remarks, "Librarian and law enforcement rarely understand each other's roles and responsibilities in case of a reported theft," a situation that should be ameliorated insofar as possible.[8] On the other hand, some preparation is possible. As one commentator remarked: "Police or security personnel and library staff must talk to one another about their common problems. It is essential to any effective proactive program to determine and share different perspectives, to understand techniques and procedures associated with each other's discipline and to grasp what may and what may not be practically accomplished by the other.... What is critical is that representatives from both areas recognize the need and importance of such communication and initiate the network without hesitation."[9] The institution's primary goal is to get somebody with arrest powers to the scene as soon as possible.[10]

As obvious a corollary as it would seem, it is vital that staff know how to summon the proper authorities to the scene. In some cases, doing so may be as simple as dialing 911. In other cases, especially on university campuses or state institutions with their own security forces, the procedure may be more complicated. One might first, for example have to contact campus security, who will in turn investigate and then contact regular law enforcement if necessary. In all cases, however, staff need to know precisely which number to dial to summon the needed assistance.[11]

5) Psychologically prepare and empower staff.

All library staff must be educated to expect theft rather than to believe it will never happen. At bottom, a uniform low level of mistrust must be imbued into all staff so that they do not commit crucial mistakes, such as allowing unwarranted exceptions for certain users, believing certain people to be above suspicion, or failing to believe the evidence of their own eyes. Staff should feel free to bring to supervisors any suspicions or concerns they may have, even about their colleagues. As Schröeder remarks, "Instilling a sense of ownership and motivation within employees can often make the difference between an attempted theft and a successful one."[12] Of course, it does not pay to instill staff with Othello's level of paranoia, but a healthy suspicion about many things can prevent mischief.[13]

6) Secretly flag extremely valuable materials. Despite the rather mundane theft discussed in the first paragraph of this chapter, some materials are truly of higher value than others and often need special protection. It is an asset to security if those materials an institution considers highly valuable can be somehow marked to alert reading room staff of their presence. Such a mark would normally take the form of an altered call number with an otherwise meaningless element that alerts staff to the material's importance or a special flag inserted with the item. Such plain language indications as "Vault" or "High Security" should be avoided and replaced with something meaningless, like ### or "Doe Collection." Special shelf marks can also be used to indicate the availability of surrogates, which might be offered instead of originals.[14]

7) Establish and maintain a marking program of both visible and secret marks. As obvious and as necessary as such a program may appear as a first defense against theft and an aid to recovery, many institutions for various reasons throw up their hands at the very idea, either for aesthetic or practical reasons. Marking programs have proven

deterrent value and have more than proven themselves when it comes to recovering materials. In the case of Smiley, who did more than $3,000,000 worth of damage, that kind of money would have paid legions of trained workers to mark the maps he stole. In Smiley's case, libraries were unable to identify and recover their property because he removed some visible marks and some maps lacked marks, a situation distressingly similar to that of Gilbert Bland, in which the same situation pertained.[15] Visibly marking materials may be shameful; losing and being unable to recover materials is even more shameful, however.

8) Have library material professionally appraised to identify high-value items and other items of commercial value. Although the majority of special collections items might not be extremely valuable, the actual cash value of an item might well influence a police officer's decision about what course to take with the suspect. Such evaluations might be obtained as part of an institution's insurance reviews.[16]

9) Compose a written security policy in which procedures, actions, and policies are clearly set out and agreed to by everyone in the repository. All staff members who are responsible for enforcing security should sign this document, both at its origination and any time it is changed; it may prove to be an important legal protection for both the institution and its staff in the event of an incident.[17] It will also serve as the basic guide for all staff confronted with a possible incident in the library.

10) Learn to think like a thief. Security measures of all kinds should be constantly tested under various scenarios to see if one can identify weak points or even defeat the system. As Mandelbaum remarks, "The ingenuity of some criminals in devising new techniques to defeat protective installations is close to incredible. Reports of their successful ruses would fill an entire volume."[18] Sadly, in the

case of special collections, their exploits do in fact fill entire volumes. As Shuman recommends, "Read the literature of library theft. Don't assume you know all the answers or have even thought of all the questions."[19]

11) Consider restricting access, both to certain classes of researchers and certain classes of materials. Some libraries will not allow researchers who are otherwise unconfirmed or unvetted to show up unannounced and be admitted to the reading room. Others allow readers to examine materials without prequalification but then do not allow unrestricted access to original materials, especially those of high value. Common sense would suggest that such policies would limit access to original materials and hence reduce thefts. In some ways, however, such policies go against the grain. It is, nevertheless, prudent for a library to examine its access policies well in advance of any potential regrets. In Blumberg's case, for example, at least two libraries refused to admit him.[20] That was probably a wise decision.

During a Theft

The chances that a special collections staff member will actually have to confront a thief directly are remote, although that does not mean one should not be prepared for the possibility. The occurrence happens so rarely that it is basically undocumented. (See Appendix I below.) In most reported cases, the thief was confronted by law enforcement or security personnel either on the spot or well after the fact. Nevertheless, in the rare instance that a person might have to confront or challenge a thief, certain considerations apply.

Reasonable Grounds / Probable Cause

Before a staff member may confront a suspected thief, s/he must usually have "reasonable grounds" or "probable cause" to believe that the person is committing theft or mutilation. In Connecticut,

that concept is defined as:

> For the purposes of this subsection, reasonable grounds shall include knowledge that a person (A) has concealed a book or other archival library materials while on the library facility premises or is removing such book or material from the library facility premises without authority or (B) has mutilated, defaced or destroyed a book or other archival library materials belonging to or deposited in a library facility. (Sec. 53–119b)

For better or worse, the concept is open to interpretation with each individual incident. A mere "hunch" that someone is doing something nefarious is not grounds to confront him or her. Some action or set of circumstances must exist to lead a reasonable person to believe that a theft is occurring, although probable cause is not the equivalent of absolute certainty. For example, when an X-Acto© blade was discovered on the floor of the Beinecke Library, that alone was sufficient to establish reasonable grounds that Smiley was stealing materials or intended to do so. When Bland fled from Johns Hopkins, he established reasonable grounds for further investigation since flight is usually taken as a sign of possible guilt. If a patron, after repeated requests not to do so, continues to arrange boxes in the work space so as to obscure the view of the reading room attendant, that action would possibly be reasonable grounds to suspect theft. In some ways, those are common-sense definitions and apply to the conclusions an ordinary, prudent person would make in the same circumstances. Gaining familiarity with this concept is an issue with which counsel or the local police can help library staff. Needless to say, that type of training should take place well before it is needed and should be repeated for newly hired staff.[21]

Reasonable Suspicion

Reasonable suspicion is a standard just below the level of reasonable grounds, and posits that if the "officer receives information, either through his own senses or from some other source, which leads him to believe criminal activity is occurring, or is about to occur, then the officer can briefly detain the individual. That detention can last until the officer has determined that no crimes are occurring or until probable cause develops, at which time the officer can arrest the detainee."[22] In most cases, it is probably wiser to await the arrival of the police, who can act on a reasonable suspicion with relative impunity. One major problem arises with third-party reports. If a volunteer, for example, states that Mr. Doe appears to be stuffing manuscripts in his pants, try to verify the suspicions for yourself. Acting on what is basically hearsay is hazardous, although the police can probably act on such a report if the officer is persuaded that he or she has a reasonable suspicion that a crime has been committed, which would give the officer leave to investigate further to see if probable cause can be established. In the absence of probable cause, an officer usually may not arrest someone without a warrant.

At the development of the incident:

- Summon a witness as soon as possible. If you believe a patron is stealing materials right before your eyes, get corroboration from another staff member. Do so discreetly.
- Contact the LSO immediately.
- If the CCTV system has the capability, focus a camera on the suspect and have someone watch the monitor. Be sure the recording equipment is working.
- If any material used by the patron has already been turned back in, immediately examine it for damage or loss.

- If you are reasonably certain that something amiss is happening, call the police or whomever institutional policy directs.

The above five points would seem appropriate to any security policy. Beyond them, however, the situation and staff actions will vary widely depending on institutional policy, the specific situation, and state laws. The points suggested below are merely offered as some scenarios and issues that a library might consider in a security policy.

If the person shows no signs of leaving:

- If the suspect shows no signs of leaving, merely summon the police. They will take care of the whole situation once they arrive. *It is pointless for library staff to confront a patron suspected of theft if there is no urgent reason to do so, even if they are actively mutilating or concealing materials.* Under no circumstances betray to the person that your suspicions are aroused.
- If an officer arrives while the suspect is still on the premises and you believe the person has secreted your materials on his or her person, try to persuade the officer to do a so-called Terry Pat (or "patdown") of the suspect. A Terry Pat is a cursory search of a person's outer garments that an officer may do for various reasons, but is usually permissible when reasonable suspicion is present. If the person is believed to be slicing materials from books, remind the officer that the person may be armed with a blade of some sort, which would then give the officer grounds to search the suspect for personal safety concerns. If the officer finds any library materials on the suspect, the case will probably at that point escalate to probable cause.

If the person is trying to leave:

- You may have little choice but to try to delay the person until the police arrive, if that is institutional policy. That course will involve direct contact with the suspect. At this point, the police should already have been summoned.

- If at all possible, try to move your conversation to a private place away from others. Keep your witness with you at all times, however.

- Be alert to the suspect's body language. One symptom to observe is the so-called Pinocchio Syndrome. Supposedly, when people are lying, blood rushes to the nose, causing it to itch. If your suspect scratches or touches his or her nose, note that fact. Also be alert to people who put a hand over the mouth, pull on an ear, or will not look you in the eye. Be aware, however, that none of those actions necessarily indicate anything specific in relation to the unfolding incident. A shy but otherwise innocent researcher who believes s/he is being doubted may display many of the same reactions.

- Be alert to your own body language. In your own case, do not use threatening gestures, such as balling your hands into fists or pointing a finger at the person. Avoid crossing your arms or putting your hands on your hips. Never lose your temper, use curse words, shout, or call the person names. No matter how upset you are, do not display any negative emotions when talking with a suspected thief. Keep your voice calm, level, and professional.

- Do not make accusations. In your conversation with the person, merely inquire if perhaps there has been some misunderstanding whereby your materials have been intermingled with personal possessions by mistake. That should be your tack even if you are sure the person is secreting your materials. Try to enlist the person's cooperation in resolving the situation.[23] Under *no* circumstances threaten the person with arrest or jail.

- If the person surrenders any library material, you will have a judgment call to make. It is possible that an innocent mistake has been made, and some state laws forgive those who unintentionally or unwillfully conceal materials. On the other hand, if you are reasonably sure a deliberate theft has occurred, do not accept denials, either, and do not necessarily let the person leave just because you have recovered your materials.[24] Do not be cowed by threats of a law suit.

- Do not touch the person without cause to do so. Although state laws or library consent policies might give you the right to search a person's belongings, usually only a police officer may conduct a physical search of a person. Even if you saw a patron put a manuscript in a coat pocket, you should not attempt to retrieve it yourself.

- If your institution retains a patron's ID card, every effort should be made to keep possession of it. (This situation is an important argument for taking photocopies of ID during the registration process.)

- If the person tries to leave the premises, the situation can become extremely problematic. Some states allow librarians to restrain a patron by using reasonable force, although such laws still do not permit a search. If your state or institution does not allow that course or you are not in a position to do so, there is little choice but to allow the person to depart. Do not be a hero.

- If you have the person actually locked in the reading room, you might end up with a very unpleasant situation on your hands, especially if there is no other avenue of escape except a controlled, locked door. If the person is actually guilty, h/she may become desperate to escape before police arrive. If the person becomes physically threatening, by all means unlock the door and allow him or her to exit. If the person attempts to escape through another means, such as a staff door or a fire escape, allow him or her to leave.

If one is faced with a serious physical threat during a theft, the first lines of defense are compliance and retreat. One's chief goal under the circumstances is to get the person to depart without anyone's being injured. Whatever the person demands should be surrendered without protest or resistance. If the person actually assaults someone, however, most jurisdictions allow a person to use reasonable force to defend her/himself or others. Again, this scenario should be reviewed with counsel and law enforcement; it is possible, for example, that the jurisdiction will require a person to retreat and offer resistance only as a last resort.

Actual violence in the U.S. committed during thefts of materials from rare book and manuscript libraries is extremely rare. One of the few such instances involved a theft at Transylvania University Library in 2004 when a librarian was physically restrained and assaulted by thieves, who were later captured and convicted.[25] Bland and a thief at the New York Public Library also refused to cooperate and resisted capture by fleeing. Other than those instances, however, such occurrences are not the norm, and most thefts are by undetected legerdemain or, as in Blumberg's and Spiegelman's cases, burglary.[26] (See Appendix I.)

- If the person actually leaves the building, s/he might be followed so long as possible, keeping in mind that you should maintain a careful distance and immediately retreat if necessary. The goal here is to gather information for the police, not to actually apprehend the person. If you are going to follow someone, do not do so alone and try to take a cell phone, a piece of paper, and something to write with. If a vehicle is involved, record its make, model, color, and license plate information. Also take careful note of the person's physique, clothing, and other identifying characteristics. If the person discards anything, be sure to note its location but do *not* retrieve it.[27] All those actions will assist the police in their efforts to resolve the problem. Again, this is not a situation that calls for the heroics of Rex Libris.[28]

- If the police actually apprehend the suspect promptly, if at all possible try to persuade them to arrest the person if probable cause can be established. This is an instance in which it would be important to know the value of materials the person supposedly stole or damaged, since that information might influence the police one way or the other, and to know your state laws about library thefts.[29] At the very least, attempt to persuade the police to hold the person long enough to confirm his or her identity. There is just enough possibility that the person may have presented a false ID that this point should be definitively cleared up. Both Bland and Blumberg, for example, used false identification on occasion. In another instance, "One Robert Bradford Murphy passed himself off as Dr. Bradford, historian and consultant in Western history for the Library of Congress, to the Georgia Department of Archives and History; as R. O. Stanhope, journalist, to the Indiana State Library; as Dr. Murphy, journalist residing in Illinois, to the National Archives."[30] Remind the officer that the possibility of false identity is very real in the situation and that the suspect's genuine identity should be established before s/he is released.

- If the police are convinced that the person should be arrested, an officer will likely ask if you wish to press charges. The answer to the question should probably always be "Yes"; however, that question should be answered only by a person authorized to make that decision. Charges may later be dropped for various reasons, but the initial stage of prosecuting the person begins at the arrest and should go forward at that point.

- Do not disturb or move anything until the police allow you to do so. Leave all papers and books on the desk, for example, exactly as they were at the time of the incident. Moving things might compromise evidence. (See Incident 7 below.)

- As soon as you can, write down your description of the incident while it is fresh in your mind. Any other staff members who had any contact with the suspect should also write down their recollections. Do not wait two weeks. It is important to be accurate, dispassionate, and detailed, and to continue to add to the document as time passes. For example, details that may not seem to matter at the time may become crucial later. The document may end up in court. As Allen remarks, "This will prove to be an invaluable record later as memory fades."[31]

After a Theft

If a theft is discovered, the library will begin to the process of recovering its materials. In some cases, the path to recovery is straight and short; in others it is neither. Recovering lost materials is treated in the next chapter.

Appendix I: True Crime
Real Stories of Real Encounters with Real Thieves in Special Collections

INCIDENT 1

THE MAN I CHASED got away from a locked room with a Defoe *System of Magick*–the old reading room–after running a substitution. After using the book (it was the second edition, not the first), he'd asked to have it held, left, and come back–without anyone realizing that, in Prints (next door) he had taken a volume of similar size and covered in the same sort of library brown off the publicly-accessible reference shelves, put it under his shirt, and come back with it. Prints was not, in those days, a "special collection"; I don't know if this sort of thing could still be done. He waited until I was out of the room working with a reader. J*** and (I believe) L*** were not there, either. The then Technical Assistant B*** was working with another reader *in* the room, so she too was distracted. When she got "the book" back, she let the thief out. But Prints class marks are very distinctive. Rare Books are one mark; Prints are something else. He did get out the door but, within 30 seconds, B*** was at the gate interrupting me with the reader I was helping. I had to chase the guy the equivalent of two blocks and down two flights of stairs. To his astonishment–and mine–I caught him; I was a LOT heavier then, and then as now rather un-fleet of foot. And–credit to the cops–they were on us as I reached him. By then he had ditched the book; it was, however, almost immediately located (atop a bookcase ornamentally located in a stairwell? I am not sure where it was) by a cop who asked him a question that, he later told me, would almost certainly push him (a) to deny that there *was* any book and (b) look in its direction–which he did (that is, he did *both* a *and* b; the cop didn't listen to him but instead watched the direction of his gaze). The guy was a rather well-dressed African-American male, probably late 20s/

early 30s (forgive my memory; it *has* been more than a quarter of a century). I probably wouldn't have chased him if he'd merely stolen my wallet; I was *really* angry that he'd stolen a book.

But I got two things out of this. (1) A long lecture from John Law. The guy looked sweet enough but his record included armed robbery, rape, and assault. Not a nice man; in fact, a dangerous one. I was informed roundly that I would never ever chase such a person in any situation even remotely similar ever, ever again. I could get dead. The guy'd apparently been hired by a scholar in Canada to steal the book. Whether he was supposed to take the second rather than the first edition, I don't know. (2) I also got an injury I still have. Going down the staircases, and without noticing it at the time, I crumpled my left knee quite severely. By the time I got off the bus in Pennsylvania around 7:45 that night, I *did* notice it, but thought it would walk off. I won't bore you with the rest of *that*, but it resulted in what seemed at the time a sizeable chunk of change from the State's workman's comp board (I didn't ask for it; all I wanted was the vacation time I'd lost sitting for about three weeks after the Library insisted I go home and see a doc and it became gruesomely apparent that I could not walk). The money is gone; but the bad knee I still have, and it's still bad.

Some months later I showed up for the arraignment downtown. The DA and I were there; the guy wasn't. And that was the last I ever heard about it or him–although it was there that the DA's rep lectured me on how stupid I had been to chase such a guy–and, by implication, *any*one–who is a nasty and able (and liable!) to do me in. I haven't had the occasion, or perhaps merely the opportunity, to test my reactions since the '70s/'80s when this incident took place...but when I consider the state of my temper I am not sure it's advice I would take now anymore than I'd have taken it then, despite the fragility and presumed wisdom both of which it is alleged come with increase of years.

(From email to author, 2007) Used by permission

INCIDENT 2

WE HAD AN INCIDENT a few years ago. Not a theft of collections, but our donation "jar". When I first arrived here, a large pickle jar for donations sat on the front entry desk. I know, a pickle jar, very tacky, plus easy to remove. It always contained money and was cleaned out by reference desk staff every week or couple of weeks, but "seed" money was left in place. At some point, we discovered the jar was missing. No one was sure when they had last seen the jar or had cleaned out the money. Not learning from this incident, another pickle jar appeared to serve as our new donation jar.

This incident occurred at the end of a day; it was a Thursday and staff were going about the closing down the library routine. We had gathered at the patron computer area each of us talking about our day and shutting down the computers. We heard the sounds of coins in a jar. Dashing around to the front desk two people, a young man and woman were exiting the building with our pickle jar of donation money under his arm. We had a security button, and immediately hit the button. This becomes the part where one should never assume anything. Believing Capitol Mall Security staff would be racing towards us, I and another staff member ran out the front door to see where our thieves were going. We were eager to share the direction the thieves were heading with the Capitol Mall Security staff that we knew were racing towards us. The thieves appeared to have vanished once they exited the building. One staff member ran one direction and I the opposite direction only to discover the thieves walking hand in hand with our pickle jar under

his arm away from the building. The other staff member ran back towards me when I motioned for her to join me.

As we continued to believe the Capitol Mall Security would arrive in nano-seconds we stood on the side walk watching our pickle jar and thieves walk away. They did turn and look at us several times but kept on walking. At some point my fellow staff member called out to them. Not a smart move. The thieves stopped and turned around with the pickle jar in full view. To this day, I don't know what compelled me to take the following action, but it was stupid. Keep in mind, Capitol Mall Security should arrive momentarily, or so we believed. I pointed to our thieves and with a finger out, motioned for them to come back. As stupidity continued to blind me, our thieves began walking in our direction. They approached us and my fellow staff member was hit with a major wave of stupidity and began to verbally lash out at the thieves, trying to shame them while demanding they had over the jar. To our surprise, without any comment, they handed over the jar, turned and began walking away. Capitol Mall Security didn't arrive for another 15 minutes. Their excuse was they thought someone had hit the panic button by mistake. These smart fellows were taken to the wood shed the following day. My fellow staff member and I, while understanding that we were caught up in the excitement of the moment, realize how stupid and lucky we were, placing ourselves in danger over a few dollars in a pickle jar.

(From email to author, 2007) Used by permission

INCIDENT 3

I HAVE AT least twice had to physically chase people who have taken things from the Reading Room and know that this has happened to other staff on reading room duty. In all cases, the person just says they made a "mistake" and the material was been returned. Nothing was done. I have suspected that items have been taken home and returned later but have never been able to prove it. The patrons in our geographical area, both students and faculty, do not like the idea of not being able to take everything out of the library; something to do with being within a large open stack library. If I had a nickel for every argument that I had on this subject, I would be quite well off.

There have been problems with people photocopying things that we specifically asked not to be photocopied, either for intellectual property or conservation reasons. Once, when a patron was barred from using the photocopier, he physically took the item out of Special Collections and copied it on a photocopier in the open stacks. A staff member returning via the open stacks saw him photocopying it; otherwise, he might have gotten away with it. Whether this counts as theft or not…. There were terrible problems with patrons not wanting to have their briefcases put out of reach on the other side of the room. Once or twice people with portable scanners were caught making hot—literally—copies of manuscripts. Due to the way the room was set up, it was very hard for staff to watch patrons, and there was never enough staff to have someone just sit and watch the reading room. The staff member whose presence was supposed to deter misuse was actually sitting behind a set of bookshelves that totally blocked his view. A newly designed reading room should help with some of this, and at least there will be lockers for patrons' property.

(From email to author, 2007) Used by permission

INCIDENT 4
WE HAD A READER who was a fairly consistent researcher of one particular collection. At one point, some staff were suggesting that we watch him a bit more carefully. While I was on the desk, I saw him shuffle a group of papers (letters) and slide one leaf underneath the others, drawing it close to him and then slide it off the table, apparently into his lap or crotch. Fortunately my colleague was there and she said she thought she saw him do something. We are prevented from directly confronting the user, so we called security. I was not sure exactly what report was made out, and I know that our reference desk staff was not alerted in a general way (probably deliberately, to keep it quiet). But on a subsequent occasion, the same person was caught and banned from the library.

I don't think the regular police were called in. I think our own security caught him based on the idea of not publicizing it too widely within the library, so that only the specific reference desk staff charged with that Special Collections area knew about him.

(From email to author, 2007) Used by permission

INCIDENT 5
ON THE AFTERNOON OF December 7, 1995, Jennifer Bryan, curator of manuscripts for the Maryland Historical Society, was doing a little research inside the grand stack room [of Johns Hopkins Peabody Library] when she started to get a bad feeling about a fellow patron. The man in question was sitting across the way from her, looking through some books that were obviously very old.

There was nothing unusual about his appearance–quite the contrary. A studious man in his midforties, wearing a blue blazer and khaki pants, he could have been mistaken for half the scholars who walk through the library's doors. He was a withdrawn, slight-framed person with a biggish nose, smallish chin, reddish hair and mustache.

Yet the man kept looking over his shoulder and flashing her "surreptitious" looks. Her suspicions soon deepened. "I just happened to look up and over in that direction and thought I saw him tear a page out of a book," she remembers. "And I thought, well, now what do I do? Do I say something, or did I just imagine that?"

As time went on, the man seemed to grow flustered by her stares. Finally, he stood up and pulled open a card catalog drawer, purposely obstructing Bryan's view. For Bryan, that was the last straw. She got up and reported him to Peabody Library officials.

A short time later, when three security officers confronted him, the man hastily gathered up his belongings and dashed out the Peabody's front door. In a scene that might have come from some odd amalgamation of *The Nutty Professor* and *The Fugitive*, the bookworm led his pursuers through downtown Baltimore, all four of them in a jog. Crossing historic Charles Street, the procession threaded past a famous statue of Washington and around another of Lafayette. Finally, after ditching a notebook in a row of bushes, the man found himself trapped on the back steps of the Walters Art Gallery.

Donald Pfouts, director of security at the Peabody Library, spoke to the man first. "I would really like to invite you back to the library," Pfouts remembers telling him, "because I think there are some issues here that we have to deal with."

The officers pulled the red spiral notebook–about the size of a steno pad–from the bushes and quickly discovered that Jennifer Bryan's suspicions had been well founded. Tucked into its pages were three maps from a rare 1763 book, *The General History of the Late War*, by John Entick, a modest trove that the library later estimated to be worth around $2,000.

From Miles Harvey, "Mr. Bland's Evil Plot to Control the World," *Outside Magazine*, (June, 1997).

Used by permission

INCIDENT 6
Edward Forbes Smiley Arrest Warrant
THE UNDERSIGNED AFFIANT, being duly sworn, deposes and says:

I, Detective Martin Buonfiglio, am a member of the Yale University Police Department, and have been a member of said Department for approximately 13 years prior to the date hereof, and at all times mentioned herein was acting as a member of said Department, and that the following facts and circumstances are stated from personal knowledge and observations, as well as information received from brother and sister officers acting in their official capacity.

That while a member of said Department, the undersigned has conducted numerous investigations regarding Larceny, made arrests and obtained convictions in a court of law.

On June 8, 2005, Ellen Cordes, Head of Public Services, for Yale University's Beinecke Library reported a suspicious incident at the Beinecke Library.

Ms. Cordes reported that Library employee Naomi Saito found an exacto blade on the floor of the Beinecke Rare Document Reading Room. This type of instrument is used to illegally remove (steal) rare documents, maps, signatures, and other authentic pages from rare books.

Ms. Cordes said that the reading room is cleaned daily and finding the knife blade at about 11:00 Am on the floor make her suspect that the person responsible for dropping the knife blade would still be there. The knife was picked up and wrapped in a white tissue for safe keeping, which was later turned over to the Police.

Ms. Cordes walked through the room and noticed a man looking at books containing rare maps. She then checked the Library register and identified the man as Edward Forbes Smiley. Ms. Cordes not knowing the man looked him up on the Internet and found that he was listed as a rare map dealer.

Ms. Cordes then called the Yale Sterling Memorial Library to ascertain if anyone there knew Mr. Smiley. Ms. Cordes was told that Smiley was suspect in a theft there, that on a prior occasion Smiley was there looking at rare documents and shortly after Smiley left the items he was looking at were missing. The incident was never reported or pursued because of lack of proof.

Ms. Cordes notified Mr. Ralph Mannarino Security Supervisor for Beinecke Library who then began a video surveillance of Smiley, as well as physically watching him. Smiley was seen by Mannarino looking at several books in the reading room and physically walking to the Library in-house computer. At one point Mr. Mannarino saw Smiley fidgeting with the inside pocket of his jacket. Mannarino then called the Police. At about 2:00 PM I responded and began this investigation.

At approximately 3:00 PM Smiley left the library and I followed. Smiley walked towards High Street carrying his briefcase and stopped, placing the briefcase on top of a wall. Smiley opened the briefcase for a moment, looked around, closed it and continued walking on High Street towards Elm Street. Smiley walked down High Street again stopping about 100 yards North of Chapel Street, placed the briefcase down and opened it and closed it. He continued to Chapel Street, across Chapel to the rear of the British Art Museum [Yale Center for British Art]. Smiley then stopped, turned around and walked backs towards Chapel Street. He then entered the Museum Store on High Street and quickly exited walking toward Chapel and down Chapel toward York Street. He then turned around and walked back toward High Street then into the British Art Museum [Yale Center for British Art].

Smiley then checked his briefcase in at the security desk and walked towards the elevator, stopping and looking around as if he didn't know where he was going. I then spoke to Smiley and introduced myself. I identified myself as a Police Detective working for Yale University and asked him if he was just at the Beinecke Library, when he replied yes.

Timothy Aylward was the Security Guard present at the time of my conversation with Smiley.

I then showed Smiley the exacto blade that was wrapped in the white tissue and asked if the blade was his. Smiley became very nervous and replied "yes it is I must of dropped it I have a cold" (the tissue wrapped around the blade was put there by library staff). I then asked Smiley if I might look in his briefcase because Yale was missing some things from the library and I just wanted to make sure that he didn't take anything by mistake. Smiley said "of course" and he retrieved the bookcase[sic] from the security desk and opened it for me to look inside. I quickly checked and located several what appeared to be rare maps and documents, and other personal items of Smiley. I then told Smiley that I wasn't sure what I was looking at and asked if he would mind returning to the Library so a curator could examine the documents I had. Lt. Holohan then arrived and Smiley accompanied us to the Beinecke Library, where we were met by Ms. Cordes and Edwin Schroeder, the head of Technical Services.

While I was gone from the Library following Smiley Ms. Cordes was able to look at the several books Smiley checked out to the reading room. One book in particular was entitled *Advertisements for the Unexperienced Planters of New England or anywhere*. Cordes found that book missing a map. She then checked the Library computer and ascertained that the map was in fact part of the book and was not attached just placed in the book.

On our arrival in the first floor lobby, Smiley removed several maps from his briefcase and displayed them for Ms. Cordes and Mr. Schroeder. Cordes told me that it would take some time to know if the documents were taken from the library. Ms. Cordes then showed Smiley the specific book Taylor 316 that was missing a map, and asked Smiley if he had the map. Smiley replied that the map was in fact rare, but did not mention anything about having the map in his possession.

Cordes and Schroeder then left to further check the documents Smiley had in his possession. Smiley told me that the maps he surrendered were his and that he took them to the Library to compare the quality of his maps to the quality of the Library's maps.

Lt. Holohan asked Mr. Smiley if he had anything belonging to the Beinecke Library. Smiley opened his blazer and removed some type of credit card form from his inside left pocket. Lt. Holohan noticed that there was still a bulge in that same pocket and asked Smiley what else was in there. Smiley then took out a map and gave it to Lt. Holohan, and said "Oh I forgot about that." I then checked with Cordes who told me that the map Smiley had in his pocket was the map missing from the books she showed Smiley just a few moments earlier.

The map is described as having a portrait of John Smith in the upper left, dated 1614, 20 x 15 CM, valued at approximately $50,000.00.

I asked Smiley where he got the map and first he told me he bought it from a dealer in London, Mr. Philip Burden. When I asked for a way to confirm the sale, Smiley told me he wasn't sure if it was Burden; it may have been someone else.

Smiley was then arrested for Larceny in the First Degree in violation of CGS 53a–122, transported to New Haven Police detention by Officer Funaro for processing.

When Smiley was arrested on June 8, 2005 he had the following maps in his possession.

1. 36.4 x 49.3 cm map, titled TYPIS ORBIS TERRARVM–Call number Taylor 188 valued at $78,000.00.

2. 32 x 44.8 cm, titled Part of America Part of China–call number Vanderbilt 57, valued at $50,000.00.

3. 42 x 55 cm, titled Vnivers Orbis sevterrani-glo–call number 1976 Folio 2, valued at $150,000.00.

4. 30 x 44.4 cm map titled Thorne map, "Septentrio vniversalis descriptio," authored by Hakluyt, Richard, 1552–1616, comp. valued at $500,000.00.

5. 30.2 x 38.8 cm, Facsimile map of New America authored by Hubbard unknown value

6. 37 x 48 cm map, titled Lac Superieur, valued at $25,000.00.

7. 37 x 51.1 cm map, titled Carte generale de la nouvelle France, authored by Le Clerc, Chrestien, ca. valued at $75,000.00.

On June 9, 2005 I was contacted by Ellen Cordes of the Beinecke Library and told that three of the seven items Smiley showed her in June 8, 2005, were the property of the Beinecke Library. Ms. Cordes said that her research of the Library records showed items 1, 2, and 3 listed above were stolen from the Library by Smiley on June 6, 2005. Ms. Cordes produced records that showed what books Smiley looked at on June 8, 2005. Those records showed call number Taylor 188, Vanderbilt 57, and 1976 Folio 2, were examined by Smiley on June 8, 2005 and were missing the maps. Those missing maps were found in Smiley's possession.

Ms. Cordes also produced a video tape of Smiley examining several books on the 8th of June. The tape shows Smiley removing the map from the 1976 Folio 2 book. There was no other video that day due to the fact security cameras were not turned on until the library was aware of the possibility of a theft in progress.

On June 15, 2005, I met with William Reese a private dealer in rare maps at the Beinecke Library. Mr. Reese is retained by Beinecke Library as a book appraiser, as well as an advisor in rare book collections. He appraised the stolen maps and identified the stolen maps as from the Beinecke Library.

The book titled *North West Fox or Fox from the North West Passage* by Luke Fox 1586–1635, was signed out by Smiley on June 8, 2005. That book was examined by Ms. Cordes after Smiley returned it and found to be missing the map titled Part of America, Part of China. That map was inventoried by Library Staff at an earlier date and found to be part of the above mentioned book. The map titled Part of America part of China was one of the seven maps surrendered by Smiley on June 8, 2005. The book's paper is described as being washed and pressed, which is sometimes done to preserve old books. The map Smiley had was also washed and pressed which would indicate that map came from Beinecke's book.

That based on the above stated facts and circumstances described in this affidavit, it is the request of this officer for the courts consideration and belief that probable cause exists for the issuance of an arrest warrant for the subject, Edward Forbes Smiley III on the violation of Connecticut General Statutes 53a–122 Larceny in the First Degree.

From Exlibris archives:

http://palimpsest.stanford.edu/byform/mailing-lists/ exlibris/2005/08/msg00188.html (Public document)

INCIDENT 7

UNITED STATES COURT of Appeals for the Sixth Circuit. United States of America v. Charles Thomas Allen, II, et al. 5 February 2008
[This opinion in part describes incidents at the theft of special collections materials from Transylvania University Library on 14 December 2004. The defendants were Charles Thomas Allen, Eric Borsuk, Warren Lipka, and Spencer Reinhard.]

Once inside the Special Collections Library, the two men [Lipka and Borsuk] wrestled Mrs. Gooch to the ground, and began zapping her in the arm with a pen-type stun gun, which caused a tingling sensation and left a small bruise, but did not cause any significant pain or lasting harm. Mrs. Gooch screamed, though she knew that no one could hear

her from that location in the library, but she did not panic. She testified that, while being subdued, she felt the tingling, heard the electric humming and popping noise, and feared that she was being zapped with a stun gun. She was particularly unnerved, however, when Lipka–whom she did not know–called her by her first name, warning her: "B. J., if you just keep on struggling, it will only hurt more. Do you want it to hurt more?" Greatly frightened by this threat, her awareness of the stun gun, and the hair-raising intimacy of the robber having used her first name so casually, Mrs. Gooch submitted and the two men bound her hands and feet with plastic zip ties. They also removed her glasses and covered her eyes with a stocking cap....

To return to the story, Lipka and Borsuk had, in a matter of minutes, collected these seven objects– except for the two *Birds of North American* volumes that they had abandoned on the pink bed sheet, and one of the three *Quadrupeds of North America* volumes, which had become stuck in its drawer–and were preparing to abscond with them. According to the (revised) plan, they would take the "employee only" elevator down to the first floor and escape through an emergency exit, where Allen was waiting in a van....

Apparently Lipka and Borsuk had some difficulty operating the elevator, however. Head librarian Susan Brown was in the library's basement at the time and, prompted by the unexpected "ding" of the elevator's opening doors, she turned her attention to see who would be using the elevator. She was startled when the door opened to reveal not employees, but Lipka and Borsuk, in their heavy coats and gloves, holdings some of the library's most prized and valuable possessions. Realizing that something was amiss, Ms. Brown started for the elevator, but Lipka and Borsuk quickly got the doors closed and the elevator moving again. Alarmed, Ms. Brown ran up the stairs to Special Collections in search of

Mrs. Gooch. Meanwhile, Mrs. Gooch had realized that, due to the department's security measures, Lipka and Borsuk could not re-enter the Special Collections Department from the elevator, and she had begun to free herself to call for help. She yelled to Susan Brown that they were being robbed, and Ms. Brown wheeled around to pursue the robbers.

She caught up with them in a stairwell where they were attempting to open the emergency exit and, surprised by her arrival and aggressive confrontation, they dropped several objects–specifically the two remaining volumes of the *Birds of North America* four-volume set (they had left two volumes atop the pink bed sheet in the Special Collections Department) and the two volumes of the *Quadrupeds* three-volume set (one of three volumes had been left behind, stuck in its drawer in the Special Collections Department). Lipka and Borsuk fled through the emergency door carrying five objects…with Ms. Brown and other librarians in hot pursuit. Lipka and Borsuk scrambled into the waiting van and Allen sped away…. Once the robbers had escaped, police were called, but before the police could document the crime scene, some librarians collected the discarded objects and returned them to their proper places.

–Pages 3–4.

http://www.ca6.uscourts.gov/opinions pdf/08a0062p-06.pdf (Public document)

INCIDENT 8

ONE DAY ABOUT 20 years ago, librarians at the state Archive had their eye on a suspicious-looking visitor who was known to have a criminal record. After he left, one of the staff members flew urgently back to the boss's office.

"He just took off with the book!"

Archive Director Fred Armstrong charged down the hallway, out the doors and down the front steps, taking each group of steps in a single, long-legged leap.

The thief had turned left toward a parking lot, in the vicinity of the current site of the Veterans Memorial.

Fred ran to the man and said something to the effect of "I need you to come back inside. That book belongs to the collection."

The man did not fight, but came back. The Archive filed charges against him. As part of a plea agreement, the man promised never to return to the Archive. He did come back a couple times, and the staff chased him out.

The book, a history of Nicholas County, was returned to the shelf. It would have cost the Archive more than $200 to replace, although the money is not the point.

Dawn Miller

Charleston (WVa) *Gazette*, 19 November 2007

Used by permission

NOTES

1. Another similar incident is also reported by Schröeder: "About 10 years ago, several research institutions were victimized by a man who was determined to steal pages from every copy of a book that disproved his theory on an abstruse point of literary criticism. He had stolen the relevant pages from some 12 copies of the 20 or so existing books before he was caught. Only a few of the 12 stolen pages made it back to their owners." Cited in Margaret Schröeder, "Special Protection for Special Collections," *Security Management On-line* (July, 2004), http://www.securitymanagement.com/library/001632.html. In Daviess County, KY, thieves targeted post-Civil War revenue stamps contained in archival documents. See: http://www.14wfie.com/Global/story.asp?S=6846954&nav=3w6o. Other thefts can be devastating even if the targets are volumes of relatively low value. A theft discovered at Western Washington University in early 2005 involved the removal of 648 leaves, almost all of them maps, from the Congressional Serial Set. See Robert Lopresti, "Map Theft News," Exlibris electronic discussion list, 11 January 2008, http://palimpsest.stanford.edu/byform/mailing-lists/exlibris/2008/01/msg00067.html. According to David Grossberg, "The Lessons of Mark Hofmann," *Autograph Magazine* (April, 2008), Hofmann stole relatively worthless blank leaves from older materials so he would have appropriate materials on which to perform his forgeries (55–56). In a similar instance, Lee Israel, *Can You Ever Forgive Me? Memoirs of a Literary Forger* (New York: Simon & Schuster, 2008) recounts that while fabricating her Louise Brooks forgeries, she came upon numerous perfectly suited leaves of blank paper in the backs of notebooks and stole them: "At the back of each of the binders I discovered a plenitude of off-white, beautifully weathered paper. Perfect canvasses for the letters of Louise…. I grabbed a generous supply and passed easily through the guards. I was carrying, after all, just some blank paper" (47). According to Philip Shenon, *The Commission: The Uncensored History of the 9/11 Investigation* (New York: Twelve, 2008), Sandy Berger was so determined to remove from NARA every copy he could locate of Richard A. Clarke's secret 2000 after-action report that he even stole a replacement copy planted by the archivists (250–51).

2. Abigail Leab, "The Saying and the Doing: A Survey of Security and Theft Prevention Measures in U.S. Archives," (Masters Thesis, April, 1988), reported based on her survey: "Over-all, the picture presented by the survey results is one of confusion, ignorance, and uncertainty at the institutional level about security" (105). One fairly well documented incident concerns Samuel R. Berger's thefts at the National Archives and Records Administration. Although the Inspector General's publicly released report is heavily redacted, it makes it clear that NARA's response to the ongoing thefts was contradictory, confused, and timid, even after staff were convinced that Berger was removing documents from the collections he was examining. (The Office of Inspector General report, 4 November 2005.)

3. Other steps may be found in the *Guidelines Regarding Security and Theft in Special Collections* (Chicago: ACRL, 2009) and Bruce A. Shuman, *Library Security and Safety Handbook: Prevention, Policies, and Procedures* (Chicago: American Library Association, 1999), 64.

4. Vincent A. Totka, Jr., "Preventing Patron Theft in the Archives: Legal Perspectives and Problems," *American Archivist* 56 (Fall, 1993), found that archivists he surveyed in Wisconsin were "largely unaware of the laws that could have an impact on their organization" (670). Alison M. Foley, "Can One Man Make a Difference? An Analysis of the Effects of the Crimes of Gilbert Bland on Rare Book and Special Collections Security Measures and a Review of the Evolution of Recommended Security Guidelines," (Masters thesis, Chapel Hill, 2005) reports that absolutely none of the libraries she surveyed had provided any formal security training for their employees (23). Leab reported, "Should a patron be suspected of stealing, only 20 of the 94 members of the sample population are certain of the relevant laws in the states where they work" (p. 105). Dennis East and William G. Myers, "Get the Thief 'Out of the Business:' Diary of a Theft," *RBMS* 13 (Fall, 1998), speaking from sad experience, counsel: "Find out about, learn, and teach the staff about the local or state shoplifting laws and their application to libraries and archives" (47). For a list of state laws concerning library thefts, see: http://www.rbms.info/committees/security/state_laws/.

5. For brief overview, see David C. Grossack, "Citizen's Arrest," *Constitutional Business* (Hull: Citizens' Justice Programs, 1994). http://www.constitution.org/grossack/arrest.htm.

6. Some thieves do, in fact, turn violent. One bookstore owner was assaulted when he tried to prevent a thief from leaving. The notorious thief James Shinn had to be tackled in the Oberlin College reading room by the late William Moffett.

7. This advice is reiterated by Warren Davis Graham, Jr., *Black Belt Librarians* (Charlotte: Purple Heart Press, 2006), 7–8.

8. "Viva Blumberg: Lessons Learned," *1999 National Conference on Cultural Property Protection Proceedings: Cultural Property Protection from the Ground Up* [Washington: Smithsonian Institution, 1999], 37–41. http://www.museum-security.org/blumberg-huntsberry.htm. East and Myers report of their investigating officer: "He had difficulty understanding that the address leaf or cover from these eighteenth- and nineteenth-century documents had historical and monetary value and that people actually collected them" (35).

9. Goshen College, Campus Crime Prevention Programs, *Library Safety & Security: A Comprehensive Manual for Library Administrators and Police and Security Officers* (Goshen: Campus Crime Prevention Programs, 1992), 1–2.

10. For the potential range of law enforcement responses, see Edward F. Clark, "Law Enforcement and the Library," in Robert K. O'Neill, ed., *Management of Library and Archival Security: From the Outside Looking In* (New York & London: Haworth, 1998), 33–47; and Don Hrycyk, "Surviving a Collection Loss: Working with Law Enforcement," *1999 National Conference on Cultural Property Protection Proceedings: Cultural Property Protection from the Ground Up* [Washington: Smithsonian Institution, 1999]. http://www.museum-security.org/donh.htm. In the case of Bland's apprehension at Johns Hopkins, university counsel explained that it was probably futile to persuade the Baltimore police to arrest Bland, which is why he was allowed to depart after paying restitution on the spot (Rare Books and Manuscripts Section, "Reading Room Security and Beyond." Workshop at 39th RBMS Preconference in Washington, DC, 22 June 1998). In Spiegelman's case, Travis McDade, *The Book Thief: The True Crimes of Daniel Spiegelman* (Westport: Preager, 2006), reports that Columbia University library staff were hardly involved at all in the criminal investigation: "The librarians at Columbia had been pretty much left in the dark for three years, picking up bits of information here and there from the police and FBI, never being in the loop. They were always glad to help…but they were almost never called upon" (89).

11. Because there is often something of a triage system in effect in various locales, the institution will need to determine in advance how certain calls will be handled. In some cases, for example, the police will not be dispatched to the scene unless the local security force requests them. In the case of burglaries, sometimes the security company will dispatch campus authorities rather than the police. On the other hand, in the case of medical emergencies, often the ambulance will first be dispatched, and the local security force alerted to that fact. All those scenarios should be well covered in a security document or a disaster plan.

12. Schröeder.

13. Berger was treated with special deference at the National Archives and Records Administration, thereby allowing him to perpetuate his thefts. Even he concluded: "After learning he was given special treatment by viewing the documents in [Mr. XXX's] office, he suggested no exceptions to the rules should be given to former National Security Advisor or others. The archives should thoroughly check people when they enter and exit the building." The Office of Inspector General report, 4 November 2005, "Memorandum or Interview of Activity," Exhibit 7, 10. http://www.fas.org/sgp/othergov/berger.pdf. Graham notes that one mental mistake sometimes made is: "'He's harmless.' Very few human beings are completely harmless under the right circumstances" (8). William E. Chadwick, "Special Collections Library Security: An Internal Audit Perspective," in O'Neill, further comments about internal thefts: "One important underlying concept which must be accepted is the reality that a fraud is possible in your organization. If you do not believe fraud is possible, you will not identify it even if it is clearly evident. Very often fraud situations are viewed as administrative errors because individuals cannot conceive of the existence of fraud, particularly in organizations where there is a longtime affiliation with coworkers" (20).

14. Any number of research libraries have long had such policies in place, apparently primarily to spare wear and tear on original documents. Providing surrogates has taken on increasing urgency as a security measure, however, a process accelerated by the rise of digitization programs.

15. The Bland maps that the FBI could not return to institutions were presented to the Library of Congress Map and Geography Division, where they will probably never be catalogued. The library is willing, however, to consider repatriation requests. Hundreds of books stolen by Blumberg could never be returned because their owners could not be identified and were eventually sold at auction. See C. Wesley Cowan, *Historic Americana Auction: Remnants of a Gentle Madness, The Stephen C. Blumberg Library of Americana* (Cincinnati: Cowan, 1999).

16. Gary L. Menges, "Security of Rare Books, Manuscripts, and Special Collections," *PNLA Quarterly* 53 (1989) for example, recommends identifying high-value items ahead of time (18). Regrettably, there can often be a disconnect concerning library materials. Whereas any shoplifter who steals a tube of lipstick will be arrested at the merchant's request, just as surely as will a thief who steals a Mercedes Benz, persuading an officer to arrest someone over a $5,000 book can be difficult. As Bruce A. Shuman, *Library Security and Safety Handbook: Prevention, Policies, and Procedures* (Chicago & London: American Library Association, 1999) points out: "Book theft is seen as distinct from such major crimes as stealing cars or computers, despite the fact that a single rare book that a skilled thief may have taken from a library may be worth more individually…than a new luxury automobile" (26)

17. Totka originally had broken his survey questions into two parts to allow for institutions that had written security policies and those that did not. He discovered that the "distinction was unnecessary; *none* of the repositories had a written security policy"

(original emphasis; 666). Foley discouragingly reports that from the libraries she reviewed for written security policies, "Of the 23 subjects interviewed for this project, including those who were Bland's targets, 5 or 22% have a formal, written security policy" (21).

18. Albert J. Mandelbaum, *Fundamentals of Protective Systems: Planning, Evaluation, Selection* (Springfield: Thomas, 1973), 6.

19. Bruce E. Shuman, *Library Security and Safety Handbook: Prevention, Policies, and Procedures* (Chicago: American Library Association, 1999), 61.

20. One of them later admitted Bland, to its regret.

21. See Appendix I for examples of various scenarios that led to reasonable suspicions being aroused. Michael F. Brown, *Criminal Investigation: Law and Practice*, 2nd ed. (Boston: Butterworth-Heinemann, 2001) states, "Probable cause exists where the facts and circumstances within the knowledge of the arresting officers and of which they had reasonably trustworthy information are sufficient in themselves to warrant a man of reasonable caution in believing that an offense has been committed or is being committed" (26).

22. Brown, 25

23. See Appendix I, Incident 5, the report of the apprehension of Bland at Johns Hopkins, for such an approach in practice. John L. Fay, ed., *Encyclopedia of Security Management*, 2nd ed. (Burlington: Butterworth-Heinemann, 2007), suggests the following scenario for confronting a shoplifting suspect: "Ideally, shoplifters should be approached with an assertive and confident posture. The tone of voice should be matter of fact but polite. Trigger words such as 'thief,' 'jail,' and 'police' should be avoided so as to better attain the cooperation of the individual. The approach should be as private as possible, should never be confrontational, and treated simply as a situation that needs resolving…. To obtain compliance, the employee should have a polite but firm business-like tone and not be diverted from the situation at hand. The employee should not take personally anything the shoplifter might say and avoid arguing or reacting negatively" (218–19).

24. The report on Berger's thefts recounts this evolution of events in recovering NARA's documents: "[Mr. XXX] was surprised when Mr. Berger returned the documents he removed in September. He knew he was caught, so he purported he must have removed the documents accidentally or inadvertently by sweeping them up with his documents. Later, Mr. Berger made a decision, on his own, to tell the truth. He said 'I realize I was giving a benign explanation for what was not benign.' Mr. Berger wanted to return everything he had taken. He realized he was returning documents he had removed in September. He did not realize he returned more than they knew he removed. Mr. Berger was aware of the consequences but he knew returning the documents was the right thing to do" (The Office of Inspector General report, 4 November 2005, "Memorandum or Interview of Activity," Exhibit 7, 9). Totka states: "If the patron claims to have made a mistake and turns the document over to the staff member, the crisis is over. This is an acceptable outcome because the first priority of the archives should be to protect the holdings" (669). Such a resolution is hardly an "acceptable" outcome. That would have allowed Smiley, for example, to continue on his merry way once Yale had recovered its pilfered maps. One institutional priority should also be to protect other institutions by causing the thief to be taken out of circulation.

25. See John Falk, "Majoring in Crime…," *Vanity Fair*, no. 568 (December, 2007): 232–246.

26. The same can hardly be said for the worlds of public libraries and museums, where assaults and thefts involving the use of weapons are distressingly common. For an older but instructive discussion of the assault problem in public libraries, see Alan J. Lincoln, *Crime in the Library: A Study of Patterns, Impact, and Security* (New York & London: Bowker, 1984), 61–63 and 153–155. As was widely reported in the press, the 2004 theft of Munch's "The Scream" from an Oslo museum was accomplished by armed robbers who held guards and visitors at gunpoint. One of the oddest armed book thefts involved a book distributor in Turin, Italy, who was robbed at gunpoint of modern books. See Richard Owen, "Cultural 'Robin Hoods' in Books Raid," Exlibris (19 July 1998): http://palimpsest.stanford.edu/byform/mailing-lists/exlibris/1998/07/msg00134.html. Although not directly connected with libraries, the case of convicted forger Mark Hofmann is chilling. He killed two innocent people with a bomb and apparently intended to try to murder a third to cover his tracks. See David Grossberg, "The Lessons of Mark Hofmann," *Autograph Magazine* (April, 2008): 54.

27. While being pursued, Bland discarded a notebook believed to be his shopping list for maps he intended to steal. It also contained several maps he had stolen from the library.

28. Rex Libris is the name of a hero librarian featured in a comic book series of the same name in which his adventures enforcing library rules are recounted. It is good fantasy reading for the frustrated librarian. For a compendium of his adventures, see *Rex Libris* (San Jose: SLG, 2007). Other librarian heroes are depicted by Jason Shiga, *Bookhunter* (Sparkplug Comics, 2007),

which is based in Oakland, California, in the 1970s. Also in the fantasy category is the "Macho Librarians with Guns" website, which indulges several fantasies, available on-line at http://maverick.brainiac.com/mwwg/mlwg.html. Finally, the teenage detective Kiki Strike investigates book thefts at Columbia's Butler Library in Kirsteen Miller, *The Columbia Conspiracy: A Story of Secret Tunnels, Mad Scientists, and Maple Syrup.* http://www.kikistrike.com/chap1.htm. Since this work is an on-line novel being written on the fly, it even includes discussion of E. Forbes Smiley in addition to the novel's map thief, Dr. Lyle Mayhew. On the other hand, the author has reports concerning librarians who apparently do carry firearms during their work time at the library. One anonymous bulletin board poster notes: "What gives you the impression that some librarians don't carry guns at work? In Florida the regulation of concealed weapons is reserved to the state, so counties and cities cannot ban them from their libraries. Some Florida librarians do carry guns at work legally" (http://lisnews.org/articles/04/09/13/1647254. shtml). A colleague reports personal knowledge of a Virginia librarian who carries a concealed weapon at work. See also Denis Lacroix, "Librarians with Guns: Guadalajara's Military Public Library," *Feliciter*, 51 (2005): 50–51, for a report of a visit to a library where guns were in ample evidence.

29. Under no circumstances should you guess about the value of materials. If you do not know exact values, merely state that the materials have market value and that you can determine that figure. Point out to the police that the suspect would probably not be stealing them if they had no commercial value.

30. Alice Harrison Bahr, *Book Theft and Library Security Systems, 1978–79* (White Plains: Knowledge Industry Publications, 1979), 105.

31. Susan M. Allen, "Thefts in Libraries and Archives: What to Do During the Aftermath of a Theft," in O'Neill, 10. If you and your document end up in court, you may be called on to review it to "refresh" your memory from it. You will not be able to introduce the document directly into evidence as testimony but will be required to furnish your own original testimony based on it. East and Myers also suggest keeping a diary of all events during and after a theft "detailing every phone call, e-mail message, event, or person related to the entire affair…. The diary…would, we were told, be extremely helpful if this matter ever went to court" (28).

Bringing It All Back Home: Recovery of Stolen Special Collections Materials

Richard W. Oram and Ann Hartley

> Possession is nine-tenths of the law.
> ~ *Traditional saying*

After a perpetrator is sentenced, victims of special collections theft may discover that their troubles are only beginning. That situation is particularly true if large numbers of stolen items reach the marketplace or if recovered books and manuscripts have been stolen from more than one library. In the 1980s, prominent theft cases involving James Shinn and Stephen Blumberg resulted in the discovery of hundreds of stolen books that could not be easily identified. Despite tireless efforts by dedicated librarians, many books never found their way back to the owners.[1] In 1994, Daniel Spiegelman was arrested for the theft of incunabula, maps, and documents from Columbia University Library's Rare Book and Manuscript Library. Numerous items were located in his safe deposit boxes and other locations, but many years after Spiegelman's conviction important items thought to have been stolen by him remain at large.[2]

Two recent cases of theft resulted in valuable materials reaching the market and required extensive recovery efforts. E. Forbes Smiley III removed at least ninety-seven maps from Yale University, Harvard University, and several other prominent collections in the U.S. and the U.K.; the thief was sentenced in 2006. In the Mimi Meyer case, some 400 books were stolen from the Harry Ransom Humanities Research Center, University of Texas at Austin; Meyer was sentenced and given three years probation in 2004.[3] (See fig 18.1) The legal concept of replevin (the right of a property owner to sue the current possessor for return of property) is often involved in the return of stolen goods to their rightful owner. However, in common archival use, the term most frequently refers to the recovery of alienated governmental records, which is not under consideration here. It is also worth noting that the scope of this chapter does not include the recovery of books and manuscripts seized by governments during wartime.

Law enforcement action in the immediate aftermath of the theft often leads to recovery of many stolen items. In the Smiley case, the thief was apprehended while in the process of removing maps from books at Yale University. A quick response by law enforcement resulted in the recovery of many other items taken from various libraries over the next few months. At the time of Smiley's conviction in July 2006, the prosecutor told the court that eighty-six of the ninety-seven stolen maps were in the possession of federal agents. A year later, most of the owners had been identified and almost all the maps had been returned. Nevertheless, subsequent institutional inventories raised questions about

Thanks to Everett C. Wilkie, Jr., David Cobb, and Michael Thompson for their helpful comments.

Figure 18.1

Materials Seized from Mimi Meyer and Returned to the Harry Ransom Humanities Research Center (Courtesy Pete Smith, Harry Ransom Center)

whether he had stolen additional missing maps.[4] In the Meyer case, the FBI, with cooperation of the thief, inventoried her Chicago apartment and confiscated some 300 books stolen from Texas, which were returned to the Ransom Center a few days after sentencing; however, not all the stolen books in her possession were found by the FBI. Later discussions between the Ransom Center and Meyer resulted in her disgorging several more books and maps. The Austin office of the FBI did not offer assistance with the recovery of around a hundred books—the exact number is still unknown—that Meyer had sold at auction from 1994 to 2000. The thefts had taken place nearly fifteen years before sentencing (as opposed to no more than eight years in the Smiley case), and some of the books reached the marketplace a full decade before the recovery began. The reason given by the FBI was that any information it obtained from the auction houses was part of a grand jury investigation, and under federal law (Rule 6, Federal Rules of Criminal Procedure) such information is confidential. Once a library becomes aware of theft, law enforcement officers can obtain a search warrant, yet if the library does

not immediately know what has been taken (which is probable without a thorough, up-to-the-minute inventory and evidence linking the suspect to the supposed theft), a search warrant cannot identify particular books to be sought. To protect citizens' constitutional rights against unreasonable searches and seizures, search warrants must not only be justified with probable cause but also limited in scope.[5]

Since many theft cases are resolved through plea bargains, institutional victims have an opportunity to obtain court-ordered restitution as part of the settlement. That money will be important in buying back any books sold to good-faith purchasers who are willing to return them for the price they paid. In the Meyer case, The U.S. District Court staff requested an accounting of the books known to have been stolen and sold at auction. The Ransom Center was also asked to provide an estimate of the cost of identification and recovery efforts (which in the final accounting proved to be much too low!). At sentencing, the judge simply set restitution as the sum of these figures, or $381,595. In the Smiley case, restitution to institutions and map dealers to cover their losses was initially set by the court at $1.9M and later raised to $2.3M, with the thief ordered to sell off some of his assets as part of a plea bargain. Since one of the reasons Smiley began stealing maps was to pay down a mountain of debt, the plaintiffs likely will not recover anything close to the full amount.[6] While financial restitution is obviously worth insisting upon, all too often the perpetrator lacks sufficient (or any) resources, after paying legal bills, fines, and court costs. After sentencing, the thief may have nothing more valuable than information to help locate the stolen items; the victim institution should definitely seek an enforceable condition in the sentencing order or judgment that obligates the thief to cooperate.

For both practical and legal reasons, it is essential to begin the recovery process as quickly as possible after the discovery that materials are at large. Generally, the more time that has passed since the materials were stolen, the more times the property will have changed hands and the more difficult the recovery effort will be. The importance of spreading the word about stolen items likely to have reached the market cannot be overstated. Informal, personal and professional contacts should be alerted, and institutional notices must also be made, listing the stolen property. Police reports, insurance claims, notices in professional publications and discussion lists, entries on trade association internet sites—all these efforts are important. The stolen items must be described in accurate, identifying detail. The theft victim needs to publish enough information so that a reasonably diligent person looking to buy a book would have notice that it has been stolen.[7] Fortunately, it is now generally accepted (at least in theory) that libraries have a clear ethical obligation to report thefts, or has Susan Allen has noted, "The question is no longer a question of whether to notify. Rather it has shifted to a question of who should do the notifying and who should be notified."[8] While administrators may resist transparency on the grounds that it may damage their institution's reputation, curators must strongly press the case for full disclosure.

Regrettably, as of 2008, all of the online registers for missing or stolen rare materials have serious limitations. For example, many auction houses typically recognize the Art Loss Register (ALR) as the definitive source of record on stolen items, including rare books and manuscripts, yet that listing is largely unknown outside the fine arts field. Further, both searching and adding records to ALR require registration and the payment of fees, unless records

are submitted through Interpol (not the easiest of tasks in practice, as the present writers discovered). The databases of the Antiquarian Booksellers Association of America (ABAA) and the International League of Antiquarian Booksellers (ILAB) are laudable in concept, but the ABAA database is still, at this writing, a relatively new effort that depends on the availability of staff time to keep the file current, and access to the ILAB database requires organizational membership.[9] The Library Security Officer (LSO) electronic mailing list and the "Incidents of Thefts" reports on the RBMS site are compiled from press reports and other sources but often do not provide detailed listings of individual stolen items. However, at this writing the future for such registers is looking brighter. In 2008 a web-based Missing Maps Database was inaugurated,[10] and curators, booktrade representatives, staff from OCLC (which maintains the WorldCat bibliographic database) and law enforcement gathered at the Getty Research Library in June 2008 to discuss the creation of a similar database for missing rare books.

Another part of the initial theft response involves an immediate report to the institution's risk management office and its insurer as well as continuing contact with them as the investigation proceeds. While many public institutions continue to "self-insure," it is becoming increasingly common for colleges and universities to take out fine arts insurance policies. Typically, those are designed to cover the institution in the event of a catastrophic loss, but there may be theft provisions as well. They will usually exclude losses resulting from "mysterious disappearance" (e.g., an inventory discloses that an item is missing from the collection but it cannot be proven to have been stolen). Even when a loss results from a provable theft, the high deductibles required to keep premiums down, together with the relatively low values of most rare books and manuscripts (at least compared to works of art), may make it infeasible to claim. A highly desirable feature of fine arts insurance policies is the "buy-back provision." If the insurer does pay a claim and the stolen item is later located and returned, the original owner has the option of returning the settlement money and reclaiming the item; otherwise, the recovered item becomes by default the legal property of the insurance company, which has the option of selling it to recover its loss.[11] The Art Loss web site of the Los Angeles Police Department notes that "Insisting upon a buy-back provision will not only ensure a victim's right to exercise this option, it will also obligate the insurance carrier to notify the victim if there is a recovery."[12]

Along with law enforcement and counsel, bookdealers are effective allies in tracking down and recovering stolen items. By and large, the booktrade has a good record in collaborating with libraries to apprehend thieves and recover books; at a 2005 symposium on the recovery of stolen books, booksellers Ken Sanders and David Szewczyk reported on their identifications of suspicious materials offered for sale, which led to the arrest of the perpetrators, and cited other dealer involvement in successful sting operations.[13] The Code of Ethics of the Antiquarian Booksellers Association of America, the largest and most prominent trade association, specifically mandates cooperation with theft recovery:

> 3(b). An Association member shall make every effort to prevent the theft or distribution of stolen antiquarian books and related materials. An Association member shall cooperate with law enforcement authorities and the Associations' Board of Governors in the effort to recover and return stolen materials, and apprehend and prosecute those responsible for the theft, including, but not limited to, providing the names of the persons involved.[14]

Ideally, booksellers and librarians should present a unified front in resistance to the further distribution of stolen rare materials. In his book about the Spiegelman/Columbia theft case, Travis McDade takes the optimistic view that the "Book Community" of dealers and collectors greatly limits thieves' options when it comes to fencing rare materials, to the extent that they are "almost without exception" found out.[15] Nevertheless, the authors' experiences, as well as those of librarians involved in the Smiley case and other recovery efforts, suggest that the trade cannot be counted upon to "do the right thing" in every instance. Regrettably, a few members of the book trade take the narrow view that library thefts are primarily the result of lax security and thus exclusively a library problem.[16] Others cite their "obligation" to protect the identity and privacy of customers from probing victims of theft, although that is based more on the firm's relationship with the consignor than any statutory requirements. More problematic is the fact that only a small portion of the trade is subject to the Code of Ethics of the ABAA, which is composed of established firms. Mom-and-pop storefronts selling used books on eBay and Amazon proliferate. Owners who have located stolen books or archival materials on online auctions have had difficulty getting the sites to intervene.[17] The laissez-faire environment of the Web thus tends to promote the unchecked distribution of stolen items, as well as those with suspect provenance. Auction houses—ineligible for ABAA membership—present a particular problem because they frequently insist on protecting their consignors' and purchasers' identity, even when there is overwhelming evidence that stolen material has passed through their rooms[18]

This is perhaps the most surprising and difficult lesson for victims of theft: owners generally have a *legal right* to return of their stolen property, but even if they are able to locate it, recovery is often problematic. If they do not know where the property is, or even that it has been stolen, it is obviously even more fraught with difficulty. Ideally, the thief would be in the position of being both fully cooperative and highly organized, having retained impeccable records about which materials were sold and to whom. If this is not the case (Meyer, though initially cooperative, suffered from severe memory lapses and had to be encouraged to remember where more stolen books in her possession were, and, as we have noted, it is impossible to be certain that Smiley identified all the maps he had taken), the library will have to approach the dealers and auction houses that can be identified. As the authors discovered, the recovery process involves complicated and highly specialized legal issues. Thus, at the outset one will wish to seek the best legal advice, beginning with in-house counsel.

Unless the case is miraculously simple, the victimized institution may face numerous legal complications. To take one example: The theft occurs at an unknown date in the past in one state, the thief lives in another state by the time recovery is undertaken in earnest, the first buyer of the stolen book is in a third state and refuses to reveal any information about the purchase of the book by its customer, alleging "privacy" concerns (date, name and address of buyer, and price are fundamental facts needed to follow the trail of a stolen item). Other complications are likely to accrue. When considerable time has passed since the theft, a limitations defense may be made against the original owner's claim. The limitations statues are unique to each state with respect to starting and tolling of the clock. In New York State, a suit for replevin must be filed within three years[19], but the clock does not start until the owner has made demand on the possessor and the possessor has refused. This application of the "discovery rule" means that the owner of stolen property has three

years after learning who possesses the property to demand return of the property and file a lawsuit if the demand is refused.[20] In California, similarly, a three-year statute of limitations "accrues upon discovery of the whereabouts of a stolen article of artistic significance."[21] A second obstacle might center on the issue of ownership, assuming the current possessor of the stolen book bought it in good faith with no reason to know it was stolen. A third obstacle, even if the first two are overcome, may be "laches," a legal doctrine providing that when a plaintiff unreasonably delays pursuit of his rights and thereby causes undue prejudice to the defendant ("sits on his rights"), the plaintiff's claim will fail. Laches also requires that the victim institution use reasonable diligence in trying to recover its stolen property, which includes public notice of the theft.

Such complications involving differences in state laws are far from uncommon and almost ensure the need for a qualified lawyer. When international recovery is in question, counsel becomes essential. Paying a retainer to an appropriate law firm (probably one that has some relevant experience and is recognized by commercial dealers) shows a commitment to recovering stolen property and will not go unnoticed. Even if litigation is not being considered, the terminology and common practices related to recovery of stolen property will be familiar to a good lawyer, who can be very helpful in drafting and negotiating agreements incidental to cooperative transactions leading to recovery. Since New York and California are major centers for the book trade, if the victim institution has lost books in (or via) these states, retained lawyers need to be licensed and experienced in their courts. Determining which law applies to which aspect of a case is not at all simple, and it is difficult to discern even basic principles that would govern all case outcomes.

Laws in continental Europe tend to favor the good-faith purchaser of stolen property rather than the original owner who is the theft victim. The American "discovery rule" generally does not apply, so the limitations period starts and continues running regardless of whether the theft victim knows where his stolen property is. Tainted provenance can be cleansed, and stolen property may return to the legal art trade. Under French law, a theft victim has three years from the day the property was stolen to claim it from the person who holds it (if the person holds it in good faith; a person holding property in bad faith must wait for thirty years before a claim from the owner will be barred by limitations, but after that, even the bad faith holder of stolen property may have good title in France.[22]) In Japan, someone who owns a stolen item for more than two years becomes the legal owner of the object. This fundamental legal and cultural conflict recently became an issue when the library of Christ Church College, Oxford, attempted to recover a stolen Vesalius that had migrated to Japan. The current owner, a Japanese school of dentistry, refused to repatriate the volume(s), citing that country's law and leading to a loud outcry in the Western world.

In common law countries, by contrast, it is commonly said that, "a thief cannot pass good title." The fact that a stolen book, for example, was bought at auction by an innocent bona fide purchaser who paid a fair price, does not clear the book's dubious provenance, and no buyer in the United States or England may obtain good title to the stolen book. However, as the saying goes, "Possession is nine-tenths of the law." While a library may have a good replevin case against a British or American collector who bought a book stolen from the library, if the library does not know who possesses the book, or how to reach the possessor, in reality there will be no lawsuit and no recovery.

Even with its current location known and the law on one's side, recovery of a stolen book may be difficult and time-consuming. Even though the thief has confessed to stealing some books, the institution may have difficulty proving particular missing books were stolen, rather than mislaid. The practical significance is that the institution may be required to show the books were stolen before they can be listed on some registries. The initial approach can be made by a letter (a certified letter from the institution's attorney, or from outside counsel, shows the institution is serious) asserting ownership and requesting the return of an item. Sometimes a formal approach will be less productive than a softer, diplomatic effort of persuasion; fear of notoriety and disgrace within professional or cultural circles may be more effective than a threatened legal challenge, especially where the challenge is weak.

An appeal for return is enhanced in most cases by an appeal to the purse. As previously noted, circumstances may not even allow for compensation of current owners. Although the Ransom Center had enough funds to compensate current owners for the amount they paid for books stolen by Meyer, the passage of time had resulted in considerable appreciation of the materials. (In one case, the current owner had purchased a book for a figure about 400% larger than the original auction hammer price received by Meyer a decade earlier.) Getting a book dealer to participate in the compensation proposal may not be easy. The dealer not only stands to lose money but also risks being discredited for having bought and sold stolen property. At one time, the ABAA adopted a "Fair Play Resolution" recommending that a bookseller who sold a stolen item split the cost of compensation 50/50 with libraries, although according to a spokesperson that is apparently no longer its official policy.[23] The 50/50 split is recommended by the Code of Conduct jointly produced by the U.K. booksellers' trade association and the Chartered Institute of Library and Information Professionals (CLIP, formerly the Library Association).[24] Obviously, that is only a guideline, and when the value of an item has risen substantially since leaving the hands of a dealer, the chances of such participation fall. If a book has changed hands several times since the theft, with a price increase at every step, the victim institution is faced with four bad choices: (1) trying to get every seller along the way to contribute to payment of the current possessor; (2) trying to persuade the first dealer who bought from the thief to split or share the price of recovery; (3) trying to persuade the current possessor to accept less than he paid for the book; or (4) paying whatever is necessary.

In the course of pursuing the Smiley maps and Meyer books, institutions discovered that while most private owners understandably had mixed feelings about returning stolen property, in the end most were happy to see the book returned to its rightful owner in exchange for the price they had paid; a few, unhappily, demanded additional compensation of one kind or another. In such cases the library will need to decide how badly it wants the book back. The present authors believe that yielding to such demands is, in general, not a good practice, but each library must make up its own mind, taking into account the importance of the individual item and the funds available for what may be extended and expensive litigation. At present, legal fees in large metropolitan areas range upwards from $500 per hour, plus expenses. Unless the victim institution seriously intends to file a lawsuit for recovery of its stolen book (after researching all relevant laws and facts), a threat to do so is unethical and will almost certainly not produce a good result.

The reader may reasonably conclude from this article that the recovery of stolen rare items is a slow, time-consuming, and sometimes frustrating and/or painful process requiring the utmost in patience and persistence.[25] Among the obstacles we have pointed to are the lack of reliable shared information about unrecovered stolen books and less than satisfactory channels of communication among the booktrade, law enforcement, and the curatorial community, as well as the lack of readily available sources of information regarding the complex legal issues. On the other hand, the experience provides curators with a fascinating, if unsought, tutorial in the law of replevin and the inner workings of law enforcement and the book trade. Those who have lived through it pray that it is a once-in-a-lifetime education.

Appendix I
FBI Application for Search & Seizure Warrant Involving a Manuscript

Case 3:09-mj-00248-BF   Document 1   Filed 08/20/2009   Page 1 of 6

U.S. DISTRICT COURT
NORTHERN DISTRICT OF TEXAS
FILED
AUG 20 2009
CLERK, U.S. DISTRICT COURT
By _____
Deputy

United States District Court

_____NORTHERN_____ DISTRICT OF _____TEXAS_____

In the Matter of the Search of
(Name, address or Brief description of person, property or premises to be searched)

Heritage Galleries and Auctioneers
3500 Maple Ave., 17th Floor
Dallas, Texas 75219-3941

**APPLICATION AND AFFIDAVIT FOR
SEARCH WARRANT**

CASE NUMBER: 3:09-MJ-248

I __John Skillestad__ being duly sworn depose and say:

I am a __Special Agent for the Federal Bureau of Investigation (FBI)__ and have reason to believe that __XX__ on the property or premises known as (name, description and/or location)

Heritage Galleries & Auctioneers, 3500 Maple Ave., 17th Floor, Dallas, TX. 75219-3941

in the _____NORTHERN_____ District of _____TEXAS_____ there is now concealed a certain person or property, namely (describe the person or property to be seized)

The original and all copies of a handwritten, undated letter from Jacqueline Kennedy to Ethel Kennedy written on or about June 8, 1968

which is (state one or more bases for search and seizure set forth under Rule 41(b) of the Federal Rules of Criminal Procedure)
property that constitutes evidence of the commission of a crime, contraband, the fruits of crime, and is, otherwise, criminally possessed, **concerning a violation of Title __18__ United States Code, Section(s) __2315__. The facts to support a finding of Probable Cause are as follows:**

(SEE ATTACHED AFFIDAVIT OF SPECIAL AGENT JOHN SKILLESTAD).

Continued on the attached sheet and made a part hereof.   XX Yes __ No

_____
Signature of Affiant
JOHN SKILLESTAD
Special Agent, FBI

Sworn to before me, and subscribed in my presence

__August 20, 2009__
Date

at _____Dallas, Texas_____
City and State

PAUL D. STICKNEY
United States Magistrate Judge
Name and Title of Judicial Officer

_____
Signature of Judicial Officer

AFFIDAVIT

The affiant, JOHN P. SKILLESTAD, having been duly sworn, states as follows:

I.

INTRODUCTION

A.   Your affiant is JOHN P. SKILLESTAD, Special Agent, FEDERAL BUREAU OF INVESTIGATION (FBI), having been so employed since August, 1990. Your affiant is currently assigned to the Dallas FBI Field Office and has been since December, 1990. Your affiant's current assignment is supervision of the Dallas Field Office's Public Corruption Squad. Previous to his current assignment, your affiant's primary investigative assignment was violent crime matters to include bank robberies, kidnappings, fugitives, and property crimes to include interstate transportation of stolen property.

B.   Based on affiant's training, experience and participation in numerous investigations, you affiant knows the following:

1.   Individuals who steal property and items of intrinsic value tend to maintain those items and rarely share information with others as to the items or their locations;

2.   Individuals who steal property and items of intrinsic value tend to secret those items so they cannot be readily detected and will maintain those items as a souvenir or trophy, or until they feel they can convert them and obtain something of value in exchange.

II.

INFORMATION OBTAINED

A.   Based on Affiant's personal investigation and interviews of witnesses, and other law enforcement investigation, he has obtained the following information:

1. On June 5, 1968, shortly after winning the California primary election, Robert Kennedy, a candidate for President of the United States for the Democratic Party, was shot and mortally wounded by an assassin (Sirhan Sirhan) in Los Angeles, CA. Robert Kennedy died the next day, June 6, 1968.

Affidavit - Page 1

Case 3:09-mj-00248-BF   Document 1   Filed 08/20/2009   Page 3 of 6

2. On June 8, 1968, a funeral for Robert Kennedy was held in New York, NY. At the time of the funeral and events surrounding the burial of Robert Kennedy at Arlington National Cemetery, Arlington, VA, Jacqueline Kennedy, the widow of President John F. Kennedy, and sister-in-law of Robert Kennedy, sent a personal, hand written, undated letter, to Ethel Kennedy, Robert Kennedy's widow, to express her thoughts to Ethel about her husband Robert Kennedy and her willingness to help with anything she may need, especially with her children.

3. During the late 1960's and into the 1970's, W.J. Bomback, Inc., a plumbing company, performed plumbing work at Hickory Hill in McLean, VA., the residence of Robert and Ethel Kennedy. One of the employees for W.J. Bomback, Inc., who worked at the Kennedy estate was Russell Thomas Nuckols.

4. On January 10, 1999, Russell Thomas Nuckols died of heart failure. Thomas Nuckols, the son of Russell Thomas Nuckols advised that he discovered the "Jackie Letter" when he was going though his father's belongings and papers. Thomas Nuckols said he was dumbfounded upon discovery of the letter because he had never seen it before and did not know how it came into his father's possession.

5. Shortly thereafter, Thomas Nuckols decided to contact the Kennedy Library or Museum in Boston, MA about this letter. Thomas Nuckols said he spoke to an unknown individual at the library or museum and advised them of his discovery. Thomas Nuckols stated the person on the telephone did not seem too interested in the letter and referred Nuckols to John Reznikoff of University Archives, 49 Richmondville Avenue, Westport, CT 06880. Nuckols did not think to call the Kennedy family.

6. Next, Thomas Nuckols contacted John Reznikoff by telephone and advised him of what he had in his possession. Reznikoff requested that Thomas Nuckols send the "Jackie Letter" via facsimile so he (Reznikoff) could determine the letter's authenticity. Upon preliminary review of the letter to confirm the signature of Jacqueline Kennedy, Reznikoff requested that Thomas Nuckols send the letter to him for further analysis. After examining the letter, Reznikoff confirmed its authenticity. Thomas Nuckols believed the letter was of some value, but had no need for the letter. Thomas Nuckols offered to sell the letter to Reznikoff. Thomas Nuckols advised he sold the letter to John Reznikoff for $6,000 dollars.

7. In approximately May 2001, John Reznikoff, owner of University Archives, subsequently sold the letter to Richard T. Newell, 11 Canterbury Crossing, Tilton, NH 03220, who has a hobby of autograph collecting , with a majority of his purchases being presidential autographs. Reznikoff sold the letter to Newell for $25,000.

Affidavit - Page 2

Reznikoff agreed to purchase Newell's President Gerald R. Ford's memorabilia if Newell agreed to make a purchase at the store (University Archives). An invoice dated May 9, 2001, from the University Companies listed the purchase of the Jackie letter for $25,000 along with three other items. The invoice also lists a credit in the amount of $18,000 for the Ford documents sold to Reznikoff. Newell sent a handwritten letter, dated May 15, 2001, to Reznikoff reminding him to send a provenance for the Jackie letter. Several months later, Reznikoff forwarded a letter of provenance to Newell regarding the Jackie letter.

8. On approximately February 5, 2004, Richard T. Newell sold the Jackie letter to Charles Thomas Jasiak, 15 Woodland Drive, Boylston MA 01505, as a part of trade to obtain a rare letter signed by President William Henry Harrison (Harrison only signed four letters during his brief presidency which lasted only thirty days). Newell paid $130,000 in cash along with the Jackie letter and a letter written by Martha Washington to Jasiak in exchange for the President Harrison letter. Newell advised that he and Jasiak agreed the combined value of both the Martha Washington letter and the Jackie letter was $30,000.

9. Approximately six months later (around August 2004), Charles Thomas Jasiak sold the Jackie letter to Richard P. Goodkin, 336 Singletary Lane, Framingham, MA 01702, as repayment of a debt owed to Goodkin by Jasiak. At the time of the transaction, Goodkin valued the letter between $25,000 and $30,000. Goodkin initially planned on keeping the Jackie letter as a part of his collection, but realized that while Kennedy memorabilia was a wanted asset, its value may diminish over time and through subsequent generations.

10. In approximately July 2006, Richard P. Goodkin consigned the Jackie letter to the Heritage Galleries & Auctioneers Galleries, 3500 Maple Avenue, 17th Floor, Dallas, TX 75219-3941. At the same time, Goodkin consigned a manuscript of "America the Beautiful" with the auction house.

11. In approximately September 2006, the Dallas Division of the FBI received information from Max Kennedy, son of Ethel and Robert Kennedy, that the Jackie letter was in possession of the Heritage Auction Galleries. Max Kennedy advised that he is the person in charge of all of his mother's and father's papers and he was the only person with the authority to loan documents outside the Kennedy family. Max Kennedy stated that he had not given authority to sell, give, or donate any papers of Ethel or Robert Kennedy to anyone. Max Kennedy advised that he had spoken with James Halperin, Co-Chairman and CEO, Heritage Auction Galleries, who advised that his business was in possession of the letter. Halperin did not indicate that he would be

Affidavit - Page 3

Case 3:09-mj-00248-BF   Document 1   Filed 08/20/2009   Page 5 of 6

willing to turn the letter over to Max Kennedy, nor did he say he would be keeping the letter.

12. On September 13, 2006, Thomas D. Slater, Director, Americana Department, Heritage Auction Galleries, was contacted by affiant regarding the Jackie letter. Slater advised his company was in possession of the letter and contended that the person (Richard P. Goodkin) who consigned the letter to them was the legitimate owner of the letter. Slater stated that Goodkin consigned an autographed manuscript of "America the Beautiful" and the Jackie letter for auction. Slater advised the manuscript would be priced at $30,000 and the letter would be priced at $15,000. Slater advised he would remove the letter from the auction site.

13. Also on September 13, 2006, Richard K. Brainerd, general counsel, Heritage Auction Galleries, advised that the Jackie letter would remain on the premises and the gallery would cooperate with law enforcement.

14. Interviews of Thomas Nuckols, John Reznikoff, Richard T. Newell, Charles Thomas Jasiak, and Richard P. Goodkin were conducted to provide the sequence of events and information regarding the transfer of the letter.

15. In October 2008, affiant spoke with Ethel Kennedy regarding the Jackie letter. Ethel Kennedy advised she remembers the letter and that it was of great sentimental value. Ethel Kennedy stated that she would never relinquish ownership of the letter for any reason. Furthermore, Kennedy advised she never gave the letter to anyone to keep and under no circumstances would anyone have the authority to transfer ownership of the letter to anyone. Ethel Kennedy advised she remembers that Russell Thomas Nuckols was a plumber from W.J. Bomback, Inc., who worked at the Kennedy residence in Virginia during the 1960s and 1970s, but that she did not give, sell, or donate the Jackie letter to Russell Thomas Nuckols or any other individual.

CONCLUSION

A.   On the basis of the entire contents of this affidavit, affiant avers there is probable cause for the issuance of a search warrant for the Heritage Auction Galleries to obtain possession of the original and all copies of the Jacqueline Kennedy hand written letter to Ethel Kennedy on the day of Robert Kennedy's burial (June 8, 1968), which is considered as a stolen good in violation of Title 18 United States Code (USC), Section 2315, Sale or Receipt of Stolen Goods.

Affidavit - Page 4

Case 3:09-mj-00248-BF   Document 1   Filed 08/20/2009   Page 6 of 6

JOHN P. SKILLESTAD
Supervisory Special Agent
FEDERAL BUREAU OF INVESTIGATION

Sworn to and subscribed before me this 20th day of August, 2009.

Paul D. Stickney
United States Magistrate Judge

Affidavit - Page 5

NOTES

1. Capsule summaries of both theft cases may be found in Nicholas A. Basbanes, *A Gentle Madness: Bibliophiles, Bibliomanes, and the Eternal Passion for Books* (New York: Holt, 1995), 465–519.

2. The list may be found on the web at http://www.columbia.edu/cu/lweb/data/indiv/rare/missing/. See also Travis McDade, *The Book Thief : The True Crimes of Daniel Spiegelman* (New York: Greenwood, 2006).

3. The Smiley map thefts received extensive national and international publicity; for links to articles see http://www.maphistory.info/smileynews.html For background on the less publicized Meyer case, see the Ransom Center press release at http://www.hrc.utexas.edu/news/press/2004/theft.html, and Margarite Annette Nathe, "A Learned Congress: A Closer Look at Book and Manuscript Thieves," Master's Thesis, School of Information and Library Science, University of North Carolina at Chapel Hill, 2005, 60–62.

4. This web page contains links to maps which were found to be missing after inventories were conducted at various institutions: http://www.nymapsociety.org/features/woram.htm

5. For an example of how documents can move rapidly and frequently in the market place and of an FBI application for a search and seizure warrant to recover such a manuscript, see Appendix I in this chapter.

6. See John Christoffersen, "Map Thief Ordered to Pay $2.3M," FoxNews.com (22 May 2007): http://www.foxnews.com/wires/2007May22/0,4670,StolenMaps,00.html

7. Suggestions for responding to thefts may be found in the "RBMS/ACRL Guidelines for Security and Theft in Special Collections" (2009) on the RBMS Security Committee web site. For a useful but now dated list of sources to notify, see Susan M. Allen, "Theft in Libraries and Archives: What to Do During the Aftermath of a Theft," *Journal of Library Administration* 25 (1998): 6–9. The RBMS Security Committee web site maintains an updated list of such resources.

8. Allen, p. 6.

9. A brief historical overview: between 1989 and the early 2000s, the ABAA distributed so-called Pink Sheets with reports of stolen books to its members and others, but the system had obvious disadvantages and was discontinued in favor of email reports to membership and the ABAA missing books database, which went live around 2005. In 1980 the BAMBAM (Bookline Alert—Missing Books and Manuscripts) computer system began as a pioneering effort to link booksellers, librarians, and law enforcement through a computer network, but it ceased to exist in 1992, before web technology became available. Some of its records are at the Grolier Club. That database was unusual in that it also accepted listings for items that were simply "missing" as opposed to being demonstrably stolen.

10. http://www.missingmaps.info. The database's principal developer is Joel Kovarsky.

11. The relevant clause in the University of Texas System fine arts policy reads: "The Insured shall have the right to repurchase from the Company any property of the Insured that is recovered for the amount paid to the Insured for the loss, plus an amount which represents loss adjustment and recovery expenses."

12. http://www.lapdonline.org/art_theft_detail/content_basic_view/1476

13. "Declared Lost," sponsored by Saving Antiquities for Everyone (SAFE) held in Boston, 29 October 2005. A similar conference was held in Wales in 2002; see Chris Fleet, "Report of the 'Responding to Theft' Seminar," Held at the National Library of Wales (http://www.maphistory.info/aberseminar.html).

14. Note that the Code stipulates cooperation with law enforcement, and not necessarily with libraries or other original owners. According to an ABAA spokesperson, that is because the Association does not wish to be drawn into ownership disputes.

15. P. 28. To be fair, McDade applies his generalization to large thefts. As a counterexample, some seven years elapsed between Mimi Meyer's first sale of stolen books and her discovery in 2001 by librarians and booksellers, despite the fact that many of the books she sold displayed obvious signs of tampering with bookplates and ownership markings. McDade's observation would be valid if he had had stated that most book thieves who fence large numbers of materials are found out—eventually.

16. At an RBMS Preconference seminar at Austin, TX, 22 June 2005, an ABAA bookseller declared in a public forum that book thefts were the fault of libraries. See Exlibris archives http://palimpsest.stanford.edu/byform/mailing-lists/exlibris/2006/09/msg00192.html. That perception is repeated by William Finnegan, "A Theft in the Library: The Case of the Missing Maps," *The New Yorker* (17 October 2005), who observed: "Dealers, in any case, habitually blame libraries for thefts. Librarians are not serious about security, they say" (89).

17. See, for example, Patrick Meighan, "Old Nashua Tax Ledger Sold on eBay Stirs up Legal Debate," *Nashua Telegraph* (6 July 2007). http://www.nashuatelegraph.com/apps/pbcs.dll/article?AID=/20070706/NEWS01/207060373. According to the reporter, "The issue has raised concerns about not only the private sale of public records, but also about whether an effective mechanism exists for stopping an inappropriate auction on the popular on-line buying and selling site."

18. The Rules and Regulations of the City of New York (6 RCNY § 2-125 [a]) specify that an auctioneer must "furnish to any buyer, consignor or owner of an article, upon request, information as to the whereabouts of that article that comes into his or her possession or that is sold or offered for sale by him or her." In addition, "an auctioneer must keep a written record of all details of each sale including copies of advertisements; lot number, quantity, description and selling price of each lot; record of disbursements; and net amount sent to persons entitled to proceeds of sale for a period of six years from the date of the auction."

19. McKinney's CPLR 214(3)

20. Where replevin is sought against the party who converted the property, the action accrues on the date of conversion (*Sporn v. MCA Records,* 58 N.Y.2d 482, 488, 462 N.Y.S.2d 413, 448 N.E.2d 1324 [1983]). Where the action is brought against a party who purchased the property in good faith, for value and without notice of the conversion, the action accrues only upon the refusal of a demand for its return (*Menzel v. List,* 22 A.D.2d 647, 253 N.Y.S.2d 43 [1964]). This is "because a good-faith purchaser of stolen property commits no wrong, as a matter of substantive law, until he has first been advised of the plaintiff's claim to possession and given an opportunity to return the chattel" (*Guggenheim Found. v. Lubell,* 153 A.D.2d 143, 145, 550 N.Y.S.2d 618 [1990], affd. 77 N.Y.2d 311, 567 N.Y.S.2d 623, 569 N.E.2d 426 [1991]), 153 A.D.2d at 147, 550 N.Y.S.2d 618).

21. Cal. Code Civ. P § 338(c)

22. See *Warin v. Wildenstein & Co.,* 13 Misc.3d 1201(A), 824 N.Y.S.2d 759 (2006), *affirmed* 45 A.D.3d 459, 846 N.Y.S.2d 153 (2007).

23. John Jenkins, *Rare Books and Manuscript Thefts: A Security System for Librarians, Booksellers, and Collectors* (New York: ABAA, 1982): Section V. This guideline is no longer in force, according to an ABAA representative (emails to Oram of 19 and 21 November 2007).

24. *Theft of Books and Manuscripts from Libraries: An Advisory Code of Conduct for Booksellers and Librarians,* U.K. Library Association and the Antiquarian Booksellers Association, Section 6.2. http://www.la-hq.org.uk/directory/prof_issues/tobam.html.

25. Paintings by Rufino Tamayo and Andy Warhol supposedly stolen over two decades ago recently resurfaced in Manhattan. See Edith Honan, "New York Gallery Sues for Return of Stolen Warhol," (Reuters, 5 February 2008). http://www.reuters.com/article/domesticNews/idUSN0528337820080205, and Melissa Grace, "SoHo Gallery Sues Unemployed Brooklyn Man, Christie's over Warhol Painting," *Daily News* (6 February 2008). http://www.nydailynews.com/news/2008/02/06/2008-02-06_soho_gallery_sues_unemployed_brooklyn_ma.html

APPENDIX I

Blumberg Survey

Created and analyzed by Susan M. Allen
Data compiled by Nicole Davis, Kelly Jensen, and Laurel Rozema

History of the Blumberg Case and the *Blumberg Survey*:

Stephen (Stevie) Carrie Blumberg was arrested on March 20, 1990, following a FBI raid on his Ottumwa, Iowa home in which almost 21,000 books valued at $20,000,000 from more than 300 libraries were recovered. Most of these books had been stolen from libraries across the United States over a 20-year period. One year later, Blumberg was brought to trial in federal court for a fraction of the thefts. He was convicted and sentenced to six years in prison, $200,000 in fines, and three years' probation following his imprisonment. The FBI was left with the job of returning the stolen goods to the libraries from which they had been taken. As this was no small matter, they enlisted OCLC and volunteers from the Creighton University Library to catalog the collection. Then they began the job of returning the loot.

Once the "Blumberg Collection" was dismantled and the books were returned to their rightful owners, it seemed a good time to try to learn something about library and special collections security from the experience. The idea of a survey was born.

In 1995 the FBI supplied a list of libraries to which it had supposedly returned books stolen by Stephen Blumberg. At that time, most libraries had no Internet presence and effective search engines were not available. Google, for example, did not even exist, and Yahoo was in its infancy. Thus, the mailing list used to send out the survey was developed from the then current, print edition of the American Library Association's *Guide to American Libraries*. In some cases, it proved impossible to identify positively some of the libraries because they had gone out of existence, merged, or had duplicate names. No surveys were sent to those libraries on the FBI list that had no address that could be identified. All libraries with addresses received surveys. A freedom of information (FOI) request to the FBI in 2008 for another copy of the original list was denied.

The sources for the FBI's original list seem to have been property markings, bookplates, or claims made by the libraries themselves. Some denied any involvement in the case and stated that the items returned by the FBI were not even theirs. (See the Survey responses.) Nevertheless, many of the libraries on the list were legitimate targets and did suffer losses, in some cases significant ones. The FBI's task was Herculean, reuniting rightful owners with nineteen tons of stolen books. It is a credit to the agency that it succeeded in any way in that task.

The Survey Methodology and Response Rate

The *Blumberg Survey*, consisting of thirteen multiple choice questions with open-ended comments sections, was mailed by Everett Wilkie with the financial support of The Connecticut Historical Society to 319 institutions in 1995/96. These institutions were all on the list of libraries the FBI used when it attempted to return the books stolen by Blumberg to their rightful institutional owners. Of the original 319 institutions, 199 returned surveys that were filled out at least partially, for a response rate of 59%. It should be noted that not all survey questions were answered by all survey takers. There was no follow-up to elicit a higher response rate or to ask respondents to answer questions they had skipped.

Survey Findings

1. Most institutions first learned of their theft by contact from the FBI after the fact.

2. One hundred respondents (53%) did not know how many books were missing from their institutions; only 36 (19%) were able to name a specific number of missing items.

3. Approximately 70% of the responding institutions recovered ten or fewer items.

4. In retrospect, 96% of the institutions reported that no staff members remembered whether Stephen Blumberg visited their libraries during business hours.

5. Most respondents (90%) did not know during what time period Blumberg removed materials from their institutions.

6. When asked whether they did regular inventories before the Blumberg theft was discovered, 71% responded that they did not.

7. At the time of the survey (1995/96), 63% still did not do regular inventories.

8. At the time of the thefts (1970s–1990), 50% of 111 respondents had cages or other locked areas in place for security. All other forms of security measures (i.e. motion detectors, proprietary keyways, security patrols, etc.) were implemented at rates ranging from 9% for electronic locks/access cards or codes to 29% for proprietary keyways. Seventeen percent reported "Tattle Tape" systems.

9. At least 73% have enhanced security since the Blumberg thefts, but they have not always done so in response to these thefts.

10. The vast majority (93%) of institutions were not under construction or being renovated at the time of the thefts.

11. Only 10% publicized their theft; 90% did not.

12. Stephen Blumberg was arrested at the University of California, Riverside in 1987. Forty-five percent indicated that his arrest did not alert staff or cause a change in procedures while 34% indicated that change(s) was made.

13. When asked to volunteer other information regarding the theft and recovery, 18% revealed that the material that was returned to them by the FBI was from the open stacks.

14. The largest numbers of institutions to which the FBI returned materials were in Iowa (24 institutions), Ohio (23), Minnesota and Texas (19 each), California and Illinois (18 each), Massachusetts (16), New York (14), Michigan (13), and Pennsylvania (10). [See 14, "Demographic Information," below.]

15. It was observed by one respondent that "when [he or she] was examining the books at the house [Blumberg's] in Ottumwa, … [he or she] saw that many of them had had new end papers added, with no bookplates present. This work was done very skillfully, leading [him or her] to wonder who might have done it, and what they might have thought about replacing endpapers, presumably having ownership plates, with new blank ones."

Conclusions

Although these data and the findings they reveal are about fifteen years old, it is likely that not much has changed since 1995. Library administrators are often in denial regarding library theft. Most such occurrences are discovered after the fact when stolen materials become known in the antiquarian book and manuscript market and/or when researchers call for materials that turn out to be missing. In spite of monitored reading rooms, motion detectors, electronic locks and access cards, theft of rare materials continues to occur. It is rare that a thief is caught in the act of stealing library materials.

Why is this so? Is it the very nature of libraries and departments of special collections that it is next to impossible to detect theft? Do large collections of rare materials, often under staffed, simply invite plunder? What might be done to deter theft? Here are four suggestions:

1. Perform regular inventories to know what may or may not be missing;
2. Report missing materials to OCLC's Missing Materials Blog (www.missingmaterials.org)
3. Communicate with peer institutions when thefts are discovered; and
4. Identify rare materials that remain in circulating collections and unsecured storage areas and transfer items to more secure areas.

The Survey

Total responses: 199, though not all questions were answered by all survey takers. Most identifiers of institutions, organizations, and individuals have been removed as well as all references to geographic locations to maintain the confidentiality of the survey and to protect participants.

1. How did you first discover that Blumberg stole books from your library? 170 responses

Books discovered missing–10
Keys discovered missing– 0
Blumberg found in secured area–1
Contacted by FBI–138
Contacted by other law enforcement agency. If so, which agency?–2

- Federal Agency–FBI?
- No one remembers anything prior to the receipt of the book.

Evidence special collections area had been broken into. If so, what evidence?–3

- Through 1984 special collections were housed in a caged area with a gap between cage and ceiling. In the Fall of 1980 someone (possibly Blumberg) was seen climbing out of the caged area. He was chased but not caught.
- Our volumes were not in special collections
- Three expensive titles were missing which triggered an article in 1989 and then an FBI visit in 1990

Other—explain.

- Beginning in 1980 active participation in the 18th-Century STC began to show that much material was missing. There were no records of material located in the special collections but, by the end of 1980, increasing concern led to creation of an inventory list of what was then on the shelf.
- News of thefts at a neighboring institution prompted a search.
- We were not burglarized! B. removed some books from the Zamorono Club library when it was at USC. It subsequently was moved to Occidental College—our facility.
- We don't know if Blumberg stole any books from us.
- One of our librarians contacted FBI upon hearing that Blumberg had been in Colorado.

- Book was returned via mail from FBI. It had not been missed.
- Found "lurking" in area—demanded access—refused and was asked to leave
- Our books were returned to us by the Michigan State University Library, which recognized our markings on books returned to them by the FBI
- All books were taken from general stacks of the graduate library. No material was lost from special collections.
- We have never been told Blumberg stole the books, Your letter is the first information with his name involved.
- We knew our volumes were "missing," but they were on open shelving and were not particularly valuable
- We sent listing of missing items to FBI, Omaha after we were alerted to the arrest in the library and OCLC press.
- Another library in state
- We contacted FBI to let them know he had been in our library and to ask about non-book material he may have stolen.
- Thru this survey and the director remembering he may have received a book from the FBI.
- No materials were stolen from Penn State University Libraries.
- Yale did not lose any material to Mr. Blumberg.
- We have no record of any of our materials being stolen.
- Member [patron] reported some lost books.
- Unaware of any books being stolen.
- We checked OCLC database of missing/stolen books against our holdings records. We found 24 missing books on the OCLC database and after visiting Omaha found 7 more.
- Coincidentally with discovering books missing, we also discovered that manuscripts were missing as well. Taken separately, these circumstances can be alarming enough. Taken

together, we concluded quickly that our problems were more than simply of a housekeeping nature—mis-shelving or mis-filing but rather reflected mis-appropriation, which in fact was the case.
- [Contacted by someone, but can't remember who, the FBI? another library?]
- We have not been involved in the Blumberg case.
- I don't believe that Blumberg stole any material from our library.
- [Do not know of any thefts]
- We have had no dealings with FBI or Mr. Blumberg.
- We don't know anything about this. You might try Beloit College Library.
- The University of Massachusetts at Boston has never had a theft by Stephen Blumberg. Another campus perhaps?
- To my knowledge…Stephen Blumberg did not steal any books from this library.
- Letter from Everett Wilkie.
- We have no evidence that a particular individual stole the books, they were simply discovered missing in an inventory that was taken in 1973.
- I have been employed here since 1980 and do not recall a book stolen by this gentleman being returned.
- Books returned by FBI.
- Book returned by FBI.
- Were unaware until this letter.
- FBI sent box with 4 vols. Had read articles in lib. lit. concerning Blumberg case and put 2 and 2 together. Books noted as missing during recent retrospective conversion project.
- Most books taken were from the Main Library collection—most were duplicates to books located in Spec. Coll. which may have been protected by being housed in a different building at the time.

- The FBI asked me to inspect the collection in the Ottumwa house after Blumberg had been arrested. The agents showed me the suitcase containing removed bookplates, one group of which was from U Iowa books.
- No evidence that Blumberg stole material from our library's special collections. All books returned by FBI were from open stacks in the main library. We did have at least one instance of a Blumberg alias using special collections; however, the item he used is still intact on our shelves.
- Book was in open stacks, not in secure area.
- *Chronicle of Higher Education* and New York *Times*.

2. Approximately how many items did you find missing? 171 responses

1. Books:
   1: 8
   2: 3
   at least 2: 1
   2–3: 1
   3: 1
   4: 1
   less than 5: 1
   at least 5: 1
   5: 1
   6?: 1
   7: 1
   8: 1
   13: 1
   15: 1
   20: 1
   23: 1
   24: 1
   25: 1
   30: 1
   32: 1
   37: 1

46: 1
51: 1
100: 1
357: 1
2. Manuscripts:
   2500: 1
3. Do not know: 100
4. None: 1
5. Comments:
   - Only 15 titles we were confident in claiming
   - We are aware of items missing but cannot say how they came to that state.

3. Approximately how many items did you recover? 178 responses

1. Books:
   1: 36 + 1 (pamphlet) + 1 book, but it was not ours
   2: 21
   2-3: 1
   3: 15
   4: 4
   5: 4
   5-8: 1
   6: 8
   7: 3
   8: 8
   10: 4
   11: 2
   12: 1
   14: 1
   15: 2
   20: 2
   23: 1
   24: 1
   25: 2
   27: 1
   28: 1
   29: 1
   30: 1
   approx. 30: 1

31: 2

34: 2

35: 3

42: 1

50: 1

51: 1

56: 1

60: 1

70: 1

121: 2

300–400: 1

343: 1

550: 1

several, but they seem not to have been ours: 1
some: 5 + some but can't remember how many
a number: 1

2. Manuscripts:

2500: 1

Comments:
- Could not confirm whether they were ours or not.
- [Were sent a pamphlet, but determined it had been deaccessioned long ago.]
- A few were mistakenly returned to us by the FBI but we sent them back.
- Unknown what and how many were returned by FBI.
- 4 books returned had U Minnesota plates.
- 5 memorabilia.
- Book was from main stacks.
- 68 pamphlets.
- Not all are ours.
- "According to our records, none."
- From circulating collections.

4. In retrospect, did any of your staff remember that Blumberg visited your library during business hours? 150 responses

Yes: 6

No: 144

Comments:
- Staff changed from the time that he was in this area.

5. Do you know when Blumberg allegedly removed materials from your institution? 154 responses

Yes: 15

No: 139

Dates:
- Late 1979–1981
- December 1988
- Sometime between 1978 and 1985
- Ca. 1985
- Summer/fall 1986
- Some material returned pre-dated at the end of 1980, some was originally added as late as 1983.
- 9/2–3/80, 12/3–4/80, 10/26/87—Data taken from Blumberg's travel log indicate he was in our city on these days.
- <1985?
- We had a reclass project from 1977 to 1989 (Dewey to LC). The classified books recovered were all Dewey.
- We know dates of when he was in our city from FBI log.
- 1986 or 1987
- We're not certain that book returned to ASU Library was ours. There was no record for the book in Special Collection's Card Catalog; nor any record online for the general collection. If it had been stolen, it would have had to have been taken from the general stacks sometime before retroconversion and before adoption of the present online system. (1986/1987).
- Possibly 1985 and 1988/1989.
- We were unable to find any cataloging data for the items sent to us, leading us to feel

the material was probably stolen prior to 1972 when we moved into our new library building.

- Most likely between June of 1987 and February of 1988, although we cannot be certain—these dates constitute the extreme outside dates.

6. Did your institution do regular inventories before you discovered the theft? 142 responses

Yes: 42

No: 101

Comments:

- Not b/w 1979–1986
- "Semi-regular"; had completed a major one in 1988
- In Special Collections only (no in Main)
- But infrequent
- Only once in 10 years
- Only partial inventories
- Only infrequently
- "Regularly"
- Not in that area

7. Do you do regular inventories now? 143 responses

Yes: 53

No: 91

Comments:

- Planning to implement an automation system.
- We are reorganizing our entire collection now and expect to have an inventory beginning either this year or next, but this depends on funding available.
- We hope to in the future.
- More or less regularly. To my knowledge, only MSS, Archives and Spec. Collections did or does anything resembling inventories of the book collections. We do not

inventory mss/archival materials.

- "Semi-regular"
- We do a regular inventory of the most important items.
- [In the late 80s we inventoried all books held by the Central Library and created an online catalog]
- We have been making a concerted effort to sort and catalog items that have not been included in our electronic data base. I regret that we do not have a really good list of items that my have disappeared with Mr. Blumberg or others.
- [Books] were discovered missing in an inventory that was taken in 1973.
- We have done one inventory in special collections.
- In some sections.
- In special collections only. Recently brought up on-line catalog and barcoded.
- Periodic shelf readings.
- In Special Collections only (no in Main).
- But potential is there when problems arise.
- But still infrequent.
- One in progress, last one 5 years ago.
- No, but collection was barcoded in 1992 and missing items were deleted from inventory.
- Except for Special Collections.
- One inventory done July–Dec. 1993.
- Partial only.
- Don't have staffing levels to carry out the inventory.
- Budget cutbacks.
- Not regular but irregular.
- "Regularly"
- In special collections.
- We do them on a rotating basis. Everything is inventoried in a 5-yr. period.
- Not in that area.

- Currently, a shortage of staff and time does not permit this.
- Not often enough.

8. What security measures did you have in place at the time of the thefts? 111 responses

1. Motion detectors—21
2. Proprietary keyways—32
3. Security patrols—28
4. Perimeter intrusion devices (i.e., contacts)—20
5. Electronic locks/access cards or codes—10
6. Cages, or other locked areas—56
7. Other (please specify)—54:
   - Checkpoint security
   - Exit security gate
   - We are in the process of revising our security procedures.
   - Checkpoint exit door security system.
   - Exit monitors and detection devices.
   - Alarmed doors.
   - Our security measures were pretty much that of appearance rather than substance. We are a closed stack library, and people have to fill in call slips and the staff fetch most material. There is a sign-in requirement, but... no requirement to prove one's identity. We don't have enough staff to steadily man a check-out station.
   - Security measures in place.
   - Sign in; monitored research; no book bags, etc allowed in study/research room.
   - None
   - security gates
   - At that point in time, the Central Library did not have a Rare Books Department, and rare items were used without adequate supervision in the various subject departments.
   - While many of the items in our 'old' collection were not even property-stamped, some of them do contain a stamped 'red star' or even a 'double red star.' The items returned to us by the FBI did contain red star stamps.
   - Manually checked bags
   - Some tattle tape
   - 3M theft detection—rare books in vault
   - 3M Tattletape
   - 3M security
   - 3M Security System was installed April 1982.
   - Checkpoint—3M system
   - Special Collections is locked when not staffed and the books in that area do not circulate.
   - In main, books are stripped. (Stolen books from main not special collections.)
   - 3m security strips
   - 3M gates
   - Book security system
   - 3M Tattletape system
   - Tattletape system
   - Yes, rare books room now has an attendant.
   - Tattle tape
   - Door guard
   - Passes provided for stack access.
   - Tattle tape
   - He stole from the general stacks, not the special collections, and the answers are based on that.
   - Exit guards checking briefcases and backpacks.
   - None
   - Checkpoint monitors at main door

- Unknown—do not know when books were stolen
- Not a secured library
- None
- Security strips in books
- "I don't know, it was before my time, but possibly cages."
- Exit security system/magnetic strips
- Relocated items to more secure room in staff only area.
- Strict registration procedures
- None
- A simple locked door
- No
- Limited access (only to staff)
- Book theft detection system
- Secured reading area
- 3M Security System
- Guard at entrance during evening and weekend hours.
- Because of the lack of cataloging data, it is difficult to determine the location of this material in the previous building—general open stacks or closed stacks.
- Tattle taped material and exit sensors.

9. Have you added to or enhanced your security systems since the thefts? Please explain. 103 responses

"No" (without explanation): 23
"Yes" (without explanation): 2
Comments:
- All special collections in locked area.
- Maintained same security—have recently changed companies and upgraded but this had nothing to do with this specific incident.
- We will be revising security procedures during 1994–1995.

- Security gate at both entrances. Staff positioned to view exits. Rare or special collection kept in locked room. Motion detectors.
- We added video cameras, but not in relation to the incident.
- No changes were made in security at the time. We are getting a card key lock at the staff entrance and possibly a video camera, but I am not sure that will be very helpful.
- Upgraded within the last 3 years
- 3M tattle tape
- Among the enhancements are proprietary keyways, perimeter intrusion devices and motion detectors.
- Yes, rare books are on lower levels now with full security and no access by the public. They are paged.
- In the new building (home of Rare Books since 1981) we have a system of multiple locks, caged areas and patrols for security. We collate books with prints and maps before and after each use by a patron. All use is under staff supervision.
- The particular collection involved has been removed from the public floor. Security system enhancements undertaken in recent years were routine and not related to Blumberg.
- Enhanced security procedures especially where we have unprocessed material but this didn't necessarily have anything to do with Blumberg.
- At that point in time [late 80s, after return of thefts by William Witherell] a Rare books Department had been created, with strict policies for use of special materials and limited access to them.
- During the last few years the management staff here has made an effort to improve both the staff and materials security. The

efforts are complicated by the fact that the building is nearly one hundred years old and was not designed for public access to the collection or for a staff of the present size. (Long ago, when staff costs became prohibitive, the collection was opened to the public; collection security has been a problem ever since.)

- We now have an electronic security system for the library which we did not have before 1990. Special Collections moved in 1990 to our new library addition and has much more secure quarters. Collections from many locations in the old building were consolidated, and we have a vault for the most valuable items. We also have security-stripped books in our open shelf reference collection and have done a comprehensive inventory of books in Special Collections. Users have to exit our reference area via a locked gate which is released by a staff member at our reception desk. Although our locks in the new building are much better than those in the old, construction has been complete for a key card system, but the system hasn't been installed yet.
- 3M book security system
- Museum/Lib. are monitored via electronic surveillance; staff are with patrons during the time they are in our facility in both the museum and lib.
- Added 3M security system in 1986 when we built an addition and renovated.
- No—We are a small town lib. (pop 342), we were blown away when we received the letter from the FBI. We have two glass cases where some of Dr. Skene's original collections are kept, plus a few treasured volumes of local interest. Footnote: Dr. Skene is regarded as the founder of Ameri-

can Gynecological medicine—he had a summer home here.
- We have installed electromagnetic security gates at the main entrance.
- In Special Coll. added motion detectors, glass breaking, perimeter intrusion, front door activates bell.
- We now have locked cases in our reference and genealogy sections with access to keys by staff only. We also have added staff and now no longer leave this area unattended by a staff member. We had 3 copies of the title recovered by the FBI and the theft went unnoticed for quite a while before a copy was reported as missing.
- No, but are seeking budget funding to do so.
- Security patrols
- We re-instituted stamping books on the last page of text with indelible ink and embossing covers.
- In 1992 Special Collection staff systematically transferred all pre-1700 imprints and rare Americana into a vault area. At that time there were no notable missing items discovered. [All returned stolen books had been taken from open stacks.]
- Have completed tattle taping the entire collection.
- No, but a security audit was undertaken.
- Automated system with all materials barcoded, primarily for inventory purposes.
- A state of the art electronic alarm system was installed.
- 3M book detection system installed in 1991.
- Collection moved from cages to unidentified locked rooms. Key security improved. Most material now tattle-taped. Doors alarmed on closing. Curator named for special collections.

- Motion detectors, perimeter intrusion devices, electronic locks/access cards or codes.
- Since the items were stolen from the open stacks, we have no additional protective systems in place for the publicly open stacks.
- A new library building is under construction (opening in Dec. 1997) which will have considerably increased security.
- No, but 3M system was added to secure the general circulating system & Special Collections installed an electronic system between the dates of the thefts and the time the thefts were called to our attention.
- Motion detectors, perimeter intrusion devices
- Installed Knogo
- Library is now closed to the general public, but not in response to thefts.
- No; though the new building does have a modern security system, with motion detectors, and though we have had security patrols out of concern for the safety of students and personnel, the books are probably no more secure than before.
- We've added a 3M security system and a motion detection system with access codes. These were not directly in response to the Blumberg theft.
- Not as a direct result of the theft. However, we have recently installed a book security system, which will not be fully functional until a larger portion of our collection is stripped.
- Staff now all have badges; no others receive stack passes; elevators to stacks works only with key.
- Yes, we have Medco keys and locks on exterior doors. Have caged additional areas.

- Toughened security of key access to the Sp. Col. area; changed security system from Sentronics to Knogo; added electronic security system to Sp. Col. and to the building.
- Special collections has motion detectors, electronic alarms and separate keys.
- We now have a vault plus restricted access to the rare book area.
- Only to the extent that rare book items are identified in our automated catalog as non-circulating.
- Special Collections has moved to a separate facility with controlled access, secure stacks, alarms and electronic locks.
- We have updated checkpoint security gates but did this because we needed to widen aisles of older system to meet ADA requirements.
- We have gathered all pre-1800 volumes and placed them in secure areas, and we also have a secure rare books room. At time of theft, book was probably a circulating item.
- We installed a 3-M system
- New library building
- Motion detectors, perimeter intrusion devices, and access codes for areas with valuable material.
- Additional motion detectors have been incorporated into the system.
- Electronic locks
- We now have cages around the archives and collection areas. Additional motion detectors have been installed. The cage areas are now alarmed and only three people have an access code to deactivate the alarms.
- In 1990, the library moved to another building (*) where all materials except a 'ready reference' collection, genealogical indexes,

and microfilm copies of local newspapers are in locked stacks. All stack material must be requested by signed call slips and most are 'signed out' to the library user (*which were renovated to our specifications).

- Books were not stolen from special collections but from the open general stacks.
- Some areas have an electronic lock or a separate security zone. Very rare items are stored in a vault constructed two years ago.
- Remodeled building with larger archives/special collections which allowed us to move items for open racks and also added 3M security system.
- 1994: Security system installed in Special Collections (motion detectors, etc.)
- We are raising funds to construct a secure vault. Many valuable items have been removed from the stacks and kept in locked storage since I started working here 2 years ago.
- The books were not from special collections.
- Motion detectors.
- Now in locked area
- 3M Tattle Tape System
- Checkpoint book target system—superficial security
- Access is more restricted than before.
- Yes. About 1988 we started a complete check of bags, purses, cases, etc. to see that all materials leaving the building are correctly checked out; not depending entirely on a "security system."
- 3M security system installed in 1994. Key access now more restricted.
- Yes—museum displays have motion detectors.
- Rare items transferred from open stacks to Rare Books.

- Yes, we are developing a more secure Special Collections area.
- Yes! Motion detectors, special keys, etc.
- New library built in 1972 with one exit (previous library had multiple exits). Patron check-in at circulation desk. Special Collections now in compact moveable shelving not open to the public; material must be pulled by staff. New Special Collections reading area with improved view of tables.
- We have installed a security system in Special Collections, which includes alarmed doors and noise sensors for the windows.
- Yes, staff development courses, security patrols, and perimeter intrusion devices, book security.

10. At the time of the thefts, was your institution under construction or being renovated? 126 Responses

Yes: 9
No: 117
Comments:
- Not sure, but not major construction/renovation since none has been done on this building.
- Do not know when book was taken.
- Not known, asbestos abatement took 3 years
- We don't know when items were taken, but our building was renovated in 1982–1983.
- Don't remember when our renovation was.
- Possibly. The Library underwent a building project in 1990–1992.
- Possibly—present structure was built '86–87.
- We don't have any idea when they were stolen.
- Do not know.
- Don't know, building was under renova-

tion in 1985–86.

- Don't know.
- Probably.
- Unknown when thefts occurred. New building in 1972.
- As we cannot pinpoint the exact time of the theft, this is just an assumption, although we have not had any recent large-scale renovations.
- Unsure.
- Don't know.
- Possibly, renovation in 1985–86.
- Perhaps, new building going up in 84–85.
- Unknown.

11. Did you publicize the theft in any way? 144 Responses

Yes: 15
No: 129
Comments:

- After the two items were returned by the FBI, we received coverage in the regional press regarding these thefts.
- Local newspaper accounts, letter to ABAA detailing eleven of the major [printout cut off].
- Posted on staff bulletin board.
- The local and campus newspapers had feature stories.
- Articles in local newspapers after items were returned.
- To the staff and other campus libraries.
- Reported on progress of checking and having books returned to mgt. groups within the library.
- Non-book thefts were reported in local press.
- *AB Bookman* Missing Books Section, Dec. 16, 1985, p. 4663; and to dealers by letter.
- Campus police, and indirectly, other West

Coast law enforcement agencies; specialist and antiquarian booksellers; local newspapers.

- Enclosed are articles including the one of 7/19/1989 almost a full year before the FBI visited us 6/4/1990. We also informed Book Alert Network.
- There was press coverage at the time materials were returned.
- There was some local publicity in the papers at the time a small collection of books was donated to our library.
- Notified faculty and staff.
- After recovering the books, we sent an article to the local paper and had the book on display for a month.

12. The arrest of Blumberg in 1987 at the University of California at Riverside was widely publicized. Did that arrest alert your staff in any way or cause you to change procedures? If so, please explain. 58 Responses.

26 people responded No; other elaborations as below.

- We were aware of the Blumberg thefts but items that were stolen from our collection were in the general collection. Subsequently, we do have a periodic review of books that should be placed in more secure areas.
- The staff did not realize the value of items held by Forsyth Library; nor were there any precautions, other than security gates.
- The arrest seemed to increase staff awareness of the possibility of theft.
- No change in procedure. The information was circulated among circulation staff, security personnel, and special collections staff.
- Not beyond the usual gossip.
- Yes, made us rethink access to closed stack areas.

- The archives/special collections reading room is more strictly monitored. Room use "check out" system improved and routine tightened.
- Special Collections has further limited number of items and increased security procedures in the search room.
- Staff more aware; procedures already in place.
- No. We just became more alert.
- We checked to see if Blumberg had visited Special Collections under any known aliases, but he had not and thus we made no changes.
- We reviewed procedures.
- Stepped up process of identifying books for transfer to Special Collections.
- Yes, adding security measures.
- Of course, it made everyone more aware in general, but not in any specific way (since at the time we did not know B. had even been here).
- The Special Collections Dept. became a closed stack environment in 1992. Books were stolen from the general stacks.
- Probably not—it was before my time.
- We note name and description of any publicized book thieves and file these in the front of our Registration Card file at Reference Desk at Special Collections.
- Not until FBI letter requesting information.
- We knew some of our old books were missing, but we could not connect him to stealing our books.
- No. We still didn't seem to think that he had been through Colorado.
- We knew about some thefts before the arrest—in libraries near us—WSU & U of O. We changed security.

- General discussion among the staff; increased awareness of the problem.
- We had a security system and were usually quite vigilant—we perhaps are more alert after reading about the arrest but had no idea it may have affected us.
- I was not here then but I do not believe the staff was aware of the arrest at that time. In 1987 I was at WSU and was aware of the arrest and did make some changes in security.
- We made efforts to tighten both our physical security and our operational procedures immediately after discovering the thefts and apart from the Blumberg incidents in California which came later.
- No notice was taken. The History Library at the Museum of New Mexico has since purchased a copy [of one of the books stolen from us] so the theft had an effect on their collection development policy.
- No changes in routine security procedures. However, Blumberg action DID prompt us to remove "rare" materials from general stacks and put in Spec. Coll. which tightly controlled access.
- Prof. librarian arrived in 1985. Staff notified of thefts described on ExLibris. Since 1985 better monitoring and records of items pulled. Better check in procedure. Removal of outside packs. Began to stamp Spec. Coll. books again.
- The KU libraries has installed the 3M security system for its circulating collections, but the installation was not related to the Blumberg case.
- We discuss security regularly in staff meetings.
- It made the reality of book thefts more genuine to staff. We have tried to follow RBMS

security guidelines, but personnel and physical plant circumstances make that difficult.

13. What other information would you like to volunteer regarding this case and the experience of your institution?

- We have encountered one persist known thief recently and try to watch for him. Many cooperate to get and be pointed with suspicious characters. We try to be careful and we do have some problems but it's a compromise. See my [Russell Maylone] piece with our intruder in the ABAA Newsletter. I am not aware of plans for changing circumstances in the main collections.

- Not until we were notified by the FBI in the Fall of 1990 did we take a full inventory of the collection. More than 800 volumes were reported missing. Since many of the books returned by the FBI were included in our original 1980 inventory, the number missing zooms into the conjecture zone. Considering the extent to which Blumberg eradicated or altered identifying marks, I am amazed that we got back as many as we did. Of those returned to us, there is only one that I have doubts about.

- The stolen materials were part of the Augsburg Seminary Collection, which was folded into our collection many years ago. The theft went undetected. The others were not part of a rare book collections; all were merely old, not rare.

- Blumberg took the book from open stacks, where there are no security measures in place. He erased all of our markings, but not a note from the donor which identified Davidson College. The book had shown up as missing in a previous inventory, but we had no reason to suspect Blumberg.

- Blumberg did not steal from our special collection repositories (Barker Center, HRC). Although those have many security systems, our main library has armed guards and a 3M security system. We do not wish to implement additional security systems for our main library (other than a locked room for some material that are considered rare), esp. not for our open stacks.

- All books recovered belonging to the Univ. of MO were from the general stacks, not Special Collections. Additionally, a few titles recovered were from the State Historical Society of MO, which is located in the same building as the main University library, but is administratively separate. Those, too, were from open stacks.

- As far as I can ascertain, no items were stolen from Smith. In the lists of the seven allegedly stolen items sent to us by the FBI, three items are still on the shelves in the general stacks. According to our catalogues and shelf lists, we never owned the other four volumes.

- The books were just on the shelves, not in a rare book or secured area. Surprised to receive the volumes in the mail. No one had noticed them missing.

- Blumberg appears to have confined his thefts here to bibliographical reference books.

- One book was returned and we are not aware of other books which were stolen.

- I would like to comment that we are sure the books returned were ours because they had an old library mark. We were also able to make out faint traces of the call numbers which had been assigned, and trace them to shelf-list cards, showing the books as missing. There had been deliberate attempts to remove library markings, but they were not entirely successful.

- When OCLC made the Blumberg data base available we searched our holdings in the database and found 2 of those items missing. We made a claim with the FBI for these items. We don't really know if Blumberg took these items or if someone else did. As I mentioned earlier the items Blumberg stole from our library were Dewey classified books—Dewey books had not yet been entered in OCLC so we wouldn't have found them thru the OCLC database search. I was able to verify through shelf list cards that all of the items the FBI sent us were ours except for one.

- Apparently B. had "cased" our facility, but because we kept our valuable items under such a low profile he did not discover the really valuable things we owned.

- FBI contacted me asking us to accept a book that appeared to be ours. We examined it but did not believe it belongs to [us]. At their request we have kept it. We have done an inventory of our archives and have not identified any missing volumes. If a rare book was on the open shelves, we may not yet know that it is missing. A Dutch Masters print collection was stolen from us in 1986. The FBI reported that Blumberg's collection did not included any paintings, drawings, etc.

- Not a problem for us. Our main stacks books are so heavily marked it is very unlikely Blumberg had more that got misdirected.

- We have only a vague memory of the whole affair, and we have not been able to locate our records regarding the return of materials from the FBI. Although we feel that the books returned were indeed

ours, we are not 100 percent certain of that because of our now vague memory of it.

- We did not receive books that are not ours and we do not believe our materials were sent to other libraries.

- His arrest alerted us the fact that he had been in Boulder. After, we checked with local police. He had been stopped for traffic violation and had library books in his car which the local police returned. We feel Blumberg came in at night and went thru our files, but we really don't know when or how theft occurred. We were told he made key impressions and then made keys. We now have Medco keys which are supposed to be more secure.

- Additional security measures are under way. These are driven by the general level of theft than by Blumberg.

- These thefts occurred when the Rare Book Room was in another building.

- This proved that theft from our general collection is very difficult to discover. Until someone else is looking for the material, we don't know it is missing.

- Our agency has very few "rare" book materials.

- We feel that the security structures and procedures for Special Collections are now fairly good, although we remain vulnerable to insider thefts. We continue to have extensive groups of valuable material in the general collections, and these remain vulnerable to Blumberg imitators. Items returned to us by the FBI were from the general collection. There is no evidence that Blumberg entered Special Collections at anytime. One appears to have been withdrawn and other may not have belonged to us.

- The consistent marking of ownership in our books was key to claiming them. Even though Blumberg attempted to obliterate property marks, one could readily tell where a stamp had been removed. I would have appreciated the opportunity to see and possibly claim some of the "homeless" volumes which were ultimately given to Creighton University.
- This happened in the old building prior to 1984.
- There was no special collections area, per se, at that time, and the librarian who coordinated at the time has since retired, making her files relating to the incident unavailable.
- The only evidence was the presence of Essex Institute bookplates in some of the volumes that were recovered. We believe that all of these items had been deaccessioned decades ago.
- We also knew about the theft and books recovered for the library after one of the local book dealers, who was called by the FBI came back and told the director. I believe he is the reason why we received at least three books—because many of our older collection do not have identifying property stamps. The older collection in general only contained book plates of the major donors and Mr. Dawson (book dealer) was familiar with these. I believe we may be missing more books that do not have property stamps and unless someone was familiar with all our various book plates we won't get them back.
- We are working on a new automation system that will allow for more security. We have had greater losses from our general public than from Blumberg. He did more

harm in the specialized historical libraries.
- I have located items that seemed to be missing from the special collections but it is very possible that other valuable titles were taken from the open stacks; some 20% of our Dewey holdings are not recorded in our online catalog, nor did we retain a shelf-list after automation. Our practice seems to have been to emboss our seal on p. 100/101 or 200/201 with our former name "Michigan State Library." One of the books returned to us had this page slashed out and then laid in again, by whom I don't know. I don't think that anything was returned to us by mistake; the likelihood is rather that we might still be missing things.
- After the FBI returned the books which they claim are from our library, I became more concerned about special collections security, but was unable to institute any change in procedure because of understaffing and transitional phase of a remodeling program. The only effect Blumberg had on us was to assure that our new special collections area has good security and to hope that when it is complete we will have increased staffing to be more security conscious when dealing with users. I don't even know what security measures will be taken in the new cataloging dept. of the library. Online catalog with barcodes should make inventorying easier, but I don't know if other depts will take advantage of that.
- The university had disposed of its rare book collection in 1986 by selling it to Georgetown University. At the time of the sale, an inventory resulted in a record of missing items being generated. These records were just placed in storage until the FBI notification. Also, once the case was in the

press, university librarians went through the stacks and relocated any titles which could be identified as "rare." So now the library has another rare book collection in a more secure area.

- We are an extremely small library and I wonder if the books were ever truly stolen from us. The book markings did have our name, but we couldn't find inventory records of them and since we had been doing extensive weeding, we even wondered if the books were some that were withdrawn and perhaps stolen from someone who had picked them up at our used book sales. If there is another Potter County Library in the U.S.A., I suspect the books may have been theirs.

- Blumberg increased awareness of the craftiness of practiced book thieves and reinforced the need to adhere to strict procedures already in place. The library's security procedures have been modified in the last few years, though not specifically because of Blumberg. CPL is a large public research library with all the inherent security concerns of such an institution, for both staff and material. Security patrols have been increased within the last few years (i.e., additional security guards added to the staff); cameras installed in some areas; emergency call buttons installed at service desks; and awareness promoted among staff of security issues and of ways to deal with problem people.

- We had no knowledge of the books being missing. When the FBI decided they were ours, we had no real way of knowing if that was so—there was no record of them. The books were of little or no value and might well have been discarded or sold after being here.

- We were very pleased with the courtesy and effectiveness of the FBI in handling our situation.

- One book the FBI returned to us had been withdrawn from our collection and was marked as such. We are not sure that it actually was "stolen" from our library. Any information I have is based on staff member's recall.

- Our books were stolen from the general stacks and not rare. The FBI sent us one book that was not ours. We mailed it to the institution indicated on the book. A historical society received one of our books and asked to retain it if we had another copy (it was a work of local history). We had another copy and agreed to donate the copy received by the historical society to them.

- We do not have a rare books room. All materials are in open stacks.

- Omaha office of FBI tried to return four books to us based on our listing sent to them. The FBI apparently couldn't understand the difference between Dewey and LC numbers for they sent two of our missing titles with the LC cataloging yet on the spines. We returned the books to Omaha and never heard any more. The two items returned to us contained none of our markings or accession numbers.

- One book FBI claims to have returned has not been; instead, they returned another book stolen from us.

- The book the FBI returned to us was no longer listed in our shelf list. It is possible Blumberg may have purchased the book.

- Would be very interested to know how Blumberg learned of the existence of our library and when visited. As well as the recovery of other material not yet identified.

- Newer building also has security gate and all material contains security strips.
- Attached sheet—recalled slight involvement in seizure of Blumberg property in Amarillo warehouse on March 20, 1990.
- We are satisfied that our losses have been accounted for.
- As our library serves mainly undergraduates we sacrifice a great deal of security in favor of easy access.
- The one volume we recovered has markings which were not commonly used in our library, but are occasionally used. Many of our older and more unusual items have come to us as gifts and/or were previously owned by another institution, making it difficult to be sure. We had two sets by James Cook (*A Voyage to the Pacific Ocean* and *A Voyage Towards the South Pole*) from the 1700's which were stolen during that time frame and fit Blumberg's interests, but could have been stolen by some other person(s). We have no direct evidence (other than our one returned volume) linking the thefts to Blumberg.
- The volumes were from our general stacks, not special collections. The books we received were ours originally. Since we are a large (million+) open stacks library, we lose a large number of volumes due to theft. There is no way we can determine if any other volumes were stolen by Blumberg.
- The books that the FBI returned to Rutgers that were not our property were returned to the FBI. They had no property stamps. We did not keep a record of the number of books returned by the FBI or the number returned to them. The books returned to us were books that were on the open shelves and not part of our Special Collec-

tions and Archives.
- We received only one book from the FBI and never could figure out why they sent the book to us. As far as we could tell, it was not a book from our collection.
- No materials were stolen from Penn State University Libraries by Stephen Blumberg. I believe that your letter was intended for the University of Pennsylvania.
- We consider ourselves very fortunate indeed to have been bypassed in his collecting trips.
- Although the FBI "returned" several books to us, they seem not to have been ours.... In addition [we] cannot recall any Blumberg-related thefts from Special Collections. Does the FBI or the people who have been examining these books have reasons—reasons that we seem to lack—indicating that Penn books *were* among those that Blumberg stole? Do Penn bookplates or ownership marks show up in books still in Omaha? Did Blumberg steal materials from other Philadelphia libraries? Is there sufficient evidence of a Penn provenance among the books at Omaha to suggest that it would be worth the time and expense for a Penn staff member to fly there and examine the books?
- I have searched my files and asked the staff if a report for missing materials was ever filed regarding Stephen Blumberg. To the best of my knowledge, we did not generate such a claim or report.
- We have no record of any of our materials being stolen.
- Mr. Blumberg is unknown to us, and to our knowledge has never visited the Masonic Grand Lodge Library and Museum of Texas. We are unaware of how Mr. Blumberg

or the FBI acquired possession of the books, but we are satisfied with their return.

- We have having difficulty locating the information you need, partly because none of us quite remembers during what time period we recovered the stolen materials. We keep a chronological file of copies of correspondence, but we can't remember which month or year all of this happened.

- Until 1979, our 19th century materials circulated to the public. I arrived in 1990 and am unfamiliar with procedures before my arrival. I wish I could be of more help, but procedures here have undergone significant change in the past five years and I cannot attest to the efficacy of procedures before 1990.

- We are unaware of any books that may have been stolen from our institution by Stephen Blumberg and have not had anything turned over to us by the FBI.

- We have consciously chosen—paradoxical as it may seem—in the interest of good public relations within the state, to give security and preservation lower priority than quick and liberal access. Given also the current stringent budgets, with no flexibility, I would say that our security is not likely to change much in the foreseeable future. Frankly, I believe it will probably take a major and obvious loss, a major horse already gone, before we would be able to gain additional funds to improve security, or be willing to clamp true security measures down on staff.

- We are quite satisfied that the books returned to us by the FBI were ours. As far as we are concerned the case is closed.

- Until your letter arrived, I never heard or knew anything about Stephen Blum-

berg and the Lathrope Library. As far as I know, nothing was ever returned to us by any source with clear indications that the item(s) had been stolen by Stephen Blumberg and were being returned to us.

- We have never experienced any losses to Stephen Blumberg.

- No one at this library is aware of materials being removed by Stephen Blumberg. We are also under the impression that nothing was returned to us by the FBI or any other agency.

- Several items on the FBI's list attributed to this collection were indeed missing, and others may not have been cataloged (i.e. Special Coll. backlog).

- We [former special collections curator and current special collections curator] both found your letter and survey to be mysterious, because neither of us is aware that Mills was one of Blumberg's victims. Do you know something that we don't? I find nothing in my files to indicate that Blumberg was here.

- Yikes! We have no recollection of how, why, etc.

- No record of this.

- Neither I nor my staff have any information regarding this topic. I have been here for almost 11 years and two other librarians have been here in excess of 22 years.

- I am not aware of any materials stolen from the Butler University Libraries by Stephen Blumberg. Thus, I am unable to provide any information requested in your survey.

- We did receive books from the FBI which had been stolen from this library.... Of course, we knew of the Blumberg case, but had no idea that these volumes were stolen by him. We are in a small college in a rather remote location, and we did not connect the receipt of the books with Mr. Blumberg's activities. We did not make note of the volumes [titles].

- All three [books returned by the FBI] were from the regular, open stacks and were in now way considered rare or unusual. We hadn't known the books were missing. We are not aware of any material missing from our Special Collections.

- I am unaware of any books left here to other libraries on a regular basis; whether any of these were materials that Mr. Blumberg took from other libraries and were left here, I cannot know.

- The FBI has neither contacted us about historical documents from our collections nor returned any documents to us. Our records do not show that Mr. Blumberg visited the Society.

- We held a theft/security workshop with Steve Huntsberry immediately after learning of the theft by Blumberg of items here—we involved 25 other academic and public libraries and got funding from the Alliance of Higher Education in North Texas and from SMU to do this. We invited librarians and campus security officers from each institution.

- As it stands now, Clarion has received all but 1 of its stolen books back. The other volumes all had our property mark.

- I believe it was 1988 around mid-year, not 1987, that Blumberg was apprehended at Cal Riverside, sometime after we believe the theft took place here, i.e. end of '87-beginning of '88. Further, I do not remember the incident in Riverside as having been highly publicized at all. In fact, I'm quite certain I found out about it from the WSU campus

policeman here...who was instrumental relatively early on in identifying "Matthew McGue," the name under which Blumberg was operating when he was arrested both at Claremont and Riverside, as really being Stephen Carrie Blumberg. (As you may remember, Blumberg went underground after the Cal Riverside incident and to the best of my recollection remained so until his apprehension by the Feds.) The publicity did not come forth until after the FBI condescended to get involved as the result of a tip-off from one of Blumberg's cohorts.

- We have not been notified by the FBI that Mr. Stephen Blumberg stole materials from our library, not are we aware of any materials that may be missing due to theft by him.

- After his arrest we went through our reader applications and found no record of his having been here.

- Apparently the Canady Center was not victimized by Blumberg, so I suppose I need more information before I can proceed with the survey. The thefts occurred before I came to the University of Toledo and my Rare Books Assistant (who was here during that time) has no recollection about the situation.

- I reviewed the University of Illinois at Urbana-Champaign's situation with Nancy Romero, Head, Rare Books and Special collections. To her knowledge, Mr. Blumberg did not steal any volumes from our library.

- We are unaware of the theft of any materials from the libraries at Baylor. If materials were removed from any other location at Baylor I would need that information to pursue a further answer to your questionnaire. At this time we can add nothing further for your investigation.

- Frankly, I first heard of Blumberg through an article that was brought to my attention. It was published in the "Enquirer" and detailed his arrest of March 20, 1990. We have several boxes of information and data relating to this case but they are not open to the public.
- Enclosed are copies of some correspondence related to this theft.
- The materials returned to the Davenport Museum of Art library actually belonged to the Putnam Museum of History and Natural Science. When I realized the materials (2 books, I think) were not ours, I returned them to the Putnam which is next door to our museum.
- Blumberg has not been in this library at least since 1980. We keep the readers registration as far as 1971.
- Sorry, but we have not been contacted or sent any materials by the FBI.
- We have no records in our files that our Library was involved in the Blumberg case.
- I am not aware of any materials returned to the MSU library from the FBI that were alleged to have been stolen by Blumberg.
- We have not been involved in the Blumberg case. He has not, as far as we know, ever been in Louisville. We did alert ABAA and the FBI in 1978 when two of our rare books were stolen from our old library building. The books were not recovered.
- No records of Blumberg stealing from HCL.
- I have checked and no one seems to know about this. I think you have the wrong library.
- I don't believe that Blumberg stole any material from our library.
- We do not show Stephen Blumberg as a patron and did not report any theft of materials by him from this institution.
- We have had no dealings with FBI or Mr. Blumberg.
- Based on the list of the titles which were found with BYU Library ownership labels and/or barcodes, supplied by the Bureau, we have inventoried the two major areas known to have been pilfered by Mr. Blumberg.
- In 1970 another thief, William Witherell, did steal many books from the library, both common and rare. Most of Witherell's thefts were returned to the library by the FBI in the late 1980s. Many were intact, but some had had the title pages removed and/or were disbound.
- Books were not stolen from our collection.
- Your letter to me was the first indication that we have had that Stephen Blumberg may have stolen anything from the Buffalo & Erie County Public Library. I have checked with William Loos, our Rare Books Curator, and his is confident that nothing was stolen from the Rare Book Room in 1987 but it does not necessarily follow that materials from the stacks were not stolen. However, we have never had any indication from the FBI that Blumberg stole any of our materials. Perhaps the FBI is in possession of bookplates which I understand Blumberg removed from volumes he stole and then kept. However, if that is the case we have no way of knowing from what books they were removed.
- It is unfortunate that previous staff members removed the cards from the public catalog and put them in the volumes that were in a restricted area in the belief that the items were less likely to be stolen "if people

don't know we have them." Consequently the cards were often gone with the titles in question. Because this is a public library, the staff here has not been highly educated in the care and maintenance of rare and/or historical materials, and we do not attempt to collect these things. The older items that we own were donations and are, generally, related to the opening of the West, the Civil War, etc. The items that were returned to us by the FBI were titles of these types.

- No materials have been returned to the College of the Mainland library. Enclosed is a list of those books reported missing to the FBI.

- I have not idea whatsoever what you are contacting me about, nor do I recall a book being returned.

- We do not have high level security for our special collections, and the lack of them concerns me to the extent that I question the acquisition of rare and valuable materials—in these times.

- FBI contacted us, stating that Blumberg said he got the 9 books from our library. We have no evidence that these books ever belonged to us. We said that to the FBI, who we might as well keep them as otherwise they would simply be deposited elsewhere. Two books had St. John's University stamps, so we returned those books. We have accessioned the remaining 7 titles, but would be happy to return them, too—if we knew where to send them. Blumberg may have taken some of our books—we can't say we ever had a big theft. We were certainly never aware that he was here. We will be moving to a new building in 1.5 yrs, and plan to have better security there.

- This correspondence was the first we have received that the Henry County Historical Society Museum was involved in these thefts. Due to personnel changes, there is no recollection or records indicating a return of stolen materials by the FBI. We would appreciate whatever information comes to light regarding what was or may have been stolen from our facility. Thank you for your help and interest. PS: A picture of Mr. Blumberg might help us for future reference.

- We were not aware that he had one or more of our books, when it was returned it was routinely reshelved.

- All items stolen were in the main (open) stacks of the Univ. Lib. All items were originally tattle-taped—a sec. measure of no problem for the likes of Blumberg. We are unsure if additional items were stolen by Blumberg, but have taken measures to increasingly review materials from the circ. coll. and transfer to Spec. Coll.

- Our books were not in a secure area. They were all published between 1850 and 1875 and are not particularly rare. In general, we keep materials published in the 18th century or earlier in Spec. Coll. We have many 19th c. works in our open stacks. These works contained many engravings. Our holdings were not in OCLC nor was our symbol listed in NUC. I did notice that the Cleveland Public Lib. also owns these titles so perhaps Blumberg couldn't get to them there so just made a circuit to other Ohio libs with old colls.

- As far as we know, we have back the only book that was missing.

- How Blumberg stumbled onto our little library in Fleischmanns is a mystery to us. We have not heard of any other library thefts in our area. The stolen book (if there were more than one we have no way of knowing) was old, but not especially valuable. We had the returned book appraised by an antiquarian book dealer/appraiser at $100–150—we tried to sell it, but had no offers.

- I was amazed at Blumberg's ability to wipe clean lib. stamps. More aware that there are rare books in our general coll. that should be transferred into spec. coll.—a future project that will be to read the main library shelf list or after retrospective conversion read by imprint dates.

- His theft was one of several, but no added precautions have been taken until last year. Special Collections is more theft conscious and reduced their hours open to the public. Other measures were recommended, but nothing really happened until we changed directors 2.5 years ago.

- When I was examining the books at the house in Ottumwa, I looked at each volume of the incunabula in his "treasure room." I saw that many of them had had new end papers added, with no bookplates present. This work was done very skillfully, leading me to wonder who might have done it, and what they might have thought about replacing endpapers, presumably having ownership plates, with new blank ones. Has anyone commented about this?

- Material stolen was from the main, open-stack collection, not from a special collection. I traveled to Omaha and collected our material. I also acted as an agent for Kansas State University and Wichita State University, each of which has items in the Blumberg Collection. Upon checking the

material more closely, I identified several items which belonged to the Kansas State Library and returned these items to them. I was not working at KU in 1987 and am unaware of what additional security measures were undertaken in the wake of Blumberg's arrest.

- We felt one reason we were not broken into in Special Collections is that we had a separate entrance from the Main Library. Only staff working full time in Special Collections had keys to Special Collections. Ms and Special Collections librarians currently working in Special Collections feel that security is a top concern for us; that in order to responsibly monitor the collections, the Library must commit itself to having well trained staff, dedicated to serving patrons, but also to preserving and securing the collections.

- Books were stolen only from the open stacks.

- None.

- The only volume received from the FBI was of a two volume set. The item was from an open stack area of old Dewey's in the process of being recatalogued to LC—we no longer had a shelf list card on the book, and we assume it was stolen sometime before the project was finished (about 1982).

- Although we have no verified thefts of material from special collections by Blumberg, we have in the past few years discovered a number of missing items in the course of a retrospective conversion project. Several of these are in the subject areas Blumberg perused.

- All materials taken from our library were in the open stacks. The area Blumberg removed items from was in an area which receives little use from undergraduate students.

- Book was in unsecured stacks but has been transferred to secure storage. No losses have been noted from secure storage.
- We believe the theft of our materials occurred during the move into a newly constructed building. Security was haphazard at best during this time. Concurrent to this move was the acquisition of the papers and

memorabilia of Senator Mark O. Hatfield. Some of those materials were stolen.

- One returned book had a withdraw stamp—it was probably from our book sale. Both books were in poor condition and were not items we needed; we discarded them.
- All titles stolen were from Circulation, not special collections.
- One book was returned to the UK that is not ours.

14. Demographic information

Number of institutions replying to the survey and number of institutions in the state to which the FBI returned materials.

Replied to Survey	Institutions on FBI list
AL – 0	1
AR – 2	1
AZ – 5	4
CA – 9	18
CO – 3	3
CT – 3	8
DC – 1	4
DE – 1	1
GA – 1	2
IA – 15	24
ID – 3	4
IL – 11	18
IN – 6	8
KS – 6	9
KY – 3	8
LA – 2	2

Replied to Survey	Institutions on FBI list
MA – 10	16
MD – 2	2
ME – 0	1
MI – 6	13
MN – 5	19
MO – 3	4
MT – 4	4
NC – 5	7
ND – 1	1
NE – 5	8
NH – 2	5
NJ – 2	3
NM – 1	1
NV – 1	1
NY – 7	14
OH – 12	23

Replied to Survey	Institutions on FBI list
OK – 2	4
OR – 6	9
PA – 5	10
RI – 1	2
SC – 1	3
SD – 3	3
TN – 2	6
TX – 16	19
UT – 1	2
VA – 0	4
VT – 1	2
WA – 4	4
WI – 3	7
WY – 1	2
Canada – 5	5

Type of Library

Academic	127	Research	21	Special	37
Public	42	Government	6	Archives & State Libraries	14

Who's Who

Daniel J. Slive

These entries briefly document the careers of some of the thieves mentioned in the text of this manual. The articles cited below the entries may be read for fuller information. Those entries without articles cited may usually be searched on the Internet for additional information.

Joseph Anastasio

Anastasio worked as a security guard at the University of Bridgeport in Connecticut between 1991 and 1993, during which time he had access to the special collections area. He removed rare documents, including letters by Abraham Lincoln, although it was not until a routine inventory in 1994 that the items were discovered missing. Lists published by the library in January, 1995, revealed that the documents had been sold throughout the country. He was sentenced to three years of probation and required to make restitution.

> "Man Gets Probation for Stealing Letters." *Hartford Courant* (27 October 1996).

Vido K. Aras

Aras attempted to steal a Gutenberg Bible from Harvard University's Widener Library in 1969. In a scheme worthy of any cat burglar and perhaps a few Hollywood movies, Aras secreted himself in the library after hours, shimmied down a rope to enter the building on a lower floor by breaking a window, and then attempted to escape by climbing back up the rope. Unfortunately for Aras, the Bible weighed far more than he was capable of handling. Being unable to climb and having a rope too short to reach the ground, he eventually fell several stories, landed on the Bible, and was discovered badly injured. He was deemed mentally incapable of understanding his actions and not prosecuted, but was out of mental confinement shortly thereafter.

> W. H. Bond. "The Gutenberg Caper." *Harvard Magazine* (March/April 1986): 42–48.

> "Charges Against Suspect in Bible Theft Dismissed." *The Harvard Crimson* (4 December 1969). http://www.thecrimson.com/article.aspx?ref=351509

Christopher Bellwood

Bellwood (using the alias Perry) visited the Helsinki University Library in 2001, from which he stole six maps in the course of two visits. Finally confronted in England, he was sent to Finland and four of the maps were recovered. Tried and sentenced to eighteen months in prison, he disappeared before serving his sentence. He apparently also stole from the Swedish Royal Library in Stockholm in 2000. Some of those maps were also recovered. He also removed maps from other libraries, such as the National Library in Wales, for which he was sentenced in 2004 to 4½ years imprisonment. Once the British sentence was completed, he was sent to Denmark, where he was sentenced for cutting eleven maps from books in the Danish Royal Library in Copenhagen in 2001.

Esko Häkli. "Paradise Lost: A Theft from Helsinki University Library." *Liber Quarterly* 12 (2002): 320–328.

Jesper During Jørgenson, "Map Thief Bellwood Sentenced." Exlibris-L discussion list (18 May 2008).

Tomas Lidman. "Thieves in Our Cultural Heritage: Crime and Crime Prevention Measures in the Royal Library, Stockholm, 2000–2002." *Liber Quarterly* 12 (2002): 309–315.

Samuel Richard ("Sandy") Berger

Sandy Berger served as President Bill Clinton's National Security Adviser from 1997 to 2001. Asked to prepare testimony for the 911 Commission, in 2003 he consulted files at the National Archives and Records Administration (NARA) in Washington, DC. Due to a series of blunders by NARA staff and deliberate deceptions by Berger himself, he managed to remove various documents from the archives. Eventually confronted, he returned some of the documents (some of which NARA staff did not even know he had taken), pled guilty to a misdemeanor, and was sentenced to community service. He admitted to destroying several documents, but the extent of his thefts has never been made clear.

John F. Harris & Allan Lengel. "Berger Will Plead Guilty to Taking Classified Paper." *The Washington Post* (1 April 2005): A01. http://www.washingtonpost.com/wp-dyn/articles/A16706-2005Mar31.html

Gilbert Joseph Bland, Jr.

Bland, also using the alias James Perry, stole an indeterminate amount of cartographical materials from various libraries in the U.S., usually by razoring the maps from bound volumes. He was finally caught doing so in 1995 at Johns Hopkins University. Although released on the spot after paying restitution, his criminal activities were halted by an Exlibris message posted by Special Collections Curator Cynthia Requardt. Once that message was posted and follow-up messages from other institutions were received, the extent of Bland's crimes became clear, he was arrested by the FBI, and a portion of the maps he had stolen were seized. Following convictions in several jurisdictions he was finally released, although some institutions victimized by Bland never pressed charges. Maps seized by the FBI but unclaimed were given to the Library of Congress Map and Geography Division, where they are kept together but will apparently never be catalogued.

Miles Harvey. *The Island of Lost Maps: A True Story of Cartographic Crime.* New York: Random House, 2000.

———. "Mr. Bland's Evil Plot to Rule the World." *Outside Magazine* (June 1997). http://outside.away.com/outside/magazine/0697/9706bland.html

Stephen C. Blumberg

Blumberg is without doubt one of the most notorious book thieves of the twentieth century in the U.S. His career came to an end when his travelling companion snitched on him. Visiting libraries across the United States, he amassed a collection of thousands of books stolen from over 300 libraries in forty-five states that he stored in his house in Ottumwa, Iowa. Many of the volumes were stolen in reading rooms or at book fairs, but others were stolen from stack areas by outright burglary. His "library," once seized by the FBI after his arrest, was processed through volunteers working for OCLC. After those books claimed by institutions had been returned, approximately 6,000 volumes remained from the nineteen tons originally seized. These were given to Creighton University, which eventually disposed of the remaining titles. Some of the books were finally auctioned by Cowan. Convicted in 1991, Blumberg served more than six years in federal prison for his crimes.

> Nicholas Basbanes. *A Gentle Madness: Bibliophiles, Bibliomanes, and the Eternal Passion for Books* (New York: Holt, 1995), 465–519.

Patrick Bucklew

A self-confessed thief, Bucklew stole a Ming scroll from the University of California's Berkeley Art Museum by removing it from behind its protective mounting, rolling it up, hiding it in his sleeve, and walking out with it. He later attempted to return the scroll to claim a $500 reward, but was instead arrested and fined $500.

> Patrick Bucklew. "How I Stole a Ming Scroll." *Time* (6 September 2004). http://www.time.com/time/magazine/article/0,9171,995033,00.html

Daniel Cevallos-Tovar

Cevallos-Tovar (aka "The Alchemist") stole nearly 300 books on the occult and alchemy from libraries at Harvard and Yale. His criminal career began to unravel, however, when his apartment caught fire. He was forced to move the stolen materials to a storage unit, for which he failed to pay the rent. The owner of the storage facility began to sell the books, and word quickly spread through the book community that fantastic bargains were available. Suspicions were also raised when some of the books were offered back to Harvard. The FBI arrested Cevallos-Tovar in 1995, and he was sentenced to approximately three months in prison but released as he had already been in custody for that period of time.

Karen Dale Churton

Churton, a rare book librarian at Massey University in New Zealand, removed six rare books from the collection in 2001 and deleted the records for these titles from the on-line catalogue. In addition to destroying the catalogue records, Churton also removed ownership marks to conceal provenance. She sold the books in 2002 through an Australian auction house. Police began looking into these thefts as part of a larger investigation into an organized crime ring that was stealing and selling rare books. Sentenced to eleven months in prison, her term was reduced to four months.

> "$1M Book Heist in NZ." Script & Print blog. March, 2007. http://scriptandprint.blogspot.com/2007_03_01_archive.html

Clive Driver

Driver was Director of the Philip H. & A.S.W. Rosenbach Foundation (later the Rosenbach Museum and Library) in Philadelphia. In committing insider thefts from this institution between 1965 and 1978, he sometimes forged deaccession authorizations and sold materials from the collection for his own financial advancement. The thefts were not revealed, however, until after he retired. He was successfully sued in 1987 by the Rosenbach in a civil suit and also convicted of a federal felony in the case.

> Douglas C. McGill. "Museum Says Ex-Chief Sold Off 30 Rare Letters." *New York Times* (22 April 1987). http://query.nytimes.com/gst/fullpage.html?res=9B0DE6DB1F3CF931A15757C0A961948260

Oliver Fallon

Fallon, a Sanskrit scholar, was convicted both in England and Scotland for stealing manuscripts. Released from an English jail, he proceeded in 2006 to the Scottish Catholic Archives in Edinburgh, where he stole and mutilated nearly 300 records. Alerted by English authorities, Scottish police soon determined with the help of the archives staff that documents were missing and Fallon was most likely the thief. He was sentenced in 2008 to 300 hours of community service for his thefts in Scotland.

> Paul Thornton. "Academic 'Falls from Grace' by Stealing Church Records." *Edinburgh Evening News* (13 May 2008).
>
> http://edinburghnews.scotsman.com/ edinburgh/Academic—39falls-from-grace39.4077609.jp

Michel Garel

Garel was the curator of Hebrew manuscripts at the Bibliothèque Nationale de France when he came under suspicion as part of a larger investigation into materials missing from the library. The first item that strongly suggested his involvement was Manuscript H52, which had been sold at Christie's New York in 2000. After a confusing series of denials and confessions, Garel was finally convicted of the H52 theft in 2006. Sentenced to two years in prison, there were strong suspicions that he had stolen and sold additional items, including 145 printed works. Upon appeal, the original sentence was increased to three years. Garel maintained that he was the victim of a conspiracy, and the library, after a long series of negotiations, recovered H52.

> Edouard Launet. "Les manuscrits volés de la BNF, suite et fin?" *Libération* (1 March 2007). http://www.liberation.fr/ culture/010192445-les-manuscrits-voles-de-la-bnf-suite-et-fin

> Michel Garel. Wikipedia. http://fr.wikipedia. org/wiki/Michel_Garel

César Ovidio Gómez Rivero

Gómez Rivero, an Argentinean citizen, set off an international manhunt when it was suspected that he stole eight maps in 2006 from the Biblioteca Nacional de España in Madrid. By the time authorities confronted him in Buenos Aires, Argentina, he had sold some of the stolen maps on the Internet to buyers in Australia and the U.S. These transactions led to additional investigations and recovery efforts in those countries. When he appeared before an Argentinean court the following year, he surrendered other maps he had in his possession.

Farhad Hakimzadeh

Between 1998 and 2005 Hakimzadeh razored leaves and maps from books in the British Library and the Bodleian Library at the University of Oxford, apparently to complete defective copies of his own books. He is thought to have vandalized approximately 150 volumes, and many of the razored leaves were discovered by police in his home in his personal copies. Still, much of the material identified as missing has never been recovered. He was sentenced in early 2009 to two years in prison. Outrage emerged following the revelation that he had earlier been caught committing similar crimes at another British library but that the incident had been hushed up.

Howard Harner

In 2005 Harner was fined and sentenced to two years in prison for stealing over one hundred documents dating from the Civil War era out of the National Archives and Records Administration (NARA) between 1996 and 2002. He was charged after an alert user spotted a suspicious document listed for sale on eBay. At the time of his sentencing, NARA had recovered only 42 documents.

Allen Weinstein. "Statement by Archivist of the United States Allen Weinstein on the Sentencing of Howard Harner." 26 May 2005. http://www.archives.gov/press/press-releases/2005/nr05-71.html

Lee Israel

Israel was a well-respected writer who, in the early 1990s, forged letters from famous twentieth-century authors. In the course of doing so, she stole blank stationery and other materials from various libraries and assembled a collection of antique typewriters to facilitate her forgeries. She also stole legitimate manuscripts from institutional collections. A suspicious bookseller initiated the process that led to her arrest and conviction, although she was sentenced only to probation and a brief period of house arrest. In most instances, she sold both her forgeries and the items she stole. Her memoir should be used with caution.

Lee Israel. *Can You Ever Forgive Me?: Memoirs of a Literary Forger.* New York: Simon & Schuster, 2008.

William Simon Jacques

Jacques was convicted of stealing books from various English libraries, including Cambridge University and the London Library. Some of the items were spectacular, such as two copies of Newton's *Principia* and works by Malthus and Galileo. The investigation into his crimes was long and tedious, and at one point Jacques transferred a large amount of money to Cuba and fled there. He resided on the island for a period before mysteriously returning to England, where he was tried, convicted, and fined in 2002. After his release, however, he jumped bail and again supposedly stole more books. Finally re-arrested, he was convicted for thefts from the Royal Horticultural Society library and jailed in

July 2010. Many of the books were recovered. He is nicknamed "Tome Raider."

Benjamin Johnson

Johnson, a University of Wisconsin-Madison student who was employed by Yale University in Summer 2001 used his position to steal autographs and books worth approximately $2,000,000 from the collections. His thefts were discovered after he offered multiple rare items to a bookseller, who became suspicious and investigated. Ironically, Yale did not realize the thefts had occurred until contacted by the Wisconsin authorities who had arrested Johnson after finding stolen materials in his dorm room. Convicted in 2002 to fifteen years, he served fewer than twelve months.

Daniel Lorello

Lorello stole items from the New York State Archives in Albany, where he was employed. He would typically come to work early and commit his thefts before his co-workers arrived. He stole a wide variety of materials, which he sold personally and on eBay. His thefts were finally discovered when somebody monitoring eBay spotted a document reportedly belonging to the archives and notified the institution of the problem in late 2007. The ensuing investigation led to Lorello's confession, in which he stated that he stole because he needed money. He was caught and convicted in 2008.

"Update: State Worker Accused of Stealing Historic Documents." *Times Union*, 28 January 2008. http://timesunion.com/AspStories/story.asp?storyID=658903&category=&BCCode=HOME&newsdate=1/28/2008

Donald Lynch

Lynch, a shoe salesman using the alias of Professor Sinclair E. Gillingham of Middlebury College, talked his way into the Chapin Library at Williams College in 1940 to research Shakespeare folios. The requested volumes were retrieved for him. Lynch then stated that he wished to bring his wife into his investigations, said he would return with her, and would be back shortly. Unnoticed by the librarian, Lynch stole a First Folio by either concealing it under a coat he had draped over his arm or in his briefcase. The theft was discovered fairly promptly, and the investigation led to Canada and unsuccessful negotiations for the book's return. Finally, a drunken Lynch surrendered. Authorities were eventually able to uncover the Buffalo, New York, ring that had organized the theft of the volume, return the book to Chapin Library, and secure convictions of the conspirators. Almost all those who were convicted were sentenced to probation.

> Mark E. Rondeau. "The Bard's Wild Ride: The Almost Forgotten Theft of a Shakespeare First Folio from Williams College." http://www.markrondeau.com/folio.html

Denning McTague

McTague was an intern at the National Archives and Records Administration (NARA) in Summer 2006, where he worked arranging Civil War documents. During his internship, he smuggled out of NARA over 160 letters and other materials concealed in a legal pad. He sold most of the documents on eBay until his criminal activities were uncovered after one item was offered for sale on the auction website and NARA was notified. He pled guilty to stealing federal property and was sentenced to fifteen months in prison. NARA recovered almost all the documents. McTague also operated a rare book and manuscript business known as Denning House, which is back in business.

> "Intern Sold Stolen Civil War Documents on

eBay." MSNBC (4 April 2007). http://www.msnbc.msn.com/id/17952733/

Dwain Edgar Manske

Manske was a professor at the University of Arkansas when he plundered several libraries. He was particularly active in Texas, where he stole extensively from the Marfa County Library and other institutions, including court house collections. Caught with numerous documents in 1995, he was only fined and continues to run his book business, South by Southwest Books, in Fayetteville, Arkansas. Although he was fined in Presidio County, his case was not more extensively pursued because his crimes were considered minor offenses rather than felonies. In addition, some jurisdictions chose not to prosecute.

> "An Arkansas Professor Is Charged with Swiping Outlaw's Documents." *The Victoria Advocate* (7 October 1996): 10A. http://news.google.com/newspapers?nid=861&dat=19961007&id=4ScKAAAAIBAJ&sjid=zEoDAAAAIBAJ&pg=7264,1178068

Ernest Medford

Medford, a custodian at the Historical Society of Pennsylvania for eighteen years, stole realia between 1987 and 1997 in an arrangement with George Csizmazia, an outside electrician working for the Society who also collected antiques. He purchased about 200 stolen items from Medford for approximately $8,000, a small fraction of their true value, and was caught only because he bragged publicly about owning one of the items. The loss amounted to approximately $2.2 million. Both were convicted and sentenced to prison terms of several years each, although they appealed and had their sentences reviewed. The appeals court decision was significant, however, in that it affirmed that the trial court was correct in also including the intangible damages done by the thieves. All the items were recovered from Csizmazia.

> United State Court of Appeals. Third Circuit. "United States of America, v. Ernest Medford, Appellant in 98-1647 United States of America, v. George Csizmazia Appelant in 98-1646." Decided 2 July 1999. http://cases.justia.com/us-court-of-appeals/F3/194/419/505162/

Anthony Melnikas

In 1995 a rare books dealer became suspicious of fourteenth-century manuscript leaves offered to him by Melnikas, an art history professor at Ohio State University. Investigation quickly revealed that the leaves had been removed from a manuscript in the Vatican Library, where Melnikas was a frequent and trusted researcher. He had also removed manuscript leaves from Spanish libraries. In 1996 Melnikas signed a written confession to the thefts and was subsequently convicted in the U.S. of violating customs laws and sentenced to fourteen months in prison. Never convicted of a theft, his case is important because he was the first criminal prosecuted for trafficking in objects of foreign origin under the Archeological Resources Protection Act. He supposedly stole to help finance his retirement.

Mimi Meyer

Meyer was a volunteer at the Harry Ransom Humanities Research Center (HRC) at the University of Texas, Austin from 1989 to 1992. She systematically stole materials from the HRC before she was dismissed for having an improperly checked out book in her workspace. The thefts were discovered after a book from the HRC was put up for sale at an auction in 2001 and brought to the library's attention. The resulting investigation revealed that she had often sold the library's materials at auction.

In 2004 Meyer was sentenced to three years probation and was required to pay restitution. Her case brought into question the vetting procedures of auction houses and the firms' willingness to help resolve cases of stolen property that had passed through their hands. Meyer died in January, 2010.

> Harry Ransom Humanities Research Center. "Perpetrator of Rare Book Theft at Harry Ransom Center Sentenced." News release, February 2, 2004. http://www.hrc.utexas.edu/press/releases/2004/theft.html

> Mark Lisheron. "Book Bandit Rocked Ransom." *Austin American-Statesman* (1 February 2004).

Frede Møller-Kristensen

Møller-Kristensen, an employee of the Danish Royal Library, stole approximately 1,500 books from the library's collections before retiring in 2000. He then began to sell the books through auction houses and other venues. After his death, his widow and son continued to sell the volumes, but suspicions regarding some of the materials were raised by a consignee. After houses belonging to the widow and son and other venues were raided, authorities recovered approximately seventy-five boxes of books belonging to the library. The widow, son, and several others were sentenced to prison terms in 2004–2005, their protestations of innocence deemed not believable. As he had died in 2003 before the thefts were solved, Møller-Kristensen was never questioned. However, it was clear that he was adept at altering materials to remove their provenance markings given evidence found in the workshop in his house.

> Jesper Düring Jørgensen. "Report on a Theft of Books, a Non-Fiction Detective Story."

Care and Conservation of Manuscripts 9: Proceedings of the Ninth International Seminar Held at the University of Copenhagen, 14th-15th April, 2005. Copenhagen: Museum Tusculanem Press, 2006. Pp. 113–124.

Charles Merrill Mount

Mount (né Sherman Suchow) was granted special research privileges at the National Archives and Records Administration that exempted him from the usual security scrutiny exercised on researchers. He was arrested in 1987 after being caught attempting to sell Civil War papers from the collections. Subsequent searches recovered additional stolen documents. He was sentenced to eight years in prison.

> Theresa Galvin. "The Boston Case of Charles Merrill Mount: The Archivist's Arch Enemy." *American Archivist* 53 (Summer 1990): 442–50.

Robert Bradford Murphy (aka George Matz)

Murphy and his wife, Elizabeth Irene, stole more than two hundred documents from the National Archives and Records Administration in 1962 during the course of several visits to the institution. They were arrested by the FBI in 1964 after suspicions were aroused when they tried to sell some of the documents to the Detroit Public Library. The stolen materials were found in various locations, including an apartment into which the couple unwittingly invited two FBI agents. Although the government's attempts at untangling the Murphys' mysterious lives were unsuccessful, the husband and wife were still sentenced to ten years each in prison.

Melvin Nelson Perry

Perry was convicted in 2002 and sentenced to eighteen months in prison for the theft of maps from Helsinki University in 2001. He had also previously been convicted in 1995 for thefts from libraries in England. In addition, suspicions were widely held that he was involved in thefts from numerous other libraries, including those in Aberystwyth, Copenhagen, Helsinki, Stockholm, and The Hague. He was believed to have accomplices that used the same aliases. He never served any time in Finland.

Walter Ploughman

Ploughman stole a considerable amount of manuscript material in the early 1980s from The Connecticut Historical Society and Connecticut State Library, both in Hartford. Although some material was recovered, a significant portion never was found and items occasionally surface in the market. He was convicted and sentenced to probation.

Alexander Polman

Polman was a trusted curator at the Dutch Army Museum in Delft, the Netherlands. When preparations were being made in 2003 for a major exhibition, it was discovered that some books had been heavily vandalized and that other materials were missing, including approximately 2,000 prints and several paintings. Polman apparently stole most of this material by arriving earlier than the rest of the staff and secreting the materials in his car. He also was involved in a network of dealers and buyers for the materials he stole. During the course of the investigation, Polman made self-incriminating statements and was arrested. He was sentenced to twenty-six months in prison in 2003, and several of his confederates were also convicted.

> Ton Cremers. *"…And the Curator Did It."* *Rogues Gallery: An Investigation into Art Theft.* AXA Art Conference, London, England, 1 November 2005. http://www.museumsecurity.org/insider-theft.pdf

James Shinn

Shinn, whose real name is James Richard Coffman, was first arrested at Oberlin College in 1981, when a search of his hotel room revealed a trove of books apparently stolen from various libraries, burglary tools, and false identification documents. Released on bond he disappeared, but was arrested again in late 1981. Believed to have stolen approximately $750,000 worth of materials from forty libraries, he was eventually convicted and sentenced to two consecutive ten-year federal prison terms but served only four years. He is the only book thief with a bathroom named after him, the so-called Shinn Room at Oberlin College's Mudd Library. Stealing only from open stacks, the ease with which he sold his stolen goods to the rare book trade shook confidence in the antiquarian book market (See Smiley).

Nicholas Basbanes. *A Gentle Madness: Bibliophiles, Bibliomanes, and the Eternal Passion for Books* (New York: Holt, 1995), 484–486.

William A. Moffett. *The Shinn Lists*. Oberlin: Oberlin College, 1982.

Edward Forbes Smiley

Smiley is the most celebrated and notorious map thief of the twenty-first century, a distinction that one hopes nobody will surpass in the next ninety years. Honing his craft in the time-honored tradition of razoring maps from books, he stole for many years from institutions on both sides of the Atlantic and sold the materials through his rare map business. Finally caught at Yale University, he confessed, cooperated with prosecutors, and was sentenced in 2006 to 3½ years in federal prison with a concurrent state sentence. His thefts rocked the rare book world to its core in several ways, and again rattled confidence in the antiquarian book trade (See Shinn) and in library security practices.

He was released from prison in January 2010.

"Forbes Smiley," Wikipedia. http://en.wikipedia.org/wiki/Forbes_Smiley. [Authoritative article]

Daniel Spiegelman

Spiegelman stole materials worth almost $2 million from Columbia University by committing a series of clever burglaries that allowed him access to Special Collections areas. He attempted to sell the items in Europe, and was captured there in 1995. He tried to avoid extradition by claiming a connection to the bombing of the Murrah Building in Oklahoma City, knowing that he would not be extradited if he faced the possibility of a capital sentence in the U.S. That ploy failed, however, and he was returned to the U.S. and convicted in 1998. The case was unusual because Judge Lewis A. Kaplan was persuaded that Spiegelman's crimes were so serious that he departed from federal sentencing guidelines and sent the defendant to jail for more time than normally recommended.

Lewis A. Kaplan. "The Cultural Value of Books: United States of America v. Daniel Spiegelman, defendant." *Gazette of the Grolier Club*, n.s. 50 (1999): 9–25.

Travis McDade. *The Book Thief: The True Crimes of Daniel Spiegelman*. Westport: Praeger Publishers, 2006.

Rebecca Streeter-Chen

Streeter-Chen was a former curator at the Rockland County Historical Society in New York. One day, accompanied by her two children, she entered the library and removed a valuable atlas from a storage area. The Society promptly notified other libraries and the book trade. When Streeter-Chen tried to sell the atlas to a bookseller, she was caught, indicted, pled guilty, and eventually sentenced in 2007 to five years' probation and community service.

Steve Lieberman. "Former Rockland County Historical Society Curator Charged in Theft of Rare Book." *The Journal News* (1 June 2007). http://forums.delphiforums.com/n/mb/message.asp?webtag=nyackhigh&msg=1813.1

José Torres-Carbonnel

Torres-Carbonnel was the husband of a Harvard University graduate student and thus had access to the University's libraries, from which he removed material worth nearly a quarter million dollars between 1994 and 1996. His criminal career ended when a bookseller in Granada, Spain, talked to Harvard Library officials and admitted that one of the items he was offering for sale had Harvard markings that had been effaced. Harvard detectives traced the items back to Torres-Carbonnel. When arrested in 1996, he was planning to leave the country for Spain that day. Ironically, he was undone by his own wife, whose request for one of the missing books set off the investigation that led to his discovery and arrest. He was sentenced in 1997 to three to four years in prison and ordered to be deported. Harvard recovered much, but not all, of its stolen material.

Transylvania University Theft

One of the very few known U.S. thefts in special collections to involve violence occurred at Transylvania University in December, 2004. Two assailants attacked, bound, and used a stun device on Special Collections librarian B.J. Gooch before stealing several valuable books from the collection. Their escape from the library was less than smooth, however, as they were pursued by librarians until they piled into a waiting van and escaped. Soon thereafter, they made an appointment at Christie's in New York City in an attempt to sell the volumes, but their plans were foiled. They were arrested, tried, convicted, and each sentenced to eighty-seven months in prison in 2005. Ironically, on appeal, the court ordered the lower court to consider *raising* the sentence. Charles Thomas Allen, Eric Borsuk, Warren Lipka, and Spencer Reinhard may be remembered as the most inept rare book thieves of the twenty-first century.

Charles Allen. *Mr. Pink: The Inside Story of the Transylvania Book Heist*. Lexington: Allen, 2010.

John Falk. "Majoring in Crime—The Untold Story of the 'Transy Book Heist' is One Part Ocean's 11, One Part Harold & Kumar: Four Kentucky College Kids Who Had Millions to Gain and Nothing to Lose." *Vanity Fair* 568 (December 2007): 232–246.

United States Court of Appeals. Sixth Circuit. "United States of America, Plaintiff-Appellee/Cross Applicant v. Charles Thomas Allen, II, et al., Defendants-Appellants/Cross-Appellees." Decided 5 February 2008.

Lester F. Weber

Weber, an archivist at the Mariners' Museum in Newport News, Virginia, removed items from the collection over the course of several years, and with assistance from his wife sold the stolen materials on eBay. Both husband and wife were convicted in 2008 of federal tax violations. Among the items sold were extremely rare documents relating to the sinking of the HMS *Titanic*. It is believed that Weber stole approximately 1,500 documents in all.

Tim McGlone. "Museum Archivist Pleads Guilty of Charges Related to Artifacts Theft." Pilotonline.com. http://hampton-roads.com/2008/06/museum-archivist-pleads-guilty-artifacts-theft

Robert Marion ("Skeet") Willingham

Willingham, curator at the Hargrett Rare Book & Manuscript Library at the University of Georgia, stole materials from the library. His insider thefts included the obliteration of ownership marks and removal of cataloguing records. Confronted and arrested in 1986, he went to trial and was convicted, partially on forensic evidence that revealed partly obliterated provenance marks on some of the materials in question. Sentenced in 1988 to fifteen years in prison, he was ordered to prison in 1991 after exhausting his appeals. He was paroled in 1993. Many of the missing materials have never been recovered.

Nicholas Basbanes. *A Gentle Madness: Bibliophiles, Bibliomanes, and the Eternal Passion for Books* (New York: Holt, 1995), 488–490.

Kathy Wilkerson

Wilkerson, an employee in Special Collections at the University of Pennsylvania, during the late 1980s and early 1990s stole materials from the department by concealing them on her person. She was finally caught after suspicious book sellers contacted university officials about a book she had offered for sale. She was sentenced to parole and fined. Some of the material she is believed to have stolen has not been recovered.

Daniel Traister. "Seduction and Betrayal: An Insider's View of Internal Theft," *Wilson Library Bulletin* 69 (September 1994): 30–33.

Stephen L. Womack

Womack was a casual-staff library employee at Harvard University's Widener Library between 1989 and 1990. During that time, he razored over 600 text blocks from their covers, leaving the covers on the shelves. Womack was finally identified and apprehended because of similar crimes he had committed at Northeastern University's Snell Library. By the time police caught Womack and discovered a microfilm laboratory in his basement, he had microfilmed most of the stolen books and discarded them. Arrested in December, 1994, he was sentenced in 1996 to between 7 and 10 years in prison.

Marvin Hightower. "Destroyer of Books Gets Stiff Sentence." *The Harvard University Gazette* (28 March 1996). http://www.news.harvard.edu/gazette/1996/03.28/DestroyerofBook.html

ACRL/RBMS Guidelines Regarding Security and Theft in Special Collections

http://www.acrl.org/ala/mgrps/divs/acrl/standards/security_theft.cfm

These guidelines identify important issues that collection administrators should address in developing adequate security measures and a strategy for responding to thefts. While directed primarily toward special collections in the U.S., many topics are also applicable to general collections and to special collections in other countries. "Special Collections" here refers to repositories containing rare books, manuscripts, archives, and other antiquarian and special materials. "Booksellers" refers to those who sell such materials. In the term "Library Security Officer," "Library" is understood to mean any special collections repository.

Part I: Security Measures

1. Introduction

Administrators of special collections must ensure that their materials remain intact and secure from theft and damage. The security of collections is now especially important since administrators' efforts to increase the use and knowledge of collections in their care can result in a greater public awareness of their value and may increase the risk of theft. Security arrangements may vary from one institution to another and are dependent on staffing, physical setting, and use.

Booksellers also must concern themselves with collection security, since thieves may offer stolen materials to them for sale. Administrators should make every effort to familiarize booksellers with the ways institutions attempt to secure and identify their materials and help them use this knowledge to lessen anyone's chances of profiting from theft.

The appointment of a Library Security Officer (LSO) and the development of a written security policy can help ensure that all staff are aware of their legal and procedural responsibilities in applying security measures.

2. The Library Security Officer (LSO)

Each institution concerned with the security of special collections materials should appoint an LSO. The LSO should be appointed by the director, should have primary authority and responsibility to carry out the security program, and should have a thorough knowledge of all repository security needs, particularly those of special collections. The LSO should not necessarily be conceived of as the general security officer, although he or she may also hold that role. The LSO is the person with principal responsibility for planning and administering a security program, which should include a survey of the collections, reviews of the physical layout of the institution, and training of the institution's staff. He or she should develop and maintain active working relationships with colleagues and seek the advice and assistance of appropriate personnel, such as institutional administrators, corporate counsel, life safety officers, as well as outside consultants from law enforcement agencies and insurance companies.

Suggestions for implementation:

- In some repositories, the LSO and the special collections administrator may be the same person.
- Special collections administrators in institutions without another official for whom the role of LSO would be appropriate are encouraged to take on this role and advocate that the institution recognize the importance of this responsibility.
- Report the name of the current LSO to the LSO-List administrator (see Appendix C: Resources Directory).

3. The Security Policy

The LSO should develop a written policy on the security of the collections, in consultation with administrators and staff, legal authorities, and other knowledgeable persons. The policy should include a standard operating procedure on dealing with a theft or other security problems. The security policy should be kept up-to-date with current names and telephone numbers of institutional and law enforcement contacts. The institution should also review the policy periodically to insure that institutional needs continue to be adequately addressed. The LSO should be involved with the development and implementation of general security measures, as these may affect the security of special collections materials. The LSO should also be involved with emergency and disaster planning.

Suggestions for implementation:

- In large institutions it may be necessary to assemble a Security Planning Group to assist the LSO in identifying problem areas and to recommend solutions. This group, made up of the LSO and other appropriate personnel, will be responsible for developing a security plan to prevent theft and a detailed plan of action to follow when a theft is discovered. The plan may be a part of the institution's disaster plan or constitute a separate plan. The plan should not be a public document (e.g., it should not be posted on a web site), but accessible only to appropriate institutional personnel.
- Institutions that lack appropriate staff resources may wish to bring in a security consultant to assist in developing a policy and in determining any major threats to the collection. When engaging a security consultant, the institution or LSO should use caution in evaluating the consultant's competence or ability to perform the work. The institution should investigate the security consultant's background and references thoroughly.

4. The Facility

The special collections building, unit, or area should have as few access points as possible. Fire and emergency exits, which should be strictly controlled and alarmed, should not be used for regular access. Within the facility itself, the public should have access only to public areas, not to work areas or stack space. Researchers should be received in a separate reception area where a coatroom and lockers should be provided for researchers' personal belongings and outerwear. A secure reading room where researchers can be continuously monitored by staff trained in surveillance should be identified as the only area in which material may be used. A staff member or security guard should check researchers' personal research materials before they enter the secure area as well as when they depart.

Keys or electronic keycards are especially vulnerable items; therefore, a controlled checkout system for all keys should be maintained. Keys to secure areas should be issued to staff only on an as-needed basis, and master keys should be secured against unauthorized access. Combinations to vaults should have limited distribution and be changed each time a staff member with access leaves his or her position. Strong consideration should be given to installing proprietary keyways (i.e., unique keys and locks available only from a single manufacturer) in locks in the special collections area. Security cameras should be installed that cover reading rooms and any access points that security professionals deem appropriate. All recordings should be retained for as long as possible, preferably permanently.

Suggestions for implementation:

- In institutions where it is not possible to hire a security guard, a designated staff member could perform the guard's function. Consideration should be given to installing a video surveillance system.
- As a precautionary policy, keys and locks to secure areas should be changed on a regular basis.
- When an institution plans to remodel, renovate space, or build a new facility for special collections materials, the LSO and the special collections administrator should ensure that all security needs are addressed in the design and planning.

5. The Staff

An atmosphere of trust and concern for the collections is probably the best guarantee against theft by staff. Nevertheless, close and equitable supervision is essential. The staff, including students and volunteers, should be chosen carefully. Careful personnel management is an ongoing necessity. Disgruntled staff may seek retribution through theft, destruction, or willful mishandling of collections. Consideration should be given to bonding employees

who work in special collections. Training the staff in security measures should be a high priority of the LSO. Such training should ensure that staff are aware of their legal and procedural responsibilities in relation to security as well as their own and the researchers' legal rights when handling breaches. Staff should be discouraged from taking personal belongings into secure areas, and such belongings should be subject to inspection by security staff when exiting.

Suggestions for implementation:

- The LSO and special collections administrators should ensure that all staff are familiar with these guidelines and the security policies in their institutions and how they may apply specifically to their institution. New staff should receive security training in a timely fashion as part of their orientation process.
- When appropriate or consistent with institutional policies, background checks and bonding of staff members should be considered.
- The LSO and special collections administrators should be familiar with the institution's personnel policies, and advocate security concerns with the institution's human resources staff.

6. The Researchers

The special collections administrator must carefully balance the responsibility of making materials available to researchers against the responsibility of ensuring the security of the materials. Registration for each researcher who uses special collections materials should be required, including the name, address, legal acknowledgment, and institutional affiliation (if any). Photo identification or some other form of positive identification is necessary to establish physical identity. Records should also be kept of projects researchers are working on and of collections they will be using. These registration records should be retained permanently.

Staff must be able to identify who has used which materials by keeping adequate checkout records, whether paper or electronic. These records should also be retained indefinitely in order to be available to law enforcement authorities if thefts or vandalism later come to light. No matter what their format, the records should unequivocally link a particular researcher to a specific item.

Special collections security plans must take into consideration institutional policies, especially those pertaining to confidentiality, of their parent institution. Access to registration and circulation records should be restricted. Institutional policies and practices, especially in the course of investigating possible thefts, should not violate applicable confidentiality laws. LSOs should be familiar with all applicable laws governing personally identifiable information about users.

Each researcher should be given an orientation to the rules governing the use of the collections. Rules should be prominently posted as well as available on the institution's web site. Researchers should legally acknowledge compliance with these regulations. Researchers should not be permitted to take extraneous personal materials into the reading areas. These include such items as notebooks, briefcases, outerwear, books, and voluminous papers. Personal computers should be removed from the case before use in the reading room is permitted. Lockers or some kind of secure space should be provided for any items not permitted in the reading room.

Staff should observe researchers at all times and not allow them to work unobserved behind bookcases, book trucks, stacks of books, or any other obstacles that restrict staff view. Research-

ers should be limited at any one time to having access only to those books, manuscripts, or other items that are needed to perform the research at hand. Staff should check the condition, content, and completeness of each item before circulating it and when it is returned after use. This checking of materials that are returned is especially important for the use of archival and manuscript collections, which often consist of many loose, unique pieces. Researchers should be required to return all materials before leaving the reading room, even if they plan to return later to continue their research. They should not be allowed to exchange items or to have access to materials brought into the room for use by another researcher.

Suggestions for implementation:

- The LSO or special collections administrator should seek the advice of the institution's legal counsel or other appropriate legal authority when developing researcher policies in order to ensure adequate legal recourse if researchers violate the use agreement.
- The institution should require that all researchers read and legally acknowledge an agreement to abide by institutional policies.

7. *The Collections*

Administrators of special collections must be able to identify positively the materials in their collections to establish loss and to substantiate claims to recovered stolen property. This process includes keeping adequate accession records, maintaining detailed cataloging records and lists in finding aids, recording copy-specific information, and keeping condition reports and records. Lists developed to fulfill the requirements of insurance policies should also be kept current. In addition, the materials themselves should be made identifiable by marking them following the Guidelines for Marking (page XX) by applying other unique marks, and by keeping photographic, digital, or microform copies of valuable items.

A recent theft or act of vandalism may give an indication of a building area, subject, or type of material that will be the target of future theft or mutilation. If appropriate, transfer materials related to those already stolen or mutilated to a more secure area. The theft or mutilation of printed books or manuscripts may indicate that other genres of materials containing similar subject matter will become the targets of thieves and vandals.

Many institutions house materials in open stack areas accessible to all users. These open stack areas may contain rare materials which are unidentified and unprotected. Materials in open stacks are most vulnerable to breaches in security. Many thieves search these areas for materials considered rare, rather than attempt to infiltrate special collections or outwit the security measures implemented in monitored reading rooms. Institutions should establish procedures for the routine review of general stacks, using the ACRL/RBMS Guidelines on the Selection of General Collection Materials for Transfer to Special Collections to assist in identifying rare materials on the open shelves in need of protection.

Suggestion for implementation:

- Items that are more valuable should be segregated from the collections into higher security areas, with more restricted conditions for staff access and researcher use.

8. Record-Keeping, Description, and Cataloging

A. Catalog all materials as fully as institutional resources and descriptive practices will allow. Stolen materials that have been described in detail are far more easily identified and recovered. Materials that have not been completely cataloged or processed should be made available to researchers only if security is not compromised and additional precautions (such as more stringent supervision of use, a reduction in the number of items dispensed at one time, and marking of items) are taken.

B. In the case of books, use the catalog record to describe copy-specific characteristics (e.g., binding, marks of previous ownership, defects) and bibliographic information that helps to distinguish among editions, issues, and states. Maintain complete acquisitions records, including antiquarian catalog descriptions. Create machine-readable records for local public access and international bibliographic databases. Participate in bibliographic projects that record detailed bibliographic descriptions.

C. Conduct regular inventories of both cataloged and uncataloged book collections and other collections when possible. This task is most effectively performed by staff members working in teams and should be conducted on a random basis. Proceeding through the collection in a predictable manner is not wise since it may allow thieves to temporarily replace stolen materials. A simultaneous reconciliation of the shelflist with the collection is also recommended. Inventories conducted even in small stages are valuable since they may reveal thefts (as well as misshelved books) and serve as a deterrent to any potential in-house thieves.

D. Maintain a shelflist, preferably in paper form for special collections, in a secure area. If the shelflist is electronic, it should be secure from tampering and a backup should be stored off-site. Since the shelflist indicates precisely where each item should be located, and because it contains copy-specific information about special collections materials, its maintenance and security are vital for detecting and recovering thefts.

E. Maintain up-to-date records of unlocated items and periodically recheck them; consider reporting missing items which are still unlocated after several searches to appropriate agencies (see II.3.B. below), noting their status as missing rather than stolen.

F. Cancel marks of ownership when deaccessioning items and keep careful, detailed records of such deaccessions. No attempt to remove ownership marks should be made.

9. Legal and Procedural Responsibilities

The administrators of special collections and the LSO must know laws relating to library and archival theft as well as institutional policies on apprehension of suspects and must convey this information to staff; they must also report thefts promptly to appropriate law enforcement agencies. Staff members must be aware of their legal rights in stopping thefts without infringing on the rights of suspects.

Suggestion for implementation:

- LSOs and/or special collections administrators should take an active role in raising the awareness of other institutional officials, e.g., institutional legal officers, public safety officers, the director, et al., regarding the serious nature of materials theft, and urge the institution to resolve security threats and breaches and to seek the strictest punishment possible for those convicted of theft or other security violations.

10. Institutional and Legislative Support

A. Work with the institutional administration to ensure their support for the prosecution of thieves. This support may range from the collection of evidence to be shared with prosecutors, to direct participation with the prosecution before and during the trial.

B. Work with appropriate institutional, local, and state groups to lobby for strengthening state laws regarding library and archival thefts and for diligent prosecution of such crimes. (See Appendix B: Draft of Model Legislation: Theft and Mutilation of Library Materials.)

Part II: Responses to Theft

1. Formulation of Action Plan

Like a disaster plan, an institutional plan for dealing with a theft will ensure a quick and well-organized response. The LSO, in concert with appropriate administrators, public relations personnel, security personnel, law enforcement (local, state, and federal, if necessary), and legal counsel should formulate a course of action that includes:

- Establishment of good working relations with law enforcement agencies—institutional, local, state, and/or federal—and determination of which agency has original jurisdiction over the institution (e.g., in-house security, local or state police, etc.) and under which circumstances they should be called. The institution should maintain a list of contacts in each level of law enforcement and discuss the plan of action with each. (See Appendix C: Resources Directory) The F.B.I., as well as U.S. Customs or Interpol, might become involved if stolen items are suspected of being smuggled into or out of the country.

- Notification of appropriate stolen and missing books databases and other appropriate networks (see Appendix C: Resources Directory)

- Notification of local and regional booksellers and appropriate specialist sellers
- Transfer of vulnerable items to a more secure location
- Arrangement of appraisals upon discovery of missing items
- Questioning of staff regarding any suspicious behavior by users or other persons
- Preparation of regular communications to staff about progress in the case, consistent with the investigation's integrity
- Preparation of news releases and responses by authorized institutional representatives to questions posed by the news media; all staff should be instructed to refer inquiries to the authorized spokesperson
- Maintenance of internal record of actions taken during the case's progress, from its discovery to its final disposition

2. Response to a Theft in Progress

If suspicions are sufficiently aroused, both a witness and the LSO should immediately be summoned and if possible the subject's actions captured on a security camera. After this point, it is necessary to follow institutional policies and applicable state laws concerning the incident. Because of wide vagaries in both those variables, more specific recommendations about potential courses of action in this situation are problematic. Whereas some actions, such as summoning security or the police may seem logical, they may in fact be counter to institutional policies.

- If there is probable cause that a theft has occurred, the appropriate library staff should request that the police officer place the suspect under arrest. (Laws regarding grounds for arrest vary from state to state, and

library staff should know the relevant state laws.) If there is evidence of theft, (e.g., materials hidden on the suspect's person), one should not agree to the suspect's release in return for the suspect's assurances that he or she will return to face charges. If the officer will not make an arrest, attempt to persuade the officer to detain the suspect until the officer can verify his/her identity and place of residence.

At the first opportunity, each person involved should describe in writing the suspect's physical appearance and obtain written accounts of the entire event from witnesses involved. This document may be needed later, especially if the case is prosecuted. Any materials the suspect has already turned back in should be immediately retrieved and inspected for loss or damage.

3. Subsequent Response

A. Gather Evidence

The LSO will notify administrative officers, institutional security personnel, as well as appropriate law enforcement personnel, and will compile a list of missing items. (This does not mean that the entire collection needs to be inventoried.) Other units and local repositories should be alerted. However, after the immediate steps listed below have been taken, it is suggested that works similar to those that have been stolen be inventoried. In consultation with the personnel previously notified, one should gather all available evidence of theft (such as those items listed below), which must not be altered in any way:

- Detailed, copy-specific descriptions of missing materials
- Any relevant video files or electronic security system logs
- Chain of custody documentation for missing materials (including call slips or copies of electronic records)

- Indications of unauthorized physical access to restricted areas
- Report of any missing cataloging or circulation records and database tampering
- Report on any indication of systematic patterns of loss of materials

B. Report to Appropriate Organizations and Agencies

The library should inform local booksellers of the institution's collecting areas and establish a procedure for quickly informing them of any theft that has occurred in the repository. Thieves sometimes try to sell stolen property quickly, and sellers with knowledge of the collections can recognize, or at least be suspicious of, these genres of materials when they are offered.

Thefts or missing items which are believed to have been stolen should be immediately reported to appropriate electronic mailing lists and national stolen and missing book databases (for a complete listing and details see Appendix C: Resources Directory). A search of auction sales records may be advisable if there is reason to believe the stolen material reached the market.

C. Assist with Prosecution

After the perpetrator is apprehended and brought to trial, the institution should establish lines of communication with the prosecution throughout the process of adjudication. This is particularly important if a plea-bargain and restitution are involved, since the institution may need to submit an account of damages. It is advisable for a representative to be present during the trial and especially during the sentencing phase, at which point the institution may wish to make a statement. This statement should refer to the seriousness of the crime, the damage to the cultural record, and its impact on the institution and its users. Such statements have been known to influence judges to impose harsher punishments.

D. Arrange for the Return of Located Materials

Once stolen materials are identified, it is necessary to confirm that they indeed belong to the institution; this process is facilitated by the record-keeping recommendations in Part I, section 8.

If the stolen materials reached the market and are in the hands of a new owner, recovery may be a difficult and time-consuming process. This is especially true if the materials are in a foreign country, where different legal systems and laws of title regarding the transfer of stolen goods are involved. Law enforcement and legal counsel will be able to provide advice on these issues. If a bookseller or auction house sold the items, its assistance should be enlisted in the recovery effort.

While in some cases authorities may be able to seize stolen items, in many cases this is not possible. Negotiation may be required, and it may prove necessary to compensate the current owner to obtain the timely return of the items. Depending on the circumstances, a bookseller or auction house should be requested to participate in the compensation, though this cannot be enforced.

Careful records of the stolen and returned items and all other aspects of the theft should be kept in perpetuity.

Appendix A: Guidelines for Marking Books, Manuscripts, and Other Special Collections Materials

I. Introduction

There has been much discussion within the special collections community regarding the appropriateness of permanently marking books, manuscripts, and other special collections materials. Failure to mark compromises security. Cases of theft show that clear identification of stolen material is vital if material, once recovered, is to be returned to its rightful owner. The following guidelines are intended to aid special collections in marking their materials, as well as to promote consistency and uniformity.

Even the most conservative marking program results in permanent alteration of materials. Choices concerning marking are likely to depend heavily on one's aesthetic judgment balanced against the need to secure materials from theft and to assist in their identification and recovery. Each repository will have to balance those competing needs. The ACRL/RBMS Security Committee recommends that libraries and other institutions use marking as part of their overall security procedures and that they attempt to strike a balance between the implications for deterrence (visibility, permanence) and the integrity of the documents (both physical and aesthetic).

II. General Recommendations

1. That markings be both:
   a. readily visible to the casual observer and
   b. hidden and difficult to detect
3. That readily visible marks be made in an approved form of permanent ink, such as that available from the Library of Congress (http://www.loc.gov/preserv/marking.html)
4. That marks which are hidden or difficult to detect never be the only or primary types of marking
5. That visible marks be placed so that they will cause significant damage to the aesthetic and commercial value of the item if they are removed
6. That marks be placed directly on the material itself and not on an associated part from which the material may be separated
7. That all marks unequivocally and clearly identify the repository

III. Discussion

1. Readily visible marks are intended to deter potential thieves; hidden marks are intended to assist in the recovery of stolen materials. If only one type of mark is to be used, it should be of the readily visible type.
2. Visible marks should be all but impossible to remove and should never consist of just a bookplate. Although not the only form of a visible mark, ink is perhaps the best medium for this purpose, so long as the ink meets current standards for permanence and conservation. There is still controversy surrounding which inks are best suited for this purpose, so a recommendation cannot go beyond urging those in charge of marking programs to be current on the latest developments in this field.
3. Hidden marks should never be used as the only form of marking, because they

are worthless in alerting others, such as booksellers, that material has been stolen. Hidden marks are intended only as supplements to visible marks.

4. Much controversy has surrounded the placement of visible marks. Given the varying nature of special collections materials and the varying nature of beliefs and sentiments concerning what is proper placement for a visible mark, it is probably futile to overly prescribe placement of marks. It is recommended, however, that no position for a mark be rejected outright. Some repositories might, for example, be comfortable stamping the verso of a title page or the image area of a map; others might reject those options. However, regardless of where the visible mark is placed, it should not be in a position that it can be removed without leaving obvious evidence of its former presence.

5. Marks of whatever type must be placed directly on the material itself. Marks placed only on a front pastedown in a book, on a portfolio that holds prints, or on some type of backing material are rendered useless if that element is separated from the item. Especially in the case of flat items, such as maps and broadsides, it is important that the marks be applied before any backing procedure is done.

6. Marks should not be generic (e.g., "Rare Book Room," "Special Collections," "University Library," etc.) but should rather make plain the repository to which they refer. It is recommended that visible marking consist of the repository's Library of Congress symbol. If a repository lacks such a symbol, the Library of Congress will supply one upon request. If the Library of Congress symbol is not used, then the name of the repository should be used, being careful that no confusion arises among repositories with similar or identical names.

IV. Other Considerations

1. Hidden marks do not have to be marks at all. They merely have to provide some positive ownership indication that is extremely difficult if not impossible to detect. Microembossers, for example, provide an extremely cheap and difficult to detect type of nearly invisible mark. Modern technology also provides non-invasive marking techniques, such as microphotography, that do not leave any mark on the item itself yet serve as positive identification. Other technologies, such as microtaggants, may also be appropriate for this purpose. It is vital if such marks are used, however, that the repository keep extremely accurate records of such marks so that they can be readily found for identification purposes if the need arises to do so. Generic secret marking systems, such as underlining a word on page 13 of every book, should be avoided as the sole means of such marks.

2. Repositories should never attempt to cancel marks, even in the event that the material is deaccessioned. No system has yet been devised for canceling marks that cannot be imitated with relative ease by thieves, and there seems to be no alternative but to assume permanent responsibility for one's mark on a book, manuscript, or other document. Permanent records should be kept of deaccessioned materials, whether marked or unmarked, and the material itself when

released should be accompanied by a document conveying ownership. It is advisable to place stamps or notes in items indicating that they have been deaccessioned, but no attempt should be made to cancel or remove previous ownership marks.

3. Marks should be applied to all items when they are accepted into the collection. It is dangerous to send unmarked items into storage or a cataloging backlog, where they may remain for years with no indication that the repository owns them. Despite the fact that some items may present extremely difficult and complicated decisions about marking, the process should never be deferred. It is strongly recommended that programs also be instituted to mark retrospectively materials already in the collections.

4. Care must be taken to ensure that all discrete or removable parts are marked. It is recommended that each separate plate, map, chart, or other such item in a printed volume be marked individually. Volumes of bound manuscripts and collections of individual manuscripts present a similar problem and each discrete item in such collections should also be marked.

Appendix B: Draft of Model Legislation: Theft and Mutilation of Library Materials

The draft of proposed legislation presented below may have to be modified in order to conform with federal and state laws regarding search and seizure. Also, the recourse to civil law that is available to a detained suspect may differ from state to state, and the draft legislation may have to be modified in order to meet such potential challenges. However, the wording of definitions should be adhered to; they have been formulated with the assistance of legal counsel. Nationwide conformity to the definition of essential terminology in criminal legislation is desirable.

Declaration of Purpose

Because of the rising incidence of library theft and mutilation of library materials, libraries are suffering serious losses of books and other library property. In order to assure that research materials are available for public use, it is the policy of this state to provide libraries and their employees and agents with legal protection to ensure security for their collections. It is the policy of this state to affirm that local, state, and federal prosecution of crimes affecting books or other library property is executed with the same degree of diligence as is exercised in prosecution of crimes affecting other forms of property. Federal statute pertaining to stolen property is designed not only to implement federal-state cooperation in apprehending and punishing criminals who utilize, or cause to be utilized, channels of interstate commerce for transportation of property of which the owner has been wrongfully deprived, but also to deter original theft.

Definition of Terms

Library: means any public library; any library of an educational, benevolent, hereditary, historical, or eleemosynary institution, organization, or society; any museum; any repository of public or institutional records.

Property: means any book, plate, picture, photograph, print, painting, drawing, map, newspaper, magazine, pamphlet, broadside, manuscript, document, letter, public record, microform, sound recording, audiovisual material in any format, magnetic or other tape, catalog card or catalog record, electronic data processing record, artifact, or other documentary, written, or printed materials, or equipment, regardless of physical form or characteristics, belonging to, on loan to, or otherwise in the custody of a library.

Proposed Wording

Section I.a.

Any person who willfully, maliciously, or wantonly writes upon, injures, defaces, tears, cuts, mutilates, or destroys any book, document, or other library property belonging to, on loan to, or otherwise in the custody of a library is guilty of a crime.

Section I.b.

The willful concealment of a book or other library property upon the person or among the belongings of the person or concealed upon the person or among the belongings of another while still on the premises of a library shall be considered prima facie evidence of intent to commit larceny thereof.

Section I.c.

The willful removal of a book or other library property in contravention of library regulations shall be considered prima facie evidence of intent to commit larceny thereof.

Section I.d.

The willful alteration or destruction of library ownership records, electronic or card catalog records retained apart from or applied directly to a book or other library property shall be considered prima facie evidence of intent to commit larceny of a book or other library property.

Section II.a.

An adult agent or employee of a library or that library's parent institution, whether or not that employee or agent is part of a security force, who has reasonable grounds to suspect that a person committed, was committing, or was attempting to commit the acts described in Section I may detain the suspect. Immediately upon detention, the library employee shall identify himself/herself and state the reason for his/her action. If, after the initial confrontation with the suspect, the adult agent or library employee has reasonable grounds to believe that at the time of detention that the person committed, was committing, or was attempting to commit the crimes set forth in Section I, said employee or agent may detain such a person for a time sufficient to summon a peace officer to the library. Said detention must be accomplished in a reasonable manner without unreasonable restraints or excessive force and may take place only on the premises of the library where the alleged crime occurred. Library premises include the interior of a building, structure, or other enclosure in which a library facility is located; the exterior appurtenances to such building structure, or other enclosure; and the land on which such building, structure, or other enclosure is located. Any person so detained by an employee or agent of a library shall promptly be asked to identify himself/herself by name and address. Once placed under detention, the suspect shall not be required to provide any other information nor shall any written and/or signed statement be elicited from the suspect until a police officer has taken the suspect into custody. The said employee or agent may, however, examine said property which the employee or agent has reasonable grounds to believe was unlawfully taken as set forth in Section I.b and/or I.c, or injured or destroyed as set forth in Section I.a and/or I.d. Should the detained suspect refuse to surrender the item for examination, a search may be made only of packages, shopping bags, handbags, or other property in the immediate possession of the person detained; no clothing worn by the suspect may be searched.

The activation of an electronic article surveillance device as a result of a person exiting the premises or an area within the premises of a library where an electronic article surveillance device is located shall constitute probable cause for the detention of such person by such library or agent or employee of the library, provided that such person is detained only in a reasonable manner and only for such time as is necessary for an inquiry into the circumstances surrounding the activation of the device, and provided that clear and visible notice is posted at each exit and location within the premises where such device is located indicating the presence of an anti-theft device. For purposes of this section, "electronic article surveillance device" means an electronic device designed and operated for the purpose of detecting the removal from the premises or a protected area within such premises, of any specially marked or tagged book or other library property.

Section II.b.

For the purposes of Section II.a, "reasonable grounds" shall include, but not be limited to, knowledge that a person has concealed or injured a book or other library property while on the premises of the library or the inability of the suspect to produce the library material for which there is a document proving that person had used but had not returned said material.

Section II.c.

In detaining a person who the employee or agent of the library has reasonable grounds to believe has committed, was committing, or was attempting to commit any of the crimes set forth in Section I, the said employee or agent may use a reasonable amount of non-deadly force when and only when such force is necessary to protect the employee or agent or to prevent the escape of the person being detained or the loss of the library's property.

Section III.

An adult agent or employee of a library who stops, detains, and/or causes the arrest of any person pursuant to Section II shall not be held civilly liable for false arrest, false imprisonment, unlawful detention, assault, battery, defamation of character, malicious prosecution, or invasion of civil rights of the person stopped, detained, and/or arrested, provided that in stopping, detaining, or causing the arrest of the person, the adult agent or employee had at the time of the stopping, detention, or arrest reasonable grounds to believe that the person had committed, was committing, or was attempting to commit any of the crimes set forth in Section I.

Section IV.

The fair market value of property affected by crimes set forth in Section I determines the class of offense: value under $500 constitutes a misdemeanor; $500–$5,000 a Class I felony; above $5,000, a Class II felony.

The aggregate value of all property referred to in a single indictment shall constitute the value thereof.

Section V.

A copy or abstract of this act shall be posted and prominently displayed in all libraries.

Section VI.

This act shall take effect upon passage.

Appendix C: Resources Directory
(current as of March 2009)

The updated directory of resources for this document is located at the RBMS website: www.rbms.info Please consult this directory for the latest information on moderators and web addresses.

I. Publications

- ACRL Code of Ethics for Special Collections Librarians (2003). http://www.rbms.info/standards/code_of_ethics.shtml.
- Association of College and Research Libraries. Guidelines on the Selection and Transfer of Materials from General Collections to Special Collections (2008). http://www.ala.org/ala/acrl/acrlstandards/selectransfer.cfm.
- Association of College & Research Libraries. Guidelines for the Interlibrary Loan of Rare and Unique Materials. http://www.ala.org/ala/acrl/acrlstandards/rareguidelines.cfm
- Association of College and Research Libraries. Guidelines for Borrowing and Lending Special Collections Materials for Exhibition (2005). http://www.ala.org/ala/acrl/acrlstandards/borrowguide.cfm
- Society of American Archivists. *Libraries and Archives: An Overview of Risk and Loss Prevention* (1994)
- Society of American Archivists. *Protecting Your Collections: A Manual of Archival Security* (1995).
- American Library Association Map and Geography Round Table. Map Collection Security Guidelines Current draft (2007) at: http://www.ala.org/ala/magert/MapSecurityGuidelines2007.pdf

- Thefts of Early Maps and Books. http://www.maphistory.info/thefts.html

II. Other Resources

International Association of Professional Security Consultants

http://www.iapsc.org . Tel: 949-640-9918; fax 949-640-9911.

Includes listing of professional security consultants with varying areas of expertise. Members of the organization cannot sell anything or represent any security firm.

Archives and Security Bibliography (Draft)

http://www.archives.gov/research/alic/reference/archives-resources/security.html

This document, dated 6/27/02, is attributed to Nicole Gordon of the Office of Regional Records Services. The page is contained within the website for the Archives Library Information Center (http://www.archives.gov/research/alic/), and is part of NARA (http://www.archives.gov/).

ACRL/RBMS Security Committee

http://www.rbms.info/committees/security/index/shtml

Current chair: Richard Oram roram@mail.utexas.edu

Exlibris Electronic Discussion List

exlibris-l@indiana.edu; subscribe at listserv@listserv.indiana.edu

Posting by subscribers only. Extensive web archives that include security topics available at http://palimpsest.stanford.edu/byform/mailing-lists/exlibris/. For further information, contact moderator Everett Wilkie at: ewilkie@ix.netcom.com

Archives & Archivists Electronic Discussion List
Often includes discussions about library security. Archives are available at http://forums.archivists. org/read/?forum=archives (September 2006 to present) and http://listserv.muohio.edu/archives/ archives.html (April 1993 to September 2006) . Address for posting is archives@forums.archivists. org. Subscription address is http://www.archivists. org/listservs/arch_listserv_terms.asp

Federal Bureau of Investigation, Art Theft Program
http://www.fbi.gov/hq/cid/arttheft/arttheft.htm

Los Angeles Police Dept. Art Theft Detail
http://www.lapdonline.org/art_theft_detail
Saving Antiquities for Everyone (SAFE)
Sponsors occasional conferences on stolen rare books.
http://www.savingantiquities.org

III. Secret Marking Technology

For more information about several of the currently available secret marking technologies, see the following web sites.

- Microembossers: http://www.microstampusa.com
- Microtaggants: http://www.microtracesolutions.com/915.htm
- Microdots: http://www.datadotdna.com

IV. Addresses for Reporting Thefts

Antiquarian Booksellers Association of America
20 West 44th St., 4th floor, New York, NY 10035-6604. 212-944-8291; (fax) 212-944-8293; email: hq@ abaa.com. The ABAA circulates reports of thefts through its electronic discussion list and maintains a stolen books database with a report form at http://www.abaa.org/books/abaa/databases/ stolen_search.html

ACRL/RBMS Security Committee
See contact information provided above.

Art Loss Register
For-profit database with charge for listing and searching entries (unless these are submitted through Interpol). http://www.artloss.com/

DeRicci Project
dericci@aol.com (for pre-1600 manuscripts only) International League of Antiquarian Booksellers (ILAB). Send theft reports and requests for database searches to: security@ilab-lila.com (Reporting and searching limited to members).

International Antiquarian Mapsellers Association
"Missing and Stolen Map Database": http://www. missingmaps.info. This is open to the public, but use of the report form does require site registration.
Interpol
Investigates international thefts of cultural property. Submit reports via Interpol liaison at state or provincial level or via F.B.I. http://www.interpol. int/Public/WorkOfArt/Default.asp

Library Security Officers List
Susan Allen, moderator. Closed non-discussion electronic list for theft reporting and limited to library security officers only. For information contact the owner at: sallen@getty.edu
Museum Security Network. http://www.museum-security.org/wordpress/. Reporting address: securma@pop.xs4all.nl. Contact the moderator at: museum-security@museum-security.org

Professional Autograph Dealers Association
c/o Catherine Barnes, P.O. Box 27782, Philadelphia, PA 19118; email: cb@barnesautographs.com; Home page: http://www.padaweb.org.
215-247-9240; fax: 215-247-4645

Society of American Archivists
527 S. Wells, Chicago, IL. 60607.
312-922-0140; fax 312-347-1452; email: sfox@archivists.org;
home page: http://www.archivists.org
This organization has several books in print on special collections/archives security. It also has a security-related round table and a discussion list at saasecurity-l@cornell.edu. This list is open only to SAA members, however.

V. Disaster Preparedness

Smithsonian Institution Staff Disaster Preparedness Procedures
Prepared by Office of Risk Management
October 1992, revised, October 1993
http://palimpsest.stanford.edu/bytopic/disasters/

Northeast Document Conservation Center
100 Brickstone Square, Andover, MA 01810-1494
978-470-1010; fax 978-475-6021
http://www.nedcc.org/home.php
They maintain a "Disaster Assistance" services page at: http://nedcc.org/services/disaster.php

About the Guidelines

This version was completed by the RBMS Security Committee in 2008 [and was approved by ACRL in 2009]. It replaces the separate "Guidelines for the Security of Rare Books, Manuscripts, and Other Special Collections" and "Guidelines Regarding Thefts in Libraries."

Guidelines on the Selection and Transfer of Materials from General Collections to Special Collections (Third edition)

http://www.acrl.org/ala/mgrps/divs/acrl/standards/selctransfer.cfm

Approved by the ACRL Board of Directors, July 1, 2008

Materials located in a library's general collections may gain, over time, special cultural, historical, or monetary value. Librarians have a responsibility to identify and transfer these materials to a special collections unit to ensure that they remain accessible and that they receive an appropriate level of preservation and security. These guidelines provide an overview of the considerations regarding selection criteria and recommend procedures for an effective transfer policy.

The first edition (1987) of the *Guidelines on the Selection of General Materials for Transfer to Special Collections* was prepared by an ad hoc committee of the ACRL Rare Books and Manuscripts Section (RBMS) chaired by Samuel A. Streit and published in *C&RL News* 48:8 (September 1987). The second edition was approved by the ACRL Standards Committee in 1994 and revised in 1999.

1.0 Introduction to the Guidelines

Many libraries intentionally acquire rare books, serials, ephemera, documents, manuscripts, media (e.g. photographs, sound recordings, moving images), and other rare or unique items. However, virtually all libraries acquire materials that, with time and changing circumstances, become rare and gain special cultural and historical value. These materials may also gain significant monetary value in the marketplace. Librarians have a responsibility

to identify the rare and valuable materials currently held in general and open stack collections and to arrange for their physical transfer to a library location that provides an appropriate level of access, preservation, and security. For many libraries the preferred transfer location is the special collections unit.

Some libraries provide environmentally sound and secure storage of rare materials in a location other than special collections, a location that provides an intermediate level of supervised access. While this transfer option is not addressed in these guidelines, it does require policy decisions similar to those considered here.

For definitions and examples of terminology used in the guidelines, please refer to Section 5.2 Bibliography.

It is worth noting a transfer action related to, but not covered in, these guidelines: the transfer of materials *out* of a special collections unit. Once identified, these items may merit relocation to other protected areas of the library, transfer into the library's general stacks, or they may be deaccessioned and transferred to another institution. (see Appendix A: Transfers from Special Collections to Other Areas in the Library)

2.0 The Selection and Transfer Program

Selection criteria and transfer policies vary from

institution to institution and depend on the nature, strength, and use of the general and special collections; staffing; and the physical setting. These guidelines are intended for general use by a range of library types and sizes, provide an overview of the considerations regarding selection criteria, and recommend procedures for an effective transfer policy to a special collections unit.

A successful selection and transfer program relies upon cooperation and coordination at every level of the library organization. In developing the program it is essential to obtain the support and approval of the library's senior administration. The written selection and transfer policy statement—hereafter referred to as the transfer policy—supports the library's mission and philosophical framework and documents the recommended procedures for everyone within the library.

The transfer policy should be written by those who are administratively responsible for the program and should receive functional support from individuals and/or departments within the library responsible for: special collections, collection development, preservation, cataloging, reference, circulation, government documents, gifts, and systems.

2.1 The transfer policy must:

1. promulgate to the public the library's definition of and policy toward rare and special collections,[1] justify the measures required to protect rare materials, and describe how implementing these measures will enhance the institution's ability to carry out its mission;
2. establish firm lines of authority to facilitate an effective and expeditious program;
3. list and document the criteria for the selection of items for transfer, which may be influenced by the nature and strengths of the library's general and special collections;

4. set forth clear procedures to implement the transfer process. These should include: selection and approval of transfers, inspection by preservation staff, physical handling and processing, updating bibliographic and circulation records, and maintenance of security throughout the process.

The library may find it helpful to contact professional consultants and colleagues from other libraries to help write the transfer policy, to refine selection criteria, and to inventory the collections. Once completed, the transfer policy should be approved by the library's senior administration and incorporated into the library's overall collection development policy.

3.0 Transfer Policy Procedures

The transfer policy has five procedural phases:

1. identification of materials that fit the selection criteria
2. review and decision to transfer
3. preservation assessment
4. cataloging review and processing, including location changes
5. physical transfer to protected collections, e.g. special collections.

3.1 Identification of Materials That Fit the Selection Criteria

Ideally, a library will systematically inventory large segments of its general collections according to the selection criteria. Few libraries, however, find such a comprehensive assessment possible. More often they choose instead to review materials and records selectively and incorporate identification into an existing library program or function. Other effective approaches include a selective review based on the history of the collection or a review that focuses on the areas of known strength. Many institutions find it worthwhile to solicit suggestions and comments from faculty, students, researchers, professional appraisers, and other experts to aid in the identification of significant materials. The library may also publicize its willingness to consider recommendations from patrons. Regardless of the scope of the identification program, the direct inspection of both individual transfer candidates and their corresponding bibliographic records is essential.

3.1.1 The identification process may include any of the following:

   a. reading the shelves (or the shelf list) in classifications likely to contain candidates for transfer

   b. examining chronological files for early imprints of particular interest and value

   c. producing review lists from the online catalog based on name, title , imprint date, classification, place of publication, literary genre, subject, provenance, or other relevant elements

   d. consulting bibliographies, databases, dealer catalogs, dealer Web sites, and other reference tools.

3.1.2 Transfer candidates may also be identified during routine handling associated with the following library functions:

   a. acquisitions

   b. binding

   c. cataloging

   d. circulation and stack maintenance

   e. collection surveys and assessments

   f. reformatting operations (digitization, photoduplication, microreproduction)

   g. gifts and exchanges

   h. identification of materials for off-site storage

   i. interlibrary loan (Note: the scarcity of an item is sometimes revealed when conducting interlibrary searches)

   j. inventory and shelf reading

   k. preparation of exhibitions

   l. preservation

   m. reference

   n. retrospective conversion and/or enhancement of existing cataloging records

   o. weeding

Transfer candidates may also be brought to the attention of library staff by patrons.

Titles identified as candidates for transfer and not yet removed from the circulating stacks can be flagged with a temporary marker, electronically "flagged" in the online catalog record, or some other method of temporary identification can be used to prevent circulation prior to review. If bar codes and other permanent identifiers are not already affixed to transfer candidates, new bar codes/identifiers should not be applied, pending the review and decision to transfer.

3.2 Review and Decision to Transfer

Not every item identified as a possible candidate will be chosen for transfer to special collections. For example, multiple copies of a title should be reviewed carefully to determine whether transfer of one or more copies is appropriate. Or, an item may be in such poor physical condition that it cannot be stabilized using standard conservation treatment, and thus loses its value as a candidate for transfer. In all cases, special collections staff (or staff assigned to this work)—in consultation with bibliographers, subject specialists, preservation staff, or faculty—should decide whether a given item merits transfer or should remain in the general collection.

3.3 Preservation Assessment

Physical changes made to an item after its original publication will diminish its value as a candidate for transfer. For this reason, a preservation assessment focusing on the physical condition of candidate materials should be conducted in consultation with special collections staff. The preservation assessment may occur either prior to the decision to transfer or after, depending on the item, the nature of the item's physical condition, and its anticipated use. For example, candidate items that are damaged or mutilated will require a preservation assessment prior to the transfer decision; the assessment will determine whether or not the damage can be remedied in order to make the item suitable for transfer. Alternatively, the preservation assessment may occur following the decision to transfer if the item has such value that it would be accepted into special collections despite its physical condition.

The preservation assessment will also include a recommendation as to when conservation treatment should occur, either before or after transfer. Treatment decisions should be made in conjunction with special collections staff and will range from minor repairs, stabilization, and protective housing to full conservation of the item.

3.4 Cataloging Review and Processing
Library users must be informed promptly when the location of an item has changed. One way to inform users is to update the catalog records to provide change of location information and adequate description. In some instances complete recataloging will be required. (See Appendix B: Changing Catalog Records)

3.5 Physical Transfer to Protected Collections
Once the decision is made to transfer an item to special collections or another protected collection within the library, it is essential that the physical transfer be completed in a timely manner and that an appropriate level of security be provided during each phase of the transfer procedure.

4.0 Transfer Criteria
The criteria for what is rare or unique are not always obvious; reasons for considering items as valuable candidates for inclusion in a special collection will vary among institutions. The transfer decision should include an evaluation of the special qualities of an item relative to the institution's collection development policies. Selection for transfer implies that all similar items in the collection (e.g., all books in original bindings printed before 1845) ought to be considered. The constraints of implementing an effective transfer policy are familiar: the institutional mission and the resources needed to carry out that mission (personnel, space, equipment, technology, and budget). The dynamic balance between mission and resources will require a realistic approach and, most likely, compromise.

Still, in most cases a combination of general criteria will apply when evaluating an item for transfer: 1. market value; 2. age; 3. physical and intrinsic characteristics; 4. condition; 5. bibliographic and research value.

It is worth noting that the application of these criteria may vary from one institution to another. The following discussion of criteria is provided for general guidance and is not meant to prescribe what ought to be transferred. (See Appendix C: Sample Transfer Criteria)

4.1 Market Value
Information on the market value and location of books and other materials in the general collections of libraries is readily available on the Internet. Therefore, library materials that have high monetary value are easily identified and especially vulnerable to theft. The transfer criteria will often include a threshold monetary value: the amount that the library defines as a "high" value for an item. Items located in the library's general collections with a market value at or above that threshold

should be identified and considered for transfer.[2] Additionally, the library's threshold value should be reviewed periodically—for example, every five years—and adjusted as needed.

4.2 Age

The longer an item survives, the more it becomes one of a decreasing number of witnesses to its own time and place, and to the technology of its creation. Examples range from books printed during the hand press era, approximately 1455 to 1855, to fire insurance maps published from 1867 to 1970. Therefore, age can be particularly useful as an initial criterion in identifying candidates for transfer.

Some libraries select a "trigger" date (threshold date) when reviewing materials for transfer, e.g. all items published before 1850 will be reviewed. Given that materials dating from 1900 are now over a century old, it is recommended that libraries relying on pre-set review dates revisit these parameters. It is possible that compelling reasons now exist to adjust the review dates.

An item's age alone is a relative factor in the decision to transfer. There are often other factors related to age which help determine value, such as regional printing history. For example, books and other printed material from a specific geographical location have significant value if published within the first years or decades after printing was established in that locality; these published materials are known as "regional incunables." The publication dates that define regional incunables will vary, for example: Pennsylvania (1685–1695), Texas (1817–1823), Alabama (1815–1825), and Oregon (1846–1856).[3]

In addition, the importance of the age of an object is relative to the development of the discipline it documents. For example, special collections that focus on modern science or medicine collect twentieth-century journals containing seminal research articles in those fields.

With regard to technology, mid-nineteenth-century publications may be valuable and scarce if they contain illustrations incorporating early photographic processes. Representatives of new media or technology may also qualify items for transfer. For example, recording media, which went through their formative stages in the early twentieth century, and "early" computer games are now being preserved at some institutions.

4.3 Physical and Intrinsic Characteristics

Library materials often have physical and intrinsic characteristics that qualify them as candidates for transfer. Some of these features may make them vulnerable to mutilation or theft and, therefore, require that they receive special protection. Library materials with qualifying characteristics for which there is wide, but not always unanimous, agreement include:

a. decorated end papers, unbound plates, vellum or publisher's bindings, and book jackets (examples of physical characteristics related to the publication process)

b. library materials with significant provenance or evidence of association

c. fine press editions

d. valuable maps, original art, original photographs,[4] or plates—especially plates with hand-applied or lithographed color—either as issued or as part of extra-illustrated volumes

e. broadsides, posters, and printed ephemera (examples of library materials in special formats)

f. materials having local interest, about local history, or by local authors

g. in-depth, subject-specific collections

h. books in unusual formats, erotica, or materials that are difficult to replace (examples of library materials requiring security)

i. books with moveable parts, pop-up books,

books having non-standard sizes or shapes (examples of library materials with artistic and/or unique structural characteristics)

j. items for which five or fewer copies are reported in the national online bibliographic database (OCLC WorldCat) or items for which only one copy is held in the geographic region (examples of library materials that are scarce or rare)

k. limited editions and small press runs

l. custom-produced books and handmade books

m. books and other objects made out of unusual materials

n. scrapbooks or photograph albums

o. handwritten or typed materials

4.4 Condition

When reviewing library materials for possible transfer, condition may be the most important criterion, since all other values—market, age, physical/ intrinsic, bibliographic/research—may be greatly affected by condition. Library materials that are badly worn, much repaired, or rebound should not automatically be transferred unless they represent a particularly scarce type of resource or present a compelling example(s) of the transfer criteria. For instance, it is now increasingly difficult for researchers to locate examples of many nineteenth- and twentieth-century printing and binding processes in fine original condition. So many volumes have been rebound that the richness of the decorative art applied to the original bindings and printed endpapers is increasingly difficult to find and study. Therefore, the reviewer must consider whether to transfer copies in less than perfect condition.

If the dust jacket is still present on a general collection copy, it should be retained when transferred. A book's dust jacket frequently contains important information including text, illustrative design, price, series, alternative titles, and biographical information about the author.

4.5 Bibliographic and Research Value

Bibliographic and research values should not be overlooked. For example, careful consideration should be given to reference works and periodicals still needed for general use since they frequently become quite valuable. Reference works and periodicals may be candidates for transfer especially if facsimile or other reprint editions are available to replace them on the open shelves. If the institution's special collections have in-depth holdings on the history of native Americans in the Midwest, for example, reference titles about native Americans published in the late nineteenth to mid-twentieth-century might be considered for transfer.

Federal, state, and local government documents are also receiving attention as their research (and market) value increase. Examples of particularly relevant government documents include: reports of nineteenth-century scientific discoveries and expeditions, government publications containing maps or plates, ethnographic reports, and documents produced during major historical events (e.g. federal regulations for World War II internment camps).

Additional factors that may affect bibliographic and research value include:

a. market value among collectors and the antiquarian book trade

b. evidence of censorship or repression

c. seminal nature of or importance to a particular field of study or genre of literature

d. production for use by a private group with no subsequent public distribution.

5.0 Selected Readings

The process of developing, refining, and updating a selection and transfer policy is ongoing and complex. It requires vision and good judgment, and profits from wide and informed reading. Although there is no literature dealing with transfer per se, the following Web sites and print publications may assist those charged with forming their library's policies. Several of the sources can be used to determine market value and scarcity.[5] In addition to the sources listed below, there are many print and Web-based bibliographies that include reference materials for specific disciplines and topics.

5.1 Web Resources

1. Association of College and Research Libraries (ACRL). January 2006. *Guidelines for the Security of Rare Books, Manuscripts, and Other Special Collections.* http://www.ala.org/ala/acrl/acrlstandards/securityrarebooks.htm (accessed 16 February 2008).

2. Association of College and Research Libraries (ACRL). January 2003. *Guidelines Regarding Thefts in Libraries.* http://www.ala.org/ala/acrl/acrlstandards/guidelinesregardingthefts.htm (accessed 16 February 2008).

3. Council on Library and Information Resources (CLIR). November 2001. *The Evidence in Hand: Report of the Task Force on the Artifact in Library Collections.* http://www.clir.org/PUBS/reports/pub103/contents.html (accessed 16 February 2008).

4. Rare Books and Manuscripts Section. Bibliographic Standards Committee. January 2008. *Directory of Web Resources for the Rare Materials Cataloger.* http://lib.nmsu.edu/rarecat/ (accessed 16 February 2008).

5. Rare Books and Manuscripts Section. Publications Committee. February 2006 (Revision 2005.2). *Your Old Books.* http://www.rbms.info/yob.shtml (accessed 16 February 2008).

5.2 Bibliography

1. *Antiquarian Books,* edited by Phillipa Bernard, Philadelphia: University of Pennsylvania Press, 1994.

2. *Book Collecting: A Modern Guide,* edited by Jean Peters, New York: R.R. Bowker, 1977.

3. G. L. Brook, *Books and Book Collecting.* London: Andre Deutsch, 1980.

4. John Carter, *ABC for Book Collectors,* Eighth edition, revised by Nicolas Barker. New Castle, DE: Oak Knoll Press, 2004.

5. John Carter, *Taste and Technique in Book Collecting; with an Epilogue.* London: Private Libraries Assoc., 1970 (1977 printing).

6. Roderick Cave, *Rare Book Librarianship,* Second edition revised, New York: R.R. Bowker, 1983.

7. Philip Gaskell, *A New Introduction to Bibliography.* New Castle, DE: Oak Knoll Press, 1995.

8. Geoffrey Ashall Glaister, *Encyclopedia of the Book,* Second edition, introduction by Don Farren. New Castle, DE and London: Oak Knoll Press / British Library, 1996.

9. Jean Peters, *Collectible Books: Some New Paths.* New York: R.R. Bowker, 1979.

10. Lawrence Clark Powell, "Rare Book Code," *College & Research Libraries* 10 (October, 1949): 308.

11. *Standard Citation Forms for Published Bibliographies and Catalogs Used in Rare Book Cataloging,* prepared by Peter VanWingen and Belinda D. Urquiza, Second edition. Washington, D.C.: Library of Congress, 1996.

12. Samuel Streit, "Transfer of Materials from General Stacks to Special Collections," *Collection Management* 7 (Summer 1985): 33–46.

13. Jim Walsh, Barbara Hulyk, George Bar-

num. *Rare and Valuable Government Documents: A Resource Packet on Identification, Preservation, and Security Issues for Government Documents Collections.* Chicago: Rare Books and Manuscripts Section [and] Government Documents Round Table [and] Map and Geography Round Table Joint Committee on Government Documents as Rare Books, American Library Association, 1993.

5.3 *Appendices*
Appendix A. Transfers from Special Collections to Other Areas in the Library
Appendix B. Changing Catalog Records

Appendix C. Sample Transfer Criteria
ACRL Rare Books and Manuscripts Section. Task Force to Review Guidelines on the Selection and Transfer of Materials from General Collections to Special Collections (2005–2008):

Emily Epstein
Janet Gertz
Ron Lieberman
Daryl Morrison
Phyllis Payne
Andrea Rolich
Bruce Tabb
Jennifer Hain Teper
Charlotte B. Brown, Chair

NOTES

1. In most cases, a general definition of and policy for rare and special collections are publicized. The selection criteria utilized by the library to identify potential rare and special materials are not publicly announced.
2. The urgency of determining market value for selected library items has increased since the guidelines were last published. Web sales of materials stolen from general library collections have occurred. Plates, maps, and other graphic materials are also subject to theft. For additional information on the security of special collection materials, see: Association of College and Research Libraries (ACRL). January 2006. *Guidelines for the Security of Rare Books, Manuscripts, and Other Special Collections.* Available online at http://www.ala.org/ala/acrl/acrlstandards/securityrarebooks.htm. (accessed 16 February 2008). For a list of publicly reported thefts of rare books and other special collections materials, see: Rare Books and Manuscripts Section. Security Committee. *Security Resources.* Available online at http://www.rbms.info/committees/security/index.shtml. (accessed 16 February 2008).
3. Roger J. Trienens, *Pioneer Imprints From Fifty States.* Washington, D.C.: Library of Congress, 1973.
4. This includes library materials containing original photographs often pasted or glued into the item.
5. Web-based resources can provide general guidelines for determining scarcity and value. Library staff are advised to consult rare book, map, and/or manuscript specialists to confirm the assessments.

Appendix A: Transfers from Special Collections to Other Areas in the Library

Items that are not rare or do not require a high level of preservation or security are sometimes located in a library's special collections unit and may merit transfer into other protected areas of the library or into the general library stacks. Examples are: 1) subject collections (e.g. books about the Napoleonic era); 2) donations containing a mixture of rare and non-rare materials; and 3) items that become out-of-scope after changes are made to the collecting emphasis of special collections. While not ideal, the decision to transfer materials out of special collections may also be influenced by space constraints.

It is recommended that the administrator in charge of special collections, in consultation with the collection development and preservation staff, give final approval for materials that are deaccessioned from the special collections unit. Donor records, including existing deeds of gift, should be consulted to determine if there is an obligation for the item to remain in special collections. The impact that the transfer might have on the physical condition of the item once it is relocated to the circulating collections, such as, loss of the dust jacket, added markings and stamps, damage during circulation, possible theft, should also be considered.

Appendix B: Changing Catalog Records

Develop a local procedure that includes: searching the local catalog; examining existing records; updating or replacing bibliographic, item, and holdings records; creating shelf dummies (as needed); and physically remarking materials with new location information. [NOTE: "record" refers to catalog cards, electronic records, or both as applicable.]

    a.   Create lists of records to be changed.

    b.   Edit catalog records according to local cataloging requirements or standards.

As appropriate, edit catalog records to meet rare book cataloging standards. Consider adding notes for provenance, printers, binding, and citations.

These steps are recommended components for a transfer program. Libraries should strive to incorporate as many of them as feasible given local or outsourcing resources and expertise.

In addition to changing their bibliographic records, some libraries may choose to make a general announcement to their users that they have transferred a broad category of materials to a special collections area. For example, all books published before 1850.

Appendix C: Sample Transfer Criteria

The following is an example of transfer criteria that might be employed by a public research university library established in the mid-nineteenth century and located in the mid-west United States:

- books published in [name of state] prior to 1835
- books published in the U.S. prior to 1850
- materials published prior to 1825
- children's books published prior to 1920
- travel books published prior to 1900
- items published in the Confederate States of America (CSA), 1860–1865
- items published in Africa prior to 1851
- items published in Latin American prior to 1851
- items having market value over $500.00
- items printed in editions of 100 copies or fewer
- publications by authors formerly residing in [name of city]

If Special Collections does not accept the item for transfer, forward the item to the subject specialist for review.

ALA Map and Geography Round Table

MAP COLLECTION SECURITY GUIDELINES

MAGERT Task Force on Library Security for Cartographic Resources

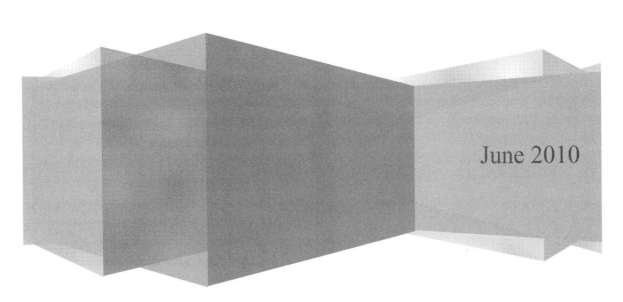

June 2010

Electronic Publication Series no.8

MAP COLLECTION SECURITY GUIDELINES
MAGERT Task Force on Library Security for Cartographic Resources
June 2010

I. Introduction

We live in a world where crime is reported daily on the front pages of newspapers and Web sites and seen each evening on the nightly news. It has been stated that after international drug trafficking the second largest category of crime is within the fine arts market. Such crime is not limited to the works of Picasso or Rubens but also includes those of Blaeu, Mercator, and Jefferson as well as nineteenth-century U.S. government documents. Now that we are in the 21st century we must realize that early 20th century materials are over 100 years old, out-of-print, and essentially irreplaceable without considerable investment. Maps in atlases and books are often very valuable and especially vulnerable as the removal of a map or two is not immediately apparent when the volume is returned; it is often difficult to know if a volume contains all of its constituent parts since few collections, if any, have the time or staff to inventory all of their maps and illustrations.

As librarians we have a responsibility to preserve the collections under our care and provide access to them in our institutional environments. Access to our collections has supported scholarship throughout the sciences, humanities, and social sciences and remains the key to intellectual freedom. We must create an environment where primary source materials are respected, handled carefully, and returned intact to the collection so that they might be studied again in the future. Institutions and librarians must reassess their collections and administrators must provide collections with an infrastructure and staffing that will allow appropriate access, preservation, and security. It is important that rare book collections, archives, and government document collections and their curators realize that thousands of valuable maps are contained in many volumes in their collections. Similarly, map collections and their curators must be more cognizant of the marketplace and the increasing prices of early maps and even early twentieth century road maps.

The following guidelines will allow librarians and curators to better assess their map collections, prepare security proposals for their administrations, and provide a more secure environment for their map collections.

II. Collections

Positive identification of materials and ownership of materials will be required when attempting to recover stolen items; librarians and library staff must be able to clearly identify materials that belong to their collections. Identification methods include marking, cataloging, and regular inventory. Digital imaging of rare and significant materials is rapidly becoming a process to increase security and identify missing items.

- *Collection Processing*

Materials should be processed (marked, indexed, cataloged, inventoried) in a space separate from areas accessible by users.

- *Marking*

All pieces should be marked with a clear property stamp. Items should be marked with an appropriate property stamp immediately upon receipt; items should not be stored in any kind of cataloging front log or backlog without a property stamp. Property stamps should indicate the institution to which the item belongs, not just the subunit which might have a generic name. Although it is possible to indicate ownership with secret or hidden marks, they should never be used alone; an obvious, visible property stamp may be a good first deterrent in preventing theft. Stamps should be placed in locations where they do not obscure graphic or textual data; this placement must also be such that the stamp cannot be cut away without leaving an obvious incision, such as in the margin. Multiple stamps may be necessary in cartographic volumes; it is important that individual maps, both folded and unfolded, included in volumes are property stamped.

- *Cataloging and Finding Aids*

Cataloging fills a number of roles. It alerts potential users that materials are available, assists in collection development decisions, and provides a framework of data that describes the extent of the collection. This framework should be fully fleshed out with descriptive data. Unique aspects of items should be considered as additions in local fields. For multi-piece titles, full holding and item records need to be constructed to create the necessary data/paper trail for inventory work. Atlases should not be described merely as "1 v." A fuller enumeration such as "1 v., including 57 maps, no. 52 missing" should be created. A marked finding aid (index map) in itself is not sufficient to tracing specific items owned because indexes rarely include information about edition or date of sheet publication or unique qualities. A finding aid should only be used for collection access.

- *Collection Inventory*

Collections should be inventoried on a regular and ongoing basis. Inventories should be dated and retained to be used as a baseline for future inventory or for comparison should a loss or theft be suspected. Significant local materials should be inventoried more regularly; however, "spot check" inventories are often beneficial if only to identify misfiling.

- *Determining Value*

Value can be defined in a number of different ways: monetary, personal/emotional, research, or contextual. Cartographic materials may be determined to have high value because of their market value, age, physical characteristics, condition, and/or research value; an item that has a high value in one location may have a relatively low value elsewhere. Some items have comparatively high values, in particular monetary, regardless of location. These items can be tracked through dealer catalogs, reports of auction results, and tools such as *Antique Map Price Record* and *American Book Prices Current*. Be aware that new publications can be as rare or expensive as old publications. Also, remember that values are not static; items which may appear to be commonplace, including early 20th century U.S. federal government publications and highway maps, are aging, becoming less common, and increasing in value.

Although it may be useful to compile an estimation of collection value and the value of especially noteworthy items based upon inventory work, especially for insurance and fundraising purposes, at no time should a "shopping list" of holdings and associated values be compiled and distributed. Monetary values placed on collection items should not be discussed with readers or visitors.

High-value materials should be transferred out of vulnerable situations (open stacks) and into closed stacks or restricted access areas such as remote storage. Transfers should be made following clearly documented procedures, and all individuals and offices involved with a transfer should know where the impacted materials are at all times.

- *Copying and Scanning*

Excellent copying and scanning areas should be provided within the cartographic collection space; when located in the map collection area self-service copying and scanning facilities reduce the need to loan materials or send materials elsewhere for duplication. Equipment needs to be placed so that use can be monitored and collection staff can provide assistance. Research collections should provide for high quality oversized scanning and printing; however, antiquarian materials should only be handled by collection staff. Collection staff must have and exert the authority to deny copying or scanning of fragile and damaged items.

Scanning done by collections/holding institutions serves multiple purposes. Like catalog records, images placed on the Web function as advertisement, drawing potential users to the collection. As the quality of images available through the Web increases and the cost of full-size, high quality color printing decreases many cartographic users' needs may be filled using digital surrogates, thus protecting valuable and fragile originals. Digital copies, especially those that capture unique aspects such as stains, marks, and/or tears, can be useful in identifying items that have strayed from the collection. Digital images should be deposited in online repositories and linked to appropriate records in the online catalog.

III. Facilities and Security

Facilities and facility organization need to be structured to maximize security while providing for the use of materials. Security protocols should be obvious to but not discussed with collection visitors and should have minimal impact on access to collections

- *Physical Configuration*

The arrangement in public areas of furniture, collection storage equipment (map cases, vertical files, shelving), walls, supporting architectural structures such as columns, and the relationship between reader and staff spaces should be such that there are no impeded lines of sight. There should be a minimal number of egress points and only a single controlled entry that is used by both readers and staff. A cloakroom with lockers should be available outside of the collection space for readers to leave belongings such as outerwear, bags and/or carrying cases, large volumes or stacks of paper. A specific area that is continuously monitored by staff, from multiple angles if possible, in which readers can consult materials should be designated. Chair backs should not be higher than the tops of the tables. There should be nothing at all in room arrangement or décor that obstructs the staff members' line of sight.

- *Monitoring Access*

Doors should be monitored by staff members that check research materials being brought into the collection by readers on their way in and out of the facility. If a staff member can not be at the door at all times, it should be locked and buzzed open by staff as needed. Additionally, the door should be alarmed with both audio and visual alarms to alert staff to any door opening. Security gates at doors are useful to detect objects that have been security stripped.

If cameras are being used for security, they must be strategically placed to cover as much of the area as possible. Signs need to be posted to tell readers that they are being recorded. If a camera is in place it must be running; "decoy" cameras are a liability.

When readers are using the collection, the staff member assigned to monitor the reading room should be doing no other task at the same time. Readers and the materials that they are using should be in clear sight of the room monitor at all times.

- *Keys, Keycards, and Passwords*

Access mechanisms such as keys, keycards, and passwords are often a weak point in collection security because they are easily lost or shared. A minimal number of keys should be issued to only those staff requiring them, and records of key distribution should be kept. All combinations, keys, and passwords should be changed on a scheduled basis and must be changed each time there is a change in staff; security should be notified of departing employees' last day.

- *Locked Spaces*

Restricted and vault areas should be securely locked at all times except if a staff member is in the space.

Offices should be locked if the assigned occupant is not present and access to the space is not required for normal operational procedures.

IV. Staff Members

Staff members are both the greatest asset in protecting a collection and potentially the largest risk to a collection. Through their work with the collection and its users staff members become intimately familiar with holdings, and may be the ones who give the alert that things are missing. However, because of this intimacy staff members have insider knowledge of what is available, what is not appropriately protected, and weaknesses in the collection's security planning. Regardless of this dichotomy, staff needs to be given the trust and told that they are trusted so that they can do the jobs they have been hired to undertake. Additionally, the importance of the each staff member's role in providing collection security should be emphasized in training and ongoing communication.

A background check should be done and all references contacted as a regular part of the hiring process. Beyond the training needed for performing assigned tasks, staff members must be trained in appropriate security measures and procedures; the training should include information on legal rights and responsibilities. All staff members should be issued and carry photographic employee identification badges.

In many library settings, there are personnel from other library operations or facilities support operations that need access to collection space. These might include preservation staff, custodial staff, facilities maintenance workers, computing systems employees from both library and non-library offices, library security forces, and contractors for construction projects. All of these individuals should be known to the collection staff and should carry appropriate identification. The schedule for regular visits to the unit by nonaffiliated staff such as custodial workers should be known, posted and monitored by a staff member or security staff; all other visits should be scheduled in advance. If non-staff members need access to secured areas of the collection they should be accompanied and monitored by a staff member at all times.

- *Staffing Levels and Numbers*

Hours should be commensurate with staffing levels and infrastructure. A minimum of two staff members are needed to have a cartographic collection open to readers; a single employee, regardless of rank or level of appointment, is not sufficient to provide appropriate collection security while serving readers or undertaking other tasks. Depending on factors such as physical configuration, line of sight, storage locations and door security measures, more staff may be required. If a sufficient number of staff members are not available, some services and portions of the collection may not be accessible.

V. Readers

When readers arrive at a collection to use materials, they should be asked to complete a user registration form including name, address, institutional affiliation as appropriate, and signature; the registration form may also include a statement of collection access and use policies. A form of photo identification should be requested. Registration forms as well as request or page slips for materials housed in restricted areas should be kept on file indefinitely. Ideally, registration would be done using an online form that would create an archival database of users.

Objects being carried into the collection should be inspected prior to entry by a staff member. Bags, carrying cases, coats/jackets, large volumes or stacks of paper should not be allowed into the collection area but instead left in an exterior locker space. Some collections may elect to not allow loose sheets of paper but instead provide colored paper for note taking that is cut or pierced in a way to facilitate checking for stray collection items when the reader leaves.

In many instances, historical cartographic collections and collections of early books with significant cartographic holdings will have closed stacks; readers will not be able to retrieve materials on their own. Access to cartographic collections should be completely moderated by a member of the staff who discusses with the reader the region needed and types of data desired.

When a map collection has open access, readers should not be allowed to carry any materials into the stacks area besides slips of paper for jotting down notes.

When leaving the collection space, readers' belongings that have accompanied them into the unit should be checked at the door by a staff member before readers are allowed to depart. Books, folders, and laptops should be opened and stacks of paper leafed through.

VI. Policies and Procedures

Policies regarding cartographic collections should be posted; all staff must be thoroughly familiar with the policies and able to articulate and enforce the policies as needed. Policies should be enforced consistently and should not be changed for unique circumstances, special readers, friends, or dealers.

- *Open and Closed Stacks Collections*

Closed stacks storage of historical cartographic materials is highly preferred over open stacks. A closed stacks policy prohibiting non-staff members from retrieving materials on their own provides greater collection security than an open stacks policy. Closed stacks policies also facilitate better collection management and preservation/conservation of materials.

There are degrees of "closed-ness". In the least restrictive, readers browse the collection with staff members and select at the drawer the items they wish to inspect; staff members do the physical retrieval, sometimes with assistance from the reader. This situation is more appropriate for newer, more common materials and for materials that are in good physical condition. Older, more valuable, less common, and physically fragile items as well as folded maps in volumes need to be held with greater protection. These items should be housed in areas restricted from reader access, and only staff members should be at the drawer or shelf browsing and retrieving items. Readers also should be prohibited from accessing areas in which unprocessed items are stored. There may be some items that are of such great value that they are housed in a vault-like situation where only specially designated staff may enter.

Regardless of policy regarding closed or open stacks, no access should be allowed to the cartographic collection unless a staff member is present. Having student employees can assist in extending collection accessibility hours but this may not necessarily include access to all parts of the collection.

- *Documenting Distribution of Keys and Passwords*

Paralleling degrees of physical access to the collection, keys and passwords should be distributed on an as-needed basis; not all employees need access to the entire collection. Records of key and password distribution should be kept and retained indefinitely. These records should include name and rank/status/position of employee, date of distribution, date of return, and circumstances or reasons for return or termination of access.

The unit head should also have a list of all other individuals or locations where keys to the unit are housed. This may include offices such as facilities and maintenance, shipping services, custodial services, and central library administration. Individual teaching and research faculty who are not unit staff member should not have access to keys.

- *Changing Locks and Passwords*

Locks and passwords should be scheduled to be changed at least annually. All individuals should be required to turn in their old keys to receive new ones. If a key is reported lost or stolen, locks should be rekeyed immediately. If there is any evidence that a password has been breached, it also should be changed immediately. Locks and passwords should also be changed when an employee is dismissed.

- *Reader Access Policies*

Readers should not have access to collection facilities unless a staff member is present. Readers should be required to follow unit policies regarding closed and open stacks areas as well as directions pertaining to areas in which materials may be consulted, which personal belongings may or may not be brought into the collection area, and restricted areas.

All readers should be required to complete a reader registration form as well as request or page slips, completed by staff members, for any materials retrieved for their use from restricted areas. These records should be kept on file in the unit indefinitely and updated on an ongoing basis for regular or repeating readers.

- *Materials Usage*

Except in open stacks situations where readers retrieve their own materials, readers should not be presented with large quantities of materials to review at one time. A sensible and track-able limit of items needs to be established that balances collection protection against research needs. The item limit may differ from area to area within the collection with the number of allowable items decreasing as the security needs of the items increase. Very rare, valuable, or fragile items should be restricted to single item use – one item viewed and then returned before another is delivered for viewing – except under special and staff monitored circumstances that require comparison of similar items. Some materials may be designated as being restricted to use in only very specific areas of the reader space. Items should be examined for physical condition and completeness prior to giving items to readers; items should be examined again upon their return. If returned materials cannot be refiled or reshelved immediately they should be placed in a secure area away from the reader space. Rare items that will be used over a period of time should not be left in public areas; a secure non-public holding area should be designated for such items.

- *Interlibrary Loan*

In general, interlibrary loan as well as exhibit and in-house research loans of original cartographic materials, including maps, aerial photographs, and older materials of all formats is not recommended; copies or high-quality scans should be used instead. Copying should be done by staff within the cartographic collection or in facilities where appropriate measures have been taken to protect, store, and transport materials safely.

Rare and/or valuable materials should be limited to significant exhibition events that can support insurance, transportation, and building security guidelines. Rare items should not be loaned or exhibited on a regular basis.

VII. Administering the Security Plan

The value of our collections, both monetarily and historically, continue to increase and our commitment to open access makes them especially vulnerable. Recognizing this vulnerability should allow us to plan a course of action that falls into place the moment an incident is verified. It is critical that an institution create a communications plan whereby all parties (administration, librarians, and staff) know how to react when a theft occurs. Most institutions have created a disaster plan and review it regularly; a similar process should include planning for an incident of theft.

Initial and immediate contacts should be with local safety officials; this includes protecting a building from a theft if it has been breached by a natural disaster or other incident. Collections should be connected to local safety officials through alarms and panic buttons so that any emergency can receive immediate attention. Once the building is declared secured, librarians and preservation staff should evaluate the situation and determine the status of the collections. Local law enforcement officials should be contacted immediately if a theft is suspected and collections sequestered for further review.

Agreed-upon channels of communication will make this process move more smoothly. Scheduling meetings after the incident to decide on a plan of action loses valuable time and provides the perpetrator additional time. It is critically important to establish an early warning system as the map trade moves much more quickly than one might imagine; the general marketplace (i.e. eBay) moves even faster.

VIII. Notifying the Community

The following Web sites and listservs are important communication devices that should be used to alert the map trade and library community of theft:

Missing and Stolen Maps Database - http://www.missingmaps.info/index.htm
Map History/History of Cartography - http://www.maphistory.info
- Thefts of Early Maps and Books - http://www.maphistory.info/thefts.html
- News About Map Thefts - http://www.maphistory.info/theftnews.html
MapHist - maphist@geo.uu.nl
Map Trade - maptrade@raremaps.com
Maps-L - maps-l@listserv.uga.edu
ExLibris-L - exlibris-l@listserv.indiana.edu

IX. Sources

Center, Clark, Jr. and Donnelly Lancaster. 2004. *Security in Special Collections*. SPEC Kit 284. Washington, DC: ACRL.

Goodbody, Margaret and Jennifer R. Evans. 2005. Protecting Access and Materials in Public Library Special Collections. Technical Services Quarterly 22(3): 19-28.

Guidelines for the Security of Rare Books, Manuscripts, and Other Special Collections 2006. http://www.rbms.nd.edu/standards/security_guidelines.shtml

Guidelines on the Selection and Transfer of Materials from General Collections to Special Collections. American Library Association. 2006. http://www.ala.org/ala/acrl/acrlstandards/selectransfer.htm

Guidelines Regarding Thefts in Libraries 2003. http://www.ala.org/ala/acrl/acrlstandards/guidelinesregardingthefts.htm

Harvey, Miles. 2000. *Island of Lost Maps: A True Story of Cartographic Crime*. New York: Random House.

Joint Statement on Access to Original Research Materials 1994. http://www.ala.org/ala/acrl/acrlstandards/jointstatement.htm

Library Security Guidelines Document, June 7, 2001. http://www.ala.org/ala/lama/lamapublications/librarysecurity.htm

Research Libraries Collection Management Group: ALA MAGERT Midwinter San Antonio, January 2006. *base line* 27(2): 19.

Thefts of Early Maps and Books. Map History/History of Cartography. http://www.maphistory.info/thefts.html

Thomas, Mark, Amée Piscitelli, and Julia Rholes. 1994. Security and Preservation of the U.S. Congressional Serial Set. *Journal of Government Information* 21(4): 351-366.

Weessies, Kathleen. 2003. The Secret Inside Your Library's Atlases. *American Libraries* 34(9): 49-51.

X. Acknowledgements

In memory of friend and colleague Jan Dixon (1952 – 2009), Map Librarian, University of Arkansas, long-time MAGERT member and chair of the Task Force on Library Security for Cartographic Resources.

Sources Consulted

Note: The hundreds of newspaper and magazine articles and Internet postings that have appeared on library thefts over the years generally are not listed.

Adams, Randolph G. "Librarians as Enemies of Books." *Library Quarterly* 7 (July 1937): 317–31.

Adams, Thomas R. "Librarians as Enemies of Books?" *College & Research Libraries*. 45 (May 1984): 196–200, 205–6.

Allen, Charles. *Mr. Pink: The Inside Story of the Transylvania Book Heist*. Lexington, KY: Allen Brothers, 2010.

Allen, Susan M. "A Costly Lesson for Librarians." *AB Bookman's Weekly* (2 September 1991): 769–73

———. "Preventing Theft in Academic Libraries & Special Collections." *Library & Archives Security* 14 (1997): 29–43. http://web.simmons.edu/~mahard/Allen%201997.pdf (accessed 2010).

———. "Theft in Libraries and Archives: What to Do During the Aftermath of a Theft." *Journal of Library Administration* 25, no. 1 (November 1998): 3–13.

———. "Theft in Libraries or Archives." *C&RL News* 51, no. 10 (1990): 939–43.

———. "Using the Internet to Report Rare Book and Manuscript Thefts." *Rare Books and Manuscripts Librarianship* 10, no. 1 (1995): 33–37.

A Plus Identification & Security. "Focus On: Access Control." http://www.aplusid.com/FOCUS-ON-Card-Access-Control-Systems-c01071.html (accessed 2010).

American National Standards Institute & Builders Hardware Manufacturers Association. *A.156.5-2001, Auxiliary Lock and Associated Products*. http://www.buildershardware.com/standards/a156_5.pdf (accessed 2010).

American Risk and Insurance Association. "Risk Management." http://www.museum-security.org/riskmanagement-insurance.html (accessed 2010).

Anderson, A. J. "The Trouble with Larry." *Library Journal* 111, no. 11 (1986): 45–47.

Anna, Cara. "Company Admits It Sold Illegal Audio Bugs." *Austin American Statesman*, 28 November 2002, D:1.

Antwi, I. K. "The Problem of Library Security: The Bauchi Experience." *International Library Review* 21 (1989): 363–72.

Ariely, Dan. *Predictably Irrational: The Hidden Forces that Shape Our Decisions*. New York: Harper, 2008.

"An Arkansas Professor Is Charged with Swiping Outlaw's Documents." *The Victoria Advocate*, 7 October 1996, 10A.

Ashton, Jean. "Picking up the Pieces." In *To Preserve and Protect*, , 109–15. Washington, DC: Library of Congress, 2002.

Association of College & Research Libraries. *Guidelines for Borrowing and Lending Special Collections Materials for Exhibition*. Chicago: ACRL, 2005. http://www.ala.org/ala/acrl/acrlstandards/borrowguide.cfm (accessed 2010).

———. *Guidelines for the Interlibrary Loan of Rare and Unique Materials*. Chicago: ACRL, 2004. http://www.ala.org/ala/mgrps/divs/acrl/standards/rareguidelines.cfm (accessed 2010).

———. *Guidelines for the Security of Rare Books, Manuscripts, and other Special Collections*. Chicago: ACRL, 2006.

———. *Guidelines on the Selection and Transfer of Materials from General Collections to Special Collections*. Chicago: ACRL, 2008. http://www.ala.org/ala/mgrps/divs/acrl/standards/selectransfer.cfm (accessed 2010).

———. *Guidelines Regarding Thefts in Libraries*. Chicago: ACRL, 2003.

———. *Guidelines Regarding Security and Theft in Special Collections*. Chicago: ACRL, 2009.

———. Library Administration and Management Association. *Library Security Guidelines Document, June 7, 2001*. Chicago: American Library Association, 2007. http://www.ala.org/ala/lama/lamapublications/librarysecurity.htm (accessed 2010).

———. MAGERT. *Map Collection Security Guidelines*. Chicago: American Library Association, 2008.

————. MAGERT. *Map Collection Security Guidelines: Administrative Summary.* Chicago: American Library Association, 2008.

Association of Research Libraries. *Special Collections in ARL Libraries: A Discussion Report from the ARL Working Group on Special Collections.* Washington, DC: ARL, 2009. http://www.arl.org/bm~doc/scwg-report.pdf (accessed 2010).

Atlas Systems. Aeon. http://www.atlas-sys.com/products/aeon/ (accessed 2010).

Babbage, Charles. *Passages from the Life of a Philosopher.* Piscataway, NJ: Rutgers University Press, 1994.

Badwey, Rick. "Heading off Replevin through 'Due Diligence'" *Manuscripts* 57, no. 2 (Spring 2005): 97–104.

Bahr, Alice Harrison. *Book Theft and Library Security Systems, 1978–79.* White Plains, NY: Knowledge Industry Publications, 1978.

————. *Book Theft and Library Security Systems, 1981–82.* White Plains, NY: Knowledge Industry Publications, 1981.

————. "The Theft in Our Midst." *Library & Archival Security* 9, nos. 3–4 (1989): 77–81.

Balas, Janet L. "Online Treasures—Security in the Library: Technology Brings a New Twist to an Old Problem." *Computers in Libraries* 23, part 5 (2003): 28–30.

Banks, Paul N., and Roberta Pilette, eds. *Preservation: Issues and Planning.* Chicago: American Library Association, 2000.

Barnard, Megan, ed. *Collecting the Imagination: The First Fifty Years of the Ransom Center.* Austin: University of Texas Press, 2007.

Barnhart, James. "Developing a Security Department." In *Cultural Property Protection from the Ground Up: Proceedings of the National Conference on Cultural Property Protection and International Conference on Museum Security, March 7–11, 1999,* 126–29. [Washington, DC: Smithsonian Institution, 1999].

Basbanes, Nicholas A. *A Gentle Madness: Bibliophiles, Bibliomanes, and the Eternal Passion for Books.* New York: Holt, 1995.

Baskes, Roger. "What Can the International Map Collectors' Society Do to Deter Map Thieves?" *Journal of the International Map Collectors' Society,* 103 (Winter 2005): 3–4. http://www.maphistory.info/baskes.html (accessed 2010).

Bass, Richard. "Collections Security." *Library Trends* 33 (1984): 39–48.

Beers, Henry Putney. *Spanish & Mexican Records of the American Southwest: A Bibliographical Guide to Archive and Manuscript Collections.* Tucson: University of Arizona / Tucson Corral of the Westerners, 1979.

Belanger, Terry. "Oberlin Conference on Theft Calls for Action." *Library Journal* 108 (15 November 1983): 2118.

Bellow, M. A. "Library Security, Materials Theft and Mutilation in Technological University Libraries in Nigeria." *Library Management* 19, no. 6 (1998): 379–83.

Berger, Sidney. "Special Collections and Security." *Focus on Security* 8 (January 1996): 8–17.

————. "What Is So Rare…Issues in Rare Book Librarianship." *Library Trends* 36 (1987): 9–22. https://www.ideals.uiuc.edu/bitstream/handle/2142/7513/librarytrendsv36i1c_opt.pdf?sequence=1 (accessed 2010).

Berkeley, Edmund, Jr. "Archival Security: A Personal and Circumstantial View." *Georgia Archive* 4, no. 1 (Winter 1976): 3–9.

Bickford, Christopher P. "Public Records and the Private Historical Society: A Connecticut Example." *Government Publications Review* 8A (1981): 311–20.

Billington, James A. "Here Today, Here Tomorrow: The Imperative of Collections Security." *American Libraries* 27, no. 7 (August 1996): 40–41.

Bingham, Karen Havill. *Building Security and Personal Safety.* Washington, DC: Association of Research Libraries, 1989. SPEC Kit 150.

Bland, Gilbert. Taped confession to the University of Delaware police. Newark, 1996. Available at Special Collections, University of Delaware, Newark.

Bond, W. H. "The Gutenberg Caper." *Harvard Magazine,* March/April 1986, 42–48.

Booth, Jennifer. "Dr. Drewe—A Cautionary Tale." *Art Libraries Journal* 28 (2003): 14–17.

Bornhofen, Frederick A. "Where Security Fits In: Behavioral Guidelines on What Is—and Is Not—Expected from a Security Department." *Security World* 15, no. 8 (August 1978): 92–93.

Boss, Richard W. "RFID Technology for Libraries." *Public Library Association Tech Notes.* 2004. http://www.ala.org/ala/pla/plapubs/technotes/rfidtechnology.cfm (accessed 2010).

————. "Security Technologies for Libraries: Policy Concerns and a Survey of Available Products." *Library Technology Reports* 35, no. 3 (1999): 271–356.

Bowers, Dan M. *Access Control and Personal Identification Systems.* Oxford: Butterworth-Heinemann, 1996.

Bowling, Mary Boone, and Richard Strassburg. "Security in the Reading Room: A Society of American Archivists Web Seminar." Web seminar presented to Society of American Archivists, Chicago, 7 June 2005. Compact disc audio recording and visual outline for a web seminar presented on 7 June 2005.

Boylan, Patrick. "Security Guidelines when Using Outside Contractors." Museums and Heritage Organization Policy Statements Series. http://www.museum-security.org/articles.html#contractors (accessed 2010).

Bozeman, Pat, ed. *Forged Documents: Proceedings of the 1989 Houston Conference.* New Castle: Oak Knoll, 1990.

Braaksma, Betty. "Zero Tolerance at the Library: The Work of the Thunder Bay Public Library's Security Task Force." *Library & Archival Security* 14, no. 2 (1998): 43–49.

Bradsher, James Gregory, ed. *Managing Archives and Archival Institutions.* Chicago: University of Chicago Press, 1989.

Brady, Eileen. "Getting the Word Out." In *Cultural Property Protection from the Ground Up: Proceedings of the National Conference on Cultural Property Protection and International Conference on Museum Security, March 7–11, 1999,* 102–6. [Washington, DC: Smithsonian Institution, 1999].

———. *Library/Archive/Museum Security: A Bibliography.* 5th ed. Moscow, ID: Catula Pinguis Press, 1995.

Brand, M. "Security of Academic Library Buildings." *Library & Archival Security* 3, no. 1 (1980): 39–47.

———., ed. *Security for Libraries: People, Buildings, Collections.* Chicago: American Library Association, 1984.

Bray, Thomas. *Proposals for the Encouragement and Promoting of Religion and Learning in the Foreign Plantations; and to Induce such of the Clergy of this Kingdom, as are Persons of Sobriety and Abilities, to Accept of a Mission to those Parts.* [London, 1696].

Brashear, J. K., J. J. Malone, and J. Thornton-Jaringe. "Problem Patrons: The Other Kind of Library Security." *Illinois Libraries* 63, no. 4 (1981): 343–51.

Bregman, Alvan. "Organizational Initiatives for Library Security: A North American Perspective." La coopération internationale au service de la sûreté des collections—Journée d'étude du 14 mai 2004. http://www.bnf.fr/PAGES/infopro/journeespro/pdf/surete/bregman.pdf (accessed 2010).

Breighner, Mary, William Payton, and Jeanne M. Drewes. *Risk and Insurance Management Manual for Libraries.* Chicago: American Library Association, 2005.

Broustas, Marios V. "Is Harvard Checking Employees' Records?" *The Harvard Crimson,* December 1994. http://www.thecrimson.com/article.aspx?ref=228062 (accessed 2010).

Brown, David. "William Shakespeare Folio Worth £15m Recovered 10 Years After Being Stolen." *Times,* 12 July 2008. http://www.timesonline.co.uk/tol/news/uk/article4316464.ece (accessed 2010).

Brown, Ellen Firsching. "What Happens when Uncle Sam Comes Calling for your Collection?" *Fine Books & Collections,* September/October 2008, 31–35.

Brown, Karen E., and Beth Lindblom Patkus. *Collections Security: Planning and Prevention for Libraries and Archives.* Preservation Leaflet 3.11 Andover: NEDCC, 2007. http://www.nedcc.org/resources/leaflets/3Emergency_Management/11CollectionsSecurity.php (accessed 2010).

Brown, Marion. *Problem Patron Manual.* Schenectady: Schenectady Public Library, 1981.

Brown, Michael F. *Criminal Investigation: Law and Practice.* 2nd ed. Boston: Butterworth-Heinemann, 2001.

Brown-Syed, C. "Some Observations on Systematic Book Theft." *Library & Archival Security* 15, no. 1 (1999): 83–89.

Bryan, Alice. "Loss Control: The Museum and Its Collections." In *Insurance and Risk Management for Museums and Historical Societies,* Hamilton: Gallery Association of New York State and Division of Educational Services of the Metropolitan Museum of Art, 1985.

Buchman, Wolf. "Preservation: Buildings and Equipment." *Journal of the Society of Archivists* 20, no. 1 (April 1999): 5–23.

Bucklew, Patrick. "How I Stole a Ming Scroll." *Time,* 6 September 2004. http://www.time.com/time/magazine/article/0,9171,995033,00.html (accessed 2010).

Bureau of Justice Assistance. Operation Cooperation: Guidelines for Partnerships between Law Enforcement & Private Security Organizations. N. p., 2000.

Burke, Robert S., and Sam A. Adeloye. *A Manual of Basic Museum Security.* Leicester: International Council of Museums, 1986.

Burns Security Institute. *National Survey on Library Security*. Briarcliff Manor: Burns Security Institute, [1973].

Cady, Susan A. "Insuring the Academic Library Collection." *The Journal of Academic Librarianship* 25, no. 3 (May 1999): 211–15.

Campbell, M. A. "Archival Security Program of the Society of American Archivists." *American Archivist* 38 (October 1975): 499–500.

Campbell, Tony. "Map History/History of Cartography: The Gateway to the Subject." http://www.maphistory.info/index.html (accessed 2010).

———. "How Should We Respond to Early Map Thefts?" http://www.maphistory.info/response.html (accessed 2010).

Canal, B. A. "Libraries Attract More Readers: Investing in Library Safety." *Indiana Libraries* 17, no. 1 (1998): 15–17.

Capel, Vivian. *Security Systems and Intruder Alarms*. Oxford: Heinemann Newnes, 1986.

Carlucci, April. "Library Security for Maps: Report on the Program Sponsored by the Map and Geography Round Table of the American Library Association, Held in Washington, DC, on Sunday, 24 June 2007." *Cartographiti: The Newsletter of the Map Curators' Group of the British Cartographic Society*, no. 79 (Summer 2007): 11–16.

Carter, Lisa. "It's the Collections that Are Special" (11 February 2009). http://inthelibrarywiththeleadpipe.org/2009/its-the-collections-that-are-special/#_edn1 (accessed 2010).

Castaing, Frédéric. "Le commerce du livre ancien et des manuscrits: la question de la provenance des oeuvres." La coopération internationale au service de la sûreté des collections—Journée d'étude du 14 mai 2004. http://www.bnf.fr/pages/infopro/journeespro/pdf/surete/castaing.pdf (accessed 2010).

CD Associates. *CCTV*. Available on-line at: http://www.business-crime.co.uk/leicestershire/cctv.html (accessed 2010).

Center, Clark, and Donnelly Lancaster. *Security in Special Collections*. SPEC kit 284. Washington, DC: Association of Research Libraries, Office of Leadership and Management Services, 2004.

Central Station Alarm Association. *A Practical Guide to Central Station Burglar Alarm Systems*. 2nd ed. Washington, DC: Central Station Alarm Association, 1997. First published as *An Insurance Guide to Selecting a Burglar Alarm System*. Washington, DC, 1993.

———. *Standards Document (CSAA GOT 1)*. Washington, DC: Central Station Alarm Association, 1998. http://www.csaaul.org/CSAAGOT1. htm (accessed 2006; now unavailable).

———. *Standards Document (CSAA STA 1)*. Washington, DC: Central Station Alarm Association, 1996. http://www.csaaul.org/CSAASTA1.htm (accessed 2010).

Cerve, Kate. "Stolen Torahs Stun Congregations, Including One Near St. Louis." *Kansas City Star*, 11 July 2008. http://www.kansascity.com/105/story/701961.html (accessed 2008; now unavailable).

Chadwick, William E. "Special Collections Library Security: An Internal Audit Perspective." *Journal of Library Administration* 25, no. 1 (November 1998): 15–31.

Chaffinch, Lynn. "Surviving and Reacting to a Collection Loss." In *Cultural Property Protection from the Ground Up: Proceedings of the National Conference on Cultural Property Protection and International Conference on Museum Security, March 7–11, 1999*, 96–99. [Washington, DC: Smithsonian Institution, 1999].

Chaney, Michael, and Alan F. MacDougall. *Security and Crime Prevention in Libraries*. Aldershot, UK: Ashgate, 1992.

"Charges against Suspect in Bible Theft Dismissed." *The Harvard Crimson*, 4 December 1969. http://www.thecrimson.com/article.aspx?ref=351509 (accessed 2010).

Charney, Noah, ed. *Art and Crime: Exploring the Dark Side of the Art World*. New York: Praeger, 2009.

Chartered Institute of Library and Information Professionals. Rare Books and Special Collections Group. Theft of Book and Manuscripts Materials from Libraries: An Advisory Code of Conduct for Booksellers and Librarians. 2005. http://www.cilip.org.uk/cgibin/MsmGo.exe?grab_id=154&EXTRA_ARG=GRAB_ID%3D149%00%26PAGE_ID%3D2559488%00%26HIWORD%3DGUIDELINE%2BTHEFTS%2Bguidelines%2Btheft&host_id=42&page_id=921088&query=thefts+guidelines&hiword=GUIDELINE+guidelines+THEFT+thefts+ (accessed 2010).

Cherry, Don T. *Total Facility Control*. Boston: Butterworth-Heinemann, 1986.

ChexSystems. "Sample Consumer Report." (2009). https://www.consumerdebit.com/consumer-info/us/en/chexsystems/SampleChexCnsrRpt.pdf (accessed 2010).

Christian, John F., and Shonnie Finnegan. "On Planning an Archive." *American Archivist* 2, no. 4 (October 1974): 573–78.

Christie-Miller, Ian Russell. "New Tools for Old Paper." *The Book Collector* 58 (Autumn 2009): 383–89.

———. "The Web Site for Watermarks." http://www.earlypaper.com/ (accessed 2010).

Christoffersen, John. "Map Thief Ordered to Pay $2.3M." FoxNews.com (22 May 2007). http://www.foxnews.com/wires/2007May22/0,4670,StolenMaps,00.html (accessed 2007; now unavailable).

Cieszynski, Joe. *Closed Circuit Television*. Oxford: Newnes, 2001.

Clarkson, William, et al. "Fingerprinting Blank Paper Using Commodity Scanners." *Proceedings IEEE Symposium on Security and Privacy* (May 2009). http://citp.princeton.edu/paper/ (accessed 2010).

Columbia Daily Tribune, 22 April 1995. http://archive.columbiatribune.com/1995/apr/19950422news13.htm (accessed 2010).

———. (24 April 1995). http://archive.columbiatribune.com/1995/apr/19950425news16.htm (accessed 2010).

The Complete Library Safety and Security Manual: A Comprehensive Resource Manual for Academic and Public Library Professionals and Law Enforcement Officers. Goshen, KY: Campus Crime Prevention Programs, 2001.

Corwin, Brook. "No Background Checks Slated despite Arrests." *Daily Tar Heel*, 30 August 2001. http://media.www.dailytarheel.com/media/storage/paper885/news/2001/08/30/University/No.Background.Checks.Slated.Despite.Arrests-1344110.shtml (accessed 2005; now unavailable).

Cox, Richard J. "Collectors and Archival, Manuscript, Rare Book Security." *Focus on Security* 26 (April 1995): 19–27.

Council for Museums, Archives, and Libraries. *Security in Museums, Archives and Libraries*. London: Resource, 2003.

Council for the Prevention of Art Theft. *Code of Due Diligence for Dealers*. (1998). http://www.findstolenart.com/Default.asp?sac=5 (accessed 2010).

Cowan, C. Wesley. *Historic Americana Auction: Remnants of a Gentle Madness, The Stephen C. Blumberg Library of Americana*. Cincinnati: Cowan, 1999.

Cravey, Pamela. *Protecting Library Staff, Users, Collections and Facilities: A How-To-Do-It Manual*. New York: Neal Schuman, 2001.

Cremers, Ton. "…And the Curator Did It." *Rogues Gallery: An Investigation into Art Theft*. AXA Art Conference, London, England, 1 November 2005. http://www.museum-security.org/insider-theft.pdf (accessed 2010).

———. Museum Security Network. http://www.museum-security.org/frameengels.html (accessed 2010).

Cummin, Wilbur B. "Institutional, Personal Collection & Building Security Concerns." In *Security for Libraries: People, Buildings, and Collections*, edited by Marvine Brand, 24–50. Chicago: American Library Association, 1984.

Cupp, Christian M. "Security Considerations for Archives: Rare Book, Manuscript, and Other Special Collections." Wright-Patterson Air Force Base, March 1989. http://www.eric.ed.gov/ERICDocs/data/ericdocs2sql/content_storage_01/0000019b/80/1f/40/1d.pdf (accessed 2006; now unavailable).

Curry, Ann, Susanna Flodin, and Kelly Matheson. "Theft and Mutilation of Library Materials: Coping with Biblio-Bandits." *Library and Archival Security* 15, no. 2 (2000): 9–26.

Curtis, Gregory. "Forgery Texas Style: The Dealers Who Buy and Sell Historic Texas Documents Move in a World of Big Money, Big Egos, and Big Mistakes." *Texas Monthly*, March 1989.

———. "Highly Suspect: A Famous Letter from the Alamo May Very Well Be a Twentieth-Century Fraud." *Texas Monthly*, March 1989.

Dahl, Edward H. "Facsimile Maps and Forgeries." *Archivaria 10: Archives and Medicine* (1980–81): 261–63.

Damjanovski, Vlado. *CCTV: Networking and Video Technology*. 2nd ed. New York: Elsevier, 2005.

Daniels, Maygene F., and Timothy Welch. *A Modern Archives Reader: Basic Reading on Archival Theory and Practice*. Washington, DC: National Archives Trust Fund Board, 1984.

DataDot Technology, Ltd. http://www.datadotdna.com/ (accessed 2010).

DeRosa, F. J. "The Disruptive Patron." *Library and Archival Security* 3, nos. 3–4 (1980): 29–37.

Dixon, Leon. "Keys & Locks: Technical Aspects of Locking Devices." In *Cultural Property Protection from the Ground Up: Proceedings of the National Conference on Cultural Property Protection and International Conference on Museum Security, March 7–11, 1999,* 130–33. [Washington, DC: Smithsonian Institution, 1999]. http://www.museum-security.org/locks-and-keys.htm (accessed 2010).

Dizard, R. "Safe and Sound: Protecting the Collections of the Library of Congress." *Library of Congress Information Bulletin* 57, no. 6 (1998): 144–45.

Dodson, Minot. "Why Choose a Contract Guard Service?" *Cultural Property Protection from the Ground Up: Proceedings of the National Conference on Cultural Property Protection and International Conference on Museum Security, March 7–11, 1999.* [Washington, DC: Smithsonian Institution, 1999]. Pp. 27–28.

Doon, Ellen. "Beinecke Library's New Processing Facility." *Manuscript Repositories Newsletter* (Summer 2007). http://www.archivists.org/saagroups/mss/summer2007.asp (accessed 2010).

Dow, C. "Library Rules, Policies, and Library Security." *Nebraska Library Association Quarterly* 31, no. 1 (1999): 16–26.

Duggar, D. C. "Security and Crime in Health Sciences Libraries in the Southern United States." *Medical Reference Services Quarterly* 18, no. 1 (1999): 37–48.

East, Dennis, and William G. Myers. "Get the Thief 'Out of the Business': Diary of a Theft." *RBMS* 13, no. 1 (Fall 1998): 27–47.

Eichorn, Martin. *Konflikt und Gefahrensituationen in Bibliotheken: Ein Leitfaden für die Praxis.* Bad Honnef: Bock & Herchen, 2006.

Ekman, Paul. *Telling Lies: Clues to Deceit in the Marketplace, Politics and Marriage.* New York: W. W. Norton, 1985.

Elliott, J. "Disturbed Clients." *Unabashed Librarian* 44 (1982): 16–17.

Ellis, Judith, ed. *Keeping Archives.* Brunswick: D. W. Thorpe & Australian Society of Archivists, 1993.

Exlibris discussion list archives. http://palimpsest.stanford.edu/byform/mailing-lists/exlibris/ (before November 2006; now unavailable) and http://www.lsoft.com/scripts/wl.exe?SL1=EXLIBRIS-L&H=LISTSERV.INDIANA.EDU (after November 2006; accessed 2011).

Falk, John. "Majoring in Crime—The Untold Story of the 'Transy Book Heist' is One Part *Ocean's 11,* One Part *Harold & Kumar:* Four Kentucky College Kids Who Had Millions to Gain and Nothing to Lose." *Vanity Fair,* December 2007.

Fay, John. *Security Dictionary.* Alexandria, VA: ASIS International, 2000.

Fay, John Jay, ed. *Encyclopedia of Security Management.* 2nd ed. Burlington: Butterworth-Heinmann, 2007.

———. *Security Management Essentials.* Oxford: Butterworth-Heinemann, 2001.

Federal Bureau of Investigation. "Stolen Treasures: The Case of the Missing Maps." http://www.fbi.gov/page2/september06/maps092806.htm (accessed 2008; now unavailable).

———. "Theft Notices & Recoveries: Isabella Stewart Gardner Museum." http://www.fbi.gov/hq/cid/arttheft/northamerica/us/isabella/isabella.htm (accessed 2008; now unavailable).

Fennelly, Lawrence J., ed. *Handbook of Loss Prevention and Crime Prevention.* 3rd ed. Boston: Butterworth-Heinemann, 1996.

———. *Museum, Archive and Library Security.* Boston: Butterworths, 1983.

Feldman, Franklin, Stephen E. Weil, & Susan Duke Biederman. *Art Law: Rights and Liabilities of Creators and Collectors.* 2 vols. Boston: Little, Brown, 1986.

Feldman, Franklin, Stephen E. Weil, & Susan Duke Biederman. *Art Law: Rights and Liabilities of Creators and Collectors. 1988 Supplement.* Boston: Little, Brown, 1988.

Fides Consulting. Provenanced.com. http://www.provenanced.com (accessed 2008; now unavailable).

Finnegan, William. "A Theft in the Library: The Case of the Missing Maps." *New Yorker,* 17 October 2005.

Fischer, Robert J., and Gion Green. *Introduction to Security.* 7th ed. Boston: Butterworth-Heinemann, 2004.

———. *Introduction to Security.* 8th ed. Boston: Elsevier Butterworth-Heinemann, 2008.

——— & Richard Janoski. *Loss Prevention and Security Procedures: Practical Applications for Contemporary Problems.* Boston: Butterworth Heinemann, 2000.

Fleet, Chris. "Report of the 'Responding to Theft' Seminar, Held at the National Library of Wales on 25 April 2002." http://www.maphistory.info/aberseminar.html (accessed 2010).

Foley, Alison M. "Can One Man Make a Difference? An Analysis of the Effects of the Crimes of Gilbert Bland on Rare Book and Special Collections Security Measures and a Review of the Evolution of Recommended Security Guidelines." Master's thesis, University of North Carolina Chapel Hill, 2005. http://ils.unc.edu/MSpapers/3048.pdf (accessed 2010).

Fondren Library. "Off-Site Shelving Appendix: Woodson Materials. Recommendations for Handling Rare Books, Special Collections, and University Archives Materials, November, 2002." http://library.rice.edu/collections/about-fondrens-collections/collection-development/collection-maintenance/appendix (accessed 2010).

———. "Selection Guidelines for Off-Site Shelving." 2002. http://library.rice.edu/collections/about-fondrens-collections/collection-development/collection-maintenance/guidelines-off-site-shelving (accessed 2010).

Foreman, Chris. "Greensburg Library Scuffle Injures Director; Police Seek Couple." *Pittsburg Tribune-Review*, 14 March 2008. http://www.pittsburghlive.com/x/pittsburghtrib/search/s_557237.html (accessed 2010).

Galvin, Theresa. "The Boston Case of Charles Merrill Mount: The Archivist's Arch Enemy." *American Archivist* 53 (Summer 1990): 442–50.

Gandert, S. R. *Protecting your Collection: A Handbook, Survey, & Guide for the Security of Rare Books, Manuscripts, Archives, & Works of Art.* New York: Haworth, 1982.

Garcia, Mary Lynn. *The Design and Evaluation of Physical Security Systems.* Boston: Butterworth-Heinemann, 2001.

Gargan, Pat. "Options for Staffing a Security Force." In *Cultural Property Protection from the Ground Up: Proceedings of the National Conference on Cultural Property Protection and International Conference on Museum Security, March 7–11, 1999*, 32–36. [Washington, DC: Smithsonian Institution, 1999].

Gavin, Robert. "Update: State Worker Accused of Stealing Historic Documents." *Times Union*, 28 January 2008. http://timesunion.com/AspStories/story.asp?storyID=658903&category=&BCCode=HOME&newsdate=1/28/2008 (accessed 2008; now unavailable).

Gibbs, Paula. "Wiscasset, State Lose; Declaration of Independence to Stay in Virginia." *Wiscasset Newspaper*, 28 February 2008. http://wiscassetnewspaper.maine.com/2008-02-28/wiscasset_state_lose.html (accessed 2008; now unavailable).

Gill, Martin. *CCTV.* Leicester: Perpetuity, 2003.

———. "Security in Libraries: Matching Responses to Risks." *Liber Quarterly* 18, no. 2 (September 2008): 101–6.

Gnissios, Todd. "R.F.I.D.—Radio Frequency Identification Systems." 13 April 2005. http://www.slais.ubc.ca/courses/libr500/04-05-wt2/www/T_Gnissios/index.htm (accessed 2010).

Goldberg, M. "The Never-ending Saga of Library Theft." *Library & Archival Security* 12, no. 1 (1993): 87–100.

Goodbody, Margaret, and Jennifer R. Evans. "Protecting Access and Materials in Public Library Special Collections." *Technical Services Quarterly* 22, no. 3 (2005): 19–28.

Gordon, Nicole. "Archives and Security Bibliography (Draft)." Washington, DC: National Archives & Records Administration, 2002. http://www.archives.gov/research/alic/reference/archives-resources/security.html (accessed 2010).

Goshen College. *Campus Crime Prevention Programs. Library Safety & Security: A Comprehensive Manual for Library Administrators and Police and Security Officers.* Goshen, KY: Campus Crime Prevention Programs, 1992.

Gothberg, H. M. "Managing Difficult People: Patrons (and Others)." *The Reference Librarian* 19 (1987): 269–84.

Government of British Columbia. Ministry of Management Services. *Privacy Guidelines for Use of Video Surveillance Technology by Public Bodies.* 2000. http://www.mser.gov.bc.ca/foi_pop/main/video_security.htm (accessed 2002; now unavailable).

Grace, Melissa. "SoHo Gallery Sues Unemployed Brooklyn Man, Christie's over Warhol Painting." *Daily News*, 6 February 2008. http://www.nydailynews.com/news/2008/02/06/2008-02-06_soho_gallery_sues_unemployed_brooklyn_ma.html (accessed 2010).

Graham, Warren. *Black Belt Librarians: Every Librarian's Real World Guide to a Safer Workplace.* Charlotte: Purple Heart Press, 2006.

Greene, Mark A., and Dennis Meissner. "More Product, Less Process: Revamping Traditional Archival Processing." *American Archivist* 68 (Fall/Winter 2005): 208–63.

Greenwood, L., and H. McKean. "Effective Measurement and Reduction of Book Loss in an Academic Library." *Journal of Academic Librarianship* 11, no. 5 (1985): 275–83.

Grimes, Andrea V. "Card Catalogs: Adaptive Reuse Suggestions." Exlibris-L electronic discussion list, 12 August 2009.

Grossberg, David. "The Lessons of Mark Hofmann." *Autograph Magazine*, April 2008, 54–59.

Guggenheim Found. v. Lubell, 153 A.D.2d 143, 145, 550 N.Y.S.2d 618 [1990], affd. 77 N.Y.2d 311, 567 N.Y.S.2d 623, 569 N.E.2d 426 [1991]), 153 A.D.2d at 147, 550 N.Y.S.2d 618.

Guthrie, Ross. "Customer Service? Balancing Security and Customer Service." In *Cultural Property Protection from the Ground Up: Proceedings of the National Conference on Cultural Property Protection and International Conference on Museum Security, March 7–11, 1999*, 71–72. [Washington, DC: Smithsonian Institution, 1999].

Hajicek, John. "Beyond All Description: A Historical Analysis of Cultural Intolerance in the Case of Missing Rare Mormon Books." http://www.mormonism.com/Outrages.htm (accessed 2010).

Häkli, Esko. "Paradise Lost: A Theft from Helsinki University Library." *Liber Quarterly* 12, no. 4 (2002): 320–28.

Hanff, Peter E. "The Story of the Berkeley Library Theft." *C&RL News* 45 (June 1984): 284–87.

Hanley, Bryan. "Crime Prevention." Australian Institute of Criminology. Art Crime, Protecting Art, Protecting Artists, and Protecting Consumers Conference, 2–3 December 1999. http://www.aic.gov.au/conferences/artcrime/hanleycp.pdf (accessed 2001; now unavailable).

"Hard Questions about Background Checks." CSO Online (March 2006). http://www.csoonline.com/read/030106/background_checks.html (accessed 2010).

Hardwick, Bonnie. *The Function and Force of Reader Registration Procedures.* Denver: Society of Colorado Archivists, 1992.

Harris, Carolyn. "The Preservation Considerations in Electronic Security Systems." *Library & Archival Security* 11, no. 1 (1991): 35–42.

Harris, John F. & Allan Lengal. "Berger Will Plead Guilty to Taking Classified Paper." *Washington Post*, 1 April 2005, A01. http://www.washingtonpost.com/wp-dyn/articles/A16706-2005Mar31.html (accessed 2010).

———, and Susan Schmidt. "Archives Staff Was Suspicious of Berger; Why Documents Were Missing Is Disputed." *Washington Post*, 22 July 2004.

Harry Ransom Humanities Research Center. "Perpetrator of Rare Book Theft at Harry Ransom Center Sentenced." News release, 2 February 2004. http://www.hrc.utexas.edu/press/releases/2004/theft.html (accessed 2010).

Hartford Courant, 27 November 1996. *See also* Martineau, Kim.

Harvey, Miles. *The Island of Lost Maps: A True Story of Cartographic Crime.* New York: Random House, 2000.

———. "Mr. Bland's Evil Plot to Rule the World." *Outside Magazine*, June 1997. http://outside.away.com/outside/magazine/0697/9706bland.html (accessed 2010).

Harwood, Emily. *Digital CCTV: A Security Professional's Guide.* Boston: Butterworth-Heinemann, 2008.

Healey, R. M. "The Borrowers: High Profile Thefts from Libraries and Dealers Appear to Be on the Increase." *Rare Book Review*, November 2006, 28–32.

Heslinga, Els Van Eijck Van. "Catch as Catch Can." *Liber Quarterly* 12 (2002): 316–19. http://webdoc.gwdg.de/edoc/aw/liber/lq-4-02/316-319.pdf (accessed 2004; now unavailable).

Hewett, David. "Good Faith Purchaser Protests City Treatment, Dover Records Returned." *Maine Antiques Digest*, June 2008, 28-A.

Hill, Justin. "Books of Mormon May Resurface if Thief Was after Cash." *Salt Lake City Tribune*, 12 April 2006. http://msn-list.te.verweg.com/2006-April/004974.html (accessed 2006; now unavailable).

Hitchcock, Robert M. "Case of a Missing Shakespeare." *Esquire*, December 1961.

Hoff-Wilson, Joan. "Access to Restricted Collections: The Responsibility of Professional Historical Organizations." *American Archivist* 46, no. 4 (Fall 1983): 441–47.

"Homeland Security: Guards, Earning Little." CBS News (29 May 2007). http://www.cbsnews.com/stories/2007/05/29/terror/main2860972.shtml (accessed 2010).

Honan, Edith. "New York Gallery Sues for Return of Stolen Warhol." Reuters, 5 February 2008. http://www.reuters.com/article/domesticNews/idUSN0528337820080205 (accessed 2010).

Honan, William H. "Ideas and Trends: Strip Search before Scholarship." *New York Times*, 28 May 1995. http://query.nytimes.com/gst/fullpage.html?res=990CE0DF103EF93BA15756C0A963958260 (accessed 2010).

Honey, Gerard. *Electronic Access Control*. Oxford: Newnes, 2000.

Honigsbaum, Mark. "Lost Worlds." *Observer Magazine*, 20 July 2003. http://observer.guardian.co.uk/magazine/story/0,11913,1001735,00.html (accessed 2010).

Hopf, Peter S. *Handbook of Building Security Planning and Design*. New York: McGraw-Hill, 1979.

Houghton, Beth. "Art Libraries as a Source of False Provenance." World Library and Information Congress: 69th IFLA General Conference and Council, 1–9 August 2003, Berlin. http://www.ifla.org/IV/ifla69/papers/047e-Houghton.pdf (accessed 2010).

Hrycyk, Don. "Surviving a Collection Loss: Working with Law Enforcement." Proceedings of the National Conference on Cultural Property Protection and International Conference on Museum Security, "Cultural Property Protection from the Ground Up." [Washington, DC: Smithsonian Institution, 1999]. http://www.museum-security.org/donh.htm (accessed 2010).

Hu, Vincent C., David F. Farriaiolo, and D. Rick Kuhn. *Assessment of Access Control Systems*. Interagency Report 7316. Gaithersburg, MD: National Institute of Standards and Technology, 2006. http://csrc.nist.gov/publications/nistir/7316/NISTIR-7316.pdf (accessed 2010).

Hulyk, Barbara, Jim Walsh, and George Barnum. *The Identification, Preservation and Security of Rare and Valuable Government Documents: A Selective Bibliography*. Rev. ed. Chicago: American Library Association, 1999. http://www.ala.org/ala/mgrps/rts/godort/godortcommittees/regp/ALA_print_layout_1_398847_398847.cfm (accessed 2010).

Huntsberry, J. Stephen. "Forged Identification: A Key to Library Archives." *Library & Archival Security* (Binghamton) 9, nos. 3–4 (1989): 69–74.

———. "Students Library Security Patrol: A Viable Alternative." *CAN* 49 (April 1992):

———. "Viva Blumberg: Lessons Learned." In *Cultural Property Protection from the Ground Up: Proceedings of the National Conference on Cultural Property Protection and International Conference on Museum Security, 7–11 March 1999*, 37–41. [Washington, DC: Smithsonian Institution, 1999]. http://www.museum-security.org/blumberg-huntsberry.htm (accessed 2010).

Inland Marine Underwriters Association and Society of American Archivists. *Libraries and Archives: An Overview of Risk and Loss Prevention*. New York: Inland Marine Underwriters Association, 1994.

"Intern Sold Stolen Civil War Documents on eBay." MSNBC, 4 April 2007. http://www.msnbc.msn.com/id/17952733/ (accessed 2010).

Israel, Lee. *Will You Forgive Me? Memoirs of a Literary Forger*. New York: Simon & Schuster, 2008.

Jackanicz, Donald W. "Theft at the National Archives: The Murphy Case, 1962–1975." *Library & Archival Security* 10, no. 2 (1990): 23–50.

Jackson, Marie. "Library Security: Facts and Figures." *Library Association Record* 93 (June 1991): 384.

"Jail for Stealing Pages from Rare Books." http://uk.news.yahoo.com/4/20090116/tuk-jail-for-stealing-pages-from-rare-bo-dba1618.html (accessed 2009; now unavailable).

Jenkins, John H. *Audubon and other Capers: Confessions of a Texas Bookmaker*. Austin, TX: Pemberton, 1976.

———. *Rare Books and Manuscript Thefts: A Security System for Librarians, Booksellers, and Collectors*. New York: Antiquarian Booksellers Association of America, 1982.

Jewish Community Relations Council of New York "Universal Torah Registry." http://www.jcrcny.org/html/torah1.html (accessed 2010).

Johansson, David. "Library Theft, Mutilation, and Preventative Security Measures." *Public Library Quarterly* 15, no. 4 (1996): 51–66.

Jones, Barbara M., comp. "Hidden Collections, Scholarly Barriers: Creating Access to Unprocessed Special Collections Materials in North America's Research Libraries" (Association of Research Libraries, 2003). http://www.arl.org/bm~doc/hiddencolls-whitepaperjun6.pdf (accessed 2010).

Jørgensen, Jesper Düring. "The Anatomy of a Crime Discovery after 25 Years: A Notable Case of Book Theft and Its Detection." *Liber Quarterly* 17 (2007)..

———. "Report on a Theft of Books, a Non-Fiction Detective Story." In *Care and Conservation of Manuscripts 9: Proceedings of the Ninth International Seminar Held at the University of Copenhagen, 14th–15th April 2005*, 113–24. Copenhagen: Museum Tusculanem Press, 2006.

Joseph, John. "UK Police Find Himmler/Churchill Archive Forgeries." http://in.reuters.com/article/worldNews/idININdia-33383120080503 (accessed 2010).

Kaempffer, William, and Natalie Missakian. "$2 Million Heist: Hamden Man Suspected in Yale Theft." *New Haven Register*, 30 November 2001.

Kahn, Miriam B. *The Library Security and Safety Guide to Prevention, Planning, and Response*. Chicago: American Library Association, 2008.

Kaplan, Fred. "Berger with a Side of Secret Documents: Is He a Criminal or a Klutz?" (21 July 2004). http://slate.msn.com/id/2104138 (accessed 2010).

Karatnytsky, Christine. "Lee Israel Article in Today's NY Times." Exlibris-L discussion list (25 July 2008).

Keiger, Dale. "An Audacious Map Thief Revealed." *Johns Hopkins Magazine*, February 2001. http://www.jhu.edu/~jhumag/0201web/arts.html#map (accessed 2010).

Keller, Steven R. *An Architect's Prize Building May Be Security's Nightmare*. Deltona, FL: Steven R. Keller, 1988.

———. *Conducting the Physical Security Survey*. Deltona, FL: Steven R. Keller, n. d.

———. "Hiring a Consultant: Clearing up Cloudy Skies" (1998). http://www.museum-security.org/consult.html (accessed 2010).

———. *The Most Common Security Mistakes that Most Museums Make*. Deltona, FL: Steven R. Keller, 1988.

———. *Security Training—Why We Have Failed*. Deltona, FL: Steven R. Keller, 1990.

———. "Understanding Risks." http://www.museum-security.org/keller/la.html (accessed 2010).

Kent, Allen, ed. "Library Theft." In *Encyclopedia of Library and Information Science* 62, supplement 25. New York: Dekker, 1998. Pp. 194–215.

King, Bob. "Know your Employee." Cornell University Cooperative Extension, Monroe County. N. d. http://counties.cce.cornell.edu/Monroe/ag/2002%20Know%20Your%20Employee.htm (accessed 2008; now unavailable).

Kinney, John M. "Archival Security and Insecurity." *American Archivist* 38 (October 1975): 493–97.

Knox Company. http://www.knoxbox.com/store/ (accessed 2010).

Korey, Marie E. "The Oberlin Conference on Theft." In *Rare Books, 1983–84*, edited by Alice D. Schreyer, 129–32. New York: Bowker, 1984.

Kovarsky, Joel. "Keeping it Safe, Keeping it Available: Theft Prevention in Special Collections." *Library Student Journal*, July 2007. http://www.librarystudentjournal.org/index.php/lsj/article/view/37/70 (accessed 2010).

Kowal, Kimberly C., and John Rhatigan. "The British Library's Vulnerable Collection Items Project." *Liber Quarterly* 18 (September 2008): 76–79. http://liber.library.uu.nl/publish/issues/2008-2/index.html?000247 (accessed 2010).

Kruegle, Herman. *CCTV Surveillance: Video Practices and Technology*. Boston: Butterworth-Heinemann, 1995.

La, Phuoc. "String of Library Thefts Dates back to '70s." *Yale Herald On-line*, 7 December 2001. http://www.yaleherald.com/archive/xxxii/12.07.01/news/p4a.html (accessed 2010).

Lacroix, Denis. "Librarians with Guns: Guadalajara's Military Public Library." *Feliciter* 51, no. 1 (2005): 50–51.

Land, Robert. "Defense of Archives against Human Foes." *American Archivist* 19 (1956): 121–38.

Lapélerie, François. "Copernic, Galilée, Ptolémée et les autres: traffics de livres précieux en Europe de l'Est." *Bulletin des bibliothèques de France* 46, no. 6 (December 2001): 6–13.

Lasilla, Kathrin Day. "Paper Trail Close-Ups—And Some Recent History of Sterling's Rare Maps." *Yale Alumni Magazine*, July/August 2007. http://www.yalealumnimagazine.com/issues/current/maps.html (accessed 2007; now unavailable).

Launet, Edouard. "Les manuscrits volés de la BNF, suite et fin?" *Libération* (1 March 2007). http://www.liberation.fr/culture/010192445-les-manuscrits-voles-de-la-bnf-suite-et-fin (accessed 2010).

Laville, Sandra. "Book World's Silence Helps Tome Raiders." *Guardian*, 2 February 2009. http://www.guardian.co.uk/uk/2009/feb/02/antiquarian-book-theft-library-crime (accessed 2010).

Lazarus, David. "Online Breach at Bancroft." *San Francisco Chronicle*, 23 November 2003.

Layne, Stevan P. *Closing the Barn Door: Dealing with Security Issues*. Nashville: American Association for State and Local History, 2002.

———. *The Cultural Property Protection Manual: The "How To" Guide for Managers/Administrators.* Rev. ed. Denver: Layne Consultants, 2002.

———. *The Official Library Security Manual.* Dillon: Layne Consultants, 1994.

Leab, Abigail, *see* Martin, Abby L.

LDP, LLC. http://www.maxmax.com/aSpecialtyInks.htm (accessed 2010).

Lehndorff, Betsy. "Denver Pharmacy Burglar Strikes from Above." *Rocky Mountain News*, 7 September 2007. http://www.rockymountainnews.com/drmn/local/article/0,1299,DRMN_15_5692592,00.html (accessed 2007; now unavailable).

Leppard, David. "Forgeries Revealed in the National Archives." *Times OnLine* 4 May 2008. http://www.timesonline.co.uk/tol/news/uk/article3867853.ece (accessed 2010).

Lerner, Ralph E., and Judith Bresler. *Art Law: The Guide for Collectors, Investors, Dealers, and Artists.* 3rd ed. New York: Practising Law Institute, 2005.

Libengood, Ronald S., and Bryan J. Perun. "The Key to Good Security: Proprietary Keyways and Electronic Locks." *Focus on Security* 2, no. 3 (April 1995): 6–16.

Library of Congress. "MARC Code List for Organizations." http://www.loc.gov/marc/organizations/ (accessed 2010).

———. "Ownership Marking of Paper-Based Materials." http://www.loc.gov/preserv/marking.html (accessed 2010).

———. Working Group on the Future of Bibliographic Control. *On the Record.* Washington, DC: Library of Congress, 2008. http://www.loc.gov/bibliographic-future/news/lcwg-ontherecord-jan08-final.pdf (accessed 2008; now unavailable).

"Library of Congress Materials 'Unaccounted For.'" *Archival Outlook* (November/December 2007): 13.

Lidman, Tomas. "Thieves in Our Cultural Heritage: Crime and Crime Prevention Measures in the Royal Library, Stockholm, 2000–2002." *Liber Quarterly* 12, no. 4 (2002): 309–15. http://webdoc.gwdg.de/edoc/aw/liber/lq-4-02/309-315.pdf (accessed 2010).

Lieberman, Ron. "Are Rubber Stamps Better than Chains? Security Concerns and the Marking of Books." *College & Undergraduate Libraries* 6, no. 1 (1999): 77–80.

———. "Security Concerns for Archival Collections." *AB Bookman's Weekly*, 14 October 1999.

Lieberman, Steve. "Former Rockland County Historical Society Curator Charged in Theft of Rare Book." *Journal News*, 1 June 2007. http://forums.delphiforums.com/n/mb/message.asp?webtag=nyackhigh&msg=1813.1 (accessed 2010).

Liemer, Ross. "Yale Map Heist Stirs University Concern." *Daily Princetonian*, 12 October 2006.

Ligue des Bibliothèques Européennes de Recherche/Association of European Research Libraries. "The LIBER Security Network of 2002—The Copenhagen Principles." *Liber Quarterly* 12 (2002): 329–32. http://webdoc.gwdg.de/edoc/aw/liber/lq-4-02/329-332.pdf (accessed 2004; now unavailable).

Lincoln, Alan Jay. *Crime in the Library: A Study of Patterns, Impact, and Security.* New York & London: Bowker, 1984.

———. "Library Legislation Related to Crime and Security." *Library & Archival Security* 10, no. 2 (1990): 103–15.

———. "Library Legislation Related to Crime and Security." *Library & Archival Security* 11, no. 1 (1990).

———. "Low Cost Security Options: Background Checks." *Library & Archival Security* 9, nos. 3–4 (1989): 107–13.

———. "Reducing Personal Crimes." *Library & Archival Security* 10, no. 1 (1990).

———. "Vandalism: Causes, Consequences, and Prevention." *Library & Archival Security* 9, nos. 3–41 (1989).

——— & Carol Zall Lincoln. *Library Crime and Security: An International Perspective.* New York: Haworth, 1987.

Lindsey, Robert. *A Gathering of Saints: A True Story of Money, Murder, and Deceit.* New York: Simon & Schuster, 1988.

Ling, Ted. *Solid, Safe, Secure: Building Archives Repositories in Australia.* Australia: Australian Archives, 1998.

Lisheron, Mark. "Book Bandit Rocked Ransom." *Austin American-Statesman*, 1 February 2004.

Lock, Carrie. "Deception Detection: Psychologists Try to Learn How to Spot a Liar." *Science News* 166, no. 5 (31 July 2004): 72. http://www.sciencenews.org/articles/20040731/bob8.asp (accessed 2005; now unavailable).

Lopresti, Robert. "Map Theft News." Exlibri-L electronic discussion list, 11 January 2008.

———. "Map Theft News 2." Exlibris-L electronic discussion list, 14 January 2008.

Lorello, Daniel. "Voluntary Statement." Rensselaer County, NY. 24 January 2008. http://blogs.timesunion.com/capitol/wp-content/uploads/2008/01/lorello.pdf (accessed 2008; now unavailable).

Lorenzen, M. "Security in the Public Libraries of Illinois." *Illinois Libraries* 79, no. 1 (1997): 21–22.

———. "Security in the Public Libraries of Missouri." *Missouri Library World* 1, nos. 3–4 (1996): 15–17.

———. *Security Issues of Ohio Public Libraries.* ERIC, ED 416907. 1998.

———. "Security Issues in the Public Libraries of Three Midwestern States." *Public Libraries* 37, no. 2 (1998): 2–4.

———. *Security Issues of Academic Libraries.* ERIC, ED 396765. 1996.

———. *Security Problems of Ohio Academic Libraries.* ERIC, ED 367341. 1993.

Los Angeles Police Department. Art Theft Detail. "Insurance Buy-Back Provision." http://www.lapdonline.org/art_theft_detail/content_basic_view/1476 (accessed 2010).

McAlister, Sheila. "Hargrett Library to Close for Renovations." Exlibris-L electronic discussion list (10 February 1999). http://palimpsest.stanford.edu/byform/mailing-lists/exlibris/1999/02/msg00135.html (accessed 2004; now unavailable).

McDade, Travis. *The Book Thief: The True Crimes of Daniel Spiegelman.* Westport: Praeger Publishers, 2006.

———. "Codifying Cultural Heritage: Why United States Criminal Law Suddenly Treats Our Rare Materials with Respect." *RBM: A Journal of Rare Books, Manuscripts, and Cultural Heritage* 9, no. 2 (Fall 2008): 205–12.

McGill, Douglas C. "Museum Says Ex-Chief Sold Off 30 Rare Letters." *New York Times*, 22 April 1987. http://query.nytimes.com/gst/fullpage.html?res=9B0DE6DB1F3CF931A15757C0A961948260 (accessed 2010).

McGlone, Tim. "Mariners' Museum Archivist Pleads Guilty to Charges Related to Artifacts Theft." *Pilotonline.com.* http://hamptonroads.com/2008/06/museum-archivist-pleads-guilty-artifacts-theft (accessed 2010).

McNally, Thomas. *Planning for Security in Academic Libraries.* Chicago: Association of College and Research Libraries, 1986.

McNeil, Beth, and Denise J. Johnson. *Patron Behavior in Libraries: A Handbook of Positive Approaches to Negative Situations.* Chicago: American Library Association, 1996.

Maclay, Kathleen. "Bancroft Library Reduces Hours in Preparation for Move, Retrofit" (18 March 2005). http://www.berkeley.edu/news/media/releases/2005/03/18_librarymove.shtml (accessed 2010).

Maclean, Norman. *Young Men and Fire.* Chicago: University of Chicago Press, 1992.

"Man Gets Probation for Stealing Letters." *Hartford Courant* 27 October 1996.

Mandel, Carol. "Hidden Collections. The Elephant in the Closet." *RBM: A Journal of Rare Books, Manuscripts, and Cultural Heritage* 5, no. 2 (2004): 106–13. http://www.ala.org/ala/acrl/acrlpubs/rbm/backissues-vol5no2/mandel.pdf (accessed 2010).

Mandelbaum, Albert J. *Fundamentals of Protective Systems: Planning, Evaluation, Selection.* Springfield: Charles C. Thomas, 1973.

Mann, Joan. "IT Education's Failure to Deliver Successful Information Systems: Now Is the Time to Address the IT-User Gap." *Journal of Information Technology Education* 1, no. 4 (2002): 253–67. http://jite.org/documents/Vol1/v1n4p253-267.pdf (accessed 2010).

MapHist electronic discussion list. http://www.maphist.nl (accessed 2010).

"Marking of Materials." *Library & Archival Security* 4, nos. 1–2 (1982): 47–53.

Marryat, Frederick. *Masterman Ready; or, The Wreck of the Pacific.* 3 vols. London: Longmans, etc., 1841–42.

[Martin, Abigail Leab] Abigail Leab. "The Saying and the Doing: A Survey of Security and Theft Prevention Measures in U. S. Archives." Master's thesis, University of British Columbia, 1998.

———. "The Saying and the Doing: The Literature and the Reality of Theft Prevention Measures in US Archives—Part 1." *Library & Archival Security* 15, no. 2 (2000): 27–76.

———. "The Saying and the Doing—Part 2: The Real World and the Future." *Library & Archival Security* 16, no. 1 (2001): 7–46.

Martineau, Kim. Series of articles on E. Forbes Smiley. *Hartford Courant*, 2007.

Mason, Philip P. "Library and Archival Security: New Solutions to an Old Problem." *American Archivist* 38, no. 4 (October 1975): 477–92.

Matchett, Alan R. *CCTV for Security Professionals*. Boston: Butterworth-Heinemann, 2003.

Matheson, Ann. "Golfiana: A Theft from the National Library of Scotland." *Liber Quarterly* 12 (2002): 303–8. http://webdoc.gwdg.de/edoc/aw/liber/lq-4-02/303-308.pdf (accessed 2003; now unavailable).

Mattox, J. Douglas. *Philatelic Gold in the Archive*. Raleigh: Mattox Coins & Stamps, 1993.

Mayo, Hope. "MARC Cataloging for Medieval Manuscripts: An Evaluation." In "Bibliographic Access to Medieval and Renaissance Manuscripts: A Survey of Computerized Data Bases and Information Services," edited by W. M. Stevens, special issue, *Primary Sources & Original Works* 1, nos. 3–4 (1991): 93–152.

———. "Medieval Manuscript Cataloging and the MARC Format." *Rare Books & Manuscripts Librarianship* 6, no. 1 (1991): 11–22.

———. "Standards for Description, Indexing and Retrieval in Computerized Catalogs of Medieval Manuscripts." In *The Use of Computers in Cataloging Medieval and Renaissance Manuscripts: Papers from the International Workshop in Munich 10–12 August 1989*, edited by Menso Folkerts and Andreas Kühne, 10–40. *Algorismus: Studien zur Geschichte der Mathematik und der Naturwissenschaften, Heft 4*. Munich: Institut für Geschichte der Naturwissenschaften, 1990.

Meighan, Patrick. "Old Nashua Tax Ledger Sold on eBay Stirs up Legal Dispute." *Nashua Telegraph*, 6 July 2007. http://www.nashuatelegraph.com/apps/pbcs.dll/article?AID=/20070706/NEWS01/207060373 (accessed 2008).

Melnichak, Marsha L. "Library's Goal of Public Safety Causes Conflict Among its Volunteers." *Northwest Arkansas Times*, 29 October 2007. http://www.nwanews.com/nwat/News/58737 (accessed 2008; now unavailable).

Menges, Gary L. "Security of Rare Books, Manuscripts, and Special Collections." *PNLA Quarterly* 53 (Winter 1989): 18.

Menzel v. List, 22 A.D.2d 647, 253 N.Y.S.2d 43 [1964].

Metcalf, Keyes. *Planning Academic and Research Library Buildings*. New York: McGraw-Hill, 1965.

———. *Planning the Academic Library*. Newcastle: Oriel Press, 1971.

Microstamp Corporation. http://www.microstampusa.com/ (accessed 2010).

Microtrace, LLC. http://www.microtracesolutions.com (accessed 2010).

Miller, Kirsteen. *The Columbia Conspiracy: A Story of Secret Tunnels, Mad Scientists, and Maple Syrup*. http://www.kikistrike.com/chap1.htm (accessed 2010).

Missing and Stolen Maps Database. http://missingmaps.info/maps.htm (Accessed 2010).

MissingMaterials.org. http://missingmaterials.org/ (Accessed 2010).

Moffett, William A. *The Shinn Lists*. Oberlin, OH: Oberlin College, 1982.

Morawski, Ed. *How to Defeat Burglar Alarms—Not!: Dispelling Hollywood Myths*. N. p., 2007.

Morris, Adam. "Gangs Put Library under Siege." *Edinburgh* (Scotland) *Evening News*, 17 March 2008. http://news.scotsman.com/latestnews/Gangs-put-library-under-siege.3884348.jp (accessed 2010).

Morris, John. *The Library Disaster Preparedness Handbook*. Chicago: American Library Association, 1986.

Mount, Charles Merrill. Statement of Charles Merrill Mount to the United States Senate Committee on the Judiciary on the Nomination of Stephen C. Breyer to the United States Supreme Court. [Washington, DC]. http://a255.g.akamaitech.net/7/255/2422/25aug20051329/www.gpoaccess.gov/congress/senate/judiciary/sh103-715/651-679.pdf (accessed 2008; now unavailable).

"Multiple Map Thief Behind Bars." *Thinkspain*, 12 August 2009. http://www.thinkspain.com/news-spain/16929/multiple-map-thief-behind-bars (accessed 2010).

Munn, Ralph. "The Problems of Theft and Mutilation." *Library Journal* 60 (1935): 589–92.

Myers, Gerald E. *Insurance Manual for Libraries*. Chicago: American Library Association, 1977.

Myers, Marcia J. *Insuring Library Collections and Buildings*. Washington, DC: Association of Research Libraries, 1991. SPEC Kit 178.

"NARA Seeks Public Assistance in Search for Stolen Papers." *Manuscript Society News* 27, no. 1 (2006): 21–22.

Nathe, Margarite Annette "A Learned Congress: A Closer Look at Book and Manuscript Thieves." Master's thesis, University of North Carolina Chapel Hill, 2005. http://etd.ils.unc.edu/dspace/bitstream/1901/187/1/master's+paper+PDF.pdf (accessed 2010).

National Archives and Records Administration. *Does That Document Belong in the National Archives?* Washington, DC: NARA, [2004?]. General Information Leaflet 74.

———. *General Records Schedule 21 Audiovisual Records*, Transmittal 8 (December 1998). http://www.archives.gov/records-mgmt/ardor/grs21.html (accessed 2006; now unavailable).

———. *National Archives II: National Archives at College Park: Using Technology to Safeguard Archival Records*. Technical Information Paper 13. [Washington, DC]: NARA, 1997.

———. "National Archives Recovers Stolen Documents." 11 February 2002. http://www.archives.gov/press/press-releases/2002/nr02-17.html (accessed 2010).

———. "Recover Lost and Stolen Documents." http://www.archives.gov/research/recover/ (accessed 2010).

———. "Statement by Archivist of the United States Allen Weinstein on the Sentencing of Howard Harner." 26 May 2005. http://www.archives.gov/press/press-releases/2005/nr05-71.html (accessed 2010)

———. Office of Inspector General. Report of 4 November 2005 on Samuel R. Berger.

National Employment Screening Services. *The Guide to Background Investigations*. 9th ed. Tulsa: National Employment Screening Services, 2000.

New York Attorney General's Office. "Attorney General Cuomo Announces Arrest of Education Department Employee for Stealing Hundreds of Historic State Artifacts." 28 January 2008 press release. http://www.oag.state.ny.us/press/2008/jan/jan28a_08.html (accessed 2008; now unavailable).

Newman, John, and Walter Jones, eds. *Moving Archives: The Experiences of Eleven Archivists*. Lanham, MD: Scarecrow, 2002.

———, and Chris Wolf. "The Security Audit." *Colorado Libraries* (Spring 1997): 19–21.

Nielsen, Erland Kolding. "Library Security Management: The Responsibility of the Chief Executive." *Liber Quarterly* 12 (2002): 296–302. http://webdoc.gwdg.de/edoc/aw/liber/lq-4-02/296-302.pdf (accessed 2005; now unavailable).

Nitecki, Danuta A., and Curtis L. Kendrick, eds. *Library Off-Site Shelving: Guide for High-Density Facilities*. Englewood, NJ: Libraries Unlimited, 2001.

Northeast Document Conservation Center. *Packing and Shipping*. Preservation Leaflet 4.12. Andover, MA: NEDCC, 2007. http://www.nedcc.org/resources/leaflets/4Storage_and_Handling/12PackingAndShipping.php (accessed 2010).

OCLC. *The Omaha Project: A Rare Book Adventure*. [Dublin: OCLC, 1990]. VHS tape.

Oftelie, Brad. "Results of the 1997 Survey of the Rare Books and Manuscript Section (RBMS). [Chicago: ACRL, 1997]. http://www.rbms.info/committees/membership_and_professional/rbms-survey97.pdf (accessed 2010).

O'Neill, James E. "Repelvin: A Public Archivist's Perspective." *College and Research Libraries* 40 (January 1979): 26–30.

O'Neill, Robert Keating, ed. *Management of Library and Archival Security: From the Outside Looking In*. New York: Haworth, 1998.

Olsen, R. J., and L. J. Ostler. "Get Tough on Theft: Electronic Theft Detection." *Library & Archival Security* 7, nos. 3–4 (1985): 67–77.

Olson, Brooke. "Material Stolen from Archives." http://www.museum-security.org/bermeo.html (accessed 2010).

"$1M Book Heist in NZ." *Script & Print* blog. March 2007. http://scriptandprint.blogspot.com/2007_03_01_archive.html (accessed 2010).

O'Toole, James M. *Understanding Archives and Manuscripts*. Chicago: Society of American Archivists, 1990.

Owen, Richard. "Cultural 'Robin Hoods' in Books Raid." Exlibris-L electronic discussion list, 19 July 1998.

Panagopulos, Bill. "More re Jefferson Davis-Transylvania U. Theft." Exlibris-L electronic discussion list, 23 May 2008.

Parfomak, Paul W. *Guarding America: Security Guards and U.S. Critical Infrastructure Protection*. Washington, DC: Congressional Research Service, 2004. http://www.italy.usembassy.gov/pdf/other/RL32670.pdf (accessed 2005; now unavailable).

Pearce-Moses, Richard. *A Glossary of Archival and Records Terminology*. Chicago: Society of American Archivists, 2005. http://www.archivists.org/glossary/index.asp (accessed 2010).

Pease, Allan, and Barbara Pease. *The Definitive Book of Body Language*. New York: Bantam, 2006.

Popa, Opritsa D. *Bibliophile and Bibliothieves: The Search for the Hildebrandslied and the Willehalm Codex*. Berlin: W. de Gruyter, 2003.

Patkus, Beth L. "Collection Security: The Preservation Perspective." *Journal of Library Administration* (1998): 67–89.

Peterson, Scott W. "Another Perspective on Replevin." *The Rail Splitter* 10, nos. 1–2 (Summer/Fall 2004): 8–10.

Pfleger, Katherine. "The Formula for Invisible Ink Will Remain Classified as Part of the CIA's Effort to Protect National Security. Really." *St. Petersburg Times*, 23 June 1999. http://www.fas.org/sgp/news/1999/06/spt062399.html (accessed 2010).

Post, Deborah Cromer. "Specifying a Security System." *Security World* 18 (February1981): 29–31.

Post, Richard. *Security Manager's Desk Reference*. London: Butterworths, 1986.

Potter, Lee Ann. "The Flip Side of History." *Prologue: The Quarterly Journal of the National Archives and Records Administration* 36, no. 44 (Winter 2004): 6–10.

———. "On the other Side: Hidden Treasures Abound on the Backsides of Historic Documents." *Social Education* 68, no. 6 (October 2004): 376–80.

Primary Research Group. *Trends in Rare Book & Documents Special Collection Management*. Dublin: Research and Markets, 2009.

Privacy Committee of New South Wales. *Invisible Eyes: Report on Video Surveillance in the Workplace*. No. 67, September 1995. http://www.austlii.edu.au/au/other/privacy/video (accessed 2010).

Purcell, A. D. "Abstractions of Justice: The Library of Congress's Great Manuscripts Robbery, 1896–1897." *American Archivist* 62, no. 2 (Fall 1999): 325–45.

Radio and Television News Directors Foundation. *Hidden Cameras, Hidden Microphones: At the Crossroads of Journalism, Ethics and the Law: News in the Next Century*. Washington, DC: Radio and Television News Directors Foundation, 1998. http://www.rtnda.org/resources/hiddencamera/contents.html (accessed 2005; now unavailable).

Rare Books and Manuscripts Section. Home Page, "Incidents of Theft." http://www.rbms.info/committees/security/theft_reports/index.shtml (accessed 2010).

———. "Reading Room Security and Beyond." Workshop at 39th RBMS Preconference in Washington, DC, 22 June 1998.

Raynor, Bob. "Replevin: The Issue of Manuscript Recovery." *The Rail Splitter* 10, nos. 1–2 (Summer/Fall 2004): 3–6.

Reed, Christopher. "Bibioklepts." *Harvard Magazine*, March-April 1997.

———. "The Slasher." *Harvard Magazine*, March-April 1997.

———. "Student, Teacher, Scholar." *Harvard Magazine*, March-April 1997.

Rendell, Ken W. "Problems of Archival Security." *AB Bookman's Weekly* 59 (June 1977): 3719–23.

"Responding to Theft." Seminar held at the National Library of Wales, 25 April 2002. http://www.maphistory.info/aberseminar.html (accessed 2010).

"RFID Zapper(EN)–22C3." http://itp.nyu.edu/everybit/blog/media/rfid-zapper.pdf (accessed 2010).

Rhodes, James B. "Alienation and Thievery: Archival Problems." *American Archivist* 29, no. 2 (April 1966): 197–208.

Rice University. Fondren Library. Woodsen Research Center. "Bird and Small Mammal Prints Theft Collection, 1859–2004." MS 544.

Ricci, Joseph. Testimony of Joseph Ricci, CAE Executive Director, National Association of Security Companies (NASCO), Before the House Homeland Security Committee Hearing on "The Direction and Viability of the Federal Protective Service." [Washington, DC, 2007]. http://homeland.house.gov/Site Documents/2007050111514-01127.pdf (accessed 2008; now unavailable).

Richards, J. H. "Missing in Action." *Journal of Academic Librarianship* 5, no. 5 (1979): 266–69.

Risk Reactor. http://www.riskreactor.com/Security_Inks/Security_Inks_Main.htm (accessed 2010).

Ritzenthaler, Mary Lynn. *Preserving Archives and Manuscripts*. Chicago: Society of American Archivists, 1993.

Roberts, M. "Guards, Turnstiles, Electronic Devices and the Illusion of Security." *College & Research Libraries* 29, no. 4 (July 1968): 259–75.

Rondeau, Mark E. "The Bard's Wild Ride: The Almost Forgotten Theft of a Shakespeare First Folio from Williams College." http://www.markrondeau.com/folio.html (accessed 2010).

Rosenbaum, Richard W. "Can We Predict Employee Theft?" *Security World*, October 1975.

Rude, Renee, and Robert Hauptman. "Theft, Dissimulation and Trespass: Some Observations on Security." *Library and Archival Security* 12, no. 1 (1989): 17–22.

Russell, Jenna. "BPL, Harvard Renew Map Quest: Inventory Taken after Thief's Plea." *Boston Globe*, 1 August 2006. http://www.boston.com/news/local/massachusetts/articles/2006/08/01/bpl_harvard_renew_map_quest/ (accessed 2010).

———. "Stolen Maps Find their Way back to Library's Collection." *Boston Globe*, 2 January 2008. http://www.boston.com/news/local/articles/2008/01/02/stolen_rare_maps_find_their_way_back_to_librarys_collection/ (accessed 2010).

Sable, Martin H. *The Protection of the Library and Archive: An International Bibliography.* New York: Haworth, 1984.

Sampson, K. J. "Disturbed and Disturbing Patrons: Handling the Problem Patron." *Nebraska Library Association Quarterly* 13, no. 1 (1982): 9–11.

Sampson, Rana, *False Burglar Alarms.* 2nd ed. Washington, DC: U. S. Department of Justice, Center for Problem-Oriented Policing, 2007. http://www.popcenter.org/problems/false_alarms/1 (accessed 2010).

Samuel, E. "Protection of Library and Archival Materials: A Case Study—New York Institute of Fine Arts." *Library & Archival Security* 2, nos. 3–4 (1978): 1.

Sanson, Jacqueline. "Stolen Manuscript: Lessons Learnt." *Liber Quarterly* 18, no. 2 (September 2008): 107–9. http://liber.library.uu.nl/publish/articles/000257/article.pdf (accessed 2010).

Sax, Joseph L. "Legal Concepts of Cultural Heritage Property." *RBM: A Journal of Rare Books, Manuscripts, and Cultural Heritage* 8, no. 1 (Spring 2007): 67–74.

———. *Playing Darts with a Rembrandt: Public and Private Rights in Cultural Treasures.* Ann Arbor: University of Michigan Press, 1999.

Scalet, Sarah D. "Good (and Bad) Background Checks." *Csooline.com*, 1 August 2004. http://www.csoonline.com/article/219483/Good_and_Bad_Background_Checks?page=1 (accessed 2010).

Scham, A. M. "Appraisals, Insurance, and Security." In *Managing Archives and Archival Institutions.* New York: Schuman, 1987.

Schneider, K. G. "Safe from Prying Eyes: Protecting Library Systems." *American Libraries* 30, no. 1 (1999): 98.

Schröeder, Margaret. "Special Protection for Special Collections." *Security Management On-line*, July 2004. http://www.securitymanagement.com/article/special-protection-special-collections (accessed 2011).

Scislowska, Monica. "Rare Books Stolen from University in Poland: Missing Manuscripts Humiliate Famous School." Seattlepi.com, 13 November 1999. http://seattlepi.nwsource.com/national/pole13.shtml (accessed 2010).

Sentry Security Systems Inc. http://www.cctvsentry.com/ (accessed 2010).

Shankle, Royce H., and Mary D. Shankle. *Comprehensive Manual of Locksmithing.* Marble Falls, TX: Shankle & Shankle, 1994.

Shenon, Philip. *The Commission: The Uncensored History of the 9/11 Investigation.* New York: Twelve, 2008.

Sheridan, L. W. "People in Libraries as Security Agents." *Library & Archival Security* 3, no. 1 (1980): 57–61.

Shiga, Jason. *Bookhunter.* Sparkplug Comics, 2007.

Shockowitz, Tonya. "Security for Archives, Rare Books and Special Collections: A Bibliographic Essay." *Current Studies in Librarianship Issues* 19, nos. 1–2 (Spring/Fall 1995): 4–12.

Shuman, Bruce A. *Case Studies in Library Security.* Westport, CT: Libraries Unlimited, 2002.

———. "Designing Personal Safety into Library Buildings." *American Libraries* 27 (August 1996)..

———. *Library Security and Safety Handbook: Prevention, Policies, and Procedures.* Chicago: American Library Association, 1999.

Smartwater. http://www.smartwater.com (accessed 2010).

Smith, F. E. "Questionable Strategies in Library Security Studies." *Library and Archival Security* 6, no. 3 (1984): 45–53.

———. "Supplementary Deterrents in Library Security." *Library & Archival Security* 6, no. 1 (1984): 49–57.

Society of American Archivists. "Archival and Special Collections Facilities: Guidelines for Archivists, Librarians, Architects, and Engineers." Chicago: SAA, 2008. Unpublished third draft.

———. *Libraries and Archives: An Overview of Risk and Loss Prevention.* Chicago: SAA, 1994.

———. *National Register of Lost or Stolen Archival Materials. List A. 1975 to Present.* Chicago: SAA, 1980.

———. *National Register of Lost or Stolen Archival Materials. List B. 1955 to 1975.* Chicago: SAA, 1977.

———. *Protecting Your Collections: A Manual of Archival Security.* Chicago: SAA, 1995.

Soete, George J. *Management of Library Security*. Washington, DC: Association of Research Libraries, 1999. SPEC Kit 247.

Sozanski, Edward J. "Theft of Confidence." *Philadelphia Inquirer Magazine*, 25 May 1999. http://www.museum-security.org/theft-of-confidence.htm (accessed 2010).

Soultrait, Vérène De. "Les maisons de vente aux enchères face au commerce des oeuvres volées." La coopération internationale au service de la sûreté des collections—Journée d'étude du 14 mai 2004. http://www.bnf.fr/fr/professionnels/anx_rel_int/a.cooperation_surete_collections.html (accessed 2010).

Spain, Norman M., and Gary Lee Elkin. "Private Security Versus Law Enforcement: There Is a Difference." *Security World* 16, no. 8 (August 1979): 32, 38, 40.

Spiel, Robert. "The Reporting Reaction—Should You or Shouldn't You?" In *Cultural Property Protection from the Ground Up: Proceedings of the National Conference on Cultural Property Protection and International Conference on Museum Security, March 7–11, 1999*, 100–101. [Washington, DC: Smithsonian Institution, 1999].

Sporn v. MCA Records, 58 N.Y.2d 482, 488, 462 N.Y.S.2d 413, 448 N.E.2d 1324 [1983].

Stack, Michael J. "Frequently Asked Questions (FAQ's) about Library Security Systems." *Library & Archival Security* 14, no. 2 (1998): 39–41.

———. "Library Theft Detection Systems—Future Trends and Present Strategies." *Library & Archival Security* 14, no. 2 (1998): 25–37.

Stafford Municipal School District. "Instructions for Making Certified/Licensed/Professional Application Position." http://www.stafford.msd.esc4.net/pdfs/SubApplication.pdf (accessed 2009).

Stalker, Laura & Henry Raine. "Rare Book Records in On-line Systems." *Rare Books and Manuscripts Librarianship* 11, no.2 (1996): 103–21.

Steele, Victoria. "Exposing Hidden Collections: The UCLA Experience." *College & Research Libraries News* 69, no. 2 (June 2008): 316–17, 331.

Stern, Gary M. "Replevin—Perspective from a Government Official Responsible for such Actions." *The Rail Splitter* 10, nos. 1–2 (Summer/Fall 2004): 6–7.

Stielow, Frederick J. "Archival Security." In *Managing Archives and Archival Institutions*, ed. by James Gregory Bradsher, 207–17. Chicago: University of Chicago Press, 1989.

Stillman, Michael. "Bookseller Sentenced to Fifteen Months for Theft, *AE Monthly* (August 2007). http://www.americanaexchange.com/NewAE/aemonthly/article.asp?f=1&page=1&id=524 (accessed 2010).

Stillwell, Margaret Bingham. *Librarians Are Human: Memories in and out of the Rare Book World, 1907–1970*. Boston: Colonial Society of Massachusetts, 1973.

Storey, Richard, A. M. Wherry, and J. F. Wilson. "Three Views on Security." *Journal of the Society of Archivists* 10 (July 1989): 108–14.

Strassburg, Richard. *Conservation, Safety, Security, and Disaster Considerations in Design*. Ithaca, NY: Cornell University Press, 1984.

———. "The Final Barrier: Security Considerations in Restricted Access Reading Rooms" In *Reference Services for Archives and Manuscripts*, ed. by Laura B. Cohen, 95–105. New York: Haworth, 1997.

———. "Security Bibliography." 2003. http://www.ferris.edu/library/SpecCollections/SAA/Security-Bibliography.pdf (accessed 2006; now unavailable).

Streit, Samuel. "Transfer of Materials from General Stacks to Special Collections." *Collection Management* 7 (Summer 1985): 33–46.

Stroup, Roger, Gary Stern, and Ivo Meisner. "Panel Discussion: Replevin." *Manuscript Society News* 26, nos. 2–3 (2005): 83–86.

Swann Galleries. *Medicine—Including Books from the Library of Doctor Henry Dolger and a Selection of Instruments; Natural History, Featuring Ornithological Books from the Watkinson Library, Trinity College, Hartford, Connecticut*. New York: Swann Galleries, 1989.

Switzer, Teri R. *Safe at Work? Library Security and Safety Issues*. Lanham: Scarecrow, 1999.

Taylor, D. "Enemies of Books." *C&RL News* 42, no. 9 (1981): 317–19.

Taylor, W. Thomas. *Texfake: An Account of the Theft and Forgery of Early Texas Printed Documents*. Austin: W. Thomas Taylor, 1991.

Texas Department of Public Safety. Bureau of Identification and Records. *Obtaining Proper Standards of Writing to Be Used for Comparison with Forged and Questioned Documents*. N. p., n. d.

Texas State Library and Archives Commission. *Missing List: Materials Missing from the Texas State Archives*. http://www.tsl.state.tx.us/arc/missingintro.html (accessed 2010).

Thomas, D. L. *Study on Control of Security and Storage of Holdings: A RAMP Study with Guidelines.* Paris: General Information Program & United Nations Education, Scientific, and Cultural Organization, February 1987. PGI-86/WS/23.

Thomas, Mark, Amée Piscitelli, and Julia Rholes. "Security and Preservation of the U.S. Congressional Serial Set." *Journal of Government Information* 21, no. 4 (1994): 351–66.

Thompson, Lawrence Sidney. *Bibliokleptomania.* Berkeley: Peacock, 1968.

Thompson, Michael. "A Legal and Ethical Look at the Making of Leaf Books." In *Disbound and Dispersed: The Leaf Book Considered*, ed. by Christopher de Hamel and Joel Silver. Chicago: The Caxton Club, 2005.

Thornton, Paul. "Academic 'Falls from Grace' by Stealing Church Records." *Edinburgh Evening News*, 13 May 2008. http://edinburghnews.scotsman.com/edinburgh/Academic—39falls-from-grace39.4077609.jp (accessed 2008; now unavailable).

Totka, Jr., Vincent A. "Preventing Patron Theft in the Archives: Legal Perspectives and Problems." *American Archivist* 56 (Fall 1993): 664–72.

Traister, Daniel. "The Rare Book Librarian's Day." *Rare Books and Manuscripts Librarianship* 1, no. 2 (Fall 1986): 93–105.

———. "Seduction and Betrayal: An Insider's View of Internal Theft." *Wilson Library Bulletin* 69 (September 1994): 30–33.

Transportation Safety Administration. "Screening Passengers by Observation Techniques (SPOT)." http://www.tsa.gov/what_we_do/layers/spot/index.shtm (accessed 2007; now unavailable).

———. "Train Police Officers to Spot Terrorist Related Activity: TSA Designs and Tests Curriculum to Train Police Officers to Spot Terrorist-Related Activity" (6 April 2006). http://www.tsa.gov/press/releases/2006/press_release_0655.shtm (accessed 2010).

Treese, William R. *Library Security: A Select, Annotated Bibliography.* N. p., 1980.

Trinkaus-Randall, Gregor. "Library and Archival Security: Policies and Procedures to Protect Holdings from Theft and Damage." In *Management of Library and Archival Security: From the Outside Looking In*, ed. by Robert K. O'Neill. New York: Haworth, 1998. Also in *Journal of Library Administration* 25, no. 1 (1989): 91–112.

———. "Preserving Special Collections through Internal Security." *College and Research Libraries* 50, no. 7 (July 1989): 448–54.

———. *Protecting Your Collections: A Manual of Archival Security.* Chicago: Society of American Archivists, 1995.

Tryon, Jonathan S. "Premises Liability for Librarians." *Library & Archival Security* 10, no. 2 (1990): 3–21.

U. K. Library Association and the Antiquarian Booksellers Association. *Theft of Books and Manuscripts from Libraries: An Advisory Code of Conduct for Booksellers and Librarians.* http://www.la-hq.org.uk/directory/prof_issues/tobam.html (accessed 2007; now unavailable).

United States Army. Information Security Program. *AR 380-5.* Washington, DC, 1988. http://www.marcorsyscom.usmc.mil/sites/ia/References/training/IASO%20Training/Army/AR%20380-5/preface.htm (accessed 2010).

United States Court of Appeals. Sixth Circuit. "United States of America, Plaintiff-Appellee, v. Robert Bradford Murphy, a/k/a Samuel George Matz, and Elizabeth Irene Murphy, a/k/a Elizabeth Irene Matz, Defendants and Appellants." 413 F.2d 1129, June 12, 1969, as Amended September 12, 1969 Certiorari Denied October 27, 1969. http://cases.justia.com/us-court-of-appeals/F2/413/1129/ and at: http://altlaw.org/v1/cases/869265 (accessed 2010).

———. "United States of America, Plaintiff-Appellee/Cross Applicant v. Charles Thomas Allen, II, et al., Defendants-Appellants/Cross-Appellees." Decided 5 February 2008. http://www.ca6.uscourts.gov/opinions.pdf/08a0062p-06.pdf (accessed 2010).

———. Laws. Code, Title 31, Subtitle IV, Chapter 51, Subchapter 2, 5112.

———. Third Circuit. "United States of America, v. Ernest Medford, Appellant in 98-1647 United States of America, v. George Csizmazia Appelant in 98-1646." Decided 2 July 1999. http://cases.justia.com/us-court-of-appeals/F3/194/419/505162/ (accessed 2010).

United States Department of Labor. "Occupations Ranked by Employment Percentage of Woman and Men." *Occupational Outlook Handbook* (2004). http://www.ocouha.com/cur/ooh130501.htm (accessed 2009).

———. "Employed Persons by Detailed Industry, Sex, Race, and Hispanic or Latino Ethnicity." *Occupational Outlook Handbook* (2008–9). http://www.bls.gov/cps/cpsaat18.pdf (accessed 2009).

United States District Court. Northern District of Texas. John Skillestad. "Application for and Affidavit for Search Warrant." Case 3:09-MJ-248. 20 August 2009. http://www.dallasnews.com/sharedcontent/dws/dn/latestnews/stories/091309dnmetkennedyletter.3ffe31b.html (accessed 2010).

University of California, Los Angeles, College of Letters and Science. "An Academic Gem Returns" (4 January 2008). http://www.college.ucla.edu/news/08/clark-library.html (accessed 2010).

Van Nort, S. "Archival and Library Theft: The Problem that Will Not Go Away." *Library and Archival Security* 12, no. 2 (1994): 25–49.

Varner, C. *The Causes, Measurements, and Prevention of Journal Mutilation in an Academic Library.* ERIC, ED 23417. 1983.

Verification Technologies, Inc. http://www.verification.com/main.htm. (Company now defunct.)

Vitale, Cammie. "The Blumberg Case and its Implications for Library Security at the Central University Libraries, Southern Methodist University." *Library & Archival Security* 12, no. 1 (1993): 79–85.

Wagner, Joyce. "Analyzing Handwriting to Select the Most Suitable Security Candidate." *Cultural Property Protection from the Ground Up: Proceedings of the National Conference on Cultural Property Protection and International Conference on Museum Security, March 7–11, 1999,* 77–81. [Washington, DC: Smithsonian Institution, 1999].

Walch, Timothy. *Archives & Manuscripts Security.* Chicago: Society of American Archivists, 1977.

Walsh, Jim, Barbara Hulyk, and George Barnum. *Rare and Valuable Government Documents: A Resource Packet on Identification, Preservation, and Security Issues for Government Documents Collections.* Chicago: American Library Association, 1993.

Walsh, R. R. "Rare Book and Security System Confidentiality." *Library & Archival Security* 2, no. 2 (1978): 71–73.

Wall, C. "Inventory What You Might Expect to Be Missing." *Library & Archival Security* 7, no. 2 (1985): 27.

Walters, William H. "Journal Prices, Book Acquisitions, and Sustainable College Library Collections." *College & Research Libraries* 69, no. 6 (November 2008): 576–86.

Warin v. Wildenstein & Co., 13 Misc.3d 1201(A), 824 N.Y.S.2d 759 (2006), *affirmed* 45 A.D.3d 459, 846 N.Y.S.2d 153 (2007).

Watkins, T. H. "The Purloined Past." *American Heritage Magazine,* August/September 1978. http://www.americanheritage.com/articles/magazine/ah/1978/5/1978_5_48.shtml (accessed 2010).

Watstein, S. B. "Book Mutilation: An Unwelcome By-product of Electronic Security Systems." *Library & Archival Security* 5, no. 1 (1983): 11–33.

Weessies, Kathleen. "The Secret Inside Your Library's Atlases: Reexamine Your Collections and How to Protect Them—Before Someone Else Does." *American Libraries* 34, October 2003.

Weiss, Phillip. "The Book Thief—A True Tale of Bibliomania." *Harper's Magazine,* January 1994.

Welch, Edwin. "Security in an English Archive." *Archivaria* 1, no. 2 (Summer 1976): 49–54.

Wilkie, Everett C. "Weighing Materials in Rare Book and Manuscript Libraries as a Security Measure against Theft and Vandalism." *RBM: A Journal of Rare Books, Manuscripts, and Cultural Heritage* 7, no. 2 (Fall 2006): 146–64. http://www.lita.org/ala/mgrps/divs/acrl/publications/rbm/7-2/wilkie06.pdf (accessed 2010).

Wilsted, Thomas. *Planning New and Remodeled Archival Facilities.* Chicago: Society of American Archivists, 2007.

Winter, K. "Entrance/Exit Design of Australian Academic Libraries since 1959." *Australian College Libraries* 3, no. 4 (1985): 167–75.

Wisner, William H. *Whither the Postmodern Library? Libraries, Technology, and Education in the Information Age.* Jefferson, NC: McFarland, 2000.

Wurzburger, M. "Current Security Practices in College and University Special Collections." *Rare Books & Manuscript Librarianship* 3 (1988): 43–57.

Wyly, Mary. "Special Collections Security: Problems, Trends, and Consciousness." *Library Trends* 36 (Summer 1987): 241–56.

"Yenching Plundered." *Harvard Magazine,* January-February 2001.

Zeidberg, David. *Collection Security in ARL Libraries.* Washington, DC: Association of Research Libraries, 1984.

Zika, J. "Library Security=Eyes Wide Open." *North Carolina Libraries* 57 (1999): 118.

CONTRIBUTORS

Susan M. Allen is Director of the California Rare Book School, a project of the Department of Information Studies at the Graduate School of Education and Information Studies, UCLA. She is a former Chair of the RBMS Security Committee.

Alvan Bregman is Associate Professor Emeritus at the University of Illinois at Urbana-Champaign and Librarian, Preservation and Collection Management Programs, University of British Columbia. He is currently Chair of the RBMS Security Committee.

Nicole Davis is Assistant Photographic Archivist & Assistant Project Archivist, Morris L. Ernst Papers, Harry Ransom Humanities Research Center, University of Texas, Austin

Ann Hartley is an attorney in the Texas Attorney General's Office, Austin.

Kelly Jensen is Head of Youth Services, Aram Public Library, Delavan, Wisconsin.

Anne Marie Lane is Faculty Curator and Head of the Toppan Rare Books Library, American Heritage Center, University of Wyoming, Laramie. She is a former co-Chair of the RBMS Security Committee.

Jeffrey D. Marshall is Director of Research Collections, Bailey/Howe Library, University of Vermont, Burlington.

Richard W. Oram is Associate Director and Hobby Foundation Librarian, Harry Ransom Humanities Research Center, University of Texas, Austin. He is a former Chair of the RBMS Security Committee.

Laurel Rozema is an archivist, Dolph Briscoe Center for American History, University of Texas, Austin

Elaine Shiner is a cataloguer in the Houghton Library, Harvard University.

Daniel J. Slive is Head of Special Collections, Bridwell Library, Perkins School of Theology, Southern Methodist University, Dallas, Texas. He is a former co-Chair of the RBMS Security Committee.

Margaret Tufts Tenney is Head of the Reading Room, Harry Ransom Humanities Research Center, University of Texas, Austin.

Everett C. Wilkie, Jr., is a former Chair of the RBMS Security Committee and an independent scholar.

INDEX

A

Access
- cards, control, 104
- code, knowledge, 74–75
- control level, representation, 50
- restriction, 216

Access control systems, 13, 47
- AHJ consent, 47–48
- circulation records, 55
- components, 48
- computers
  - interaction, 53
  - requirement, 56
- configurations, 53–54
- contracts, 55–56
- contrast, 52–53
- cost, 55
- daisy chain problem, 54
- degraded mode, 53
- disadvantages, 55
- elements, 48
- function, 47
- intrusion detection system, relationship, 54
- patron registration, 55
- ring problems, 54
- sophistication, 50–51
- testing, 54–55
- trunk problems, 54

Accession records, 149–150
- arrangement/recordation, 150
- sample, 150f

Acoustic glass break detectors, 64

Acquisitions, 141

Action plan, formulation, 292–293

Active device (photoelectric device), 65

After-hours stacks, security guard access, 125

Air movement, HVAC (impact), 66

Alarms
- circuits, bypassing, 73, 74
- codes
  - control, 104
  - impact, 43
- company, phone number (accuracy), 76
- false alarms, sources, 65–66
- initiating devices, 62
  - normally open/normally closed (phrase), 62
- interpretation, human element (removal), 66
- silencing, 73
  - responsibility, 73
- supervisory alarms, central station monitoring, 77
- system, security guards arming/disarming knowledge, 124–125

Alarm systems, 46, 59
- DC power, usage, 68
- protection, 35

Allen, Charles, 284

Allen, Susan M.
- security argument, 1
- theft report, 8

American Library Association Map and Geography Round Table, 301

Analog CCTV
- cameras, frame output, 85
- system, digital CCTV system (contrast), 92–93

Anastasio, Joseph, 275

Annunciation devices, 67–68
- installation, 68
- mounting, 68
- powering, 68

Antiquarian Booksellers' Association of America (ABAA)
- book theft report, 114
- Code of Ethics, 236
- databases, usage, 235
- Fair Play Resolution recommendation, 238–239
- thefts, reporting, 302

Antiquarian book trade
- auction house (subgroup), 3
- library contact, 3

Applegate, Shannon, 199

Applicants
- FICO score, 13
- hires, education, 12